# Money, Banking , and Credit

Dwight M. Jaffee

# Money, Banking, and Credit

WORTH PUBLISHERS, INC.

*"There are three faithful friends—an old wife, an old dog, and ready money."*

**Benjamin Franklin** (Poor Richard's Almanac for 1738)

**Money, Banking, and Credit**

Copyright © 1989 by Worth Publishers, Inc.

All rights reserved

Library of Congress Catalog Card Number: 88-51476

ISBN: 0-87901-408-3

Printed in the United States of America

Printing: January 1989

Editor: Toni Ann Scaramuzzo

Production: Sarah Segal

Design: Malcolm Grear Designers

Art Director: George Touloumes

Layout design: Patricia Lawson

Line art: York Graphic Services, Inc.

Typography: Techna Type, Inc.

Printing and binding: Von Hoffman Press

Photo Credits: Front cover: AMERICAN EXPRESS Card Design® and Gladiator Head® are registered service marks of American Express and are used with permission.

VISA, CLASSIC and THE DIAMOND DESIGN are service marks of Visa International Service Association and are reproduced with permission.

All coins: Frank Lawrence Stevens/Nawrocki Stock Photo

Back cover: detail from One Shilling and Six Pence note: Frank Lawrence Stevens/Nawrocki Stock Photo

Photo credits appear on page 685, which constitutes an extension of the copyright page.

Worth Publishers, Inc.

33 Irving Place

New York, New York 10003

# Preface

No other area of the economy, or of economics, has undergone changes as extensive as those that have transformed money, banking, and credit during the last fifteen years. *Deregulation* has obliged banks and other financial firms to operate in highly competitive markets in which only the most efficient and innovative are likely to prosper. *Technological advances* have introduced new management methods and financial instruments, which in turn have opened up new markets. And recently developed *tools of economic analysis* have sharpened our understanding of these developments and their short- and long-term implications.

As a result of such major changes—and those that are likely to continue into the 1990s—a money and banking textbook that emphasizes only how financial firms and markets work is not sufficient. A modern money and banking text must show students how to analyze the behavior of financial firms and markets as the environment changes. This book does just that; it develops and applies a systematic framework for analyzing how individuals, firms, and government agencies make *rational decisions* in a changing world based on the information available to them and their expectations of future values.

My experiences as a research economist, a consultant and a board member for financial institutions, and as a long-time teacher of the course indicate that an understanding of economic and financial theory is critical for developing coherent answers to the key questions in the money and banking field. To transmit this knowledge to students, a text must develop basic principles in a simple and organized fashion, with exciting and provocative applications. This will enable students to learn how to apply the key principles in a changing world, instead of learning only specific facts that may become rapidly outdated. In preparing this book, then, I have worked with three prime goals in mind: to provide a *modern text*, which encompasses recent developments in economic, financial, and monetary theory; to provide an *accessible text*, even for students with only a modest background in economic principles; and to provide an *interesting text*, which applies modern theory to current developments and policies. I have also attempted to provide a *flexible text*, so that instructors can easily mold it to meet the needs of specific courses.

# Content

The text is divided into seven parts (with the six chapters of Part I serving to introduce the remaining parts). This organization is intended to allow instructors maximum flexibility in course design.

## Part I: Basic Concepts

Part I introduces the basic principles and concepts of money, banking, and credit. A modern theory of the medium of exchange and the store of value is used to introduce money with special emphasis on the gains from trade, money illusion, and real wealth effects. Financial institutions are analyzed as firms that provide check-clearing, borrowing, and lending services. Financial markets are discussed with regard to how security prices and interest rates are determined. The concept of "making a market" is a unifying concept for financial institutions and financial markets. Such an approach gives students a flexible tool for analyzing the changes that are occurring in money and banking markets.

## Part II: Financial Decisions and Markets

Uncertainty concerning future interest rates, security prices, and related variables is a fundamental issue for most financial decisions. Before analyzing financial institutions and monetary policy, it is therefore essential to study how uncertainty affects financial decisions and how portfolios are selected. To this end, the chapters in Part II develop the basic principles of risk preferences, portfolio selection and term structure theory, and futures and options contracts and show how these principles are applied by financial investors and institutions.

## Part III: Financial Institutions

In today's deregulated banking markets, successful institutions must provide low-cost and innovative services. The chapters in Part III show how microeconomic and financial principles are used to manage financial firms in a deregulated environment. The discussion of banking institutions focuses on their decisions regarding loan and deposit interest rates, quantities, and maturities, loan quality, and bank liquidity. The discussion of nonbank institutions highlights how mutual funds—an important group of bank competitors—operate.

## Part IV: Money Supply and Money Demand

Although money supply theory and money demand theory are treated separately in most texts (with money demand theory deferred until after monetary policy), in this book they are treated together, just before the discussion of monetary policy. A key benefit of this arrangement is that when students reach the discussion of monetary policy, they will be able to apply the money demand/money supply theory of interest rates and the knowledge of what factors shift the demand curve for money.

## Part V: Monetary Policy and the Federal Reserve System

The analysis of monetary policy in Part V is based on the concepts of financial theory, financing institutions, and money demand and supply developed in the earlier parts. The Federal Reserve's policy goals, methods and techniques, and practical experiences in coping with diverse economic conditions are covered, with special emphasis on the problems of (and the solutions for) the lags and uncertainty in the effects of monetary policy. Federal Reserve policy statements and directives are used to illustrate how monetary policy works in practice.

## Part VI: International Trade and Finance

Given the large international trade deficit of the United States and the impact it has on U.S. interest rates and the economy—discussed throughout the book—it is critical that students be familiar with the factors that determine exchange rates, including how the purchasing power and interest rate parity theories of exchange rates are based on international arbitrage. The placement of these topics in Part VI, rather than at the end of the book, is intended as an extension of the discussion of monetary policy in Part V.

## Part VII: Monetary Theory

The treatment of monetary theory provides a balanced consideration of the various factors that determine macroeconomic relationships, rather than emphasizing specific doctrines or "schools." Macroeconomic relationships are developed with the use of three key models. The IS/LM model is used to study the relationships between monetary and fiscal policies and to examine the alternative methods that are available for financing a government budget deficit. The aggregate supply/aggregate demand model is used to study monetary policy and inflation. And rational expectations models of monetary policy are used to illustrate the central role of information and expectations in modern macroeconomics.

# Special Content Features

To help students in their study of money, banking, and credit, the book incorporates a number of distinctive topics, and uses innovative approaches to other topics.

## Money and Banking in the Payments System

Most textbooks pay only perfunctory attention to the basic roles that money and banking play in an economy's payments system. In contrast, this book carefully develops the costs and benefits of alternative payments system at the outset (in Chapter 2), and then applies the principles throughout. The value of this approach is apparent when discussing, for example, how banks set their fees and interest rates for checking accounts (Chapter 6); how payments system factors influence the demand for money (Chapter 15); and how commodity arbitrage works in international trade (Chapter 21).

## Consumption, Saving, and Capital Investment Decisions

Although most textbooks indicate that interest rates adjust to match the demand and supply of savings, they do not emphasize how interest rates affect consumption, saving, and capital investment decisions over time. In this book, the principles of how decisions are made over time are developed using the two-period model of Irving Fisher (in Chapter 3). This approach gives the student an understanding of the role of interest rates in consumer decisions (such as the demand for money) and in policy issues (such as the government deficit and the international trade deficit).

## The Theory of Interest Rates

Alternative theories of interest rates are introduced throughout the book, reinforcing the basic concepts and bringing in additional concepts as they are needed. The fundamental determinants of interest rates are introduced in Chapters 3 and 4 by combining the Irving Fisher two-period model with the loanable funds model. The term structure and risk structure of interest rates are developed in Part II as part of finance theory. The money supply/money demand theory of interest rates is introduced as part of the discussion of money supply and money demand in Part IV. The relationships among these alternative theories are developed in Chapters 3, 15, and 26.

## Asset Demand and Portfolio Selection

Using the concepts of wealth, capital, and portfolios (introduced in Chapter 4) and of decision making under uncertainty (developed in Chapter 7 and expanded in the rest of Part II), this book offers a distinctively comprehensive treatment of asset demand and portfolio selection. These theories are then applied to the portfolio decisions of banks and non-bank intermediaries (Chapters 11 to 13) and to asset theories of money demand (Chapter 15).

## Adverse Selection, Moral Hazard, and Credit Rationing

Recent loan losses among commercial banks and the failure of many thrift institutions dramatically highlight both the loan market effects of adverse selection and moral hazard and the potential role of credit rationing in offsetting these effects. These concepts are developed as an integral part of decision making under uncertainty (in Part II) and are then applied, for example, to failing thrift institutions (Chapters 10 and 13), bank loan losses (Chapter 12), and the Federal Reserve's discount window policies (Chapter 18).

## Integrated Treatment of International Trade and Finance

The increasing importance of international trade and finance for the U.S. financial system and economy requires that these topics be covered in an integrated fashion throughout the book. Accordingly, these topics are introduced in Part I, with regard, for example, to the determinants of interest rates (Chapter 3) and to the net wealth position of the U.S. (Chapter 4). They are then applied throughout the book, including, for example, the discussions of mutual fund portfolios based on foreign stocks (Chapter 13), international banking operations (Chapter 21), and exchange rate policy as a part of monetary policy (Chapter 22).

## Innovative Use of Demand and Supply Analysis

This book uses demand and supply analysis extensively to illustrate how equilibrium prices and interest rates are determined in various markets. This approach is particularly valuable because the microeconomic foundations developed in Part I are used to derive the factors that shift demand and supply curves in the various markets (such as for money and for loanable funds). Also, demand and supply analysis is integrated with the concept of "making a market," by introducing bid and ask prices for security markets (Chapter 5) and the spread between loan and deposit interest rates in financial intermediary markets (Chapter 6).

## Combining Theory with a Real World Focus

Throughout the book, microeconomic theory and financial theory are applied to real world problems and developments—such as the stock market crash of 1987 and the current federal deposit insurance crisis—thereby encouraging students to seek coherent answers to exciting questions. The learning aids described below (such as tables and graphs and boxed discussions of recent developments) are also critical for this purpose.

## Learning Features

Special care has been taken to make the discussion clear and interesting. Important pedagogical aids include the following.

**Part and Chapter Introductions**. Each part begins with an introductory preview of the main points to be developed in the following chapters. Each chapter opens with a short scenario that provides an application of the upcoming material.

**Special Topic Boxes**. The text discussion is augmented with over a hundred special topic boxes. Each of the four categories of boxes— Money Matters, Banking Briefs, Credit Checks, and In Depth—provides an application of money, banking, or credit, or an in-depth discussion of a key topic.

**Figures and Tables**. An unusually large number of figures and tables are provided to illustrate and extend the text discussion. All figures have carefully written captions that reinforce the major points.

**Chapter Summary, Key Terms, Glossary**. Each chapter has a succinct summary that reviews the main concepts of the chapter. Key terms, which are shown in boldface in the text, are listed at the end of each chapter for review. Definitions of these terms are also provided in the glossary at the back of the book.

**Study Questions**. At the end of each chapter there are ten questions or problems that cover the chapter's material. Answers to even-numbered questions are provided at the end of the book.

**Recommended Reading**. Each chapter concludes with an annotated bibliography for further reading. The listings include especially interesting and clearly written books and articles, as well as the "classics" of the field.

**Flexibility in Designing a Course**. The text is organized to provide the instructor with a wide variety of options in coverage and organization. A course emphasizing financial markets, for example, might include Part II but exclude Part III, whereas a course emphasizing financial institutions might do just the opposite. Also, some instructors may choose to omit Chapter 9 dealing with futures and options contracts or the parts of Chapters 23 and 24 dealing with the IS/LM model. Courses emphasizing monetary theory and policy might skip Parts II and III since Chapters 5 and 6 cover the basics of the financial system and the banking industry.

## Supplements

A particularly well-conceived package of supplements to this textbook is available.

## Study Guide

The *Study Guide* was written by Walter H. Kemmsies of Memphis State University. Each chapter of the *Study Guide* contains an overview of the material covered in the text chapter. This is followed by a list of key terms and fill-in questions, which together constitute a quick review of the text chapter. Then, a series of analytical questions provides students with practice in using the key concepts developed in the chapter. A self-check test of 20 multiple-choice questions lets students practice for exams. Finally, for those chapters where it is appropriate, a section entitled "Common Misconceptions" describes typical conceptual errors about which students should be forewarned.

## Instructor's Manual

The *Instructor's Manual* was written by Peter Locke of Tulane University and Robert McLeod of the University of Alabama. Each chapter contains a detailed lecture outline of the topics covered in the text chapter. Also included in the *Instructor's Manual* are the complete answers to the study questions in the text (students are given only the odd-numbered answers in the text). Each chapter concludes with a set of transparency masters showing key graphs from the text.

## Test Bank and Computerized Test-Generation System

Forty multiple-choice and five essay questions have been written by Peter Locke of Tulane University and Robert McLeod of the University of Alabama for each chapter of the textbook. Answers to the essay questions are also included. These questions in the print version of the *Test Bank* are also available on diskette (for use with an IBM PC, Macintosh, or Apple II family microcomputer). Instructors can add their own questions, edit the questions, and print out as many as nine different versions of an exam.

## Computer Tutorials and Simulation

*Mastering Money, Banking, and Credit: Interactive Tutorials, Exams, and Simulations* has been prepared by William Gunther of University of Alabama and Irene Gunther of Systematic Research Inc. to accompany the text. Students can use this interactive software throughout the course. The eight topic modules cover Basic Concepts and Payments System, Finance Theory, The Banking Firm, The Determinants of Interest Rates, International Finance, Monetary Policy, Monetary Theory, and Money Demand and Supply. There are four programs for each of these eight topic modules: Tutorials, Glossary, Exams, and Simulations.

- *Tutorials* introduce and develop concepts, present problems, and monitor students as they solve problems. A performance evaluation concludes the program.

- *Glossary* is a dictionary resource students can access as needed (to find a concept, definition, or relationship) when using the other programs.
- *Exams* offer multiple-choice, problem-solving, and analysis questions from the Study Guide to help students explore the depth of their understanding. Incorrect answers prompt a hint and an opportunity to access the "Help" program.
- *Simulations* are real-world scenarios where students must assume decision-making roles for the Federal Reserve, banks, and other financial institutions.

## Acknowledgments

I am indebted to a large number of people who have helped to shape and to produce this book. From beginning to end, Paul Shensa and his coworkers at Worth Publishers have encouraged and helped me to make the book interesting and accessible without compromising intellectual integrity. Editorial and production assistance was provided by many people, principally Toni Ann Scaramuzzo, George Touloumes, Pat Lawson, and Sarah Segal.

The comments and suggestions of experienced teachers and insightful reviewers were received and gratefully incorporated. I list those colleagues here with respect and appreciation:

David A. Aschauer, University of Michigan
Scott Freeman, Boston College
Mary Gade, Oklahoma State University
Beverly Hadaway, University of Texas, Austin
Arnold A. Heggestad, University of Florida
Arthur P. James, Texas A&M University
Nancy Ammon Jianakoplos, Michigan State University
Walter H. Kemmsies, Memphis State University
Jeffrey M. Lacker, Purdue University
Peter Locke, Tulane University
Robert W. McLeod, University of Alabama
W. Douglas McMillin, Louisiana State University
Douglas K. Pearce, North Carolina State University
Robert Schweitzer, University of Delaware
Case Sprenkle, University of Illinois

In particular Nancy Jianakoplos of Michigan State University and Walter Kemmsies of Memphis State University went well beyond the call of duty. The same is true for the many Princeton students who suffered through, but helped to improve, mimeographed drafts of the book.

# Contents in Brief

# Contents

## CHAPTER 11 The Banking Firm and Liquidity Management

## CHAPTER 15 Theories of Money Demand

# Basic Concepts

Money, banking, and credit play a key role in two basic types of economic transactions: the purchase and sale of goods and services, and the borrowing and lending of money. In Part I, we introduce and apply the basic tools of economic and financial theory to examine how money, banking, and credit provide benefits to an economy.

In Chapter 1, we will look at basic concepts and principles: how the money supply is used to purchase goods and services and to store wealth over time, how bank deposits are used to make payments by check and to accumulate savings, and how the financial system provides a range of facilities (including money and banking) to expedite borrowing and lending. We will also look at policy issues that currently affect money, banking, and credit.

The organization of the economy's system for buying and selling goods (and services) plays a pivotal role in determining the quantity and type of goods that are produced and who receives them. In Chapter 2, we will evaluate some alternative trade and payments systems. As an aid in this evaluation, we will use a "standard trading problem" to measure how well the alternative systems—barter, commodity money, paper money, and bank deposits—perform. We will see that efficient payments systems generally use paper money or bank checking deposits as the medium of exchange.

The interest rate is a key variable that people refer to in deciding how much of their income to save or to consume, and how much money they need to borrow or can afford to lend. The interest rate is also a factor in determining how much capital investment is carried out in the economy. In Chapter 3, we will use Irving Fisher's model of consumption and saving to identify the fundamental factors that cause people to save and invest their income, as well as to borrow or lend money. We will then develop a theory of interest rates—the loanable funds theory—on the basis of these factors.

Wealth is the focus of Chapter 4, where we study such topics as how people determine their portfolios of assets and liabilities, the effect of a changing price level or inflation rate on the economy, and the distinctions between expected and unexpected inflation and between nominal and real interest rates. This analysis is closely related to the material in Chapter 3 because (1) wealth is the accumulated amount of saving and (2) capital is the accumulated amount of (tangible) investment.

The credit and financial system of the economy provides the overall structure in which lending and borrowing takes place. In Chapter 5, we will examine each component of the financial system—securities, financial institutions, and financial markets—and analyze how security prices and interest rates are determined. Among other things, we will see how brokers, dealers, and financial exchanges manage the financial markets (including how dealers "make the market" for a security).

The services of the banking system are used both when people purchase goods and services and when they borrow or lend money. In Chapter 6, we will look at the structure of the banking industry and at the two main services it provides—checking accounts for making payments, and intermediation facilities for borrowing and lending money. We will also see that banks "make the market" for loanable funds just as security dealers "make the market" for a security. We use commercial banks as a case study in Chapter 6, anticipating that most financial institutions operate in the same basic fashion, as we will confirm in Part II.

# Introduction to Money, Banking, and Credit

*"Money is what you keep score with."*

**Andrew Carnegie**

When you look at the front page of the morning newspaper nowadays, it is not startling to find that a major bank has failed or that the stock market just dropped 100 points. The business or financial section of the paper may have further reports: that a rapidly growing money supply is creating fears of inflation, that escalating interest rates are disrupting the credit markets, or that the foreign exchange value of the dollar is gyrating because of the foreign trade deficit.

These news reports mean that money, banking, and credit are intruding on our everyday life in a major way. Why this intrusion? A hard question to answer precisely, but here are some ideas to think about.

- *Computers* and related technological developments have dramatically changed how money, banking, and credit function. Most banks now use automated-teller machines, which allow people to withdraw cash or to examine their bank account balance at almost any time. Banks also use computers to "wire" large amounts of money around the economy, and to keep track of all of the different types of accounts they offer. Even stock market trading is automated with computers—in fact, computer-based trading has been blamed for the stock market crash of October 1987.

- *Deregulation*—reducing the extent of government rules—occurred for money, banking, and credit services at about the same time it occurred for the airlines and the telephone companies. With deregulation, banks and other financial firms can offer products and techniques that previously were prohibited.

- *Competition* in the markets for money, banking, and credit is now more aggressive, reflecting in part the new opportunities provided by computers and deregulation. Increased competition is generally beneficial for consumers, although it may also create new problems for the government agencies that regulate the money, banking, and credit markets.

We will be seeing the effects of these changes throughout this book.

In this chapter, we will start to examine the basic principles of money, banking, and credit. We will distinguish between microeconomic principles—that pertain to individuals and firms—and macroeconomic principles—that pertain to the overall economy. We will first look at some of the principles that govern the use of money.

## Money

People often think about how much—or how little—money they have. The amount of money can be measured either as the amount people hold at a moment in time—money at rest, which is the money supply—or as the rate at which money is changing hands—money on the move, which is the velocity of money.

### Money at Rest: The Money Supply

The available quantity of money at a moment in time is called the **money supply. Currency,** consisting of coins and dollar bills of various denominations, is a familiar part of the money supply. But there is more to the money supply than currency; in fact, as illustrated in Figure 1.1, there is more than one definition of the money supply.

#### The M1 Money Supply

The **M1 money supply** (or **M1**) consists of money that can be directly used to purchase goods and services. Specifically, M1 equals the sum of currency held by the public (that is, outside of banks), travelers checks, and transaction deposits. **Transaction deposits** is the formal name for bank *checking deposits*—which people use to write checks to transfer money to other people. Box 1.1 explains why the term "transaction deposits" was adopted.

Both the currency and transaction accounts components of the M1 money supply are very large. In 1987, there was $197 billion of currency in the U.S. economy, which translates to over $800 per person. Right now I have $15 of currency in my pocket, and you probably do not have

The M1 money supply, consisting of currency, travelers checks, and transaction deposits (checking account balances) can be directly used to pay for the purchases of goods and services. The M2 money supply represents a broader definition that includes nontransaction deposits.

**Source:** *Federal Reserve Bulletin,* Table 1.21, Board of Governors of the Federal Reserve System, 1988.

FIGURE 1.1
**The Money Supply of the United States**
At year-end 1987 (Dollars in billions)

| The M2 Money Supply = $2,901 | |
|---|---|
| Nontransaction deposits | $2,150 |
| M1 Money Supply | 751 |

| The M1 Money Supply = $751 | |
|---|---|
| Currency | $197 |
| Travelers checks | 7 |
| Transaction deposits | 547 |
| [Demand deposits, $288 + other checkable deposits, $259] | |

## BOX 1.1 MONEY MATTERS

### Transaction Deposits

Figure 1.1 shows that the M1 money supply includes two types of checking accounts—demand deposits and other checkable deposits. **Demand deposits**—bank accounts from which funds can be withdrawn immediately (on "demand")—were once the only type of checking account. Legislation passed by Congress in 1933 prohibited banks from paying interest on demand deposits. (In contrast, funds could not be withdrawn immediately from *time deposits*, but some interest could be paid on these deposits.)

Starting in the early 1970s, as the level of interest rates in the economy rose, pressure developed to allow banks to pay interest on demand deposits. When Congress resisted, regulators started to allow banking institutions to pay interest on special types of checking accounts—originally called negotiable orders of withdrawal (or *NOW accounts*)—that circumvented the prohibition of interest on demand deposits. In 1980, Congress granted the regulators wider powers to allow interest-paying checking accounts.

Checking accounts on which interest can be paid are now generically called **other checkable deposits,** to distinguish them from demand deposits on which interest is still prohibited. The name *transaction deposits* is now used to refer to all accounts with transaction privileges—that is, to all checking accounts.

much more. So other people in the economy must be holding a large amount of currency.

Some of this extra currency is being held by people in the **underground economy** who deal in illegal activities, as described in Box 1.2.

## BOX 1.2 MONEY MATTERS

### Money in the Underground Economy

People in the underground economy deal in activities that are illegal—such as the drug trade, loan-sharking, and income tax evasion. Unlike most of us, people in the underground economy must be careful about depositing their money in bank checking accounts. Banks keep accurate records of all amounts deposited and are required to report the identity of customers depositing more than $10,000 in cash. The Internal Revenue Service (IRS) could try to use these records to determine how much money a person actually had earned.

People in the underground economy try to use currency for most of their transactions, but they prefer to use checks to pay for big-ticket items such as new cars—it arouses suspicion to pay for a car with a wad of $100 bills. So they have to use special techniques—called **money laundering**—to "clean" their money before depositing it in a checking account at a U.S. bank.

For example, people in the underground economy might first deposit their money in a bank on a Caribbean island that keeps the names of its depositors secret and does not ask questions about the source of their money. A check can then be written on the Caribbean bank to open a regular checking account at a U.S. bank. This way the IRS will have trouble tracing the source of the money.

Currency in circulation is the amount of currency that has been issued by the U.S. government, primarily by the Federal Reserve, the central bank of the United States. The diagram shows the value of the money that was in circulation for coins and each denomination of dollar bills at the end of 1987. The large amount of $100 bills suggests that a good part of the currency is being used in the underground economy or is being hoarded for safety.

Source: *Treasury Bulletin*, U.S. Department of the Treasury, 1988.

FIGURE 1.2

**Currency in Circulation by Denomination**
At year-end 1987 (Dollars in billions)

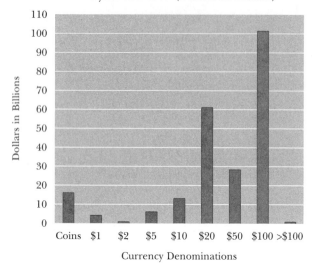

Currency Denominations

Other currency has been lost or misplaced—there is no way to find out how much has disappeared in this way—or is being hoarded. It is interesting to observe in this regard that the value of $100 bills in circulation is almost the same as the combined value of all the other currency denominations in circulation, as shown in Figure 1.2.[1] It is a good guess that these $100 bills are not being used to buy the morning newspaper.

The transaction deposit component of the M1 money supply is almost three times as large as the currency component, amounting to over $2,200 per person in the United States. Who holds this part of the money supply? Because banks keep accurate records of their deposits, there is a more definite answer here than for currency. The proportion of total transaction deposits held in each *sector* of the economy—business, household, financial institutions, foreign, and other—is shown in Table 1.1. We can see that over half of all transaction deposits are held by business firms. This makes sense because business firms pay almost all of their bills with checks.

### Broader Definitions of the Money Supply

The M1 money supply, which is the sum of currency and transaction deposits, is the most "narrow" of the U.S. money supply definitions—it includes the smallest number of items. The broader M2 money supply is the sum of the M1 money supply and various nontransaction bank

---

[1] Currency in *circulation* includes currency held by banks, whereas the M1 money supply only includes currency held by the public. This is why the total amount of currency in Figure 1.2 is somewhat larger than the $197 billion of currency shown as part of M1 in Figure 1.1.

**TABLE 1.1**
**Transaction Deposits by Sector of The Economy**

| At Year-End (Percentage of total) | |
|---|---|
| Business | 55 |
| Household | 26 |
| Financial institutions | 11 |
| Foreign | 1 |
| Other | 7 |
| All holders | 100 |

**Source:** *Federal Reserve Bulletin,* Table 1.21, Board of Governors of the Federal Reserve System, 1988.

deposits and related items. At times, the Federal Reserve has used money supply definitions numbered as high as M7: the higher the number, the "broader" the definition, and the more items it includes. We will look at the nontransaction deposits that are included in the M2 money supply shortly.

## Money on the Move: the Velocity of Money

Most people would rather spend their money than hold it. Money moves around the economy as people receive it, hold it briefly, and then spend it. There is much we can learn from the velocity of money as it circulates through an economy. But before we look at those matters, we have to be more precise about how to measure the velocity of money.

The **annual income velocity of money** represents the amount of income that is produced in the economy per dollar of average money supply. In 1987, for example, U.S. income was $4,486 billion and the M1 money supply was $751 billion, so the velocity of money was about 6 ($4,486/$751). How can a $751 billion supply of money support $4,486 billion of income? Only if each dollar circulates—changes hands—about six times a year on average. We can thus express the annual income velocity of money in a simple equation:

$$V = \frac{Y}{M},\tag{1.1}$$

where $Y$ = annual income,
 $M$ = the money supply,
 $V$ = the annual income velocity of money.

The velocity of money is computed on the basis of a specific measure of income—such as GNP (gross national product)—and of the money supply—such as the M1 money supply. Thus the annual GNP velocity of the M1 money supply is expressed as:

$$V = \frac{GNP}{M1}.$$

FIGURE 1.3

**The Annual GNP Velocity of the M1 Money Supply**

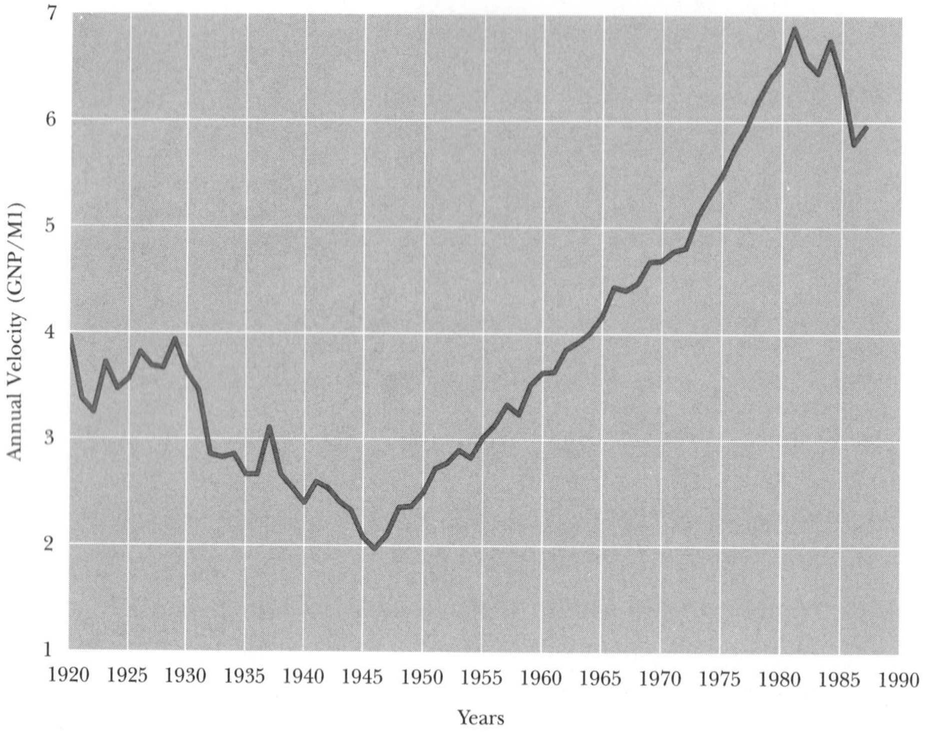

The annual GNP velocity of the M1 money supply—the ratio of annual GNP (Gross National Product) to the average level of the M1 money supply—has had two major trends since 1920, a negative trend that lasted through the end of World War II, and a positive trend that lasted until 1980. Since 1980, another negative trend may be developing.

The GNP velocity of the M1 money supply is graphed from 1920 to 1987 in Figure 1.3. The graph shows two major trends: velocity falling until 1946, and then rising until 1980. Since 1980, another falling trend may be developing. As we just calculated, the velocity of money was about 6 in 1987, just below its highest level of almost 7 in 1980. When we discuss the demand for money in later chapters, we will see that the velocity of money depends on such factors as the level of interest rates and income, and on how payments are made in the economy.

Each time a person goes through a cycle of receiving and spending income, the money involved turns over two times. Therefore, if people are paid monthly, and spend all of their income, then their *monthly* income velocity of money is 2, and their *annual* income velocity of money is 24 (12 × 2). Many people are paid more often than monthly, so their income velocity of money is even higher. In comparison, as illustrated in Figure 1.3, even at its highest value the annual GNP velocity of money just approached 7.

One reason for the relatively low measured GNP velocity of money is that some types of transactions are excluded from GNP. For example, activity in the underground economy is excluded from GNP as a matter of principle. Since GNP is in the numerator of the velocity formula, a lower value for GNP creates a lower value for velocity. Intermediate transactions—such as goods sold by wholesalers to retailers—and purchases and sales of assets are also excluded from GNP, which similarly reduce the measured value for the velocity of money.

A second reason for the relatively low measured GNP velocity of money is that there are really two types of money balances: *active balances* that circulate in the normal fashion, and *hoarded balances* that have a velocity near zero. The measured GNP velocity of money represents an average of the higher velocity of the active balances and the lower (or even zero) velocity of the hoarded balances.

## The Microeconomic Functions of Money

The concepts of money on the move and money at rest represent the two basic functions of money. When money is on the move, it serves as the **medium of exchange**—expediting the exchange of goods and services in the economy. When money is at rest, it serves as a **store of value**—a way that people hold wealth over time.

Money also has two *accounting* functions. The monetary unit (the *dollar* in the United States) is normally used to measure prices and wealth in the economy. This function of money is called the **unit of account.**[2] The monetary unit is also normally the unit in which debt is measured. If you take out a loan, for example, the amount you promise to repay is usually stated in dollars. This accounting function of money is called the **standard of deferred payment.**

These four functions of money—medium of exchange, store of value, unit of account, and standard of deferred payment—represent its microeconomic uses. We will study the **microeconomic** uses of money in Chapters 2, 3, and 4.

## The Macroeconomic Consequences of Money

**Macroeconomics** studies how the economy operates in terms of aggregate variables such as national income and the average level of prices. The total money supply is also an aggregate variable, and, as we shall see, it is a key determinant of national income and the price level.

---

[2] It is possible for the medium of exchange and the unit of account to refer to different items. For example, in the American colonies before 1776, Spanish silver coins called "dollars" were often the medium of exchange, but prices were usually stated in pounds sterling (the British unit of account).

BOX 1.3 IN DEPTH

## Irving Fisher

Irving Fisher (1867–1947) was an economics professor at Yale University during the first third of this century. During his career, Fisher was the author of more than 2,000 titles, covering a wide range of topics, but focusing on money, banking, prices, capital, and interest rates. Nevertheless, Fisher was not an "ivory tower" economist. Among other things, he became a millionaire by founding a company based on a card index system that he had invented. Unfortunately, he later lost his fortune in the stock market crash of 1929.

In this book, we will make use of a number of Irving Fisher's contributions to economics. In this chapter, we are starting with his quantity equation of exchange. In Chapter 3, we will use Fisher's model of consumption and saving to identify some of the key variables that determine interest rates. In Chapter 4, we will look at the Fisher effect, a theory of how interest rates in the economy adjust to changes in the expected rate of inflation. And in Chapter 16, we will examine Fisher's theory of the demand for money and the velocity of money.

The macroeconomic consequences of money are illustrated by an important equation in economics—**the quantity equation of exchange (QEE)**. This equation was developed by Irving Fisher in his 1911 book, *The Purchasing Power of Money*. Many consider Irving Fisher to have been the greatest American economist; some of his accomplishments are described in Box 1.3.

### The Quantity Equation of Exchange

The quantity equation of exchange is derived from the definition of the income velocity of money by solving equation (1.1), $V = Y/M$, for income $Y$:

$$MV = Y,$$

or in a more expanded form,

$$MV = Py, \tag{1.2}$$

where $M$ is the money supply,
      $V$ is the income velocity of money,
      $Y$ is the value of nominal income,
      $P$ is the price level,
      $y$ is the value of real income.

Equation (1.2) represents the value of *nominal income Y* in terms of the product of two components, the *price level P* and *real income y*. Box 1.4 reviews the concepts of nominal income, real income, and the price level.

BOX 1.4 IN DEPTH

## Nominal Income, Real Income, and the Price Level

Let us suppose that your annual **nominal income**—the amount you are currently paid in dollars—is initially $20,000 a year and you are spending all of it. Let us also suppose that you are being offered a 10 percent raise for next year, so that your nominal income would rise by $2,000 to $22,000. Your feelings about this raise will depend on your expectations about next year's prices. For example, if you expect the **price level**—the average level of prices in the economy—to rise by only 5 percent, then you will be better off next year because you will be able to buy a larger quantity of goods and services.

The concept of **real income** is used to measure how well off people are after their nominal income and the price level both change. Since real income $y$ equals nominal income $Y$ divided by the price level $P$, or $y = Y/P$, real income $y$ will rise whenever the increase in nominal income $Y$ exceeds the increase in the price level $P$. In the example, your initial real income of $20,000 (nominal income $20,000/price level 1.0) would rise the next year to $21,000 (nominal income $22,000/expected price level 1.05). (The price level of 1.05 is 5 percent higher than the initial price level of 1.0.)

Since it is important to distinguish between nominal and real variables, we will denote nominal variables as uppercase letters—such as nominal income $Y$—and real variables as lowercase letters—such as real income $y$.

The quantity equation of exchange can be illustrated by a simple example based on actual, but rounded, 1987 values.

Money supply $M$ = $750 (billion).

Nominal income $Y$ = $4,500 (billion).

Annual velocity of money $V$ = 6.

Price level = 3.0 (based on 1970 value = 1.0).

Real income $y$ = $1,500 (in billions of 1970 dollars).

We can confirm that these values satisfy equation (1.2):

$$M \times V = \quad Y \quad = P \times y.$$

$$\$750 \times 6 = \$4,500 = 3 \times \$1,500.$$

Now suppose that the money supply $M$ doubles to $1500, while velocity $V$ is unchanged at the value of 6. Nominal income $Y$ will then double to $9,000 ($Y = MV = (\$1,500 \times 6)$). Nominal income $Y$ can be represented by any price level $P$ and real income $y$ with a product that is equal to $9,000. For example, since $9,000 = 4.5 \times \$2,000$, the price level $P$ would be 4.5 if the real income $y$ were $2,000.

In applying the quantity equation of exchange (QEE), we should be aware that it is an *identity*—it is true because we have defined the velocity of money to be the ratio of nominal income to the money supply. Nevertheless, the equation is instructive for illustrating the possible effects of an increase in the money supply on nominal income $Y$, real income $y$, and the price level $P$. Specifically, we can consider three special *cases* by holding different variables constant:

### QEE Case (1.1): Control of Nominal Income

*If*: the velocity of money $V$ is constant,

*Then*: a change in the money supply $M$ will cause a proportionate change in nominal income $Y$.

*Example*: If the money supply doubles from $750 billion to $1,500 billion, then nominal income will double from $4,500 billion to $9,000 billion, given that the velocity of money is constant.

### QEE Case (1.2): Control of the Price Level

*If*: *a.* the velocity of money $V$ is constant, and
  *b.* the value of real income $y$ is constant,

*Then*: a change in the money supply $M$ will cause a proportionate change in the price level $P$.

*Example*: If the money supply doubles from $750 billion to $1,500 billion, then the price level will double from 3 to 6, given that the velocity of money and the value of real income are constant.

### QEE Case (1.3): Control of Real Income

*If*: *a.* the velocity of money $V$ is constant, and
  *b.* the price level $P$ is constant,

*Then*: a change in the money supply $M$ will cause a proportionate change in real income $y$.

*Example*: If the money supply doubles from $750 billion to $1,500 billion, then real income will double from $1,500 billion to $3,000 billion, given that the velocity of money and the price level are constant.

Each QEE case follows directly from the QEE equation (1.2), depending on which variables—$V$, $P$, or $y$—are constant.

### Monetary Policy

The QEE cases help illustrate how the **Federal Reserve** (or the **Fed**, as it is commonly known)—the central bank of the United States—uses **monetary policy** to achieve such macroeconomic goals as a high growth rate of real income and a stable price level (that is, a low inflation rate). Specifically, the QEE cases indicate how the money supply—a main indicator of monetary policy—is linked to the policy targets of real income and the price level.

Taken at face value, the QEE cases might even suggest that monetary policy is easy to implement. Based on Case 1.2, for example, a lower money supply should lead directly to a lower price level, and based on

Case 1.3, a higher money supply should lead directly to higher real income. However, monetary policy is not at all easy to implement in practice.

The practical problem is that other conditions must be satisfied for the QEE cases to hold:

- The Federal Reserve must be able to control the money supply.
- The velocity of money should be constant.
- Real income should be constant for Case 1.2. The price level should be constant for Case 1.3.

If these conditions are violated, the QEE cases will be violated. The results of monetary policy then become more complicated, and it is even possible that the actual result could be just the opposite of what the Fed intended.

The practical difficulty of implementing monetary policy is illustrated in Figure 1.4, which shows the annual growth rates between 1978 and 1987 of the M1 money supply, nominal GNP, the price level, and real GNP. In panel A, we can see that M1 grew by over 16 percent in 1986, indicating that sometimes the Federal Reserve cannot control the M1 money supply. Indeed, the Fed stopped trying to control M1 in 1987. Panel A also shows that the growth rates of M1 and of nominal income can be quite different, which means that the velocity of money is changing (remember the velocity of money is equal to nominal GNP divided by the money supply). Indeed, this is why velocity fell in 1986 but rose in 1987, as shown in Figure 1.3.

FIGURE 1.4
**Growth Rates of Macroeconomic Variables**
A. Growth Rate of M1

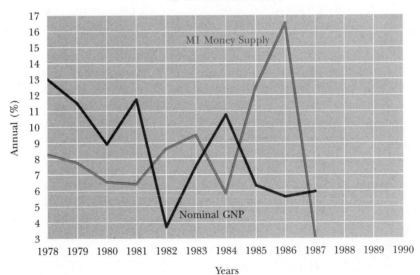

The large gyrations in the M1 growth rate during 1986 and 1987 suggest that the Federal Reserve was not able to control the money supply. A change in the velocity of money is also indicated whenever the growth rates of M1 and nominal GNP are not equal.

FIGURE 1.4
B. Growth Rates of the Price Level and Real GNP

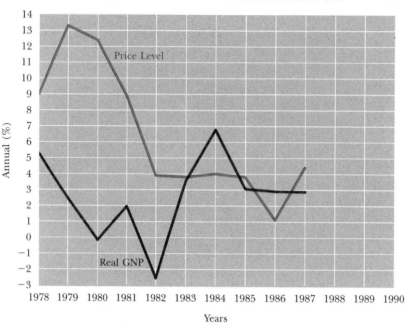

Between 1979 and 1982, the Federal Reserve was successful in reducing the inflation rate (the growth rate of the price level) by reducing the growth rate of the money supply. However, the policy also had the undesired side effect of temporarily reducing the growth rate of real income. **Source:** Economic Report of the President, February, 1988.

Panel B of Figure 1.4 shows the growth rates of the price level and real GNP. The period between 1979 and 1982 is particularly interesting because the Federal Reserve was trying very hard at that time to reduce the growth rate of the money supply so as to reduce the inflation rate. We can see that the growth rate of real income was also temporarily depressed through 1982—an unintended effect of the anti-inflation policy.

In Part V, we will look at how the Fed tries to deal with such problems as it carries out monetary policy.

### Macroeconomics and Monetary Theory

**Monetary theory** is the part of macroeconomics that examines how changes in the money supply affect aggregate variables such as income and the price level. Theories differ in their predictions of what will happen when the money supply increases. In discussing the QEE cases, we have covered the most common predictions—the price level alone rises (Case 1.2), real income alone rises (Case 1.3), or both rise—nominal income increases (Case 1.1). In Part VII of the book, we will look at the specific assumptions and models that are the basis of alternative macroeconomic and monetary theories.

## Banking Institutions

Most people are familiar with *commercial banks,* having used them to deposit money or to borrow money. Commercial banks are members of a larger group of institutions called **financial intermediaries,** which intervene—or intermediate—between investors and borrowers—by providing investment and lending services. Commercial banks and *thrift institutions* (including savings and loan associations, savings banks, and credit unions) are specifically called **depository intermediaries** because they raise money by providing *deposits.* There are also **nondepository intermediaries** (including mutual funds, insurance companies, and pension funds) that raise money by issuing financial instruments other than deposits.

The importance of commercial banks and other financial intermediaries can be gauged by their large share of the total amount of credit extended to individuals and nonfinancial firms that need to borrow. As shown in Table 1.2, as of year-end 1987, a total of $8.4 trillion of credit had been extended to borrowers, of which all financial intermediaries accounted for 78% and commercial banks alone accounted for 28%.

**TABLE 1.2**
**Sources of Credit**

| | **At Year-End 1987** | |
| | **$ Billions** | **Percentage** |
|---|---|---|
| Financial intermediaries: | | |
| Commercial banks | $2,301 | 28 |
| Thrift institutions | 1,437 | 17 |
| Nondepository intermediaries | 2,796 | 33 |
| Total | 6,534 | 78 |
| Private direct lending: | 1,037 | 12 |
| Federal agency and foreign lending: | 791 | 10 |
| Total credit extended to borrowers | $8,362 | 100 |

**Source:** *Flow of Funds Accounts,* Direct and Indirect Sources of Funds to Credit Markets (Levels), Board of Governors of the Federal Reserve System, 1988.

### The Banking Industry

The banking industry employed about 2.5 million people, or about 2.5% of total U.S. payroll employment, in 1987. Banking firms are generally operated and managed today under the same principles as other business firms. However, there are also many special aspects of banking, as indicated by the following list of topics we will be studying:

- *Bank services* (Chapter 6).
- The *maturity of assets and liabilities*—the time until a deposit or loan is repaid (Chapters 8 and 9).

- *Banking regulation and deregulation* (Chapter 10).
- *Liquidity management*—how banks manage their cash and other assets to meet deposit withdrawals (Chapter 11).
- *Credit risk*—the risk that a borrower defaults on a loan (Chapter 12).
- *Nonbank intermediaries* (Chapter 13).
- *International banking* (Chapter 21).

All financial intermediaries provide **intermediation services**—they raise money with deposits or other instruments, and they make loans or purchase securities. In addition, depository intermediaries (commercial banks and thrift institutions) provide **transfer services**—they offer transaction deposits which people use to write checks.

## Bank Assets, Liabilities, and Balance Sheets

A bank operates as if it has two doors: money comes in one door—as deposits or in similar forms—and goes out the other door—as loans or payments for securities. The deposits coming in represent the bank's **liabilities**—the bank has to return this money later. The loans going out represent the bank's assets—this money will later be repaid to the bank.

A generic bank **balance sheet**—a listing of bank assets and liabilities—is illustrated in Table 1.3. The balance sheet is based on a system of **double-entry accounting.** This means that each time a net change is made on the asset side of the balance sheet, a corresponding change must be made on the liability side of the balance sheet. As a result total assets equal the sum of total liabilities and bank capital.

### TABLE 1.3
### Generic Bank Balance Sheet

| Assets | Liabilities |
|---|---|
| Cash assets | Deposits |
| Investments |   Transaction accounts |
| Loans |   Investment accounts |
| Other assets | Other liabilities |
|  | Total liabilities |
|  | Bank capital |
| Total assets |   Total liabilities and bank capital |

The *liability side* of the balance sheet includes two types of bank deposits—**transaction accounts** and **investment accounts.** In Box 1.5, we compare the features of investment deposits with those of transaction deposits, which we discussed earlier in Box 1.1. Both types of deposits are *federally insured* up to $100,000 per account, so most depositors are

BOX 1.5 MONEY MATTERS

## Investment Deposits

Banks offer special types of nontransaction deposit accounts for investment purposes. *Savings deposits* are meant for small investors—the interest rate is usually quite low, but the money can generally be withdrawn whenever the depositor wishes. *Time deposits* are meant for larger investors—the interest rate is usually higher, but a deposit cannot be withdrawn until its specified maturity date.

The Federal Reserve used to set ceilings that limited the interest rates that banks could pay on savings and time deposits. These interest rate limits were known as **Regulation Q ceilings,** since they were based on Regulation Q of the Federal Reserve Act. Congressional legislation phased out the ceilings in 1980. However, during the 1970s, the Fed had already responded to the demands of institutions and allowed a number of new categories of investment accounts that were not subject to the ceilings.

The result is that there are now various types of nontransaction accounts, but there is not a standard name for all of them. Since they are all held for investment purposes, we will refer to them as *investment accounts.* They are also sometimes called "time deposits" or "nontransaction" accounts.

guaranteed that they will receive back the amount they deposited. In addition to deposits, banks issue other securities—other liabilities—to raise money, but these liabilities are not federally insured.

*Bank capital* is also represented on the liability side of the bank balance sheet. Most commercial banks in the United States are owned by shareholders. Each bank's capital is equal to the sum of the amount invested by the original shareholders and the amounts that have been added or subtracted later, as the bank retained profits or suffered losses. The discussion in Box 1.6 illustrates how a bank uses its capital to *write off* losses on bad loans.

**Bank assets** are shown on the left side of the balance sheet in Table 1.3. *Cash assets* are used when a depositor makes a cash withdrawal or transfers an amount by check. *Investments* are mainly securities that can be sold if the bank needs additional cash to meet withdrawals. *Loans*—made to individuals, business firms, and other borrowers—are the main earning assets of banks. *Other assets* include bank offices and equipment.

### A Microeconomic Issue in Banking

Loan losses now represent a major microeconomic issue for banking. Bank loan problems have been front-page news for some time, including a number of large banks that failed after suffering losses on loans they had made to foreign borrowers, the oil industry, or farmers. As we

BOX 1.6 BANKING BRIEFS

## Bank Capital and Loan Losses

When a bank (or a bank examiner) decides that a loan is not likely to be repaid, the bank has to write off the loan—remove it as an asset from its balance sheet. In double-entry accounting, if an asset item is reduced, an item on the liability side of the balance sheet must be reduced by the same amount. When a loan loss occurs, bank capital is the corresponding liability-side item that is reduced.

Alternatively, a bank can anticipate future loan losses by setting aside part of its capital as a **loan loss reserve**. For example, Citibank—the largest bank in the United States—added $4 billion to its loan loss reserve in 1987—the largest increase ever recorded—in anticipation of future losses on its loans to borrowers in Latin American countries. When a loan is later determined to be a loss, it is written off by deducting the amount from the loan loss reserve.

A bank can report a more stable stream of earnings over time when it uses a loan loss reserve. This is because the bank's profits are reduced each time an addition is made to the loan loss reserve, so that no further reduction in profits occurs when a bad loan has to be written off. Thus, by making steady additions to its loan loss reserve, a bank can avoid the large fall in earnings that would otherwise occur each time it sustains a substantial loan loss.

describe in Box 1.6, banks reduce their capital when they write off bad loans. If a bank's capital actually becomes negative, then the bank is insolvent and it must be closed or merged with a healthy bank.

Table 1.4 shows how the number of banks closed due to financial difficulties has been growing. More than 160 banks a year were closed in 1986 and 1987, and the number is rising. Over 1,500 banks were classified as **problem banks** at the end of 1987—meaning that there is

TABLE 1.4

Banks Closed Due to Financial Difficulties[a]

|  | 1951–1960 | 1961–1970 | 1971–1980 | 1981–1985 | 1986–1987 |
|---|---|---|---|---|---|
| Average number of banks closed *per year* | 4 | 6 | 8 | 60 | 161 |
| Number of problem banks[b] | [c] | [c] | 217 | 1,140 | 1,575 |

[a] Commercial banks and savings banks insured by the Federal Deposit Insurance Corporation (FDIC).
[b] Banks identified as "problem banks" by the FDIC, at year-end 1980, 1985, and 1987, respectively.
[c] Figures on problem banks were not recorded during these periods.
**Source:** *1987 Statistical Abstract of the United States,* Table 810, U.S. Department of Commerce, and *Annual Report,* Federal Deposit Insurance Corporation.

a distinct chance they will fail. The situation does not approach the calamity of the Great Depression, when over 4,000 banks failed in 1933 alone. But it is the most serious banking crisis since then.

Loan losses and failing banks create pressure on the policymakers—Congress, the Fed, and other banking regulators—to rectify the situation. The federal deposit insurance agencies also face serious financial problems as a result of bank failures. There are no simple solutions, but we will look at the possibilities when we discuss bank regulation and deregulation in Chapter 10.

## A Macroeconomic Issue in Banking

The main macroeconomic issue for banking concerns how banks affect monetary policy. In order to see the connection, suppose that the Federal Reserve tries to raise the money supply $M$ with the goal of increasing nominal income $Y$. If there were no banking system, then the money supply would consist only of currency—the quantity of which can be directly controlled by the Federal Reserve. Thus, based on the quantity equation of exchange, $MV = Y$, the Fed would reach its target for nominal income $Y$ as long as the velocity of money $V$ was constant, or at least predictable.

Taking the banking system into account, the Federal Reserve faces two further complications: the money supply may become harder to control; and the velocity of money $V$ may become harder to predict. Each of these complications makes it more difficult for the Fed to reach a specific target for nominal income.

A banking system makes it more difficult for the Fed to *control the money supply* because bank transaction deposits make up the greater part of the M1 money supply. A change in bank transaction deposits might thus cause the money supply to change by a different amount, or even in a different direction from what the Fed desires.

A banking system makes the *velocity of money fluctuate* unexpectedly when people shift their deposits between transaction accounts and investment accounts, the two main categories of bank deposits. Since transaction deposits are part of M1, but investment deposits are not, these shifts affect the M1 velocity of money.

If banking institutions make it more difficult for the Fed to carry out monetary policy, a solution might be for the Fed to regulate how banks affect both the money supply and the velocity of money. However, there is a possible cost to more regulation, since the banking system may then not provide its services as efficiently. This trade-off between the microeconomic efficiency of banking and the macroeconomic effectiveness of monetary policy played a role in the 1980 deregulation of the banking system: the deregulation may have made the banking system more efficient, but it has also made monetary policy harder to manage effectively.

## Credit Facilities and the Financial System

Money and banking are important components of the total spectrum of securities, institutions, and markets that encompass the *financial system*. The overall purpose of the financial system is to transfer *credit*, from people and firms who want to lend or invest money, to other people and firms who want to borrow it.

### Interest Rates

An **interest rate** measures the cost of borrowing money as a percentage of the amount borrowed. For example, if you borrow $1,000 for a year, and repay the loan with a single payment of $1,100 at the end of the year, the interest cost is $100 ($1,100 − $1,000) and the interest rate is 10% ($100/$1,000). An interest rate also measures the return earned from lending or investing money. For example, if you invest $1,000 in a one-year bank time deposit at a 6% annual interest rate, at the end of the year you will have accumulated $1,060 ($1,000 x 1.06).

There are literally thousands of different interest rates in the U.S. economy, each one referring to a particular type of loan or security which individuals or firms use to borrow or lend money. Even at your local bank, you are likely to find a dozen or more interest rates:

- Each type of deposit account generally has a different interest rate. Transaction deposits tend to earn lower interest rates, while investment deposits (time deposits) usually earn higher rates. Longer-term investment deposits—for which you have to leave your money for a longer period of time—generally earn the highest interest rate.
- Each type of loan may also have a different interest rate. Banks generally charge their lowest interest rates on loans to high-quality business borrowers because these borrowers are very likely to repay their loans. Relatively low interest rates are also charged on mortgage loans (for home purchases) and auto loans (for car purchases) made to individuals, because a bank can take over the house or the car if the borrower fails to repay the loan. In contrast, banks generally charge their highest interest rates on credit card loans, since borrowers fail relatively often to repay these loans.

Since all interest rates tend to rise and fall together over time, economists often refer to **the market interest rate,** as if the economy had a single representative interest rate. The interest rate on U.S. Treasury securities—securities issued by the U.S. Treasury to finance the federal government's budget deficit—is a good example of such a representative interest rate. However, there are actually many Treasury security interest rates, each reflecting a different maturity date (at which the Treasury will repay the amount borrowed). Two of these interest rates—the **Treasury bill rate** (referring to short-term Treasury securities) and the **Treasury bond rate** (referring to long-term Treasury securities)—are illustrated in Figure 1.5.

FIGURE 1.5
**Interest Rates on U.S. Treasury Securities**

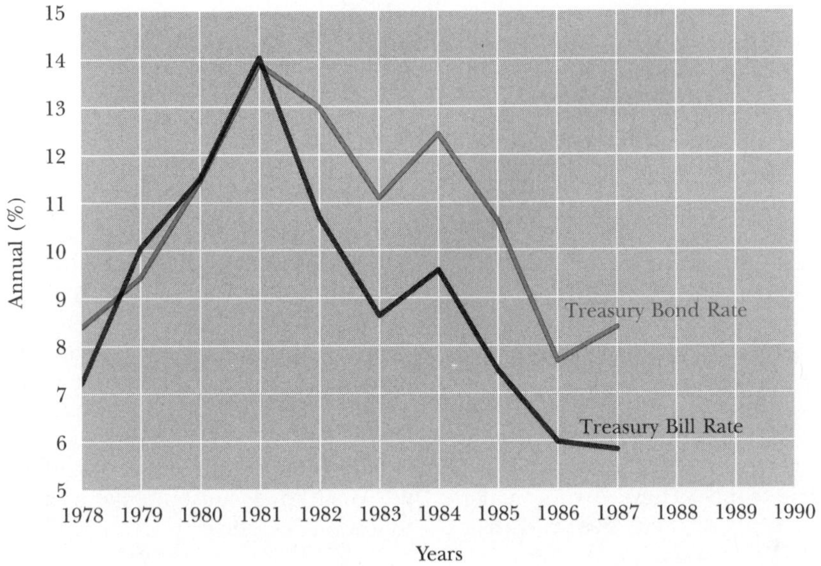

The Treasury bill interest rate refers to short-term (1 year or less) securities issued by the U.S. Treasury. The Treasury bond interest rate refers to long-term (over 1 year) securities issued by the U.S. Treasury. **Source:** *Economic Report of the President*, February, 1988.

It is evident from the figure that interest rates have fluctuated substantially in recent years. Many factors—including monetary policy, the rate of inflation, and the growth rate of real GNP—have caused the interest rates to change in this fashion. One of our early tasks is to consider how interest rates are determined, which we will do in Chapters 3, 4, and 5.

## Financial Markets

**Financial markets** expedite credit transactions between lenders and borrowers. Lenders and borrowers could transact directly between themselves, but the cost of finding a suitable partner and designing a loan or security is generally very high. Financial markets therefore arise to carry out credit transactions efficiently and inexpensively. Various financial markets specialize in trading different types of securities—for example, bonds (such as Treasury bonds) are traded in bond markets, while common stocks are traded in stock markets.

The financial markets are managed and organized by several groups of institutions. The commercial banks and other financial intermediaries we just discussed are one such group. Security exchanges, such as the New York Stock Exchange, are a second group of institutions that op-

## The Banking System During the Crash of 1987

On October 19, 1987, the financial system of the United States received an enormous shock: a one-day stock market decline of over 500 points in the Dow-Jones Index, meaning that stockholders lost about 25%, or almost $1 trillion, of their stock values. Many feared the financial system was about to suffer "meltdown." But it did not, and one reason was that the banking system performed very well during the crisis.

The stock market crash created immediate fears that firms serving the stock market—such as stockbrokers—might become bankrupt. These firms make stock investments of their own, and they lend a lot of money to other firms and people who buy stocks. The fear was not only that these firms might fail, but also that there might be a chain reaction with failures causing further failures. To avert a chain reaction, the banking system made huge loans available to stockbrokers, with the result that no major stockbrokers failed.

After the crash, investors remained fearful of further declines in stock prices, so they continued to switch some of their investments to safer assets. The obvious choice was federally insured bank deposits, which grew substantially in the weeks following the crash.

erate financial markets. Brokers and dealers, who transmit and act on buy and sell orders for securities, are a third group of institutions. Of course, these groups also interact: an interesting example arose during the stock market crash of October 1987, as discussed in Box 1.7.

We will look at the financial system in Chapter 5, including how security prices and interest rates are determined.

## The Market for U.S. Treasury Securities

We can get a preliminary glimpse of how a financial market operates by looking at the market for U.S. Treasury securities. This market performs the microeconomic functions of distributing Treasury securities to investors and of determining prices and interest rates for the securities. The market also serves a macroeconomic function related to the money supply, as we will now see.

The Treasury security market is active because the securities are safe and there are lots of them. The federal government has been running large deficits in recent years and new issues of Treasury securities are the primary means of financing these deficits. The outstanding amount of this debt was about $2 trillion at the end of 1987.

Table 1.5 shows how the market for Treasury securities functioned during 1987. The Treasury issued $142 billion of new securities—close to the government's deficit for the year. Foreign investors were the largest group of buyers, followed by households and the two types of financial intermediaries.

**TABLE 1.5**

**The Market For U.S. Government Securities**

**Calendar Year 1987 (Dollars in billions)**

| | |
|---|---|
| Supply (net new issues) | 142 |
| Demand (by type of buyer) | |
| Foreign | 37 |
| Households | 28 |
| Depository intermediaries | 25 |
| Nondepository intermediaries | 24 |
| Federal Reserve | 11 |
| Business | 10 |
| Other | 7 |

**Source:** *Flow of Funds Accounts*, Release Z.1, Board of Governors of the Federal Reserve System, 1988.

Purchases and sales of Treasury securities by the Federal Reserve are the key connection between the credit markets and monetary policy. The Fed's control of the money supply is based largely on its ability to buy and sell Treasury securities. For example, the Federal Reserve purchases of Treasury securities during 1987 contributed to a larger money supply. The connection is that the Fed pays for its security purchases with currency or the equivalent, which either counts directly as part of the M1 money supply, or is the basis for the transaction deposits component of the money supply. We will examine the steps in this process in detail when we study in Part IV how the money supply is determined.

## Chapter Summary

1. There are various definitions of the money supply. The narrow definition, the M1 money supply, is the sum of currency, travelers checks, and bank transaction accounts (checking account balances). The annual income velocity of money equals income divided by the average value of the money supply.

2. Money serves four microeconomic functions. As the medium of exchange, money expedites the exchange of goods and services, and as the store of value, money provides a means of holding wealth. It serves as the unit of account for measuring prices and wealth, and as the unit of deferred payment for loans.

3. Commercial banks, part of the group of institutions known as financial intermediaries, offer two basic services. They provide intermediation services by attracting money (as deposits) and by lending money to other people who need to borrow. They provide transfer services through transaction deposits, which people use to write checks.

4. Money and banking serve both microeconomic functions—the efficient exchange of goods and the allocation of credit to borrowers—and macroeconomic functions—the determination of such aggregate variables as nominal income, real income, and the price level.

5. The Federal Reserve, as the central bank of the United States, operates monetary policy. The goals of monetary policy include the growth of real income and price level stability. The Fed uses its control of the money supply to achieve these goals.

6. The quantity equation of exchange shows how the money supply, income, and the price level are linked together. An increase in the money supply may cause changes in nominal income, real income, or the price level, depending on how each of the variables responds. Monetary the-ory studies the macroeconomic process through which the money supply determines the price level and real income.

7. Money and banking operate as components of the financial system consisting of securities, institutions, and markets. Interest rates represent the cost of borrowing money, and the return to be made in lending or investing it. The financial markets, which include security exchanges, brokers and dealers, and financial intermediaries, expedite borrowing and lending transactions.

## Key Terms

Balance sheet

Bank assets and liabilities

Bank intermediary and transfer services

Currency

Depository and nondepository financial intermediaries

Double-entry accounting

Federal Reserve (the Fed)

Financial markets

Interest rates:

Market

Treasury bill

Treasury bond

Investment and transaction deposits

M1 and M2 money supply

Macroeconomics and microeconomics

Monetary policy

Monetary theory

Monetary functions:

Medium of exchange

Standard of deferred payment

Store of value

Unit of account

Price level

Real and nominal income

Quantity equation of exchange

Velocity of money

## Study Questions

1. Why are both currency and bank transaction deposits included in the M1 money supply? What are some differences between them?

2. Why is there so much currency in circulation per person in the United States? Why are there so many transaction deposits per person?

3. The value of $100 bills in circulation is very high, and it is interesting to compare their rate of growth with the rate of growth of economic activity. Which has been

growing faster? What might your answer indicate about the growth of the underground economy? Below are some data to work with.

| Year | $100 Bills ($ Billions) | GNP ($ Billions) |
|------|-------------------------|------------------|
| 1970 | 12.1 | 1,015.5 |
| 1975 | 23.1 | 1,598.4 |
| 1980 | 49.3 | 2,732.0 |
| 1983 | 67.5 | 3,405.7 |
| 1987 | 100.4 | 4,486.2 |

4. What is your own income velocity of money? Show what you are assuming and how you have calculated it.

5. What is the *annual* income velocity of money for a household that earns $4,000 a month, is paid twice a month, and spends all of its income each month?

6. Why is the quantity equation of exchange (QEE) an identity? What information is needed to use it to analyze how an increase in the money supply might affect real income.

7. An economy initially has a money supply of $800 billion, a price level of 1.0, and an annual GNP velocity of money of 5. What is the current annual value of GNP? If the money supply rises by 10%, while the price level and the velocity of money are unchanged, by how much will GNP rise?

8. Starting again with the initial situation in Question 7, suppose that the money supply rises by 10%, and that the price level and real income each rise by 3%. What is the resulting value for the velocity of money?

9. In what sense does a bank balance sheet have to balance? If a bank suffers a loan loss and must write the loan off as an asset, what other item in the balance sheet has to change?

10. Suppose you invest $5,000 for one year in a bank time deposit at a 6% annual interest rate. How much interest will you earn during the year? What will be the total amount in your account at the end of the year?

## Recommended Reading

*There are many popular and instructive books about money and banking. Here are some good ones:*

Martin Mayer, *The Bankers*, Ballantine, New York, 1976.

Martin Mayer, *The Money Bazaars*, Mentor, New York, 1984.

Adam Smith, *The Money Game*, Random House, New York, 1976.

Adam Smith, *Paper Money*, Random House, New York, 1968.

Adam Smith, *Super-Money*, Popular Library, 1972.

*There are also several books in which papers and readings on money and banking have been collected together:*

Donald Fraser and Peter Rose, *Financial Institutions and Markets in a Changing World*, Business Publications Inc., Plano, Tex., 1984.

Thomas Havrilesky and Robert Schweitzer, *Contemporary Developments in Financial Institutions and Markets*, Harlan Davidson, Arlington Heights, Ill., 1983.

Thomas Havrilesky, Robert Schweitzer, and John Boorman, *Dynamics of Banking*, Harlan Davidson, Arlington Heights, Ill., 1985.

Murray Polakoff and Thomas Durkin, *Financial Institutions and Markets*, 2nd edition, Houghton Mifflin, Boston, 1981.

James A. Wilcox, *Current Readings on Money, Banking, and Financial Markets*, Little, Brown, Boston, 1987.

*Two books by Irving Fisher to look at are:*

Irving Fisher, *The Purchasing Power of Money*, Macmillan, New York, 1911.

Irving Fisher, *The Theory of Interest*, Macmillan, New York, 1930.

# Trade and Payments Systems

*"The two most beautiful words in the English language are 'check enclosed.'"*

**Dorothy Parker**

Money and banking are almost always involved when people use trade to exchange goods and services with other people. Consequently, a clear understanding of why people trade, and how trade and payments systems are arranged, is useful for studying the basic functions of money and banking.

To see how trade works, let us start by imagining that a person has to manage his economic affairs without the benefit of trade. To illustrate this, we will use—with an occasional twist—Daniel Defoe's story of Robinson Crusoe, a lone, shipwrecked sailor on an uninhabited island. After landing on the island, one of Crusoe's first priorities is to organize his economic life. This involves finding resources, choosing the best production techniques, and deciding which goods to consume. The result is that Crusoe produces apples and bacon (from hogs), but not much else. So, although he uses his resources well, Crusoe's economic life is quite dismal without trade.

Then Crusoe discovers a neighboring island, with another shipwrecked sailor—we will call her Friday—who is in a similar state. Fortunately, it turns out that Friday's island has different resources, so Crusoe can specialize in producing apples and Friday can specialize in producing bacon. They then use barter trade—exchanging apples for bacon—so that each consumes larger amounts of the goods than either could produce alone.

Later, Crusoe discovers there are many similar islands close by. Since other goods are produced on these islands, and each island produces one good at a relatively low cost, there are opportunities for further trading. Crusoe, of course, wants to buy goods from the islands that sell them at the lowest prices and to sell his apples and bacon to the islands where he can obtain the highest prices. But he needs a better system for trading: the simple system of barter, which worked acceptably well between Crusoe and Friday, is too cumbersome when there are many traders.

**To handle more complex trade, it would behoove Crusoe to introduce money and banking for the island economies. This would further expand the benefit derived from trade. In this chapter, we will investigate exactly how money and banking perform this valuable function.**

We will start with a demonstration that trade allows people to consume more goods and services, or a more varied selection. (Hereafter, when we say goods, we will mean goods and services.) Then we will evaluate the costs and benefits of different trading systems. In the process, we will follow the stages of development, from barter to money, and from money to money and banking. The main goal is to see why trading with money and banking is generally more efficient than any of the alternatives.

## The Principles of Trading Systems

A basic purpose of an economy is to determine how goods are produced, consumed, and traded. These all represent economic activities because scarce resources limit production, while people usually desire unlimited consumption. We will first look at how people make decisions regarding production, consumption, and trade. To do so, we will review three important tools of microeconomic analysis: the *production possibility frontier, consumer indifference curves,* and the *market trading line.*

### Production Decisions

The combinations of goods that can be produced in an economy are illustrated by a **production possibility frontier.** As an example, we will look at the combinations of apples and bacon that Crusoe can produce on his island. Crusoe's production possibility frontier is illustrated in Figure 2.1, where the curve $P'P$ shows the best combinations of apples and bacon that Crusoe can produce, given his labor, land, raw materials, and technology. For example, at point $P_0$ Crusoe produces 12 units of apples and 16 units of bacon.

The production possibility frontier has a negative slope because there is a *trade-off in production*—if more resources (labor, land, raw materials) are used for apple orchards, then fewer resources are left for pig sties, and conversely. For example, 20 units of apples are produced if all the resources are allocated to apple production (point $P'$), whereas 20 units of bacon are produced if all the resources are allocated to bacon production (point $P$).

The curve *P'P* shows the best combinations of apples and bacon that can be produced. If no bacon is produced, then 20 units of apples are produced at point *P'*. If no apples are produced, then 20 units of bacon are produced at point *P*. Between these extremes, there is a trade-off in production: if more apples are produced, then less bacon can be produced.

FIGURE 2.1
**The Production Possibility Frontier**

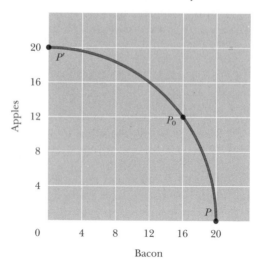

The production possibility frontier also becomes flatter proceeding from right to left. This means that each successive unit of foregone bacon production yields a smaller gain in apple production. This is a common feature of production because, as the output of a good (apples) rises, the increase in its production is derived from poorer quality resources (the best resources having been used first).

## Consumption Decisions

The level of satisfaction—or what economists call **utility**—that a person receives from consuming alternative combinations of goods is represented by the person's **indifference curves.** As an example, we will look at the utility that Crusoe receives from consuming various combinations of apples and bacon. Crusoe's indifference curves are illustrated in Figure 2.2, where each curve shows the combinations of apples and bacon that provide Crusoe with the indicated level of utility. For example, at point $C_0$, Crusoe obtains utility level II by consuming 12 units of apples and 16 units of bacon.

The negative slope of each indifference curve indicates there is *a trade-off in consumption*—on a given indifference curve (which means the utility level is constant), if more bacon is consumed, then fewer apples can be consumed. The level of utility rises in the northeast direction in the diagram, since more of both goods is preferred to less. Therefore, indifference curve III is at a higher level of utility than II, and II is higher than I. A person would maximize his or her utility by choosing a combination of apples and bacon located on the highest possible indifference curve.

Each indifference curve represents the various combinations of apples and bacon that provide the indicated level of utility. For example, each of the indicated points on curve II provides the same level of satisfaction. But any combination of apples and bacon on curve III is preferable to every combination on curve II. That is, utility levels rise in the northeast direction, so indifference curve I represents the lowest utility and indifference curve III represents the highest.

FIGURE 2.2
**Indifference Curves**

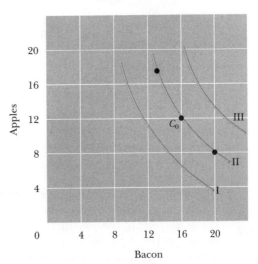

## Production and Consumption Without Trade

Without trading partners, a person can only consume what he or she produces. To see how Crusoe determines his production and consumption of apples and bacon without trade, we combine the production possibility frontier of Figure 2.1 and the indifference curves of Figure 2.2, as illustrated in Figure 2.3. Point $E_0$—corresponding to point $P_0$ in Figure 2.1 and point $C_0$ in Figure 2.2—is Crusoe's best choice for production and consumption. That is, the combination of 12 units of apples and 16 units of bacon provides Crusoe the highest possible utility, be-

Without trading opportunities, an individual chooses the point along the production possibility frontier that provides the highest level of utility. This occurs at point $E_0$, where the production possibility frontier is tangent to indifference curve II.

FIGURE 2.3
**Production and Consumption Without Trade**

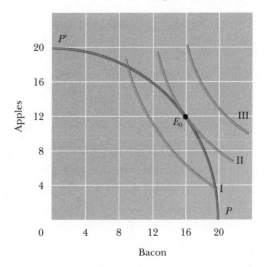

cause point $E_0$ lies on the highest possible indifference curve along his production possibility frontier. This is true because production possibility frontier $P'P$ and indifference curve II are tangent at point $E_0$, indicating that the trade-off in production (the slope of $P'P$) and the trade-off in consumption (the slope of curve II) are equal for the two goods at point $E_0$.[1]

## Trading Decisions

Market trading allows people to produce different combinations of goods than they consume, so they can obtain higher levels of utility. The combinations of goods available for consumption with trading are illustrated by a **market trading line** (also called a budget line). Crusoe's market trading line $T'T$ is illustrated in Figure 2.4, for the case where Crusoe produces at point $P_1$ (16 units of apples and 12 units of bacon). Line $T'T$ is tangent to the production possibility frontier at point $P_1$. Among the points on the trading line, Crusoe chooses to consume at point $C_1$ (10 units of apples and 20 units of bacon). By moving down the trading line from point $P_1$ to point $C_1$, selling 6 units of apples and buying 8 units of bacon, Crusoe exchanges a combination of produced goods for a more satisfactory (higher utility) combination of goods to consume.

A trading line must touch (or pass inside) the production possibility frontier at the combination of goods produced, such as at point $P_1$ in Figure 2.4. The slope of the trading line is negative because there is a *trade-off in trading:* the person has to sell one good (apples) in order to buy the other good (bacon). Moreover, the slope of the trading line

---

[1] If this tangency condition did not hold at point $E_0$, then Crusoe could improve his situation. For example, suppose indifference curve II were steeper than the production possibility frontier at point $E_0$. Then Crusoe could obtain a higher level of utility by moving production to the right, producing fewer apples and more bacon.

The market trading line shows the trading possibilities that are available. To move from point $P_1$ to point $C_1$, Crusoe must sell one good (6 units of apples) in order to buy the other good (8 units of bacon). The slope of the market trading line represents the relative price of bacon in terms of apples—the amount of apples sold relative to the amount of bacon received.

FIGURE 2.4
**The Market Trading Line**

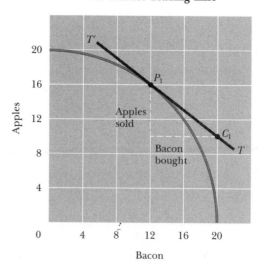

represents the *relative price of bacon in terms of apples*—how many apples Crusoe must sell to obtain one unit of bacon. A flatter trading line would indicate a lower relative price for bacon—Crusoe would have to sell fewer apples to obtain a unit of bacon. A lower relative price for bacon is equivalent to a higher relative price for apples.

## Production and Consumption with Trade

We can now see why Crusoe's welfare is enhanced with a trading partner. We will assume that Crusoe's trading partner, Friday, will buy apples at a high relative price and will sell bacon at a low relative price. Crusoe may therefore raise his utility by selling apples to Friday at the high relative price, while buying bacon from her at the low relative price.

The trading is illustrated in Figure 2.5, where the trading opportunities available to Crusoe are determined by the slope and position of the trading line $T'T$. Since Friday will trade at a low relative price for bacon, the slope of the trading line is relatively flat. Crusoe would prefer to position the trading line as far to the northeast as possible (to reach the highest possible level of utility), but the line still must touch the production possibility frontier at one point—Crusoe must produce at least the amount of apples he wants to sell.

Crusoe's trading line is therefore tangent to the production possibility curve at the desired point of production, point $P_1$. Crusoe chooses point $P_1$ because it provides him with the best trading possibilities. Responding to the high relative price of apples, Crusoe produces more apples at point $P_1$ with trade (16 apples) that he would produce at point $E_0$ without trade (12 apples).

Given that production occurs at point $P_1$, Crusoe may consume at any point along the trading line $T'T$. The best choice for consumption—which maximizes utility—occurs at point $C_1$, where the *trade-off in con-*

With trading opportunities, Crusoe chooses point $P_1$ for production, while he chooses point $C_1$ (beyond the production possibility frontier) for consumption. The slope of the trading line is determined by the relative price of bacon in terms of apples. The trading line is positioned as far to the northeast as possible, but it must touch the production possibility frontier at the point of production, point $P_1$. Since point $C_1$ provides the highest possible level of utility along the trading line, Crusoe sells apples and buys bacon to move from point $P_1$ (production) to point $C_1$ (consumption).

FIGURE 2.5
**Production and Consumption with Trade**

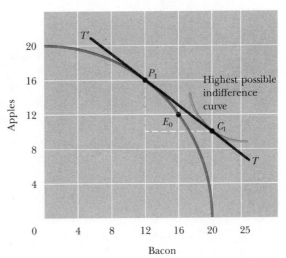

*sumption* (the slope of the indifference curve) equals the *trade-off in trading* (the slope of the trading line). The result is that trading allows Crusoe to *separate* the production decision (at point $P_1$) from the consumption decision (at point $C_1$).

## The Gains from Trade

There are **gains from trade** because Crusoe is better off when he consumes at point $C_1$ (with trade) than he was at point $E_0$ (without trade). In other words, trade allows the consumption point $C_1$ to lie outside of Crusoe's production possibility frontier. These gains arise because Crusoe sells high-priced apples, while he buys low-priced bacon.

The gains from trade are reflected, of course, in everyday experience: most people specialize in the production of one or a small number of goods, then trade to obtain a wide range of goods for consumption. Similar considerations apply in international trade, where countries produce and export certain goods (such as wine, cars, or computers), while they import a wider set of goods from abroad.

Box 2.1 provides a numerical example that summarizes our main results for production, consumption, and trade.

## The Costs of Trade

Our discussion of Crusoe and his gains from trade has so far treated the costs of trade as if they were zero. In practice, trade usually involves costs, often significant ones. Crusoe, for example, has to spend time, energy, and resources finding trading partners on other islands.

Trading costs reduce the gains from trade because they alter the slope of the trading line. This is illustrated in Figure 2.6, where $Y'P_1Y$ is a

Trading costs alter the slope of the trading line, from the "free" trading line $T'P_1T$ to the "costly" trading line $Y'P_1Y$. The vertical distance between the two lines represents the trading costs measured in terms of apples. This distance widens further from point $P_1$ because as trade increases so do trading costs.

FIGURE 2.6
**Production and Consumption with Costly Trading**

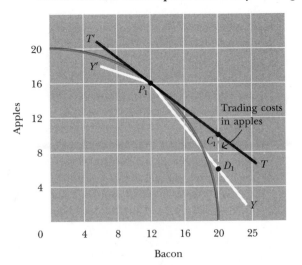

BOX 2.1 IN DEPTH

## A Numerical Example of Production, Consumption, and Trade

### Production and Consumption Without Trade

The production possibility frontier is expressed as:

$$A^2 + B^2 = 400, \tag{2.1}$$

where $A$ is the amount of apples produced (or consumed) and $B$ is the amount of bacon produced (or consumed). The production of apples $A$ and bacon $B$ can include such combinations $\{A, B\}$ as $\{20, 0\}$, $\{16, 12\}$, $\{12, 16\}$, and $\{0, 20\}$. Without trade, the combination that provides the highest level of utility is chosen for production and consumption. For example, in Figure 2.3, this is the combination $\{12, 16\}$.

### Production and Consumption with Trade

The market trading line is expressed as:

$$A = 25 - \left(\frac{3}{4}\right) B \tag{2.2}$$

where $A$ is the amount of apples consumed and $B$ is the amount of bacon consumed. The coefficient of $B$ (the slope of the line), $-3/4$, indicates that 3 units of apples have to be exchanged for every 4 units of bacon. As illustrated in Figure 2.5, the $\{A, B\}$ combination $\{10, 20\}$ is consumed. Given that Crusoe produces the $\{A, B\}$ combination $(16, 12)$, this means he sells 6 units of apples and buys 8 units of bacon. There are gains from trade because Crusoe could not produce the $\{A, B\}$ combination $\{10, 20\}$ himself.

"costly" trading line that takes the costs of trade into account, while $T'P_1T$ is the "free" trading line represented in the preceding discussion. The trading costs, measured in terms of apples, equal the vertical distance between the free trade line $T'P_1T$ and the costly trading line $Y'P_1Y$. This distance widens as Crusoe consumes further from point $P_1$ because the volume of trade rises.[2] At point $P_1$, the two trading lines coincide because there is no trade (production and consumption coincide), and therefore there are no costs of trade.

The altered slope of the costly trading line $Y'P_1Y$ reduces Crusoe's gains from trade. Crusoe is worse off—he gets fewer apples—if he has to consume at point $D_1$ on the costly trading line rather than at point $C_1$ on the free trade line. This is why it is important to take trading costs into account when making trading plans.

[2] Of course, Crusoe will try to arrange his trade so as to minimize trading costs. We are assuming that these considerations are already reflected in the position of the costly trading line $Y'P_1Y$.

We will next look at two specific types of trading costs: search costs and trading system costs.

### Search Costs

Imagine that you have moved to a new town and must decide where to buy your groceries. You will have to invest time and energy, and perhaps money, to find the grocery store that offers the best selection and prices. Or imagine that you are a laid-off worker having trouble finding a new job in a recession. The costs of searching for work in this case may be so high that you give up and withdraw from the labor force altogether, in effect deciding not to trade. Both of these examples illustrate the **search costs** of trading—the costs of finding a trading partner and arriving at a mutually satisfactory price. The costs may be represented by wasted time, demanding negotiations, or cash expenses.

### Trading System Costs

When the exchange of goods makes use of public facilities that are available to everyone in a trading system, then there will also be **trading system costs**—the costs of providing the public facilities. People are usually willing to pay the costs of public facilities if their search costs are reduced by a larger amount. Markets and a medium of exchange represent two key public trading facilities.

*Markets* can take many forms, ranging from the trading fairs of medieval times to modern shopping centers. Their common feature is that they reduce search costs by placing all of the buyers and sellers in one area. The rentals paid for market locations represent trading system costs.

A *medium of exchange* is a commodity that serves as the means of payment in an economy. One trading system cost of a medium of exchange is that the commodity used for trading is not available for production or consumption. For example, gold used as a medium of exchange cannot be used in jewelry or in industrial applications.

## Trading Systems

Economies generally have large numbers of people and firms who wish to engage in trade. **Trading systems** represent the set of arrangements, laws, and conventions that determine how trade is carried out. Trading systems have usually evolved through an increase in public trading facilities—mostly markets and a medium of exchange. Public facilities were adopted because they reduced total trading costs (substituted low trading system costs for high search costs). Moreover, as more effective commodities were introduced as the medium of exchange, there were further reductions in trading costs.

Trading systems can be distinguished in various ways. One distinction is between *multilateral trade*—which always involves three or more traders—and *bilateral trade*—which involves precisely two traders. Another distinction is between *barter trade*—where commodities are exchanged only for other commodities—and *monetary exchange*—where the medium of exchange is "money." We will see that bilateral trade based on monetary exchange is dominant in most modern payments systems.

## The Standard Trading Problem

To evaluate the advantages and disadvantages of various trading systems, we need a standard of comparison. We will use the **standard trading problem,** illustrated in Table 2.1, for this purpose.

The *problem* is that the four traders—A, B, C, and D—have each produced 1 unit of a specific good—trader A has produced 1 unit of apples, trader B 1 unit of bacon, and so on—but each wants to consume a different good—trader A wants to consume 1 unit of bacon, trader B wants 1 unit of corn, and so on.

A *solution* to the standard trading problem is a set of transactions that allows the traders to exchange the goods they have produced for the goods they want to consume. For example, a transaction in which trader A ships one unit of apples to trader D—thus satisfying trader D's consumption choice—will be presented as:

$$\{A, 1 \text{ apple}, D\}.$$

By looking at the transactions carried out in each trading system, and at how well each trading system solves the standard trading problem, we will have a basis for comparing the alternative systems.

We have used several assumptions to simplify the standard trading problem.[3] For one thing, each trader produces just one good and consumes just one good. For another thing, the price of each good equals $1 per unit of that good. This way, trade is balanced whenever a trader delivers one unit of a good and receives one unit of another good.

---

[3] See Jurg Niehans, *The Theory of Money*, The Johns Hopkins University Press, Baltimore, paperback edition, 1980, for a more general development of the standard trading problem.

**TABLE 2.1**
**The Standard Trading Problem**

|  | Production | | | | Desired Consumption | | | |
|---|---|---|---|---|---|---|---|---|
|  | Apples | Bacon | Corn | Dates | Apples | Bacon | Corn | Dates |
| Trader A | 1 | 0 | 0 | 0 | 0 | 1 | 0 | 0 |
| Trader B | 0 | 1 | 0 | 0 | 0 | 0 | 1 | 0 |
| Trader C | 0 | 0 | 1 | 0 | 0 | 0 | 0 | 1 |
| Trader D | 0 | 0 | 0 | 1 | 1 | 0 | 0 | 0 |

Each trader initially has one unit of the good listed in his or her row under the heading *production*. Each trader wants to consume one unit of the good listed in his or her row under the heading *desired consumption*. For example, trader A has produced one unit of apples, but wants to consume one unit of bacon. The problem is to arrange trade so that all of the traders obtain their desired consumption.

## Multilateral Trade

**Multilateral trade** occurs when trader A sells a good to trader B, but is paid with a good from some third trader, say trader C. Multilateral trade thus necessarily involves at least three traders. In early American history, for example, multilateral trade occurred with ships that left southern American ports with cotton, which was traded in England for manufacturing equipment, which was later sold in northern American ports for manufactured goods, which were brought back to the South.

Multilateral trade must have **overall balance:** all goods shipped by traders must be received by other traders. However, multilateral trade *does not have* **bilateral balance** for each pair of traders: when trader A sends a good to trader B, trader B may not send a good to trader A.

Multilateral trades that solve the standard trading problem are shown in Table 2.2. To verify that these trades are a solution, return to Table 2.1 and notice that each transaction allows one trader to exchange the good he or she produces for the good he or she consumes. We can also see that multilateral trade has overall balance, but it is not balanced on a bilateral basis between any pair of traders.

The solution in Table 2.2 illustrates a key advantage and a key problem of multilateral trading. The advantage is that trade occurs with the *minimum number of transactions*—in this case, four—so other things being equal, trading costs will be low. The problem is that *someone must monitor the system* to make sure that all of the transactions occur. Otherwise, trader D, having received a unit of apples from trader A, might not ship his dates to trader C (although this is required in transaction 4). In the jargon of financial markets, trader D is then guilty of **nonperformance.**

You might think that nonperformance could be eliminated with laws that require each trader to fulfill his or her obligation. However, laws can be enforced only if the culprit is identified. The monitoring problem of multilateral trade arises because it is hard to identify the culprit. In Table 2.2, for example, if trader C fails to receive her dates, although she has sent corn to trader B, she might think trader B is responsible, even though trader D is really the culprit.

The upshot is that multilateral trade must be monitored by a central agency which knows what each trader is supposed to ship. Since cen-

---

**TABLE 2.2**

**The Multilateral Solution to the Trading Problem**

| Transaction | | Result |
| --- | --- | --- |
| Transaction 1: | {A, 1 apple, D} | D is satisfied |
| Transaction 2: | {B, 1 bacon, A} | A is satisfied |
| Transaction 3: | {C, 1 corn, B} | B is satisfied |
| Transaction 4: | {D, 1 date, C} | C is satisfied |

In transaction 1, trader A sends 1 unit of apples to trader D. Since trader D wanted to consume apples, trader D is satisfied. Similarly, in transaction 2, trader B sends 1 unit of bacon to trader A, and this satisfies trader A. The transactions represent a solution to the standard trading problem because each of the traders is satisfied by one of the transactions. The transactions represent multilateral trade because trade is *not* balanced between any pair of traders. For example, trader B sends 1 unit of bacon to trader A, but trader A does not send any good back to trader B. Trader A, however, does send 1 unit of apples to trader D, so the overall trade is balanced.

tralized monitoring is costly to arrange, multilateral trading systems are uncommon in the markets for goods and services. Multilateral trading is more common in financial markets because trading is centralized and regulated on financial exchanges, such as the New York Stock Exchange.

## Bilateral Trade

To deal with the monitoring problem, most markets for goods and services use **bilateral trading,** consisting of two transactions, one in which trader A sends a good to trader B, and a balancing transaction in which trader B sends a good to trader A. Thus,

$$\{A, 1 \text{ apple}, B\} \text{ and } \{B, 1 \text{ bacon}, A\}$$

is a bilateral trade. Bilateral balance characterizes most trades: when people buy things, they normally pay for them. The item used to make payment is sometimes called the **quid pro quo** (this for that). In barter trading systems, the quid pro quo is another commodity, whereas in monetary exchange systems, the quid pro quo is money.

Bilateral trade is monitored on a *decentralized* basis—each trader monitors his or her own trades. So if there is nonperformance, the culprit is known, and laws can be enforced to make the culprit pay. This is why bilateral trade (with decentralized monitoring) tends to be less costly than multilateral trade (with centralized monitoring).

## Barter Trade

We will now look at barter trade to illustrate how bilateral trading works. In all barter systems, commodities are exchanged only for other commodities. More specifically, we will begin with **direct barter**—in which all commodities received through trade are *consumed* directly. Using our standard trading problem, we will see that direct barter is usually an inefficient trading system.

### Direct Barter

For direct barter to occur, there must be a **double coincidence of wants**—each trader must want to consume the good that another trader wants to sell. This feature of direct barter was emphasized by W. S. Jevons (1835–1882) in his classic study, *Money and the Mechanism of Exchange*. Jevons' point was that direct barter is an inefficient form of exchange because the need for a double coincidence of wants reduces the opportunities for trade. In other words, the search costs of finding a suitable trading partner tend to be very high with direct barter.

The inefficiency of direct barter is illustrated clearly in the standard trading problem of Table 2.1. In fact, direct barter is so inefficient that it cannot even solve the trading problem—the traders cannot obtain their desired consumption. For example, trader A wants to consume the bacon produced by trader B, but trader B does not wish to consume the apples produced by trader A. So traders A and B do not have a double coincidence of wants, and therefore they cannot trade with direct barter. The same situation exists for each pair of traders in Table 2.1—so none of them can trade with direct barter.

BOX 2.2 MONEY MATTERS

## Tax Distortions of Trading Systems

Many techniques are used to avoid the payment of income taxes. A common one is to use barter, so monetary income is not earned or reported to the Internal Revenue Service (IRS).

The usefulness of barter for this purpose is reflected in the appearance of **barter clubs.** Barter clubs are cooperative ventures in which members trade goods or services through the club's facilities. Many of the clubs use computer-accessed "electronic bulletin boards" to list offers

to buy and to sell. Sellers then receive "credits," which they can use to purchase goods or services from other members.

Originally, members were not reporting the "credits" they earned as taxable income. Later, the IRS caught on; it now requires people to pay taxes on their barter credits. Accordingly, barter clubs are becoming less popular: without the tax benefit of barter trade, people prefer to choose from the wider variety of goods available in regular markets.

---

Of course, there are special circumstances in which direct barter may be used in practice. For example, a plumber and a carpenter may exchange their services, the plumber fixing the carpenter's pipes, and the carpenter fixing the plumber's furniture. However, the motivation for modern barter trade is often just tax avoidance, as discussed further in Box 2.2.

### Indirect Barter

In contrast to direct barter, with **indirect barter** people may accept certain commodities in trade because they expect to sell them later for other commodities they wish to consume. The result is that indirect barter does not require a double coincidence of wants, and thereby it provides more trading opportunities than direct barter. In fact, indirect barter can solve the standard trading problem in many ways. A specific example is shown in Table 2.3.

In Table 2.3, each trade consists of two transactions: (1) the first trader sends a good to the second trader, and (2) the second trader sends a good to the first trader. Each trade therefore represents bilateral balance. The three trades—six transactions—solve the standard trading problem

---

TABLE 2.3

Indirect Barter with an "Active Trader"

| | | | |
|---|---|---|---|
| Trade 1: {A, 1 apple, D} | and | {D, 1 date, A} | D satisfied |
| Trade 2: {A, 1 date, C} | and | {C, 1 corn, A} | C satisfied |
| Trade 3: {A, 1 corn, B} | and | {B, 1 bacon, A} | A and B satisfied |

Trader A is the active trader because he participates in every trade. The solution is indirect barter because trader A does not always consume the commodity he receives in trade; for example, he obtains dates in trade 1, but then sells them in trade 2.

BOX 2.3 MONEY MATTERS

## Trading Pepsi Cola for Vodka

Trade between the residents of countries that use different currencies—such as U.S. dollars and Japanese yen—usually requires that at least one of the traders convert the foreign currency (say yen) into the domestic currency (say dollars). This is not a serious problem if the currencies are freely convertible—can be freely exchanged, one for the other, in a market for foreign exchange.

But some countries prohibit the free exchange of their currency with foreign currencies. For example, the Soviet Union allows the exchange of Russian rubles into U.S. dollars only at grossly distorted exchange rates (in favor of rubles). This is one reason it has been hard for U.S. firms to trade with the Soviet Union.

However, U.S. firms are starting to use **countertrade**—essentially indirect barter—to carry out trade when the other currency is not convertible. For example, Pepsico now exports Pepsi to the Soviet Union, but receives payment not in dollars or rubles, but in Russian vodka. Pepsico then sells the Russian vodka in the United States, so that it ultimately earns its profits from the transaction in dollars.

because each trader eventually receives the good that he or she wants to consume. The particular arrangement, with trader A active in every trade, might be advantageous if trader A's costs of trading are particularly low, perhaps because he is centrally located in the trading system. For example, trader A might own the general store located at the main crossroads.

Box 2.3 discusses a current example in which indirect barter is sometimes used in international trade.

## Commodity Exchange Systems

Indirect barter is also the basis of trading systems in which a specific commodity serves as a medium of exchange. These are called **commodity exchange systems** and the commodity used is the **commodity medium of exchange** or **commodity money.**

A commodity exchange system is illustrated in Table 2.4. Apples are the commodity medium of exchange because apples appear in every

TABLE 2.4
Indirect Barter with a Commodity Medium of Exchange

Trade 1: {A, 1 apple, B}  and  {B, 1 bacon, A}   A satisfied
Trade 2: {B, 1 apple, C}  and  {C, 1 corn, B}   B satisfied
Trade 3: {C, 1 apple, D}  and  {D, 1 date, C}   C and D satisfied

The special feature is that apples are part of each trade, so apples are the commodity medium of exchange. For example, trader B accepts apples as payment in trade 1, but then uses them in trade 2 to pay for the corn that he wants to consume.

trade. For example, in trades 1 and 2, traders B and C accept apples as payment, but each then sells the apples in a later trade. This is precisely the character of a medium of exchange—and since apples are a commodity, they are a commodity medium of exchange.

Commodity exchange systems evolved because they provided lower trading costs than the existing barter systems. However, a commodity exchange system will have a lower cost only if the commodity money is convenient and inexpensive to use. For example, since perishable commodities like apples rot, they would make a bad commodity money. Instead, most commodity exchange systems used gold (or another precious metal) as the medium of exchange:

1. Gold is *durable*, so it can be used over and over.
2. Gold is *portable*, so it can be moved during trade.
3. Gold is *valuable*, per unit volume, so it can be used for large trades.
4. Gold is *divisible*, so it can also be used for small trades.

However, a gold exchange system also has drawbacks:

1. Gold used for trading is not available for consumption (jewelry) or production (industrial uses of gold).
2. Gold is heavy and risky to ship over long distances.
3. Governments may *debase*—reduce the gold content—of minted coins. (Box 2.4 discusses the minting of coins.)
4. The happenstance of new gold discoveries may limit the amount of gold available for rising amounts of trade.

## Fiat Money

The drawbacks of gold exchange systems encouraged people to develop more flexible trading systems. An important advance was to deposit gold in a warehouse and to use the deposit *receipts* as the medium of exchange. This reduced the problems of shipping gold and of using gold coins. But as long as the receipts were fully *convertible* into gold—people could exchange the receipts for gold—the warehouse had to hold physical gold, and the system still relied on a commodity money.

Another possibility was to use items of *symbolic value*, instead of items that were useful for production or consumption, as the medium of exchange. Indeed, such diverse and otherwise not useful items as woodpecker skulls and large boulders have been used at one time or another as the medium of exchange.

But *paper money* was the real breakthrough. Paper money has all of the advantages of commodity money as a medium of exchange, but its value is only symbolic—valuable resources are not diverted from consumption or production. We will now look more closely at how fiat money—the formal name for paper money—functions as part of a modern payments system.

BOX 2.4 MONEY MATTERS

## Seignorage Profits and Debasing the Currency

The right of a government to mint coins is called **seignorage,** and *seignorage profits* equal the exchange value of a gold coin minus the market value of the gold it contains. So if the mint can reduce the amount of gold in each coin—*debase the currency*—seignorage profits will rise.[4]

The opposite result may occur if the market price of gold rises, so that gold coins become more valuable as gold than as coins: people will then *melt down* coins to make bars of gold bullion. This was recognized by Sir Thomas Gresham (1519–1579) and is now known as **Gresham's law:** bad money (whatever replaces gold coins) drives good money (gold coins with high bullion value) out of circulation as the medium of exchange.

A second metal was also sometimes used to mint coins, as part of a *bimetallic system.* For example, the nineteenth-century "free silver" movement lobbied for the United States to mint silver coins as part of a bimetallic system. (Their leader, William Jennings Bryan, captured attention with his famous "cross of gold" speech in 1896 supporting silver coinage—". . . you shall not crucify mankind upon a cross of gold.") *Gresham's law* also has a role in a bimetallic system: the coins with the higher relative bullion value—gold or silver—tend to be melted down, leaving only the "bad" money in circulation.

[4] Individuals may also debase the currency by shaving or clipping a bit of gold from coins. Some coins are minted with notched edges to make this practice easier to detect.

## Establishing a Fiat Money System

*Fiat money* consists of paper money or coins that are accepted in trade even though the intrinsic value of the paper or metal is negligible. An immediate question is: why do people accept fiat money in trade? A simple answer is that governments force people to use fiat money through *legal tender laws*—that is, by fiat.[5]

Legal tender laws do not, however, explain why people use fiat money *willingly*. The complete answer is that fiat money becomes established as the medium of exchange when *traders are confident that other traders will accept it.* This explanation may seem circular, but the use of fiat money actually is based on *self-fulfilling expectations*. That is, a person uses fiat money because he or she *expects* that other people will use it too—accept it in trade. If everyone shares this expectation, then everyone will accept fiat money in trade, so the expectation is fulfilled.

Of course, it may be that no one shares this expectation, in which case no one will use fiat money. Thus if a government wants people to use its fiat money, then it has to create the "right" expectations. Legal tender laws help the government to do this. It is also helpful if the fiat money system is introduced into the economy gradually.

[5] Some governments also required that all taxes be paid in fiat money. Although the governments did not thereby force people to use fiat money, almost everybody paid taxes, so it had the same effect.

## The Introduction of Fiat Money in the United States

The United States holds a substantial amount of gold—currently worth about $16 billion—much of it in Fort Knox. What is the purpose of this gold? The right answer has changed over time, reflecting the evolution of our payments system from a gold exchange system to fiat money. As recently as 1933, U.S. paper money was *fully backed* by the U.S. gold reserves; so people could convert their paper money into gold just by requesting it. The paper money was thus really gold commodity money. However, the gold backing for the paper money was eliminated over time, leaving the fiat money we now have.

### The Gold Backing of U.S. Fiat Money

Throughout most of U.S. history, paper money was convertible into gold (or silver)—gold reserves "backed" paper money, and people were free to exchange paper money for gold whenever they wished. The United States last eliminated gold convertibility in 1933, when, during the Great Depression, President Franklin Roosevelt ordered that all gold coins and convertible money be exchanged for a new paper money. Although the new paper money continued to have gold backing (at a 50% rate), people could not convert their paper money into gold. Indeed, they could not even hold gold—so for them the gold backing was only symbolic. (Foreign central banks, however, could convert dollars into gold for international trade transactions.)

Over time, Congress eliminated even the symbolic gold backing of the paper money. Since this was done gradually, no one paid much attention, and when the gold backing was completely eliminated in 1968, nothing happened. More recently, people have again been allowed to hold gold, and this remains true today. But gold is now just a commodity, although it still has symbolic importance due to its historical role as a commodity money.

Why, then, do we still keep gold in Fort Knox? Actually, the United States has started to sell its gold reserves—in the form of newly minted "American Eagle" gold coins. But there is no rush to sell all of the gold. Some people even propose a return to a gold standard for international trade, as we will discuss in Chapter 22.

## The Overissue of Fiat Money

A government can pay for its purchases of goods in three basic ways: it can collect taxes, it can borrow money, or it can print new money. Given the ease of printing money, the difficulty of collecting taxes, and the interest expense of borrowing money, it is no wonder that governments are frequently tempted to pay for goods by printing fiat money.

However, the **overissue** of fiat money—issuing too much of it—runs the risk of creating inflation. That is, prices will rise if people try to use the new money to purchase more goods than are available for sale. In contrast, taxation and borrowing recycle the existing stock of money, so they tend to be less inflationary. That is, with taxation or borrowing, the government takes in money with one hand (by collecting taxes or issuing debt), and then returns it with the other hand (by purchasing goods).

## Banking Systems

We have seen that gold exchange systems were subject to various practical problems, including the safekeeping of gold and the shipment of gold over long distances. In resolving these problems, banking institutions started to evolve.

The first step was that gold merchants accepted gold "deposits" from people to solve the problem of safekeeping. A trader received a receipt as verification of a deposit, and could then transfer the receipt to another party as payment for a purchase. The gold merchant's receipt thus physically circulated, replacing gold itself as the medium of exchange, and eliminating many gold shipments.

### Transfer Agent Banks

The gold merchants were starting to function as simple banks, although they were not yet making loans. We will refer to the gold merchants who provided the receipts that served as the medium of exchange as **transfer agent banks.** They earned income by charging fees for the transfer agent services of holding and transferring gold.

As the number of banks grew, an efficient mechanism for settling accounts between transfer agent banks became necessary. The problem was that trader A with gold in bank A might want to transfer gold to trader B who kept his gold in bank B. Gold then had to be transferred between the two banks. This was the origin of **clearinghouses,** which were developed to facilitate the transfer of gold between banks in the same city. Banks that owed gold to other banks in the city would transfer the amount to the clearinghouse, while banks that were owed gold would receive the amount from the clearinghouse. Clearinghouses thus avoided many of the gold shipments between banks by settling the accounts on a multilateral basis.

It was still necessary at times to make physical deliveries of gold to distant cities. Since the transportation of gold was costly and risky, techniques also developed in which a group of banks in different cities each agreed to make gold payments in their own city at the request of other participating banks. As long as these requests were roughly balanced, relatively small shipments of gold were required to balance accounts between banks. Banking families with banks managed by family members in different cities were particularly effective in this regard because the family relationship created trust that the accounts would be settled equitably. Box 2.5 discusses the Rothschilds, a famous banking family that started out this way.

## The Banking Rothschilds

Rothschild is still a potent name in banking; members of this venerable family have maintained banking operations in New York, London, Paris, and elsewhere for many years. The Rothschilds started as bankers in Frankfurt in the eighteenth century by making loans to the rulers of the smaller kingdoms and principalities that existed at the time. The rulers had to depend on the banks that had connections in the major financial centers. The Rothschilds, with family banks in many of these centers, were able to transfer and lend gold wherever the demand (and interest rate) was highest.

Centuries before "information" became a buzzword, the Rothschilds employed an army of correspondents in the financial and political centers of Europe, who rushed intelligence to the banks by the fastest means available—couriers, then carrier pigeons, and later the telegraph. By using carrier pigeons, for example, the Rothschilds were the first to receive the news that Britain had won the Battle of Waterloo in 1815. They were thus able to buy British government securities at low prices before anyone else knew of the victory. When couriers later spread the good news in England, there was a boom in the market price of the securities and the Rothschilds made a fortune.

The balance sheet of a transfer agent bank is illustrated in Table 2.5. The assets represent the amount of physical gold the bank holds as **reserves**—in readiness to repay people who want to withdraw their gold. The liabilities represent the value of gold receipts—or deposits—that the bank issued as gold was deposited. As long as the bank held all of its gold as reserves, its **reserve ratio,** the ratio of reserves to deposits, was 100%.

## The Origins of Fractional Reserve Banking

Transfer agent banks noticed, of course, that most of their gold stood unused. Even a busy agent found that the net transfer of gold each day was small relative to his total gold reserves. The unused resources thus represented a golden opportunity waiting to be realized.

### TABLE 2.5
### Transfer Agent Bank Balance Sheet

| Assets | Liabilities |
|---|---|
| Gold reserves $100 | Gold deposits $100 |

When a transfer agent bank received a gold deposit of $100, it held the gold as reserves—a bank asset—and issued the depositor a receipt—a bank liability. As long as the bank held all of the gold as reserves, its reserve ratio—gold reserves divided by gold deposits—was 100%.

So transfer agent banks expanded into the new business of lending unused gold reserves, while of course charging interest on the loans they made. Banks that operate in this way are called **fractional reserve banks**—after they lend out some of their gold reserves, their reserve ratio is a fraction of 100%. Table 2.6 shows the balance sheet of a fractional reserve bank with a 20% reserve ratio, which can be compared with the 100% reserve ratio of the transfer agent bank in Table 2.5.

Because a fractional reserve bank earned loan interest, its total income would exceed the income of a similar transfer agent bank that earned only service fees. However, a fractional reserve bank also faced two sources of additional costs:

1. It could suffer losses on bad loans.

2. If too many depositors withdrew their gold deposits at the same time, it could run out of gold reserves (because its gold reserves were only a fraction of its gold deposits).

A fractional reserve bank that runs out of gold reserves is in big trouble because it must **suspend convertibility**—it must stop redeeming its deposits with gold. Such a situation also means big trouble for depositors, since they lose access to their gold, and might lose their gold completely. For this reason, other things being the same, depositors would prefer to deal with a transfer agent bank that makes no loans and maintains a 100% reserve ratio. (As mentioned in Chapter 1, depositors in U.S. banks are now protected by deposit insurance up to $100,000 per account.)

Fractional reserve banks therefore have to compensate their depositors for accepting the risk that the bank might fail. Usually they do so by paying interest on deposits. Fractional reserve banks thus face two special costs: losses suffered on bad loans, and interest paid on deposits. The profits of a fractional reserve bank will then exceed the profits of a corresponding transfer agent bank only if the loan interest received by the fractional reserve bank exceeds its loan loss and deposit interest costs.

Fractional reserve bankers did not really know until they tried it whether their type of banking would be profitable. In other words, it was unclear whether fractional reserve banking would really work. As it has turned out, *fractional reserve banking is dominant around the world,* indicating that loan interest income generally exceeds the costs of running fractional reserve banks.

| TABLE 2.6 | |
|---|---|
| **Fractional Reserve Bank Balance Sheet** | |
| **Assets** | **Liabilities** |
| Gold reserves $20<br>Loans $80 | Gold deposits $100 |

After the fractional reserve bank has used $80 of its gold reserves to make loans, its reserve ratio is only 20% ($20 of gold reserves divided by $100 of deposit liabilities).

## Fiat Money and Fractional Reserve Banking

The payments system now used in the United States (and in most other countries) combines fiat money and fractional reserve banking. The result is that the United States has two different types of monetary aggregates—the monetary base and the M1 money supply. These are illustrated in Figure 2.7.

The **monetary base,** representing the fiat money of the U.S. economy, consists of two components: (1) *currency outstanding*—currency held by people and firms (but not banks)—and (2) *bank reserves*—currency and its equivalent held by banks. The amount of the monetary base is determined by the Federal Reserve, which can print fiat money and create bank reserves. The monetary base was $261 billion at the end of 1987.

FIGURE 2.7
**The Monetary Base and M1 Money Supply for the United States**
At year-end 1987

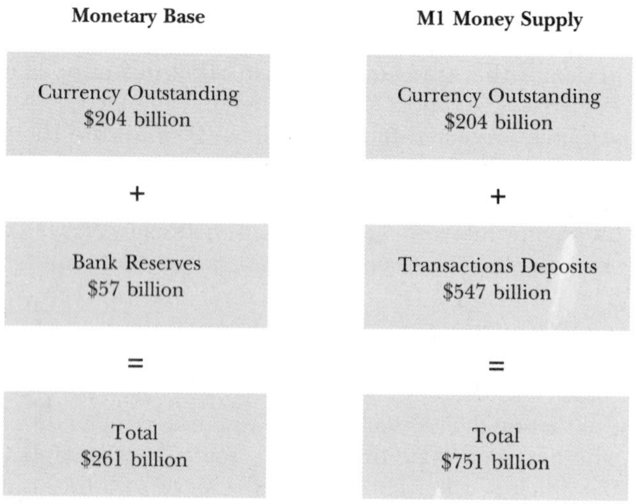

| Monetary Base | M1 Money Supply |
|---|---|
| Currency Outstanding $204 billion | Currency Outstanding $204 billion |
| + | + |
| Bank Reserves $57 billion | Transactions Deposits $547 billion |
| = | = |
| Total $261 billion | Total $751 billion |

The monetary base—the fiat money in the U.S. economy—equals the sum of currency outstanding (currency outside of the banking industry) and bank reserves. The M1 money supply—the medium of exchange in the U.S. economy—equals the sum of currency outstanding (including travelers checks) and transaction deposits.

The **M1 money supply** (or M1), as we saw in Chapter 1, represents the medium of exchange—the amount of money available for payments purposes. The M1 money supply also consists of two components: (1) *currency outstanding,* and (2) *transaction deposits,* the type of bank deposits used for payments purposes. The M1 money supply was $751 billion at the end of 1987, with transaction deposits representing the larger part.

Because bank deposits are only convertible into fiat money (the monetary base), banks rarely have to suspend convertibility. A bank in need of additional reserves usually can borrow the necessary amount from the Federal Reserve. The Fed is able to meet such requests because it controls the monetary base—it issues the fiat money.

Federal Reserve control of the monetary base also means that it has some control over the M1 supply. In particular, each component of the monetary base is related to a component of the M1 money supply: (1) the currency component of the monetary base is itself a component of M1; and (2) the bank reserve component of the monetary base is used by banks in part to back their transaction deposits. Consequently, the Federal Reserve can try to control M1 by controlling the monetary base.

## Chapter Summary

1. The best combination of goods for an individual to produce and consume without trading partners is determined by the point where his or her production possibility frontier is tangent to an indifference curve. Individuals with trading partners can move along a market trading line that is tangent to their production possibility frontier to obtain better consumption opportunities. Gains from trade allow people to obtain larger amounts and wider choices of consumption goods.

2. Trading systems represent the rules, regulations, and conventions the economy uses in organizing transactions. The costs of trading include search costs and trading system costs (such as the costs of maintaining markets and using a medium of exchange). Systems of exchange may be arranged on a centralized basis with multilateral trading, but decentralized systems with bilateral trading are generally more practical.

3. With barter trading, goods are exchanged only for other goods. With *direct* barter, goods are traded only for the direct purpose of consumption. With *indirect* barter, goods may be traded with the intention of later reselling them. Goods purchased for the purpose of later resale represent a commodity medium of exchange or a commodity money. Gold frequently served this purpose.

4. Modern payments systems reduce trading costs by using fiat money—paper money and coins—as one form of the medium of exchange. Fiat money is usually issued by governments. People accept fiat money in trade basically because they expect other people to accept it as well.

5. Banks first appeared as transfer agents who maintained 100% reserve ratios—their gold reserves were equal to their gold deposits. Fractional reserve banks developed later when banks started to make loans, reducing their gold reserves and their reserve ratio. Fractional reserve banks are now the dominant form of banking.

6. Fiat money is currently represented in the U.S. economy by the monetary base, consisting of currency outstanding and bank reserves. The medium of exchange is represented by the M1 money supply, consisting of currency outstanding and bank transaction deposits. The Federal Reserve controls the monetary base, and thereby has some control over the M1 money supply.

## Key Terms

Bank reserves

Bilateral balance

Bilateral and multilateral trade

Clearinghouse

Commodity exchange system

Direct and indirect barter

Double coincidence of wants

Fiat money (paper money)

Fractional reserve bank

Gains from trade

Indifference curves

Legal tender laws

M1 money supply (M1)

Market trading line

Medium of exchange

Monetary base

Production possibility frontier

Reserve ratio

Search costs and trading system costs

Transfer agent bank

## Study Questions

1. Consider a lone individual with the choice of consuming figs ($F$) and grapes ($G$), and with a production possibility frontier given by:

$$F^2 + G^2 = 100.$$

Sketch the frontier by calculating the specific values for $F$ and $G$ when: (a) only $F$ is produced, (b) only $G$ is produced, (c) $G$ is equal to 6, and (d) $G$ is equal to 8. Would the person be willing to consume the $\{F, G\}$ combination $\{6, 6\}$?

2. Suppose the individual of Question 1 can now trade with others along the market trading line:

$$F = 12.5 - 0.75 \, G.$$

What is the maximum amount of $F$ that could be consumed? What is the maximum amount of $G$ that could be consumed? Why do these results indicate there are gains from trade?

3. Consider the following set of trades that are suggested as a solution to the standard trading problem of Table 2.1:

Trade 1: {B, 1 bacon, C}
and {C, 1 corn, B}

Trade 2: {C, 1 bacon, D} and
{D, 1 date, C}

Trade 3: {D, 1 bacon, A} and
{A, 1 apple, D}

Does this set of trades provide each trader with his or her desired consumption? Is this an example of bilateral or multilateral trade? What is special about bacon?

4. The examples in Tables 2.2 and 2.4 demonstrate that multilateral trade can provide the same outcome as trading with a medium of exchange. Why then is multilateral trading used so infrequently in practice?

5. The example of a medium of exchange in Table 2.4 indicates that six different transactions are necessary to solve the standard trading problem. The example of multilateral trade in Table 2.2 indicates that only four transactions are necessary for a solution. How can a medium of exchange system be more efficient even though it requires more trades?

6. Why would it be unusual to find an economy in which, at one moment, some people used fiat money, while others refused to use it. What might the government do to motivate everyone to use the fiat money?

7. When the market value of gold was $20 an ounce, the United States minted $20 gold coins that weighed 1 ounce. But 1 ounce of gold is now worth several hundred dollars. If you owed someone $20, would you want to pay them with one of these coins? What principle does this illustrate?

8. In a fiat money / fractional reserve banking system, the balance sheet of the First National Fractional Reserve Bank appears as follows:

| Assets | Liabilities |
|---|---|
| Reserves, $60<br>Loans, $40 | Deposits, $100 |

What reserve ratio is maintained by the bank? If the bank decided to reduce its reserve ratio to 20%, what amount of new loans would it make? Write out the bank's balance sheet after the loans are made.

9. Why might depositors consider a fractional reserve bank more risky than a transfer agent bank? How might depositors respond if they become especially concerned about this?

10. Why does the Federal Reserve have more complete control over the monetary base than over the M1 money supply?

## Recommended Reading

An economic and anthropological study of how money is used in primitive settings:

Paul Einzig, Primitive Money, Eyre and Spottiswoode, London, 1948.

The classic economic history of the United States from a monetary standpoint:

Milton Friedman and Anne Schwartz, A Monetary History of the United States 1867–1960, Princeton University Press, Princeton, N.J., 1963.

This book discusses the basic features of money, including the standard trading problem:

Jurg Niehans, The Theory of Money, The Johns Hopkins University Press, Baltimore, paperback edition, 1980.

An important study showing how a commodity medium of exchange develops when a monetary medium of exchange is not available:

R. A. Radford, "The Economic Organization of a POW Camp," Economica, November 1945, pp. 189–202.

This book illustrates the relationships between the great gold discoveries (the Americas in the sixteenth century and the gold rushes of Australia, California, and South Africa):

Pierre Vilar, A History of Gold and Money, Verso, London, 1984.

# 3

# The Determinants
# of Interest Rates

*". . . the rate of interest as determined by the impatience to spend income and the opportunity to invest it"*

**Irving Fisher**

We revisit Robinson Crusoe to consider the role of interest rates on his island economy. Crusoe is now producing more goods each day than he needs for his immediate survival. So by saving and storing some of the goods, Crusoe can take time off from work once in a while. But each vacation has to be short due to the poor storage conditions on the island.

Later, Crusoe discovers that, instead of storing the saved goods, he can *lend* them to Friday and other trading partners who live on nearby islands. One benefit of lending goods is that the borrowers return fresh goods. Another benefit is that they return an additional amount of goods, representing interest. Higher interest rates thus allow Crusoe to take longer vacations.

Crusoe also discovers that by *borrowing* goods he can solve two other problems. First, at times he wants to take a vacation even though he has not yet saved up enough goods. The solution is to borrow the goods he needs for the vacation, then to repay the loan later. Second, he wants to construct a factory to produce more goods. The solution is to use borrowed goods, as well as saved goods, to build it. Of course, he has to repay each loan with interest, but this is possible because Crusoe will eventually be able to produce more goods with his factory. The relationships between interest rates, saving and investing, and lending and borrowing are the basis of the loanable funds theory of interest rates, the main focus of this chapter.

According to the loanable funds theory, interest rates settle at a level where the supply of loanable funds—the amount of money available for lending—equals the demand for loanable funds—the amount of money people want to borrow. The supply of loanable funds comes from people who are saving and are willing to lend their money to others. The demand for loanable funds comes from people who want to consume or invest more than their income allows, and thus need to borrow money.

We begin with an overview of saving and investment and the connections between them. That leads us to consider the factors that determine the amounts that people decide to save and invest. We will then develop the loanable funds theory of interest rates in conjunction with what we learned about saving and investment. Keep in mind as you read this chapter that we are assuming the price level remains unchanged.

## Saving and Investment in the United States

We start by developing the concepts of saving—keeping current outlays below current income—and investment—purchasing durable assets. We will first look at household saving and investment to illustrate the basic principles. We will then look at the saving and investment of each sector of the U.S. economy—household, business, finance, government, and foreign—and of the economy as a whole.

### Household Saving and Investment

The total saving and investment of households in the United States during 1987 is summarized in Table 3.1. The data come from the Federal Reserve's **Flow of Funds accounts**, which tabulate all financial transactions that occur *between* sectors of the U.S. economy.[1] We can analyze these accounts as though they referred to a single household.

[1] Transactions *within* a sector cancel each other out. For example, there is no net change in the value of homes owned by the household sector of the economy when one household just buys a home from another household.

**TABLE 3.1**
**Household Saving and Investment**[a]

| Calendar year 1987 (Dollars in billions) | | | |
|---|---|---|---|
| **Saving** | | **Investment** | |
| Disposable personal income $Y$ | $3,675 | Capital investment $I^C$ | $ 636 |
| Consumption $C$ | −2,948 | Financial investment $I^F$ | + 91 |
| Total Saving $S^b$ | $ 727 | Total investment $I$ | $ 727 |

[a] Households, personal trusts, and nonprofit organizations.
[b] The Flow of Funds accounts often reflect statistical discrepancies such that saving does not precisely equal total investment for the household sector. Disposable personal income ($Y$) and saving ($S$) have been adjusted to balance the accounts for this table.
**Source:** *Flow of Funds Accounts*, Release Z.1, Board of Governors of the Federal Reserve System, March 11, 1988.

**Disposal personal income** $Y$ is the annual income the household receives and has available for spending. We will simply call this "income." Income includes wages and salaries, interest and dividends, and other amounts received by household members, minus the taxes they have to pay (income used to pay taxes is not "disposable" for other purposes).

**Consumption** $C$ is the amount the household spends during the year for nondurable goods. Most households tend to spend most of their income this way.

**Saving** $S$ is the part of the household's income that is not consumed. That is, saving is income minus consumption ($S = Y - C$).

**Total investment** $I$ is the sum of the two types of nonconsumption outlays the household can make—capital investment and financial investment.

**Capital investment** $I^C$ is the amount the household spends on durable, tangible assets, such as houses, cars, and refrigerators. These outlays represent capital investment because the assets last over a period of time.

**Financial investment** $I^F$ is the sum of two components, one with a positive value and the other with a negative value. The positive component equals the loans made and the securities purchased—such as bank deposits, corporate bonds, and common stocks—by the household. The negative component equals borrowing by the household.

**Lending** money and purchasing securities are treated as positive financial investment because—like consumption and capital investment—they represent *uses* of the household's income. **Borrowing** money is treated as negative financial investment because it represents a *source* of funds (other than income) to cover current outlays.

As shown in Table 3.1, households both saved and invested $727 billion during 1987. Indeed, the terms are defined so that the amounts of saving and of total investment are always equal. That is, the part of income that is not consumed—saving—must equal total investment.[2] Box 3.1 clarifies why this must be true. The box also warns about different meanings of the term "investment."

Although saving, capital investment, and financial investment each have a positive value for the household sector, one or more of these items often have a negative value for an individual household:

- A negative value for saving merely means that consumption spending exceeds income, hardly an unusual situation; negative saving is also called **dissaving.**

---

[2] Some of the definitions used in the Flow of Funds accounts differ from the definitions used in the **National Income accounts**—the accounts that measure GNP and its components. For example, the Flow of Funds definitions of saving and capital investment correspond to what are called *gross* saving and investment in the National Income accounts.

BOX 3.1 IN DEPTH

## Saving Equals Total Investment for Households

Saving equals total investment for households because of the way terms are defined:

1. Disposable income $Y$ has to be spent on consumption $C$, financial investment $I^F$, or capital investment $I^C$:

$$Y = C + I^F + I^C.$$

2. Income not consumed, $Y - C$, and the two components of investment, $I^F + I^C$, are therefore equal:

$$Y - C = I^F + I^C.$$

3. Saving $S$ is the part of income $Y$ that is not consumed $C$:

$$S = Y - C.$$

4. Total investment $I$ is the sum of financial investment $I^F$ and capital investment $I^C$:

$$I = I^F + I^C.$$

5. From equations 2, 3, and 4, saving $S$ equals total investment $I$:

$$S = I.$$

*Note* Most people think of investing as purchases of securities—that is, as financial investment. Economists, on the other hand, usually think of investing as purchases of tangible capital assets—that is, as capital investment. To avoid confusion, in this chapter we will always specify the type of investment.

■ If saving is negative, then at least one of the two components of total investment must be negative. A negative value for financial investment means the household is borrowing money on balance, while a negative value for capital investment means the household is selling capital assets on balance—for example, selling a used car or a house.

## Saving and Investment for Each Sector and for the Economy

The amount of saving and investment during 1987 for each sector and the whole economy is shown in Table 3.2. Each sector is represented in a column and each type of transaction is represented in a row. The rest of the world is included as a sector—the foreign sector—that contributes to U.S. saving and investment. The household, business, and foreign sectors each generated large and positive amounts of saving during 1987. Only the government sector had negative saving, mainly due to the federal government's budget deficit.

Saving and Investment for Each Sector and for the Whole Economy

**Calendar year 1987 (Dollars in billions)**

| | House-hold | Business | Financial | Government Federal | Government State & Local | Foreign | Whole Economy |
|---|---|---|---|---|---|---|---|
| Saving[a] | 727 | 406 | 12 | − 184 | − 9 | 153 | 1,105 |
| Total | | | | | − 9 | 153 | 1,105 |
| investment | 727 | 406 | 12 | − 184 | | | |
| **Total investment** | | | | | | | |
| Financial | 91 | − 49 | − 5 | − 181 | − 9 | 153 | 0 |
| Capital | 636 | 455 | 17 | − 3 | 0 | 0 | 1,105 |
| **Capital investment** | | | | | | | |
| Residential | | | | | | | |
| construction | 205 | 23 | 0 | 0 | 0 | 0 | 228 |
| Consumer | | | | | | | |
| durables | 414 | 0 | 0 | 0 | 0 | 0 | 414 |
| Plant and | | | | | | | |
| equipment | 17 | 384 | 17 | 0 | 0 | 0 | 418 |
| Other | 0 | 48 | 0 | − 7 | 0 | 0 | 45 |

[a] The Flow of Funds accounts often reflect statistical discrepancies such that saving does not precisely equal total investment for each sector and that financial investment is not precisely zero for the whole economy. The amount of saving has been adjusted to balance the accounts for this table.

**Source:** *Flow of Funds Accounts,* Release Z.1, Board of Governors of the Federal Reserve System, March 11, 1988.

The household sector invested in both financial and capital assets, the latter primarily in homes (residential construction) and consumer durables. The business sector had a large amount of capital investment in manufacturing plants and equipment, some of it financed with negative financial investment—that is, by borrowing money. The foreign sector is represented with only financial investment because foreign capital investment—also called foreign direct investment—is treated as financial investment in the Flow of Funds accounts.

The amounts of saving and investment for the whole economy, the sum of the activities for all six sectors, are shown in the last column of Table 3.2. The aggregate amounts of saving and total investment were each equal to $1,105 billion during 1987. That is, saving equals total investment for the whole economy, just as for each sector.

Financial investment for the whole economy during 1987 was zero. This is always true because each financial transaction has a lender—for whom the transaction represents positive financial investment—and a borrower—for whom the transaction represents negative financial investment. When the positive financial investment of lenders and the negative financial investment of borrowers are combined, as they are for the whole economy, financial investment must be zero.

Because financial investment is zero for the whole economy, *saving and capital investment are equal for the whole economy.* This result is also

BOX 3.2 IN DEPTH

## Saving Equals Capital Investment for the Economy

It is readily confirmed that saving equals capital investment for the whole economy:

1. For each sector of the economy, and for the whole economy, saving $S$ equals the sum of financial investment $I^F$ and capital investment $I^C$:

$$S = I^F + I^C.$$

2. Financial investment is zero for the whole economy:

$$I^F = 0 \text{ for the whole economy.}$$

3. It follows from equations 1 and 2 that saving $S$ must equal capital investment $I^C$ for the whole economy:

$$S = I^C.$$

verified in Table 3.2: saving and capital investment both equal $1,105 billion. Box 3.2 summarizes why saving and capital investment must be equal for the whole economy.

We will now look at the factors that determine how much saving and capital investment people choose to carry out. We will start with the decision to save.

## The Decision To Save

The saving rate in the United States—domestic personal saving relative to disposable personal income—has been considered low for many years. Box 3.3 shows just how low the U.S. saving rate is compared to saving rates in other countries. A low domestic saving rate is a serious concern because it means the U.S. economy depends on funds from the foreign sector to maintain a high level of capital investment.

The theory of saving and consumption developed by Irving Fisher, in his book *The Theory of Interest,* provides insights into why the U.S. saving rate is so low. Fisher viewed saving as the result of two basic forces:

1. The impatience to consume income, which reduces saving.

2. The opportunity to invest income, which increases saving.

An impatience to consume income is one key reason the U.S. saving rate is so low. We will now examine Fisher's model more closely to identify other variables that may influence the amount of saving.

BOX 3.3 IN DEPTH

## Saving Rates in the United States and Abroad

Are Americans saving too little? Comparisons of saving rates in various countries suggest this might be true. In 1985, the latest year for which comparative figures are available, the United States had the lowest domestic saving rate—the ratio of domestically generated personal saving to disposable personal income—among the six large industrialized countries shown in the table below.

This is a serious problem because the amount of domestic saving is the basis for an economy's capital investment. Although the United States has been successful in augmenting the amount of its amount of capital investment by borrowing funds from abroad, this is not sustainable in the long run. To rectify the situation, Americans will have to consume less because less consumption means more saving.

**Domestic Saving Rates[a]**

| | | | |
|---|---|---|---|
| Japan | 18.0% | United Kingdom | 7.7% |
| West Germany | 9.6 | France | 6.2 |
| Italy | 7.7 | United States | 3.7 |

[a] The comparative saving rates are based on the National Income account concept of domestic personal saving relative to disposal personal income.

**Source:** *Economic Outlook, Historical Statistics,* Organization for Economic Cooperation and Development, 1987.

## The Fisher Model of Saving and Consumption

The Fisher model focuses on how a person consumes and saves over a horizon of two time periods: a current period, period 1, and a future period, period 2. During period 1, the person receives current income $Y_1$, consumes the current amount $C_1$, and saves the amount $S$ $(Y_1 - C_1)$. For period 2, the person anticipates receiving future income $Y_2$ and consuming the future amount $C_2$. There is no saving in period 2 because this consumption plan does not extend beyond period 2. This means that consumption $C_2$ in period 2 must equal the sum of $Y_2$ and $S$, plus or minus any interest earned or paid on $S$. (In practice, of course, a person could formulate a new plan at the beginning of period 2 to cover consumption for periods 2 and 3 and saving for period 2.)

The amount of saving $S$ $(= Y_1 - C_1)$ can be zero, positive, or negative. These cases are illustrated in Table 3.3 by three families—the Whites, Greens, and Browns—that have the same current income $(Y_1 = \$1,000)$ and expected future income $(Y_2 = \$1,500)$, but save different amounts. Specifically, the Whites have no saving, the Greens save $500, and the Browns dissave $500. We will also assume, to simplify matters, that the interest rate $r$, equal to 10%, applies both to lending (for families that save) and to borrowing (for families that dissave). We will further assume that none of the families has any capital investment.

**TABLE 3.3**

**Income, Consumption, and Saving for Three Families**

|  | **(In dollars)** | | |
| --- | --- | --- | --- |
|  | **Whites** | **Greens** | **Browns** |
| **Period 1** | | | |
| Current income $Y_1$ | 1,000 | 1,000 | 1,000 |
| Saving $S$ | 0 | 500 | −500 |
| Current Consumption $C_1$ (= $Y_1 - S$) | 1,000 | 500 | 1,500 |
| **Period 2** | | | |
| Future income $Y_2$ | 1,500 | 1,500 | 1,500 |
| Use of saving $S$ | 0 | 500 | −500 |
| Interest ($rS$): | | | |
| Earned when lending ($S > 0$) | 0 | 50 | 0 |
| Paid when borrowing ($S < 0$) | 0 | 0 | −50 |
| Future consumption $C_2$ (= $Y_2 + S + rS$) | 1,500 | 2,050 | 950 |

**Note:** Current income $Y_1$ equals the sum of current consumption $C_1$ and saving $S$: $Y_1 = C_1 + S$. This can also be expressed as $C_1 = Y_1 - S$, or as $S = Y_1 - C_1$. Each family has current income of $1,000 and future income of $1,500. The Whites have no saving so their consumption equals their income in both periods. The Greens have positive saving, which reduces their current consumption but raises their future consumption. The Browns have negative saving, which raises their current consumption but reduces their future consumption.

Since the Whites have no saving ($S = Y_1 - C_1 = 0$), their consumption must equal their income each period: $C_1 = Y_1 = \$1,000$, and $C_2 = Y_2 = \$1,500$. The Whites therefore have neither extra funds to lend nor any need to borrow.

Since the Greens save $500 ($S = \$500$), their current consumption is only $500 (current income $1,000 − saving $500). The Greens use the amount they save to increase their future consumption. In addition, by lending their saving to someone else during period 1 (for example, to the Browns), the Greens earn interest of $50 ($rS = 10\%$ of $500). So the future consumption of the Greens is $2,050 (future income $1,500 + saving $500 + interest earned $50).

Since the Browns dissave $500 ($S = -\$500$), their current consumption can be $1,500 (income $1,000 + dissaving $500). However to dissave this amount, the Browns have to borrow $500 during period 1. The $500 loan is then repaid during period 2, along with an interest payment of $50 (10% of $500). So the future consumption of the Browns is $950 (future income $1,500 − dissaving $500 − loan interest $50).

**The Budget Line**

As illustrated in Table 3.3, the amount of future consumption $C_2$ that is affordable depends on future income $Y_2$, saving $S$, and interest earned or paid $rS$:[3]

$$C_2 = Y_2 + S + rS = Y_2 + (1 + r) S. \tag{3.1}$$

Because saving $S$ equals the difference between current income $Y_1$ and current consumption $C_1$, $S = Y_1 - C_1$, equation (3.1) can also be expressed as:

$$C_2 = Y_2 + (1 + r)(Y_1 - C_1). \tag{3.2}$$

---

[3] When saving has a positive value ($S > 0$), the term $rS$ represents interest earned ($rS > 0$). When saving has a negative value ($S < 0$), the same term $rS$ represents interest paid ($rS < 0$).

Equation (3.2) is referred to as the **budget equation** because it indicates the amount of future consumption $C_2$ that is affordable, given current income $Y_1$, future income $Y_2$, the interest rate $r$, and current consumption $C_1$.

A **budget line** that represents equation (3.2) graphically is shown in Figure 3.1. The budget line is similar to the trading line we introduced in Chapter 2 (in Figure 2.4). However, the earlier trading line referred to the exchange of two goods (apples and bacon), whereas the current budget line refers to the exchange of two sets of goods (current consumption and future consumption).

FIGURE 3.1
**The Decision To Save**

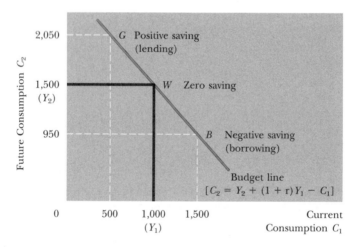

The budget line is a graph of equation (3.2), representing the affordable combinations of current and future consumption {$C_1$, $C_2$}. The position of the budget line is determined by the amounts of current income $Y_1$ ($1,000) and future income $Y_2$ ($1,500). The slope of the budget line is determined by the interest rate, a higher interest rate determining a more steeply sloped budget line. The points $W$, $G$, and $B$ refer to the consumption and saving of the three families—the Whites (no saving), Greens (positive saving), and Browns (negative saving), respectively—described in Table 3.3.

The position of the budget line is determined by the amounts of current income $Y_1$ ($1,000) and future income $Y_2$ ($1,500). The slope of the budget line is $-(1 + r)$, indicating that a family can exchange 1 unit of current consumption $C_1$ for $(1 + r)$ units of future consumption $C_2$ (the negative sign means the family reduces $C_1$ to increase $C_2$). One unit of forgone current consumption converts into a larger amount of future consumption because interest is earned—at the rate $r$—on the amount saved (remember that lower current consumption means higher saving).

This process also works in the opposite direction: a family can convert $(1 + r)$ units of future consumption for 1 unit of current consumption. This conversion is unfavorable—$(1 + r)$ units of $C_2$ convert to just 1 unit of $C_1$—because interest must be paid—at the rate $r$—on the amount that is borrowed (to increase current consumption).

Because points on the budget line in Figure 3.1 correspond to different combinations of current and future consumption $\{C_1, C_2\}$, they also correspond to different amounts of saving. This is illustrated by the points for the three families: point $W$ for the Whites (no saving), point $G$ for the Greens (positive saving), and point $B$ for the Browns (negative saving). The three families can be represented on the same budget line because all three have identical current and future incomes. If a family decides to move down the budget line to the right, current consumption $C_1$ rises, saving $S$ falls, and future consumption $C_2$ falls. Below point $W$, saving is negative—there is dissaving.

### Time Preference

The particular point that each family chooses on the budget line depends on the extent of its *time preference*—its preference regarding current consumption relative to future consumption. A family that consumes exactly the same amount as its income each period has *neutral time preference* (relative to the amounts of current and future income), while a family that prefers relatively less current consumption has *low time preference*, and a family that prefers relatively more current consumption has *high time preference*.

On this basis, we can see in Figure 3.1 that the Whites have *neutral time preference*—they choose point $W$ with no saving, so they consume exactly the same amount as their income in each period.

In contrast, the Greens save a positive amount at point $G$, lowering their current consumption, while raising their future consumption. Since the Greens *forgo current consumption* to increase future consumption, they have *low time preference*.

Finally, the Browns dissave (save a negative amount) at point $B$, raising their current consumption, while lowering their future consumption. Since the Browns *forgo future consumption* to increase current consumption, they have *high time preference*.

### Summary of Consumption and Saving

The Fisher model identifies four variables that play a key role in determining a family's desired amount of consumption and saving: current income $Y_1$, future expected income $Y_2$, time preference $TP$, and the market interest rate $r$:

- **Current income** $Y_1$ determines the family's *current consumption* unless the amount is reduced by saving or raised by dissaving.

- **Future income** $Y_2$ determines the *future consumption* unless the amount is raised by earlier saving or is reduced by earlier dissaving.

- **Time preference** $TP$ indicates the extent of a family's preference for current consumption $C_1$ over future consumption $C_2$. A family with high time preference is impatient to consume, so it will tend to raise current consumption, even though this means lowering future consumption.

- The **market interest rate** $r$ determines the interest expense of a family that raises its current consumption (by dissaving) and the interest income of a family that lowers its current consumption (by saving).

## Desired Saving

**Desired saving** is the amount of saving a family chooses based on its current and future income, the market interest rate, and the extent of its time preference. In brief, desired saving is current income minus the chosen amount of current consumption ($S = Y_1 - C_1$). In this section, we will summarize the key variables that determine desired saving.

To focus on a specific case, we will continue the example of the White family. The White family's budget line is reproduced in Figure 3.2 from Figure 3.1, based on the family's current income of $1,000, its future income of $1,500, and the market interest rate of 10%. Given its neutral time preference, the Whites initially choose point $W_0$, where consumption equals income each period, so there is no saving.

We will now look at how a higher value for each of the variables— time preference $TP$, current income $Y_1$, future income $Y_2$, and the interest rate $r$—affects the family's desired saving. The main results are summarized for easy reference in Box 3.4.[4]

---

[4] Although our discussion focuses on household saving, the saving decisions of business firms and governments should reflect similar considerations. After all, firms are owned, and governments are elected, by household members.

### FIGURE 3.2
### Income, Time Preference, and Desired Saving

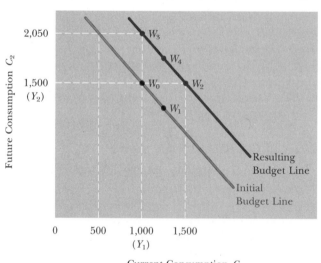

Based on its current income of $1,000, its future income of $1,500, its neutral time preference, and a 10% interest rate, the White family chooses point $W_0$ on the initial budget line.

An increase in its time preference causes the family to move to a point such as $W_1$ on the initial budget line, representing more current consumption $C_1$ and less future consumption $C_2$.

A $500 increase in current income causes the budget line to shift rightward to the resulting budget line, while a $550 increase in future income causes an equivalent upward shift to the same resulting budget line. After either shift, the family would normally move to a point such as $W_4$, thus distributing the increase in income between higher current consumption and higher future consumption. The result is that saving increases if current income rises and decreases if future income rises.

## Variables That Determine Desired Saving

Result 1.  If time preference $TP$ rises, then saving $S$ falls.

Result 2.  If current income $Y_1$ rises, then saving $S$ rises.

Result 3.  If expected future income $Y_2$ rises, then saving $S$ falls.

Result 4.  If the market interest rate $r$ rises, then saving $S$ rises.

**Note:** Results 2 and 3 assume that consumption is *normal*: that an increase in either current or future income causes both current consumption and future consumption to rise, but neither one as much as income.

Result 4 assumes that any "positive income effect" of a higher interest rate does not exceed "the substitution effect," as discussed in the text and Appendix 3.1.

### Higher Time Preference Reduces Saving

Starting with the White family at point $W_0$ on the initial budget line in Figure 3.2, we will first suppose that the family's time preference rises. An increase in time preference indicates that the family wishes to raise current consumption, so it will choose a new point with higher current consumption on the initial budget line, as illustrated by point $W_1$. Since the family's current income $Y_1$ is unchanged, but its current consumption $C_1$ rises, saving $S$ ($= Y_1 - C_1$) falls. This confirms Result 1 in Box 3.4.

### Higher Current Income Raises Saving

Next, we will suppose that Mr. White receives an unexpected bonus of $500, raising the family's current income from $1,000 to $1,500. This shifts the family's budget line to the right by $500, as shown in Figure 3.2. The Whites must then decide how to adjust their consumption from point $W_0$ on the initial budget line to a point on the resulting budget line.

An extreme case is that the Whites move to point $W_2$, using the entire increase in current income for *current* consumption. In this case, current income $Y_1$ and current consumption $C_1$ rise by the same amount, so saving $S$ ($= Y_1 - C_1$) is unchanged.

Another extreme case is that the Whites move to point $W_3$, using the entire increase in current income for *future* consumption. In this case, current income $Y_1$ rises, but current consumption $C_1$ is unchanged, so saving $S$ ($= Y_1 - C_1$) rises by the full amount of the change in current income.

The normal case—referred to as *normal* consumption in Box 3.4—is that the Whites shift to a point such as $W_4$, sharing the increase in current income between current and future consumption. In this case, current consumption $C_1$ rises, but by less than the increase in current income

$Y_1$, so saving $S$ $(= Y_1 - C_1)$ rises (although by a smaller amount than the increase at point $W_3$). This confirms Result 2 in Box 3.4: saving rises when current income rises (as long as consumption is *normal*).

### Higher Future Income Reduces Saving

Now we will suppose that Mrs. White receives a salary increase of \$550, to be effective in the following period, so the family's expected future income rises from \$1,500 to \$2,050. This shifts the family's budget line upward by \$550, which is also illustrated by the resulting budget line in Figure 3.2 (the change is now interpreted as an upward shift of \$550 instead of the previous rightward shift of \$500).

The family again may consume at any point on the resulting budget line. The same principle applies to an increase in future income as to an increase in current income: as long as consumption is *normal*, the family will move to a point such as $W_4$, so that current consumption and future consumption both rise. In this case, current income is unchanged, while current consumption $C_1$ rises, so saving $S$ $(= Y_1 - C_1)$ falls. This confirms Result 3 in Box 3.4: saving falls when future income rises (as long as consumption is *normal*).

### A Higher Interest Rate Raises Saving

Lastly, we will suppose that the market interest rate rises. Referring now to Figure 3.3, a higher interest rate causes the family's initial budget line to rotate clockwise through point $W_0$ to the resulting budget line. The segment of the budget line above point $W_0$ rises because, when the family is saving, it earns a larger amount of interest, which can be applied to additional current or future consumption. The segment of the budget line below point $W_0$ falls because, if the family is dissaving, it will have

The White family initially consumes at point $W_0$, as in Figure 3.2. An increase in the market interest rate rotates the budget line clockwise through point $W_0$, providing the family incentive to move up the budget line to a point such as $W_1$. Lower current consumption is now more advantageous because the family earns interest at a higher rate when it saves.

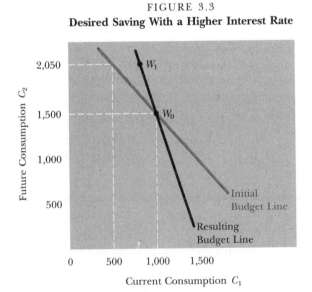

FIGURE 3.3
**Desired Saving With a Higher Interest Rate**

to pay a larger amount of interest, which reduces the affordable amount of consumption. The initial point $W_0$ is unaffected by the change in the interest rate because the family is neither saving nor dissaving at this one point.

After the budget line rotates, the family may move from the initial point $W_0$ to any point on the resulting budget line. The family has incentive to move to a point above $W_0$, such as point $W_1$, because it will now obtain a larger amount of future consumption for postponing some of its current consumption. Since the family's current income is unchanged, but its current consumption $C_1$ falls, saving $S$ $(= Y_1 - C_1)$ rises. This confirms Result 4 in Box 3.4, also referred to as the *substitution effect*: a higher interest rate causes future consumption to be substituted for current consumption.

The substitution effect is the only effect of a higher interest rate for a family, such as the Whites, that is initially neither saving nor dissaving. However, many families may initially be either saving or dissaving. In these cases, a higher interest rate also creates *income effects,* which complicate the relationship between a higher interest rate and the amount of saving. While we will focus on the substitution effect of higher interest rates—that saving rises when the interest rate rises—Appendix 3.1 discusses how our results are modified by income effects.

## The Decision To Invest

We will now look at the variables that determine the amount of capital investment. We have seen that the total investment of each sector of the economy has two components: financial investment and capital investment. However, financial investment is zero for the whole economy, so we will focus here on capital investment. (Financial investment is discussed further in Chapter 5.) Important categories of capital investment include housing, consumer durables, and plant and equipment.

The theory developed in this section is based on the profits that a person or firm can earn by investing in additional capital. Although we will emphasize the capital investment in plant and equipment made by business firms, capital investments in housing, and consumer durables are also covered by this theory to the extent that they are based on similar profit considerations. The special factors of risk and uncertainty that apply to investment decisions are studied in Part II of this book.

### The Marginal Return on Capital Investment

Capital investment is an activity in which currently available resources are invested for the purpose of generating a larger amount of goods for future consumption. The *productivity* of a capital investment is measured by its *marginal rate of return*—the incremental amount of goods produced relative to the incremental amount invested.

To start with a specific example, we will return to Robinson Crusoe and his plans to construct a factory. Since Crusoe wants a simple factory, we can analyze it in quite simple terms. His situation is illustrated by the **investment possibility frontier** $P'P$ in Figure 3.4, which is similar to the production possibility frontier we introduced in Figure 2.1 of Chapter 2. However, whereas the earlier production possibility frontier referred to the quantities of two goods that Crusoe could produce (apples and bacon), the investment possibility frontier refers to the available amounts of current and future consumption when there is capital investment.

The investment possibility frontier shows the alternative combinations of current and future consumption that are available, depending on the amount of capital investment. Point $P$ represents Crusoe's initial endowment of $2,000 of goods. Capital investment is then measured on the horizontal axis going to the left from point $P$. For example, between points $P$ and $Q$, Crusoe invests $500 (reducing current consumption by this amount) to produce $800 of goods for future consumption.

FIGURE 3.4

**The Decision To Invest**

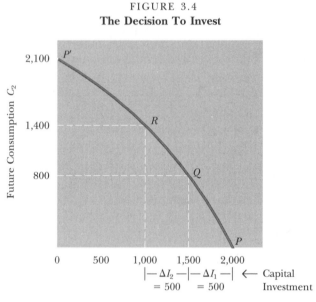

Current Consumption $C_1$

Specifically, Crusoe initially has an endowment of $2,000 of goods, as represented at point $P$ on the investment possibility frontier. He could just consume the $2,000 of goods currently. But given that he can make a productive capital investment, Crusoe prefers to invest some of his initial endowment, as represented by a movement up and along the investment possibility frontier from point $P$. He then has less current consumption but will have more future consumption.

The amount invested is measured on the horizontal axis in the leftward direction from point $P$. For example, if Crusoe invests the amount $\Delta I_1$ equal to $500, moving from point $P$ to point $Q$ on the frontier, current consumption $C_1$ falls to $1,500, but future consumption $C_2$ rises to $800. And if he invests an additional amount $\Delta I_2$, moving further along the frontier to point $R$, current consumption falls $500 more, to $1,000, but future consumption rises an additional $600, to $1,400.

Following this pattern, each incremental investment $\Delta I$ produces a corresponding incremental amount of future consumption $\Delta C_2$. The **marginal return on investment** $m$ is computed as the gain in future consumption $\Delta C_2$ minus the amount invested $\Delta I$ relative to the amount invested $\Delta I$:

$$m = \frac{\Delta C_2 - \Delta I}{\Delta I}.$$

For example, in moving from point $P$ to point $Q$ in Figure 3.4, Crusoe invests $500 and increases his future consumption by $800, so the marginal return on investment $m$ is 60% ([$800 − $500]/$500). Similarly, in moving from point $Q$ to point $R$, Crusoe invests $500 and increases his future consumption by $600, so the marginal return on investment $m$ is 20% ([$600 − $500]/$500).

As illustrated by these two calculations, the marginal return on investment falls as the total amount of investment rises. It does so because each successive increment in investment $\Delta I$ produces a smaller increment in future consumption $\Delta C_2$. This is generally true because, as illustrated by the investment possibility frontier in Figure 3.4, the frontier becomes flatter moving from right to left. The decline in the marginal return limits the amount of capital investment it is worthwhile to undertake.

## Desired Investment

Two basic variables determine the amount of capital investment a firm will wish to undertake:

1. The investment's productivity is measured by the marginal return on investment $m$.

2. The financing cost is measured by the market rate of interest $r$.

If a firm's managers are evaluating separate capital investment projects, then—all other factors being equal—all projects for which the marginal return exceeds the market interest rate should be carried out. If they are deciding the scale of a particular capital investment, such as the size of a factory, then they should increase the scale as long as the marginal return exceeds the market interest rate. In either case, as long as the marginal return exceeds the market rate of interest, the firm will raise it profits by continuing to invest.[5]

However, remember that the marginal return falls as the amount of capital investment rises. Since the marginal return will be relatively high at low levels of investment, some investment is likely to be warranted. But since the marginal return falls as investment rises, a level of capital investment will eventually be reached at which the marginal return *exactly equals* the market interest rate. This represents the best level of capital

---

[5] Firms with excess funds may carry out capital investment without borrowing. But the invested funds still have an *opportunity cost*: the funds could have been used to purchase financial assets that earn the interest rate $r$.

investment for the firm. At any higher level of investment, the marginal return would be less than the interest expense, so profits would fall.

Based on this approach, changes in two key variables raise the amount of desired capital investment:

- *Lower market interest rates r* raise capital investment because the interest rate represents the financing cost.

- *Higher marginal returns on investment m* raise capital investment because the marginal return determines the expected earnings from a project.

More detailed theories of capital investment identify more specific variables that determine the marginal return on investment. For example, lower tax rates raise the after-tax profits of a firm, while a fast-growing economy raises the likelihood that produced goods will be sold. Both of these factors raise the marginal return on investment, so they both raise the desired amount of capital investment. Expectations of future developments—such as changes in the demand for a product, new competition, or new technology—also affect the expected return and therefore the amount of investment.

Box 3.5 provides a summary of the variables that determine desired capital investment.

---

BOX 3.5 IN DEPTH

## Variables That Determine Desired Capital Investment

1. Capital investment is carried to the point where the marginal return on investment $m$ equals the interest rate $r$.
2. Variables that raise the marginal return on investment—such as lower taxes, higher income, and new technology—increase the desired amount of capital investment.
3. Lower market interest rates, which reduce the cost of financing, also increase the desired amount of capital investment.

---

## The Loanable Funds Theory of Interest Rates

According to the **loanable funds theory of interest rates,** interest rates adjust toward an equilibrium level where the supply and demand for loans are equal. In a market for auto loans, for example, some people need to borrow money for car purchases, while other people (or banks) are willing to lend money for this purpose. According to the loanable funds theory, the interest rate for auto loans should reach an equilibrium level where the supply and demand for auto loans are equal.

## The Market Interest Rate

In practice, there are hundreds of different types of loans and debt securities which people, firms, and governments use when borrowing and lending money. For example, people use mortgage loans to borrow money to buy homes, firms issue corporate bonds (and other debt securities) to borrow money to purchase new manufacturing equipment, and the U.S. Treasury issues securities to finance the federal government's budget deficit.

The loanable funds theory is particularly useful when it is applied to the overall market for loanable funds. Among other things, by focusing on the overall market, we can temporarily put aside factors that affect only the interest rate for a specific type of loan—such as the borrower's riskiness, the time that remains before the loan must be repaid, and other special factors. (We will look at individual loans and securities in Chapter 5.)

The *Treasury bill rate* is a good indicator of *the* market interest rate—the interest rate that balances demand and supply in the overall market for loanable funds. **Treasury bills**—the main securities issued by the U.S. Treasury for short-term borrowing—are representative of the many types of loans that are made, and securities that are issued, in the U.S. economy. The pattern of Treasury bill rates since 1950 is shown in Figure 3.5. It is apparent that Treasury bill rates have varied sub-

FIGURE 3.5
**The Treasury Bill Rate**

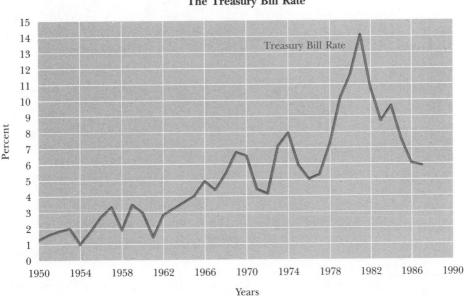

The figure shows three-month Treasury bill rates—the annual interest rates on Treasury bills issued by the U.S. Treasury that mature in three months. Treasury bill rates represent a basic measure of interest rates for the United States. **Source:** *Economic Report of the President,* February, 1988.

stantially over time, falling below 2% during the early 1950s, and rising above 14% during the early 1980s.

Changing expectations for inflation are one reason that Treasury bill rates vary so much. However, in developing the loanable funds theory, it is helpful to focus first on variables other than inflation that cause interest rates to vary. This is why we have been assuming in this chapter that there is no inflation. (We will look at the effect of expected inflation on interest rates in Chapter 4.)

## The Supply and Demand for Loanable Funds

The loanable funds theory is illustrated in Figure 3.6. The supply curve of loanable funds is positively sloped as a function of the interest rate because people tend to lend larger amounts as the interest rate—the return to lending—rises. The demand curve for loans is negatively sloped because people tend to borrow larger amounts as the interest rate—which is also the cost of borrowing—falls.

The market for loans is initially in equilibrium at the 8% interest rate, where the initial supply and demand curves intersect. If the supply curve of loans shifts to the right as illustrated, then the equilibrium interest rate falls to 2%. If the demand curve for loans shifts to the right as illustrated, then the equilibrium interest rate rises to 14%.

FIGURE 3.6
**Loan Supply and Loan Demand**

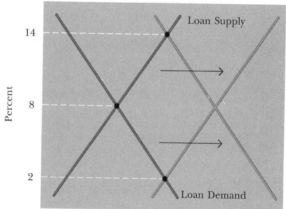

Loanable Funds

The **equilibrium interest rate** is determined where the supply and demand curves intersect, at an 8% interest rate in the figure. At lower interest rates, the loan demand exceeds loan supply, so the interest rate must rise to balance demand and supply. At higher interest rates, the loan supply exceeds the loan demand, so there is pressure for the interest rate to fall. The location of the supply and demand curves thus determines the equilibrium interest rate.

Shifts in the supply and demand curves cause the equilibrium interest rate to change. For example, if the supply curve shifts to the right to the extent shown, then the equilibrium interest rate falls to 2%. This is sensible because a rightward shift in the supply curve means that more loans are supplied at each interest rate, so the interest rate must fall to restore the balance between demand and supply. Similarly, if the demand curve shifts to the right as illustrated, then the equilibrium interest rate rises to 14%.

To know why the interest rate might change, we must therefore identify the variables that might cause the demand curve or supply curve for loanable funds to shift. Because borrowing and lending are closely related to saving and capital investment, the supply and demand curves for loanable funds shift as a result of changes in the same variables that determine desired saving and capital investment. We will now look at the relationship between loanable funds, saving, and capital investment.

## Loanable Funds, Saving, and Investment

The supply of loanable funds refers specifically to what we have been calling positive financial investment. Households with positive financial investment make loans and purchase securities on balance—that is, they supply loanable funds. Similarly, the demand for loanable funds refers specifically to negative financial investment. Households with negative financial investment borrow money on balance—that is, they demand loanable funds.

Moreover, we saw earlier that saving equals the sum of capital investment and financial investment:

$$S = I^C + I^F,$$

or equivalently,

$$I^F = S - I^C. \tag{3.3}$$

Based on equation (3.3), if a variable raises the amount of desired saving, it then raises the amount of financial investment—corresponding to an increase in the *supply* of loanable funds. Similarly, if a variable raises the amount of desired capital investment, it then reduces the amount of financial investment—corresponding to an increase in the *demand* for loanable funds. This is why desired saving can be associated with the supply of loanable funds and desired capital investment can be associated with the demand for loanable funds.

## The Equilibrium Interest Rate

The equilibrium condition for the loanable funds theory can thus be expressed in terms of the variables that determine desired saving and capital investment:

Supply of loanable funds = Demand for loanable funds, or

$$S[\overset{+}{Y_1}, \overset{-}{Y_2}, \overset{-}{TP}, \overset{+}{r}] = I^C[\overset{+}{m}, \overset{-}{r}], \tag{3.4}$$

where $S$ = desired saving,
$\quad Y_1$ = current income,
$\quad Y_2$ = future income,
$\quad TP$ = time preference,
$\quad r$ = the interest rate,
$\quad I^C$ = desired capital investment,
$\quad m$ = the marginal return on capital investment.

The brackets in equation (3.4) mean "function of," indicating that desired saving $S$ and desired capital investment $I^C$ depend on the listed variables. The positive or negative sign, $+$ or $-$, above each variable indicates the effect a change in that variable has on $S$ or $I^C$. For example, the plus sign above the current income variable $Y_1$ in the $S$ term indicates that desired saving rises when current income rises. The variables in equation (3.4)—$Y_1$, $Y_2$, $TP$, $m$, and $r$—are, of course, the same ones we discussed earlier regarding desired saving and desired capital investment.

The complete loanable funds theory is illustrated in the three panels of Figure 3.7.

## Changes in the Equilibrium Interest Rate

Changes in the variables—other than the interest rate $r$—that determine desired saving cause the supply curve to shift, as illustrated in panel B. A change in the marginal return that determines desired capital investment causes the demand curve to shift, as illustrated in panel C. (Note that a plus sign above any variable, other than the interest rate $r$, means that an increase in the variable shifts the curve to the right, while a negative sign means that an increase in the variable shifts the curve to the left.)

The equilibrium interest rate $r^*$ will change if either the supply or demand curve shifts as the result of a change in any of the other variables that determine saving or capital investment. This can be illustrated with two examples, the first applying to the supply curve and the second to the demand curve:

■ Suppose that people become less impatient to consume currently— that is, time preference $TP$ in the economy falls. This raises the desired amount of saving, and shifts the supply curve to the right, as illustrated in panel B of Figure 3.7. The equilibrium interest rate falls as a result.

■ Suppose that a technological breakthrough raises the marginal return on capital investment. This raises the desired amount of capital investment, and shifts the demand curve to the right, as illustrated in panel C of Figure 3.7. The equilibrium interest rate rises as a result.

## Four Scenarios Involving Interest Rates

We can now apply the loanable funds theory as a general theory of interest rate determination. The position of the demand and supply curves is determined by the variables $Y_1$, $Y_2$, $TP$, and $m$, as expressed in equation (3.4), and as illustrated in Figure 3.7. So if we start in equilibrium—as illustrated in panel A—but one of these variables changes, this causes the supply or demand curve to shift, and the interest rate must then adjust to restore equilibrium. Box 3.6 summarizes how the interest rate adjusts. The following scenarios give specific examples.

The equilibrium interest rate $r^*$ is determined at point $E$ where the supply and demand curves for loanable funds intersect. The variables that affect desired saving determine the position of the supply curve, while the variables that affect desired capital investment determine the position of the demand curve.

FIGURE 3.7

**The Loanable Funds Theory of Interest Rates**

A. The Equilibrium Interest Rate

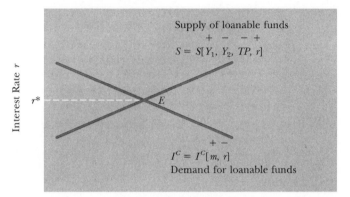

Loanable Funds

The supply of loanable funds will shift to the right if current income rises, future income falls, or time preference falls. The result is that the equilibrium interest rate falls from $r^*$ to $r'$.

B. A Rightward Shift in the Supply Curve

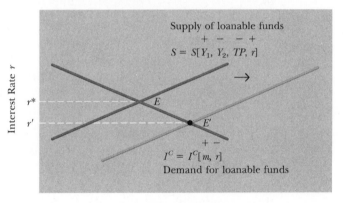

Loanable Funds

The demand for loanable funds will shift to the right if the marginal return on capital investment rises. The result is that the equilibrium interest rate rises from $r^*$ to $r'$.

C. A Rightward Shift in the Demand Curve

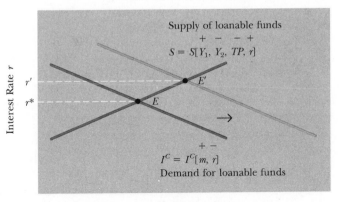

Loanable Funds

BOX 3.6 IN DEPTH

## Variables That Determine the Interest Rate

| Variable That Rises | Curve That Shifts | Effect on the Interest Rate |
|---|---|---|
| Current income $Y_1$ | Supply curve shifts to right | $r^*$ falls |
| Future income $Y_2$ | Supply curve shifts to left | $r^*$ rises |
| Time preference $TP$ | Supply curve shifts to left | $r^*$ rises |
| Marginal return on investment $m$ | Demand curve shifts to right | $r^*$ rises |

**Note:** These results assume everything else is unchanged. In practice, two or more variables may change at the same time, or a change in one variable may also cause a change in another variable. These possibilities are illustrated by the scenarios in this section.

### Scenario 1: New Technology Creates an Investment Boom

Suppose that technological developments (such as new computer chips) create investment opportunities with a high marginal rate of return ($m$ rises). Assuming that a firm is in equilibrium initially, its capital investment will rise, the demand curve for loanable funds will shift to the right, and the interest rate will rise.

However, additional capital investment may also raise current income ($Y_1$ rises). As current income rises, the supply curve for loanable funds will shift to the right, and the interest rate will fall. The overall change in the interest rate then depends on which of the two effects is larger.

### Scenario 2: Young People Are Impatient To Consume

As people graduate from college and enter the labor force, they are impatient to consume—they have a high time preference. However, their income does not yet reflect their aspirations. Since they want to consume more, but do not have enough income, they need to borrow. Their demand curve for loanable funds will thus shift to the right, and the interest rate will rise.

The increased consumption demand may also cause the pace of economic activity to pick up ($Y_1$ rises). As current income rises, saving increases, so a larger supply of loanable funds is available to finance some of the additional demand. This change moderates the initial increase in interest rates.

### Scenario 3: The Federal Government's Budget Deficit

In recent years, the federal government has run large budget deficits, forcing the Treasury department to borrow (issue securities) to finance the deficits. Higher government deficits shift the demand curve for loanable funds to the right, and the interest rate will rise on this account.

However, higher government expenditures also stimulate the economy, raising the level of current income ($Y_1$ rises). Since higher current income shifts the supply curve of loanable funds to the right, the interest rate will fall on this account.

Given that these two aspects of a government deficit have opposite effects on the interest rate, it is not surprising that the overall effect of government deficits on interest rates is much debated in economics.

### Scenario 4: Foreign Lending to the United States

We have seen that the United States depends upon foreign lending to augment domestic saving. Among the variables that foreigners consider when deciding to lend in U.S. dollars are: (1) the relative stability of the United States compared to other countries, (2) changes in the expected foreign exchange value of the dollar relative to other currencies, and (3) the level of U.S. interest rates relative to the rates available in other countries.

If these variables tend to be favorable for the United States, then the foreign supply of lending to the United States may rise. This will shift the overall supply curve of loanable funds to the right, causing the U.S. interest rate to fall. If the assessment of these variables is unfavorable for the United States, then the foreign supply of lending may be reduced, and U.S. interest rates will rise.

## The Money Demand / Money Supply Interest Rate Theory

In closing this discussion of the determinants of interest rates, we should also note that we will be looking at an alternative theory of interest rates—the money demand/money supply (MD/MS) theory—in Chapter 16 after we discuss money demand and money supply. According to the MD/MS theory, the market interest rate is determined by the equilibrium condition that money demand and money supply are equal. We will see that the MD/MS theory is logically related to the loanable funds theory. This is sensible since the demand and supply for loanable funds are, after all, a demand and supply for money.

## Chapter Summary

1. For a household, saving is the amount by which income exceeds consumption spending. Households have positive saving when they consume less than their income. Households have negative saving—they dissave—when they consume more than their income. For each sector of the economy, saving equals the sum of financial investment and capital investment. For the economy as a whole, financial investment is zero, so saving equals capital investment.

2. Saving allows households to allocate their current and future income between current and future consumption. The amount of future consumption that is affordable is determined by a budget line that depends on current and future income, the interest rate, and current consumption. A household chooses a specific point on the budget line on the basis of its time preference—its desire for current consumption relative to future consumption. Household saving generally rises as:

   a. Current income rises.
   b. Future income falls.
   c. Time preference falls.
   d. The market interest rate rises.

3. Capital investment opportunities are represented by an investment possibility frontier that determines the marginal return on investment. The market rate of interest represents the cost of financing capital investments. Capital investment should be carried out to the point where the marginal return equals the market rate of interest. Capital investment generally rises when:
   a. Factors such as new technology raise the marginal return.
   b. Falling interest rates reduce the financing cost.

4. According to the loanable funds theory, interest rates settle at the equilibrium level where the demand and supply of loanable funds are equal. The demand and supply of loanable funds depend on the factors that determine saving and capital investment. As a result, interest rates rise as:
   a. Current income falls.
   b. Future income rises.
   c. Time preference rises.
   d. The marginal return to investment rises.

## Key Terms

Borrowing and lending

Budget line

Capital and financial investment

Current and future income

Desired capital investment and saving

Flow of Funds accounts

Investment possibility frontier

Loanable funds theory of interest rates

Marginal return on investment

Market rate of interest

Saving and dissaving

Time preference

## Study Questions

1. The following is a table of hypothetical data from the Flow of Funds accounts for an economy. Fill in the missing values.

| | Sector 1 | Sector 2 | Economy |
|---|---|---|---|
| Saving | 1,000 | ? | ? |
| Capital investment | 7,000 | 4,000 | ? |
| Financial investment | ? | ? | ? |

2. In Question 1, if someone in sector 1 now buys an existing home from someone else in sector 1 for $10,000 and pays for it by issuing a $10,000 mortgage to the seller, how would the accounts change?

3. Individuals A and B have the same current and future income, but A has a higher time preference. Which person consumes more $C_1$? more $C_2$?

4. A person has current income $Y_1 = 1,000$ and future income $Y_2 = 1,100$, and the interest rate is 10%. Write out the equation for the budget line that shows how much future consumption $C_2$ the person can obtain. What is the maximum amount of future consumption $C_2$ the person can have? The maximum amount of current consumption $C_1$?

5. Using the budget equation of Question 4, for each of the following cases, indicate whether the indicated consumption combination $\{C_1, C_2\}$ is feasible (that is, whether the person can reach the combination by moving along the budget line). Also indicate how much the person is saving or dissaving for those cases where the consumption combination is feasible.

| | Current Consumption | Future Consumption |
|---|---|---|
| | $C_1$ | $C_2$ |
| Case (a) | 1,000 | 1,100 |
| Case (b) | 1,100 | 1,000 |
| Case (c) | 500 | 1,650 |
| Case (d) | 1,600 | 440 |

6. Using case (a) of Question 5 as the starting point, will saving rise or fall in response to each of the following changes (taking them one at a time)?
   a. Current income $Y_1$ rises by 100.
   b. Future income $Y_2$ rises by 100.
   c. The market interest rate rises to 15%.
   d. The person's time preference rises.

7. In drawing the budget line in Figure 3.1, we assumed that a household earns 10% interest if it lends money and that it pays 10% interest if it borrows money. How would the amount of saving and dissaving change if a household earns only 8% interest if it lends money, while it pays 12% interest if it borrows money?

8. A firm's investment possibility frontier is based on the following:

| Situation | When the Investment Level is: | The Value of Future Production Is: |
|---|---|---|
| A | 1 | 1.50 |
| B | 2 | 2.75 |
| C | 3 | 3.85 |
| D | 4 | 4.90 |

What is the marginal return to 1 unit of investment in moving from each situation to the next? What important feature of the marginal return is illustrated by your results? If the market rate of interest rate is 10%, what is the best level of investment for the firm to select?

9. Why is financial investment zero for the whole economy? Why can individuals in the economy still borrow and lend?

10. Indicate for each of the following how the demand and supply curves for loanable funds shift and whether the equilibrium interest rate rises or falls:
   a. Current income $Y_1$ rises.
   b. Future income $Y_2$ rises.
   c. Time preference $TP$ rises.
   d. The marginal return on investment $m$ rises.

## Recommended Reading

*The following Federal Reserve booklet provides all you are likely to want to know about the Flow of Funds accounts:*

Board of Governors of the Federal Reserve System, *Introduction to Flow of Funds*, 1980.

*These standard macroeconomic and microeconomic texts discuss the decisions to save and to invest in detail:*

Robert E. Hall and John B. Taylor, *Macro-Economics*, 2nd edition, Norton, 1988.

Walter Nicholson, *Microeconomic Theory*, 2nd edition, especially chapter 17 "Capital Theory."

*The classic work that discusses the determinants of interest rates is:*

Irving Fisher, *The Theory of Interest Rates*, Macmillan, 1930.

*A thorough text that discusses the determinants of interest rates:*

J. Hirshleifer, *Investment, Interest, and Capital*, Prentice-Hall, 1970.

*A recent discussion of the causes and effects of the low U.S. saving rate:*

Lawrence Summers and Chris Carroll, "Why is U.S. National Saving So Low?" *Brookings Papers on Economic Activity*, 1987, 2, pp. 607–642.

*Two well-known studies of the effect of interest rates on saving in the United States:*

Michael J. Boskin, "Taxation, Saving, and the Rate of Interest," *Journal of Political Economy*, April 1978, pp. 3–28.

E. P. Howrey and S. H. Hyman, "The Measurement and Determination of Loanable-Funds Saving," *Brookings Papers on Economic Activity*, 1978, pp. 655–705.

## Appendix 3.1
## The Income Effects of Higher Interest Rates

In addition to the *substitution effect* of a higher interest rate—that saving rises when the interest rate rises—there are *income effects* for families that are initially borrowing or lending. When the interest rate rises, a family that is initially borrowing money suffers a negative income effect, while a family that is initially lending receives a positive income effect.

We will illustrate the basis of these income effects with the cases of two families—the Greens and the Browns—that we discussed earlier in Table 3.3. The Browns are initially borrowing $500, so based on a 10% interest rate, they have an interest expense of $50. The Greens are initially lending $500, so based on a 10% interest rate, they have interest income of $50.

Now let us suppose the interest rate rises to 15%. The interest expense of the Browns will then rise to $65 (15% of $500), effectively reducing the income they have available for consumption by $15 ($65 − $50). This is the *negative income effect* of higher interest rates for *borrowers*. It means that the Browns have to cut back their consumption—both current and future consumption, given that consumption is *normal*—by $15. Since current consumption $C_1$ falls, but actual current income $Y_1$ is unchanged, their saving $S$ ($= Y_1 − C_1$) rises. The negative income effect for *borrowers* thus reinforces the substitution effect of higher interest rates—both cause saving to rise when the interest rate rises.

Comparably, when the interest rate rises to 15%, the interest income earned by the Greens rises to $65, effectively raising the income they have available for consumption by $15. This is the *positive income effect* of higher interest rates for *lenders*. It means that the Greens can increase their consumption—both current and future consumption, given that consumption is *normal*—by $15. Since current consumption $C_1$ rises, but actual current income $Y_1$ is unchanged, saving $S$ ($= Y_1 − C_1$) falls. A positive income effect thus works in the opposite direction of the substitution effect of higher interest rates. This is why Result (4) in Box 3.4 has the qualification regarding positive income effects.

# Wealth, Portfolios, and Prices 4

*"A billion here, a billion there—pretty soon it adds up to real money."*

*Senator Everett Dirksen*

Imagine that you are a Wall Street deal maker and are asked to determine the value of the United States; the whole country is up for sale and you stand to make a whopping commission. A farfetched exercise? Yes, but not entirely, considering the recent trend toward large sales of American assets to foreign investors.

How would you determine the value of the United States? The main thing is to add up the value of all of its capital assets—physical, tangible, items having a value that endures over time. Capital assets include *structures* (such as manufacturing plants, office buildings, and homes), *equipment* (such as machinery and computers), *consumer durables* (such as cars and refrigerators), and *infrastructure* (such as tunnels, bridges, and roads). The value of *land* (and natural resources) should also be included.

Human capital is another component of the country's worth, reflecting the value of its people—professors and football players alike—based on their skills, experience, education, and so forth. Human capital is as real as physical capital, but since people cannot be bought and sold (there are laws prohibiting slavery), we will exclude the value of human capital from this notion of the purchase price of the United States.

Loans and securities that constitute borrowing and lending between Americans are also excluded from the purchase value of the United States, but for a different reason. Although each loan or security represents an asset for the lender, it also represents a liability for the borrower, so there is no net value for the economy as a whole. A country's value will, however, include the net amount of its foreign financial assets; this currently lowers the value of the United States because the country is now a net debtor to the rest of the world.

Putting aside human capital and net foreign assets, the wealth of the United States consists of the value of its capital stock—structures, equipment, consumer durables, infrastructure, and land. On this basis, the United States is currently worth over $14 trillion.

A country's wealth is composed of its capital assets—its capacity to produce goods (and services) now and in the future. We will first look at how wealth is accumulated and at how it is allocated to different types of capital assets. We will then consider how inflation affects economic decisions, especially those involving wealth. Among other things, we will learn to avoid "money illusion" by taking into account the effect of the price level and the inflation rate on the value of goods and assets.

## The Sources and Uses of Wealth

People can accumulate wealth in basically two ways. They can inherit or otherwise acquire *existing wealth*. Or they can earn income and *save* some of it. (We include here capital gains income—appreciation in the value of previously accumulated wealth—as a type of saving.) The two basic ways to accumulate wealth can be expressed in a simple equation:

$$W_t = W_{t-1} + S_t, \tag{4.1}$$

where $W_t$ = the amount of wealth at the current date $t$,

$\quad W_{t-1}$ = the amount of wealth at an earlier date $t - 1$,

$\quad\quad S_t$ = the amount of saving between dates $t - 1$ and $t$.

Positive saving $S_t$ causes the amount of wealth to rise over time, while negative saving causes the amount of wealth to fall. With negative saving, a person's total wealth can even become negative (the person becomes a debtor on balance).

### Stocks and Flows

The relationship between wealth and saving illustrates the distinction made in economics between **stocks and flows.** *Stocks are quantities that are measured in terms of their level at a moment in time.* For example, wealth is a stock because the level of wealth is measured at a specific date. The amount of money in your pocket at this moment is also a stock. The time at which the measurement is made is essential. Tomorrow you are likely to have a different amount of money in your pocket.

*Flows are quantities that are measured in terms of their rate of change over a time interval.* If a person saved $1,000 during a year, then $1,000 was the annual flow of saving. It would not be sufficient to state that $1,000 was saved—the time *interval* is essential to the meaning of a flow.

A stock variable and the corresponding flow variable are related in two ways:

- If the flows of a variable over a number of time intervals are added together, the resulting accumulation is a stock. This is why the stock of wealth is the accumulation of the flow of saving.

- The change in the stock of a variable between two dates is a flow. For example, current wealth exceeds previously acquired wealth by an amount equal to the flow of saving.

## Wealth and Portfolios

People use their wealth to buy capital assets and financial assets. **Capital assets** are tangible, physical items, such as manufacturing plants and equipment, houses, and consumer durables. **Financial assets** are securities, such as stocks, bonds, and money. There are also **financial liabilities**—the debts of people who have borrowed money to buy goods or assets. **Net financial assets** equal financial assets minus financial liabilities. (There are no capital liabilities because a negative capital asset has no meaning.)

A **portfolio** represents the specific combination of capital assets, financial assets, and financial liabilities that a person holds. The *size of a portfolio*—the person's wealth $W$—equals the sum of the capital assets $K$ and the *net* financial assets (financial assets $A$ minus financial liabilities $L$):

$$W = K + A - L. \tag{4.2}$$

The size of a portfolio—wealth—is increased by saving because the excess of income over consumption is used to buy capital assets $K$ and financial assets $A$, or to reduce (repay) financial liabilities $L$. Similarly, the size of a portfolio is decreased by dissaving because the deficiency of income relative to consumption is financed by selling assets or taking out loans (adding to financial liabilities).

The *composition of a portfolio* can be adjusted without changing its size. This may involve buying certain capital or financial assets, while selling others. Or it may involve buying assets, while issuing financial liabilities (taking out loans). For example, when a family purchases a house—a capital asset—and finances it with a mortgage loan—a financial liability—of the same value, then the capital assets $K$ and the financial liabilities $L$ in equation (4.2) rise by the same amount, leaving wealth $W$ unchanged.

People control the level and the composition of their wealth with two types of decisions:

1. The *saving decision* determines the level of wealth—the size of the portfolio.

2. The *portfolio decision* determines the composition of wealth—the specific assets and liabilities held in the portfolio.

## Portfolio Selection

The process by which the composition of the assets and liabilities in a portfolio is determined is called *portfolio selection*. Portfolio selection theory is a major topic we will discuss in Part 2 of the book. Here we will introduce some of the key factors that are considered in selecting portfolios. Everything else being equal:

- Financial and capital assets with higher *expected rates of return* are generally preferred as investments. Financial liabilities with lower rates of interest are preferred for financing purchases of goods and assets.

- Assets with lower levels of *risk* are generally preferred.

■ Portfolios usually should be *diversified*—they should consist of a relatively large number of individual assets.

■ Portfolios generally include some *liquid assets*—assets that can be rapidly sold at fair prices to raise money. The *maturity* of the assets—the time until the invested amount is returned—may also matter for this reason.

## The Wealth of U.S. Households

The aggregate portfolio of the household sector of the U.S. economy is shown by the balance sheet in Table 4.1. The data are from the Federal Reserve's Flow of Funds accounts for the end of 1987 (the same source we used in Chapter 3).

**TABLE 4.1**

**Wealth and Capital for the Household Sector**

|  | At year-end 1987 (Dollars in billions) | | |
|---|---|---|---|
| Financial Assets *A* | | Financial Liabilities *L* | |
| Deposits | $ 2,967 | Home mortgages | $ 1,897 |
| Credit market instruments | 1,242 | Consumer credit | 753 |
| Common stock | 2,143 | Other liabilities | 330 |
| Unincorporated business | 2,428 | Total liabilities | 2,980 |
| Life insurance and pension funds | 2,594 | | |
| Other financial assets | 279 | | |
| Capital Assets *K* | | Net worth (Wealth) | 14,776 |
| Residential structures | 2,942 | | |
| Consumer durables | 1,657 | | |
| Land | 1,280 | | |
| Other | 279 | | |
| Total assets | $17,756 | Total liabilities and net worth | $17,756 |

Source: *Balance Sheets for the U.S. Economy*, Flow of Funds Accounts, Release C.9, Board of Governors of the Federal Reserve System, 1988.

The assets owned by households are shown on the left side of the balance sheet. Financial assets, *A*, include bank deposits, credit market instruments (such as government and corporate bonds), common stock, unincorporated (family-owned) businesses, and life insurance and pension funds. Capital assets, *K*, consist primarily of homes (residential structures), consumer durables (including autos), and land.

Financial liabilities, *L*, on the right side of the balance sheet, include home mortgages, consumer credit, and other debts. Wealth is the amount by which total financial and capital assets exceed total liabilities. This is referred to in the table as **net worth**—the accounting term used to denote wealth. The household sector's net worth (or wealth) was over $14 trillion at the end of 1987.

## Capital as the Use of Wealth

For the whole economy, financial assets $A$ equal financial liabilities $L$ because there must be a lender for every borrower. This means that *net financial assets* $(A - L)$ equal zero for the whole economy. It then follows from equation (4.2), $W = K + A - L$, that wealth $W$ equals the capital stock $K$ for the whole economy, $W = K$.

The capital stock grows when people add capital investment to the existing stock of capital:[1]

$$K_t = K_{t-1} + I_t, \tag{4.3}$$

where $K_t$ = the capital stock at the current date $t$,

$K_{t-1}$ = the capital stock at an earlier date $t - 1$,

$I_t$ = the capital investment between dates $t - 1$ and $t$.

(From now on, we will refer to "capital investment" simply as *investment*: this is the standard economic terminology, and we will be careful not to confuse it with financial investment.)

Capital is thus accumulated through investment. Earlier we saw that wealth is accumulated through saving. In fact, these concepts are closely related for the whole economy: *saving equals capital investment* and *wealth equals capital.*

## The Wealth of the U.S. Economy

The relationship between wealth (accumulated saving) and capital (accumulated investment) is further clarified by looking at the data from the Flow of Funds accounts for the main sectors of the U.S. economy and for the economy as a whole.

The wealth of each sector is shown in Table 4.2. It is apparent that the *household sector* holds most of the wealth of the United States. However, the *business* and *financial institution* sectors are more important than they might appear: about $5 trillion of the household sector wealth is made up of the ownership of business and financial firms.

[1] The investment $I_t$ in equation (4.3) is *net investment*. Net investment equals gross investment (the actual amount of new capital purchased) minus depreciation (the amount of capital used up during the period).

TABLE 4.2
Wealth and Capital for the U.S. Economy

At year-end 1987
(Dollars in billions)

| Wealth by Sector | | Capital Assets | |
|---|---|---|---|
| Household | $14,776 | Residential structures | $ 4,037 |
| Business | 621 | Plant and equipment | 4,085 |
| Financial institutions | 424 | Land | 3,441 |
| Government (financial assets less liabilities) | − 1,922 | Consumer durables | 1,656 |
| Foreign sector (net claims on U.S. assets) | 285 | Inventories | 944 |
| | | U.S. gold and other | 21 |
| Total wealth | $14,184 | Total wealth | $14,184 |

**Source**: *Balance Sheets for the U.S. Economy*, Flow of Funds Accounts, Release C.9, Board of Governors of the Federal Reserve System, 1988.

The *government sector* is the only sector with negative wealth—the result of past federal budget deficits. However, this is also not quite as it appears because the measured wealth of the government sector is based only on its financial assets and liabilities. (Government-owned capital assets—such as bridges and roads—are not counted in the accounts because their market value cannot be determined accurately.)

The *foreign sector* represents the net claims of foreigners on U.S. assets—the value of U.S. assets owned by foreigners minus the value of foreign assets owned by Americans. As shown, foreigners now own $285 billion of U.S. assets on balance. Box 4.1 discusses the significance of this recent development.

BOX 4.1 CREDIT CHECK

## The Selling of America

The cover of an issue of the British weekly, *The Economist* (April 30, 1988) showed Paul Revere shouting, "The British are coming, and the Japanese, and the Germans, and the Canadians. . . ." His warning was not about soldiers with red coats, but about foreign investors with green dollars. After decades of buying up foreign assets around the world, it seems that Americans are suddenly selling assets instead of buying them.

Federated Department Stores (which owns Bloomingdale's among other stores) was sold to Robert Campeau, a Canadian investor (Canadian ownership of New York City now equals 1 square foot per Canadian citizen). Brooks Brothers, the venerable men's clothing store, was purchased by the British firm Marks and Spencer's. And so on down the list, which even includes some large U.S. banks.

This is all happening because the United States had large *trade deficits* throughout the 1980s—the amount of foreign goods imported into the United States exceeded the amount of U.S. goods exported abroad (in some years by as much as $150 billion). To pay for the trade deficits, Americans either have to borrow money from abroad (which we have been doing steadily during the 1980s) or they have to sell assets to foreigners (as we are now seeing). We will look at this process further in Chapters 21 and 22 when we discuss international finance and international monetary systems.

Capital assets are another way of looking at the wealth of the U.S. economy, as shown on the right side of Table 4.2. Residential structures, plant and equipment, and land are the three primary types of capital assets, each with a value of about $4 trillion. Thus, whichever way you look at it—as the combined wealth of the individual sectors, or as the total value of the capital stock, the total wealth of the United States was just over $14 trillion at the end of 1987.

## Wealth and Prices

Although we assumed in Chapter 3 that the **inflation rate**—the rate of change of the price level—was zero, we know that inflation rates can be high and can fluctuate widely. The rate of inflation in the United States reached "double-digit" levels as recently as 1980, then later declined to low levels. The basic concepts of price levels and inflation rates have important ramifications with regard to wealth and income.

### Price Levels and Inflation Rates

The **price level** represents the average level of prices in an economy at a given date. A **price index** is the price level for a particular group of goods. The **consumer price index** (*CPI*) is the price level of a typical U.S. consumer's "basket" of goods. Box 4.2 shows the weights accorded different consumption categories in computing the CPI.

---

BOX 4.2 FINANCIAL NEWS

## The Consumer Price Index

The consumer price index (CPI) for the United States is collected and tabulated by the Bureau of Labor Statistics (BLS), a government agency. This is a big job because prices for all categories of consumption have to be sampled across the country every month. The BLS, moreover, has to keep updating the weights—called **relative importance**—accorded the different categories of consumption as people change their buying patterns. The following table shows how the CPI is reported and how the BLS changed the weights in 1987.

| Expenditure Category | Average Expenditure | Relative Importance |
|---|---|---|
| All items | $19,362.65 | 100.000 |
| Food and beverages | 3,454.36 | 17.840 |
| Food at home | 1,962.94 | 10.138 |
| Food away from home | 1,189.82 | 6.145 |
| Alcoholic beverages | 301.60 | 1.558 |
| Housing | 8,255.57 | 42.637 |
| Apparel and upkeep | 1,263.23 | 6.524 |
| Transportation | 3,620.03 | 18.696 |
| New vehicles | 1,064.36 | 5.497 |
| Used vehicles | 246.08 | 1.271 |
| Motor fuel | 929.49 | 4.800 |
| Public transportation | 269.67 | 1.393 |
| Medical care | 928.58 | 4.796 |
| Entertainment | 848.02 | 4.380 |
| Other goods and services | 992.85 | 5.128 |

**Note:** Annual expenditures by urban consumer units in the seven major categories and selected subcategories for the Consumer Price Index. Many factors contributed to the need for revision, including differences in consumer buying habits as well as prices, population shifts in age and location, new technology and products and new category definitions.

**Source**: Bureau of Labor Statistics.

The CPI index shown in panel A of Figure 4.1 begins at 1.0, an arbitrary value selected for the year 1970. The year 1970 is called the *base year* of the index, and the initial value of 1.0 is called the *base value*. (A base value of 100 is also commonly used.) The price levels for other years are measured relative to the base value.

The corresponding annual inflation rate for the CPI index is shown in panel B of Figure 4.1. The annual inflation rate $\pi$ is the annual proportionate increase in the price level $P$:

$$\pi = \frac{P_t - P_{t-1}}{P_{t-1}}, \tag{4.4}$$

where $P_t$ = the price level at the end of the current year $t$,

$P_{t-1}$ = the price level at the end of the previous year.

To calculate the inflation rate for the year 1980, for example, we see from panel A that the CPI index in 1980 was 2.16 and in 1979 it was 1.92. Using equation (4.4), we calculate the annual inflation rate in 1980 to be 12.5% [(2.17 − 1.91) ÷ 1.91], and this is confirmed in panel B.

Inflation rates are generally measured *as annual rates*, the percentage change in the price level over a year. If the time interval is a period other than one year, then the inflation rate calculated for that period has to be adjusted so it can be expressed as an annual rate. For example, if the inflation rate were measured to be 1% for 1 month, then the equivalent annual rate would be 12% inflation.

Although we will generally use the consumer price index to illustrate and measure the price level in this book, there are actually many price indexes, including the GNP deflator and the producer price index. For a given application, the proper price index depends on the relevant category of goods.

### The GNP Deflator

The **GNP deflator** covers the prices of all the goods included in GNP (gross national product), so it tends to be more comprehensive than the CPI (which just covers consumption goods). However, the CPI includes *imported* consumption goods, whereas the GNP deflator covers only domestically produced goods. Each component of GNP receives a weight in the GNP deflator based on its share of total GNP. The annual average increase in the GNP deflator between 1970 and 1987 was about 6%, while the comparable increase in the CPI was about 6.5%. This indicates that the prices of consumption goods rose a bit more rapidly than the prices of GNP goods during this period. In a given year, of course, the situation might be reversed.

### The Producer Price Index

The **producer price index** (*PPI*)—which was called the wholesale price index until 1978—refers to the prices of goods that are used to produce other goods. It includes, for example, the prices of raw materials, commodities, and semifinished goods. The PPI measures the prices of goods at an earlier stage of the production and distribution cycle than the CPI.

FIGURE 4.1
**The Consumer Price Index and Inflation Rate**
A. The Consumer Price Index

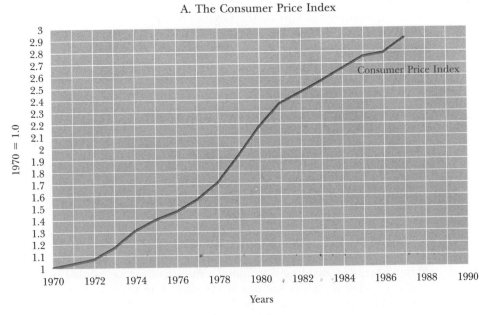

The consumer price index (CPI) measures the price level of a standard "basket" of consumer goods. The price index shown in the figure uses 1970 as the *base year* and 1.0 as the 1970 *base level*. Price levels in other years are stated *relative* to the base level.

B. The Annual Inflation Rate Based on the Consumer Price Index

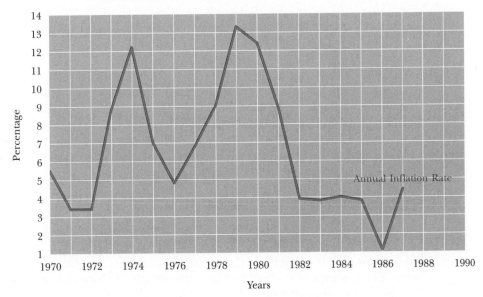

The annual inflation rate is computed as the percentage change in the price level during each year. The figure shows that the inflation rate for the CPI index has recently been as high as 13.3% (in 1979) and as low as 1.1% (in 1986).

For this reason, a change in the PPI is sometimes used as a "leading indicator" of a forthcoming change in the CPI. The average annual increase in the PPI between 1970 and 1987 was about 5.5%, a lower level than either the CPI or the GNP deflator.

## Nominal and Real Variables

Economic variables can be measured in either **nominal** or **real** terms. Variables measured in nominal terms are expressed in dollars (or dollar prices). Variables measured in real terms are expressed in quantities, such as the number of units by weight or volume. In reporting an amount of fish purchased, for example, you might refer to either $10 worth (in nominal terms) or 2 pound's worth (in real terms), given a $5 per pound price of fish.

A nominal variable can be converted to a real variable by dividing the nominal variable by its price:

$$\text{Real value} = \frac{\text{Nominal value}}{\text{Price}} = \frac{\$10 \text{ of fish}}{\$5 \text{ per pound}} = 2 \text{ pounds of fish.}$$

The process of dividing a nominal value by its price to obtain its real value is called **deflating the nominal value.** The price used is called the **price deflator** (hence the origin of the name "GNP deflator").

A nominal value can also be deflated by a price index, such as deflating the nominal value of fish by a food price index. The resulting real value is then stated in terms of prices for the base year of the index. If the food price index has a current value of 2.5 relative to a base value of 1.0 for 1970, and someone now buys $10 of fish, the real value of fish could be expressed as:

$$\text{Real value of fish} = \frac{\$10 \text{ nominal price}}{2.5 \text{ price index}} = \$4.0 \text{ in 1970 food prices.}$$

Many economic data series are expressed in nominal terms, including the data for wealth and capital in Tables 4.1 and 4.2. In an inflationary economy, it can be misleading to compare current and past nominal values of a variable such as wealth: a large part of the increase may simply reflect an increase in the price level over time, not—as might be thought—an increase in real wealth. In these circumstances, real values—derived by deflating the nominal values—must be compared. We will look at an example of this shortly.

## Nominal and Real Interest Rates

Interest rates must also be converted from nominal to real values to account for inflation. Most interest rates—the 6% that a bank pays on its deposits, or the 10% that it charges on auto loans—are **nominal interest rates.** The corresponding **real interest rate equals the nominal interest rate minus the expected rate of inflation.** If the nominal interest rate is 10% for example, and the expected inflation rate is 6%, then the real interest rate is 4%.

This relationship can be expressed as:

$$\rho = r - \pi^e, \tag{4.5}$$

where $\rho$ = the real interest rate,
$\quad r$ = the nominal interest rate,
$\quad \pi^e$ = the expected inflation rate.

When the inflation rate $\pi^e$ is expected to be 5% over the next year, for example, the real interest rate $\rho$ on a one-year $1,000 bond with an annual, nominal, interest rate $r$ of 8%, is 3% ($\rho = r - \pi^e = 8\% - 5\%$).

Equation (4.5) provides a useful basis for computing real interest rates, but it overlooks the fact that inflation erodes the value of the interest payment as well as the principal repayment. As shown in Box 4.3, however, this does not represent a serious problem as long as the inflation rate is not too high.

## Computing Ex Post and Ex Ante Real Rates

When the rate of inflation is known it is a simple matter to calculate the real rate of interest. In 1987, for example, the nominal interest rate for one-year Treasury bills was 6% and the actual inflation rate was 4%, so

---

**BOX 4.3 CREDIT CHECK**

### The Precise Computation of Real Interest Rates

We can illustrate the precise computation of real interest rates with the example of an investor who buys a one-year bond with an annual, nominal, interest rate of $r$, and who expects the inflation rate to be $\pi^e$ over the next year. It simplifies matters to assume that the price level is 1.0 on the date that the investor buys the bond, so that—based on the expected inflation rate $\pi^e$—the expected price level one year later when the bond matures is $(1 + \pi^e)$. For each dollar invested, the investor receives a total *nominal repayment* (including both principal and interest) of $(1 + r)$ dollars one year later. The *real repayment*—determined by deflating the nominal repayment $(1 + r)$ by the expected price level at the end of the year $(1 + \pi^e)$—is $(1 + r)/(1 + \pi^e)$. Denoting the expected real interest rate as $\rho$, we then have:

$$(1 + \rho) = \frac{(1 + r)}{(1 + \pi^e)}, \text{ or, solving for } \rho,$$

$$\begin{aligned} \rho &= \frac{(1 + r)}{(1 + \pi^e)} - 1 \\ &= \frac{(1 + r) - (1 + \pi^e)}{(1 + \pi^e)} \\ &= \frac{r - \pi^e}{1 + \pi^e}. \end{aligned}$$

This reduces to equation (4.5) when the expected inflation rate $\pi^e$ is small enough to treat the amount $(1 + \pi^e)$ in the denominator as approximately equal to 1.0. When $r = 8\%$ and $\pi^e = 5\%$, for example, equation (4.5) gives the real interest rate $\rho$ as 3, while the more precise formula (with 1.05 in the denominator) gives it as 2.86%.

we can readily compute that the real interest rate was 2%. Real interest rates derived from actual inflation rates are called **ex post real interest rates** (*ex* = from, *post* = afterward).

Investment decisions generally look forward in time, however, to the receipt of interest payments in the future. Given that future inflation rates cannot be known, how do we determine a value for the expected inflation rate? We could refer to the most recent rate of inflation and the current state of the economy to estimate the real interest rate. Or we could use the forecast of an organization that specializes in these matters. Such estimates are called **ex ante real interest rates** (*ex* = from, *ante* = before).

Comparisons of *ex post* and *ex ante* real rates are illustrated in Table 4.3 for a period—1980 to 1983—during which there were especially large changes in nominal interest rates and inflation rates. The nominal interest rate is available to an investor on a one-year Treasury security as of the first day of each year, for example 12% on January 1, 1980. The *ex ante* real interest rate is the nominal interest rate minus the expected inflation rate. The *ex post* real interest rate is the nominal interest minus the actual inflation rate, for example 12% − 12% = 0%. Of course,

**TABLE 4.3**

**The Computation of Real Interest Rates**

| | Annual Percentage | | | |
|---|---|---|---|---|
| | **1980** | **1981** | **1982** | **1983** |
| Nominal interest rate | 12 | 15 | 13 | 9 |
| Expected inflation rate | 9 | 10 | 9 | 5 |
| Actual inflation rate | 12 | 9 | 4 | 4 |
| Ex ante real interest rate[a] | 3 | 5 | 4 | 4 |
| Ex post real interest rate[b] | 0 | 6 | 9 | 5 |

The nominal interest rate is the one-year Treasury bond rate at the beginning of each year.

The expected inflation rate is the inflation rate forecast each year in *Economic Outlook USA,* Survey Research Center, The University of Michigan.

The actual inflation rate is the percentage increase in the consumer price index during the year.

[a]Determined by subtracting the expected inflation rate from the nominal interest rate.
[b]Determined by subtracting the actual inflation rate from the nominal interest rate.

**Source**: Data adapted from *Federal Reserve Bulletin,* Board of Governors of the Federal Reserve System, 1988; *Economic Outlook USA,* Survey Research Center, The University of Michigan, 1988; and *Economic Report of the President,* 1988.

on the first day of 1980, neither borrowers nor lenders could have known that there was going to be 12% inflation that year.

The corresponding *ex ante* and *ex post* real interest rates for a longer period of time, from 1970 to 1987, are illustrated in Figure 4.2. Panel A shows the nominal interest rates and actual inflation rates for this period. Panel B shows the ex post real rate (based on the actual inflation rate) and the ex ante real rate (based on an expected inflation rate). The ex-

FIGURE 4.2
**Real Interest Rates**
A. The Nominal Interest Rate and the Inflation Rate

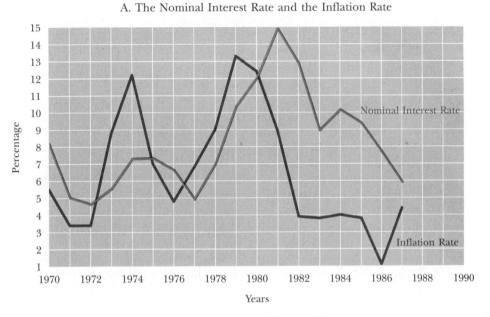

The nominal interest rate shown is the rate on one-year Treasury bills
The inflation rate is based on the consumer price index.

B. Ex Ante and Ex Post Real Interest Rates

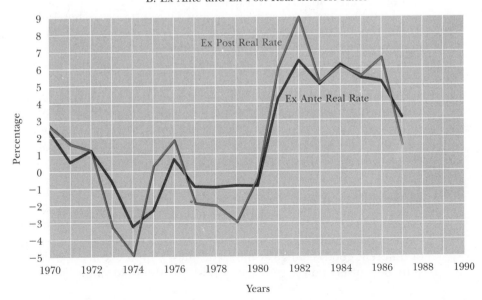

The ex ante real interest rate for each year is based on an expected inflation rate that was computed by averaging the actual inflation rates for that year and the previous year. **Source**: Data adapted from *Federal Reserve Bulletin*, Board of Governors of the Federal Reserve System, 1988; *Economic Outlook USA*, Survey Research Center, The University of Michigan, 1988; and *Economic Report of the President*, February 1988.

pected inflation rate for each year was computed by averaging the actual inflation rates for that year and the previous year (because consistent inflation rate forecasts are not available for the full period).[2] The figure illustrates two key effects of rising inflation rates on real interest rates.

First, *when inflation rates rise, ex post real interest rates tend to be low.* Although the nominal interest rate generally rises when the inflation rate rises, it often rises by a smaller amount especially if the inflation is unexpected, so the ex post real interest rate—the nominal interest rate minus the actual inflation rate—tends to be low. This is illustrated in Figure 4.2 between 1976 and 1980, a period of rapidly rising inflation. By the same token, when inflation fell dramatically after 1980, the ex post real interest rate was high.

Second, *when inflation rates rise, ex ante real rates tend to exceed ex post real rates.* Although the expected inflation rate generally rises when the actual inflation rate rises, the expected inflation rate tends to rise less—it usually takes time for people to revise their expectations fully. Consequently, the *ex ante* real rate tends to be higher than the *ex post* real rate, which is also illustrated between 1976 and 1980 in Figure 4.2. Comparably, when the inflation rate fell after 1980, inflation expectations remained high for a while, so the *ex ante* real rate generally was lower than the *ex post* real rate.

## Money Illusion

A common error in financial situations is to base a decision on a nominal variable—like nominal wealth or a nominal interest rate—when it should be based on a real variable. Decision makers who are mislead by using nominal variables suffer from **money illusion.**

For example, let us suppose that the price level, a person's nominal income, and the nominal amount of his consumption purchases, all rise at exactly the same rate, so that the real amount of his consumption purchases is unchanged. If the person feels better off because he is consuming a larger nominal amount of goods, then he has money illusion. It is the *real quantity* of goods consumed, not the *nominal value* of goods consumed, that should matter to a consumer.

### Money Illusion and Relative Prices

Although it might seem an easy matter to avoid this type of money illusion, the matter becomes more difficult in practice because the prices of different goods change at different rates. Suppose, for example, that your boss offers you a 10% salary raise for the following year, during

---

[2] Expectations that are formed in this way are called *adaptive expectations*, meaning that the expected inflation rate adapts to the actual inflation rate in a steady fashion.

which you expect a 10% inflation rate. If you have no money illusion, you may complain that the raise provides no real benefit. However, your boss may respond—based on an expected 3% inflation rate for the items that *she* consumes—that you are receiving a real raise of 7% (10% nominal raise minus 3% expected inflation). So who has money illusion?

The point is that all prices in the economy generally do not rise at the same rate. Therefore, not only must you avoid money illusion, but you must use the proper price index to reckon where you stand in real terms.

When the price of a good changes at a rate that differs from the overall inflation rate in the economy, the good's **relative price**—its price relative to the overall price level—is changing. Specifically, if $P_i$ is the price of good $i$, and $P$ is the overall price level in the economy, then the relative price of good $i$ is $P_i/P$. The nominal price $P_i$ for good $i$ can then rise in three different ways:

1. In line with the price level $P$ (so the relative price $P_i/P$ is unchanged).

2. Faster than the price level $P$ (so the relative price $P_i/P$ is rising).

3. Slower than the price level $P$ (so the relative price is falling).

A relative price usually changes because the demand or supply conditions in the market for that good change. For example, if consumers raise their demand for a good, then its relative price will rise. Overall inflation, however, refers to the aggregate change in the price level of all goods. Money illusion can then arise because people may have trouble sorting out a relative price change—which calls for a change in the amount demanded or supplied of the particular good—from overall inflation—which may call for quite different changes.

## Money Illusion Over Long Periods of Time

Money illusion tends particularly to distort decisions that are based on nominal values extending over long periods of time, because the effects of inflation accumulate. For example, Figure 4.3 shows that the **nominal wealth** of the United States rose from about $3 trillion in 1970 to about $14 trillion in 1987, an increase of about 350% ([$14 − $3]/$3). By how much did the country's real productive capacity grow over this period? Someone with money illusion would focus on the nominal magnitudes and answer that it increased 350%.

However, as we saw in Figure 4.1, the price level tripled over the same period, from a base value of 1.0 in 1970 to a relative value of 3.0 in 1987. And we know that an increase in productive capacity has to be judged on the basis of **real wealth,** computed by deflating nominal wealth by a price index. In 1970, real wealth in 1970 prices was the same as 1970 nominal wealth, $3 trillion ($W/P$ = $3 trillion/1.0). In 1987, real wealth in 1970 prices was $4.7 trillion ($W/P$ = $14 trillion/3.0). Thus, real wealth rose by a little over 50% ([$4.7 − $3.0]/3.0) between 1970 and 1987.

FIGURE 4.3
**Nominal and Real Wealth for the United States**

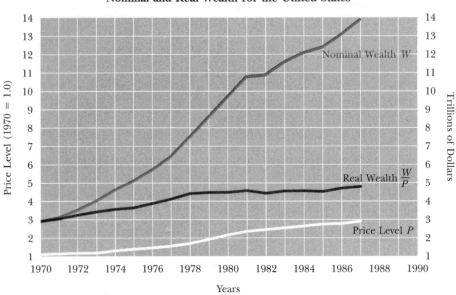

The nominal wealth W of the United States is based on the market value of the capital stock in each year, the value of which rose by about 350% between 1970 and 1987. That is equivalent to a growth rate of about 9.5% each year. However, the consumer price index nearly tripled over the same period.

Therefore, the value of real wealth, the deflated value of nominal wealth, rose by only a little over 50%. That is equivalent to a regular annual growth rate of just under 3%. **Source:** *U.S. Economy,* Flow of Funds Accounts, Release C.9, Board of Governors of the Federal Reserve System, 1988.

## Money Illusion and Real Rates of Interest

Money illusion can also arise with regard to interest rates when decisions are based on nominal instead of real rates. Nominal interest rates are often used in practice, mainly because people fail to take the time to compute the real rates. This does not introduce an error when the returns on investments are compared over the same time period—computing real returns by subtracting the same inflation rate (expected or actual) from the nominal returns does not change the ranking of the returns.

However, money illusion will arise if the nominal return on an investment is thought of as a real return. Suppose a couple retiring in 1970, for example, made an investment that was comparable to investing in the growth potential of the United States. If they then based their retirement spending plans on an expected 9.5% annual rate of return on this investment, the result can be evaluated using the graph of nominal and real wealth in Figure 4.3.

*Nominal* wealth for the United States grew at an annual rate of about 9.5% between 1970 and 1987. The consumer price index, however, grew at an annual rate of about 6.5% between the same years. Thus the *real* annual return on the investment was 3.0% (9.5% − 6.5%). Given an initial investment of $100,000, the retired couple expected an annual income of $9,500—in 1970 dollars—each year (based on a 9.5% annual return). By 1987, however, the $9,500 nominal return on their investment could purchase only goods they could have bought for $3,000 in 1970. (Box 4.4 shows how the same principle applies to the 1626 sale of Manhattan Island for $24.)

---

**BOX 4.4 MONEY MATTERS**

## Money Illusion and the Sale of Manhattan Island

All Americans learn in elementary school that Peter Minuit, the agent for the Dutch West Indies Company, founded New Amsterdam (later New York City) by purchasing Manhattan Island from the local Indians for $24 in 1626. It is usually implied that the Indians got the worst of the deal. But was this really such a bad trade for them? Remember, the purchase price of $24 represented goods valued in 1626 prices, not in current prices. So, to check this out directly, we should convert the 1626 price of $24 into a current price. But, unfortunately, existing price indexes do not go back that far.

However, we can calculate how much the Indians would have accumulated had they invested the $24 purchase price in a savings account earning a 6% annual interest rate for the last 363 years (to 1989). On this basis, they would now have accumulated about $37 billion ($[1.06]^{363}$), not much less than the current assessed valuation of New York City. Of course, this assumes that the Indians were able to invest the $24. Not having that alternative available to them, they presumably consumed it, and so the sale left them with no wealth at all. (Minuit also did not end up all that well—he was lost at a sea in a hurricane in 1638.)

---

### The Fisher Effect

Because inflation reduces the real return earned on an investment, people who expect higher inflation rates may require higher nominal interest rates when they invest. For example, if a bank offers a 6% interest rate on a one-year savings deposit, and you expect a 2% inflation rate during the next year, then the corresponding real rate is 4%. On the other hand, if you expect 6% inflation, and still want to earn a 4% real rate, then you will have to find a security offering a 10% nominal rate.

This notion is the basis of the **Fisher effect** theory—named after its originator Irving Fisher—that nominal interest rates change in precise step with changes in the expected rate of inflation. This is easily expressed as an equation:

$$r = \rho + \pi^e. \tag{4.6}$$

In other words, as long as the real interest rate $\rho$ is unchanged, an increase in expected inflation $\pi^e$ will create an equal increase in the nominal interest rate $r$.

FIGURE 4.4
**The Fisher Effect**

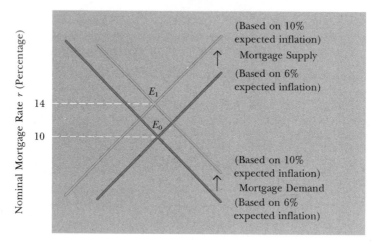

The supply curve of mortgages represents mortgage loans supplied by lenders, while the demand curve for mortgages represents mortgage loans demanded by borrowers. The equilibrium nominal mortgage rate is initially 10% at point $E_0$.

We will illustrate the Fisher effect by applying the loanable funds theory of interest rates (developed in Chapter 3) to mortgage loans (used to finance home purchases). The demand and supply curves for mortgage loans are shown in Figure 4.4. The upward-sloping supply curve indicates that lenders will supply additional mortgage loans as the nominal mortgage interest rate $r$ rises, everything else being unchanged. The downward-sloping demand curve indicates borrowers will demand fewer mortgage loans as the nominal mortgage interest rate rises. The equilibrium nominal mortgage rate is then 10% at point $E_0$. If the expected inflation rate is 6%, this corresponds to a real mortgage rate of 4%.

Now suppose the expected inflation rate rises from 6% to 10%. Were the nominal mortgage rate to remain unchanged at 10%, then the real mortgage rate—the nominal mortgage rate minus the expected inflation rate—would become zero. This would provide borrowers with a powerful incentive to demand more mortgages, so the demand curve would shift rightward (or upward). At the same time, a zero real rate would provide lenders with a powerful incentive to supply fewer mortgages, so the supply curve would shift leftward (or upward). The resulting equilibrium then occurs at point $E_1$, where the new demand and supply curves intersect.

You can see that the equilibrium nominal mortgage rate increases as the demand and supply curves shift upward. Not only is the new mortgage rate higher, but as shown in the diagram, its new value is 14%, so the mortgage rate has increased by exactly the same amount as the expected inflation rate. This represents the Fisher effect—the nominal mortgage rate and the expected inflation rate rise by the same amount, given that the real interest rate is unchanged.

The Fisher effect occurs as long as the demand and supply curves both shift upward by exactly the amount of the increase in expected inflation (four percentage points in the case illustrated). There are good reasons for expecting this to happen. For borrowers, a higher price level reduces the real value of their debt, so they might be willing to pay a higher nominal interest to the extent that they expect higher inflation. For lenders, a higher price level reduces the real value of the loan repayment they will receive, so they might require a higher nominal interest rate to compensate for higher expected inflation.

Put another way, when borrowers and lenders have no money illusion, the *real* interest rate is the key variable that balances the *real* demand and supply of loans. If the expected inflation rate rises, and the nominal interest rate rises by the same amount, then the real interest is unchanged, so the real demand and supply of loans will remain balanced.

## Price Level and Inflation Rate Neutrality

Since real economic variables, such as real wealth and real interest rates—play a key role in the economy, it is important to know how changes in the price level and the inflation rate affect them. Economists call a situation *neutral* when real variables are *unaffected* by changes in the price level or inflation rate. Specifically, we will call a situation **inflation rate neutral** when changes in the expected inflation rate do not affect *ex ante* real interest rates, and we will call a situation **price level neutral** when changes in the price level do not affect such real variables as real wealth or real income.

Price level neutrality had been understood by classical economists at least since Adam Smith in the eighteenth century. Inflation rate neutrality—which is illustrated by the Fisher effect—was analyzed by Irving Fisher at the beginning of this century. Generally speaking, an economy will be neutral with respect to inflation and prices as long as there is no money illusion and there are no impediments to changing prices or interest rates.

A neutral economy is sometimes described as operating with a *monetary veil*. This means that changes in the price level and inflation rate affect only other nominal variables, not any real variables. Although a monetary veil is an intriguing and sometimes useful feature for an economy, there are many reasons why the U.S. economy probably does not operate in this manner. We will now examine some of the ways that the price level and the expected inflation rate can affect the real sphere of the economy.

## Exceptions to the Fisher Effect

The Fisher effect requires that the demand and supply curves for mortgages each shift by the amount of any change in the expected inflation rate. An exception to the Fisher effect occurs whenever factors cause the demand curve or supply curve *not* to shift by this amount. This possibility can be expressed with a more general formulation of equation (4.6):

$$r = \rho + a(\pi^e). \tag{4.7}$$

The coefficient $a$ determines the extent to which an increase in the expected inflation rate $\pi^e$ is reflected in an increase in the nominal rate of interest $r$. The full Fisher effect thus requires that the coefficient $a = 1$; otherwise, there is an exception to the Fisher effect.

Here are some common reasons why the Fisher effect may be violated following an increase in the expected inflation rate:

- *Money illusion* may cause the demand curve or the supply curve to shift upward by less than the increase in expected inflation. The nominal mortgage rate will then rise by less than is required for the full Fisher effect.

- *Relative price changes* may affect how much the mortgage demand or supply curves shift. For example, if borrowers expect house prices to rise more slowly than the overall price level, then the demand curve for mortgages may shift upward by a smaller amount, leading to a smaller change in the nominal mortgage rate.

- *Usury ceilings*—state laws that set maximum limits on nominal mortgage interest rates—have sometimes restricted how much lenders could raise mortgage rates. (However, all usury ceilings on mortgage loans were eliminated by federal law in 1980.)

- *Taxes* affect the demand and supply curves for mortgages because the *after-tax* mortgage rate is what should really matter to borrowers and lenders. For example, tax law changes during the 1980s limited the amount of mortgage interest that borrowers could deduct from their income tax, which reduced the demand for mortgage loans.

## Real Wealth Effects

**Real wealth effects** are another possible source of nonneutrality in an economy. Real wealth effects occur through a two-step process in which (1) an unexpected increase in the price level causes real wealth to fall and (2) lower real wealth causes real saving to rise. An increase in the price level may reduce real wealth because real wealth equals nominal wealth divided by the price level. People may then raise their real saving in an attempt to restore their real wealth to its initial level.

As an example of how this works, imagine that you are trying to save $10,000 to buy a new car. You have already accumulated $5,000 in your bank deposit, and so are halfway to your goal. Your financial wealth is represented by the $5,000 bank deposit. Now suppose that unexpected inflation causes both the price level and the price of the car to rise suddenly.

The increase in the car price will force you to save more, in both nominal and real terms. In *nominal* terms, as the price of the car rises, you will obviously have to save more to buy it. In *real* terms, the real value of your $5,000 bank deposit falls when the price level rises. So even if the real cost of your car is unchanged—its nominal price rises in line with the price level—you have to save an additional amount to offset your loss in real wealth.

Unexpected increases in the price level operate in just the opposite way for people with negative net financial wealth. These people are net debtors, and the real value of their wealth is negative. Therefore, an increase in the price level reduces the real value of their debt, which is to say that their wealth position improves. Consequently, these people will carry out *less real saving when the price level rises.*

We can see how this works by altering our example. We now assume that you actually purchase the $10,000 car immediately, paying for it with your $5,000 deposit and a $5,000 loan from the bank. This makes your financial wealth −$5,000, representing your $5,000 debt to the bank. Now an unexpected spurt of inflation is good news for you. Since you already have the car, the only effect of the higher price level is to reduce the real value of your bank loan. You will therefore need less real saving to repay the loan (assuming that your interest rate does not rise in line with the inflation rate).

Real wealth effects can also influence other economic decisions, such as the particular goods that are purchased or the amount of money that is held. Box 4.5 describes how unexpected inflation affects money holdings.

BOX 4.5 MONEY MATTERS

## The Inflation Tax on Money Balances

The **inflation tax** refers to the reduction in the purchasing power of money (how many goods and services it can buy) that occurs when the price level rises. The inflation tax applies primarily to the monetary base—fiat money issued by the government. There is no equivalent inflation tax on debt securities because, whatever amount is lost to inflation by the lender, the same amount is gained from inflation by the borrower. The inflation tax also does *not* apply to bank deposits because, although bank depositors suffer a loss from inflation, bank borrowers (or bank shareholders) gain to the same extent.

To obtain a measure of the inflation tax,

recall from Chapter 2 that the monetary base at the end of 1987 was about $260 billion. So an annual inflation rate of 10% would reduce the purchasing power of the monetary base by about $26 billion in the course of a year.

Of course, if people expect that inflation is about to occur, then they may try to avoid the inflation tax by spending their money more rapidly. But this activity is also costly—and not very productive—because people will have to spend time and energy keeping their money balances as low as possible. Furthermore, if everyone tries to do this, the velocity of money will rise, so the inflation rate in the economy may just rise further.

## Real Wealth Effects for Sectors of the Economy

Price level changes can also affect the real saving of entire sectors of the economy, depending on whether the sector is a net lender or net borrower. When the sector is a net lender, and there is an unexpected rise in the price level, the real value of its financial wealth falls. This is why *unexpected inflation harms lenders.* As a result, a lending sector may *increase its saving* to rebuild its wealth.

On the other hand, when a sector is a net borrower (financial liabilities $L$ exceed financial assets $A$), and there is a sudden rise in the price level, the real value of its debt falls, and thus its real financial wealth rises. This is why *unexpected inflation helps borrowers.* As a result, a borrowing sector may *decrease its saving.*

The net effect for the economy will depend on whether one side is dominant; that is, whether there is a net change in real saving for the overall economy. For the overall economy to be neutral to price level changes, the increased real saving of the lending sectors must offset the decreased real saving of the borrowing sectors, so that the *net* real wealth effects are zero. It is currently a matter of debate in economics whether there are significant net real wealth effects for the economy as a whole.[3]

---

[3] A major issue concerns whether people increase their real saving when the real value of government debt falls as the result of a higher price level.

## Chapter Summary

1. Wealth is accumulated by retaining existing wealth from an earlier period or as the result of saving (including capital gains on previously accumulated wealth).

2. Wealth is used to buy capital assets—such as equipment, structures, and consumer durables—and to buy financial assets—such as stocks, bonds, and money. People may also issue financial liabilities—debt—to buy assets or consumption goods. The wealth of each sector of the economy is measured by its net worth—the excess of its capital and financial assets over its financial liabilities. The wealth of the economy as a whole equals the stock of capital (because financial assets offset financial liabilities).

3. A person's portfolio may consist of capital assets, financial assets, and financial liabilities (the latter as negative items). The size of a portfolio is expanded through saving. The composition of a portfolio is changed by buying some assets and selling others (or by issuing additional financial liabilities). People will consider expected rates of return, risk, and liquidity in deciding how to allocate specific assets and liabilities to a portfolio.

4. The price level is the average level of prices in an economy, and the annual inflation rate is the percentage increase in the price level during a year. Nominal magnitudes are measured in terms of current prices. Real magnitudes are calculated by deflating nominal values by the current price level. Real interest rates equal nominal interest rates minus the inflation rate. Real interest rates derived from *actual* inflation rates are called ex post rates; those derived from *estimates* of what inflation will be are called ex ante rates.

5. Money illusion occurs when economic decisions are made on the basis of nominal magnitudes when they should have been made on the basis of real magnitudes.

6. Price level neutrality is a situation where a change in the price level has no effect on any real magnitude. Inflation rate neutrality is a situation where a change in the expected inflation rate has no effect on real interest rates. The Fisher effect—where a change in the expected inflation rate results in an equal change in the nominal interest rate—illustrates inflation rate neutrality. However, many factors—such as money illusion, income taxes, the inflation tax on money holdings, and real wealth effects—may cause the U.S. economy not to respond in a neutral fashion to unexpected changes in the price level or inflation rate.

## Key Terms

Capital assets
Consumer price index
Deflating a nominal value
Financial assets
Financial liabilities
Fisher effect
GNP deflator
Inflation rate

Inflation tax
Interest rates:
  Nominal
  Real (ex ante)
  Real (ex post)
Money illusion
Net financial assets
Net worth

| Neutrality: | Price: |
|---|---|
| Inflation rate | Level |
| Price level | Index |
| Nominal and real magnitudes | Producer price index |
| Nominal and real wealth | Real wealth effects |
| Portfolio | Relative price |
| | Stocks and flows |

## Study Questions

1. At each birthday, a child receives a gift of $10 and spends an amount equal to her age. What wealth has the child accumulated after her fifth birthday?

2. In Chapter 3 we learned that saving is equal to capital investment for the overall economy. In this chapter, we have learned that wealth is equal to the stock of capital for the overall economy. How are these two results related?

3. At dates $t = 1$, 2, and 3, a person has the following combinations of financial assets $A$, financial liabilities $L$, and capital $K$:

| | $t = 1$ | $t = 2$ | $t = 3$ |
|---|---|---|---|
| Financial assets $A$ | 100 | 75 | 100 |
| Financial liabilities $L$ | 50 | 50 | 100 |
| Capital $K$ | 0 | 50 | 100 |

What is the person's wealth at the three dates? How much is saved between dates 1 and 2? Between dates 2 and 3?

4. Why do people have to save to increase the size of their portfolio? Specifically, what is wrong with just buying additional capital assets or financial assets?

5. Should human capital be included in the real wealth of the United States? Why does measured real wealth generally exclude it?

6. Babe Ruth's annual salary in 1927 was $100,000, while Reggie Jackson's salary in 1987 was $500,000. The consumer price index for 1927 was 50, while the CPI for 1987 was 350 (both based on 1967 = 100). Which player had the higher real salary? What was Reggie's salary in 1927 prices? What error is made in comparing directly the nominal salaries of the two players?

7. Compute the indicated real rates of interest based on the following information:

| | Year | | |
|---|---|---|---|
| | (1) | (2) | (3) |
| Nominal interest rate | 5% | 6% | 7% |
| Expected inflation rate | 4 | 5 | 6 |
| Actual inflation rate | 4 | 4 | 8 |
| Ex post real interest rate | ? | ? | ? |
| Ex ante real interest rate | ? | ? | ? |

8. Referring to Question 7, does the Fisher effect hold between years (1) and (2)? Between years (2) and (3)?

9. Suppose that you are planning the future level of your consumption on the basis of the interest rate you are earning on a bank savings deposit. Why might this reflect *money illusion*?

10. Indicate which cases are consistent with a *neutral* economy, and which cases are consistent with a *nonneutral* economy. Briefly explain the basis of each answer.

*Case a*: An unexpected increase in the price level affects borrowers and lenders differently.

*Case b*: A rise in the price level, reducing the real quantity of money, affects the behavior of people holding the money, but does not affect the behavior of the Federal Reserve that supplies the money.

*Case c:* An increase in the inflation rate, accompanied by an equal change in the nominal interest rate, causes the stock market to fall.

*Case d:* Taxes affect the relationship between an increase in the inflation rate and the corresponding change in the nominal interest rate.

## Recommended Reading

*The topics of wealth and capital, and the price level and inflation are covered in macroeconomics texts, of which several alternatives are listed here:*

Rudiger Dornbusch and Stanley Fischer, *Macroeconomics*, 4th edition, McGraw-Hill, New York, 1987.

Robert Gordon, *Macroeconomics*, 4th edition, Little, Brown, Boston, 1988.

Robert Hall and John Taylor, *Macroeconomics*, 2nd edition, Norton, New York, 1988.

*Useful readings on nominal and real interest rates include:*

A. Steven Holland, "Real Interest Rates: What Accounts for Their Recent Rise," *Review*, Federal Reserve Bank of St. Louis, December 1984, pp. 18–29.

G. J. Santoni and Courtenay C. Stone  What Really Happened to Interest Rates? A Longer-Run Analysis," *Review*, Federal Reserve Bank of St. Louis, November 1981, pp. 3–14.

Herbert Taylor, "Interest Rates: How Much Does Expected Inflation Matter?" *Business Review*, Federal Reserve Bank of Philadelphia, July/August 1982, pp. 3–12.

# 5

# The Financial System: Security Prices and Interest Rates

*"A person who can't pay, gets another person who can't pay, to guarantee that he can pay."*

**Charles Dickens**

**You want to make a special trip, but do not have enough money to pay for it. You could borrow the money at a local bank, but are apprehensive about applying for a loan. A friend tries to reassure you, saying that borrowing money at a bank is just like buying a hamburger at McDonalds. But you know that this is not really true.**

**If you have the purchase price, you can always get a hamburger. But will the banker accept your promise to repay the loan? How will your credit worthiness be determined? How long will you have to repay the loan? What will it cost?**

**Loans differ from ordinary commodities in that the borrower *promises* to pay the lender at a *later date*. As we will see in this chapter, that is the main reason the financial system is more complicated than the system used for buying standard commodities like hamburgers.**

We will focus on three main aspects of the financial system in this chapter:

First, we will look at the *structure* of the financial system: the *securities* that are traded within it, the *institutions* that operate it, and the *markets* in which credit transactions are carried out.

Second, we will analyze how securities are valued. Because a security represents a promise (or intention) to make a payment in the future, it actually has two values: a *future value*, which is the *amount* of the promised future payments, and a *present value*, which is the *current value* of the future payments.

Third, we will study how security *prices* and *interest rates* are determined. In particular, we will see that the demand and supply curves for loanable funds, which we studied in Chapter 3, can be applied to determine security prices and interest rates.

## Securities

A **security** is formally a document or contract that represents the terms under which a *borrower* (or *issuer*) will make future payments to a *lender* (or *holder*). There are three main types of securities—debt securities, equity claims, and contingent claims.

A **debt security** represents the obligation (or promise) of the borrower to make specified payments on specified dates to the lender. Loans, corporate bonds, and Treasury securities are all examples of debt securities.

An **equity security** represents a *residual claim* by the holder on the assets of the issuer (after all debts have been paid). Equity securities thus represent ownership; the shareholders—the owners of the common stock—of a corporation own the portion of the company represented by their shares. The holders of equity securities may receive *dividends*—voluntary payments made by the issuer (such as by a corporation to its shareholders). (There are also hybrid securities that combine the features of debt and equity.)

A **contingent security** represents a claim by the holder if some specified event occurs. For example, a life insurance policy provides a specified sum to the beneficiary of the policy when the insured person dies.

### Debt Securities

Most banking institutions, including the Federal Reserve, deal primarily in debt securities—principally loans and government securities. Consequently, this type of security will be the focus of our discussion, and when we refer to "securities" we will mean loans and other debt securities. However, the points we will be making generally apply to equity and contingent securities as well.

To negotiate a loan (or other debt security), many matters have to be settled: the agreement on these matters constitutes the loan contract—the security. The interest rate is a basic issue because it determines the amount that will be repaid in the future. The number and the timing of the payments are also important: for example, a loan might be repaid with just one large payment at the end of the loan period; or it might be gradually repaid with a sequence of payments. In addition, a collateral requirement might be specified—something of value owned by the borrower that the lender can sell, if necessary, to obtain repayment. Debt contracts may also refer to a variety of other, more technical, matters, such as whether the borrower is permitted to repay the borrowed amount prior to the agreed upon date.

Box 5.1 describes the pertinent characteristics of securities that we will now summarize.

## Basic Characteristics of Securities

### Cashflow Pattern

*Payment Dates and Amounts*
The sequence of cash payments and payment dates agreed upon by the borrower and lender comprises a security's *cashflow pattern*. The payments include principal—the amount initially borrowed—and interest—the amount paid for using the borrowed money.
*Maturity Date*
The final date by which all payments must be made. The *maturity* refers to the time remaining until the maturity date.

### Credit Risk

*Default Risk*
The possibility that the borrower will default—fail to make the promised payments.
*Security Ratings*
Classifications that indicate the likelihood that a borrower will default. For example, the Standard and Poor's ratings range from AAA (highest quality, essentially no credit risk) to D (lowest grade, high risk of default).
*Collateral*
Assets pledged by borrowers to reduce or eliminate the lender's loss if default occurs.

### Liquidity

The ability to sell a security on short notice at a price close to its full market value.

### Other Characteristics

*Types of Securities*
On debt securities—such as loans and bonds—the borrower is obligated to make the cashflow payments. On equity securities—such as common stock—dividend payments by the issuer are voluntary. On contingent securities, the cashflow payment requires that a specific event occur—such as the death of the insured on an insurance policy.
*Ancillary Privileges*
Privileges such as prepayment options that give borrowers the opportunity to repay the principal on a loan or bond before the maturity date.
*Tax Status*
The interest payments on some securities—such as state and local bonds—are exempt from federal (and sometimes also state) income taxes.

## The Cashflow Pattern

The **cashflow pattern** is the sequence of cash payments and payment dates agreed upon by the borrower and lender. The total amount to be repaid by a borrower can be separated into two parts: principal and interest. The *principal* is the borrowed amount, which, of course, must be repaid. The *interest* is an additional amount that represents the charge for using the borrowed money. The amount of interest is determined by the interest rate negotiated when the loan is taken out. Although it can be important for some purposes—such as tax deductions—to distinguish between payments for interest and principal, the *cashflow pattern* refers only to the total amount of the actual payments.

Although almost any cashflow pattern is possible, most debt securities are based on one of three established patterns, illustrated by the *time line diagrams* in Figure 5.1. Time is represented along the horizontal axis—the time line—and the amount of each cashflow payment is shown as the height of the vertical line at each payment date.

FIGURE 5.1
**Time Line Diagrams of Cashflow Patterns**
A. Zero-Coupon Bond

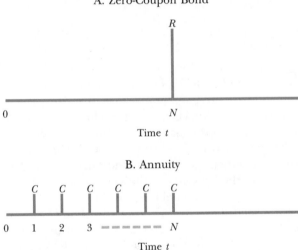

B. Annuity

C. Coupon Bond

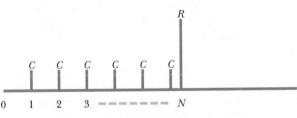

Time line diagrams show the cashflow payments made by the borrower to the lender. The loan is taken out (or the security is issued) at time $t = 0$, and the dates of the cashflow payments are indicated on the horizontal axis. The amount of each payment is indicated by its vertical height. A zero-coupon bond has a single payment $R$ at date $N$. An annuity consists of a sequence of regularly spaced payments $C$. A coupon bond combines an annuity and a zero-coupon bond.

Panel A shows the simplest security—a **zero-coupon bond**—which has precisely one payment, the amount $R$ at date $N$.

Panel B shows an *annuity*—which consists of a series of equal payments that occur at regular intervals in the amount $C$.

Panel C shows a more complicated security—a **coupon bond**—which combines the payment patterns of a zero-coupon bond and an annuity. The series of payments $C$ are the *coupon payments* that represent the interest paid on the security; the single, larger, payment $R$ at date $N$ is the *redemption payment*—the repayment of the amount borrowed (the principal).

The **maturity** of a security is the elapsed time between the moment an amount is borrowed ($t = 0$ on the time line) and the *maturity date*—when the last payment is made. Each security in Figure 5.1 has a maturity of $N$ periods. Securities with a maturity of one year or less are called **short-term**—or **money market**—**securities**; those with a maturity greater than one year are called **long-term**—or **capital market**—**securities**. Although most securities have a specific maturity date, there are some exceptions. For example, a *perpetuity* is an annuity that pays a fixed amount at regular intervals forever.

## Credit Risk

**Credit risk** refers to the possibility that a borrower will fail to make a promised payment. Such a borrower is *delinquent* and will be so notified by the lender. If the payment is still not made—the check is *not* in the mail—then a court will certify that the loan is in *default*. If the borrower still does not pay, this usually means the borrower is *bankrupt*—does not have the money to make the payment. A bankruptcy judge will then determine a settlement between the borrower and the lender, which often includes the *liquidation*—the sale—of most of the borrower's assets to repay as much of the debt as possible.

*Risk-free* securities have *no credit risk*. The U.S. Treasury is the only possible issuer of truly risk-free securities in the United States, because only the federal government has the power to raise taxes or to print money in order to repay its debts. However, even the holders of U.S. Treasury securities face *inflation risk* (the real return on the security might be reduced by inflation) and *interest rate risk* (a higher return might have been earned by purchasing the security at a later date). So risk-free securities are free only of credit risk, not of inflation risk or of interest rate risk.

*Information* regarding credit risk is obviously useful to lenders. For example, special firms—such as Moody's or Standard and Poor's—prepare *security ratings* for bonds traded in the financial markets. A common system is that (nearly) risk-free bonds are rated AAA, while bonds with a high degree of credit risk—now called *junk bonds*—are rated B or lower. Lenders may require higher interest rates on riskier securities, or they may require that borrowers provide *collateral* (assets that revert to the lender if default occurs) or a *cosigner* (a person or institution who guarantees the loan).

## Liquidity

A security is **liquid** when it can be sold for a price close to its full market value even when a sale is made on short notice. On this basis, currency is perfectly liquid, given that it is accepted in trade at full face value. Checks can also be highly liquid—a bank will immediately cash a check drawn on one of its accounts—although this may not be true for out-of-town checks. At the other extreme, a home is an illiquid asset given that it generally takes time to find a buyer willing to pay a price equal to the full market value.

The liquidity of a security often depends on such factors as its cashflow pattern—especially its maturity—its credit risk, and the volume of trading activity. Short-term, risk-free securities tend to be more liquid because buyers can rapidly ascertain their value. Securities traded in active markets are more liquid because there is a good chance of quickly finding a buyer who will pay the full market value.

# Financial Institutions

Although people can borrow money from their friends, it is often preferable to use a financial institution—like a bank—if credit risk, large amounts of money, or unusual payment schedules are involved. It is also generally safer for people to *lend* their money through a financial institution, such as with a bank deposit.

Financial institutions are thus convenient and flexible places for both borrowing and depositing money. The major groups of financial institutions, which we will now describe, are listed in Box 5.2. As you can see, the term "institutions" is applied broadly to include brokers, dealers, and financial exchanges, as well as financial intermediaries.

## Brokers and Dealers

**Brokers** bring borrowers and lenders, or buyers and sellers of securities, together. *Stockbrokers*, for example, bring the purchase and sale orders of their customers to security exchanges where the transactions are carried out. *Investment banks*—not to be confused with commercial banks—arrange mergers and other large financial transactions for corporations, thus also bringing buyers and sellers together.

The cost and the inconvenience of finding a buyer or a seller without a broker are generally high. That is why most people use a broker even though a commission will have to be paid for his or her services. A broker may also be able to complete a transaction at a more advantageous price than the person alone could obtain. Box 5.3 discusses *discount brokers*, a recent development that has reduced the cost of using a broker for security transactions.

BOX 5.2 IN DEPTH

## Financial Institutions

*Brokers* bring buyers and sellers together.
(Examples: Stockbrokers, investment bankers, and real estate brokers)

*Dealers* "make markets" by buying and selling securities.
(Examples: New York Stock Exchange specialists and Treasury bond dealers)

*Financial exchanges* provide centralized trading facilities.
(Examples: New York Stock Exchange, National Association of Security Dealers Automated Quotations, and Chicago Board of Trade)

*Financial intermediaries* both issue and purchase debt securities. There are two kinds of financial intermediaries—depository and nondepository.

*Depository intermediaries* are banking institutions that accept deposits and make loans and purchase securities.
(Commercial banks and thrift institutions)

*Nondepository intermediaries* are other firms that issue debt or equity securities and purchase securities or make loans.
(Examples: Mutual funds, pension funds, and insurance companies)

BOX 5.3 CREDIT CHECK

## Discount Brokers

It used to be that investors had no choice but to place all of their security orders through established brokerage firms such as Merrill Lynch. The firms charged quite high commission rates, often 5% of the value of an order, partly to cover the cost of the advisory services—such as stock reports and recommendations—they provided to their customers. However, the high commissions were actually enforced by the New York Stock Exchange (NYSE). Members of the NYSE—which included all the large brokerage firms—had to charge the fixed commission rates set by the NYSE for all stocks traded on the Exchange.

In 1975, under pressure from the Securities and Exchange Commission—the federal agency that regulates security markets—the NYSE gave up its fixed commission rates. As a result, the established firms lowered their commission rates to a degree, and a new group of *discount brokers*—such as the Charles Schwab firm—started to compete with the established companies. The commission rates of the discount brokers are now as low as 1% of the value of an order—a major saving for investors. Of course, the discount brokers have also had to eliminate some of the special advisory services. But for investors who make their own decisions, the discount brokers provide an efficient and low-cost method for buying and selling stocks.

**Dealers** play an even more basic role in financial transactions than brokers. Dealers "make a market" in a security by standing ready both to buy the security from potential sellers and to sell it to potential buyers. Thus, dealers do more than expedite a transaction, *they are* the other buyer or seller. We will look further at dealer activities later in this chapter.

## Financial Exchanges

Most transactions in bonds and stocks (but not in loans) are carried out on **financial exchanges** that organize and centralize trading. Three major financial exchanges in the United States are the New York Stock Exchange (NYSE), the National Association of Security Dealers Automated Quotation (NASDAQ) System, and the Chicago Board of Trade (CBOT). Each illustrates a different type of trading.

The NYSE uses the *specialist system* for its trading. Trading takes place on the floor of the Exchange, and each of the listed stocks is traded at a designated location. A specialist, who is a member of the NYSE, "makes the market" for each security, a process we will describe shortly.

The NASDAQ system is operated by a network of participating dealers spread out across the country. This is called an *over-the-counter market* because there is not a centralized physical location for the trading. Brokers communicate with the dealers by telephone or through video consoles to bring the buy and sell orders to the market.

The CBOT represents a third form of security trading, this one using an *open outcry auction*. In this system, different securities are assigned specific areas of the trading floor called *trading pits*. Trading takes place in the fashion of an auction, with buyers and sellers shouting out their bids. The financial instruments that are traded in this fashion, futures contracts, will be described shortly.

Each financial exchange must provide *settlement procedures*—established rules which specify how and when traded securities are delivered by the seller to the buyer and how and when payment is made. Established settlement procedures reduce the amount of *nonperformance*—when the buyer fails to make payment or the seller fails to deliver the securities. Standardized and enforced settlement procedures are an important advantage of exchange trading.

## Financial Intermediaries

The most common way to carry out a financial transaction is simply to go to a **financial intermediary**. There are two kinds of financial intermediaries—depository and nondepository. *Depository intermediaries* are chartered banking institutions—commercial banks and thrift institutions—that accept deposits, make loans, and purchase securities. *Nondepository intermediaries* are other firms—mutual funds, pension funds, and insurance companies—that issue debt or equity securities, and purchase securities or make loans.

Financial intermediaries combine the features of brokers, dealers, and financial exchanges: they bring borrowers and lenders together (the brokerage function); they make a market in loanable funds, raising money on the one hand, and making loans or purchasing securities on the other (the dealer function); and they centralize financial transactions (the financial exchange function). Financial intermediaries do all of these things because they carry out transactions simultaneously in two classes of securities: the funds they raise represent their *liabilities*; and the loans they make and the securities they purchase represent their *assets*.

The term *intermediation* is used because the institutions intervene— intermediate—between people who want to invest or lend money and people who want to borrow it. Without intermediaries, lenders would have to make loans directly to borrowers, bearing the costs of finding borrowers and evaluating their credit risk. With financial intermediaries, lenders can leave the task of finding borrowers and evaluating their credit risk to the institution. In fact, in the case of depository interme- diaries, depositors can rely on federal deposit insurance (up to $100,000 per account), so they do not have to worry at all about the creditwor- thiness of the institution or its borrowers. This is a major reason why banks and other depository intermediaries are so important in the fi- nancial system.

We will look further at the services provided by commercial banks in Chapter 6 and by other financial intermediaries in Chapter 13, and at how these institutions are managed and operated in other chapters of Part III.

## Financial Markets

**Financial markets** are the markets in which securities are traded. Specific financial markets, such as stock markets, bond markets, and so on, trade specific types of securities. Table 5.1 summarizes the main classifications of financial markets. Since we have already covered the basis for the first three classifications, the parts of the financial system are coming together. We will now look at the last two classifications.

The **settlement date**, set after the transaction price has been deter- mined, indicates the day by which payment must be made by the buyer and the security delivered by the seller. Most financial transactions settle on a *cash*, or *spot*, basis—"for cash on the spot"—which, in practice, means that about five business days are allowed for checks to clear and securities to be delivered.

In contrast, with **futures trading**, settlement is deferred until a later time, up to a year. On a house sale, for example, after the buyer and seller agree on a price, the actual settlement (or *closing* as it is called in real estate transactions) does not occur until the seller is ready to move out and the buyer is ready to pay for the house. We will discuss the economic function of trading on futures exchanges further in Chap- ter 8.

The last distinction is between **primary markets**, in which new se- curities are issued, and **secondary markets**, in which previously issued, or "seasoned," securities are traded. Most trading occurs in secondary

---

**TABLE 5.1**
**Financial Markets**

| Classification | Example |
|---|---|
| Type of Security | |
|   Loan markets | Business and consumer loans |
|   Other debt security markets | Treasury bonds |
|   Equity markets | Common stocks |
|   Contingent security markets | Insurance policies |
| Maturity of security | |
|   Money markets | Short-term securities |
|   Capital markets | Long-term securities |
| Trading System | |
|   Auction (open outcry system) | Chicago Board of Trade |
|   Specialist (single dealer) | New York Stock Exchange |
|   Over-the-counter (competing dealers) | NASDAQ |
| Settlement Date | |
|   Cash—or spot (prompt settlement) | New York Stock Exchange |
|   Future (deferred settlement) | Chicago Board of Trade |
| Seasoning of Security | |
|   Primary markets | Newly issued securities |
|   Secondary markets | Existing securities |

---

markets because the quantity of outstanding securities is much greater than the annual quantity of new issues. **Investment banks** act as brokers and dealers in the primary markets to distribute newly issued securities. We saw earlier that investment banks also operate as brokers on mergers and acquisitions. Indeed, most large Wall Street investment banking firms have a number of divisions to carry out their various activities.

## Investment Decisions

We will now look at how lenders and investors evaluate and select specific loans and securities. To focus on certain points, we will make some simplifying assumptions:

■ We assume that *each security has the cashflow pattern of a zero-coupon bond* (as shown in panel A of Figure 5.1). Annuities and coupon bonds—securities with more complicated payment patterns as illustrated in Figure 5.1—are discussed in Appendix 5.1.

■ At first, we also assume *the zero-coupon security has a one-year maturity*—the issuer or borrower makes the single payment one year after the security is issued.

■ We assume *each security is risk free*—that there is no credit risk—and that the investors' decisions are not affected by any other features of the security.

Of course, in practice, the credit risk, maturity, and liquidity features of a security or loan may be of crucial importance to investors. These features are being put aside right now so that we can focus on how investors determine a security's price and interest rate on the basis of its cashflow pattern. In Part II of this book, we will look carefully at how investors evaluate these other security features when making their portfolio selections.

## Present Value and Future Value

Given the opportunity, people generally like to be paid as soon as possible. This reflects the fact that money can be invested and grow in value. The increase in the value of invested money is called the **time value of money**; on debt securities, this is represented by the interest earned by investors.

The time value of money is illustrated in Figure 5.2, which shows a time-line diagram for a one-year zero-coupon security. As an example, the security could be a one-year *Treasury bill*—a short-term zero-coupon security issued by the U.S. Treasury. On each such Treasury bill, the U.S. Treasury is obligated to repay the fixed amount of $1,000 at the maturity date. This amount represents the **future value**, $FV$, as shown at $t = 1$ in Figure 5.2. Box 5.4 shows how interest rates are reported on Treasury bills and other money market securities.

The **present value** of the security, at the initial date $t = 0$, represents the amount an investor is willing to invest currently in order to obtain the future value $FV$ in one year. The difference between the future value ($1,000) and the present value ($909) represents the time value of money.

Investors receive the time value of money as the amount of *interest*:

future value = present value + time value of money.
$FV$    =        $PV$    + amount of interest.

It is convenient to compute the amount of interest as a percentage of the present value. If the annual interest rate is $d$ (stated as a decimal, such as $d = 0.10$), then the amount of interest is $(d)(PV)$, and we have:

$$FV = PV + (d)(PV) = (1 + d)\ PV. \tag{5.1}$$

FIGURE 5.2
**The Time Value of Money for a One-Year Zero Coupon Security**

Time $t$ (in years)

The diagram illustrates a zero-coupon security issued at the current time, $t = 0$, with a one-year maturity. The $1,000 payment that occurs at time $t = 1$ is its future value $FV$. For the case illustrated, the present value of the security, at $t = 0$, is $909. The future value exceeds the present value by the time value of money—that is, by the amount of interest.

## BOX 5.4 FINANCIAL NEWS

## Money Market Securities and Interest Rates

Short-term securities (with maturity no more than one year) are called *money market securities* and their interest rates are called *money market rates*. The *Wall Street Journal* publishes current interest rates on these securities each day, as shown here. Treasury bills (short-term securities issued by the U.S. Treasury) are actively traded, so the *Treasury bill rate* is the basis for many other money market rates.

Many money market interest rates in-

volve banks. The *prime rate* is the basic interest rate that banks charge business borrowers, the *Federal funds rate* is the rate that banks charge other banks when lending them money, and the **discount rate** is the rate that the Federal Reserve charges banks when lending them money. We will look further at money market securities and interest rates when we discuss the banking industry in Chapter 6 and later.

---

### MONEY RATES

**Wednesday, July 27, 1988**

The key U.S. and foreign annual interest rates below are a guide to general levels but don't always represent actual transactions.

**PRIME RATE:** 9½%. The base rate on corporate loans at large U.S. money center commercial banks.

**FEDERAL FUNDS:** 7⅝% high, 7% low, 7¼% near closing bid, 7½% offered. Reserves traded among commercial banks for overnight use in amounts of $1 million or more. Source: Fulton Prebon (U.S.A.) Inc.

**DISCOUNT RATE:** 6%. The charge on loans to depository institutions by the New York Federal Reserve Bank.

**CALL MONEY:** 8¾% to 9%. The charge on loans to brokers on stock exchange collateral.

**COMMERCIAL PAPER** placed directly by General Motors Acceptance Corp.: 7¾% 30 to 59 days; 7.80% 60 to 89 days; 7.85% 90 to 119 days; 7.80% 120 to 149 days; 7¾% 150 to 179 days; 7.70% 180 to 270 days.

**COMMERCIAL PAPER:** High-grade unsecured notes sold through dealers by major corporations in multiples of $1,000: 7.80 30 days; 7.85% 60 days; 7.925% 90 days.

**CERTIFICATES OF DEPOSIT:** 7.35% one month; 7.46% two months; 7.63% three months; 7.84% six months; 8.02% one year. Average of top rates paid by major New York banks on primary new issues of negotiable C.D.s, usually on amounts of $1 million and more. The minimum unit is $100,000. Typical rates in the secondary market: 7.90% one month; 8⅛% three months; 8.40% six months.

**BANKERS ACCEPTANCES:** 7.73% 30 days; 7.78% 60 days; 7.92% 90 days; 7.93% 120 days; 7.97% 150 days; 8.02% 180 days. Negotiable, bank-backed business credit instruments typically financing an import order.

**LONDON LATE EURODOLLARS:** 8⅛% to 8% one month; 8 3/16% to 8 1/16% two months; 8⅜% to 8¼% three months; 8⅜% to 8¼% four months; 8 7/16% to 8 5/16% five months; 8 9/16% to 8 7/16% six months.

**LONDON INTERBANK OFFERED RATES (LIBOR):** 8⅛% one month; 8⅜% three months; 8⅝% six months; 8 13/16% one year. The average of interbank offered rates for dollar deposits in the London market based on quotations at five major banks.

**FOREIGN PRIME RATES:** Canada 10.75%; Germany 6.25%; Japan 3.375%; Switzerland 5%; Britain 10.50%. These rate indications aren't directly comparable; lending practice vary widely by location.

**TREASURY BILLS:** Results of the Monday, July 25, 1988, auction of short-term U.S. government bills, sold at a discount from face value in units of $10,000 to $1 million: 6.88%, 13 weeks; 7.09%, 26 weeks.

**FEDERAL HOME LOAN MORTGAGE CORP.** (Freddie Mac): Posted yields on 30-year mortgage commitments for delivery within 30 days. 10.36%, standard conventional fixed-rate mortgages; 7.50%, 2% rate capped one-year adjustable rate mortgages. Source: Telerate Systems Inc.

**FEDERAL NATIONAL MORTGAGE ASSOCIATION** (Fannie Mae): Posted yields on 30 year mortgage commitments for delivery within 30 days (priced at par). 10.32%, standard conventional fixed rate-mortgages; 9.40% 6/2 rate capped one-year adjustable rate mortgages. Source: Telerate Systems Inc.

**MERRILL LYNCH READY ASSETS TRUST:** 6.81%. Annualized average rate of return after expenses for the past 30 days; not a forecast of future returns.

**Source:** *Wall Street Journal*, 28 July, 1988.

---

This shows how the accumulated future value *FV* after one year is related to an initial investment of the present value *PV*. The term $(1 + d)$ is called the *interest factor*—when it is multiplied by the present value *PV*, it determines the future value *FV*.

Equation (5.1) can also be solved to determine the present value *PV* as a function of the future value *FV* and the rate *d*:

$$PV = \frac{FV}{(1 + d)}.$$  (5.2)

This shows how the present value *PV* (the amount invested currently) is related to the future value *FV* that will accumulate in one year. This computation is called **time discounting**, $1/(1 + d)$ is the *discount factor*, and *d* is the **discount rate**.[1]

Investors use time discounting to determine the present value of a security. For example, if an investor's discount rate is 10% ($d = 0.10$) and the security provides a $1,000 payment in one year ($FV = \$1,000$), then based on equation (5.2), $PV = FV/(1 + d)$, the present value is $909 ($PV = \$1,000/1.10$).

## The Discount Rate

The process of time discounting requires a discount factor, and therefore a discount rate. Where does the discount rate come from? The **discount rate** represents the *opportunity cost* of money—the interest rate that would be earned if the purchase price of a security were put to some alternative use. Based on our earlier discussion of saving and investment in Chapter 3, there are three main alternative uses of money: current consumption, capital investment, and financial investment. Each of these provides an alternative measure of the discount rate:

- *Time preference* represents the trade-off between current and future consumption, so here the opportunity cost is based on the time preference for consuming goods currently.

- The *marginal return on investment* represents the trade-off between resources invested and goods produced, so here the opportunity cost is based on the marginal return earned by investing resources currently.

- The *market rate of interest* represents the rate available on other securities, so here the opportunity cost is the interest rate earned by buying one of these other securities currently.

The discount rate can thus be measured as the rate of time preference, the marginal return on investment, or the market interest rate on alternative securities.

*Question*: Which rate best measures the discount rate?

*Answer*: The *highest* of these three rates should be used because that is the rate that will provide the *best* alternative use of the funds.[2]

## Long-Term Bonds

The present value and future value are also readily computed for a long-term zero-coupon security, for which the maturity exceeds one year. If

---

[1] This use of the term "discount rate" should not be confused with the *Federal Reserve* discount rate—the specific interest rate that the Federal Reserve charges when making loans to banking institutions. We will discuss the Federal Reserve's discount rate in Chapter 18.

[2] From the discussion of saving and investing in Chapter 3, we also know that the three rates are actually equal for a consumer in equilibrium. In this case, any one of them properly measures the discount rate.

a security has an $N$-year maturity (with $N > 1$), we will denote its future value as $FV_n$ and its present value as $PV_n$. The equations for the future value and present value are then:

$$FV_n = PV_n (1 + d)^N, \tag{5.3}$$

$$PV_n = FV_n/(1 + d)^N. \tag{5.4}$$

Equation (5.3) shows the accumulated amount after $N$ years, $FV_n$, based on an initial investment of $PV_n$. Equation (5.4) shows the initial investment, $PV_n$, that is needed to accumulate a given future value, $FV_n$, after $N$ years. These equations are equivalent to equations (5.1) and (5.2) when the maturity $N$ is one year.

In equations (5.3) and (5.4), the term $(1 + d)^N$ is called the **compound interest factor**. With compound interest, the accumulated interest consists of two components: (1) interest earned on the original amount invested—the principal; and (2) interest earned on interest accumulated from previous periods. Compound interest, in other words, includes "interest on interest." The simple algebra of compound interest is developed in Box 5.5.

---

BOX 5.5 IN DEPTH

## The Derivation of the Compound Interest Formula

Compound interest—the accumulation of "interest on interest"—is illustrated by following the steps that indicate how the future value $FV$ of an investment is accumulated. If the initial investment is $PV$, then from equation (5.1), after one year the accumulated amount $FV_1$ is:

$$FV_1 = PV(1 + d) = PV + (d)(PV).$$
$$\quad\quad\quad\quad\quad\quad (1) \quad\quad (2)$$

Term (1) is the invested amount. Term (2) is the interest earned during the first year—the interest rate $d$ times the invested amount $PV$. There is no compound interest so far because we have only considered the first year.

If the amount $FV_1$ is now invested for another year, then the accumulated amount, after the second year, $FV_2$, is:

$$FV_2 = FV_1(1 + d) = PV(1 + d)(1 + d)$$
$$= PV + (d)(PV) + (d)(PV) + (d)(d\,pV).$$
$$\quad (1) \quad\quad\quad (2) \quad\quad\quad (3) \quad\quad\quad (4)$$

Term (1) shows the repayment of the principal $PV$. Terms (2) and (3) show the interest earned during years 1 and 2 on the initial principal. Term (4) is "interest on interest"—interest earned at the rate $d$ during year 2 on the interest earned during year 1 ($d\,PV$). Equation (5.3) in the text is derived by continuing this process for $N$ years.

Compound interest is illustrated in Figure 5.3, which shows that a $1,000 present value $PV$ grows to a larger future value $FV$, the longer the maturity $N$ and the higher the discount rate $d$. When the annual discount rate is 4% (the lower curve), the future value reaches $2,000 in eighteen years. When the annual discount rate is 8% (the upper curve), the future value reaches $2,000 in nine years and $4,000 in eighteen years.[3]

FIGURE 5.3
**The Power of Compound Interest**

The future value $FV_n$ of a security is determined by its present value $PV_n$, the discount rate $d$, and its maturity $N$ with the formula: $FV_n = PV_n(1 + d)^N$.

The A curve shows the growing value of a security with a present value of $1,000 and a 4% annual discount rate. The B curve is based on an 8% annual discount rate. When the discount rate is higher, more interest is earned, and the future value accumulates more rapidly.

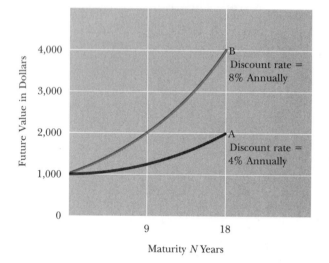

The reverse process—time discounting—is illustrated in Table 5.2, which shows, for each maturity $N$ (on the basis of equation [5.4]), the present value of a future payment of $1,000. Columns (2) and (3) of the table both show that the present value is lower, the longer the maturity—the longer the time before the $1,000 future value is received.

The table also shows that the present value based on a 8% discount rate (column 2) is less than the present value based on a 4% discount rate (column 3). This happens because a higher discount rate indicates a higher rate of time preference—the person places less value on the future payment. Column (4) shows the percentage gain in present value from a lower discount rate. The percentage gain is larger as the maturity $N$ lengthens because the difference between the two discount rates applies over a longer time.

The relationships between present and future value in equation (5.3) (and Figure 5.3) and in equation (5.4) (and Table 5.4) are summarized in Box 5.6. These results indicate the amount that would be accumulated (the future value) based on a given investment (the present value).

[3] This can also be computed using a mathematical quirk called **the rule of 72**. The value 72/d% closely approximates the number of years required for an investment to double in value. For example, at an 8% discount rate, a $1,000 investment doubles to a $2,000 future value in nine years (72/8). Also, 72/N equals the discount rate that is required for a present value to double in N years. For example, an investment will double in value in six years if the discount rate is 12% (72/6).

BOX 5.6 IN DEPTH

## Present and Future Value

**A. Future Value $FV_n$ Depends on Present Value $PV_n$:**

1. Future value $FV_n$ varies in direct proportion with present value $PV_n$.

2. Future value $FV_n$ rises as the annual discount rate $d$ rises or the maturity $N$ rises.

**B. Present Value $PV_n$ Depends on Future Value $FV_n$:**

1. Present value $PV_n$ varies in direct proportion with future value $FV_n$.

2. Present value $PV_n$ falls as the annual discount rate $d$ rises or as the maturity $N$ rises.

3. The percentage change in present value $PV_n$, resulting from a change in the discount rate $d$, is greater the longer the maturity $N$.

In part A of Box 5.6, based on an investment $PV_n$, the *amount accumulated ($FV_n$) will be greater*:

- The more that is invested, $PV_n$.
- The higher the discount rate, $d$.
- The longer the term of the investment, $N$.

In part B of Box 5.6, to accumulate an amount $FV_n$, the *amount that must be invested ($PV_n$) will be less*:

- The smaller the amount to be accumulated, $FV_n$.
- The higher the discount rate, $d$.
- The longer the term of the investment, $N$.
- As the discount rate rises, the amount to be invested ($PV$) falls more, the longer the maturity.

TABLE 5.2

Present Value of Zero-Coupon Bonds by Maturity

**Future value = $1,000**

| (1) Maturity N Years | (2) Present Value Based on Annual Discount Rate of 8% | (3) Present Value Based on Annual Discount Rate of 4% | (4) Percentage Appreciation Due to Lower Discount Rate $\frac{(3) - (2)}{(2)} \times 100\%$ |
|---|---|---|---|
| 1 | $926 | $962 | 4 |
| 2 | 857 | 925 | 8 |
| 5 | 681 | 822 | 21 |
| 10 | 463 | 676 | 46 |
| 20 | 215 | 456 | 112 |
| 50 | 21 | 141 | 571 |
| 100 | 0.5 | 20 | 3,900 |

## Decisions To Buy or Sell a Security

The *future value FV* (the promised payment) and the *maturity N* of a security are normally set at the time the security is issued. These terms then cannot be altered. The *market price P*—the price at which the security trades—is then determined by the demand and supply of individual investors. Investors determine their demand or supply on the basis of the security's *present value PV*, computed using their personal discount rates. The result is that some people may want to buy a security while others want to sell it.

We will first look at the decision of an investor who is deciding whether or not to purchase a particular security. The investor knows the security's market price, and computes its present value using his or her discount rate. The market price $P$ represents the *cost* of buying the security, while the present value $PV$ represents the *benefit* of owning it. Therefore, the investor should buy the security if the present value $PV$ (the benefit of owning it) exceeds the price $P$ (the cost of buying it):

**If $PV > P$, buy the security.**

If the market price falls, more investors will find that the condition $PV > P$ is satisfied, so more investors will want to buy the security. This is why the market demand for a security rises as its price falls, as shown by the demand curve in Figure 5.4.

Similar considerations apply to the supply of a security. A security can be supplied either by investors who own it and want to sell it, or by firms or government agencies who are issuing it to raise money. For a supplier, the market price $P$ is the amount of money that will be received, and the present value $PV$ is a current measure of the burden of repaying the debt. Therefore, the security should be sold if the price (the money received) exceeds the present value (the burden of later repayment):

**If $P > PV$, sell the security.**

The demand for a security rises as the price falls because more investors find that their present value exceeds the market price. The supply of a security rises as the price rises because more investors (or firms) find that the market price exceeds their present value. The market for the security is in equilibrium at point $E_0$ where demand and supply are equal. The equilibrium price is $P_0$ ($22) and the equilibrium quantity is $Q_0$.

FIGURE 5.4
**The Demand and Supply for a Security**

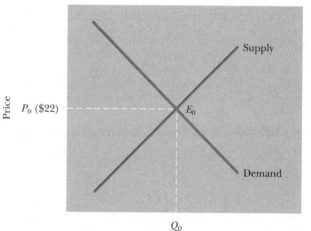

Quantity Outstanding

Following this rule, more securities are issued or sold as the market price rises. The sellers' actions are indicated by the postively sloped supply curve in Figure 5.4.

## Security Prices and Interest Rates

Security prices are determined by market trading based on the demand and supply curves. In particular, a market is in equilibrium when demand and supply are equal, as shown at point $E_0$ in Figure 5.4, where the equilibrium price is $P_0$ ($22) and the equilibrium quantity outstanding is $Q_0$. More precisely, this represents a *perfect market equilibrium* because the fees and commissions charged by brokers and dealers have not yet been included in the price.

### Equilibrium in Security Markets with Dealers

Using the perfect market equilibrium of Figure 5.4 as a starting point, we can now examine how dealers manage a security market by **making the market**. To make a market, a dealer holds an inventory of the security and quotes a **bid price**—the price at which he is willing to buy more of the security—and an *ask price*—the price at which he is willing to sell some of his inventory of the security. The ask price minus the bid price is the **bid-ask spread**, which represents the dealer's fee for managing the security market. A dealer will earn profits as long as his ask price exceeds his bid price.

This is illustrated in Figure 5.5, where the demand and supply curves are the same as in Figure 5.4. The dealer's bid price is represented as

The demand and supply curves for the security are the same as in Figure 5.4. The quantity $Q_1$ is demanded at the ask price $P^a_1$ ($24) and is supplied at the bid price $P^b_1$ ($20), so $Q_1$ is the equilibrium quantity traded at these bid and ask prices. The quantity demanded will rise as the ask price falls, and the quantity supplied will rise as the bid price rises, so the quantity traded will rise as the bid-ask spread narrows. This is why markets are more efficient, the smaller the bid-ask spread. In the extreme case, the bid-ask spread becomes zero and the perfect market equilibrium is attained at point $E_0$.

FIGURE 5.5
**Security Demand and Supply with Bid and Ask Prices**

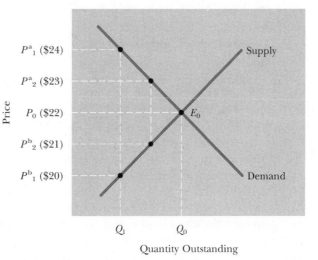

$P^b_1$ ($20) and the dealer's ask price is represented as $P^a_1$ ($24). Given these prices, the quantity $Q_1$ will be bought by security demanders from the dealer at the $24 ask price; and the same quantity $Q_1$ will be sold by security suppliers to the dealer at the $20 bid price. Since the same quantity—$Q_1$—is being bought and sold, this is an equilibrium. We will refer to this specifically as a *dealer equilibrium* since it is based on the $4 bid-ask spread ($24 − $20) set by the dealer.

We can see in Figure 5.5 that as a result of the bid-ask spread, the equilibrium quantity in the dealer market $Q_1$ is less than the equilibrium quantity $Q_0$ of a corresponding perfect market (where the demand and supply curves intersect). This happens because the $4 bid-ask spread represents the cost of using a dealer market: traders buying the security have to pay the dealer $24, while traders selling the security receive only $20 from the dealer.

The *efficiency* of dealer markets can be gauged by the size of the bid-ask spread, smaller spreads representing more efficient markets. In Figure 5.5, suppliers are better off when the bid price is $P^b_2$ instead of $P^b_1$ ($21 instead of $20), and demanders are better when the ask price is $P^a_2$ instead of $P^a_1$ ($23 instead of $24). In other words, both suppliers and demanders are better off with the smaller bid-ask spread $P^a_2 − P^b_2$.

It is also apparent in Figure 5.5 that the smaller bid-ask spread results in a larger quantity being traded, which is another measure of a more efficient market. Indeed, in the extreme case—when the bid-ask spread becomes zero—we have the perfect market equilibrium where demand and supply curves intersect at the equilibrium price $P_0$ ($22).

When several dealers operate in the same market, then competition tends to reduce the bid-ask spread, making the market more efficient. This happens because people buying a security look for the dealer with the lowest ask price, and people selling the security look for the dealer with the highest bid price. This is also the reason why investors often use brokers to locate the dealer with the best price.

Bid-ask spreads vary across different types of security markets. Everything else being equal, a security market will have a *lower* bid-ask spread when:

- The dealers are more competitive.
- The trading volume is greater (so dealers can spread their fixed costs across more trades).
- The security's price fluctuates less (so dealers face a smaller risk of losing money on their inventory should the security's price fall).

## Discount Rates and Security Prices

We will now look at how a security's price is affected by changes in the discount rates. To simplify matters, we will return to the case of a perfect market equilibrium, (similar considerations apply when dealer bid-ask spreads are included). In a perfect market, we know the equilibrium price depends on the location of the demand and supply curves, which in turn depends on the discount rates used by investors. As a result, the

The initial demand and supply curves intersect at the equilibrium point $E_0$, corresponding to the same point in Figure 5.4. When all discount rates rise, all computed present values fall. This shifts the demand curve leftward (or downward) and the supply curve rightward (or downward). The new equilibrium point $E_1$ results in a lower equilibrium price $P_1$. Thus higher discount rates lead to lower security prices. The equilibrium quantity is unchanged if the curves shift by the same amount.

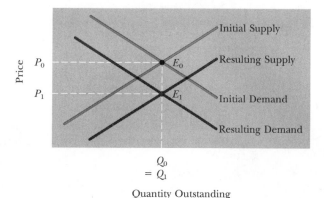

FIGURE 5.6
**Discount Rates and Security Prices**

equilibrium price will change in just the opposite direction of any change in the personal discount rates.

This can be represented by a simple experiment, illustrated in Figure 5.6, in which the discount rates used by the buyers and sellers of the security are all assumed to rise. As the discount rates all rise, the computed present values all fall. For buyers of the security, for whom the present value must exceed the price, this leads to a reduction in demand, so the demand curve shifts leftward (or downward). For sellers, for whom the price must exceed the present value, this leads to an increase in supply, so the supply curve shifts rightward (or downward). These shifts in the demand and supply curves reduce the equilibrium price of the security. Thus, *higher discount rates lead to lower market prices.* (The quantity is unchanged if the two curves shift by the same amount, as shown.)

## Interest Rates and Security Prices

We can now consider the relationship between the price and the interest rate for a security. This relationship can be easily understood if one basic concept is kept in mind: The *price* represents the *present value* of a security computed using the *interest rate* as the *discount rate*.

This concept is represented in the relationship between the price $P$ and the interest $r$ on a zero-coupon security with a future value $FV_n$ and maturity $N$:

$$P = \frac{FV_n}{(1 + r)^N}.$$

(5.5)

Comparing equation (5.4), $PV_n = FV_n/(1 + d)^N$, with equation (5.5), it is clear we have just substituted the price $P$ for the present value $PV_n$ and the interest rate $r$ for the discount rate $d$.

Because equations (5.4) and (5.5) have the same form, the relationship between the present value and the discount rate, summarized in Box 5.6, can be readily restated as a relationship between the market price and market interest rate, as summarized in Box 5.7.

## The Market Price and Market Interest Rate

1. The market price $P$ of a security varies in direct proportion to its future value $FV_n$ (its cashflow payment).

2. The market price $P$ of a security rises as the market interest rate $r$ falls (given the cashflow payment).

3. The percentage change in the market price $P$, resulting from a change in the market interest rate $r$, is greater on securities with longer maturities $N$.

Because the price and the interest rate for a security are tied together by equation (5.5), the price and the interest rate are alternative but equivalent ways to state a security's market value:

- From a market standpoint, the price is often more useful because an order to buy or sell a security is stated in terms of the market price. But the interest rate can always be computed from the market price using equation (5.5).

- In contrast, from an economic standpoint, the interest rate is often more useful because it can be readily compared with other rates, such as the rate of time preference and the marginal return on investment. But the market price can always be computed from the interest rate using equation (5.5).

Thus, in either view, prices and interest rates are just two sides of the same coin (or equation).

## THE Market Interest Rate

We have seen how to use present value and time discounting to determine market prices and interest rates for *individual securities*. However, when people refer to interest rates in the financial markets, they frequently mean *the* market interest rate—as if there were a single interest rate for all financial markets. We will now consider two different—but equivalent—approaches to thinking about *the* market interest rate.

The first approach—the *discount rate approach*—simply applies the discount rate analysis to the market as a whole. Imagine that there is a generic security—what economists call a *representative security*—which stands for the market as a whole. If the discount rates of all investors rise, then the present value of the representative security will fall, so its market price will fall, and its interest rate will rise. In this sense, *the* market interest rate is the representative discount rate of all investors.

The second approach—the *loanable funds* approach—uses the loanable funds theory, which we studied in Chapter 3, to analyze the market interest rate. Recall that individuals and firms base their demand and supply of loanable funds on the amounts that they want to save and to invest. Equilibrium in the market for loanable funds—when the demand and supply of loanable funds are equal—then determines the market interest rate.

To see that the discount rate and loanable funds approaches to determining the market interest rate are equivalent, we should first recognize that both approaches are based on demand and supply curves—the demand and supply of a representative security in the case of the discount rate approach; and the demand and supply of loanable funds in the case of the loanable funds approach. So if the demand and supply curves of the two approaches amount to the same thing, then the market interest rates they determine will be the same.

In fact, the demand and supply curves of both approaches are determined by the same basic factors: time preference and the marginal return on capital investment.[4] For the loanable funds theory, we saw in Chapter 3 that time preference and the marginal return on investment determine saving and investing, and thus the demand and supply curves for loanable funds. While for the discount rate approach, we have seen in this chapter that time preference and the marginal return on investment determine personal discount rates, and thus the demand and supply curves for a security.

Although the loanable funds and discount rate approaches are two equivalent ways of thinking about the market rate of interest, the two approaches have different applications. The loanable funds theory is convenient to apply in problems concerning interest rate levels for the economy as a whole, because aggregate demand and supply curves for loanable funds can be used. On the other hand, the discount rate approach is essential for analyzing the present value, and thereby the market price and interest rate, of a particular security.

## Market Interest Rates in Practice

Market interest rates are measured in terms of the **yield to maturity**—the annual rate of return an investor obtains by purchasing a security at the market price $P$ and holding it until it matures, receiving the cashflow payments in the process. In the case of a zero-coupon security, given the size of the cashflow payment $FV_n$, the yield to maturity is obtained by solving equation (5.5), $P = FV_n/(1 + r)^N$, for $r$:

$$(1 + r)^N = \frac{FV_n}{P}, \text{ or}$$

$$r = \left(\frac{FV_n}{P}\right)^{(1/N)} - 1. \tag{5.6}$$

[4] The expected inflation rate is also an important factor determining the nominal interest rate.

For example, suppose that a zero-coupon security, which will pay $1,000 ($FV_n$) in two years ($N$), has a current market price of $900 ($= P$). Then the (annual) yield to maturity $r$ can be computed as:

$$(1 + r)^N = \frac{FV_n}{P} = \frac{\$1,000}{\$900} = 1.11, \text{ or}$$

$$r = (1.11)^{1/2} - 1 = 1.054 - 1 = 0.054 = 5.4\%$$

The same concept applies to annuities and coupon bonds, as discussed in the appendix to this chapter. Box 5.8 shows how the *Wall Street Journal* displays the market price and the yield to maturity for U.S. Treasury securities. The yield to maturity can also be readily computed with low-cost financial calculators.

BOX 5.8 FINANCIAL NEWS

## The Yield to Maturity on Treasury Bonds

Because of the need to compress information in a limited space, the *Wall Street Journal* reports market prices and interest rates for Treasury and other securities, with special, shorthand descriptions. You have to know the code, but it is easy to learn. One general point is that each security is assumed to have a redemption value—final payment—of $100.

Since these are coupon bonds, the first column—labeled *rate*—shows the annual cashflow payment (the coupon payment) of the bond. The first bond has a coupon rate of 6⅝%, meaning that the annual coupon is $6.625 per bond of $100 redemption value.

The second column, labeled *mat. date*, gives the year and month of the bond's maturity. Thus, the first bond in the table matures during July 1988.

The third and fourth columns—labeled *bid* and *ask*—represent the dealer bid and ask prices for the bond. By tradition, the fractional parts represent 32nds. So the bid price of the first bond is $99 29/32.

The fifth column shows the change in the bid price relative to its value the previous day.

The last column shows the bond's yield to maturity.

### TREASURY BONDS, NOTES & BILLS

Wednesday, July 27, 1988
Representative Over-the-Counter quotations based on transactions of $1 million or more as of 4 p.m. Eastern time.
Hyphens in bid-and-asked and bid changes represent 32nds; 101-01 means 101 1/32. a-Plus 1/64. b-Yield to call date. d-Minus 1/64. k-Nonresident aliens exempt from withholding taxes. n-Treasury notes. p-Treasury note; nonresident aliens exempt from withholding taxes.
Source: Bloomberg Financial Markets

### Treasury Bonds and Notes

| Rate | Mat. Date | Bid | Asked | Bid Chg. | Yld. |
|---|---|---|---|---|---|
| 6⅝ | 1988 Jul p | 99-29 | 100 | ..... | 6.42 |
| 6⅛ | 1988 Aug p | 99-27 | 99-30 | ..... | 6.44 |
| 9½ | 1988 Aug p | 100-02 | 100-05+ | 01 | 6.07 |
| 10½ | 1988 Aug n | 100-02 | 100-05− | 01 | 7.00 |
| 6⅜ | 1988 Sep p | 99-25 | 99-28+ | 01 | 6.95 |
| 11⅜ | 1988 Sep p | 100-19 | 100-22− | 01 | 7.13 |
| 15⅜ | 1988 Oct n | 101-21 | 101-24− | 05 | 6.85 |
| 6⅜ | 1988 Oct p | 99-21 | 99-24 | ..... | 7.25 |
| 6¼ | 1988 Nov p | 99-15 | 99-18− | 01 | 7.49 |
| 8¾ | 1988 Nov n | 100-10 | 100-13 | ..... | 7.23 |
| 8⅝ | 1988 Nov p | 100-06 | 100-09− | 01 | 7.53 |
| 11¾ | 1988 Nov n | 101-04 | 101-07 | ..... | 7.41 |
| 10⅝ | 1988 Dec p | 101-02 | 101-06− | 01 | 7.67 |
| 6¼ | 1988 Dec p | 99-09 | 99-13− | 01 | 7.66 |
| 6⅛ | 1989 Jan n | 99-05 | 99-09 | ..... | 7.59 |
| 14⅝ | 1989 Jan n | 103-06 | 103-10− | 01 | 7.22 |
| 8 | 1989 Feb p | 100 | 100-04− | 02 | 7.75 |
| 6¼ | 1989 Feb p | 99-01 | 99-05− | 01 | 7.72 |
| 11⅜ | 1989 Feb n | 101-25 | 101-29− | 01 | 7.75 |
| 11¼ | 1989 Mar p | 102-05 | 102-09 | ..... | 7.68 |
| 6⅜ | 1989 Mar p | 98-31 | 99-03− | 01 | 7.76 |
| 7⅛ | 1989 Apr p | 99-10 | 99-14− | 01 | 7.88 |
| 14⅜ | 1989 Apr n | 104-21 | 104-25+ | 01 | 7.35 |
| 6⅞ | 1989 May p | 99-03 | 99-07− | 01 | 7.88 |
| 9¼ | 1989 May n | 100-29 | 101-03 | ..... | 7.78 |
| 8 | 1989 May n | 99-29 | 100-01− | 02 | 7.94 |
| 11¾ | 1989 May n | 102-26 | 102-30− | 01 | 7.85 |

**Source:** *Wall Street Journal*, 28 July 1988.

The yield to maturity assumes the investor holds the security until it matures. Of course, in practice investors may sell a security before that. In this case, it is appropriate to compute the **holding period return**— the yield obtained while holding the security. Equation (5.6) is also applied for this purpose, but the actual sales price $S$ replaces the cashflow payment $FV_n$, and the sales date $M$ replaces the maturity date $N$:

$$r = \left(\frac{S}{P}\right)^{(1/M)} - 1. \tag{5.7}$$

Equation (5.7) is easy to apply after the security is sold and therefore the sales price is known. However, at the time a transaction is initiated, the investor can only compute an *expected* holding period return based on the *expected* sales price.

## Chapter Summary

1. The financial system consists of three components: securities that represent the terms under which a borrower (or issuer) will make payments in the future to the lender (or holder); financial institutions that facilitate the trading of securities; and financial exchanges that centralize and organize security trading.

2. The cashflow pattern, credit risk, and liquidity are three basic characteristics of a security. The cashflow pattern is the set of payments that the borrower makes to the lender. Credit risk is the possibility that the borrower will fail to make the promised payments. Liquidity is the extent to which the full market value can be realized when the security is sold at short notice.

3. The financial system is managed and operated by brokers, dealers, financial exchanges, and financial intermediaries. Brokers expedite security trading by helping to bring buyers and sellers together. Dealers "make" financial markets by standing ready both to buy the security (at the bid price) and to sell the security (at the ask price). Financial exchanges are groups of brokers and dealers who centralize and organize the trading of similar securities. Financial intermediaries borrow (raise) funds by accepting deposits and issuing securities and they use the funds to purchase loans and other securities.

4. The time value of money is the amount of interest that accumulates on a security between an initial date and a future date. The value of the security at the initial date is its present value, and the value at the future date is its future value. A future value is converted into a present value by time discounting. The personal discount rate used for time discounting may be based on time preference, the marginal return on investment, or the interest rate on other securities.

5. The procedure for time discounting can be applied to any cashflow pattern including zero-coupon bonds, annuities, and coupon bonds. In all cases, the present value of the security varies directly with the cashflow payments. The present value of a security is inversely related to the discount rate and to its maturity. The percentage change in present value resulting from a change in the discount rate is larger on longer-term securities.

6. Investment decisions depend on the present value and the market price of a security, with demand rising and supply falling as the market price falls relative to the present value. The equilibrium price of a security is determined when demand and supply are equal. A security's interest rate and its market price are alternative but equivalent ways to state its market value.

## Key Terms

Bid and ask prices

Brokers

Compound interest

Dealers

Debt security

Discount rate

Financial exchanges

Financial intermediaries

Financial markets

Holding period return

Investment banks

Making a market

Present value and future value

Primary markets

Secondary markets

Securities:

   Annuity

   Coupon bond

   Long-term (capital market)

   Short-term (capital market)

   Zero-coupon bond

Security characteristics:

   Cashflow pattern

   Credit risk

   Liquidity

   Maturity

Settlement date

Time discounting

Yield to maturity

## Study Questions

1. What is the special feature of the cashflow pattern of a zero-coupon bond? Of an annuity? Of a coupon bond?

2. As a possible investor in a security, indicate whether the following factors would *raise, reduce,* or *leave unchanged* the *present value* of the security:
   a. The security has a greater future value (cashflow payment).
   b. The security has a longer maturity.
   c. Your personal discount rate rises.

3. As a possible investor in a security, indicate whether the following factors would *raise, reduce,* or *leave unchanged* the price you might be prepared to pay for it, holding everything else unchanged:
   a. The security has a greater amount of credit risk.
   b. The security provides a greater amount of collateral.
   c. The borrower has a prepayment option.
   d. The interest payments on the security are tax-exempt.

4. What factors should you consider in determining your discount rate? How would you choose among these factors in determining a specific numerical value for your discount rate?

5. Compare and contrast the roles that brokers, dealers, financial exchanges, and financial intermediaries play in expediting financial transactions.

6. Why are markets generally considered to be more efficient when the bid-ask spread is smaller? Why is the volume of trading also likely to be higher when the bid-ask spread is smaller? Why is this a good thing?

7. If you invested $1,000 in a zero-coupon security at an 8% annual interest rate, what total amount (interest and principal) would have accumulated after 1 year? After two years? After nine years? After eighteen years? (Use Figure 5.3 for the last two questions.)

8. Assuming you can earn 8% on a zero-coupon security, how much do you have to invest now in order to accumulate $1,000 after one year? To accumulate $1,000 after two years?

9. On a zero-coupon bond with a given maturity and cashflow payment, why does the market price of the security fall when its market interest rate rises? Why does the market interest rate for the security rise when its market price falls?

10. Following up on Question 9, what other factors might also determine the market price for this security?

---

## Recommended Reading

*There are many textbooks and books of readings that deal specifically with the financial system. Some standard references include:*

Tim Campbell, *Financial Institutions, Markets, and Economic Activity*, 2nd edition, McGraw-Hill, New York, 1988.

Thomas Havrilesky and Robert Schweitzer, *Contemporary Developments in Financial Institutions and Markets*, Harlan Davidson, Arlington Heights, Ill., 1983.

Robert W. Kolb, *Principles of Finance*, Scott, Foresman, Glenview, Ill., 1988.

S. Peter Rose, and Donald R. Fraser, *Financial Institutions*, 3rd edition, Business Publications, Plano, Tex., 1988.

*More advanced books include:*

William Sharpe, *Investments*, 3rd edition, Prentice-Hall, Englewood Cliffs, N.J., 1985.

Kenneth Garbade, *Securities Markets*, McGraw-Hill, New York, 1982.

---

# Appendix 5.1
# Prices and Interest Rates for Other Securities

Although it was convenient to focus the text discussion on zero-coupon securities, they represent a small, although growing, part of the financial markets. We will now look at how present value is computed for annuities and coupon bonds, traded actively in financial markets.

## Annuities

Recall from Figure 5.1, panel B, that an annuity provides a series of cashflow payments equal in amount and regularly spaced over time. An $N$-year annuity thus has the same cashflow pattern as a series of zero-coupon bonds with maturities that range from one year to $N$ years, each bond having a future value of $C$. If we look at it this way, then the present value of an annuity $PV_A$ equals the sum of the present values of each of the respective zero-coupon bonds:

$$PV_A = \frac{C}{(1 + d)} + \frac{C}{(1 + d)^2} + \frac{C}{(1 + d)^3} + \cdots\cdots + \frac{C}{(1 + d)^N},$$

or, in mathematical shorthand, using the summation sign $\Sigma$,

$$= \sum_{t=1}^{N} \frac{C}{(1 + d)^t}. \tag{5.8}$$

The relationship between present value and a discount rate, given in Box 5.6, applies directly to annuities with the payment $C$ substituted for the future value $FV_n$. The price/interest rate relationship given in Box 5.7 for zero-coupon securities also applies to annuities.

The cashflow pattern of annuities is commonly used for *consumer loan* and *mortgage loan* contracts. The amount borrowed is the present value, because the lender immediately pays the borrower this amount in cash. The lender then holds the security—the loan contract—and is repaid by the series of cashflow payments. Payment of the last of the specified cashflows terminates the borrower's obligation.

## Coupon Bonds

Coupon bonds are issued by corporations and government agencies, including the U.S. Treasury. The cashflow pattern of a coupon bond with a maturity of $N$ years is shown in panel C of Figure 5.1. The cashflow consists of two parts, one part being an annuity, and the other part being a zero-coupon bond. The annuity part consists of a series of equal payments $C$, one in each period; these are the bond's *coupon payments* representing the payment of interest. The zero-coupon part consists of a single payment $R$ in the last year; this is the *redemption payment,* representing the repayment of the *principal* (the amount borrowed).

The present value of a coupon bond $PV_C$ is determined by adding together the present value of the two parts. Based on equation (5.2) for the zero-coupon security part, and on equation (5.8) for the annuity part, the present value of a coupon bond $PV_C$ is:

$$PV_C = \left( \sum_{t=1}^{N} \frac{C}{(1 + d)^t} \right) + \frac{R}{(1 + d)^N} . \tag{5.9}$$

Since a coupon bond combines the features of a zero-coupon bond and an annuity, the relationship between its present value, its discount rate, and its maturity can be expressed:

1. The present value of a coupon bond varies directly with the size of the coupon payments $C$ and the redemption value $R$.

2. The present value of a coupon bond rises as the discount rate $d$ falls.

3. The percentage change in a coupon bond's present value, resulting from a change in the discount rate $d$, is greater the longer the maturity $N$ of the bond.

The price/interest rate relationship given in Box 5.7 for zero-coupon securities also applies to coupon bonds.

# The Banking Industry: Structure and Services

**6**

*"Banking establishments are more dangerous than standing armies."*

**Thomas Jefferson**

Banks expedite two sets of transactions—transfers of money from buyers to sellers of goods, and from lenders to borrowers. Basic as these functions are, we can imagine an economy operating without banks. Currency would then be the only medium of exchange, and loans would be made directly between borrowers and lenders.

The Great Depression of the 1930s dramatically illustrates what can happen in an economy without banks. Between 1929 and 1933, almost 10,000 commercial banks in the United States failed, cutting their number almost in half. This sharply reduced banking services, and people were understandably reluctant to deposit their money in the banks that remained.

According to one current theory, the failure of the banking system early in the Great Depression turned what might have been a normal recession into an economic catastrophe. The Great Depression was so severe, and lasted so long, the theory holds, precisely because there was no place in the economy where borrowers could obtain loans. People and firms then could not obtain the money and credit they needed to follow through with their consumption and investment plans. The level of economic activity remained weak as part of a vicious circle that lasted for a decade, right up until World War II.

---

In this chapter, we will look at commercial banks—the most important type of financial intermediaries in modern economies—as a case study typifying all financial intermediaries. We will focus on the two main services that commercial banks provide: intermediation services and transfer services.

**Intermediation services** are provided to expedite the transfer of loanable funds from lenders to borrowers, *intermediation* meaning that banks intervene between lenders and borrowers. Without bank intermediation, people (and business firms and government agencies) who now deposit money in interest-bearing bank accounts would instead have to lend their money directly to borrowers.

**Transfer services** are provided by banks as part of the economy's payments system for goods and services. Bank checks are used to make most of the payments in the economy: money is deposited in a checking account so that it can be transferred to a specified payee by writing a check.

## Commercial Banks and Other Financial Intermediaries

Although our discussion will focus on commercial banks, they are *not* the only institutions that provide intermediation or transfer services. Table 6.1 shows the total assets at the end of 1987 for all of the major categories of financial intermediaries. They all operate under one common principle: they attract funds by issuing deposits or similar instruments, and they make loans or purchase securities. Commercial banks represent a particularly useful example because they are the single largest group, and there are ample data sources to describe their broad range of activities. We will look in detail at the nonbank intermediaries— thrift institutions (savings and loan associations, savings banks, and credit unions) and nondepository intermediaries—in Chapter 13.

**TABLE 6.1**
**The Major Classes of Financial Intermediaries**

### At year-end 1987 (Dollars in billions)

| Type of Intermediary | Total Assets | Special Activities |
|---|---|---|
| Depository intermediaries | | |
| Commercial banks | 2,721 | Business and other loans |
| Savings and loan associations[a] | 1,262 | Mortgage loans |
| Savings banks | 259 | Mortgage loans |
| Credit unions | 184 | Consumer loans |
| Nondepository intermediaries | | |
| Pension funds | 1,559 | Retirement investments |
| Insurance companies | 1,394 | Insurance policies |
| Mutual funds | 771 | Financial investments |
| Finance companies | 448 | Consumer loans |

[a]Savings and loan associations include those savings banks insured by the Federal Savings and Loan Insurance Corporation.

**Source:** *Financial Assets and Liabilities*, Flow of Funds Accounts, Board of Governors of the Federal Reserve System, 1988.

### Commercial Banks

There are currently about 14,000 commercial banks in the United States, with total assets of over $2.5 trillion, so the average bank has assets of about $175 million. However, their size distribution is highly skewed, so that there are more than one hundred banks that individually have total assets of over $1 billion. Almost all commercial banks are shareholder-owned, meaning that they are structured in the same way as corporations, with shares of common stock, a board of directors, and executive managers.

Commercial banks are regulated in a number of ways. First, all commercial banks must obtain a charter—a license to operate—either at the state level (from the state banking commissioner) or at the federal level (from the Comptroller of the Currency). Second, the deposits of almost all commercial banks in the United States are insured by the Federal Deposit Insurance Corporation (FDIC). Third, various state and federal agencies, including the Federal Reserve, determine the regulations under which banks operate, and they supervise and examine the banks to make sure they are meeting the regulations. We will look in detail at bank regulation (and deregulation) in Chapter 10.

The most basic feature of banking is to raise money in one set of markets (by attracting deposits as liabilities) and to lend it in another set of markets (by making loans and buying securities as assets). The liabilities (mainly deposits) and assets (mainly loans) of a bank are related for two reasons. First, the sum total of a bank's liabilities and its capital represents the total amount of money that the bank has available for acquiring assets. Second, the interest a bank earns on its assets is its main source of income for paying interest on its liabilities.

The balance sheet of all commercial banks in the United States, shown in Tables 6.2 and 6.3, provides a quick way to see how banks are operated.

| TABLE 6.2 |
| --- |
| **Commercial Bank Liabilities** |

**December 1987**

| | $ billions | Percentage of total |
| --- | --- | --- |
| Deposits | | |
|   Transaction accounts: | | |
|   Demand deposits | 452 | 18 |
|   Other checkable deposits | 187 | 7 |
|   Total transaction accounts | 639 | 25 |
|   Investment accounts: | | |
|   Savings accounts | 524 | 20 |
|   Time deposits | 493 | 19 |
|   Certificates of deposit ($100,000 or more) | 298 | 12 |
|   Total investment accounts | 1,954 | 51 |
| Nondeposit liabilities | 445 | 17 |
| Total liabilities | 2,386 | 93 |
| Bank capital | 178 | 7 |
| Total liabilities and bank capital | 2,564 | 100 |

**Source:** *Federal Reserve Bulletin,* Table 4.22, Board of Governors of the Federal Reserve System, June 1988.

**TABLE 6.3**
**Commercial Bank Assets**

### December 1987

|  | $ billions | Percentage of total |
|---|---|---|
| Cash assets |  |  |
| Currency and coin (vault cash) | 25 | 1 |
| Balances due from other depository institutions | 225 | 9 |
| Total cash assets | 250 | 10 |
| Securities | 479 | 19 |
| Loans |  |  |
| Real estate | 574 | 22 |
| Commercial | 478 | 19 |
| Individual | 313 | 12 |
| Other | 207 | 8 |
| Total loans | 1,564 | 61 |
| Other assets | 258 | 10 |
| Total assets | 2,564 | 100 |

**Source:** *Federal Reserve Bulletin,* Table 4.22, Board of Governors of the Federal Reserve System, June 1988.

## Bank Liabilities

Banks attract various types of deposits, and also issue various securities as nondeposit liabilities, so that they will have money to lend and invest. The amounts and types of deposits and nondeposit liabilities for commercial banks in the United States at the end of 1987 are shown in Table 6.2.

There are two main classes of deposits: transaction accounts and investment accounts. **Transaction accounts,** commonly called checking accounts, are held by depositors primarily so that they can transfer money by check. As we discussed in Box 1.1 of Chapter 1, *demand deposits* are a type of checking account, mainly held by business firms, on which no interest is paid. *Other checkable deposits* include other types of checking accounts—such as NOW accounts (Negotiable Orders of Withdrawal)—that are mainly held by consumers, and on which interest is usually paid.

**Investment accounts,** also called *time deposits* or *nontransaction deposits,* are held by depositors to earn interest. As we discussed in Box 1.5 of Chapter 1, investment accounts include various types of time deposits and *savings accounts.* Time deposits include *certificates of deposit*—deposits with a fixed maturity that are represented by a certificate—and *money market deposit accounts*—which allow a small number of checks to be written each month.

Interest is paid on interest-bearing deposits at the rate and terms that were set at the time the deposit was made. At the maturity date of the deposit, the bank also repays the principal amount that was invested. Interest is paid and the principal is repaid on deposits without regard to the bank's earnings on its loans and securities. Although a bank can fail to meet its obligations, **federal deposit insurance** guarantees depositors the return of their principal up to $100,000.

Although deposits are their main source of money, banks also issue securities—nondeposit liabilities—in the capital markets, as shown in Table 6.2. These securities are similar to deposits in most respects, but they are issued in large denominations and are not covered by federal deposit insurance. A bank will use these securities to raise money when they represent a less costly source of funds than deposits or when it is difficult to attract deposits of a particular maturity. To simplify matters in this chapter, we will refer to bank deposits as if they were the only bank liabilities. However, we will look at nondeposit liabilities further in Chapter 11 when we discuss bank liquidity management.

The last item in Table 6.2—**bank capital**—is the amount invested directly in a bank by its shareholders plus the amount of retained profits (profits less shareholder dividends) or losses the bank has accrued over time. We discussed in Box 1.6 of Chapter 1 how banks use their capital to write off loan losses.

## Bank Assets

A bank's managers will consider many factors in deciding which loans to make and which securities to buy. Other things being equal, they will want the bank to earn the highest possible rate of return on its investments. However, as we will see, other things are often not equal.

As shown in Table 6.3, **cash assets** are held by banks as vault cash and as deposits at other banks. Indeed, the Federal Reserve requires banks to keep a minimum percentage of their deposits in vault cash or in a special account at the Federal Reserve. Cash assets provide a bank with *liquidity,* which can be used when depositors wish to withdraw funds from the bank. Since transaction deposits are withdrawn with a much higher frequency than investment deposits, banks with a higher proportion of transaction deposits usually maintain a comparably higher proportion of cash assets.

**Bank securities** consist mainly of U.S. Treasury securities and municipal bonds (securities issued by state and local governments). Banks benefit from holding U.S. Treasury securities because they are highly liquid, and they benefit from holding municipal bonds because their interest is exempt from federal (and sometimes state) taxation. Federal and local governments may also require banks to hold their securities as backing for government deposits. However, commercial banks are *not* allowed to hold corporate bonds or common stock.

**Loans** represent almost two-thirds of commercial bank assets. In order of importance, there are real estate (mortgage), commercial (business), and individual (consumer) loans. Banks make a large number of relatively small loans, one reason being that a bank cannot lend more than 15% of its capital to any single borrower.

*Other assets* held by banks include their offices and equipment, as well as various items of collateral they receive from bankrupt borrowers. For example, Texas banks received large amounts of oil-drilling equipment in the early 1980s from bankrupt oil companies after the price of oil fell abruptly.

## Asset and Liability Management

Bank managers consider five key factors—expected return, maturity balance, regulations, liquidity, and credit risk—when selecting bank assets and liabilites. Although each factor is discussed in a later chapter, it is useful to have a preliminary look at them now.

**Expected Return** (Chapter 7)

The expected return is the rate of return the bank expects to earn on an asset or to pay on a liability.

**Maturity Balance** (Chapters 8 and 9)

A bank with unequal amounts of loans and deposits at any given maturity is subject to *interest rate risk*—the risk that the bank's profits will change if interest rate levels unexpectedly change. To avoid this risk, banks may:

Match the amounts of loans and deposits at each maturity.

Use futures and options contracts to hedge the interest rate risk.

**Regulations** (Chapter 10)

Banking regulations prohibit banks from dealing in certain assets and constrain their portfolios in other ways.

**Liquidity Management** (Chapter 11)

Banks manage the liquidity of their assets and liabilities to ensure that they can meet deposit withdrawals.

**Credit Risk** (Chapter 13)

Credit risk reflects the likelihood that a borrower will default on loan payments. To deal with credit risk, bank managers will:

Estimate the level of risk based on available information.

Charge interest rates commensurate with the estimated risk.

Hold diversified portfolios—with large numbers of small loans.

It is not surprising that in dealing with all of these factors, banks frequently face trade-offs—they can improve their portfolio in one dimension, but only at the cost of making it worse in another. For example, assets that offer a high expected return generally also involve one or more of the following:

- Long-term maturity.
- Regulatory restrictions.
- Low liquidity.
- High credit risk.

A main task of bank managers is to balance these factors.

## Bank Competition

Another main task of management is to deal with the competition banks face when either raising money—attracting deposits—or investing money—making loans. Competition comes from other banks, as well as from thrift institutions and nondepository intermediaries. When banks issue securities in the capital markets to raise nondeposit funds, they also compete with the corporations and government agencies that use these markets.

Competition may force banks to pay higher interest rates or to offer more services in order to attract deposits. Generally speaking, bank deposits offer the advantages of safety, convenience, and special services. As a result, bank deposit interest rates tend to be somewhat lower than the rates available on other securities. However, Box 6.1 discusses a new group of bank competitors—money market funds—that have been successful in competing with bank deposits by offering higher interest rates.

Increased competition may also force banks to accept lower interest rates on the loans they make and the securities they purchase. The competition for capital market securities—such as U.S. Treasury bills and bonds—is particularly fierce because no special expertise is needed to invest in these low-risk securities. Instead, banks have specialized in making loans where the competition is less fierce because expertise is important in evaluating a borrower's credit worthiness. Box 6.2 discusses the types of loans for which banks compete most successfully.

---

### BOX 6.1 BANKING BRIEFS

## Competition for Deposits

Safety and convenience have always been an advantage of bank deposits over the securities offered by other intermediaries. However, since the late 1970s, *money market funds* have offered securities that often pay higher rates of interest than bank deposits, yet provide many similar features.

Individuals and firms invest in money market funds (MMFs) by mail; the MMFs then invest the money in capital market securities such as Treasury bills. As a result of their lower operating costs, MMFs can often pay higher interest rates than commercial banks. For example, to manage $1,000 of deposits, it may cost a bank $20 (2% of the funds), whereas it may only cost a MMF $5 (0.5% of the funds). In addition, until recently, Regulation Q ceilings limited the interest rates that banks could pay on deposits (see Box 1.5 in Chapter 1).

Although most money market funds do not provide the convenience of local offices, they can provide their customers with checking account services. They do this by allowing each customer to write checks (up to the amount invested in the MMF) on a special account that the fund maintains at a commercial bank. This is a key reason that money market funds represent such tough competition for commercial banks. We will look at MMFs further in Chapter 13 when we discuss nondepository intermediaries.

## BOX 6.2 BANKING BRIEFS

### Competition for Loans

Banks have to compete against other lenders in terms of loan rates charged, the flexibility or repayment schedules, and other terms specified in loan contracts. Banks generally fare especially well in competing for *moderate risk* loans, because they have specialized in evaluating the credit worthiness of these borrowers. Also, once a bank and a borrower have an established relationship, it is hard for other lenders to gather enough information to compete. Banks fare less well in the markets for very high-risk and very low-risk loans.

For *high-risk loans*—especially to consumers—lenders may have to use relatively tough tactics to collect overdue payments from delinquent borrowers. Banks are reluctant to do this because it may harm their reputation with depositors and other borrowers. So high-risk loans tend to be made by specialized lenders such as finance companies.

For *low-risk loans*, the problem is that there is little need for special expertise to evaluate a borrower's credit worthiness. So low-risk firms may be able to obtain lower-cost loans from other lenders—such as insurance companies—or they may issue corporate bonds directly in the capital markets. Banks still actively participate in the markets for low-risk loans, but the profit margins are likely to be low.

We can see how banks have fared in their competition with thrift institutions and nondepository intermediaries by looking at how the total assets of each type of institution have grown. For the period 1970 to 1987, as shown in Figure 6.1, commercial banks held their own against thrift institutions, but they have grown more slowly, especially in recent years, compared to nondepository intermediaries. The growth of money market funds (discussed in Box 6.1) is one factor that is responsible for these trends, and we will look at other factors when we discuss regulatory issues in Chapter 10 and nonbank intermediaries in Chapter 13.

### Bank Profits

Some time ago, banking was facetiously called a 1-2-3 business—loan interest rates were 3%, deposit interest rates were 2%, and management hit the golf course by 1. But this jibe at the simplicity of the banking business is no longer true: fluctuating interest rates, increased competition for loans and deposits, high rates of loan defaults, and intense regulation have now combined to make managing a bank as complex as running any business firm.

There are two main sources of **bank revenue:** interest earned on assets and service fees paid by customers. There are three main components of **bank costs:** interest paid on liabilities, general operating expenses, and provisions for loan losses. As an example, Box 6.3 shows the revenue, costs, and profits of Citicorp, the holding company of Citibank—the largest commercial bank in the United States—for two years: 1986 when it *earned* $1.1 billion; and 1987 when it *lost* $1.1 billion.

FIGURE 6.1
**Total Assets of Commercial Banks and Other Intermediaries**
Trillions of dollars of credit claims

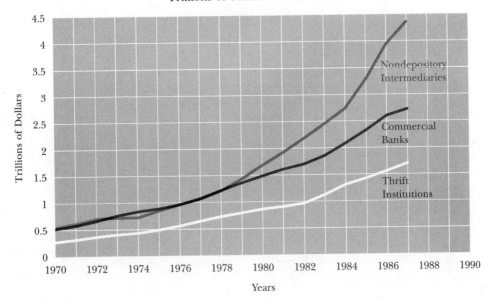

Commercial bank assets have grown in step with those of thrift institutions, but they have not grown as rapidly as the assets of nondepository interme-diaries. **Source:** *Financial Assets and Liabilities*, Flow of Funds Accounts, Board of Governors of the Federal Reserve System.

## Intermediation Services

Many people prefer to invest their money in bank deposits than in capital market securities, because bank deposits provide safety, convenience, and special services. People also frequently prefer to use banks (or other financial intermediaries) when they borrow money. Although in principle people could borrow money by issuing securities in the capital markets, the amounts they want to borrow are usually too small and their credit risk is too high to make this practical.

Consequently, most people use the intermediation services of banks (and other intermediaries) to deposit and borrow money. Indeed, we can think of the process of intermediation as if banks were "making a market" in loanable funds—the same process we described for security dealers in Chapter 5. That is, banks bid for loanable funds by offering to pay an interest rate on deposits, and they offer loanable funds by setting a different (higher) interest rate on loans.

Even though banks may appear to be an *alternative* to investing or borrowing money in the capital markets, it is more accurate to think of banks as an indirect means through which people obtain *access* to the capital markets. One factor is that banks make some of their investments

BOX 6.3 BANKING BRIEFS

## Citicorp Profits (1986) and Losses (1987)

The profit statements below show Citicorp's main revenue and cost items for 1986 and 1987 in billions of dollars and as a percentage of Citicorp's total assets at the end of each year. In 1986, Citicorp earned an effective interest return of 9.8% on its assets. It paid an effective interest rate of 6.7% on its deposits and other liabilities, and its operating expenses were 3.5% of its total assets. Over-

all, it earned $1.1 billion after taxes.

In most respects, Citicorp's results in 1987 were very similar to those in 1986. However, there was the big difference that Citibank contributed $4.4 billion to its loan loss reserve in 1987, whereas it only contributed $1.8 billion in 1986. This change accounted for the entire swing from profits of $1.1 billion in 1986 to losses of $1.1 billion in 1987.

### Citicorp Profits, 1986 and 1987

|  | 1986 | | 1987 | |
|---|---|---|---|---|
|  | $ billions | Percentage of assets | $ billions | Percentage of assets |
| Interest revenue | 19.2 | 9.8 | 22.0 | 10.8 |
| Fees and other revenue | 4.2 | 2.2 | 6.0 | 2.9 |
| Total revenue | 23.4 | 12.0 | 28.0 | 13.7 |
| Interest expense | 13.1 | 6.7 | 15.5 | 7.6 |
| Operating expense | 6.8 | 3.5 | 8.3 | 4.1 |
| Provision for loan losses | 1.8 | 0.9 | 4.4 | 2.2 |
| Total expense | 21.7 | 11.1 | 28.2 | 13.9 |
| Income before taxes | 1.7 | – | −0.2 | – |
| Minus income taxes | 0.6 | – | 0.9 | – |
| Net income | 1.1 | – | −1.1 | – |

**Source:** Citicorp *Annual Report*, 1986 and 1987.

in capital market securities; so some of the money that people deposit in banks ends up being invested in capital market securities. Another factor is that banks raise some of their money by borrowing it in the capital markets; to this extent, the capital markets are a source of the money that banks lend.

## A Graphical Analysis of Intermediary Services

We will now develop a simple graphical analysis of bank intermediation services—how banks "make the market" in loanable funds. We will focus on the equilibrium for a competitive banking industry, and will assume that all banks (1) offer one kind of time deposit, (2) make one kind of low-risk loan, and (3) have the same operating expenses. The purpose of these assumptions is to put aside issues relating to credit risk, the maturities of assets and liabilities, regulations, and liquidity, since these matters will be studied in detail in Part III.

In Figure 6.2, the supply curve $F^s$ represents the amount of deposits—the supply of loanable funds—that the banking industry attracts. This supply curve is positively related to the interest rate paid on bank deposits, the *deposit rate* $r_D$. Similarly, the demand curve $F^d$ represents the demand for bank loans—the demand for loanable funds—by borrowers. This demand curve is negatively related to the interest rate charged on bank loans, the *loan rate* $r_L$.

Point $E_0$ in the Figure 6.2 presents the equilibrium that occurs in a *perfect market*, which assumes there are no costs to operating banks. Point $E_0$ has the following features:

- The equilibrium interest rate $r_0$ represents both the deposit rate and the loan rate.
- The demand and supply of loanable funds are equal.
- The quantity of lending and borrowing is $Q_0$.

FIGURE 6.2
**Bank Equilibrium**

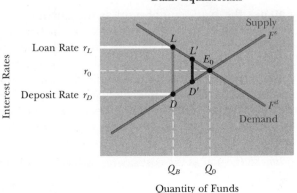

The supply of funds—deposits—is represented as a positively sloped curve $F^s$ with respect to the rate paid for deposits, $r_D$. The demand for funds—loans—is represented as a negatively sloped curve $F^d$ with respect to the rate charged on loans, $r_L$. The *perfect market equilibrium* occurs at point $E_0$, where demand and supply are equal at the quantity $Q_0$ and the equilibrium interest rate $r_0$ represents both the deposit rate and the loan rate.

The *bank equilibrium* occurs at the quantity of funds $Q_B$. At this quantity, the supply of funds at the deposit rate $r_D$ and the demand for funds at the loan rate $r_L$ are equal. The rate spread is the difference between the loan rate and the deposit rate, $r_L - r_D$. The efficiency of intermediation is measured by the rate spread—the length of the line segment $LD$ in the diagram. A more efficient banking industry has the lower rate spread $L'D'$.

Although the equilibrium of a perfect market is an idealized situation, it provides a useful starting point and standard of comparison for our discussion.

A more realistic case is shown in Figure 6.2 by the **bank equilibrium**. At this equilibrium, the loan rate is $r_L$, the deposit rate is $r_D$, and the total amount of borrowing and lending—that is, the *quantity of intermediation*—is $Q_B$. This is an equilibrium because the amount of loanable funds demanded (at the loan rate $r_L$) and the amount of loanable funds supplied (at the deposit rate $r_D$) are equal—even though $Q_B$ is not the quantity at which the demand and supply curves intersect. The features of this equilibrium are:

- Banks pay the deposit rate $r_D$ and charge the loan rate $r_L$.
- The demand and supply equal the quantity $Q_B$ at these rates.
- The *rate spread*, $r_L - r_D$, covers bank operating expenses and shareholder profits.

You can now see why financial intermediation is analogous to "making a market" in loanable funds. The deposit rate $r_D$ represents the *bid price* that banks pay to obtain or buy funds, while the loan rate $r_L$ represents the *ask price* that banks charge to provide or sell funds. So the **rate spread**—the difference between the loan rate and the deposit rate—is comparable to the *bid-ask spread* that a security dealer uses in making the market for a security. In fact, Figure 6.2 has the same structure as Figure 5.5 in Chapter 5, which we used to illustrate security dealer bid and ask prices.

## More Efficient Intermediation

What differentiates the bank equilibrium at the quantity $Q_B$ from the perfect market equilibrium at the quantity $Q_0$ is that the bank equilibrium takes into account the costs of carrying out intermediation—that is, the expenses of operating banks. These costs are the basis of the rate spread, the difference between the loan rate $r_L$ and the deposit rate $r_D$. Smaller rate spreads reflect more efficient intermediation—depositors are paid higher deposit rates and/or borrowers are charged lower loan rates.

Factors that might allow—or force—banks to operate with lower rate spreads include:

- *Lower operating costs,* such as the cost savings achieved with automated-teller machines.
- *Increased competition,* which may force banks to pay higher deposit rates (to deter depositors from investing their money elsewhere) or to charge lower loan rates (to deter borrowers from obtaining loans elsewhere).
- *Deregulation*—removing bank regulations, which may allow banks to operate more efficiently.

The results of more efficient intermediation—lower rate spreads—are illustrated in Figure 6.2 by comparing the line segment $LD$, which measures the initial rate spread $r_L - r_D$, with the shorter line segment $L'D'$ which measures a smaller rate spread. The lower rate spread illustrates three major features of more efficient intermediation:

1. The interest rate charged on loans is lower.

2. The interest rate paid on deposits is higher.

3. The quantity of lending and borrowing is higher.

More efficient intermediation therefore helps both borrowers and lenders. The extreme case of efficient intermediation is represented in Figure 6.2 by point $E_0$, the perfect market equilibrium.

## Shifts in the Demand and Supply of Loanable Funds

We know that in standard markets the quantity of a good produced will increase if there is a rightward shift in either the demand curve or the supply curve. We also know that the price of the good will rise if it is the demand curve that shifts to the right, whereas the price will fall if it is the supply curve that shifts to the right. The same considerations apply to the market for bank intermediation, as illustrated in Figure 6.3.

Factors that allow banks to attract more deposits—that is, that shift the supply curve of bank deposits rightward—include:

- An increase in income, which causes the overall amount of saving to rise.

- A decrease in capital market interest rates, which causes people to shift from capital market investments to bank deposits.

- A higher assessment of the risk of capital market investments, which causes people to hold more bank deposits. (Recall from Box 1.7 of Chapter 1 how people shifted their investments from the stock market to bank deposits after the stock market crash of October 1987.)

Factors that might cause the demand curve for bank loans to shift rightward include:

- An increase in capital investment, causing firms to borrow more money.

- An increase in consumption, causing individuals to borrow more money.

- An increase in capital market interest rates, causing firms to demand more bank loans.

The quantity of borrowing and lending—that is, intermediation—rises when either the demand curve or the supply curve of loanable funds shifts rightward. If it is the demand curve that shifts, then interest

The initial (perfect market) equilibrium occurs at point $E_0$. After the supply curve of deposits $F^s$ shifts rightward (or downward), the resulting equilibrium occurs at point $E_1$. Given that the rate spread remains constant, the line segment $LD$ will shift rightward to $L'D'$ and the resulting loan rate and deposit rate (determined by the end points of the line segment $L'D'$) will both be lower. Using the same technique, it is apparent that an increase in the demand for funds would shift the demand curve for loans rightward, creating an increase in both of the interest rates and in the quantity of intermediation.

FIGURE 6.3

**An Increase in the Supply of Loanable Funds**

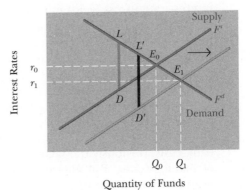

Quantity of Funds

rates—generally both loan rates and deposit rates—will rise. If it is the supply curve that shifts, then both of these interest rates will generally fall.

A rightward shift in the supply curve of funds, which could be the result of an increase in the aggregate amount of saving, is illustrated in Figure 6.3. When the supply curve shifts rightward, the equilibrium interest rate for a perfect market falls, from $r_0$ to $r_1$. If the rate spread between the loan rate and the deposit rate remains constant—so that the line segment $LD$ just shifts rightward to $L'D'$—then the loan rate and deposit rate will both fall.

Thus, a rightward shift in the *supply curve of deposits* has the following effects:

1. The interest rate charged on loans falls.
2. The interest rate paid on deposits falls.
3. The quantity of borrowing and lending—intermediation—rises.

Similarly, a rightward shift in the *demand curve for loans* has the following effects:

1. The interest rate charged on loans rises.
2. The interest rate paid on deposits rises.
3. The quantity of intermediation rises.

## Profits from Intermediation Services

The profits that banks earn from intermediation services reflect their interest income, interest costs, and operating expenses. This can be expressed in a simple equation:

$$\pi = (r_L - c_L) - (r_D + c_D), \qquad (6.1)$$

where $\pi$ = the profit rate (as a percent of total assets),
   $r_L$ = the loan rate (the gross yield on assets),
   $c_L$ = the expense ratio for loans (as a percent of total loans),
   $r_D$ = the deposit rate (interest cost),
   $c_D$ = the expense ratio of deposits (as a percent of total deposits).

The first term in parentheses represents the *net yield on assets*—the loan interest rate (gross yield) minus the operating expenses associated with making loans (expressed as a percentage of total assets). The second term in parentheses represents the *net cost of funds*—the sum of the deposit interest rate and the operating expenses associated with deposits (expressed as a percentage of total assets). The *profit rate* equals the net yield on assets minus the net cost of funds.

In applying this accounting framework, it is necessary to allocate the overall costs of running the bank to the specific activities of making loans and accepting deposits. This is straightforward for many categories of bank costs: obviously the salary of a bank loan officer is one of the costs of making loans. But allocating other costs can be more difficult: for example, how much of the bank president's salary should be allocated as a cost of making loans? And what part of the expenses of running the bank's computer center should be allocated as a cost of making loans?

**Functional cost accounting** is a technique used to estimate and allocate costs and revenues in such situations. In particular, the Federal Reserve carries out an annual **Functional Cost Analysis (FCA)** which helps participating banks to allocate their costs and revenues; the Fed then publishes the average results for participating banks.

Table 6.4 shows the FCA data for commercial bank intermediation services during 1987, the most recent year for which data are available. The net yield on assets is the gross yield minus the associated operating expenses. The net cost of funds is the sum of interest cost and associated operating expenses. The profit rate is the net yield on assets minus the net cost of funds. Although the gross yield on assets and the interest cost of deposits are the dominant factors, the operating expenses for assets and deposits are substantial—taken together they are much larger than the profit rate.

Table 6.5 shows the yields that the banks earned on specific classes of assets during 1987. *Securities* had a relatively low gross yield, but also the lowest expense ratio. In comparison, *credit card loans* had the highest gross yield, but also the highest expenses (including loan losses). Al-

---

**TABLE 6.4**

**Banks Profits from Intermediation Services**

**Calendar year 1987**
**(Percentage of total assets)**

| | |
|---|---|
| Yield on assets | |
| Gross yield | 9.32 |
| Operating expenses | − 1.44 |
| Net yield | 7.88 |
| Cost of funds | |
| Interest cost | 4.78 |
| Operating expenses | + 1.29 |
| Net cost | 6.07 |
| Profit rate | |
| Yield on assets | 7.88 |
| Cost of funds | − 6.07 |
| Profit rate | 1.81 |

**Source**: Functional Cost Analysis, 1987 Average Banks, Board of Governors of the Federal Reserve System, 1987. Data are for banks with assets over $200 million, and operating expenses for assets include loan losses.

---

**TABLE 6.5**

**Yields on Bank Assets**

**Calendar year 1987**
**(Percentage of invested funds)**

| | |
|---|---|
| Securities | |
| Gross yield | 8.93 |
| Operating expenses | .17 |
| Net yield | 8.76 |
| Installment loans | |
| Gross yield | 11.57 |
| Operating expenses | 3.11 |
| Net yield | 8.46 |
| Mortgage loans | |
| Gross yield | 10.59 |
| Operating expenses | 1.38 |
| Net yield | 9.21 |
| International loans | |
| Gross yield | 9.14 |
| Operating expenses | 0.48 |
| Net yield | 8.66 |
| Commercial and other loans | |
| Gross yield | 9.52 |
| Operating expenses | 1.99 |
| Net yield | 7.53 |
| Credit card loans | |
| Gross yield | 23.37 |
| Operating expenses | 12.39 |
| Net yield | 10.95 |

**Source**: Functional Cost Analysis, 1987 Average Banks, Board of Governors of the Federal Reserve System, 1987. Data are for banks with assets over $200 million, and operating expenses for assets include loan losses.

though the net yields vary across assets, the differences are mostly due to short-term factors that affected the markets in the particular year. In the long run, banks (and other lenders) would enter markets that had high expected net yields and would leave markets that had low expected net yields, thus causing all of the net yields to converge eventually to roughly the same value.

Table 6.6 shows the cost of specific sources of bank funds. In each category, the interest cost reflects the effective interest rate—interest paid divided by the amount of funds in that category. Comparing transaction deposits with investment deposits, transaction deposits have a lower interest rate, but higher expenses. We will see the significance of these differences as we now turn to our discussion of bank transfer—checking account—services.

### TABLE 6.6
### The Costs of Attracting Funds

**Calendar year 1987**
**(Percentage of fund balances)**

| | |
|---|---|
| Transaction deposit accounts | |
|    Interest cost | 1.92 |
|    Operating expenses | +2.83 |
|      Total cost | 4.75 |
| Investment deposit accounts | |
|    Interest cost | 6.12 |
|    Operating expenses | +0.85 |
|      Total cost | 6.97 |
| Nondeposit funds | |
|    Interest cost | 4.63 |
|    Operating expenses | +0.74 |
|      Total cost | 5.37 |

**Source**: Functional Cost Analysis, 1987 Average Banks, Board of Governors of the Federal Reserve System, 1987. Data are for banks with assets over $200 million, and operating expenses for assets include loan losses.

## Transfer Services

Checks are the most important means of transferring money within the U.S. payments system. Depository intermediaries, mostly commercial banks, maintain checking accounts and manage the system used to transfer checks.

Consider the example of person A with an account at bank A, who wants to transfer an amount of money to person B with an account at bank B. Overall, the transfer is made by subtracting the amount of A's check from his account at bank A, while adding this amount to B's account at bank B. The specific steps involved are:

1. A gives a check to B who deposits it in her account at bank B.
2. Bank B uses the Federal Reserve's *check clearing system* to return the check to bank A.
3. Bank A verifies the check, subtracts the amount from A's account, and reimburses bank B.
4. Bank B then credits the amount of the check to B's account.

Historically, commercial banks were the only institutions with access to the Federal Reserve's check clearing system, so they were the only institutions that were able to transfer checks. In 1980, thrift institutions were also granted access to the check clearing system, so all depository intermediaries can now provide transfer services. Commercial banks still have a dominant position in checking accounts, but thrift institutions are starting to gain a share of the market. Nondepository intermediaries do not have direct access to the check clearing system, but they can provide transfer services in conjunction with banks (see Box 6.1).

## The Transfer Service Business

Banks operate their transfer service business by maintaining checking accounts that allow customers to make payments by check. In principle, this is a business like any other, having costs, revenues, and profits.

Banks face two main costs in providing transfer services. First, there are operating costs (offices, equipment, and personnel) for accepting deposits, maintaining accounts, and making transfers. Second, interest may be paid on transaction account balances.

Banks also receive two forms of revenue on transaction accounts. First, they may charge fees for making transfers (clearing checks). Second, they earn interest by investing transaction account balances.

To the extent that banks invest the transaction account balances in loans and securities, the transfer service also involves an intermediation service. But because depositors can withdraw their transaction account balances "on demand" (whenever they wish), at least part of the deposits must be kept in cash assets on which no interest is earned or in highly liquid assets on which relatively little interest is earned. As a result, banks earn less interest on transaction account balances than on investment account balances.

The Federal Reserve's Functional Cost Analysis provides a useful summary of the costs, revenues, and profits of commercial bank transfer services during 1987, as shown in Table 6.7. (Notice that the percentages in Table 6.7 refer to funds used for transfer services, whereas the percentages in the earlier Tables 6.4, 6.5, and 6.6 referred to funds used for intermediation services.)

The *costs of providing transfer services*—operating expenses and interest costs—are shown at the top of Table 6.7. The annual operating expense for an average account was $175. (This cost can be further separated into a $70 annual fee for maintaining the account and a cost of $1.86 for each transfer.) These costs are high because the business remains highly

| TABLE 6.7 | | |
|---|---|---|
| The Transfer Service Business | | |
| | **Calendar year 1987 Average (%) of Deposit Balance** | **Dollars per Account** |
| Costs | | |
| Operating expenses[a] | 3.74 | 175 |
| Interest costs | 1.97 | 92 |
| Total costs | 5.71 | 267 |
| Revenue | | |
| Service fees | 1.21 | 57 |
| Investment income | 6.60 | 309 |
| Total revenue | 7.81 | 366 |
| Profits | | |
| Total revenue minus total costs | 2.10 | 99 |

[a]Operating expenses consist of $70 for annual account maintenance and $1.86 per transfer.

**Source**: Functional Cost Analysis, 1987 Average Bank, Board of Governors of the Federal Reserve System, 1987. Data are for banks with assets over $200 million, and operating expenses for assets include loan losses.

labor-intensive—remember, checks are still written on paper. The annual interest credited for an average account was $92. Thus the total annual cost of providing transfer services was $267 for an average account.

The *revenue items earned from transfer services*—service fees and investment interest (on invested account balances)—are shown in the middle of Table 6.7. For the average account annually, service fee income was $57 and investment income was $309, for a total revenue of $366.

Subtracting the costs from the revenues, the net profits from transfer services were $99 per account annually (total revenue of $366 minus total costs of $267). Stated as a percentage of average transaction account balances, the profit rate was 2.10%.

## The Pricing of Transfer Services

The prices banks charge for maintaining transaction accounts and making transfers are a key factor in determining the amount of transfer services consumers use. *Higher* prices correspond either to *higher* service fees charged or to *lower* interest rates paid. Specifically, consumers will make fewer transfers, the higher the fee per transfer, and they will maintain smaller transaction account balances, the lower the interest rate paid on these balances.

The amount of transfer services used by consumers is important from an economy-wide perspective because the more these services are demanded, the greater the amount of resources that have to be allocated to providing them—including personnel, offices, and equipment—all of which could be used for other purposes. According to microeconomic theory, the "right" amount of resources will be allocated to transfer services when banks charge a price that reflects the marginal cost of providing the services. If banks charge a price that is below the marginal cost, for example, then consumers will demand too many transfers and too many resources will be allocated to this sector of the economy.

The incentives created by profits and competition should ensure that banks charge the "right" price for transfer services. A bank that charges a price that is too low will earn low or negative profits, so it will have an incentive to raise its price or to stop providing the service. And a bank that charges a price that is too high will lose customers to competing banks or to new banks that might enter the industry.

However, because the price of transfer services has two components— the service fees charged for transfers and the interest paid on transaction account balances—there is a complication. A bank could be charging the "right" price *averaged over the two components*, but the price of one component could be too low, while the price of the other component could be too high.

In fact, the service fee component of the price has usually been too low, while the interest component has been too high (the interest rate paid on transaction account balances has been too low). This is evident in Table 6.7:

- For the average account, annual operating expenses were $175, whereas the service fees charged were only $57. Thus, there was a net subsidy of about $118 per account annually for transfers. This subsidy provided consumers with an incentive to use a larger quantity—too large a quantity—of transfer services.

- For the average account, banks received annual investment income of $309, but paid deposit interest of only $92. This provided consumers an incentive to spend time and resources to keep their balances low.

This way of pricing transfer services originated when banks were prohibited from paying interest on transaction accounts. Given that banks could not compete in terms of the interest rate, they had to charge low service fees and to provide high levels of service. This is one reason we have so many branch bank offices in the United States.

Put another way, we have had a situation of **cross subsidization**— meaning that a high price charged for one product subsidizes the low price charged for another product. With transfer services, due to low service fees, banks use too many resources—too many offices, people, and machines—to carry out the large number of transfers that consumers demand. And due to low deposit interest rates, consumers use too many resources—too many trips to the bank and too many nights carefully balancing their checkbooks—to maintain small balances.

In an efficient system of transfer services, consumers would receive market interest rates on their deposit balances and they would pay the full marginal cost of the transfer services they use. This would require that banks pay higher interest rates on transaction account balances, and charge higher fees for each transfer. With this pricing structure, customers would have the proper incentive to economize on the number of transfers, but not on the balances they leave on deposit.

With deregulation, banks can now pay competitive interest rates on most transaction accounts. Therefore, we are starting to see higher deposit interest rates and higher service fees, a step toward the elimination of cross subsidization. A better allocation of resources will result if this trend continues.

## Other Bank Services

If commercial banks can profitably provide services in addition to intermediation and checking accounts, then of course they will want to do so. Since banks already know a good deal about the financial position of some of their customers, they may have cost, informational, and other strategic advantages for supplying other services. Bank credit cards are a particularly interesting example that combines intermediation and transfer services.

### Bank Credit Cards

In addition to currency and checks, **credit cards** now represent a third common means of payment for consumer purchases. Cardholders receive a plastic credit card and a credit limit that sets the maximum amount of purchases they can make each month with the card. Most families have at least one credit card, and many have more than one (see Table 6.8).

**TABLE 6.8**
**Credit Cards Held**

| (Percentage of all families) | |
| --- | --- |
| Bank | 42 |
| Travel and entertainment | 10 |
| Retail | |
|    Gasoline | 28 |
|    National retailer | 48 |
|    Other retailer | 37 |
|    Other | 5 |

**Source**: *Survey of Consumer Finances, 1983*, Board of Governors of the Federal Reserve System, 1983.

There are three major categories of credit cards:

- Bank credit cards such as MasterCard and Visa.
- Travel and entertainment cards such as American Express.
- Retail credit cards for such specific retail uses as department stores, airlines, and gasoline companies.

---

**BOX 6.4 CREDIT CHECK**

## The Benefits and Costs of Credit Cards

For consumers, the benefits of credit cards include convenience, up to a 45-day period without payments, and access to credit as needed. The period without payments exists because the card company holds the receipt slips until the monthly bill date (for an average of 15 days) and the bill is then due one month later. This represents an interest-free loan to cardholders when the credit option is not used. If a credit option is available and is used, interest is charged on the loan amount, usually including the initial 45-day period.

For merchants, credit cards provide benefits that include safety (credit card receipts have no intrinsic value), the elimination of bad checks (the card company guarantees payment if procedures have been followed), and the competitive advantage of providing consumers with the option to use their credit card. Credit card companies, however, charge merchants a fee—the *discount fee*—usually 1% to 4% of the face amount of each sales slip. Thus on a $100 sale, the merchant might receive $97 from the card company, reflecting a 3% discount fee. Merchants could offset the discount fee by charging customers higher prices on credit card purchases, but few actually do this.

Income for credit card companies consists of the annual fees many charge their customers, discount fees paid by merchants, and interest paid by cardholders who use the credit option. This income must cover the operating costs of the card company and its losses on accounts where consumers fail to pay. Retailer credit card plans are also thought to promote customer loyalty and to provide a useful mailing list of active customers.

---

In each case, the cardholder receives a monthly bill from the card company for the accumulated amount of the purchases made. The monthly bill can be paid in full, or many of the cards offer a credit option that can be activated. With the credit option, interest is charged on the loan balance until full payment is made. Box 6.4 discusses the benefits and costs of credit cards further.

### Electronic Funds Transfer

The payments system is always evolving as new technology and new ideas create more convenient and lower-cost payment methods. Banks have been particularly active in the development of electronic funds transfer.

**Electronic funds transfer (EFT)** refers to the use of electronic and computer-based techniques to manage the payments system. EFT was originally supported by banks as an alternative to checking accounts and credit cards because transfers of paper—checks and credit card slips—are cumbersome and costly for the banking system to manage. In addition, paper transfers take time, and this increases the chance that a check will bounce or that the cardholder will default on payment.

These problems caused the banking industry to turn to computers as early as the 1960s, in looking for a low-cost alternative to the paper transfer system. The idea also captured the attention of the media, which focused on the "checkless" society—a payments system without paper. While banks did automate many of their accounting and check-sorting functions, the high expectations for EFT were not achieved. In good part, this happened because it turned out that people were attached to their credit cards, and were even willing to pay annual fees and relatively high interest rates for the convenience of using them. Nevertheless, there are two important EFT developments.

## Wire Transfers

**Wire transfers** are used by banks and their large customers to transfer money *instantaneously* to other banks and their customers. The transfers can be carried out because all banks keep a certain amount of money in special accounts at the Federal Reserve. So if a bank wants to transfer money to another bank, it can ask the Fed to transfer the desired amount from its account to the account of the other bank. And if a bank's customer wants to transfer money to the customer of a second bank, the same process is used, with the second bank depositing the money in the account of the customer who is to receive it.

In a sense, the Federal Reserve is acting just as a bank clearinghouse— an old idea. What is special about wire transfers is that communication and verification are carried out instantaneously. The volume of transfers over the Federal Reserve's system—called FedWire—and similar private systems is already immense and is still growing.

## Automated-Teller Machines and Related Developments

*Automated-teller machines* (ATMs) are the most evident and successful of the consumer-oriented EFT innovations. These machines perform the basic deposit and withdrawal tasks of tellers, and are now dependable and accepted by most consumers. Some consumers even prefer ATMs to talkative and error-prone human tellers. ATMs have higher investment costs, but lower running costs, than human tellers. So ATMs are the low-cost way to deliver transaction services at high-volume locations. ATMs also can be installed in remote locations and can operate 24 hours a day.

*Point of sale* (POS) terminals based on *debit cards* represent an EFT innovation that banks are currently trying to introduce. POS terminals are placed in retail outlets and are connected directly to bank computers. The customer gives his plastic debit card (like a credit card) to the merchant, the merchant uses the terminal to register the purchase, and the purchase amount is subtracted from the customer's bank account and added to the merchant's account. With the transaction completed instantly and electronically, the two major drawbacks of the current check and credit card system are eliminated for banks: there is no flow of paper and no time lag.

## New Services

Banks in the United States have also been trying to enter such diverse areas as insurance, accounting, and even travel agency services. However, banking regulations limit the range of services that commercial banks (and other depository intermediaries) can provide. The following list indicates some of the other services that banks are currently allowed to provide:

- Traveler's checks, money orders, and certified checks.
- Safe deposit boxes.
- Foreign exchange (foreign currency) transactions.
- Trading in government securities.
- Trust banking—administering trusts and estates.

We will discuss the regulations that limit bank services, and how banks are currently trying to expand the list of allowable activities, in Chapter 10.

# Chapter Summary

1. Financial intermediaries raise funds, invest in loans and securities, and provide various services to their customers. Commercial banks, the case study in this chapter, primarily provide intermediation and transfer services.

2. Commercial banks provide intermediation services by attracting deposits and issuing securities—bank liabilities—to raise money, and by making loans and purchasing investing securities—bank assets—to use the money. Bank deposits and other liabilities are evaluated by customers in terms of their rate of return, safety, and convenience.

3. More efficient intermediation reduces the rate spread—the difference between loan rates and deposit rates—and increases the quantity of intermediation—borrowing and lending. Shifts in the supply and demand curves for loanable funds also affect the quantity of intermediation and the level of deposit and loan interest rates. For example, a rightward shift in the supply curve of loanable funds increases the

quantity of intermediation and causes both loan rates and deposit rates to fall.

4. Bank transfer services allow people to make payments by check. Bank revenues from transfer services include the service fees they charge and the interest they earn from investing transaction account balances. Bank costs of providing transfer services include their operating expenses and the interest paid on transaction deposits.

5. Transfer services currently involve an element of cross subsidization because the service fees charged and the deposit interest paid are both too low. This situation encourages customers to make too many transfers while maintaining low balances in their transaction accounts.

6. Bank credit cards combine a credit function with a payments system function. Electronic funds transfer is a recent development in which banks are trying to use computers and related electronic systems to replace the paper-based checking account and credit card systems.

## Key Terms

Bank:
  Capital
  Costs
  Equilibrium
  Revenue
Bank assets:
  Cash assets
  Loans
  Securities
Bank liabilities:
  Investment accounts

Transaction accounts
Credit cards
Cross subsidization
Electronic funds transfer (EFT)
Federal deposit insurance
Functional cost accounting
Functional Cost Analysis (FCA)
Intermediation services
Rate spread
Transfer services
Wire transfers

## Study Questions

1. Compared with capital market securities such as stocks and bonds, what are the attractions of financial intermediaries for depositing and borrowing money?

2. Briefly describe why banks are so good at providing intermediation services, being sure to indicate what the services are, who uses them, and how they are paid for.

3. Briefly describe why banks are so good at providing transfer services, being sure to indicate what the services are, who uses them, and how they are paid for.

4. In Figure 6.2, what factors are excluded from the hypothetical "perfect market" equilibrium, but are included in the more realistic "bank" equilibrium?

5. Why is the rate spread a measure of the efficiency of financial intermediation? Explain why more efficient intermediation is created by (a) increased competition, (b) lower operating costs, and (c) less regulation.

6. Why does more efficient intermediation lead to higher deposit rates, lower loan rates, and a greater quantity of intermediation?

7. Why does an increase in the supply of funds (deposits) lead to lower deposit rates, lower loan rates, and a greater quantity of intermediation?

8. Why does an increase in the demand for funds (loans) lead to higher deposit rates, higher loan rates, and a greater quantity of intermediation?

9. What are the main components of bank income and costs in providing intermediation services? In providing transfer services? Why are the operating costs for transfer services higher than for intermediation services?

10. Bank operating expenses for transfer services exceed the fees they charge for these services. Why does this not mean that banks generally lose money in providing these services? Why does this lead to a misallocation of resources? What is the solution?

## Recommended Reading

*There are many textbooks, books of readings, and books of case studies that describe the banking industry. Some of the most current are:*

Mona J. Gardner and Dixie L. Mills, *Managing Financial Institutions*, The Dryden Press, Chicago, 1988.

Benton E. Gup and Charles Meiburg, *Cases in Bank Management*, Macmillan, New York, 1986.

Thomas M. Havrilesky, Robert Schweitzer, and John T. Boorman, *Dynamics of Banking*, Harlan Davidson, Arlington Heights, Mass., 1985.

Timothy W. Koch, *Bank Management*, The Dryden Press, Chicago, 1988.

*Some books and articles on new bank services such as electronic funds transfers include:*

Mark J. Flannery and Dwight M. Jaffee, *The Economic Implications of Electronic Monetary Transfer Systems*, Lexington Books, Lexington, Mass., 1973.

"Displacing the Check," *Economic Review*, Federal Reserve Bank of Atlanta, March 1983, pp. 15–33.

"The Revolution in Retail Payments," *Economic Review*, Federal Reserve Bank of Atlanta, July/August 1984, pp. 46–48.

"The Automated Clearing House in a New Light," *Economic Review*, Federal Reserve Bank of Atlanta, March 1986, pp. 4–33.

# Financial Decisions and Markets

Financial investments—stocks and bonds bought by individuals, and loans made by banks—represent a means of providing money to someone else. In Chapter 5, we studied the role of the interest rate—the time value of money—for investment decisions. In this part, we focus on other factors that investors and banks consider when making financial investment decisions.

Most importantly, we will study the role of *risk*. In a general sense, risk arises whenever investment results are *uncertain*—investors are unsure of the rate of return they will earn. In this part, we look at two specific types of risk: *credit risk*—that borrowers default on loans; and *interest rate risk*—that interest rates change unexpectedly.

We will begin, in Chapter 7, by looking at how people make decisions under uncertainty—how they respond to risk. We will see that people have different *preferences regarding risk*: *risk-neutral* people look only at the expected return; *risk-averse* people try to avoid risk; and *risk-loving* people try to obtain risk. We will study how people apply their risk preferences to investment, gambling, and insurance decisions. We will also consider how they use risk pooling and risk trans-

fer to reduce, or even eliminate, risk. *Risk pooling* means holding a *diversified portfolio* consisting of a large number of investments with independent risks. *Risk transfers* involve selling risk to someone else.

In Chapter 8, we will study the *term structure of interest rates*—how interest rates vary on securities with regard to *maturity* (the time remaining until the last cash flow payment). Term structure theories are based on alternative investment strategies. Individuals must decide between, say, one-year bank time deposits at a 5% interest rate and three-year time deposits at a 7% interest rate. Banks deal with interest rate risk—that their profits will change when interest rates change unexpectedly—by considering the maturities of both their assets and liabilities.

In Chapter 9, we turn to a set of financial instruments—*futures contracts and options contracts*—used for arbitrage, speculation, and hedging. We will focus on a set of new contracts—financial futures and options—based on debt securities (U.S. Treasury bills), equities (common stocks), and related assets. Investors often use these contracts to speculate on the future course of stock prices and interest rates. Banks use them to hedge their interest rate risk.

In Part III, we will look more closely at how financial institutions operate and at the special role they play in the financial system.

# Investment Decisions Under Uncertainty

*"Which ever you please, my little dear. You pays your money and you takes your choice."*

**Punch (1846)**

Whenever you say, "I'll take my chances," you are making the equivalent of an investment decision. You have decided against a sure thing—such as keeping your money—in favor of an uncertain outcome. People recognize that putting money into insured bank deposits is certain (safe) and that putting it into the common stock of a fledgling biotech or computer company is uncertain (risky). The key feature of a risky investment is that it has a range of possible outcomes, some good, some bad.

People vary, of course, in their willingness to bear risk. People can be risk averse, risk lovers, or risk neutral. Some people appear to be inconsistent in their behavior toward risk. They act as risk averters in buying insurance (to protect against the risks of fire, theft, and illness), but they act as risk lovers in gambling (betting on horses and purchasing lottery tickets). In this chapter, we will study how people make decisions under uncertainty.

---

We begin the chapter by examining the decisions of people who are indifferent to risk. As we will see, their decisions reflect a criterion called expected value. We will then look at the investment criteria used by risk-averse and risk-loving investors. Later, in Chapter 12, we will look at how banks apply such criteria to investment and portfolio decisions.

---

## Expected Value Investment Decisions

People who are risk neutral have no particular preferences for or against risk. Consider a person who bets $10 on the flip of a coin. The payoff is $20 if heads appears and $0 if tails appears. Risk-neutral people are indifferent to playing this game. They recognize that there is a 50% chance they will gain $10 and a 50% chance they will lose $10. (We will see later that risk averters will never play such a game, while risk lovers will always want to play.)

## Decisions Made Under Certainty

Even in a simple coin flipping game, a criterion or strategy is needed to make decisions. We will first look at how this works in a situation where the investment outcome is certain—there is no risk to worry about. Take an investor who is evaluating a debt security that will pay out the amount $V$ after one year, based on an initial investment $P$. Recalling our discussion of securities in Chapter 5, we can interpret $V$ as the cash flow payment (or the future value) of the security and $P$ as the market price of the security. The rate of return $r$ on the security is the rate at which the price appreciates to the future value $V$:

$$V = P(1 + r),$$

and by solving for the rate of return $r$,

$$r = \frac{V - P}{P}.$$

Similar concepts apply to longer-term and more complex securities, such as coupon bonds, on which there is a stream of cash flow payments. However, for the purposes of this chapter we need only recognize that given the outcome, the rate of return can be calculated for any security. We will also make the further simplification that the investor is comparing securities of the same maturity. In Chapter 8, we will study the special issues that arise when comparing securities of different maturities.

How does an investor decide which security or securities to buy among the large number that are available? The answer is simple when the rate of return $r$ on each security is known with *certainty*:

*The investor will chose the security that provides the highest rate of return $r$.*

This ensures that the highest value $V$ will be accumulated on the basis of any given investment $P$.

## Measuring Uncertain Investment Outcomes

We will now look at the more difficult task of making investment decisions when there is **uncertainty** regarding the outcomes, such as for equity investments where it is hard to foresee whether the outcomes will be good or bad. For an investment in an umbrella manufacturing firm, for example, success or failure might depend on the amount of rain that falls. For a biotech company, the critical condition might be whether a vaccine under development actually works. Often, complex combinations of factors have to be considered. For a computer manufacturer developing a new product, the outcome may depend on whether a new technology will work, how competitors respond, and on the size of the market.

The cost of a particular security is given by its market price $P$; its final value $V$ and rate of return $r$ depend on which outcome, among the possibilities, actually occurs. To illustrate this, suppose there are three possible outcomes—$V_1$, $V_2$, and $V_3$—each indicating the value of the investment when a particular outcome occurs (the value incorporates whatever dividends or interest payments are made). Based on the possible outcomes $V_1$, $V_2$, and $V_3$, we can compute the corresponding rates of return, $r_1$, $r_2$, and $r_3$.

Because there are a number of possible outcomes and rates of return, it is helpful to base investment decisions on an overall measure of the security's rate of return. To do this, we need to know the probabilities— $p_1$, $p_2$, and $p_3$—that are associated with the outcomes $V_1$, $V_2$, and $V_3$, respectively. Each probability represents the investor's assessment of the likelihood that a particular outcome will occur. Examples of how people obtain these probabilities will be given as we proceed. If we have considered all possible outcomes, then one of them must occur, so the probabilities must sum to 1.0.

These ideas are summarized in part A of Box 7.1, which shows the data an investor might collect to evaluate a one-year investment in the ABC Umbrella Company. The initial price of the security is 100. There are three possible outcomes, numbered $V_1$, $V_2$, and $V_3$, which we can think of as representing no rain, little rain, and lots of rain, respectively. The outcome values are 100, 110, and 120, respectively, and the corresponding rates of return are 0%, 10%, and 20%. Regarding the probabilities of these outcomes, a little rain is the most likely event (probability

BOX 7.1 IN DEPTH

## A One-Year Investment in the ABC Umbrella Company

### A: Information Needed for the Investment Decision

Security price $P = 100$.
Security maturity $N = 1$ year.

| Possible outcomes | Outcome value $V$ | Rate of return $r$ | Probability $P$ |
|---|---|---|---|
| $V_1$ (No rain) | 100 | 0% | 1/4 |
| $V_2$ (Little rain) | 110 | 10 | 1/2 |
| $V_3$ (Lots of rain) | 120 | 20 | 1/4 |

### B: Computations of Expected Return and Expected Outcome

Expected return: $\quad r_e = p_1 r_1 + p_2 r_2 + p_3 r_3$
$$= (1/4)(0\%) + (1/2)(10\%) + (1/4)(20\%)$$
$$= 10\%.$$
Expected outcome: $V_e = p_1 V_1 + p_2 V_2 + p_3 V_3$
$$= (1/4)(100) + (1/2)(110) + (1/4)(120)$$
$$= 110.$$

1/2), but there is a chance of no rain (probability 1/4) and a chance of a lot of rain (also probability 1/4). The weather bureau, of course, would be an obvious source of information for obtaining these probabilities.

## Expected Rates of Return and Expected Outcomes

The information in part A of Box 7.1 is summarized in a single measure called the security's **expected return**. The expected return is a weighted average of the rates of return associated with the possible outcomes, the weights being the probabilities of the outcomes. In other words, the expected return equals the sum of a series of terms, each one representing a particular rate of return (based on a particular outcome) multiplied by the probability of that rate of return occurring.

The formula for the expected return $r_e$, given three possible rates of return, is:

$$r_e = p_1 r_1 + p_2 r_2 + p_3 r_3.$$

Based on the values shown in Box 7.1, the expected return on the investment is 10%.

The same technique is used to determine the **expected outcome**, which is a weighted average of each of the possible outcomes. That is, the expected outcome equals the sum of a series of terms, each one representing a particular outcome multiplied by the probability of that outcome occurring. The formula for the expected outcome $V_e$, given three possible outcomes, is:

$$V_e = p_1 V_1 + p_2 V_2 + p_3 V_3.$$

Based on the values shown in Box 7.1, the expected outcome for the investment is 110.

The technique we have been using to calculate the expected return and the expected outcome is known as *expected value*. It can always be applied when there is a series of rates of return or possible outcomes, as long as we can determine the associated probabilities. The value calculated—the **expected value**—is just the average value, taking the probabilities into account.

The concept of expected value is illustrated for three different securities, each with an expected return of 10%, in Figure 7.1:

*Security A* has just one possible outcome—a return of 10%—so the expected return is *certain* (it occurs with a probability of 1.0). Therefore the security is *risk free* (free of uncertainty).

*Security B* has three possible outcomes—returns of 5%, 10%, and 15%, each occurring with a probability of 1/3—so its expected return is also 10% ([1/3][5%] + [1/3][10%] + [1/3][15%]).

*Security C* also has three possible outcomes—returns of 0%, 10%, and 20%, each occurring with a probability of 1/3—so again its expected return is 10% ([1/3][0%] + [1/3][10%] + [1/3][20%]).

Clearly, the same expected return can be generated by quite different patterns of outcomes.

FIGURE 7.1
**Three Securities with an Expected Return of 10%**

Security Returns (in percent)

Each security has an expected return of 10%. The 10% return on security A is certain: its one outcome, 10%, occurs with a probability of 1.0. Securities B and C have three possible outcomes, each with a probability of 1/3. Security C has the largest range between its highest and lowest return.

## Expected Value Decisions Under Uncertainty

When investment outcomes are *certain*, an investor would choose the security that offers the *highest rate of return*. When investment outcomes are *uncertain*, the corresponding decision rule is for an investor to choose the security with the *highest expected rate of return*. We will refer to decisions made in this way as **expected value decisions**. Expected value decisions involve three main steps:

1. For each security, the investor obtains information on the rates of return and the associated probabilities, as illustrated in part A of Box 7.1.

2. The investor then computes the *expected rate of return* for each security, as illustrated in part B of Box 7.1.

3. After steps 1 and 2 are completed, the investor chooses the security with the *highest* expected rate of return.

Table 7.1 illustrates these steps for an investment decision involving three securities, each with a one-year maturity. Security A is risk free because it has the same 10% return for all three outcomes. Securities B and C, in contrast, are uncertain. On the basis of expected value, security C is chosen because it has the highest expected return. The returns on the three securities are illustrated graphically in Figure 7.2.

From Table 7.1 and Figure 7.2, we can see that it would be a statistical fluke if more than one security provided the same highest expected return. Thus, with decisions based on expected value, *investors usually buy only a single security*—the one with the highest expected return. In practice, however, investors typically hold diversified portfolios—consisting of many securities with different expected returns. So, it would seem that most people *do not use an expected value investment strategy*. In a moment, we will look at alternative ways to describe investment decisions that are more consistent with actual behavior.

| | | Rate of Return on Security | | |
|---|---|---|---|---|
| **TABLE 7.1**<br>Investment Decisions Under Uncertainty | | | | |
| Outcome # | Probability of Outcome | Security A | Security B | Security C |
| 1 | 1/3 | 10% | 0% | 0% |
| 2 | 1/3 | 10 | 0 | 20 |
| 3 | 1/3 | 10 | 20 | 20 |
| Expected rate of return | | 10.0% | 6.7% | 13.3% |

FIGURE 7.2
**Three Securities with Unequal Expected Returns**

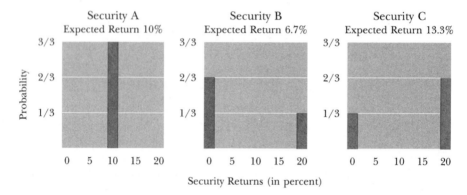

Security A has an expected (and certain) return of 10%. Security B has an expected return of 6.7%, representing the expected value of its returns, 0%, 0%, and 20%, each occurring with a probability of 1/3. Security C has an expected return of 13.3%, representing the expected value of its three returns, 0%, 20%, and 20%, each occurring with a probability of 1/3. Investors using expected value will chose security C because it has the highest expected return.

## Applications to Insurance and Gambling

Expected value can also be applied to insurance and gambling decisions, where people make choices involving uncertain outcomes. For gambling, the certain thing is just to keep your money, while the uncertain alternative is to gamble. For insurance, the certain thing is to buy insurance, while the uncertain alternative is to take your chances with being robbed, having a fire, or becoming ill. Thus for both gambling and insurance, people can make expected value decisions by comparing the value of the certain thing with the expected value of the uncertain outcomes.

### Insurance

The application of expected value to insurance decisions is illustrated with a simple example of theft insurance. Suppose you always carry $100 in cash with you, and that from past experience you know there is a 5% chance you will be robbed of your $100 one time during the year. The *expected loss* is therefore $5 (5% of $100), representing the probability of

## BOX 7.2 CREDIT CHECK

### Setting Insurance Premiums

Insurance companies set the price, or premium, of a policy at a level that they expect will cover their insurance claims, operating expenses, and profits. Should the companies find they are paying larger claims than anticipated, then they will raise the premiums they charge.

As an example of how this works, a few years ago companies providing malpractice insurance for doctors were hit with a great many large claims. It seemed that the courts were finding many more doctors guilty of malpractice and were setting higher settlements. As a result, the insur-

ance premiums charged on malpractice insurance skyrocketed. Indeed, the premiums became so high that some doctors decided to switch to medical specialties with lower insurance rates.

Quite a different situation exists with life insurance, where claims are much more predictable. Actuaries for large life insurance companies can readily compute the likely amount of claims each year using data from standard government mortality tables. The life insurance companies then use the expected claims to set their premiums.

being robbed multiplied by the amount of the loss. As an alternative, you can buy theft insurance that will return any money stolen. The insurance company, of course, charges a price—the *insurance premium*— for providing this insurance. Box 7.2 describes how insurance premiums are determined.

On an expected value basis, the decision whether or not to buy insurance depends on which is larger, the expected loss ($5 in this case) or the insurance premium. There are three possible cases, depending on whether the insurance premium is less than the expected loss (called **favorable insurance**), equal to the expected loss (called **fair insurance**), or greater than the expected loss (called **unfavorable insurance**). A simple decision rule can then be used to buy insurance:

- *Buy favorable insurance* (the insurance premium is less than the expected loss).

- *Do not buy unfavorable insurance* (the insurance premium exceeds the expected loss).

- *Be indifferent to fair insurance* (the insurance premium just equals the expected loss).

In fact, most insurance is *unfavorable* because insurance premiums must be high enough to cover a company's operating expenses and profits, as well as its claims. Therefore, people who buy unfavorable insurance must be using a criterion other than expected value.

### Gambling

Expected value is particularly well suited for gambling decisions because the probabilities of success and failure are based on objective factors.

Generally, a fee is paid, or a bet is placed, and then the payoff is determined. Gambling decisions involve a choice between a certain value (the amount bet) and a set of uncertain outcomes (the possible payoffs). The **expected value of the payoff** is compared with the amount bet to decide whether to take the gamble.

For example, would you want to bet $4 on the following gamble? A single die will be thrown and the dollar payoff will equal the number of spots on the die. The possible outcomes are, of course, 1, 2, 3, 4, 5, and 6, each with a probability of 1/6, so the expected value of the outcome is $3.50 ([1/6][$1 + $2 + $3 + $4 + $5 + $6]). You should not take this gamble on the basis of expected value: its expected value ($3.50) is less than the amount bet ($4.00).

Gambles and games of chance are rated as **favorable, fair,** or **unfavorable,** as the expected payoff exceeds, equals, or falls below the amount bet. Based on expected value, people should:

- Always take *favorable gambles* (the odds are favorable).
- Never take *unfavorable gambles* (the odds are unfavorable).
- Be indifferent to *fair gambles* (the odds are exactly even).

In practice, people are often willing to take unfavorable gambles. On bets at racetracks, for example, the expected payoff is usually only 80% to 85% of the amount bet because there are taxes and the tracks must cover their operating expenses. Yet millions of people bet on the horses. State lotteries are even more unfavorable—the expected payoff may be less than 50% of the price of a ticket—yet here too, millions of people buy lottery tickets (perhaps they are the same people). Box 7.3 describes how state lotteries work.

---

**BOX 7.3 CREDIT CHECK**

## State Lotteries

Although gambling is illegal in most of the United States—two exceptions are Las Vegas and Atlantic City—many states now run state lotteries to raise revenue in a way that is voluntary and may seem less painful to people than paying taxes. However, whether they realize it or not, people buying lottery tickets are contributing a substantial part of the ticket price to the state because all state lotteries represent highly unfavorable gambles.

In a typical situation, a state might sell 5 million tickets for which it charges $1 each. The winning ticket holder than receives $1 million, another $1 million goes to the ten holders of second-place tickets, and a third $1 million is distributed among the large number of smaller prizes. Overall, then, the state takes in $5 million for tickets, pays out $3 million as prizes, and keeps $2 million (less operating costs) as revenue—obviously a good business for the state.

But not a good gamble for those buying lottery tickets: they receive an expected payoff of 60 cents ($3 million in prizes/5 million tickets = $0.60 per ticket) on a $1 ticket. We will see later in the chapter why people might nevertheless choose to take such unfavorable gambles.

So we see that for gambling, as well as for investing and insuring, *many people seem not to base their decisions on expected value.*

## The Problem with Expected Value Decisions

Why people do not follow the rules of expected value in making their decisions has perplexed mathematicians and economists for centuries. For example, Daniel Bernoulli (1700–1782), a member of a famous family of Swiss mathematicians, constructed a coin flipping game—called the *Bernoulli Game*—that has an expected payoff of *an infinite amount of money*, yet most people will not even pay $25 to play it. If this intrigues you, you can read about the Bernoulli Game in the chapter appendix.

So, just what is the problem with expected value? It seems that actual decisions reflect *an aversion to the range of uncertain outcomes*—a factor not taken into account by expected value. Aversion to the range of outcomes means that, everything else being equal, people prefer situations where the range of outcomes is small.

For example, suppose that you are to invest in one of the following two securities: security A has a certain return of 24%, while security B has uncertain returns of 0% and 50%, each with a probability of 1/2, so its expected return is 25%. Most people would select security A. True, security B has a slightly higher expected return, but it has the disadvantage of the possibility of the very bad outcome of 0% even though this is more than balanced in an expected value sense by the possibility of the good outcome of 50%.

Securities with a range of outcomes are described as *risky*—the risk being that the bad outcome might occur. For this reason, expected value decisions are called **risk neutral**—meaning that they ignore the risk created by the range of possible returns. We will now turn to decisions that are *risk averse* or *risk loving*—these being alternative criteria to the risk-netural character of expected value. In both cases, the criteria are distinguished from expected value by the fact that the range of outcomes (risk) figures explicitly in the decision.

## Risk-Averse and Risk-Loving Behavior

People who are **risk averse** prefer the investment with the *smallest range of outcomes*, given a choice among alternatives with the same expected return. For example, among the securities with equal expected returns in Figure 7.1, a risk-averse investor would choose the risk-free security A. A risk-averse investor, in fact, may be inclined to buy a security with a lower expected return if it offers less risk than the alternatives. For example, referring to Figure 7.2, a risk-averse investor might prefer security A over security C, even though C has the higher expected return.

On the other hand, people who are **risk lovers** prefer the investment with the *largest range of outcomes*, given a choice among alternatives with the same expected return. A risk lover would prefer security C in Figure 7.1 because of its greater range of returns. A risk-loving investor, in fact, may be inclined to buy a security with a lower expected return if it offers more risk than the alternatives. This is why risk-loving people are willing to buy lottery tickets that provide one huge payoff, even though the expected payoff is less than the cost of the ticket.

We will now look at investment decision in terms of risk-averse and risk-loving behavior. Expected value remains a key part of the decision, but the range of returns or outcomes is also considered. In this sense, risk-averse and risk-loving behavior provide a more general framework than expected value for analyzing how people make decisions.

## The Measurement of Risk

The range of outcomes provides an accurate measure of risk when the *probabilities* of all outcomes are the same (as will be the case for most of the examples in this book.) However, the range of outcomes would overstate the risk for an investment with one extremely bad outcome, if there is a small probability that the bad outcome will actually occur. To deal with this problem, economists often measure risk as the **variance of outcomes**—a statistical measure of the distribution of outcomes that takes both the range of outcomes and their probabilities into account. Box 7.4 shows how variance is defined.

## Indifference Curves and Risk Preferences

We will use a special type of indifference curve to illustrate risk-neutral, risk-averse, and risk-loving behavior graphically. So that we can draw the indifference curve diagrams in only two dimensions, we will assume that the uncertain outcomes can be adequately measured by just two factors:

1. *Expected return E* measures the average outcome.

2. The *range of outcomes* $\sigma^2$ (or variance) measures the risk.

In this case, each security is described by a pair of values $\{E, \sigma^2\}$, $E$ *measuring the expected return* and $\sigma^2$ *measuring the risk*. Investment decisions regarding uncertain outcomes can then be analyzed with indifference curves that show an investor's preferences regarding expected return $E$ and risk $\sigma^2$.

In Figure 7.3, each indifference curve shows the alternative combinations of expected return and risk $\{E, \sigma^2\}$ to which an investor is indifferent. The basic idea is illustrated in panel A, where the *horizontal lines* are the indifference curves of a *risk-neutral* investor. Securities A and B have the same expected return, so the investor is indifferent between them (risk does not matter to a risk-neutral investor), and therefore both securities lie on the same indifference curve (II). In contrast, security C is on the higher indifference curve III because it has a higher expected return, while security D is on the lower indifference curve I because it has a lower expected return.

BOX 7.4 IN DEPTH

## Variance as a Measure of Risk

The statistical notion of variance provides a more general measure of risk than the range of returns when there are uncertain outcomes. The higher the variance, the greater the risk. The formula for computing variance—which we are denoting as $\sigma^2$—is

$$\sigma^2 = \sum_{i=1}^{M} p_i(r_i - r_e)^2,$$

where $\sigma^2$ = the variance of the rate of return,
$p_i$ = the probability of each outcome $i$,
$r_i$ = the rate of return associated with each outcome $i$,
$r_e$ = the expected rate of return,
$M$ = the number of possible outcomes.

The amount $(r_i - r_e)$ represents the deviation of each possible rate of return $r_i$ from the expected rate of return $r_e$. The formula for variance is thus a weighted average of the squared deviations, the weights being the probabilities of the respective outcomes.

As an example, we will compute the variance of returns for security C in Table 7.1. That security had three outcomes ($M = 3$), each with a probability ($p_i$) of 1/3 and with rates of return of 0%, 20%, and 20%, so that its expected return was 13.3%. As a result, the variance $\sigma^2$ is:

$$\sigma^2 = (1/3)(0 - 13.3)^2 + (1/3)(20 - 13.3)^2 + (1/3)(20 - 13.3)^2$$
$$= 88.59.$$

This diagram illustrates the preferences of risk-neutral, risk-averse, and risk-loving people in terms of expected return $E$ and risk (variance) $\sigma^2$. The preference ordering rises from indifference curve I (the lowest) to curve III (the highest) for each person. The slopes of the indifference curves for each type of person indicate the attitude toward risk. Each panel shows how the investor rates the four securities—A, B, C, and D.

FIGURE 7.3

**Indifference Curves and Risk Preferences**

A. Risk Neutral

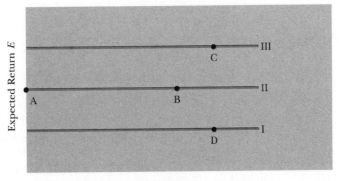

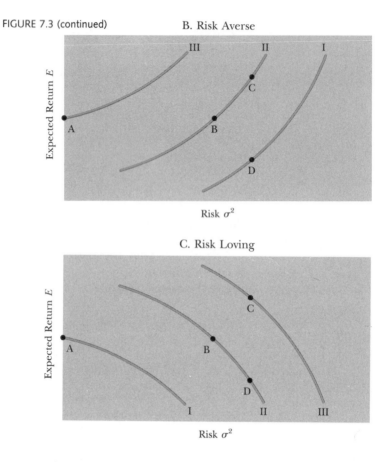

FIGURE 7.3 (continued)

B. Risk Averse

C. Risk Loving

In panel B, the *upward-sloping indifference curves* represent a *risk-averse* investor who prefers higher expected return and lower risk. The investor is thus indifferent between securities B and C (on curve II), the higher expected return of security C offsetting its higher risk. Also, this investor prefers the lower risk of security A and dislikes the higher risk of security D.

In panel C, the downward-sloping indifference curves show a risk-loving investor who prefers higher expected return and higher risk. This investor is indifferent between securities B and D, the higher risk of security D offsetting its lower expected return. In addition, this investor prefers the higher risk of security C and dislikes the lower risk of security A.

## Investment Decisions and Risk Preferences

Table 7.2 summarizes the investment decision of the three types of investors in Figure 7.3—for the case in which they choose between a *risk-free security with a certain return* (such as security A in the figure) and a *risky security with uncertain returns* (such as securities B, C, and D in the figure). The table shows three different cases for the risky security—**favorable, fair** or **unfavorable**—as its expected return exceeds, equals, or is less than the certain return on the risk-free security.

TABLE 7.2
Investment Decisions and Risk Preferences

| | Decision to Buy the Risky Security | | |
|---|---|---|---|
| | Risk Neutral | Risk Averse | Risk Loving |
| Expected return of risky security[a] | | | |
| Favorable | Always buy | May buy | Always buy |
| Fair | Indifferent | Never buy | Always buy |
| Unfavorable | Never buy | Never buy | May buy |

[a]The expected return on the risky security is favorable, fair, or unfavorable as it exceeds, equals, or is less than the certain return on the risk-free security.

*Risk-neutral investors* will compare the expected return on the risky security with the certain return on the risk-free security. They prefer the risky security, prefer the risk-free security, or are indifferent between them, as the expected return on the risky security is favorable (it exceeds the return on the risk-free security), is unfavorable (it is less than the return on the risk-free security), or is fair (the two returns are equal). In all cases, the level of risk on the risky security is of no consequence.

*Risk-averse investors* choose the risky security only if its expected return is sufficiently favorable to compensate for its risk. Otherwise, risk-averse investors buy the risk-free security.

*Risk-loving investors* choose the risk-free security only when its expected return is sufficiently high to compensate for its lack of risk. Otherwise, risk-loving investors buy the risky security.

## Applications to Insurance and Gambling

Insurance and gambling decisions can also be analyzed using the expected return–risk $\{E, \sigma^2\}$ indifference curves.

With *insurance,* the risk-free strategy is to purchase insurance, while the risky alternative is to be uninsured. As discussed earlier, insurance is fair, favorable, or unfavorable, as the insurance premium equals, falls below, or exceeds the actuarial cost of the loss. On this basis, Table 7.3 provides a summary of insurance decisions for the three classes of risk preferences. Three principles are apparent in these results:

TABLE 7.3
Insurance Decisions and Risk Preferences

| | Decision to Buy Insurance | | |
|---|---|---|---|
| | Risk Neutral | Risk Averse | Risk Loving |
| Nature of insurance[a] | | | |
| Favorable | Always buy | Always buy | May buy |
| Fair | Indifferent | Always buy | Never buy |
| Unfavorable | Never buy | May buy | Never buy |

[a]Insurance is favorable, fair, or unfavorable as the insurance premium is less than, equals, or exceeds the expected loss (the expected insurance claims).

1. Risk-neutral people evaluate insurance entirely in terms of the fairness of the insurance premium.

2. Risk-averse people shy away from gambles, taking only particularly favorable gambles.

3. Risk-loving people prefer risky outcomes, and so, other things being equal, they prefer to be uninsured.

With *gambling*, the risky thing is to gamble, the safe thing is not to gamble. Gambles are fair, favorable, or unfavorable, as the expected value of the payoff equals, exceeds, or falls below the amount of the bet. On this basis, Table 7.4 provides a summary of gambling decisions for the three classes of risk preferences. Three principles are apparent in these results:

1. Risk-neutral people evaluate gambles in terms of the fairness of the bet, favorable bets being accepted.

2. Risk-averse people shy away from gambles, taking only particularly favorable gambles.

3. Gamblers always take favorable and fair gambles, and they may even take unfavorable gambles.

**TABLE 7.4**

**Gambling Decisions and Risk Preferences**

|  | Decision to Gamble | | |
|---|---|---|---|
|  | **Risk Neutral** | **Risk Averse** | **Risk Loving** |
| Nature of gamble[a] |  |  |  |
| Favorable | Always buy | May buy | Always buy |
| Fair | Indifferent | Never buy | Always buy |
| Unfavorable | Never buy | Never buy | May buy |

[a]Gambles are favorable, fair, or unfavorable as the expected payoff exceeds, equals, or is less than the amount bet.

# Market Principles of Risk Analysis

We have so far concentrated on how people make investment, insurance, and gambling decisions under uncertainty. In this section, issues of risk and uncertainty are considered from a broader market perspective. We begin by looking at how risk is transferred between people.

## Risk Transfers

Most financial, insurance, and gambling markets function in part as *markets for risk*. For example, people buy insurance to get rid of risk, while people gamble to obtain more risk. Security transactions also serve to transfer risk. Consider an individual who owns a new firm that has good, but risky, prospects. The owner can transfer a part of this risk by selling shares in the firm to other investors for cash. Of course, the owner then receives only a part of the profits.

When risk is transferred, one party is selling a risk and the other party is buying it. Between risk-averse and risk-loving people, for example, the risk averse should be the sellers of risk and the risk lovers should be the buyers. However, if most people are risk averse—which seems to be the case—there might be an overabundance of risk sellers and not enough risk buyers, which creates a problem of balancing the demand and the supply of risk.

This problem is handled by the market price of risk. The *market price of risk* is the amount the seller of risk must pay the buyer to take on the risk. If sellers of risk outnumber buyers at a zero price, then the market price of risk must rise to a positive value to attract more buyers. For securities, a positive price of risk means that a risky security must provide a higher expected return than a less risky security. In this way, the demand and supply of risk can be balanced.

Markets for risk operate with a demand for, a supply of, and a price of risk, as illustrated in Figure 7.4. Insurance markets provide a good example: insurance companies set the price of risk—the amount by which the insurance premium exceeds the expected claims—to cover their expenses and provide for profits. Insurance markets simultaneously provide benefits to the individuals who sell the risks and profits to the insurance companies that buy these risks.

In a market for risk, risk-averse people are the suppliers (sellers) of risk, and less risk-averse—or risk-neutral and risk-loving—people are the demanders of risk. The market reaches equilibrium at the price of risk $P^*$ that balances the demand and supply. In financial markets, the price of risk is measured by the difference between the expected return on a risky security and the expected return on a risk-free security. In insurance markets, the price of risk is measured by the difference between the insurance premium on a policy and its expected claims.

FIGURE 7.4
**A Market for Risk**

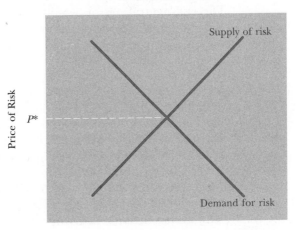

Quantity of Risk

A risk transfer between a risk-averse person and a risk-neutral person is illustrated in Figure 7.5. The *risk-neutral person* initially owns a *risk-free security*, as indicated by point $F$ on his indifference curve $N_1$. The *risk-averse person* initially owns a *risky security*, as indicated by the point $R$ on her indifference curve $A_1$.

FIGURE 7.5
**The Benefits of Risk Transfer**

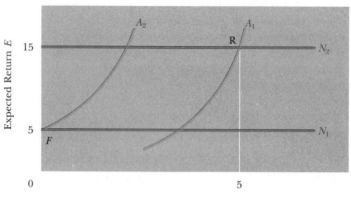

Risk $\sigma^2$

The risk-averse person initially owns the risky security R on her indifference curve $A_1$, while the risk-neutral person owns the risk-free security F on his indifference curve $N_1$. Risk transfer involves trading security F for security R, one for one, so that the risk-averse person ends up with the risk-free security F on her indifference curve $A_2$, and the risk-neutral person ends up with the risky security R on his indifference curve $N_2$.

The market price of risk equals the difference in expected return between the risky security and the risk-free security, relative to the difference in risk. For the two securities, the difference in expected return is 10% (15% − 5%) and the difference in risk is 5% (5% − 0%), so the market price of risk is 2 (10%/5%).

The risk-neutral person would be better off with a security located on his indifference curve $N_2$; similarly, the risk-averse person would be better off with a security located on her indifference curve $A_2$. They achieve this result if they simply trade security F for security R, one for one. The risk-neutral person then owns the risky security R—now interpreted as on curve $N_2$—and the risk-averse person owns the risk-free security F—now interpreted as on curve $A_2$. Both parties thus reach higher indifference curves by trading—by transferring risk.

The **market price of risk** is the difference in expected return between a risky security and a less risky security, relative to the difference of their risks. In Figure 7.5, the difference in expected return between security R and security F is 10% (15% − 5%) and the difference in their risk is 5% (5% − 0%), so the market price of risk is 2 (10%/5%). This means the risk-averse investor is giving up—and the risk-neutral investor is receiving—an expected return of 2% for each 1% of risk that is transferred.

*Summary.* Mutually beneficial **risk transfers** can occur between a risk-averse seller and a less risk-averse buyer: the seller pays a price—the market price of risk—to the buyer to transfer the risk. The market price of risk equals the difference in expected return between a risky security and a less risky security, relative to the difference in their risk.

## Risk Pooling

With **risk pooling,** people reduce the risk level of their portfolios by holding a large number of small investments. Risk pooling works better when the risks tend to be *independent*—a bad outcome on one investment does not make it more likely that a bad outcome will occur on another investment.

Risk pooling is applied by investors who hold **diversified portfolios** that consist of many small investments with independent risks. A portfolio consisting of three oil company stocks would not be well diversified. The number of securities is too small and their risks are not independent—the profits of all oil companies depend on the price of oil. In contrast, a portfolio consisting of thirty stocks in twenty-five different industries is likely to be well diversified. Both a *large number of securities* and *independent risks* are required for risk pooling to be effective.

### Risk Pooling and the Number of Securities

Table 7.5 illustrates the *benefit of increasing the number of securities*. For the situation shown, the investor has a choice of four equally priced securities, A, B, C, and D. Each of the securities offers a rate of return between 1% and 4%, depending on which outcome occurs. For example, security A earns 1% with outcome 1, 2% with outcome 2, 3% with outcome 3,

**TABLE 7.5**
**The Gains from Diversification with More Securities**

| | Rate of Return for Each Possible Outcome (in percent) | | | | Range of Rates of Return |
|---|---|---|---|---|---|
| | Outcome 1 | Outcome 2 | Outcome 3 | Outcome 4 | |
| **Individual securities** | | | | | |
| Security A | 1% | 2% | 3% | 4% | 1%–4% |
| Security B | 2 | 3 | 4 | 1 | 1–4 |
| Security C | 3 | 4 | 1 | 2 | 1–4 |
| Security D | 4 | 1 | 2 | 3 | 1–4 |
| **Diversified portfolios** | | | | | |
| Portfolio 1: 1/2 Security A + 1/2 Security B | 1.5 | 2.5 | 3.5 | 2.5 | 1.5–3.5 |
| Portfolio 2: 1/3 Security A + 1/3 Security B + 1/3 Security C | 2 | 3 | 2.7 | 2.3 | 2–3 |
| Portfolio 3: 1/4 Security A + 1/4 Security B + 1/4 Security C + 1/4 Security D | 2.5 | 2.5 | 2.5 | 2.5 | 2.5–2.5 |

and 4% with outcome 4. Obviously, if the investor holds just *one of the securities*, then the range of possible outcomes will be between 1% and 4%—a simple, but adequate, measure of risk in this situation. The table then shows what happens when the investor holds a *diversified portfolio* consisting of two or more securities.

*Portfolio 1* contains 1/2 security A and 1/2 security B, so the rate of return on the portfolio is an average of the rates of return on the two securities. For example, for outcome 1, portfolio 1 has a return of 1.5% because security A yields 1% and security B yields 2%. Overall, the range of outcomes for portfolio 1 (1.5% to 3.5%) is smaller than the range for each individual security (1% to 4%). This is the benefit of diversification.

*Portfolio 2*—containing 1/3 security A, 1/3 security B, and 1/3 security C—has outcomes that range between 2.0% and 3.0%. This is a smaller range than for portfolio 1, showing how diversification reduces risk when more securities are held.

*Portfolio 3*—containing 1/4 each of securities A, B, C, and D—has no risk at all because the return of 2.5% occurs for each outcome. Portfolio 3 thus shows that diversification can even provide a *certain return*, although each security, judged individually, is risky.[1]

### Risk Pooling and Independent Risks

Table 7.6 illustrates how the benefit of diversification rises if the securities have outcomes with low correlations—if, that is, their risks tend to be independent. Here the investor has a choice of three equally priced securities, each one with a range of outcomes between 1% and 3%.

*Portfolio 1*—containing 1/2 security A and 1/2 security B—also has a range of outcomes between 1% and 3%, so there is *no gain from diversification*. The problem is that the returns on securities A and B are *perfectly correlated*. That is, for outcome 1, security A does poorly—a return of 1%—and security B also does poorly—a return of 1%. In outcomes 2 and 3, the returns also follow exactly the same pattern. This shows that diversification provides no benefit if the returns on the securities follow exactly the same pattern.

*Portfolio 2*—containing 1/2 Security A and 1/2 Security C—in contrast, provides *perfect diversification*, a certain return of 2% for all outcomes. The key feature here is that the returns on securities A and C are perfectly *negatively correlated*: in outcome 1, when security A does poorly—a return of 1%—security B does well—a return of 3%—and vice versa for outcome 3.

Investors use a variety of methods to obtain diversified portfolios of securities with independent risks:

- Combine credit securities such as bonds with equity securities such as common stocks.

- Combine securities of firms in different industries.

- Combine securities of firms located in different regions of the country, or even in different countries.

---

[1] A certain return may be difficult to obtain in practice. In the example, the certain return of 2.5% is obtained with only four securities because there are only four possible outcomes.

**TABLE 7.6**

**The Gains from Diversification with Independent Risks**

| | Rate of Return for Each Possible Outcome (in percent) | | | Range of Rates of Return |
|---|---|---|---|---|
| | Outcome 1 | Outcome 2 | Outcome 3 | |
| Individual securities | | | | |
| Security A | 1% | 2% | 3% | 1%–3% |
| Security B | 1 | 2 | 3 | 1–3 |
| Security C | 3 | 2 | 1 | 1–3 |
| Diversified portfolios | | | | |
| Portfolio 1 1/2 Security A + 1/2 Security B | 1 | 2 | 3 | 1–3 |
| Portfolio 2 1/2 Security A + 1/2 Security C | 2 | 2 | 2 | 2–2 |

Small investors can acquire diversified portfolios by purchasing small amounts of many different securities, but the transactions costs of doing so are high. A lower cost technique is to purchase shares in a mutual fund—an investment company that itself holds a highly diversified portfolio. A mutual fund has a large portfolio and purchases *large* amounts of each security, so its average transactions costs tend to be low. There are even mutual funds—called *index funds*—that invest in all of the stocks of the widely followed stock indexes. Box 7.5 describes how they work.

**BOX 7.5 CREDIT CHECK**

## Stock Index Mutual Funds

Stock market investors often use indexes of common stocks, such as the Dow-Jones Index or the Standard & Poor 500 Index, to keep tract of stock market trends. To obtain a well-diversified portfolio, an investor might want to invest in exactly the stocks that make up one of these indexes. However, it may be impractical to do so because it is costly to purchase shares in small quantities.

In response to the need for diversified portfolios, there have developed *index funds*—mutual funds with portfolios that consist of precisely the same stocks as one of the stock indexes (usually the Standard & Poor 500). Because the overall size of a mutual fund portfolio can be $100 million or more, it becomes economical to buy shares in all of the companies that make up the index. Individual investors then purchase prorated shares of the overall portfolio—sometimes in amounts as low as $1,000 each. Although a fee is paid to the company that manages the mutual fund, this still represents an excellent way for small investors to obtain the benefit of a diversified portfolio.

## Problems with Asymmetric Information

In discussing risk transfers and risk pooling, we have so far assumed that information regarding risk is equally available to buyers and sellers. This information includes the magnitude of possible losses and the probabilities that the losses will occur. Realistically, however, there is often an asymmetry in the information available to the two parties—usually, the seller has more accurate information of risk than the buyer.

Sellers of risk are likely to be better informed because they initially "own" or control the risk. For example, the borrower on a loan (the risk seller) generally has better information than the lender (the risk buyer) regarding the chances of default on the payment. Loan markets and other markets for risk transfer may not operate efficiently as a result of such asymmetric information.

### The Market for Lemons

The market for low mileage used cars illustrates the problem that is created by asymmetric information. Owners of new cars soon learn whether they have received a *good car* or a *lemon*—a car that never operates well. The owner of a lemon naturally wants to sell the car in order to avoid the frustration and cost of trying to operate it.

The buyers of used cars will therefore try to determine whether a particular car is a lemon, while the sellers of lemons will try to conceal this information. The result may be that buyers simply assume that all low mileage used cars are lemons. Sellers of *good*—nonlemon—used cars then suffer a loss: the prices offered for their cars will be unfairly low because buyers have assumed incorrectly that all the cars are lemons. In this sense, asymmetric information causes the market for *good* used cars to function inefficiently.

### The Effects of Asymmetric Information

Asymmetric information creates two important effects in insurance markets: adverse selection and moral hazard.

*Adverse Selection.* Adverse selection arises when customers representing "bad" risks—high prospects for claims—tend to buy insurance and customers representing "good" risks—low prospects for claims—tend not to buy insurance. An insurance company therefore obtains a pool of insurance customers biased toward the bad risks. A company might raise its premium on this account, but some of the remaining good risks may then cancel their insurance—so, only the bad risks—the lemons—may be left in the market to buy insurance. Adverse selection thus reduces the benefits that are provided by insurance markets. Box 7.6 illustrates how this works for life annuities, a type of insurance.

*Moral Hazard.* Moral hazard arises when people change their behavior and raise their risk level when they obtain insurance. For example, people with accident insurance may pursue more hazardous activities such as mountain climbing and skiing, instead of safer pursuits—like studying money and banking. The effects of moral hazard are similar to those of adverse selection: the insurance company obtains an insurance pool that is riskier than the average level of all consumers.

BOX 7.6 CREDIT CHECK

## Life Annuities and Adverse Selection

Life annuities are a type of insurance that has limited use in the United States today because of adverse selection. A *life annuity* is an insurance policy for which people pay a single initial premium, and then receive monthly payments for the rest of their life, no matter how long they live. This insurance is valuable for elderly people because it allows them to obtain a guaranteed income even if they live an extremely long life. Insurance companies set the premiums for such insurance based on the expected claims computed by their actuaries.

Insurance companies that offer life annuities find that their customers tend to live longer than the average person, with the result that the annuity payments are made for longer periods than would be true for the average person. The reason for this is obvious: people who expect to live for a relatively long time tend to be the ones who buy life annuities. So, insurance companies, seeing the difference in life expectancy between their customers and the average person, have raised their life annuity premiums. The result is that most people do not buy life annuities because this insurance is expensive for someone with an average life expectancy.

### Loan Markets

Problems of adverse selection and moral hazard also arise in loan markets. Adverse selection arises in lending because—not surprisingly—the bad risks are often the ones most eager to borrow. Moral hazard occurs in lending when borrowers change their behavior after receiving a loan, the extreme case being that the borrower skips town. This adds to the asymmetry of information between borrowers and lenders, and loan markets operate less efficiently as a result. We will look at how banks deal with risky loans and asymmetric information in Chapter 12.

## Chapter Summary

1. Investment decisions are made under uncertainty when there are various possible outcomes for an investment. When there is uncertainty, the expected value can be computed as a summary number representing the expected return for each security. On the basis of expected value, the security providing the highest expected return is chosen.

2. Expected value may be used in deciding whether or not to buy insurance. Insurance is fair, favorable, or unfavorable, depending on whether the insurance premium equals, falls below, or exceeds the expected value of the claim. Using expected value, insurance is not purchased if the premium is unfavorable.

3. Expected value may also be applied to gambling. Gambles are favorable, fair, or unfavorable as the expected value of the payoff exceeds, equals, or falls below the amount bet. Using expected value, gambles are not taken if the expected value of the payoff is unfavorable.

4. Risk is the possibility that a bad outcome may occur in situations where various outcomes are possible. Decisions that take risk into account can be illustrated with indifference curves that represent the trade-off between expected return and the risk—the range (or variance) of outcomes.

5. Risk-averse people tend to avoid risky choices. This means buying less risky investments, buying insurance, and not gambling. In contrast, risk-loving people tend toward risky choices.

6. Risk transfer (the exchange of risk from one party to another) may benefit both parties as long as the buyer is less risk averse than the seller. Such exchanges occur in markets for securities, insurance, and gambling. Risk transfer is hampered when risk sellers have more accurate information than risk buyers—that is, there is asymmetric information. In this case, problems of adverse selection and moral hazard may arise.

7. Risk pooling is accomplished through diversified portfolios that consist of a large number of securities with independent (uncorrelated) risks. The risk of such a portfolio is less than the average risk of each component.

## Key Terms

Adverse selection
Diversified portfolios
Expected loss (for insurance)
Expected outcome
Expected payoff (for a gamble)
Expected return (for an investment)
Expected value (decisions)
Gambles:
 Fair
 Favorable
 Unfavorable
Insurance:
 Fair
 Favorable
 Unfavorable

Investments:
 Fair
 Favorable
 Unfavorable
Market price of risk
Moral hazard
Range of outcomes and returns
Risk preferences:
 Averse
 Neutral
 Loving
Risk pooling
Risk transfers
Uncertainty
Variance of outcomes

## Study Questions

1. What behavior of investors, gamblers, and insurance purchasers indicates they are not using expected value?

2. Compute the expected rate of return for each of the following securities. Based on expected value, which security should be selected?

| Outcome | Probability | Rate of Return | | |
|---|---|---|---|---|
| | | A | B | C |
| $V_1$ | 0.2 | 0% | 0% | 10% |
| $V_2$ | 0.3 | 0 | 10 | 10 |
| $V_3$ | 0.5 | 20 | 20 | 10 |
| Expected Rate of Return | | ? | ? | ? |

3. Excluding the security selected in Question 2, which of the remaining securities would be the natural choice of a risk-averse investor and which the choice of a risk-loving investor?

4. Many people are observed buying unfavorable insurance *and* taking unfavorable gambles. How might such behavior be explained?

5. How does Figure 7.1 illustrate that an investment strategy based on expected value does not incorporate considerations of risk?

6. Indicate whether the following statements are true or false. If a statement is false, indicate what would be the proper statement.
   a. Risk-neutral people never take fair gambles.
   b. Risk-averse people never take fair gambles.
   c. Risk-averse people never buy fair insurance.
   d. Risk pooling is particularly useful for risk lovers.
   e. Risk transfers occur between risk-averse and risk-loving people.

7. Why do horizontal lines represent the indifference curves for a risk-neutral person?

8. Why do positively sloped lines represent the indifference curves for a risk-averse person?

9. What benefit is provided by diversified portfolios?

10. Why does asymmetrical information limit the amount of risk transfer that occurs?

## Recommended Reading

*The theory of investment decisions is studied in detail in courses called investments, corporate finance, or similar names. Some standard textbooks include:*

Richard Brealey and Steward Meyers, *Principles of Corporate Finance*, 2nd edition, McGraw-Hill, New York, 1984.

Eugene F. Fama, *Foundations of Finance*, Basic Books, New York, 1976.

Eugene F. Fama and Merton H. Miller, *The Theory of Finance*, Holt, Rinehart and Winston, New York, 1982.

Kenneth Garbade, *Securities Markets*, McGraw-Hill, New York, 1982.

Frank K. Reilly, *Investment Analysis and Portfolio Management*, 2nd edition, The Dryden Press, Hinsdale, Ill., 1985.

William Sharpe, *Investments*, 3rd edition, Prentice-Hall, Englewood Cliffs, N.J., 1985.

*Books of readings include:*

Stephen H. Archer and Charles A. D'Ambrosio, *The Theory of Business Finance*, 3rd edition, Macmillan, New York, 1983.

Frank J. Fabozzi, *Readings in Investment Management*, Richard D. Irwin, Homewood, Ill., 1983.

---

# Appendix 7.1: The Bernoulli Game

The Bernoulli Game provides an intriguing example of the fact that people do not use expected value in making decisions.

The rules of the game are simple. There is a player and a banker; you are the player. The banker flips a coin until the first *heads* appears. Then the game stops, and the number of the flip is recorded as $i$: if the first *heads* appears on flip 3, for example, then $i = 3$. Whatever the case, the banker pays you the amount $\$2^i$. For example, with $i = 3$, you earn $\$2^3 = \$8$. If you are luckier, and get a high $i$ value, say $i = 25$, you earn $\$2^{25} = \$33,554,432$ (that's right, $33 million).

How much would you pay to play the game?

In the worst situation, *heads* comes up on the first flip and you receive $\$2^1 = \$2$. So you obviously would pay the banker at least $2 to play. Presumably you would pay more, since there is a chance of winning more money, and there is at least some chance of winning many millions. So how much would you be willing to pay to play?

Expected value is one way of determining how much you might pay—you might be willing to pay the expected payoff to play. If the banker allows you to play for any smaller fee, then the game is favorable and you should definitely play. If the banker charges a higher fee, then the game is unfavorable and you should not play.

The expected payoff of the Bernoulli Game is calculated as follows. Expected value is always computed as a weighted average of all possible outcomes, using the probabilities of the outcomes as the weights. An outcome in the Bernoulli Game is $2^i$ where $i$ is the number of the flip on which *heads* first appears. The probability that you obtain a particular value of $i$ is $(1/2)^i$ because the probability that *heads* will appear on any flip, including the specific flip $i$, is $1/2$.

Therefore, the expected payoff of the game, $V_e$, can be calculated as the weighted average of all possible outcomes:

$$V_e = \sum_{i=1}^{\infty} p_i V_i = \sum_{i=1}^{\infty} (1/2)^i (2)^i = \sum_{i=1}^{\infty} (1)^i$$

$$= 1^1 + 1^2 + 1^3 + \cdots 1 = 1 + 1 + \cdots = \infty \text{ (infinity)}.$$

Since the expected value of the Bernoulli Game is infinity, players should be willing to pay an infinite amount, or at least close to that, to play. If you try this out on people, however, you will find few who are willing to pay even $25. Most people, in fact, feel they are stretching matters even to pay $10 to play. This is the *Bernoulli paradox:* people are not willing to pay large sums to play a game that has an expected payoff of infinity. Various practical matters have been suggested as solutions to the Bernoulli paradox:

- Who would be able to make the huge payoffs to very lucky players
- Is there enough time for a fabulously lucky player to receive an infinite number of flips?

More theoretical explanations include:

- People might pay more to play the game if they could play it more than one time.
- People must be using some other decision rule.

The last suggestion lead to the development of the principles of risk-averse behavior described in this chapter.

# The Term Structure
# of Interest Rates

*"There are two times in a man's life when he should not speculate:*
*when he can't afford it, and when he can."*

*Mark Twain*

Investors must consider the time period over which money is to be
invested, as well as uncertainty regarding the rate of return (which we
studied in Chapter 7). As a case in point, suppose you have managed
to save some money and want to invest it in a safe and easy way, in a
time deposit account at your local bank. At the bank, the teller points
to the following table and asks which maturity you want:

### Time Deposits: Maturities and Interest Rates

| Maturity | Interest Rate |
|----------|---------------|
| 1 year   | 5%            |
| 2 years  | 7%            |
| 3 years  | 9%            |

On what factors do you base such a decision? An obvious factor is how
long you wish to leave your money invested in the bank. A more subtle
factor is whether you expect interest rates to change in the future. If
you expect interest rates to rise substantially during the coming year,
for example, then you might buy the one-year deposit, planning on
reinvesting the money at higher rates in future years.

You will confront a similar issue if you inquire about car loans: the
lending officer, pointing to his table of loan rates by maturity, will
want to know which maturity you prefer:

### Auto Loans: Maturities and Interest Rates

| Maturity | Interest Rate |
|----------|---------------|
| 1 year   | 8%            |
| 2 years  | 10%           |
| 3 years  | 12%           |

Similar factors affect loan decisions and deposit decisions. In this
chapter, we will study how these factors are reflected in the decisions
that people make when selecting maturities for loans and deposits.

The interest rates on debt securities that differ only with regard to their maturity—as in the two tables on page 181—represent the term structure of interest rates. In this chapter, we will see how people make investment decisions regarding maturity and how their decisions are reflected in theories of the term structure of interest rates. We will also look at how banks deal with the maturities of their loans and deposits. This discussion continues in Chapter 9, where we will analyze two related financial instruments—futures and options contracts.

## Theories of the Term Structure of Interest Rates

The **term structure of interest rates** represents the interest rates paid on different maturities of a given type of debt security. For example, we have seen that bank time deposits may pay 5% at a one-year maturity, 7% at two years, and 9% at three years. On the basis of such interest rates, people make borrowing and lending decisions, and their actions, in turn, determine the term structure of interest rates. In this section, we will see how this works.

### Yield Curves

A **yield curve** is a graphical representation of the term structure of interest rates for a given type of security. Each point on a yield curve represents the interest rate paid on a specific maturity of the security. For example, panel A in Figure 8.1 shows the yield curve for the bank time deposit interest rates that we just considered.

Yield curves can have distinctly different slopes, as shown in Figure 8.1. Panel A shows the most common slope, *an ascending yield curve*—the longer the maturity of the security, the higher its interest rate. Panels B and C show less common slopes: panel B shows a *descending yield curve*—the longer the maturity, the lower the interest rate; and panel C shows a *horizontal yield curve*—all maturities pay the same interest rate. Later, we will examine a yield curve with a more complicated shape.

For yield curves to be useful, the securities involved should be identical in all respects except for their maturity. Otherwise, factors other than maturity—such as varying amounts of credit risk—might influence the shape of the curve. Securities issued by the U.S. Treasury are particularly useful in this regard because the securities are all free of credit risk. In the rest of this discussion, we will refer only to U.S. Treasury securities, in order to put aside questions of credit risk.

Yield curves are also more accurate when they are based on *zero-coupon securities*, because the maturity of these securities is precisely determined by the *single date* on which all payments (principal and interest) occur. In contrast, the precise maturity of coupon bonds is difficult to compute because these bonds make a *series* of interest payments at different dates. We will refer only to zero-coupon securities in our main discussion, but we will look at coupon bonds in Appendix 8.1.

Each point on a yield curve represents the interest rate paid on a specific maturity of a given type of security. The figure shows how yield curves are distinguished on the basis of their slopes.

FIGURE 8.1
**Yield Curves**

A. An Ascending Yield Curve

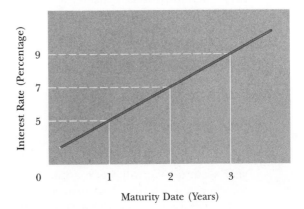

B. A Descending Yield Curve

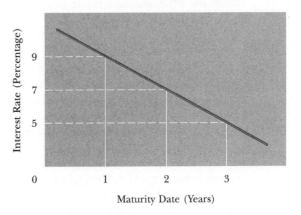

C. A Horizontal Yield Curve

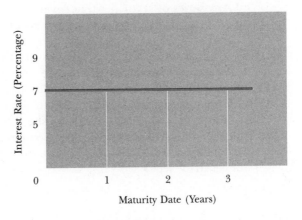

## Holding Period Returns and Security Sequences

To illustrate how investors take maturity into account when making investment decisions, consider a person who has decided to invest some money for three years in a zero-coupon security. The period of time the money is invested is called the **holding period;** so, in this example, we are talking about a three-year holding period.

The investor must then decide which particular maturity of the security to buy. It might seem that the only option is to invest in a zero-coupon security with a three-year maturity—which provides a single payment at the end of the third year (representing the repayment of principal and the interest). But it is also possible to invest in a series of securities, such as three one-year securities, or a one-year security followed by a two-year security, or a two-year security followed by a one-year security. We will see in a moment that there may be good reasons for choosing a series of securities.

We will assume that the first investment can be made in one of only three ways: a security that matures in one year, two years, or three years from the date the investment is made. We will refer to these as securities $S_{0,1}$, $S_{0,2}$, and $S_{0,3}$, respectively; the first subscript, 0, refers to the date at which the investment is made (date 0); and the second subscript refers to the date at which the security matures (dates 1, 2, or 3).

Security $S_{0,3}$—with a three-year maturity—represents the simplest investment strategy, because the investor just buys the security and holds it for the three-year holding period. Securities $S_{0,1}$ and $S_{0,2}$ represent more complicated strategies because their maturities—one and two years, respectively—do not cover the full holding period, so the investor has to link them with other securities to cover the holding period.

For example, if a person buys security $S_{0,2}$—which provides its cash payment after two years—then he or she must invest in an additional security for the remaining year of the holding period. We will refer to this additional security as $S_{2,3}$, the first subscript indicating the date on which the security is purchased (date 2 relative to the first investment date 0), and the second subscript indicating the date on which the security matures (date 3 relative to date 0). Taken together, securities $S_{0,2}$ and $S_{2,3}$ cover the three-year holding period, security $S_{0,2}$ covering the first two years and security $S_{2,3}$ covering the last year.

Any series of securities that covers a holding period—such as $S_{0,2}$ and $S_{2,3}$ in this example—represents a **security sequence** for that holding period. We will denote security sequences in the form $\{S_{0,2}|S_{2,3}\}$. The security sequence $\{S_{0,1}|S_{1,3}\}$ also covers the three-year holding period: $S_{0,1}$ matures after one year; and the cash payment is then reinvested for the remaining two years of the holding period in $S_{1,3}$.

Investors sensibly evaluate alternative security sequences on the basis of how much interest is earned. The interest earned on a security sequence is measured by the *holding period return*—the total interest earned per dollar initially invested. For example, the holding period return for the security sequence $\{S_{0,3}\}$ is $3\ r_{0,3}$—the security being held for three years and its annual interest rate being $r_{0,3}$. (In this case, of course, the security "sequence" is just the single three-year security.)

The calculation of a holding period return such as $3\ r_{0,3}$ is based on *simple interest,* computed by summing the interest earned on the initial investment for each of the years of the holding period. Although we will continue to use simple interest, the more precise calculations that result from *compound interest* are discussed in Appendix 8.2. Compound interest includes "interest earned on interest," as we discussed in Chapter 5.

## Spot Securities and Forward Securities

A complication arises in calculating holding period returns on security sequences that involve two or more securities. For example, with the sequence $\{S_{0,1}|S_{1,3}\}$, the interest rate the investor will earn on the second security—$S_{1,3}$—is not known at date 0 when the initial investment is made in $S_{0,1}$. To deal with this, it is necessary to distinguish between spot securities and forward securities.

**Spot securities**—such as $S_{0,1}$, $S_{0,2}$, and $S_{0,3}$, with 0 as the first subscript—trade in security markets as of date 0. Therefore, the interest rates on these securities—$r_{0,1}$, $r_{0,2}$, and $r_{0,3}$, respectively—are known at date 0. The yield curve as of date 0 consists of the interest rates on only the spot securities, as shown in Figure 8.2.

The yield curve at a given date consists of the interest rates on *spot securities* that are traded in security markets as of that date. At date 0, these are securities such as $S_{0,1}$, $S_{0,2}$, and $S_{0,3}$. The interest rates on these securities are $r_{0,1}$, $r_{0,2}$, and $r_{0,3}$, respectively. The common case of an *ascending* yield curve is illustrated in this diagram.

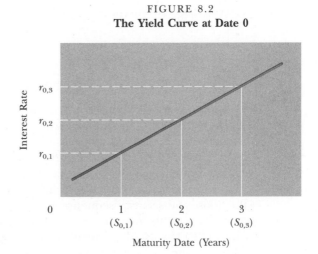

FIGURE 8.2

**The Yield Curve at Date 0**

Interest Rate

Maturity Date (Years)

In contrast, **forward securities**—such as $S_{1,3}$ or $S_{2,3}$, without 0 as the first subscript—do not exist and are not traded as of date 0. Investors thus do not know what interest rates will apply to forward securities until they begin to trade later—at date 1 for $S_{1,2}$, and at date 2 for $S_{2,3}$.

Even at date 0, however, for security sequences that include forward securities, investors can determine **expected holding period returns** based on **expected interest rates**—the interest rates that investors *expect* they will earn when the forward securities do trade. We will use the symbol *e* to refer to expected interest rates: $e_{1,2}$ is the expected interest rate on the forward security $S_{1,2}$, and $e_{1,3}$ is the expected interest rate on the security $S_{1,3}$. (Later in this chapter we will look at how investors might form expectations of future interest rates.)

As an example, for the security sequence $\{S_{0,2}|S_{2,3}\}$, the expected holding period return is $2\,r_{0,2} + e_{2,3}$. The first term, $2\,r_{0,2}$, is the interest earned for two years on the spot security $S_{0,2}$. The second term, $e_{2,3}$, is the expected interest on the forward security $S_{2,3}$ during the last year of the holding period. In the same way, the expected holding period return on the security sequence $\{S_{0,1}|S_{1,3}\}$ is $r_{0,1} + 2\,e_{1,3}$. Table 8.1 summarizes expected holding period return formulas for various security sequences based on a three-year holding period.

**TABLE 8.1**
**Expected Holding Period Returns**

**Based on simple interest for a three-year holding period**

| Security Sequence | Expected Holding Period Return |
| --- | --- |
| $S_{0,3}$ | $3\,r_{0,3}$ |
| $S_{0,2} + S_{2,3}$ | $2\,r_{0,2} + e_{2,3}$ |
| $S_{0,1} + S_{1,3}$ | $r_{0,1} + 2\,e_{1,3}$ |
| $S_{0,1} + S_{1,2} + S_{2,3}$ | $r_{0,1} + e_{1,2} + e_{2,3}$ |

## The Pure Expectations (PE) Theory

In Chapter 7, we discussed *expected return* as a criterion investors might use when credit risk or similar factors create uncertainty regarding investment outcomes. We will now see that expected returns—more specifically, *expected holding period returns*—can also be used in selecting security sequences, where uncertainty arises because interest rates on forward securities are not known initially. Using this criterion, investors will choose the security sequence that offers the *highest expected holding period return*. This investment criterion is the basis of the **pure expectations (PE) theory** of the term structure of interest rates.

The PE theory requires two basic assumptions about how investors select securities by maturity:

1. Investors buy securities only in the sequence that offers the highest expected holding period return.

2. Investors all form the same expectations concerning interest rates on forward securities. (These expectations are therefore referred to as the *market expectations*.)

## Equilibrium Conditions for the Pure Expectations Theory

In equilibrium—when all investors have selected their desired security sequences—the assumptions of the PE theory have a powerful implication:

> *Expected holding period returns will be equal for all sequences covering a given holding period.*

This is the result of **maturity arbitrage**—a process in which investors buy and sell securities of different maturities in order to earn the highest possible return.

For example, consider the case where investors have two-year holding periods and two alternative security sequences are available:

a. $\{S_{0,2}\}$ with holding period return $2\, r_{0,2}$;

b. $\{S_{0,1}|S_{1,2}\}$ with expected holding period return $r_{0,1} + e_{1,2}$.

Also assume that initially the sequence $\{S_{0,2}\}$ has a higher expected holding period return than the sequence $\{S_{0,1}|S_{1,2}\}$:

$$2\, r_{0,2} > r_{0,1} + e_{1,2}.$$

Maturity arbitrage will then eliminate the difference between the two expected holding period returns.

Maturity arbitrage begins as a result of assumption 1 of the PE theory: given that security $S_{0,2}$ has a higher expected return, all investors will buy security $S_{0,2}$ and none will buy security $S_{0,1}$ (the first security in the sequence $\{S_{0,1}|S_{1,2}\}$). Additionally, investors who were holding security $S_{0,1}$ will try to sell it and buy $S_{0,2}$ instead.

Maturity arbitrage thus *increases the demand* for the first security in the sequence that offers the higher expected holding period return ($S_{0,2}$), and *increases the supply* of the first security in the sequence that offers the lower expected holding period return ($S_{0,1}$). The buying pressure on $S_{0,2}$ will cause its market price to rise, and therefore its interest yield, $r_{0,2}$, will fall. Similarly, the selling pressure on $S_{0,1}$ will cause its market price to fall, and therefore its interest yield, $r_{0,1}$, will rise.

The resulting changes in the two interest rates—$r_{0,2}$ falling and $r_{0,1}$ rising—will cause the expected holding period returns on the two security sequences to converge. In fact, maturity arbitrage will stop only when the two expected holding period returns are equal:

$$2\, r_{0,2} = r_{0,1} + e_{1,2}. \tag{8.1}$$

This is how maturity arbitrage equalizes expected holding period returns.

The same idea can be applied to any holding period and to any pair of security sequences. For example, for a three-year holding period, investors have a choice between the security sequences $\{S_{0,3}\}$ and $\{S_{0,2}|S_{2,3}\}$. In equilibrium, the expected holding period $3\, r_{0,3}$ on $\{S_{0,3}\}$ and $2\, r_{0,2} + e_{2,3}$ on $\{S_{0,2}|S_{2,3}\}$—are again equal:

$$3\, r_{0,3} = 2\, r_{0,2} + e_{2,3}. \tag{8.2}$$

Equilibrium conditions of this type are the core of the pure expectations theory. We will now look at some of the implications of these conditions.

### Yield Curves and the Pure Expectations Theory

A main implication of the PE theory is that a yield curve is determined by just two factors:

1. The *short-term interest rate* $r_{0,1}$—the rate on $S_{0,1}$, the shortest-term security we are considering—determines the height of the first point on the yield curve.

2. *Expected short-term interest rates* such as $e_{1,2}$ and $e_{2,3}$—the expected rates on the short-term forward securities $S_{1,2}$ and $S_{2,3}$—determine the height of the yield curve beyond the first point.

For example, the second point on the yield curve—the rate $r_{0,2}$ on security $S_{0,2}$—is determined from equation (8.1):

$$r_{0,2} = \frac{r_{0,1} + e_{1,2}}{2}. \tag{8.3}$$

The rate $r_{0,2}$ is thus an average of the short-term interest rate $r_{0,1}$ and the expected short-term interest rate $e_{1,2}$.

Similarly, the third point on the yield curve—the rate $r_{0,3}$ on security $S_{0,3}$—is determined from equation (8.2) as:

$$r_{0,3} = \frac{2 \, r_{0,2} + e_{2,3}}{3}, \tag{8.4}$$

or, using equation (8.1) to replace $2 \, r_{0,2}$:

$$r_{0,3} = \frac{r_{0,1} + e_{1,2} + e_{2,3}}{3}. \tag{8.5}$$

This shows that $r_{0,3}$ is an average of the short-term interest rate $r_{0,1}$ and the expected short-term interest rates $e_{1,2}$ and $e_{2,3}$.

Continuing in this manner, interest rates corresponding to all the points on a yield curve can be determined as averages of the short-term interest rate $r_{0,1}$ and expected short-term interest rates such as $e_{1,2}$ and $e_{2,3}$. In other words, the height of the first point on the yield curve is determined by the one-year rate $r_{0,1}$, while the *shape* of the yield—the height of the curve at other points—is determined by the *expected* short-term interest rates such as $e_{1,2}$ and $e_{2,3}$ (hence the name "pure expectations theory"). This is how a yield curve is constructed according to the PE theory.

### Yield Curves and Market Expectations of Future Interest Rates

Let us now suppose that at date 0 you are asked to determine the short-term interest rate expected for next year—in other words, to determine a value for $e_{1,2}$. The pure expectations theory can be very helpful in this regard—all you have to do is solve equation (8.1), $2 \, r_{0,2} = r_{0,1} + e_{1,2}$, for $e_{1,2}$:

$$e_{1,2} = 2 \, r_{0,2} - r_{0,1}.$$

For example, we looked earlier at a yield curve with $r_{0,1} = 5\%$ and $r_{0,2} = 7\%$. We can now see that this yield curve implies that $e_{1,2} = 2 \, r_{0,2} - r_{0,1} = 2 \, (7\%) - 5\% = 9\%$.

More generally, the equilibrium conditions of the pure expectations theory can be used to calculate any expected interest rate that falls within a given holding period. For example, Box 8.1 shows the procedure that would be used to calculate the expected interest rates $e_{1,2}$, $e_{2,3}$, and $e_{1,3}$ that fall within a three-year holding period:

BOX 8.1 IN DEPTH

## Deriving Market Expectations of Interest Rates*

**Part A: Equilibrium Conditions**
(Expected holding period returns are equal for all security sequences)

From sequences $\{S_{0,2}|S_{2,3}\}$ and $\{S_{0,1}|S_{1,2}|S_{2,3}\}$:

$$[1]\ 2\ r_{0,2} + e_{2,3} = r_{0,1} + e_{1,2} + e_{2,3}.$$

From sequences $(S_{0,3})$ and $\{S_{0,2}|S_{2,3}\}$:

$$[2]\ 3\ r_{0,3} = 2\ r_{0,2} + e_{2,3}.$$

From sequences $(S_{0,3})$ and $\{S_{0,1}|S_{1,3}\}$:

$$[3]\ 3\ r_{0,3} = r_{0,1} + 2\ e_{1,3}.$$

**Part B: Formulas for Expected Interest Rates**
From equation [1]:

$$[1']\ e_{1,2} = 2\ r_{0,2} - r_{0,1}.$$

From equation [2]:

$$[2']\ e_{2,3} = 3\ r_{0,3} - 2\ r_{0,2}.$$

From equation [3]:

$$[3']\ e_{1,3} = (3\ r_{0,3} - r_{0,1})/2.$$

**Part C: Computing Expected Interest Rates**
From the yield curve of panel A, Figure 8.1, we have:

$$r_{0,1} = .05$$
$$r_{0,2} = .07$$
$$r_{0,3} = .09.$$

From equation [1']:

$$e_{1,2} = (2)(.07) - .05 = .09 = 9\%.$$

From equation [2']:

$$e_{2,3} = (3)(.09) - 2(.07) = .13 = 13\%.$$

From equation [3']:

$$e_{1,3} = ((3)(.09) - .05)/2 = 11\%.$$

*(Based on a three-year holding period)

- Part A shows the relevant *equilibrium conditions* for a three-year holding period.
- Part B shows the equations for *expected interest rates* that are derived from the equilibrium conditions.
- Part C provides a *numerical example* based on the yield curve shown in panel A of Figure 8.1.

### Yield Curves and Changes in Interest Rates

The direction of expected *changes* in interest rates are readily determined from just the slope of the yield curve. The following rule is used:

> As the yield curve is ascending, descending, or horizontal, short-term interest rates are expected to rise, fall, or remain unchanged.

We can illustrate this rule with the yield curve: $r_{0,1} = 5\%$, $r_{0,2} = 7\%$, and $r_{0,3} = 9\%$. Because this yield curve is ascending in its range between $r_{0,1}$ and $r_{0,2}$, we know that interest rates next year are expected to rise. And because the yield curve is ascending in its range between $r_{0,2}$ and $r_{0,3}$, we know that interest rates are expected to rise in the following year as well.

We can see the basis of the rule by referring again to equation (8.3), $r_{0,2} = (r_{0,1} + e_{1,2})/2$. The yield curve will be ascending ($r_{0,2} > r_{0,1}$) only if the short-term interest rate is expected to rise ($e_{1,2} > r_{0,1}$); and vice versa for a descending yield curve. The yield curve will be horizontal ($r_{0,2} = r_{0,1}$) only if the short-term interest rate is expected to remain unchanged ($e_{1,2} = r_{0,1}$). The same principle can be applied to determine expected interest rate changes further in the future.

### The Accuracy of Interest Rate Forecasts Based on the PE Theory

Since the market's expectations of future interest rates can be computed from the yield curve according to the PE theory, the yield curve can be used to *forecast* interest rates. However, caution suggests that we look first at how well the PE theory actually works before applying it in this way.

Unfortunately, statistical tests indicate that interest rate forecasts based on the PE theory are not very accurate. In fact, it seems these forecasts are actually *biased*—they deviate in a systematic way from the actual interest rates observed later. The bias of the forecasts is reflected in the fact that yield curves are ascending most of the time. According to the PE theory, an ascending yield curve should mean that the market expects interest rates to rise. However, interest rates do not actually rise with anywhere near the frequency with which we observe ascending yield curves. So something is obviously wrong with the PE theory.

One possibility is that the "market" simply does not form accurate forecasts of future interest rates. However, most economists consider it implausible that the market's interest rate forecasts would be so inaccurate as to be biased. (In this regard, Box 8.2 discusses some ways that investors forecast interest rates.)

Another possibility is that, contrary to the PE theory, investors may be influenced by the uncertainty associated with expected holding period

## How Investors Forecast Future Interest Rates

Most investors—and economists—agree that forecasting future changes in interest rates is a very difficult task. Indeed, the best wisdom in this area is probably to know enough not to try it. However, investment decisions involving maturities do have to be based on *something*.

The loanable funds theory of interest rates that we discussed in Chapter 3 is a good starting point. There we saw that interest rates are determined by desired saving and desired capital investment— or, equivalently, by desired borrowing and desired lending. For example, if you knew that new technologies were about to increase desired capital investment (or, equivalently, desired borrowing), then you might expect that interest rates would rise in the future. However, there are at least three problems with this approach:

1. Other people have probably had the same idea, and they may have already acted on it—by selling long-term securities. Therefore, this information may already be reflected in market in-

terest rates, and so it would not be a basis for forecasting how interest rates are likely to *change*. In other words, to forecast interest rate changes, you generally need *new* information.

2. When people talk about forecasting market interest rates, they usually mean *nominal interest rates*—the quoted interest rates on debt securities. But as we saw in Chapter 4, changes in the *expected rate of inflation* are actually the major source of changes in nominal rates. So, to forecast changes in interest rates, you also have to forecast changes in expected inflation—itself not an easy task.

3. Government policy—fiscal policy as determined by Congress and the administration, and monetary policy as determined by the Federal Reserve— also may affect future interest rate levels. We will discuss precisely how this works later in the book. But you can take it for granted that it is never easy to predict how government policy will affect interest rates.

returns. Remember, the PE theory assumes that investors refer only to expected holding period returns in selecting security sequences. Based on our discussion in Chapter 7 concerning investment decisions, this means that the PE theory really assumes that investors are *risk neutral*— that they ignore considerations of risk in making their decisions. (The risk that is relevant here pertains to a security's maturity, not its credit risk. We will clarify this concept further in a moment.)

If factors related to the uncertainty of holding period returns actually influence investor decisions, then these factors will also affect the yield curve. Specifically, if investors tend to buy short-term securities on this account, then the prices of those securities will be higher, and their interest rates will be lower. These changes in interest rates will be reflected in the yield curve. We will now look at theories that specifically consider how factors related to uncertainty in holding period returns might affect the yield curve.

## The Liquidity Preference (LP) Theory

According to the **liquidity preference (LP) theory**, investors prefer holding short-term rather than long-term securities, other things being equal. This is referred to as *liquidity preference*, because the shorter the term of a security, the more readily it can be converted into cash. Investors prefer short-term securities because they are considered to be less risky than long-term securities:

- Investors anticipate that unforeseen problems may force them to sell a security before its maturity date; the chances of this happening are less, the shorter the term of the security.

- If an investor does have to sell a security before its maturity date, there is then the risk that its price may be low at the time of the sale. This risk is less, the shorter the term of the security, because for a given change in interest rates, prices vary less on short-term securities than on long-term securities.

### Yield Curves and the Liquidity Preference Theory

The fact that investors with liquidity preference tend to hold shorter-term securities than they would otherwise do has an important implication for the yield curve. To see this, consider a group of investors who expect *interest rates to remain unchanged* over a three-year holding period. This means that their expected short-term interest rates, $e_{1,2}$ and $e_{2,3}$, equal the current short-term interest rate, $r_{0,1}$:

$$r_{0,1} = e_{1,2} = e_{2,3}.$$

According to the pure expectations theory, the investors would then be indifferent among all security sequences and the yield curve would be horizontal, as shown in Figure 8.3. In contrast, investors with liquidity preference would want to *buy the short-term security* ($S_{0,1}$) and to *sell the long-term security* ($S_{0,3}$). Their purchases would raise the price of $S_{0,1}$ and lower its interest rate $r_{0,1}$. Similarly their sales would lower the price of $S_{0,3}$ and raise its interest rate $r_{0,3}$.

FIGURE 8.3
**Yield Curves When Interest Rates
Are Not Expected To Change**

When interest rates are not expected to change, the yield curve of the pure expectations (PE) theory is horizontal, while the yield curve of the liquidity preference (LP) theory is ascending. Liquidity premiums—measured by the vertical distance between the LP and PE theory yield curves—are positive on long-term maturities and are negative on short-term maturities.

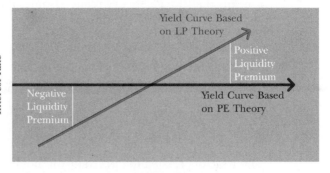

Maturity Date

The resulting changes in interest rates—the rate $r_{0,1}$ falling and the rate $r_{0,3}$ rising—cause the yield curve in Figure 8.3 to rotate counter-clockwise from the horizontal position (reflecting the PE theory) to the ascending position (reflecting the LP theory). Although we have analyzed this only for the case where interest rates were expected to remain unchanged, a corresponding result holds quite generally:

> *Given any expectations of future interest rates, the yield curve implied by the liquidity preference theory will be more sharply ascending than the corresponding yield curve implied by the pure expectations theory.*

### Liquidity Premiums

This result can be interpreted in terms of **liquidity premiums**—the vertical distance between the LP theory yield curve and the PE theory yield curve at each maturity. As shown in Figure 8.3, liquidity premiums are positive—the LP yield curve is above the PE curve—at long-term maturities, because investors with liquidity preference require that they be compensated for holding long-term securities. Similarly, liquidity premiums are negative at short-term maturities, because LP investors will accept lower interest rates on short-term securities.

There is no longer a simple relationship between expected interest rates and the shape of the yield curve when a yield curve contains liquidity premiums. The problem is that interest rate expectations and liquidity premiums are combined in the yield curve, and there is no way to separate them unless you already know one of them.

The ascending yield curve of Figure 8.3 illustrates the problem. As that curve is labeled, it represents the LP theory when market interest rates are expected to remain unchanged. However, the same yield curve could represent the PE theory when market interest rates are expected to rise. Just by looking at a yield curve, we cannot tell which theory it represents, and therefore we cannot determine how interest rates are expected to change.

## The Preferred Habitat Theory

The liquidity preference theory indicates that, other things being equal, investors prefer to hold short-term (liquid) securities. The **preferred habitat theory** generalizes this concept to the notion that investors prefer to hold securities of the same maturity as their "preferred habitat." For example, investors might want to hold long-term securities if they are saving for a specific long-term goal, such as paying for the college education of a newly born child. Alternatively, they might want to hold medium-term securities—with three- to five-year maturities—if they are saving to buy a home in a few years. Or, if they have liquidity preference, they might want to hold short-term securities.

When many investors share the same preferred habitat, their demand will force prices up—and interest rates down—for securities of that maturity. These investors may also sell securities of other maturities, forcing their prices down and their interest rates up. These interest rate changes then affect the shape of the yield curve, shifting it down over the preferred maturity range, and up over the undesired range.

A *hump-shaped yield curve*—shown in Figure 8.4—may result from the preferred habitat theory. Hump-shaped yield curves are ascending over the range of short-term maturities and descending over the range of long-term maturities. According to the preferred habitat theory, the "humped" region of the yield curve represents the undesired range of maturities. Similarly, the other regions of the yield curve, where the interest rates are low, represent the preferred habitats. (A hump-shaped yield curve may also arise under the PE theory when interest rates are expected first to rise and then to fall.)

Hump-shaped yield curves are ascending in the range of shorter-term maturities and are descending in the range of longer-term maturities. Interest rates tend to be lower in the preferred habitats and higher in the undesired maturities.

FIGURE 8.4
**A Hump-Shaped Yield Curve**

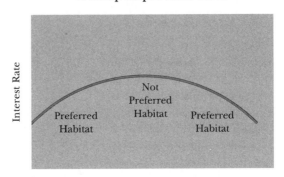

## The Market Segmentation Theory

According to the **market segmentation theory**, investors *do not* compare expected holding period returns on alternative security sequences in deciding which securities to buy. The theory is thus the opposite of the pure expectations theory. Instead, investors are assumed to deal only in the spot market security that corresponds to their holding period, such as security $S_{0,3}$ for a three-year holding period. The market segmentation theory thus implies that each spot market security trades in a separate— or segmented—market, with the interest rate for the security being determined by demand and supply in that market alone.

Because the market segmentation theory treats each maturity as if it were a separate market, the theory provides no information about the yield curve—the relationship between interest rates on securities of different maturities. Although this limits the value of the segmentation theory, it does serve as a useful reminder that short-term securities and long-term securities do trade in different markets. Therefore, it is possible that a large supply of securities of a particular maturity—such as may result from a large new issue—may temporarily alter the shape of the yield curve from what it otherwise would be.

## Applications of Term Structure Theory

Many investors and traders in security markets are well informed about term structure theory, and they have developed investment and trading strategies that combine elements from all of the theories. We will discuss two examples here.

### The Investment Strategy of Riding the Yield Curve

Consider an investor who is deciding which security to buy to cover a two-year holding period, at a time when the yield curve is ascending. She might decide on a strategy called **riding the yield curve**—buying a security with an initial maturity longer than the holding period and selling it at the end of the two-year holding period. For example, she might buy a four-year security, hold it for two years, and then sell it. Given that the yield curve is ascending, she will earn a higher interest rate with the four-year security than she would with a shorter-term security. We will now examine how well the strategy works under the pure expectations and the liquidity preference theories.

Under the *pure expectations theory*, expected holding returns are equal for all security sequences covering a given holding period. In particular, the expected return obtained by buying a four-year security and selling it after two years should just equal the expected return from any other security sequence that covers the holding period. Thus, according to the PE theory, *there is no advantage to riding the yield curve*. The fact that the four-year security has a high interest rate only means that interest rates are expected to rise in the future: so the security's price will fall and the investor will suffer a loss when selling it. In fact, the expected loss from selling the security should just balance the higher interest rate that is earned while holding it.

Under the *liquidity preference theory*, in contrast, investors can earn higher holding period returns by investing in longer-term securities—such as the four-year security—because these securities provide a liquidity premium. So if an investor *without* liquidity preference is investing in a market where other investors *have* liquidity preference, then riding the yield curve is a sensible strategy. However, in pursuing this strategy, the investor should consider that the liquidity preference of other investors could reflect factors that also apply to her—for example, that the security will end up being sold at an unexpectedly low price if interest rates rise unexpectedly.

If an investor does decide to ride the yield curve, the potential gain from the strategy depends on the degree to which the yield curve is ascending. Box 8.3 discusses two actual cases, one where the yield curve is descending (an unusual event) and the strategy is counterproductive, and another where the yield curve is sharply ascending and the potential profits of the strategy are high.

### The Monetary Policy of Bills Only

In carrying out monetary policy, the Federal Reserve often buys U.S. Treasury securities in an attempt to lower market interest rates—re-

**BOX 8.3 CREDIT CHECK**

## Riding the Yield Curve

The yield curves for U.S. Treasury securities shown here illustrate two alternative cases for riding the yield curve.

The descending yield curve in panel A—for June 30, 1981—occurred during a difficult economic period for the United States. The period combined a deep recession, high inflation, and the first of the large budget deficits that continued throughout the 1980s. As a result, short-term interest rates rose to over 15%. Long-term interest rates were somewhat lower, about 14%, perhaps reflecting expectations that interest rates would fall. So, there was *no* incentive to ride the yield curve—investors obtained higher yields by buying short-term securities.

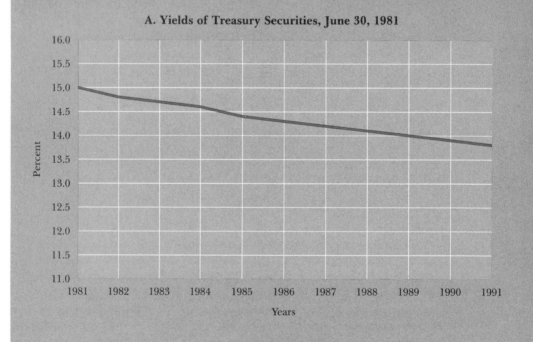

A. Yields of Treasury Securities, June 30, 1981

member, additional demand will raise the price of securities, and thus lower their interest yields. In doing so, the Fed has to consider whether it wants to buy *short-term* securities—Treasury bills—or *long-term* securities—Treasury bonds. Two considerations may affect this choice:

■ The Federal Reserve prefers buying *Treasury bills* because they are traded in particularly active markets, so it is easier to carry out large transactions. Indeed, at times the Fed has had a policy of purchasing *only* Treasury bills—called **Bills Only**.

■ The Federal Reserve prefers buying *Treasury bonds* if its goal is to stimulate capital investment and if it is thought that capital investment is mainly influenced by long-term interest rates.

The ascending yield curve in panel B—for June 30, 1987—occurred in the midst of a good economic situation. Real economic growth was reasonably strong and inflation rates were low. But there was concern that higher inflation rates might arise later. As a result, short-term interest rates were low, about 6%, but long-term rates were higher, close to 8.5%. In this situation, riding the yield curve would work well, assuming that interest rates do not rise during the time the long-term securities are held.

**Source**: *Treasury Bulletin*

**B. Yields of Treasury Securities, June 30, 1987**

The Federal Reserve might be able to meet both these objectives—buying Treasury bills, but influencing Treasury bond interest rates—if changes in Treasury bill rates cause comparable changes in Treasury bond rates. Whether this will occur or not depends on the applicable theory of the term structure of interest rates. Under the market segmentation theory, for example, the Treasury bill and the Treasury bond markets are completely separated, so Treasury bill rates will not influence Treasury bond rates—a policy of Bills Only will not work. In contrast, under the pure expectations theory, if Treasury bill rates fall, then maturity arbitrage will ensure that Treasury bond rates will also fall—Bills Only will work.

# The Interest Rate Risk of Banking Institutions

We have so far only considered how individual investors choose securities with regard to maturity. We will now look at the comparable decision for banks. We saw in Chapter 6 that banks offer intermediation services, making loans (or purchasing other assets) on the one hand, and raising deposits (or issuing other liabilities) on the other. In providing these intermediation services, banks have to consider, among other things, the maturities of their loans and deposits.

Bank decisions regarding maturity are more complicated than those of individual investors because loan and deposit maturities should be considered together. Indeed, banks that fail to have equal amounts of loans and deposits at every maturity level may face **interest rate risk**—their profits may change if interest rates unexpectedly change.

To illustrate how interest rate risk works, consider a bank that has *only* short-term deposits and long-term loans. Since the deposits will mature first, the bank will have to replace them with new deposits until the loans also mature. If interest rates unexpectedly rise during this period, then the bank will have to pay higher-than-expected interest rates on the new deposits, causing its profits to fall. This is the basis of interest rate risk.

## Maturity Gaps as a Measure of Interest Rate Risk

More generally, the interest rate risk of a bank is a function of the maturity balance between its loans and deposits. The greater the difference in maturity between loans and deposits, the greater its interest rate risk. **Maturity gaps**—the difference between the amount of loans and deposits at each maturity level—are often used to measure the interest rate risk of banks, as illustrated in Figure 8.5.

The first step in constructing maturity gaps is to designate the *maturity tiers*—the maturity ranges used to measure the maturity gaps. In Figure 8.5, the maturity tiers are under one year, one to five years, five to ten years, and ten to fifteen years. (This assumes the bank does not deal in loans or deposits with maturities exceeding fifteen years. Also, loans or deposits with unspecified maturities—such as checking deposits—have to be assigned arbitrary, but sensible, maturities.)

Panel A of Figure 8.5 shows the *loans* (L) and *deposits* (D) that mature within each of the maturity tiers.

Panel B shows the *maturity gaps*—loans minus deposits for each maturity tier.

Panel C shows the *cumulative gaps*—the sum of the maturity gaps for each tier and all shorter tiers.

In panel B, we can see that the bank has a *negative gap* at the two short-term maturity tiers and a *positive gap* at the two long-term tiers. This is normally the case for banks: short-term deposits tend to exceed short-term loans, while long-term loans tend to exceed long-term deposits. As a result, the cumulative gaps are negative until the last tier,

Panel A represents the amount of bank loans and deposits at each maturity tier. The bank shown has $1 million in total loans, balanced by $1 million in total deposits.

FIGURE 8.5

**Bank Maturity Gaps**

A. Loans (L) and Deposits (D)

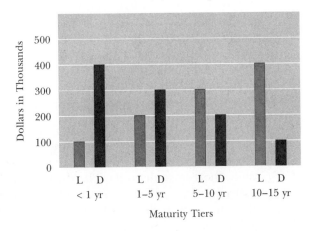

Panel B shows the maturity gaps —the amount of loans minus the amount of deposits in each maturity tier.

B. Maturity Gaps (Loans Minus Deposits)

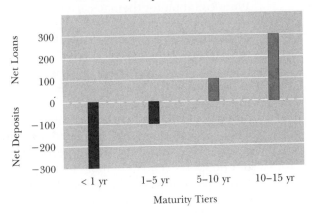

Panel C shows the cumulative maturity gaps—the sum of the maturity gaps for each maturity tier and all shorter maturity tiers.

C. Cumulative Maturity Gap

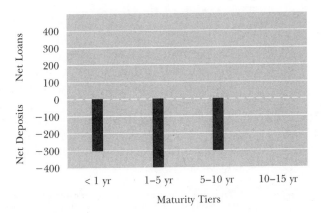

the last cumulative gap being zero because total loans equal total deposits.[1]

The more negative a bank's short-term maturity gaps, the more it is exposed to the risk of rising interest rates. This is true because a negative short-run gap means that the bank has to issue new deposits to replace maturing deposits. The decline in profits that results when interest rates unexpectedly rise will be larger the more new deposits the bank has to issue and the more that interest rates rise.

## The Thrift Institution Disaster from Interest Rate Risk

Thrift institutions (primarily savings and loan associations and savings banks) historically represented the extreme case of interest rate risk among banking institutions—they made very long-term loans based on quite short-term deposits. The thrifts mainly made long-term mortgage loans, because most of their borrowers wanted long-term loans to finance their home purchases. Additionally, thrift institutions could not raise a sufficient volume of long-term deposits to match their long-term mortgage loans.

Thrift institutions actually did well in this situation for many years. It was common for them to earn interest rates of about 8% on mortgages, while they paid interest rates of about 5% on deposits. Thus, as long as deposit interest rates were stable, the institutions earned profits by riding the yield curve—earning higher interest rates on their long-term loans than they paid on their short-term deposits.

Starting in the late 1970s, however, interest rates rose sharply, and most thrift institutions suffered huge losses on this account. In fact, hundreds of them were forced out of business. The nature of the problem is obvious from the yield curve for June 30, 1981, illustrated in Box 8.3. It shows that short-term interest rates reached levels above 15% at the time. To refinance their maturing deposits, the thrift institutions had to pay interest rates that were about this level, while they continued to earn interest only at about 8% on the mortgage loans they had made earlier. This created a disaster for the industry. Even in the late 1980s, many thrift institutions still suffered from the effects of this trauma.

## Tier-Matched Portfolios and Interest Rate Risk

The disaster that struck thrift institutions raises the question of how banking institutions can avoid interest rate risk. The most basic way is to eliminate the maturity gap at each maturity tier—this is called **tier matching**. A tier-matched bank has equal amounts of deposits and loans maturing each year, and since it does not have to attract new deposits to replace maturing deposits, its profits are not affected by unexpected changes in interest rates—it has no interest rate risk. If the bank in Figure 8.5 had practiced tier matching, each bar in panels B and C would be zero.

---

[1] This is true because we are excluding shareholder capital from the analysis. If shareholder capital were included as a source of funds for bank assets, then it would also need to be included, with an assumed maturity, among the bank's liabilities.

Since most depositors prefer short-term deposits and most borrowers prefer long-term loans, banks must take special actions to obtain tier-matched portfolios. A bank can offer higher interest rates on long-term deposits to make them more attractive. And it can charge lower interest rates on short-term loans to increase their attractiveness. But both these solutions cut into profits—raising the cost of deposits or reducing the revenue from loans. As a result, banks face a **risk-return trade-off** when they use tier-matched portfolios: their interest rate risk is low, but this is achieved at the cost of lower profits.

Consequently, banking institutions vary in the degree to which they actually use tier-matched portfolios. Commercial banks normally maintain portfolios that are nearly tier-matched. They can do this because their main customers—business and consumer borrowers—will usually accept relatively short-term loans. In contrast, the mortgage customers of thrift institutions are more reluctant to take short-term loans. However, as described in Box 8.4, thrift institutions now use *adjustable-rate mortgages* to achieve the same effect that would be achieved with short-term mortgages.

There also exist other techniques that banks can use to eliminate, or to hedge, their interest rate risk. These include interest rate futures and options contracts, which we will discuss in Chapter 9. As we will see, these techniques achieve the same effect as tier matching, but they are more flexible under some circumstances.[2]

---

[2] Banks can also achieve results similar to tier matching by matching the *average maturities* of their assets and liabilities over the entire portfolio. This is called *duration matching*—"duration" referring to the average maturity of a portfolio—and is discussed further at the end of Appendix 8.1.

---

## BOX 8.4 BANKING BRIEFS

### Adjustable-Rate Mortgages

Following the thrift institution disaster with interest rate risk, a new type of mortgage—an adjustable-rate (AR) mortgage—was introduced to deal with the problem. The key feature of an AR mortgage is that its interest rate adjusts over time in response to changes in market interest rates.

AR mortgages represent a major benefit to thrift institutions that make mortgage loans with the funds provided by short-term deposits. When market interest rates rise, the institutions' interest costs for new deposits rise, but this is balanced by the higher interest rates the institutions earn on AR mortgages, so profits need not fall. However, the relationship between deposit interest rates and AR mort-

gage rates is not always perfect. In particular, legal restrictions—enacted to protect borrowers—limit how much and how quickly AR mortgage rates may rise. Nevertheless, AR mortgages are a major help for thrift institutions in dealing with their interest rate risk.

Other things being equal, mortgage borrowers, of course, still prefer traditional—fixed-rate—mortgages. As a result, mortgage lenders have to provide borrowers an inducement to take AR mortgages. The main inducement is a lower initial interest rate. So AR mortgages, like tier-matched portfolios, still impose a cost on banking institutions that are trying to avoid interest rate risk.

# Chapter Summary

1. The "term structure of interest rates" refers to the set of interest rates on securities that differ only with respect to their maturity. A yield curve is a graph of the term structure of interest rates.

2. A holding period is the time an investor holds a particular security or a sequence of securities. The holding period return is the amount of interest accumulated per dollar initially invested. Expected rates are the interest rates that are expected to apply to securities—called forward securities—that will begin trading in security markets at later dates. Expected holding period returns are based on the expected interest rates on these securities.

3. The pure expectations (PE) theory assumes that all investors expect the same future interest rates and that they all select the security sequence providing the highest expected holding period return. As a result, in equilibrium, expected holding period returns are equal for all sequences of securities that cover a given holding period. Also, ascending, descending, and horizontal yield curves imply, respectively, that interest rates are expected to rise, fall, or remain unchanged.

4. The liquidity preference (LP) theory maintains that the yield curve is also determined by liquidity premiums—amounts that compensate investors for their liquidity preference. In this case, the shape of a yield curve does not necessarily indicate the market's expectations of future interest rates.

5. Term structure theories are used to evaluate investment strategies and monetary policy. The investment strategy of riding the yield curve, buying long-term securities and selling them prior to their maturity, can be profitable under the LP theory but not under the PE theory. The Federal Reserve's use of Bills Only—buying only Treasury bills for monetary policy—works best under the PE theory.

6. Banking institutions face interest rate risk when the maturities of their loans and deposits are not balanced. Typically, banks have relatively short-term deposits and relatively long-term loans. In this situation, if interest rates rise, bank profits fall, because the deposits will have to be refinanced at the new, higher interest rates.

7. Banks can tier match their portfolios—maintain equal amounts of loans and deposits at each maturity tier—to deal with interest rate risk. In this case, their profits are not affected by unexpected changes in interest rates.

# Key Terms

Bills Only
Expected holding period returns
Expected interest rates
Forward and spot securities
Holding period and holding period return
Interest rate risk
Liquidity premiums

Maturity:
  Arbitrage
  Gaps
Riding the yield curve
Risk-return trade-off
Security sequences
Term structure of interest rates

Term structure theories:

  Liquidity preference (LP)

  Market segmentation

  Preferred habitat

Pure expectations (PE)

Tier matching

Yield curve

## Study Questions

1. Suppose that, as of the current date 0, the yield curve contained the following interest rates:

    Security $S_{0,1}$: $r_{0,1} = 8\%$

    Security $S_{0,2}$: $r_{0,2} = 10\%$

    Security $S_{0,3}$: $r_{0,3} = 8\%$.

    Are these *spot* or *forward securities*? What is the shape of this yield curve?

2. An investor with a three-year holding period is deciding in which securities to invest. He expects the following future short-term interest rates:

    Security $S_{1,2}$: $e_{1,2} = 8\%$

    Security $S_{2,3}$: $e_{2,3} = 8\%$.

    Based on the yield curve information given in Question 1 and the expected interest rates given here, calculate the *annual expected* holding period returns the investor would obtain on the following security sequences:

    a. $\{S_{0,3}\}$,  b. $\{S_{0,2}|S_{2,3}\}$,  c. $\{S_{0,1}|S_{1,2}|S_{2,3}\}$.

3. Which of the security sequences in Question 2 would be chosen by an investor making his investment decision according to the *pure expectations theory*? Briefly explain your answer.

4. Which security sequence in Question 2 might be chosen by an investor making his investment decision according to the *liquidity preference theory*? Briefly explain your answer.

5. Explain why an investor using the *preferred habitat theory* might choose the security sequence in Question 2 that you did not discuss in Questions 4 or 5.

6. Suppose that all the investors in the market have the following expectations for future short-term interest rates:

    $$e_{1,2} = 8\%; \; e_{2,3} = 10\%.$$

    Suppose also that the current short-term interest rate, $r_{0,1}$, is 6%. Based on the pure expectations theory, what are the equilibrium values for the interest rates $r_{0,2}$ and $r_{0,3}$?

7. Based on the information in Question 6, if the term structure of interest rates was determined according to the liquidity preference theory, would you expect each of the following interest rates to be lower, higher, or basically unchanged, relative to its value in Question 6:

    $$r_{0,1}, \; r_{0,2}, \text{ and } r_{0,3}.$$

8. For the interest rate information in Question 6, indicate whether *riding the yield curve* would work under:

    a. the pure expectations theory

    b. the liquidity preference theory.

9. Show a bank balance sheet with total loans and deposits of $100, and with some loans and deposits at each of the following maturity tiers: one, two, and three years.

10. Referring to Question 9, discuss what happens to the bank's profits if, immediately and unexpectedly, interest rates on both loans and deposits rise by one percentage point, and remain at that level.

## Recommended Reading

*More detailed discussions of the theory of the term structure of interest rates—in increasing order of difficulty—include:*

C. Alan Garner, "The Yield Curve and Inflation Expectations," *Economic Review*, Federal Reserve Bank of Kansas City, September/October 1987, pp. 3–15.

James C. Van Horne, *Financial Market Rates and Flows*, 2nd edition, Prentice-Hall, Englewood Cliffs, N.J., 1984.

Burton Malkiel, *The Term Structure of Interest Rates*, Princeton University Press, Princeton, N.J., 1966.

Richard Roll, *The Behavior of Interest Rates*, Basic Books, New York, 1970.

J. Cox, J. Ingersoll, and S. Ross, "A Re-examination of Traditional Hypotheses About the Term Structure

of Interest Rates," *Journal of Finance*, September 1981, pp. 769–800.

*The interest rate risk of banks is discussed in the following articles:*

George Kaufman, "Measuring and Managing Interest Rate Risk," *Economic Perspectives*, Federal Reserve Bank of Chicago, January/February 1986, pp. 16–29.

Donald G. Simonson and George H. Hempel, "Improving Gap Management for Interest Rate Risk," *Journal of Bank Research* 13, Summer 1982, pp. 109–15.

Alden L. Toevs, "Gap Management: Managing Interest Rate Risk in Banks and Thrifts," *Economic Review*, Federal Reserve Bank of San Francisco, Spring 1983, pp. 20–35.

## Appendix 8.1: Yield Curves, Coupon Bonds, and Duration

Our discussion of yield curves used zero-coupon bonds as the example. However, *coupon bonds*—with a cash flow pattern that consists of a series of coupon (interest) payments and a final principal payment—remain the dominant debt security in the financial markets. Yield curves for coupon bonds are complicated because a distinction must be made between the bond's *formal maturity*—the time remaining until the principal amount is repaid—and its *effective maturity*—or *duration*—that takes account of the coupon payment dates.

The duration of a coupon bond is calculated as a weighted average of the time until each cash flow payment is received—counting both coupon payments and principal payments—the weights being the present value of each cash flow payment relative to the total present value of the security. The duration of a zero-coupon bond is equal to its formal maturity because there is just one cash flow payment (combining interest and principal). But for any security with more than one payment, such as a coupon bond, its duration is necessarily less than its formal maturity.

The distinction between the duration and the maturity of a coupon bond is important for investors. Suppose an investor is choosing between two coupon bonds, for example, both of which pay their principal amount of $100 in ten years, but one bond has an annual coupon of $5 (a coupon rate of 5%) and the other has an annual coupon of $10 (a coupon rate of 10%). Based on the maturity date for the principal, both bonds have a maturity of ten years. However, the bond with the 10% coupon rate has the shorter effective maturity—the shorter duration—because a larger percentage of its cash flow payments are represented by interest coupons, most of which are received prior to the date of the principal payment.

The portfolio decisions of banking institutions provide another important application of duration. The tier-matched strategies we discussed in the chapter are restrictive in that they require an exact matching of loans and deposits at each maturity tier. **Duration matching**—matching the duration of total loans and deposits—represents a more flexible strategy. Duration matching provides almost the same level of protection against unexpected interest rate fluctuations as tier matching, but it does not require that the bank exactly balance the amount of loans and deposits at each maturity tier.

---

# Appendix 8.2: Term Structure Theory with Compound Interest

The main text used simple interest to compute holding period returns. In this appendix, we will look at how these returns are computed more precisely with compound interest.

As an example, with compound interest, the total amount accumulated by holding security $S_{0,2}$ is $(1 + r_{0,2})^2$: the amount $(1 + r_{0,2})$ is accumulated by the end of the first year, and the amount $(1 + r_{0,2})(1 + r_{0,2}) = (1 + r_{0,2})^2$ is accumulated by the end of the second year. Similarly, the amount accumulated after two years on the security sequence $\{S_{0,1}|S_{1,2}\}$ is $(1 + r_{0,1})(1 + e_{1,2})$. (The holding period returns based on compound interest include the return of principal as well as accumulated interest.)

So the equilibrium condition of the pure expectations theory—that the two expected holding period returns be equal—would be written:

$$(1 + r_{0,2})^2 = (1 + r_{0,1})(1 + e_{1,2}).$$

This can be solved for the expected interest rate $e_{1,2}$:

$$e_{1,2} = \frac{(1 + r_{0,2})^2}{(1 + r_{0,1})} - 1.$$

For example, if the current yield curve has $r_{0,1} = 5\%$ and $r_{0,2} = 7\%$, then $e_{1,2} = 9.04\%$ ($= [(1.07)^2 / 1.05] - 1$). In contrast, using simple interest, the formula derived in the text for $e_{1,2}$ was:

$$e_{1,2} = 2\,r_{0,2} - r_{0,1}.$$

So under the same yield curve conditions, the result would be $e_{1,2} = 2(7\%) - 5\% = 9.00\%$. Therefore, the difference between simple interest and compound interest for calculating $e_{1,2}$ is only 0.04 percent (9.00% versus 9.04%).

In practice, the difference between simple and compound interest becomes more significant only if the interest rates or the time periods are rather large. To take another example, suppose we were trying to calculate the expected interest rate $e_{9,10}$ based on a known value for $r_{0,9}$ of 9% and a known value for $r_{0,10}$ of 10%. The simple interest formula is:

$$e_{9,10} = 10\,r_{0,10} - 9\,r_{0,9} = (10)(10\%) - (9)(9\%) = 19.00\%.$$

The compound interest formula is:

$$e_{9,10} = \frac{(1 + r_{0,10})^{10}}{(1 + r_{0,9})^9} - 1 = \frac{2.59}{2.17} - 1 = 19.35\%.$$

# 9

# Futures and Options Contracts

*"There was a time when a fool and his money were soon parted, but now it happens to everyone."*

**Adlai Stevenson**

Many new opportunities exist for investors because of *stock index futures contracts*. The main feature that distinguishes trading in stock index futures—a relatively recent development—from traditional stock market trading is the settlement date. Settlement on stock market trades is *immediate* (or within a few days)—buyers promptly pay for their purchases, and sellers promptly deliver stock certificates. In contrast, settlement on stock index futures trades is deferred until a future date—hence the name "futures" contracts. Stock index *options contracts* are similar to futures contracts, but the option holder has the choice of whether or not to complete the transaction.

A trading method based on stock index futures, called *programmed trading*, is blamed by some for the stock market crash of October 1987. People engaged in programmed trading buy or sell stock index futures contracts, while simultaneously doing just the opposite in the stock market. Such *arbitrage* trades will be profitable if the purchases are made in the market with the lower price, while the sales are made in the market with the higher price. Stock index futures were probably not the cause of the stock market crash, but they may have contributed to it, because they allow people to sell large amounts of stock rapidly.

In this chapter, we will study how futures contracts and options contracts are used for the purposes of arbitrage, speculation, and hedging.

---

Futures contracts and options contracts are available for agricultural commodities, common stocks and stock indexes, precious metals, foreign currencies, and securities (such as U.S. Treasury bills and bonds). In this chapter, we will look at the general features of these contracts, and at how banking institutions use the contracts for U.S. Treasury and related securities to hedge their interest rate risk—the risk caused by the maturity imbalance between assets and liabilities that we looked at in Chapter 8.

# Futures Contracts

**Futures contracts** are financial instruments traded in special **futures markets.** Their **settlement date**—the date at which the seller delivers the item and the buyer pays for it—is deferred, sometimes for as long as a year. Futures markets, in effect, represent "a deal to make a deal" in that the price is determined immediately, but the transaction is settled—completed—later. In contrast, in **spot markets** (or cash markets), like the stock market, settlement takes place immediately (or as soon as the paperwork is completed).

Consider a construction company that needs lumber for building homes. If the company needs the lumber immediately, the owner might go down to the local lumber yard, pay for the wood, and take it away. This is a spot market transaction. In contrast, if the construction company is going to need the lumber at a later date, then the owner could enter into a futures contract that would specify the price and the delivery date for the lumber. When that date arrives, the lumber is delivered and the contract price is paid.

Prices in futures markets are determined by demand and supply, in the same fashion as for any other security or commodity. There is also a *term structure* of futures prices, like the "term structure of interest rates" that we looked at in Chapter 8. The "term structure of futures prices" is the relationship between the futures market price for a commodity and the spot market price for the same commodity. This relationship is based on the maturity of the contract—the amount of time that remains until the settlement date.

## Futures Markets

Futures trading for agricultural products originally developed during the nineteenth century to protect farmers against unexpected fluctuations in the prices of their crops. Recently, futures trading has been extended to **financial futures**—for precious metals, foreign currencies, and debt and equity securities. Figure 9.1 shows that financial futures, especially futures contracts in securities, are now the fastest-growing type of futures contracts.

## Functions of Futures Markets

A trader who purchases a futures contract has a **long position**—the obligation to take delivery of the commodity at the settlement date, paying the price agreed on when the contract was originally purchased. A trader with a long position essentially owns the commodity (even though its delivery does not occur until the settlement date), and therefore earns a profit if the price of the commodity rises, and suffers a loss if the price falls.

FIGURE 9.1
**The Trading Volume of Futures Contracts**

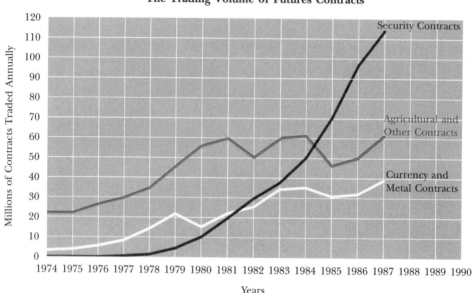

Financial futures contracts—based on securities, foreign currencies, and precious metals—are now growing in trading volume much faster than other futures contracts. **Source:** *Annual Reports*, Commodity Futures Trading Commission, 1988.

A trader who sells a futures contract has a **short position**—the obligation to deliver the commodity at the settlement date for the previously agreed-upon price. If the price of the commodity *falls*, the trader earns a profit relative to the price he would receive from a current spot market sale. By the same token, if the price rises, he suffers an effective loss.

Futures contracts are used for transactions that cannot be efficiently carried out in the spot market; these may include arbitrage, speculation, and hedging. As examples of these three types of transactions, we will consider gold futures contracts. We will assume that the price of gold in the spot market is $400 per ounce, while the price of gold in a one-year futures market—where delivery and payment occur one year later—is $450 per ounce.

### Arbitrage

**Arbitrage transactions** occur when traders seize opportunities to lock in sure profits by buying or selling in futures markets while balancing their positions with opposite transactions in the corresponding spot markets. In our gold futures example, a trader engaging in arbitrage might buy gold in the spot market (for $400 per ounce), while simultaneously selling it in the futures market (for $450 per ounce). The gold is then held for one year, at which time it is delivered to fulfill the futures contract. Although this transaction appears profitable, the expenses of holding gold for a year (which are discussed below) must also be considered.

### Speculation

The goal of **speculation** is to profit from an anticipated change in a commodity's price. In our gold futures example, a speculator might expect that the price of gold will rise to $500 per ounce in one year. Obviously, she should buy gold, either in the spot market or in the futures market. Although the price in the spot market is initially lower ($400 versus $450 per ounce), the difference mainly represents the expense of holding gold for a year. In fact, many speculators favor futures markets over the corresponding spot markets, because no immediate payment is required on futures market purchases.

### Hedging

**Hedging** means taking a position in one market in order to offset an exposure to price changes that results from an existing position in another market. **Futures hedging,** in particular, means taking a position in a futures market in order to offset an existing spot market position.

Consider the owner of a gold mine who is not sure whether the price of gold will rise or fall. He would be happy to sell his gold at the current spot market price of $400 per ounce, but he has to wait until he has accumulated a full bar. To hedge against the risk that the price of gold might fall in the meantime, he would sell gold futures contracts (at $450 per ounce). He would then accumulate gold and deliver it at the end of the year to settle the futures contract. He is compensated for waiting a year to receive his payment by the fact that the futures market price ($450) is higher than the spot market price ($400).

Although arbitrage, speculation, and hedging in futures markets can be distinguished conceptually, the differences between them are often blurred in practice. After all, as we have just seen in the gold trading examples, traders enter into each type of transaction with the hope of profiting in one way or another.

## Some Features of Futures Market Trading

The time lag between the transaction date and the settlement date is the special aspect of futures contracts. We will now look at some of the features of futures market trading that result from this time lag.

### Trading Facilities

Most futures exchanges use "open outcry" auctions for trading—traders in "pits" on the exchange floor shout out offers to buy and to sell. A trade is completed when a buyer and seller are matched at the same price. Since trades will be settled later, an important task of futures exchanges is to keep the **record of open interest**—the record of completed trades that remain to be settled. An example is shown in Table 9.1. (Also see Box 9.1, which shows how futures market trading is reported in the financial press.)

## BOX 9.1 FINANCIAL NEWS

# Reports of Futures Trading

For each futures contract, the type of commodity, the exchange (such as CBT for the Chicago Board of Trade), and the quantity per contract are identified in the heading. The trading prices shown are based on the month that each contract expires. The price of the opening trade of the day is followed by the day's high, low, and closing (settle) prices. Other information includes the high and low prices since the contract started trading ("lifetime"), the amount of open interest, and the trading volume.

## FUTURES PRICES

### —GRAINS AND OILSEEDS—

| | Open | High | Low | Settle | Change | Lifetime High | Lifetime Low | Open Interest |
|---|---|---|---|---|---|---|---|---|
| **CORN (CBT) 5,000 bu.; cents per bu.** | | | | | | | | |
| Sept | 287 | 293 | 278 | 279¾ | − 7¾ | 364 | 180¾ | 62,430 |
| Dec | 296½ | 301½ | 285 | 287 | − 7½ | 370 | 184 | 130,227 |
| Mr89 | 302 | 306½ | 292 | 293½ | − 5¾ | 370 | 193½ | 25,422 |
| May | 301 | 307 | 294 | 295 | − 5 | 369 | 207½ | 11,819 |
| July | 296 | 302 | 292 | 292½ | − ¾ | 360 | 233 | 6,413 |
| Sept | 273 | 277 | 270 | 271½ | + 2½ | 317¾ | 245 | 1,283 |
| Dec | 260 | 263 | 257 | 259½ | + 2 | 295 | 235 | 6,635 |

Est vol 65,000; vol Tues 54,009; open int 244,231, −1,894.

| | Open | High | Low | Settle | Change | Lifetime High | Lifetime Low | Open Interest |
|---|---|---|---|---|---|---|---|---|
| **OATS (CBT) 5,000 bu.; cents per bu.** | | | | | | | | |
| Sept | 254 | 259 | 247½ | 249 | + 5 | 394 | 143 | 2,398 |
| Dec | 258 | 265½ | 254 | 255 | + 4½ | 389¼ | 162 | 3,252 |
| Mr89 | 265 | 270 | 258 | 260 | + 5 | 367¾ | 161 | 1,067 |
| May | 258 | 263 | 252 | 255 | + 7 | 340 | 187 | 347 |
| July | 232 | 243 | 232 | 238 | + 8 | 277 | 230 | 269 |

Est vol 2,000; vol Tues 2,614; open int 7,333, −57.

### —METALS & PETROLEUM—

| | Open | High | Low | Settle | Change | Lifetime High | Lifetime Low | Open Interest |
|---|---|---|---|---|---|---|---|---|
| **COPPER (CMX) 25,000 lbs.; cents per lb.** | | | | | | | | |
| July | 97.50 | 97.50 | 94.80 | 95.55 | − 1.75 | 110.70 | 62.30 | 1,200 |
| Sept | 94.80 | 95.20 | 93.20 | 94.95 | + .95 | 103.70 | 59.45 | 16,459 |
| Dec | 89.80 | 90.50 | 88.30 | 90.45 | + 1.45 | 96.50 | 64.70 | 7,438 |
| Mr89 | 87.00 | 87.70 | 86.30 | 87.45 | + .95 | 93.00 | 66.50 | 2,261 |
| May | 85.50 | 85.60 | 85.50 | 86.25 | + .75 | 89.00 | 73.15 | 452 |
| July | 86.50 | 86.50 | 85.50 | 85.25 | + .75 | 86.50 | 77.50 | 349 |
| Sept | 85.00 | 85.00 | 85.00 | 84.25 | + .75 | 85.00 | 76.00 | 294 |
| Dec | ... | ... | ... | 83.25 | + .75 | 83.10 | 77.45 | 366 |

Est vol 6,000; vol Tues 8,217; open int 28,919, −1,201.

| | Open | High | Low | Settle | Change | Lifetime High | Lifetime Low | Open Interest |
|---|---|---|---|---|---|---|---|---|
| **GOLD (CMX) 100 troy oz.; $ per troy oz.** | | | | | | | | |
| July | ... | ... | ... | 433.30 | + 2.20 | 467.50 | 430.00 | 20 |
| Aug | 430.90 | 434.10 | 430.60 | 433.50 | + 1.80 | 527.00 | 425.00 | 30,790 |
| Oct | 436.00 | 439.50 | 436.00 | 439.00 | + 1.60 | 533.50 | 429.00 | 14,244 |
| Dec | 441.50 | 445.10 | 441.40 | 444.50 | + 1.50 | 546.00 | 430.00 | 44,402 |
| Fb89 | 449.50 | 450.50 | 449.30 | 450.20 | + 1.50 | 549.50 | 445.40 | 10,580 |
| Apr | 454.50 | 455.80 | 454.50 | 456.00 | + 1.50 | 550.00 | 451.00 | 8,089 |
| June | 462.00 | 463.00 | 462.00 | 461.90 | + 1.50 | 570.00 | 455.50 | 12,947 |
| Aug | 467.00 | 467.00 | 467.00 | 468.00 | + 1.50 | 575.00 | 463.30 | 5,622 |
| Oct | 473.80 | 474.50 | 473.80 | 474.00 | + 1.50 | 575.50 | 466.30 | 7,055 |
| Dec | 478.00 | 478.00 | 478.00 | 480.10 | + 1.50 | 514.50 | 472.50 | 7,208 |
| Fb90 | 486.00 | 486.00 | 486.00 | 486.30 | + 1.50 | 516.00 | 485.00 | 3,102 |
| Apr | 491.00 | 491.00 | 491.00 | 492.60 | + 1.50 | 525.80 | 486.00 | 1,376 |

Est vol 61,000; vol Tues 69,524; open int 145,438, −3,088.

### —FINANCIAL—

| | Open | High | Low | Settle | Change | Lifetime High | Lifetime Low | Open Interest |
|---|---|---|---|---|---|---|---|---|
| **BRITISH POUND (IMM) 62,500 pds.; $ per pound** | | | | | | | | |
| Sept | 1.6978 | 1.7300 | 1.6974 | 1.7220 | + .0166 | 1.9012 | 1.6506 | 15,685 |
| Dec | 1.7890 | 1.7190 | 1.6890 | 1.7120 | + .0166 | 1.9000 | 1.6394 | 2,186 |

Est vol 11,627; vol Tues 9,443; open int 17,942, +1,204.

| | Open | High | Low | Settle | Change | Lifetime High | Lifetime Low | Open Interest |
|---|---|---|---|---|---|---|---|---|
| **AUSTRALIAN DOLLAR (IMM) 100,000 dlrs.; $ per A.$** | | | | | | | | |
| Sept | .7943 | .8065 | .7940 | .8063 | + .0025 | .8160 | .7008 | 5,194 |

Est vol 168; vol Tues 522; open int 5,243, +147.

| | Open | High | Low | Settle | Change | Lifetime High | Lifetime Low | Open Interest |
|---|---|---|---|---|---|---|---|---|
| **CANADIAN DOLLAR (IMM) 100,000 dlrs.; $ per Can $** | | | | | | | | |
| Sept | .8228 | .8283 | .8225 | .8279 | + .0020 | .8358 | .7307 | 25,827 |
| Dec | .8200 | .8253 | .8195 | .8252 | + .0020 | .8332 | .7390 | 4,165 |
| Mr89 | .8205 | .8225 | .8205 | .8225 | + .0020 | .8300 | .7570 | 242 |

Est vol 4,706; vol Tues 13,375; open int 30,288, −1,419.

| | Open | High | Low | Settle | Change | Lifetime High | Lifetime Low | Open Interest |
|---|---|---|---|---|---|---|---|---|
| **JAPANESE YEN (IMM) 12.5 million yen; $ per yen (.00)** | | | | | | | | |
| Sept | .7548 | .7657 | .7546 | .7643 | + .0044 | .8485 | .7075 | 44,575 |
| Dec | .7620 | .7723 | .7616 | .7713 | + .0045 | .8530 | .7115 | 2,442 |
| Mr89 | .7767 | .7780 | .7685 | .7781 | + .0046 | .8590 | .7560 | 692 |
| June | | | | .7859 | + .0047 | .8400 | .7630 | 159 |

Est vol 29,747; vol Tues 26,862; open int 47,868, −1,215.

| | Open | High | Low | Settle | Change | Lifetime High | Lifetime Low | Open Interest |
|---|---|---|---|---|---|---|---|---|
| **SWISS FRANC (IMM) 125,000 francs-$ per franc** | | | | | | | | |
| Sept | .6464 | .6582 | .6462 | .6548 | + .0028 | .8120 | .6415 | 25,443 |
| Dec | .6529 | .6650 | .6529 | .6621 | + .0031 | .8210 | .6472 | 1,270 |
| Mar | | | | .6688 | + .0033 | .7735 | .6550 | 182 |

Est vol 26,810; vol Tues 24,238; open int 26,895, −189.

| | Open | High | Low | Settle | Change | Lifetime High | Lifetime Low | Open Interest |
|---|---|---|---|---|---|---|---|---|
| **W. GERMAN MARK (IMM) 125,000 marks; $ per mark** | | | | | | | | |
| Sept | .5361 | .5465 | .5361 | .5440 | + .0027 | .6555 | .5310 | 43,883 |
| Dec | .5405 | .5510 | .5400 | .5482 | + .0026 | .6610 | .5351 | 3,566 |
| Mar | | | | .5524 | + .0026 | .6240 | .5400 | 213 |

Est vol 27,405; vol Tues 24,356; open int 47,662, −1,440.

| | Open | High | Low | Settle | Chg | Discount Settle | Discount Chg | Open Interest |
|---|---|---|---|---|---|---|---|---|
| **TREASURY BILLS (IMM) $1 mil.; pts. of 100%** | | | | | | | | |
| Sept | 92.93 | 92.96 | 92.81 | 92.82 | − .14 | 7.18 | + .14 | 16,497 |
| Dec | 92.69 | 92.71 | 92.56 | 92.56 | − .15 | 7.44 | + .15 | 3,880 |
| Mr89 | 92.95 | 92.66 | 92.52 | 92.52 | − .14 | 7.48 | + .14 | 658 |
| June | 92.45 | 92.50 | 92.35 | 92.35 | − .14 | 7.65 | + .14 | 708 |
| Sept | ... | ... | ... | 92.25 | − .14 | 7.75 | + .14 | 174 |
| Dec | ... | ... | ... | 92.19 | − .13 | 7.81 | + .13 | 144 |

Est vol 6,659; vol Tues 3,260; open int 22,069, +362.

### —INDEXES—

| | Open | High | Low | Settle | Chg | High | Low | Open Interest |
|---|---|---|---|---|---|---|---|---|
| **MUNI BOND INDEX (CBT) $1,000; times Bond Buyer MBI** | | | | | | | | |
| Sept | 87-10 | 87-26 | 87-06 | 87-11 | − 7 | 88-11 | 81-02 | 10,956 |
| Dec | 85-10 | 85-18 | 85-00 | 85-03 | − 8 | 86-30 | 80-16 | 1,012 |
| Mr89 | 83-13 | 83-15 | 83-00 | 83-01 | − 9 | 85-05 | 78-25 | 652 |
| June | 81-16 | 81-18 | 81-01 | 81-03 | − 10 | 82-20 | 77-06 | 781 |
| Sept | | | | 79-08 | − 10 | 79-27 | 78-06 | 199 |

Est vol 5,000; vol Tues 3,055; open int 13,600, +83.
The index: Close 89.02; Yield 8.19.

| | Open | High | Low | Settle | Change | Lifetime High | Lifetime Low | Open Interest |
|---|---|---|---|---|---|---|---|---|
| **S&P 500 INDEX (CME) 500 times index** | | | | | | | | |
| Sept | 266.20 | 266.70 | 262.55 | 262.95 | − 3.20 | 343.50 | 193.00 | 104,632 |
| Dec | 268.80 | 269.00 | 265.00 | 265.30 | − 3.20 | 282.10 | 252.20 | 4,770 |
| Mr89 | 270.80 | 271.00 | 267.15 | 267.45 | − 3.20 | 283.50 | 253.90 | 1,505 |

Est vol 39,277; vol Tues 34,634; open int 110,909, −610.
Indx prelim High 265.83; Low 262.48; Close 262.50 −2.69.

| | Open | High | Low | Settle | Change | Lifetime High | Lifetime Low | Open Interest |
|---|---|---|---|---|---|---|---|---|
| **NYSE COMPOSITE INDEX (NYFE) 500 times index** | | | | | | | | |
| Sept | 150.50 | 150.80 | 148.40 | 148.65 | − 1.70 | 158.10 | 128.50 | 5,576 |
| Dec | 151.95 | 151.95 | 149.95 | 150.05 | − 1.65 | 159.20 | 137.95 | 977 |
| Mr89 | | | | 151.35 | − 1.60 | 159.45 | 144.25 | 298 |

Est vol 7,119; vol Tues 4,152; open int 6,866, −169.
The index: High 150.35; Low 148.72; Close 148.74 −1.29.

**Source:** Wall Street Journal, 28 July 1988.

| TABLE 9.1 The Record of Open Interest | | |
|---|---|---|
| **Trade and Day** | **Long Position** | **Short Position** |
| 1 | L1 bought at 60 | S1 sold at 60 |
| 2 | L2 bought at 65 | S2 sold at 65 |
| 3 | L3 bought at 60 | S3 sold at 60 |

The open interest that results from three futures trades, made on three consecutive days, is shown here. On the first day, trade 1 takes place at a price of 60 between buyer L1 and seller S1. On the following days, trades 2 and 3 take place at different prices between different buyers and sellers.

## Margin Requirements

Futures exchanges face a potential problem with *nonperformance*, which occurs if the short position fails to make delivery or the long position fails to pay for the delivery, at the settlement date. The risk of nonperformance is enhanced by the fact that prices may change dramatically between the trade date and the settlement date, creating large losses for one or the other of the traders.

To guard against nonperformance, futures exchanges set **margin requirements**—amounts of money that traders are required to keep on deposit with the exchange or with their brokers (who act as agents for the exchange). There are two types of margin requirements: "initial" margin and "mark to market" margin.

*Initial margin*—required when traders open new contract positions—represents a security deposit that is returned when the transaction is completed. Initial margin is typically 5% to 10% of the value of a contract.

*Mark to market margin* is computed each day. It equals a trader's theoretical gain or loss from changes in the price of the futures contract during that day's trading. (No actual gain or loss will occur until the settlement date.) Traders with theoretical losses deposit the amount lost as mark to market margin, while traders with theoretical gains receive that amount. This process is called *marking the positions to market*, meaning that each trader's account is kept current with respect to the gains and losses that occur each day.

## Delivery and Closing Transactions

**Delivery** on the settlement date is one method of completing a futures contract. The short position, following the rules of the exchange, delivers the commodity to the long position and is paid for it. However, only a small percentage of futures contracts are actually completed in this way.

Instead, most contracts are completed by traders carrying out a second futures trade, called a **closing transaction**, that offsets the initial trade. For example, referring back to Table 9.1, trader L1—with a long position—would carry out a closing transaction by selling a futures contract—creating a short position—in a new transaction. If trader L1 sells a contract to a new buyer, L4, at the price of 65, then the following entry would be made in the record of open interest:

| **Trade and Day** | **Long Position** | **Short Position** |
|---|---|---|
| 4 | L4 bought at 65 | L1 sold at 65 |

Trader L1 would then notify the exchange (or his broker) that he wants trade 4 to be treated as a *closing transaction*; accordingly, the exchange would cancel his long position in trade 1 against his short position in trade 4.

### Futures Market Regulation

Futures trading has a reputation for questionable practices and so it is closely regulated by the federal Commodity Futures Trading Commission (CFTC). This reputation is based on earlier practices and may no longer be deserved, but peculiar things do keep happening, as illustrated in Box 9.2.

## The Term Structure of Futures Prices

The price of a futures contract is determined by the demand and supply of the traders in the futures market. However, the futures market price is not independent of the spot market price of the same commodity. In particular, *arbitrage* trading promotes a close relationship between the spot market price and the futures market price.

The **basis** is the amount by which the futures market price of a commodity, $P_f$, exceeds its spot market price, $P_s$:

$$P_f = P_s + \text{basis}.$$

---

BOX 9.2 CREDIT CHECK

## Cornering the Silver Market

The worst scandal in a generation racked the futures markets when the Hunt family of Texas tried to corner the market in silver during 1979 and 1980. To *corner a market*, a trader amasses almost the total supply of the commodity available in the spot market, and in addition buys large numbers of long positions in the futures market. Then, as the settlement date for the futures contracts approaches, the perpetrator executes a *short squeeze*, forcing traders with short positions to pay a high price to be relieved of their obligation to deliver the commodity. At this point, these traders have nowhere else to turn to obtain the commodity.

The Hunts bought large quantities of silver futures contracts and all the silver they could get in the spot market. To other traders, it seemed that the demand for silver was high and the supply was low, so the price rose dramatically—from under $10 an ounce to nearly $50 an ounce—in both the spot and futures markets.

However, it was then discovered by the futures exchange that the Hunts had broken the rules limiting the number of futures contracts that one group is allowed to control. When this was made public, the price of silver plummeted and the Hunts were forced to sell their silver at a huge loss.

## The Cost of Carry

The *cost of carry* is the main variable affecting the difference between the spot market price $P_s$ and the futures market price $P_f$ for a commodity. The cost of carry consists of three main components:

cost of carry = interest cost
             + storage cost − dividend yield.

*Interest cost* is the opportunity cost of the funds used to buy the commodity in the spot market. The interest cost is usually determined by the short-term interest rate.

*Storage cost* refers to the cost of storing the commodity over the holding period. For agricultural commodities, these costs can be high, particularly right after a harvest when silo space is at a premium. However, for most financial futures contracts, even the precious metals, these costs are small.

*Dividend yield* is the return traders earn from the commodity while holding it. For example, arbitrage traders receive dividends on the common stocks they hold when carrying out spot-to-futures arbitrage in stock index futures. This dividend income reduces the cost of carry.

For most commodities, moreover, the basis equals the **cost of carry**—the expense of holding the commodity until it is delivered. Box 9.3 discusses the factors that determine the cost of carry. The **spot price parity** is defined as the futures market price that is equal to the spot market price $P_s$ plus the cost of carry:

$$P_f = P_s + cost\ of\ carry = spot\ price\ parity. \qquad (9.1)$$

### How Arbitrage Affects Futures Prices

Arbitrage trading generally forces the spot price parity relationship of equation (9.1) to hold.[1] *Spot-to-futures arbitrage*—buying the commodity in the spot market and selling it in the futures market—occurs if the futures price $P_f$ exceeds the spot price parity:

$$P_f > spot\ price\ parity\ (= P_s + cost\ of\ carry).$$

Arbitrage traders buy the commodity in the spot market at price $P_s$ and simultaneously sell it in the futures market at price $P_f$. The commodity is then held until the settlement date for the futures contract at which point it is delivered and payment is received at price $P_f$. The arbitrage purchases in the spot market cause the spot market price to rise, and the arbitrage sales in the futures market cause the futures price to fall. These pressures eliminate the original difference between the futures price and the spot price parity.

[1] The spot parity relationship may not hold for certain *perishable* agricultural commodities, because these commodities deteriorate too rapidly to allow for arbitrage. Instead, the futures price is determined simply by the demand and supply for futures contracts.

Arbitrage in the opposite direction, *futures-to-spot*, occurs if the futures price $P_f$ is below the spot price parity:

$$P_f < \text{spot price parity } (= P_s + \text{cost of carry}).$$

In this case, arbitrage traders will buy in the futures market and sell in the spot market. Their futures market purchases cause the futures price $P_f$ to rise and their spot market sales cause the spot market price $P_s$ to fall, thus again forcing the futures price toward the spot price parity.

However, futures-to-spot arbitrage can be difficult to carry out if the spot market transaction is a *short sale*—the trader is selling a commodity he does not have. To make a short sale, the trader has to *borrow* the commodity, and this can be difficult and expensive to arrange. There-fore, futures prices sometimes remain below the spot price parity because there is not enough futures-to-spot arbitrage to eliminate the difference.

Of the two main factors that determine a futures price for a com-modity—the spot market price and the cost of carry—unexpected changes in the spot market price are the more important in causing unexpected changes in the futures price. Changes in the cost of carry normally account for only a small part of the overall fluctuations in futures prices. The result is that *spot markets and futures markets are basically just two parts of the same overall market*—only the settlement dates are different. Due to arbitrage, a change in the price in one of these markets is generally promptly reflected in a price change in the other market. In fact, this is a main purpose of the programmed trading in the stock market that we discussed at the beginning of the chapter.

## Interest Rate Futures and Bank Hedging

Futures contracts based on securities like U.S. Treasury bills—called *interest rate futures*—are among the new financial futures contracts in-troduced in recent years. We will now look at how banks use interest rate futures contracts to hedge their interest rate risk. We will focus on **Treasury bill futures contracts** because these contracts are actively used by banks for hedging interest rate risk.

### The Treasury Bill Futures Contract

We will first consider the Treasury bill itself. Following the notation we used in Chapter 8, the current one-year Treasury bill—trading in the *spot market* on the current date 0—is $S_{0,1}$, the first subscript indicating that it trades in the spot market as of date 0, and the second subscript indicating that it matures at date 1. The annual interest rate on this Treasury bill is denoted $r_{0,1}$. Each Treasury bill is a zero-coupon security that will pay \$1,000 at its maturity date. Thus, we can calculate the market price $P_{0,1}$ of security $S_{0,1}$ as the present value of $1,000, using the Treasury bill interest rate $r_{0,1}$ as the discount rate:

$$P_{0,1} = \frac{1,000}{(1 + r_{0,1})}. \tag{9.2}$$

For example, when $r_{0,1}$ is 6%, then $P_{0,1}$ is $943.40 (that is, $1,000/1.06).

We can now look at the futures contract. We will assume that each futures contract refers to one Treasury bill, like the one just described, except that the Treasury bill must become available for futures contract delivery at date 1.[2] We will refer to this Treasury bill as $S_{1,2}$, the first subscript indicating that it becomes available at date 1 and the second subscript indicating that it matures at date 2. As we discussed in Chapter 8, $S_{1,2}$ is a *forward security*—its price, $P_{1,2}$ and interest rate, $r_{1,2}$, are not known as of date 0 because the security only begins trading in the spot market at date 1.

However, futures market trading at date 0 will determine a *futures price $F_{1,2}$* for Treasury bill $S_{1,2}$. There will also be a corresponding *futures interest rate $f_{1,2}$*. The relationship between the futures price and futures interest rate is:[3]

$$F_{1,2} = \frac{1,000}{(1 + f_{1,2})}. \tag{9.3}$$

By comparing equation (9.3) with equation (9.2), we can see that $F_{1,2}$ is related to $f_{1,2}$ in the same way that $P_{0,1}$ is related to $r_{0,1}$. So, if the futures interest rate is 6%, then the futures price will be $943.40, just as would be the case for the Treasury bill itself.

## Interest Rate Futures and Interest Rate Risk

As explained in Chapter 8, banks face interest rate risk if they have maturity imbalances between their assets and liabilities. Suppose, for example, that a bank makes $1 million of loans with a two-year maturity and a 10% annual interest rate, while it has $1 million of deposits with a one-year maturity and a 6% annual interest rate. The bank then earns profits of $40,000 (4% of $1 million) in the first year.

However, interest rates could be higher at the end of the first year, at date 1, when the bank has to refinance its $1 million of deposits for another year. If the bank has to pay an additional one percentage point of interest (7% versus the original 6%) on the new deposits, for example, then its profits during the second year would fall by $10,000 ($10,000 = 1% of $1 million). This is the bank's interest rate risk.

[2] Actual Treasury bill futures contracts are based on larger units, such as $100,000 of Treasury bills.

[3] The futures interest rate, $f_{1,2}$, is related to the expected interest rate, $e_{1,2}$, that applies to the security $S_{1,2}$, as discussed in Chapter 8. Indeed, these two rates will be equal unless investors in the futures market are risk averse.

Fortunately for banks, they can sell (take a short position in) Treasury bill futures contracts to hedge—to offset or even eliminate—their interest rate risk. We will now look at how this works and at some of the problems.

## Futures Contract Hedging and Interest Rate Risk

The source of interest rate risk is the possibility that interest rates may be higher in one year when the bank has to refinance its deposits. The risk would be avoided if the bank could fix currently (at date 0) the interest rate it will have to pay on the new deposits.

Selling a Treasury bill futures contract at date 0 immediately determines the interest rate the bank will effectively pay to refinance its deposits at date 1. This works because selling a Treasury bill is akin to issuing additional bank deposits. So, by selling a Treasury bill futures contract, the bank fixes its interest rate currently, even though the transaction will be completed one year later.

Just before the futures contract matures, the bank will repurchase it as a closing transaction. In this process, the bank will earn profits—given that interest rates actually rise—because it will have sold the futures contract for more than the repurchase price. (Remember, when the Treasury bill interest rate rises, the price of a Treasury bill futures contract falls.)

The futures contract position is a hedge against interest rate risk because the profits earned on the futures contract cancel the higher interest rate the bank has to pay on its new deposits. Thus, by using futures contracts, it is *as if* the bank were able to refinance its deposits at the original (low) deposit rate.

## Hedging Interest Rate Risk: A Numerical Example

These concepts can be clarified by a numerical example in which we evaluate the effectiveness of a futures contract hedge against an increase in interest rates.

### Initial Situation at Date 0

Assume again that the bank initially makes $1 million of 10% loans that mature in two years and that it has $1 million of 6% deposits that mature in one year. The Treasury bill rate ($r_{0,1}$) and the futures market interest rate ($f_{1,2}$) are both 6% at date 0. This implies that futures market traders do not expect the Treasury bill rate to change over the year.

Referring to equation (9.3), the futures price $F_{1,2}$ will be $943.40 per contract when the futures interest rate $f_{1,2}$ is 6%. To sell $1 million worth of Treasury bill futures contracts at this price, the bank will sell 1,060 contracts ($1 million/$943.40), each representing one Treasury bill.

### The Increase in Interest Rates

Now assume that the Treasury bill rate, the futures interest rate, and the rate the bank has to pay on new deposits all rise from 6% at date 0 to 7% at date 1. As a result, the futures contract price $F_{1,2}$ will fall to $934.58 ($1,000/1.07). The bank buys the futures contracts at this price to close its position. Its profit per contract is $8.82 ($943.40 − $943.58), so the profit on 1,060 contracts is $9,349. The bank earns a profit on its futures contracts because it had a short position and the futures price went down (because the interest rate went up). If these profits are invested for one year at a 7% annual interest rate, then the final futures contract profits accumulated by date 2 will equal $10,000 ($9,349 × 1.07).

### Overall Effect on Bank Profits

To have a complete picture, we have to look at how the bank makes out both on its futures market contracts and on the interest cost of its deposits. A rise in deposit interest rates of 1% costs the bank $10,000 (1% of $1 million). However, we have just seen that by date 2 the bank will have earned futures contracts profits of $10,000. So, overall, bank profits are not affected. This is the benefit of hedging interest rate risk with futures contracts.

## Three Problems of Hedging with Futures Contracts

We will now look at three problems that may arise when banks use futures contracts to hedge interest rate risk.

### Futures Contract Hedges When Interest Rates Fall

The hedging of interest risk with futures contracts also works when interest rates fall rather than rise, but it works in just the opposite direction. That is, the bank will have a *loss* on the futures contract position, but it will earn *additional profits* from the lower interest cost of deposits. So the bank's profits are still unaffected by the interest rate change.

However, if interest rates fall, the bank will regret that it carried out the futures hedge: had it not hedged, it would not have a loss on the futures contract, and it would still have the benefit of lower deposit interest rates. Unfortunately, there is no way to avoid this consequence of hedging interest rate risk with futures contracts. The gain or loss on the futures contracts always cancels the gain or loss on deposit interest, whichever way interest rates change. Later, we will see that options contracts provide one way of dealing with this problem.

### Futures Hedging and Expected Interest Rate Changes

A second problem with futures contract hedges concerns the initial futures contract interest rate. In our numerical example, the initial futures contract interest rate $f_{1,2}$ and the initial Treasury bill interest rate $r_{0,1}$ were both 6%. The result was that the futures contracts provided a basically cost-free method of hedging interest rate risk.

But suppose the initial futures interest rate had been 7%, even though the initial Treasury bill rate was 6%. This would indicate that the market expects the Treasury bill interest rate to rise to 7% by date 1. In our example, interest rates did rise by one percentage point, so these expectations would have been correct.

Given that the initial futures interest rate is 7%, this rate will not change when the Treasury bill rate rises to 7% at date 1. Therefore, the price of the futures contracts will not change and the bank will not earn profits on its contracts, so the contracts will fail to act as a hedge for the bank's higher deposit interest costs.

This means that a bank can hedge its profits by selling futures contracts only when the increase in interest rates is *not already expected* by traders. This aspect of hedging interest rate risk also makes sense: the market will no more allow a trader to hedge against an interest rate increase that is expected to happen than an insurance company will sell fire insurance on a home that it expects is about to burn down.

### The Relationship of Treasury Bill Rates and Deposit Rates

The third problem associated with futures contract hedging is that *Treasury bill rates and bank deposit rates do not necessarily change by the same amount.* As illustrated in Figure 9.2, bank deposit rates follow the basic pattern of Treasury bill rates, but deposit rates often change by a smaller amount. This means that profits (or losses) on futures contracts may be larger than the corresponding losses (or profits) that result from changes in bank deposit rates.

Banks can try to deal with this problem by selling a smaller number of futures contracts to hedge their interest rate risk. But given that the

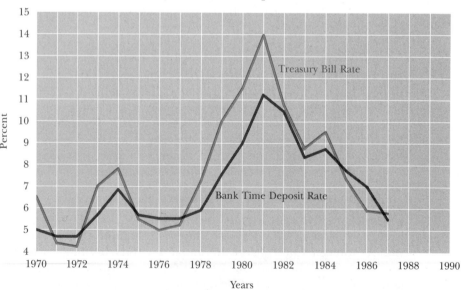

FIGURE 9.2
**Treasury Bill and Bank Deposit Interest Rates**

Bank deposit rates follow the pattern of Treasury bill rates closely enough that banks can use Treasury bill futures contracts to hedge the risk of changes in deposit rates. The two rates can nevertheless change by different amounts. **Source:** *Sourcebook*, U.S. League of Savings Institutions, 1988.

relationship between the Treasury bill rate and the deposit rate can change unpredictably, the bank may still find at times that it has sold the wrong number of futures contracts.

### In Conclusion

We have seen that future contracts have limitations as instruments for hedging interest rate risk. Nevertheless, they are being used by banks— especially by large banks—to an increasing extent, because interest rate risk is such a serious problem.

## Synthetic Loans

Banks also use futures contracts to construct **synthetic loans**. This means that a bank changes the nature of a loan by combining it with a futures contract. We will look at two examples—synthetic adjustable-rate loans and synthetic fixed-rate loans.

### Synthetic Adjustable-Rate Loans

Box 8.4 in Chapter 8 indicates that thrift institutions are using *adjustable-rate (AR) mortgages* to deal with their maturity imbalances between long-term mortgages and short-term deposits. However, because mortgage borrowers generally dislike AR mortgages, the thrift institutions have had to offer lower initial interest rates on AR mortgages, making them a costly means of reducing maturity imbalances.

An alternative approach is for a bank (or thrift institution) to make a traditional, long-term, fixed-rate mortgage, but then to sell futures contracts to transform the transaction into a **synthetic adjustable-rate loan**. Remember that the problem with fixed-rate mortgages is that the bank's interest earnings do not rise if market interest rates rise—the loan rate is fixed. However, the bank can combine a fixed-rate mortgage loan with a short position in a financial futures contract—on which it earns a profit if interest rates rise. Therefore, its income on the combination of the fixed-rate mortgage and the futures contract—the synthetic adjustable-rate mortgage—will change *as if* the bank had made an AR mortgage loan.

### Synthetic Fixed-Rate Loans

The same idea can be applied by banks to create **synthetic fixed-rate loans**. A need for these loans arises when banks choose to make adjustable-rate (AR) loans, even though their borrowers prefer fixed-rate loans. Instead of offering lower interest rates on AR loans, banks can construct synthetic fixed-rate loans for their borrowers. The technique again involves selling Treasury bill futures contracts.

The desired effect is to keep the borrower's loan cost unchanged, even when interest rates rise. If interest rates do rise, the actual AR loan rate will rise; but the profits the borrower earns on the futures contract cancel the effect of the higher loan rate. This the basis of a synthetic fixed-rate loan.

The problems we just discussed with regard to hedging interest rate risk with futures contracts also apply to synthetic loans. Nevertheless, synthetic loans are being widely used because they can be helpful for both the lender and the borrower.

# Options Contracts

We have seen that futures contracts impose contractual *obligations* on traders: traders with short positions *must* make delivery of the commodity on the settlement date; and traders with long positions *must* accept delivery of the commodity and pay for it. In contrast, with *options contracts*, as their name suggests, traders have choices. Holders of *call option* contracts can decide whether they want to take delivery. Holders of *put option* contracts can decide whether they want to make delivery. Options contracts are therefore more complicated than futures contracts, but they provide traders a wider range of investment opportunities.

## Call Options

A **call option** contract, like a futures contract, consists of two trading positions: the *option holder has the long position* and the *option writer has the short position*. The term "call option" derives from the fact that the option holder can "call" the commodity, forcing the option writer to sell it to him at an established price. The **option holder** can therefore **exercise** the option to buy the commodity any time until the **option expiration date** at a set price—called the **strike price**.

Option holders want the price of the commodity to rise so that it is profitable to exercise the option or to sell it to someone else. But if the price of the commodity falls, option holders lose only the market price they paid for the option—that is, they just do not exercise their option.

The **option writer** is the seller of the option and must make delivery of the commodity whenever the holder decides to exercise the option. For taking on this obligation, the option writer is paid the option's market price—also called the *option premium*—by the option holder. Option writers want the price of the commodity to fall or to remain unchanged so that the option will not be exercised. If the price of the commodity actually rises and the option is exercised, the option writer is then in the unhappy position of having to sell the commodity for a price—the strike price—that is less than its market price at the time.

## The Market Price of Call Options

Options contracts are traded in the United States for many of the commodities and securities for which futures contracts are traded. Options contracts on common stocks are the most actively traded, so we will use them to illustrate our discussion. As our example, consider a call option on the common stock of MBA Inc., with a strike price of $20 per share and six months remaining before it expires. The holder, by exercising this option, can buy shares of MBA at $20 a share until the option expires.

### The Value of Call Options at Expiration

The market price of a call option—the option premium—is determined by option market trading. Figure 9.3 illustrates how the price of the MBA call option is determined. We will start by considering the value of the call option *just before it expires*. This value is illustrated by the red line in Figure 9.3 labeled *option value at expiration*.

The value of the option at expiration depends on the market price of MBA stock at that time. If the price of a share of MBA stock in the stock market is $20 or less—equal to or less than the strike price of the option—then the value of the option is zero. In this case, the option holder would do as well or better buying MBA stock directly in the stock market. So there is no value to owning or exercising the option.

FIGURE 9.3

**The Market Price (Premium) of a Call Option**

Call Option for MBA Inc. with Strike Price of $20 per Share

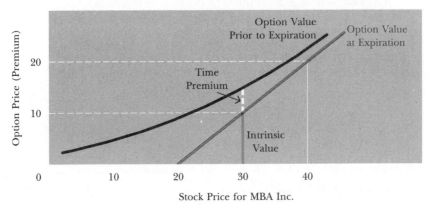

The line labeled *option value at expiration* reflects the value of the option just before it expires. This also equals the option's *intrinsic value*—the difference between the market price of the stock and the strike price of the call option (or zero, if the difference is negative).

The line labeled *option value prior to expiration* represents the price of the option when time remains until it expires. The option price is the sum of the intrinsic value and the *time premium*—the value to the option holder of having time to decide whether or not to exercise the option. The time premium approaches zero as the expiration date approaches.

However, if the price of MBA stock is above $20 per share, then the option's premium at expiration will reflect, dollar for dollar, the difference between the price of MBA stock and the option's $20 strike price. For example, if MBA stock is selling at $30 per share, then the option premium at expiration would be $10 a share, as indicated in Figure 9.3.

The value of a call option at its expiration date is also described as the option's *intrinsic value*—the difference between the stock price and the option's strike price—as long as the difference is positive (otherwise, the intrinsic value is zero). For example, when the stock price is $30 and the option's strike price is $20, the option has an intrinsic value of $10 per share. On the expiration date, the option's premium will precisely equal its intrinsic value.

### The Value of Call Options Prior to Expiration

We can now look at the more general question of the value of a call option when time remains before it expires. For this case, the market price of the MBA call option is represented in Figure 9.3 by the brown line labeled *option value prior to expiration*. Prior to the expiration date, the option's total value exceeds its intrinsic value by the *time premium*. The time premium reflects the possibility that the stock price will rise before the expiration date.

The time premium of a call option will be greater:

1. The more volatile the stock price is expected to be.

2. The more time that remains until the expiration date.

If the stock price is expected to be more volatile, then the chances are greater that by the expiration date the stock price will exceed the option's strike price by a large amount. The chances of this happening are greater the more time that remains until the option expires.

## Investment Applications with Call Options

Options contracts are used for the same speculative and hedging purposes as futures contracts. Speculators are generally the holders (buyers) of call options, and hedgers are generally the writers (sellers) of call options.[4] Box 9.4 discusses how options are also often included as part of securities, such as bonds and mortgages.

[4] Arbitrage trades can also be carried out between an options market and the corresponding spot market or futures market. Such arbitrage will keep the option price in line with the corresponding spot market or futures market price.

---

**BOX 9.4 CREDIT CHECK**

## Options as Components of Securities

Some financial instruments—like bonds and mortgages—incorporate call option features. The "call features" of corporate and municipal bonds, for example, give bond issuers the right to prepay their debts before the scheduled payment dates. Consequently, interest rates on callable bonds are higher than rates on comparable noncallable bonds, the higher rates representing the option premium paid by the issuer to have the privilege of calling the bond. Most mortgage borrowers also have the option to repay the debt prior to its stated maturity.

### Speculators as Holders of Call Options

A speculator who expects the price of MBA stock to increase significantly would consider buying an MBA call option. His cash outlay would be the market price paid for the option. If the MBA stock price then soars, either he can exercise the option, buying MBA stock at the lower strike price, or he can sell the option, realizing a profit because the option's premium will rise in step with its greater intrinsic value.

Call options can be more attractive for speculators than futures contracts or stock market purchases because, if the stock price falls, the loss for an option holder is limited to the premium (the option's market price) paid. And the premiums paid for options are not very high. The premium on a six-month option, for example, with a strike price equal to the current stock market price of the stock, is usually between 5% and 10% of the stock price. The speculator can lose no more than that.

### Hedgers as Writers of Call Options

Large institutional investors such as pension funds frequently write call options for hedging purposes. If a pension fund fears that the price of a stock it is holding will soon fall, the fund could simply sell the stock, but this might be expensive or inconvenient to do. Instead, the fund might write a call option against the shares it holds. The fund then receives the premiums paid by the option holders. How well the fund makes out with this strategy depends on what happens to the price of the stock:

- If the stock price is unchanged at the expiration date of the option, then the option will not be exercised and the option premium will represent profits for the fund.
- If the stock price falls, then again the option will not be exercised. In this case, there will be a loss on the stock, but the premium received for the option serves to offset (hedge) this loss.
- If the stock price rises, then the option will be exercised by the holder, so the fund will receive less for the stock than the market price. Nevertheless, it is better off (by the value of the premium received) than it would be if it had sold its stock at the lower initial price.

## Put Options

**Put options** are the opposite of call options, in that they give the option holder—now the short position—the right to sell the optioned stock to the option writer—now the long position—at the strike price. The put option holder pays the option writer the option premium for this privilege.

Figure 9.4 illustrates how premiums are determined for put options, again using MBA stock as the example. The line labeled *option value at expiration* represents the premium of an MBA put option with a strike price of $20 per share just before it expires. Put options are valuable when the market price of the stock is *less* than the strike price—the price at which the holder can sell stock to the option writer. This is why the value line has a negative slope, with the option's value rising, the lower the price of MBA stock.

The intrinsic value of a put option equals the strike price of the option minus the market price of the stock, just the opposite of a call option. If the market price of the stock is above the strike price, the put option has no value, and it will not be exercised.

FIGURE 9.4
**The Market Price of a Put Option**
Put Option for MBA Inc. with Strike Price of $20 per Share

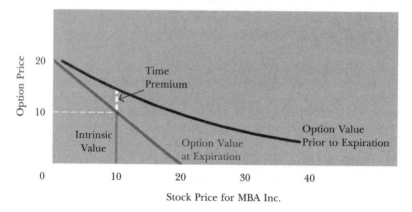

Stock Price for MBA Inc.

The line labeled *option value at expiration* reflects the value of the option just before it expires. This also equals the option's *intrinsic value*—the difference between the strike price of the put option and the market price of the stock (or zero, if the difference is negative).

The line labeled *option value prior to expiration* represents the price of the option when time remains until it expires. The option price is the sum of the intrinsic value and the *time premium*—the value to the option holder of having time to decide whether or not to exercise the option. The time premium approaches zero as the expiration date approaches.

The line labeled *option value prior to expiration* in Figure 9.4 shows the market value of the put option when there is time remaining before it expires. As with call options, the market price of a put option includes a time premium which is larger for more volatile stocks and when more time remains before the option expires.

The holder of a put option profits if the stock price falls, but suffers no loss beyond the premium paid for the option if the stock price rises. Thus, investors with volatile stock holdings might purchase put options as insurance against a decline in the value of their stocks. The option premium represents the cost of buying the downside protection. Put option writers are paid the option premium for taking the risk that the stock price will fall and the option will be exercised (stock will be "put" to them). If, instead, the stock price rises, then the option will not be exercised, and the option writer keeps the premium as profit.

## Interest Rate Options

Options contracts on securities such as Treasury bills provide a solution to one of the problems mentioned earlier regarding futures contracts—that banks will regret having hedged their interest rate risk if it turns out that interest rates fall. Instead, to hedge their interest rate risk, banks can purchase Treasury bill *put option* contracts.

If Treasury bill rates then rise, so Treasury bill prices fall, the put option will appreciate in value, just as would a short futures contract position. So a put option provides the same hedge against rising interest rates as a futures contract. Moreover, if interest rates fall, then the put option can just be allowed to expire unused. In contrast, we saw that a bank will suffer a loss if it sells futures contracts and interest rates fall. This is the advantage of using put options to hedge interest rate risk.

On the other hand, put options contracts also have a cost—the option premium—that does not arise with futures contracts. The option premium is the price the bank has to pay to induce someone to take on the obligation of being the option writer. The option premium therefore represents the cost of using interest rate options for hedging. In addition, the other practical problems that we discussed with regard to futures contracts also apply, by and large, to options contracts.

Overall, there is no simple rule for whether banks should use futures contracts or options contracts for hedging interest rate risk. Individual banks come to different decisions, depending on whether they are willing to pay an up-front fee (options contracts) or are willing to accept lower profits if interest rates fall (futures contracts).

## Chapter Summary

1. Futures contracts are financial instruments for which the settlement of trades is deferred, sometimes for as long as a year. Futures markets have long existed for agricultural commodities. "Financial futures" have developed more recently for debt instruments, precious metals, foreign currencies, and stock indexes. Futures contracts are used for transactions involving arbitrage, speculation, and hedging.

2. Arbitrage transactions involve making two trades simultaneously, one in the spot market and the other in the futures market for the same commodity. Arbitrage transactions force the futures price of a commodity to equal its spot market price plus the cost of carrying the commodity from the current date until the settlement date of the futures contract.

3. Futures market speculation involves buying or selling a futures position in order to profit from an anticipated price change. Futures market hedging arises when a trader has an initial spot market position in the commodity and then takes the opposite position in the futures market in order to eliminate the risk of unexpected price changes.

4. Banks use interest rate futures contracts—based on Treasury bills and similar securities—to hedge the interest rate risk that results from imbalances in the maturities

of their assets and liabilities. Synthetic adjustable-rate and synthetic fixed-rate loans can also be created using interest rate futures.

5. Options contracts differ from futures contracts in that option holders have the right, but not the obligation, to take or make delivery of the commodity. There are two kinds of options contracts: call options and put options. Options contracts are used for the same arbitrage, speculation, and hedging purposes as futures contracts, but option holders have the flexibility of deciding to use the contract only when it is profitable to do so. In particular, banks can use interest rate options contracts to hedge their interest rate risk.

## Key Terms

**Futures contracts:**
   **Closing transactions**
   **Delivery**
   **Long position**
   **Margin requirements**
   **Open interest**
   **Settlement**
   **Short position**
   **Treasury bill**
**Futures prices:**
   **Basis**
   **Cost of carry**
   **Spot price parity**
**Futures transactions:**
   **Arbitrage**

**Hedging**
**Speculation**
**Markets:**
   **Financial futures**
   **Futures**
   **Spot**
**Options contracts:**
   **Call**
   **Exercise date**
   **Expiration date**
   **Put**
   **Strike price**
**Synthetic loans:**
   **Adjustable rate**
   **Fixed rate**

## Study Questions

1. Why might a candy company producing chocolate bars worry about fluctuations in the price of cocoa? How would it use the futures market in cocoa to hedge its risk?

2. How would a country exporting coffee hedge its risk with regard to changes in the price of coffee? Why could these transactions also be interpreted as speculating on the price of coffee?

3. Suppose the S&P 500 stock index is currently 200, while the price of the futures contract based on the S&P 500 index, for settlement one year later, is 210. The annual one-year interest rate is 10% and the stocks in the S&P index pay an average 5% dividend rate. Show why these conditions indicate that the futures price equals the spot price parity.

4. Referring to Question 3, suppose that the

futures price rises to 220, everything else being unchanged. Describe the type of arbitrage transactions that are profitable in this situation. What effect will these transactions have on the price of the stock index futures contracts? On the stock market itself?

5. How do the obligations of the long positions on a futures contract and on a call option contract differ with respect to taking delivery of the commodity?

6. Suppose a bank has $1 million of one-year loans at a 10% interest rate and $1 million of two-year deposits at a 6% rate. (This is just the opposite of the normal case discussed in the text.) What happens to the bank's profits if interest rates unexpectedly rise by one percentage point at the end of the first year? What futures contract position should the bank take to hedge its interest rate risk?

7. Referring to Question 6, what are the advantages and disadvantages of the bank

using interest rate *options*, instead of interest rate *futures*, to hedge this interest rate risk?

8. Referring again to Question 6, how could the bank use interest rate futures contracts to create a synthetic adjustable-rate deposit to hedge its interest rate risk?

9. The common stock of M&B Inc. is currently $25 per share. A *call option* on M&B stock has a strike price of $20 and has six months to go before it expires. The market price (total premium) of the call option is $7 per share. What is the intrinsic value of the call option? What is the time premium of the call option?

10. The common stock of M&B Inc. is still $25 per share. A *put option* on M&B stock has a strike price of $20 and has six months to go before it expires. The total premium of the put option is $2 per share. What is the intrinsic value of the put option? What is the time premium of the put option?

## Recommended Reading

*An accessible introduction to futures markets:*

Robert W. Kolb, *Understanding Futures Markets*, Scott, Foresman, Glenview, Ill., 1985.

*A thorough, accurate, and readable survey by the staff of the Federal Reserve:*

Myron L. Kwast, *Financial Futures and Options in the U.S. Economy*, Board of Governors of the Federal Reserve System, Washington, D.C., 1986.

*The following articles discuss interest rate futures contracts and their use by banking institutions:*

Elijah Brewer, "Bank Gap Management and the Use of Financial Futures," *Economic Perspectives*, Fed-

eral Reserve Bank of Chicago, March/April 1985, pp. 12–22.

G. D. Koppenhaver, "Futures Options and Their Use by Financial Intermediaries," *Economic Perspectives*, Federal Reserve Bank of Chicago, January/February 1986, pp. 18–30.

Anatoli Kuprianov, "Options on Short-Term Interest Rate Futures," *Economic Review*, Federal Reserve Bank of Richmond, November/December 1986, pp. 12–26.

Anatoli Kuprianov, "Short-Term Interest Rate Futures," *Economic Review*, Federal Reserve Bank of Richmond, September/October 1986, pp. 12–26.

# Financial Institutions

Financial institutions that borrow and lend money are called financial intermediaries. They include depository intermediaries (banking institutions)— that accept deposits—and non-depository intermediaries—including mutual funds, pension funds, and insurance companies. In this part, we will study why financial intermediaries are so important in an economy—why so many people place their money in financial intermediaries and borrow money from them.

We begin by looking at banking regulation and deregulation—the removal of banking regulations—in Chapter 10. Banking has the dubious honor of being perhaps the most regulated—and the longest regulated—industry in the United States. This reflects how wary Americans have always been—and still are—of powerful banks and of unsafe banks. The first part of Chapter 10 shows how this has evolved. However, in 1980, the trend was dramatically reversed— suddenly there was a substantial amount of deregulation. The second part of Chapter 10 discusses this deregulation, including several key regulatory issues— federal deposit insurance, interstate banking, and competition between commercial banks and investment banks— that are still to be resolved.

We then look at how banking firms are managed and operated in view of regulations and related matters. The discussion in Chapter 11 emphasizes that banking firms, like manufacturing firms, are operated to maximize profits, subject to the constraints of competition and regulation. This is reflected in the interest rates and quantities that bank managers select for deposits and loans. It is also reflected in bank liquidity management—how banks maintain an adequate reservoir of cash and other liquid assets to meet deposit withdrawals.

In Chapter 12, we will see how risk preferences, risk pooling, and risk transfers affect how banks deal with *credit risk*— the risk that borrowers may default— and at how banks evaluate risky loans and set interest rates on them. Given the recent losses of banks on loans to the farming sector and oil industry, and the potential losses they still face on loans to developing countries, this is obviously a timely topic.

In Chapter 13, we look at *nonbank intermediaries*—financial intermediaries other than commercial banks. These institutions provide intermediation services that compete with and supplement the services provided by commercial banks (as discussed in Chapter 6). Using these intermediaries, borrowers can obtain special types of loans (such as mortgage loans from savings and loan associations and savings banks), investors can buy special portfolios of securities (such as diversified portfolios from mutual funds), and consumers can obtain special services (such as insurance from insurance companies and the management of their retirement investments by pension funds).

# Banking Regulation and Deregulation

*"The Congress shall have power . . . to regulate Commerce with foreign Nations, and among the several States . . . [and] to coin Money [and] regulate the Value thereof."*

**Article I, Section 8 of the U.S. Constitution**

Banks have been regulated in the United States since America's colonial days, reflecting the continuing desire of people to control the power of banks and to ensure the safety of the money they keep in banks. Banking regulation was also tied in with battles for political power, first between the colonies and England (and the Bank of England), and later between the new state governments and the new federal government.

Banking and financial regulation originally rested solely with the individual states. But Congress soon came to share this responsibility, based on its power to regulate international and interstate commerce and to coin money and regulate its value. As a result, regulatory agencies at both the federal and state levels now monitor and control banking and related financial activities.

Like banking regulation, monetary policy is implemented at the federal level under the constitutional power of Congress to coin money and regulate its value. However, after the Federal Reserve—the central bank of the United States—was founded in 1913, Congress delegated to it the task of monetary policy and a part of banking regulation. The Congressional thinking was that these responsibilities would be best executed by a politically independent and professionally expert central bank.

Even though the Federal Reserve both operates monetary policy and regulates banking and financial activity, the two activities are generally differentiated from each other. We will study banking and financial regulation in this chapter. Monetary policy is studied in Part V.

We will begin this chapter with an overview of the history of banking and financial regulation in the United States. A historical review is an aid to understanding current issues and even to predicting future ones. And you may find U.S. banking history interesting and colorful. Then we will look at current topics in banking regulation, with in-depth coverage of federal deposit insurance, new financial services (commercial banking versus investment banking), interstate banking, and the organization of banking regulation.

## Banking Regulation in the United States

The history of banking regulation in the United States has three main themes: (1) sound currency; (2) bank safety; and (3) bank services. Box 10.1 outlines the main developments.

### From the Colonies to the Civil War

Right from the beginning, the American colonies were dissatisfied with the amount of gold and currency the Bank of England was supplying them. As a result, a good part of the trade of the colonies was based on barter. As we discussed in Chapter 2, barter limits the amount of trade and the gains derived from trading.

After Independence, the states began chartering banks, but slowly, since each charter required a separate legislative act. These early banks accepted deposits of gold coins and gold bullion, deposits which were convertible into—could be redeemed for—gold. The banks also issued **bank notes**—paper money—when they made loans (see Figure 10.1). The bank notes served as a medium of exchange and were convertible into gold. So, using the concepts introduced in Chapter 2, this was a fractional reserve banking system based on gold reserves.

The interest earned on loans gave banks an incentive to issue as many bank notes as possible. Of course, the provision that bank notes could be redeemed for gold limited the quantity of notes a bank could safely issue relative to its gold reserves. But many banks went beyond the bounds of safety and then failed when too many of their notes were redeemed.

**FIGURE 10.1**  An early bank note.

## The Major Developments in U.S. Banking Regulations

**The First (1791–1811) and Second (1816–1836) Banks of the United States**
These early central banks served as the fiscal agent for the federal government, helped to control the amount of bank notes issued by state banks, and promoted trade. After the Second Bank was closed in 1836, there was no central bank in the U.S. until 1913.

**The Free Banking Era (1837–1863)**—During this period—sometimes called the "wildcat banking" era—banks were chartered only by the states.

**National Banking Act (1864)**—This act provided for a uniform national currency and for the federal chartering of commercial banks.

**Federal Reserve Act (1913)**—This act created the Federal Reserve system—still today the central bank of the United States—to make the amount of currency responsive to the needs of trade.

**McFadden Act (1927)**—This act affirmed that state laws regarding branch offices would apply equally to state and national banks.

**Banking Act of 1933 (Glass-Steagall)**—Passed in the Depression, this act created federal deposit insurance, prohibited interest on demand deposits, and separated commercial banks (dealing in loans and deposits) from investment banks (dealing in securities).

**Banking Act of 1935**—This Act gave the Federal Reserve the power, among other things, to set ceilings for bank deposit interest rates (called Regulation Q ceilings).

**Bank Holding Company Acts of 1956 and 1970**—These acts set the rules regulating bank holding companies.

**Bank Merger Act of 1960 and PNB Supreme Court Case of 1963**—This act and court decision determined the rules for bank mergers.

**Depository Institutions Deregulation and Monetary Control Act of 1980**
This act eliminated many regulations (including Regulation Q ceilings), increasing bank powers. Also, all depository institutions became subject to various Federal Reserve requirements.

**Depository Institutions Act of 1982 (Garn-St. Germain)**—This act extended the 1980 legislation and specifically dealt with the problem of failing thrift institutions.

**The Competitive Equality Banking Act of 1987**—This act revised the rules for "nonbank" banks and provided additional funding for the Federal Savings and Loan Insurance Corporation.

## The First and Second Banks of the United States

A central bank was added to the banking system when the Federalists, under Alexander Hamilton, succeeded in 1791 in chartering the *First Bank of the United States*. The Bank served as the fiscal agent for the federal government, acted to control the number of bank notes issued by state banks (by frequently presenting their notes for redemption in gold), financed trade between regions of the country, and even tried to stabilize the economy. Its headquarters was in Philadelphia, making this the financial center of the United States until the 1830s, and it maintained branch offices in other major cities.

The *Second Bank of the United States*, created after the charter of the first bank had expired, was aggressively managed by its president, Nicholas Biddle, and was considered the most advanced central bank of its time. However, by forcing state banks to redeem their notes in gold, Biddle and his bank were drawn into a continuing battle for political power between the federal government and the states.

Although the merchant and commercial interests in the country were pleased with the Second Bank, the agricultural interests and populist sentiments were set against it. The conflict was over whether the price level should remain roughly constant (good for the merchants) or should rise (good for the farmers). A long debate ensued in 1836 on whether to renew the bank's charter. In the end, Andrew Jackson vetoed the charter renewal and the central bank was dissolved. New York then became the financial center of the country and the career of enigmatic Nicholas Biddle ended in financial ruin.

## The Free Banking Era

Without the discipline and competition provided by the Second Bank of the United States, state-chartered banks proliferated after 1836. Many states enacted **free banking** statutes—meaning that bank charters were "freely" available upon application. Box 10.2 describes why this period is also known as the *wildcat banking era*. Although economic historians once thought free banking was responsible for the many bank failures of the period, recent research indicates that general economic problems may have been at fault.[1]

The free banking era ended with the Civil War. To finance the war, the U.S. Treasury in 1862 issued large quantities of bonds and **greenbacks**, the currency's color distinguishing it from the bank notes of commercial banks (see Figure 10.2). Greenbacks were actually a form of fiat money because the government, "as a question of hard necessity," had followed the example of the commercial banks and suspended convertibility. As more and more greenbacks were issued to provide for the expenses of the war, the notes depreciated in value, and at the lowest were worth only 35 cents on the dollar. The physical condition of bank notes eventually became so bad that counterfeiting was rife—people had to refer to "bank note reporters" to determine the market value of each specific bank note.

---

[1] See Arthur J. Rolnick and Warren E. Weber, "The Free Banking Era: New Evidence on Laissez-Faire Banking," *American Economic Review* 73, December 1983, pp. 1080–91.

## Wildcat Banking

It was profitable for banks to issue bank notes during the free banking era as long as the notes were rarely redeemed for gold. But people were understandably wary of banks, so they frequently redeemed their notes.

A banker with fraudulent intentions could, however, limit note redemptions by moving his bank to a remote location, out among the wildcats so to speak—hence the name *wildcat banking*.

FIGURE 10.2  A greenback.

## The National Banking Act of 1864

The **National Banking Act of 1864** was passed by Congress to deal with the currency problems. The Act established two key principles—*a uniform national currency* and *federally chartered banks*—which are still part of American banking today. The Office of the **Comptroller of the Currency** was created within the Treasury Department to distribute the new currency and to charter the new banks. The new federally chartered banks were known as *national banks* and the word "national" had to appear in each bank's name—still a feature in many bank names today. The currency was uniform because it was printed by the Comptroller of the Currency in Washington, D.C. (see Figure 10.3).

FIGURE 10.3  Currency from the National Banking Act.

The new currency was safe because only national banks could issue it, and each bank had to back its notes with securities deposited with the Comptroller. At the same time, a tax was imposed on state bank notes, the intention being to drive the state banks out of business. However, state banks were able to continue to operate because *checking deposits* soon arose as an alternative medium of exchange, and state banks began to specialize in this form of banking.

So state banks (offering deposits) and national banks (offering bank notes) existed side by side. The system of separate state and national banks—called the **dual banking system**—is still part of American banking. Overall, the National Banking Act successfully met its goals for a uniform national currency and a safer banking system. Indeed, the currency and banking system contributed to the rapid growth of the U.S. economy during the last third of the nineteenth century.

However, a conflict over currency still existed between the rural agricultural sectors and the urban manufacturing sectors of the economy. It arose because the new currency was not *elastic*—sufficiently responsive—*to the needs of trade*. The problem was that demand for currency in the agricultural sector of the economy was seasonal. It was high when farmers needed money for the spring planting and it was low when they deposited money in the bank after the fall harvest. So large amounts of currency had to flow each year from the cities to the rural areas and back again. This process did not always go smoothly and, as a result, a series of major financial panics occurred in 1873, 1884, 1893, and 1907.

## The Federal Reserve Act of 1913

In 1908, a National Monetary Commission was established to deal with the currency problem. The result was the **Federal Reserve Act of 1913**, creating the Federal Reserve system. The main innovation was that the Federal Reserve offered a facility—called the *discount window*—where banks could borrow currency or other reserves. For the Federal Reserve to lend money, it needed, of course, to have its own currency—hence Federal Reserve notes (see Figure 10.4).

The Federal Reserve Act was superimposed on the National Banking Act. National banks continued to be chartered as before, but they were

**FIGURE 10.4** An early Federal Reserve currency note.

also required to become members of the Federal Reserve. Membership was optional for state-chartered banks. Federal Reserve membership gave banks access to Federal Reserve services, principally its check-clearing network and the discount facility. But membership also imposed costs, as member banks had to adhere to Federal Reserve regulations.

## Locating Bank Offices

The location of banking offices has always been an issue for American banks because banks chartered in one state have always wanted to expand their market by opening offices in another state. But attempts at interstate banking were usually rejected by banking regulators. State regulators wanted to protect their banks from out-of-state competition and federal regulators did not want to be involved in interstate battles. There were actually two different, but related, issues—branch banking and interstate banking.

### Branch Banking

Most states had laws regulating the number of **branch offices** a bank could maintain. Some states allowed statewide branching, while others limited banks to just one office.[2] The question for federally chartered banks was: need a National bank abide by state laws that limited branch banking? This question was answered in neither the National Banking Act of 1864 nor the Federal Reserve Act of 1913.

So the Comptroller of the Currency had to determine a branch banking policy for national banks. Most Comptrollers simply prohibited all branch banking for national banks. This avoided a confrontation with the states, but it actually placed the national banks at a competitive disadvantage in states where branch banking was otherwise allowed. Ultimately, **The McFadden Act of 1927** provided a better solution: each national bank was to follow the branch banking rules of the state in which it operated.

### Interstate Banking

**Interstate banking**—banks that operate in two or more states—raised a question similar to branch banking: need national banks abide by state laws that restrict interstate banking? In response, the principle of the McFadden Act was also applied to interstate banking, meaning that interstate banking was available only when it was allowed by state laws. Most states prohibited interstate banking, and attempts failed during the 1920s to have the states liberalize their laws in this regard.

## The Banking Crisis of the Great Depression

The questions of branch banking and interstate banking addressed by the McFadden Act in 1927 were soon replaced with questions of bank survival during the Depression of the 1930s. Figure 10.5 shows the

---

[2] The extreme case was Illinois, where all bank operations had to be under one roof. Overhead bridges that connected buildings to satisfy this one-roof law are still apparent in downtown Chicago.

FIGURE 10.5

**Bank Survival During the Great Depression**

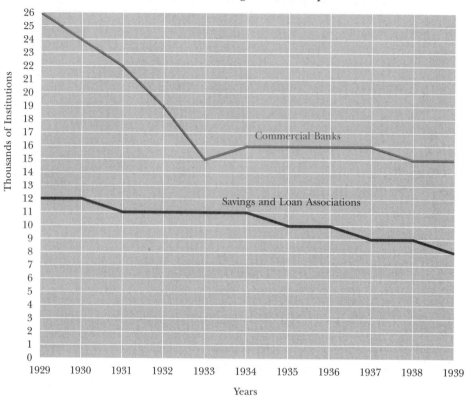

Between 1929 and 1939, more than 10,000 commercial banks and 4,000 SLAs failed in the United States.

**Source:** *Historical Statistics of the United States: Colonial Times to 1970*, U.S. Department of Commerce, Bureau of the Census, 1975.

devastating effect the Depression had on banking—the number of commercial banks was cut to almost half. The problem was that banks were caught in a vicious circle:

- *Depositors*, needing money, withdrew deposits.
- *Banks*, facing unexpected withdrawals, tried to increase their liquidity by cancelling loans, even in cases where loan renewals had previously been automatic.
- *Borrowers*, required to make unexpected loan repayments, had to default and declare bankruptcy.
- *More depositors*, seeing banks fail due to loan losses, withdrew their deposits.

### The Bank Runs of the Depression

This pattern usually leads to a *bank run*, which is always a possibility in a fractional reserve banking system if depositors suspect that a bank is in trouble. News about troubled banks spreads quickly, and everyone wants to be the first in line to withdraw their deposits, because a fractional reserve bank will eventually run out of currency. Box 10.3 gives a bank-

## Inside a Bank Run

Marriner Eccles was the manager of a Utah bank facing a run during the Depression. In his biography, *Marriner S. Eccles* by Sidney Hyman, the following description is given of what happened. Eccles not only saved his bank, but later became chairman of the Federal Reserve system.

[Eccles told his staff,] "We can't break this run today. The best we can do is to slow it down. You are going to pay them. But you are going to pay them very slowly. It's the only chance we have to deal with the panic. You know a lot of depositors by sight, and in the past you did not have to look up their signatures. But today when they come here with their deposit books to close out their accounts, you are going to look up every signature card. And take your time about it. Another thing. When you pay out, don't use any big bills. Pay out in fives and tens, and count slowly." [Later, Eccles mounted a counter,] "Many of you have been in line for a considerable time. . . . I just wanted to tell you that instead of closing at the usual hour of three o'clock, we have decided to stay open just as long as there is anyone who wants to withdraw his deposit or make one. You people who have just come in can return later this afternoon or evening if you wish. . . . As all of you have seen, we have just had brought up from Salt Lake City a large amount of currency that will take care of all your requirements. There is plenty more where that came from. And if you don't believe me, I have Mr. Morgan Craft, one of the officers of the Federal Reserve Bank, who has come up in the armored car from Salt Lake City."

(Sidney Hyman, *Marriner S. Eccles*, Stanford University Press, 1976.)

er's account of what happens inside the bank when depositors all try to withdraw their money at the same time.

A bank run is logical if a bank has serious problems and really *is* about to fail. However, a bank run can also occur as part of a self-fulfilling expectation: if depositors *think* a bank is in trouble, their deposit withdrawals create a bank run and cause the bank to fail, even though the bank initially may have been sound. The self-fulfilling feature of bank runs is particularly relevant when depositors lose confidence in the banking system as a whole, and the system fails as a result. This is what happened during the Great Depression (see Figure 10.6).

### The Federal Reserve and the Great Depression

What was the Federal Reserve doing during the bank runs of the Depression? Unfortunately, the Fed was convinced that the bank failures were an *effect* of the Depression, and that it could do nothing to help the banks short of solving the Depression.

What the Fed failed to understand was that the bank failures were as much a *cause* of the Depression as an *effect*. Had the Fed recognized this, it might have taken action to break the vicious circle. Specifically, it could have used its discount window to lend as much currency as necessary to save the banks. Ironically, this was probably also the best action it could have taken to save the economy.

**FIGURE 10.6**  The bank run of 1930.                    United Press International

There was another reason the Federal Reserve did not use the discount window: at the time the discount window was used only to lend money to banks that needed it to make loans to their customers. Banks during the Depression were cancelling loans, not making them. We will discuss this method of managing the discount window—called the Real Bills Doctrine—in Chapter 18 when we consider monetary policy. Among other things, we will see that the Federal Reserve learned its lesson—now when there is a financial disaster, the Fed promptly makes the discount window available to all banks that need it.

## The Banking Legislation of the Depression

Action to help the banks was finally taken when, on March 6, 1933, President Franklin Roosevelt euphemistically declared a *bank holiday*, closing all banks and requiring them to remain closed until their operations stabilized. A temporary closing, of course, was great news for a bank at the time. The banks reopened to a new era in banking regulation, inaugurated by the *Banking Act of 1933*, more commonly known as the **Glass-Steagall Act**, named after the bill's sponsors. It covered three main areas: federal deposit insurance, deposit interest rate ceilings, and investment banking.

### Federal Deposit Insurance

The Glass-Steagall Act provided for the immediate introduction of *federal deposit insurance* by the **Federal Deposit Insurance Corporation (FDIC)**, operating under the Comptroller of the Currency. All national banks had to join the FDIC, and state banks were allowed to join if they met FDIC standards. Since the FDIC could borrow money from the U.S. Treasury, depositors in insured banks felt their deposits were safe. Most banks joined gratefully.

Deposit insurance had a remarkable effect in stopping the bank runs. It worked so well because, when self-fulfilling expectations are the basic problem, the bank run stops once depositors change their expectations. Indeed, if deposit insurance is trusted, the insurance agencies should face very few claims, because very few banks should fail. The system actually worked this way—with few claims—until the 1980s. But then banks started to fail for quite different reasons—such as bad loans— which we will discuss later.

### Investment Banking by Commercial Banks

A second part of the Glass-Steagall Act also required that *commercial banks cease their investment banking activities*. Until that time, most large **commercial banks** (which accepted deposits and made loans) had also operated as **investment banks**. That is, they would underwrite—help firms issue—securities to finance new capital investments.

Investment banking was henceforth prohibited for commercial banks because there was evidence that some banks had underwritten new securities for nearly bankrupt firms, while failing to inform investors in the securities of this fact. Even worse, the firms had used some or all of the money raised to repay loans to the very banks that had underwritten the securities, so when the firms later declared bankruptcy, the banks had no loan losses. (Despite the value of these reforms at the time, the Glass-Steagall separation of commercial and investment banking is now being reconsidered, as we will discuss later in this chapter.)

### Interest Prohibitions on Demand Deposits

A third part of the Glass-Steagall Act prohibited *interest payments on demand deposits (checking accounts)*. It was thought at the time that high deposit interest rates had forced banks to adopt risky lending policies, thus causing them to fail. Research later showed, however, that there was little relationship between the banks that failed and the interest rates paid on deposits. Although the prohibition of interest on demand deposits remains, interest is now allowed on new types of checking accounts, as we will discuss later.

### Other Banking Legislation of the Depression

The *Banking Act of 1935* expanded Federal Reserve powers in a number of ways. The Federal Reserve Act lists the Federal Reserve's powers by lettered paragraphs, starting with Regulation A, the discount facility. The 1935 Act created a **Regulation Q**, which allowed the Federal Reserve to set ceilings on time-deposit interest rates. The purpose was similar to that of the prohibition of interest on demand deposits.

*Savings and loan associations (SLAs)*, hurt almost as badly as commercial banks by the Depression, were helped separately by legislation between 1932 and 1934 that created the **Federal Home Loan Bank System (FHLBS)** and the **Federal Savings and Loan Insurance Corporation (FSLIC)**. The FHLBS was set up as a consolidated regulatory agency for SLAs, combining the activities of the various federal banking regulators. The FSLIC provided federal deposit insurance for SLAs.

## Regulation Since World War II

Banking entered a much calmer period after World War II. The Depression banking legislation worked extremely well, providing nearly fifty years without a banking crisis. However, regulatory changes still occurred in areas covering bank holding companies, bank mergers, thrift institutions, consumer protection, and international banking.

### Bank Holding Companies

The growth of **bank holding companies** (BHCs)—corporations that own one or more banks—was a major development. BHCs had existed previously—indeed, Marriner Eccles's bank described in Box 10.3 was owned by one—but BHCs expanded more rapidly during the early

---

BOX 10.4 IN DEPTH

## Bank Holding Companies

Major activities that are permitted and denied under Section 4(c)8 of Federal Reserve Regulation Y.

**Permitted Activities** (Closely Related to Banking)
Loan offices for business, consumer, and mortgage loans.
Trust (managing estates and other trusts) activities.
Investment or financial advising.
Bookkeeping or data processing services.
Insurance for loan borrowers.
Courier services.
Selling money orders, travelers checks, and U.S. Savings Bonds.
Real estate appraisals.
Dealer operations in gold and silver bullion and coin.
Underwriting certain federal, state, and municipal securities.
Discount stock brokerage.
Purchases of failing savings and loan associations.

**Denied Activities** (Not Closely Related to Banking)
Insurance (other than for loan borrowers).
Real estate brokerage.
Computer output microfilm services.
Travel agent operations.

**Source:** *Economic Review*, Federal Reserve Bank of Atlanta, September 1982, and George Kaufman, Larry R. Mote, and Harvey Rosenblum, "The Future of Commercial Banks in the Financial Services Industry," Staff Memorandum 83-5, Federal Reserve Bank of Chicago, 1983.

1950s when they were used to avoid regulations concerning branching and interstate banking. Today, holding companies are the predominant form of bank ownership.

Bank holding companies can carry out a wider range of activities than banks. Specifically, the holding companies can carry out activities *closely related to banking*. Of course, the Federal Reserve has to interpret the term "closely related to banking," and Box 10.4 shows some of the results. In contrast, banks (even banks owned by holding companies) can carry out only *banking business*—usually interpreted to mean accepting deposits and making loans.

Congress gave the Federal Reserve regulatory power to control the activities of BHCs. The Bank Holding Company Act of 1956 applied to *multi-bank holding companies*—holding companies that own 25% or more of two or more banks—and the Bank Holding Company Act of 1970 applied to *single-bank holding companies*. Figure 10.7 shows the rapid growth of these two types of holding companies—single-bank and multi-bank. The Douglas Amendment to the 1956 Act prohibited interstate banking for holding companies (except in states that otherwise allow it). However, it did not preclude BHCs from doing their nonbanking business on an interstate basis.

FIGURE 10.7
**Growth in the Number of Bank Holding Companies**

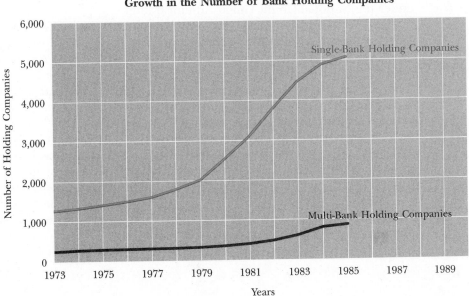

Single-bank holding companies are companies that own just one bank, whereas multi-bank holding companies own two or more banks. Bank holding companies now represent the dominant form of bank ownership in the United States. **Source:** *Statistical Digest,* Board of Governors of the Federal Reserve System, 1987.

### Bank Mergers

**Bank mergers** have been frequent since World War II, in good part reflecting the growth of bank holding companies. Bank mergers have to be approved by the banks' regulatory agencies, based on criteria that include *the needs of the community* and *bank safety*. In addition, starting with the *Bank Merger Act of 1960*, the Justice Department could object to bank mergers if they violated the antitrust laws. The larger the market share of the surviving bank or the greater the concentration of large banks in any one area, the more likely the Justice Department was to challenge the merger.

The Supreme Court, in the Philadelphia National Bank (PNB) case of 1963, set a precedent by ruling that banking is a *unique line of commerce*. As a result, the Justice Department could narrowly interpret a banking "market" as the local area for loans and deposits, with the implication that bank mergers within a city or county might violate the antitrust laws. This slowed merger activity for a while, although in the 1980s the Justice Department has challenged only mergers that involve large banks.

### Other Regulatory Developments

*Thrift institutions*. Regulations regarding thrift institutions were adjusted periodically, to keep them in line with those for commercial banks. For example, the Interest Rate Adjustment Act of 1966 applied interest rate ceilings to Savings and Loan Association deposits—comparable to the Regulation Q ceilings for commercial banks. The National Credit Union Act of 1970 provided federal chartering and insurance for credit unions under the National Credit Union Administration.

*Consumer protection*. Many laws were passed during the 1960s and 1970s to protect consumers. These included the *Truth in Lending Act of 1968*, which required lenders to disclose loan terms fully, the *Fair Credit Billing Act of 1974*, creating Federal Reserve Regulation Z (the Federal Reserve then had a full alphabet of regulatory powers) indicating how consumer complaints regarding credit cards are to be handled, and various housing and mortgage acts.

*International banking*. The international activities of U.S. banks were first regulated under the 1919 *Edge Act*, which was recently updated to allow for international banking facilities. The U.S. activities of foreign banks were first systematically regulated in the *International Banking Act of 1978*, which placed U.S. and foreign banks operating in the United States on equal terms. We shall have more to say about the regulation of international banking in Chapter 21.

## Deregulation Since 1980

From the National Banking Act of 1864 until 1980, the regulations on banks continued to accumulate. By the 1970s, however, pressure was developing to reverse the process—to **deregulate** some aspects of banking. Many factors contributed to the need for deregulation, but two were predominant:

1. High market interest rates conflicted with Regulation Q ceilings on deposit interest rates.
2. Declining Federal Reserve membership limited the Fed's regulatory power.

We will now look at each of these factors and then at the results of the deregulation legislation that passed in 1980.

### Regulation Q Ceilings

Starting in the 1960s, commercial banks (and thrift institutions) had been hampered by Regulation Q ceilings on the interest rates they could pay for deposits. Capital market interest rates had started a long upward trend, and because of the ceilings, people could often obtain substantially higher interest rates by investing their money outside of banks. Nonbank intermediaries, especially mutual funds, took particular advantage of this situation and the banks had trouble attracting deposits.

In response, the banks were always trying to circumvent the Regulation Q ceilings. A game of cat and mouse was played between the banks (trying to escape Regulation Q) and the Federal Reserve (trying to enforce it). The banks would find a loophole in the regulations—so they could pay higher interest rates and attract more deposits—and shortly thereafter the Fed would close the loophole. Then the banks would find another loophole. And so on. An annotated list of these developments is provided in Table 10.1.

---

**TABLE 10.1**
**Steps Toward Removing Regulation Q Ceilings**

| Year | Development | Objective |
|------|-------------|-----------|
| 1961 | Large denomination certificates of deposit (CDs) | To circumvent the Regulation Q ceilings |
| 1968 | Eurodollar deposits | To obtain funds in Europe where Regulation Q did not apply |
| 1972 | NOW accounts | Interest-paying transaction accounts first introduced in New England |
| 1973 | Wild Card experiment (operated for 4 mo.) | To exempt small denomination CDs from Regulation Q |
| 1978 | Money market certificates (6-mo. CDs) | Not subject to Regulation Q ceilings |
| 1980 | Small saver certificates (2½ yr CDs) | Not subject to Regulation Q ceilings |
| 1980 | DIDMCA | Set 1986 for the removal of *all* Regulation Q ceilings |
| 1981 | NOW accounts | Authorized nationwide |
| 1982 | Money market deposit accounts | Authorized as another type of bank deposit not subject to Regulation Q |
| 1983 | Super NOW accounts | Extended the NOW account concept of paying interest on transaction accounts |
| 1986 | Regulation Q ceilings removed | |

**Source:** Adapted from Daniel J. Vraback, "Recent Developments at Banks and Nonbank Depository Institutions," Federal Reserve Bank of Kansas City, *Economic Review*, July–August 1983, and Kerry Cooper and Donald R. Fraser, *Banking Deregulation and the New Competition for Financial Services*, Ballinger, Cambridge, Mass., 1986.

During the late 1970s, interest rates rose sharply, and so did competition for bank deposits from money market funds (MMFs), nonbank intermediaries which we will describe in Chapter 13. The MMFs attracted nearly $75 billion by 1980 and over $200 billion deposits by 1982. In this setting, the Federal Reserve became more sympathetic to the view that Regulation Q ceilings imposed an unfair burden on commercial banks. The low deposit rates enforced by Regulation Q were particularly unfair to small savers who had no practical investment option other than bank deposits. Business firms and wealthier people, in contrast, were able to avoid the Regulation Q ceilings by investing directly in capital market securities or money market funds. In the end, the Federal Reserve had only two choices: either regulate the money market funds or deregulate the banks.

### Federal Reserve Membership

While the Federal Reserve was grappling with that choice, it also had to deal with a decline in Federal Reserve membership. As shown in Figure 10.8, membership decreased steadily from 1970, and the decline accelerated during the late 1970s. The decline reflected the fact that the costs of membership—such as reserve requirements—often exceeded the benefits—such as access to the Federal Reserve's discount facility and check-clearing system. In response, state-chartered banks simply dropped their Federal Reserve membership, while federally chartered banks first switched to state charters—using the dual banking system—and then dropped their Federal Reserve membership.

FIGURE 10.8
**All Insured Commercial Banks and Federal Reserve Member Banks**

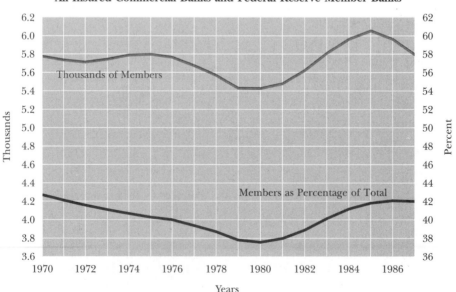

Starting in the late 1970s, large numbers of state-chartered banks withdrew from Federal Reserve membership, perceiving that the benefits of membership were not worth the cost of meeting the Federal Reserve's regulations. This lead to the passage of the Depository Institutions Deregulation and Monetary Control Act of 1980.

### The Depository Institutions Deregulation and Monetary Control Act of 1980

The difficulties with Regulation Q ceilings and with Federal Reserve membership, and a generally positive public attitude toward deregulation (reflected in the deregulation of other industries such as airlines and telephone services), prompted passage of the path-breaking (and jaw-breaking) **Depository Institutions Deregulation and Monetary Control Act (DIDMCA)** in 1980. As a result:

- The Regulation Q ceilings were phased out from 1980 to 1986.
- All depository institutions had to meet the Fed's reserve requirements, and, in return, were given access to Federal Reserve services (such as check-clearing and the discount window).

Other regulatory changes included in the DIDMCA are summarized, together with the provisions of the 1982 Financial Institutions Act, in Box 10.5. The 1982 Act, often called the Garn-St.Germain Act after its sponsors, dealt primarily with the thrift institution crisis, which we introduced in Chapter 8. This crisis remains an issue for deposit insurance, which is discussed on page 248.

---

**BOX 10.5 IN DEPTH**

## The Major Provisions of Deregulation Legislation

**Depository Institutions Deregulation and Monetary Control Act (1980)**
- Regulation Q ceilings eliminated by 1986.
- Uniform reserve requirements imposed on all depository institutions.
- Federal reserve services available to all depository institutions.
- NOW and other interest-paying transaction accounts allowed.
- Federal deposit insurance raised to $100,000 per account.
- Lending powers for thrift institutions expanded.
- State usury ceilings eliminated on mortgage loans.

**Financial Institutions Act (1982)**
- Authorized regulators to rescue failing institutions (including thrift institutions) by promoting mergers with healthy institutions (including commercial banks) on an interstate and intercharter (between different types of institutions) basis.
- Deposit and lending powers of thrift institutions expanded.
- Lending limits for banks raised to 15% of bank capital.
- Federal charters created for stockholder-owned savings banks.

**Source:** *Federal Reserve Bulletin*, 1981.

## Current Issues for Banking

Four major problems are on the current agenda for banking regulation or deregulation:

1. Federal deposit insurance.
2. Commercial banks, investment banks, and Glass-Steagall.
3. Interstate banking
4. Regulating the regulators.

We will look at each of these issues.

### Federal Deposit Insurance

The Federal deposit insurance agencies (FDIC and FSLIC) worked extremely well for nearly fifty years. In fact, the only substantive change made over the years was to raise the insurance limit per account to the current level of $100,000. However, serious problems are now apparent in the insurance agencies.

#### The Operation of Deposit Insurance

In some respects, the insurance agencies operate like private insurance companies. Insured banks pay regular premiums equal to one-twelfth of 1% (about 0.08%) of all deposits. The collected premiums—called reserves—are then invested until they are needed to pay claims. For many years, fraud was the only real source of claims—managers stealing money from their bank. Since this did not add up to much, premiums exceeded claims each year, and in some years the banks received premium rebates.

The FDIC and FSLIC suffered heavy losses for the first time during the early 1980s. The FDIC was hurt primarily by banks that failed as a result of losses on energy and agricultural loans. The Continental Illinois Bank in Chicago—involved in billions of dollars of bad loans to oil drillers—was the largest case (see Box 10.6). The FSLIC problems arose from SLAs that suffered large losses when interest rates rose sharply in the late 1970s and early 1980s. These institutions made long-term mortgage loans on the basis of short-term deposits, so their profits tumbled when the deposits had to be reissued at sharply higher interest rates. More recently, the FSLIC has also had to deal with many cases of fraud.

#### The Procedures for Failing Institutions

The process for *dealing with a failing institution* is shown as a flow diagram in Figure 10.9. An institution generally must be closed when the value of its capital reaches zero—the institution is then insolvent. However, the FDIC and FSLIC can either hasten or delay that event. A bank might be closed before its capital is depleted if the insurance agency is confident that it will become insolvent. On the other hand, the insurance agencies have techniques—such as not making a bank write off its bad loans—that can keep a virtually insolvent bank in business.

FIGURE 10.9
**How Failing Institutions Are Handled**

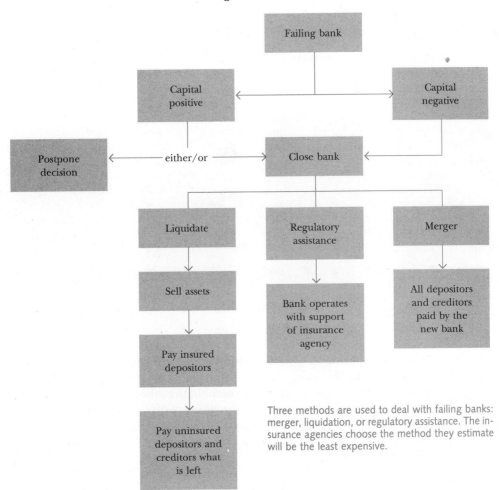

Three methods are used to deal with failing banks: merger, liquidation, or regulatory assistance. The insurance agencies choose the method they estimate will be the least expensive.

Once a decision is made to close a bank, this is done with the least costly of three main methods—merger, liquidation, or assistance.

The *merger method*—combining a failing bank with a healthy one—is most common. Bids are made by healthy banks for the right to merge with the failing one. The acquiring bank then takes on all the obligations of the failing bank, so there are no losses for either depositors or holders of uninsured liabilities. The size of the bids depends on:

- The amount of capital the failing bank has left.
- The *going concern value*—the value of the customer base—of the failing bank.
- The eagerness of the acquiring bank to enter the market area of the failing bank. (The Financial Institutions Act of 1982 encouraged this by allowing banks to buy out-of-state savings and loan associations.)

BOX 10.6 BANKING BRIEFS

## The Collapse of the Penn Square and Continental Illinois Banks

The largest U.S. bank failure occurred on July 26, 1984, when the FDIC announced that it was taking over the Continental Illinois National Bank of Chicago. Later, it was reported that Continental had gotten into trouble by buying hundreds of millions of dollars of bad oil industry loans made through a small Oklahoma bank, the Penn Square.

The FDIC used the *liquidation* method (to be explained shortly) to pay off the insured depositors of the *Penn Square Bank*. The uninsured depositors (with deposits of more than $100,000), including a number of credit unions, suffered substantial losses. However, *Continental Illinois* was much too large to either merge or liquidate. So the FDIC took over the bank: it assured *all* depositors and creditors that they would be paid, it agreed to buy over $3 billion of Continental's worst loans (so the bank would be in sound condition), and it installed its own group of managers. This assistance plan seems to be working reasonably well: Continental is now profitable and the situation seems quite stable. However, the FDIC is unlikely to recover all of its money.

Mergers are often the best solution for the insurance agencies because the bids reflect the going concern value and the value of entry into a new market. These elements are not present in the other methods for dealing with failing banks. Nevertheless, the bids are often negative numbers—representing a payment to be made *to* the acquiring bank by the insurance agency, and therefore a loss for the agency—if the failing bank's capital is very negative.

*Liquidating the institution*—selling off the failing bank's assets to raise money—is quite a different method. The money raised—plus, if necessary, additional funds from the insurance agency—is first used to pay off the insured depositors. Then, uninsured depositors and other creditors are paid with any money that remains. The FDIC and FSLIC believe that liquidation is generally *not* the best method—because the going concern value of the failed bank is lost—so it is used only when the bids received are inadequate or little value is left in the failing bank.

*Regulatory assistance*—by which the failing bank continues to operate under the control and management of the insurance agency—is used primarily for very large banks where neither merger nor liquidation is feasible. The case of the Continental Illinois Bank discussed in Box 10.7 is a prime example. The problem with regulatory assistance is that it is not a permanent solution—the insurance agency will want to use elsewhere the money it has invested in the failing bank. So the objective of regulatory assistance is only to stabilize the situation until either the bank recovers or a merger can be arranged.

### Who Insures the Insurers

As a result of many large losses, the reserves of both the FDIC and the FSLIC are low. The FDIC is still solvent, but its future status depends critically on the outcome of the very large loans banks have made to developing countries. The FSLIC is already insolvent; its available reserves are far short of the estimated $20 billion to $50 billion that it needs to deal with the pending SLA cases.

Moreover, the FSLIC problems are multiplying because it has proceeded slowly in closing institutions. In the meantime, many of these institutions make a last ditch effort at recovery, by making risky loans at high interest rates, even though these attempts usually fail and therefore add to the FSLIC's costs. To get its finances back in order, the FSLIC now requires all insured SLAs to pay supplementary premiums. Congress has also allowed the FSLIC to borrow about $10 billion.

Even with this additional money, however, it is doubtful the FSLIC will be able to solve its problems. An alternative is to merge the FSLIC into the healthier FDIC, but both sides may be unhappy with this marriage. More likely, when all else has failed, Congress will authorize government funds—taxpayer money—to bail out the FSLIC. After all, only the taxpayers insure the insurance agencies.

### The Future of Federal Deposit Insurance

Beyond these immediate problems, the insurance agencies must monitor banks in a better way. Two methods—market monitoring and risk-based insurance premiums—are being considered, but it is doubtful that either will work.

---

**BOX 10.7 BANKING BRIEFS**

## How Six Regulators May Regulate a Bank

A bank or bank holding company can be regulated in one way or another by: the Comptroller of the Currency, the Federal Reserve, the Federal Deposit Insurance Corporation, a state banking commissioner, and, if it owns a savings and loan association, the Federal Home Loan Bank Board (regulating thrift institutions) and the Federal Savings and Loan Insurance Corporation. And this does not count the regulators of credit unions.

A bank holding company that owns a federally chartered bank, a state-chartered bank, and a savings and loan association illustrates how complex the web of jurisdictions can be. The bank holding company itself is regulated by the Federal Reserve. Among the institutions owned by the holding company, the Comptroller of the Currency regulates federally chartered banks, state banking commissioners regulate state-chartered banks, and the Federal Home Loan Bank Board regulates the savings and loan associations. Finally, federal insurance is provide by the FDIC and the FSLIC.

### Market Monitoring

The idea of *market monitoring* is to expose all of the people involved with a bank—depositors, other creditors, and stockholders—to financial risk if the bank should fail. The reasoning is that if all involved would suffer a loss, they would have an incentive to exert pressure on the bank's management to operate more safely.

One way to do this for depositors would be to *reduce the amount that is insured* below the current level of $100,000 per account. This would increase the number of uninsured depositors, who would then have a keen interest in the bank being run safely. If these depositors withdrew their money, the bank's managers and the insurance agency would be alerted to trouble. In contrast, most depositors now have little stake in how well their bank is managed.

*Higher capital ratios*—requiring that banks maintain larger amounts of stockholder capital in relation to their assets—is another possible method of market monitoring. Since shareholders lose all or a portion of their capital investment when a bank fails, they might act more vigorously to see that the bank is managed safely if they had more capital at risk. This method has the advantage that shareholders, more than depositors, may be knowledgable about bank operations and in a position to influence management. However, it has the drawback that it is hard for weak banks to raise additional capital.

### Risk-Based Insurance Premiums

*Risk-based insurance premiums*—connecting the amount of the deposit insurance premium to the risk level of a bank—penalizes banks that engage in risky tactics. However, this technique appears well suited only for risks that can be objectively measured. For example, it might work well in giving banks incentive to match the maturities of their assets and liabilities. But it might not reduce the risk of loan losses, given that the evaluation of loans is intrinsically qualitative.

## Commercial Banks, Investment Banks, and the Glass-Steagall Act

Banks and nonbank institutions compete with each other in three main areas: deposits, loans, and other financial services. We have already discussed how competition for deposits led to the removal of the Regulation Q ceilings. We will now look at how the intensified competition for loans and other financial services is creating pressure to remove the Glass-Steagall Act separation between commercial banking and investment banking.

### The Expansion of Nonbank Firms

Nonbank firms that compete with banks for loans and financial services include investment banks, major retailers such as Sears Roebuck, the big three U.S. auto companies, and many others. These firms have long operated in special loan markets. The auto companies have made auto loans through subsidiaries such as the General Motors Acceptance Corporation (GMAC), the retailers have offered credit plans for purchases, and investment banks have provided loans for corporate takeovers.

The growing competition of these firms with commercial banks is based on both a deepening and a widening of their traditional loan markets. Sears, for example, is trying to introduce a new credit card as a competitor to bank credit cards; and it also owns a large savings and loan association. GMAC has become one of the major mortgage lenders in the United States. And investment banks, such as Merrill Lynch, have combined money market funds and stock market loans into *cash management accounts* that can be more convenient for some people than even bank transaction accounts.

### Nonbank Banks

Nonbank *firms* have also tried to form **nonbank banks**. Banking regulations generally define a bank as an institution that accepts transaction accounts *and* makes loans. An institution can thus be a nonbank bank as long as it does just one of these two activities. The advantage of a nonbank bank is that it may operate in some, or most, respects like a bank, but without the restrictive regulations that "real" banks face. Congress has been sympathetic to the claim by (real) banks that nonbank banks represent unfair competition, and has temporarily restricted the formation of nonbank banks.

### The Expansion of Commercial Banks

Partly in retaliation to the threat of nonbank banks, banks have taken the offensive by challenging investment banks and other competitors on their own turf. Bank holding companies (BHCs) have been the main instrument used by the banks. For example, many bank holding companies now offer discount stock brokerage services. Banks have also tried, with some success, to obtain regulatory authority to underwrite securities, and to carry out related investment banking activities that are prohibited by the Glass-Steagall Act.

For the time being, nonbank firms are continuing to try to form nonbank banks, while the banks are challenging the Glass-Steagall restrictions that keep them out of investment banking. The political and economic forces appear reasonably balanced between the banks and the nonbank firms, so it is difficult to predict how this will turn out. If public sentiment remains favorable toward deregulation, then both sides might receive additional powers; otherwise, the status quo might be retained.

## Interstate Banking

Pressure to allow interstate banking has increased directly as a function of the expanding competition between banks and nonbank firms. Nonbank firms, of course, have no geographic restrictions on where they can operate. Banks therefore claim they need interstate operations to achieve a competitive balance. Economies of scale also play a role, since new electronic technology may make large size essential for efficiency.

To be sure, bank holding companies are already allowed to provide their *nonbank services* on an interstate basis. For example, BHCs have maintained lending offices in many states. These offices are *not* considered banks—if they were, the interstate banking laws would be violated—because they do not accept deposits. Citicorp, the holding company for Citibank, the largest bank in the United States (and twenty-eighth largest in the world), operates about 1,000 lending and similar offices across the country.

Federal banking regulators have generally approved of interstate banking; it is state laws that prohibit it. However, the states now appear more sympathetic. Most states now participate in *regional compacts*—agreements that allow interstate banking within a specified region. Some states also have *unlimited bilateral compacts*—they allow interstate banking with any other state that reciprocates the offer.

A complex pattern of interstate banking linkages is arising from the regional compacts. To simplify this system, federal banking regulators and Congress have announced plans to declare a national policy on interstate banking, which would override the state compacts. Thus, the entire country will probably have interstate banking by the early 1990s.

## Regulating the Regulators

Deregulation simplified banking regulations, but it is actually complicating the regulatory system. For example, the growth of bank holding companies represented a step toward deregulation. However, the bank holding companies must then deal with as many as six different agencies (see Box 10.7 for the head count). Most observers now think the regulatory system itself should be simplified.

Competition among the regulators is another reason for modifying the regulatory system. Based on the dual banking system, institutions may choose the regulator most favorable for their needs. And regulators that compete with each other—to have more member institutions—may lose sight of the common goal of bank safety. Some people think this has already happened: that regulators now attract institutions by offering less onerous regulations—a *competition in laxity* among the regulators.

A consolidation of this regulatory web was considered in 1980. Under one proposal, the Federal Reserve was to be the single surviving regulator, carrying out both bank regulation and monetary policy; under another proposal, there was to be a new consolidated *Federal Banking Regulator*. However, because regulators rarely agree to go out of business, these proposals were never introduced as legislation. Without agreement from the banking regulators, the system is unlikely to be changed unless a major event forces a future Congress or presidential administration to take action on its own.

## Chapter Summary

1. The history of banking and banking regulation in the United States reflects a continuing concern to control the power of banks to ensure the safety of the money in their care. Banking regulation is carried out under the constitutional power of Congress to coin money and regulate its value, and laws and regulations now affect most banking activities.

2. The First Bank of the United States, the country's first central bank, was chartered in 1791. The charter of its successor, however, was not renewed in 1836. The free banking era followed: state-chartered banks operated with little regulation and control. The National Banking Act was passed at the end of the Civil War. This legislation created federal charters for national banks and created a uniform national currency. The national banking system was generally successful, but a series of financial panics indicated that the amount of currency was not sufficiently responsive to the needs of trade. The Federal Reserve system was created in 1913 as a solution, with its discount facility to be used to lend currency and reserves to banks.

3. Some of the worst effects of the Great Depression occurred in the banking sector, the number of commercial banks was cut almost in half between 1929 and 1933. The Federal Reserve did relatively little about this. Banking legislation, passed in 1933 and 1935, featured the creation of the FDIC and the FSLIC, Regulation Q ceilings on deposit interest rates, and the separation of investment banking from commercial banking.

4. Branch banking within states and interstate banking have been issues throughout U.S. banking history. Each state has been allowed to set its own rules for branch banking, with the result that some states allow only single office banks while others allow statewide branching. States also set the rules for interstate banking, and for the most part they have prohibited it. The McFadden Act of 1927 further required that each federally chartered bank abide by the branch and interstate banking rules of the state in which it operates.

5. Bank holding companies (BHCs) were an important banking development after World War II. BHCs are corporations that own more than a 25% interest in one or more banks. They are allowed to carry out approved activities that are "closely related to banking." Bank holding companies are now the dominant form of bank ownership.

6. Pressure for banking deregulation developed in the 1970s, as Regulation Q ceilings severely hampered banks and a declining membership hampered the Federal Reserve. Deregulation legislation included the Depository Institutions Deregulation and Monetary Control Act (DIDMCA) of 1980 and the Financial Institutions Act of 1982. Beside removing Regulation Q ceilings and requiring that all depository institutions meet the Fed's reserve requirements and be given access to the Fed's services, the legislation provided expanded lending and deposit powers for banks, eliminated usury ceilings on mortgages, and gave bank regulators greater power to merge failing banks.

7. The Federal deposit insurance agencies are suffering large losses for the first time in their history, as bad loans cause commercial banks to fail, and as losses created by previously high interest rates cause savings and loan associations (SLAs) to fail. There are several proposals to restructure the insurance funds and to avoid future problems.

8. Competition between commercial banks and investment banks is another unresolved issue for banking deregulation. Nonbank firms, for example, wish to form nonbank banks that either make loans or accept deposits, but not both. Banks wish to regain the investment banking powers they lost as a result of the Glass-Steagall Act. It is unclear how this issue will be solved. However, there is a developing consensus that interstate banking should be allowed, and this is likely to occur by the early 1990s.

## Key Terms

**Bank:**

    **Holding company (BHC)**

    **Mergers**

    **Notes**

**Banking Legislation:**

    **Depository Institutions Deregulation and Monetary Decontrol Act (1980)**

    **McFadden Act of 1929**

    **Federal Reserve Act (1913)**

    **Glass-Steagall Act (1933)**

    **National Banking Act (1864)**

**Branch Banking**

**Commercial Banking**

**Comptroller of the Currency**

**Deposit insurance:**

    **Federal Deposit Insurance Corporation (FDIC)**

    **Federal Savings and Loan Insurance Corporation (FSLIC)**

**Deregulation**

**Dual banking system**

**Federal Home Loan Bank System (FHLBS)**

**Free banking**

**Greenbacks**

**Interstate banking**

**Investment banking**

**Nonbank bank**

**Regulation Q ceilings**

## Study Problems

1. Bank notes issued during the free banking era were replaced by a uniform national currency under the National Banking Act. What were the problems with bank notes during the free banking era and how were these solved? What problem with the uniform national currency remained until the Federal Reserve was established?

2. How did the management of the Federal Reserve's discount facility respond to the problem of the National Banking system? How well did this mechanism work during the Great Depression?

3. What is the dual banking system? Why is it responsible for banks in different states operating under different rules regarding branch offices and interstate banking?

4. What are bank holding companies? Why have they become the dominant form of bank ownership in the United States?

5. How did rising interest rates in the United States create a need for banking deregulation by the early 1980s?

6. The following are major developments in bank deregulation during the early 1980s.

What problem did each one solve?

a. All depository institutions must meet the Federal Reserve's required reserve ratios.

b. The Regulation Q ceilings on bank deposit rates were eliminated.

c. State usury ceilings on mortgage loans were eliminated.

d. Bank regulators were given increased powers to merge failing banks.

7. What are the current problems of the Federal Deposit Insurance funds? What are some possible solutions?

8. Why did the Glass-Steagall Act of 1933 separate the activities of investment banks and commercial banks?

9. How are investment banks and commercial banks each now encroaching on the traditional markets of the other?

10. What are nonbank banks, and what is their significance?

## Recommended Reading

*Friedman and Schwartz argue that the Federal Reserve was largely reponsible for the severity of the Depression. In response, Peter Temin argues that other macroeconomic forces were equally important:*

Milton Friedman and Anna Jacobson Schwartz, *A Monetary History of the United States, 1867–1960*, Princeton University Press, Princeton, N.J., 1963.

Peter Temin, *Did Monetary Forces Cause the Great Depression?* Norton, New York, 1976.

*Hammond provides a colorful history of U.S. banking:*

Bray Hammond, *Banks and Politics in America, From the Revolution to the Civil War*, Princeton University Press, Princeton, N.J., 1957.

*This paper challenges the tradition that the banking system operated poorly under free banking during the nineteenth century:*

Arthur J. Rolnick and Warren E. Weber, "The Free Banking Era: New Evidence on Laissez-Faire Banking," *American Economic Review* 73, December 1983, pp. 1080–91.

*The Continential Illinois bank failure is described somewhat humorously in the first book and seriously in the second:*

Mark Singer, *Funny Money*, Knopf, New York, 1985.

Irvine H. Sprague, *Bailout*, Basic Books, New York, 1986.

*There are now many good books describing the recent banking deregulation and the new competition for financial services:*

Thomas F. Cargill and Gillian G. Garcia, *Financial Reform in the 1980s*, Hoover Institution, Stanford University, Stanford, Calif., 1985.

Kerry Cooper and Donald R. Fraser, *Banking Deregulation and the New Competition in Financial Services*, Ballinger, Cambridge, Mass., 1986.

Carter H. Golembe and David S. Holland, *Federal Regulation of Banking, 1986–1987*, Golembe Associates, Washington, D.C., 1986.

Kenneth Spong, *Banking Regulation: Its Purposes, Implementation and Effects*, Federal Reserve Bank of Kansas City, 1985.

*The biography of Marriner Eccles discussed in Box 10.3 is:*

Sidney Hyman, *Marriner S. Eccles*, Stanford University Press, Stanford, Calif., 1976.

# The Banking Firm and Liquidity Management

*"The buck stops here . . ."*

*Harry Truman*

Managers of manufacturing firms choose prices and quantities for the goods they sell based on the demand for the goods and the costs of producing them. Managers of banking firms make similar decisions. They choose interest rates and quantities for their loans and deposits, depending on the demand for loans, the supply of deposits, and their operating expenses. In both cases, the degree of competition is also an important factor.

Certain issues, however, are more important for banking firms than for manufacturing firms—government regulations, for example. Matters of liquidity are also more fundamental for banking firms: while a business firm can always place the blame for a late payment on its bank, for a bank, the buck—or liquidity—stops there.

This chapter takes the perspective of a banking *firm* in analyzing bank management decisions. This contrasts with Chapter 6, where we looked at the services of the banking *industry*. We will study commercial banks in particular, but the concepts developed here apply quite generally to all depository intermediaries.

First we will examine how a bank considers operating expenses, regulations, and the degree of competition in determining its interest rates and the quantities of its loans and deposits. Then we will look at liquidity management—the policies that banks follow regarding their assets and liabilities in view of unanticipated deposit withdrawals.

## The Banking Firm

We will use as our example a banking firm that is running an intermediation business. We will *not* discuss the following topics at length because they are covered in other chapters:

- We will assume our bank's only income is the interest on loans, thus putting aside service fee income (Chapter 6).
- We will assume that our bank balances the maturities of its assets and liabilities, thus putting aside questions of interest rate risk (Chapter 8).
- We will assume our bank's loans are risk free, thus putting aside issues of credit risk (Chapter 12).

In addition, we will defer consideration of bank regulations regarding capital and reserve requirements until later in this chapter, and we will at first assume that all banks have the same operating costs as a percentage of their total assets (we will modify this assumption later). In brief, we will first look at a banking firm that attracts one class of deposits, makes one class of (risk-free) loans, and is managed to maximize its profits, given its operating expenses.

## Bank Profits

We begin with the bottom line—bank profits. Given the assumptions we have made, a bank's profits will equal the interest it earns on loans, minus the interest it pays on deposits, and minus its **operating cost ratio** (its operating expenses as a percentage of deposits):

$$\pi = (r_L L) - (r_D D) - (cD) \tag{11.1}$$

where $\pi$ = bank profits,

$L$ = the quantity of bank loans,

$r_L$ = the interest rate earned on bank loans,

$D$ = the quantity of bank deposits,

$r_D$ = the interest rate paid on bank deposits,

$c$ = the operating cost ratio.

The quantity $(r_L L)$ is the interest the bank earns on loans, the quantity $(r_D D)$ is the interest it pays on deposits, and the quantity $(cD)$ is its operating expenses.

A bank has to satisfy a **balance sheet constraint**—in our simplified case, the constraint is that total loans equal total deposits:

$$L = D \tag{11.2}$$

The balance sheet constraint can be incorporated directly into the profit equation by substituting $D$ for $L$ in equation (11.1):

$$\begin{aligned} \pi &= (r_L L) - (r_D D) - (cD) \\ &= (r_L D) - (r_D D) - (cD) \\ &= (r_L - r_D - c)D. \end{aligned} \tag{11.3}$$

Bank profits are thus proportional to the **profit margin**, income minus costs per dollar of deposits $(r_L - r_D - c)$. Given the operating cost ratio and any other constraints a bank faces, the bank's managers will set its loan rate, its deposit rate, and its size (deposits, which also equal loans), so as to maximize its profits.

## Banking Competition

Of course, if a bank's managers were free to do so, they could maximize the bank's profits by setting the loan interest rate very high, the deposit interest rate very low, and the bank's size very large. But competition obviously prevents this. Indeed, as we saw in Chapter 10, banks face competition from many quarters, including other banks and nondepository intermediaries. Here we will focus on competition within the banking industry, which will be sufficient to illustrate our main points. The *degree of banking competition* determines the latitude a bank has in setting its interest rates.

### A Competitive Banking Industry

As we will use the term, a **competitive banking industry** has **free entry and exit for banks**—new banks can enter, and old banks can leave, the industry without special costs. They will decide to enter or leave depending on the level of profits. The industry is in *equilibrium* when banks are neither entering nor leaving the industry. This will occur when bank profits are zero—or equivalently, the profit margin is zero. Equilibrium thus requires a *zero profit condition* for the profit margin:

$$r_L^* - r_D^* - c = 0, \qquad (11.4)$$

where $r_L^*$ = the equilibrium interest rate for loans,

$r_D^*$ = the equilibrium interest rate for deposits.

Equation (11.4) indicates that banks earn zero profits—apparently not a very profitable business. However, we should keep two aspects of bank operating costs in mind.

First, the operating cost ratio $c$ in equation (11.4) should include the *minimum return that shareholders require* to keep the bank operating. This minimum return reflects the opportunity cost of the funds that shareholders have invested in the bank. Given that this minimum return is included in $c$, equation (11.4) really means that *economic profits*—profits above the minimum return required by shareholders—will be zero in a competitive banking industry.

The second factor to keep in mind is that *operating costs vary among banks.* In particular, the operating cost ratio $c$ in equation (11.4) applies only to a *marginal bank*—a bank that is just on the margin of leaving (or entering) the banking industry. Banks that are active in the industry will generally have lower cost ratios, and therefore they will be earning positive profits.

In summary, in a competitive banking industry, a bank on the margin of leaving the industry will earn zero economic profits. The shareholders in active banks should receive a minimum return on their investment, and they will receive positive economic profits if the cost ratio of their bank is less than the ratio of the marginal bank.

### Perfect Competition

We can provide a graph of a competitive banking industry if we make the further assumption—which we will call **perfect competition**—that each bank is small. The situation of a bank operating in such a perfectly competitive industry is illustrated in Figure 11.1. Perfect competition implies that each bank faces an unlimited demand for loans and an unlimited supply of deposits, at the equilibrium interest rates for loans and deposits, respectively. This is represented by the horizontal lines in Figure 11.1.

With perfect competition for loans, each bank can make whatever quantity of loans it wishes at the market loan rate $r_L*$. With perfect competition for deposits, each bank can attract whatever quantity of deposits it wishes at the market deposit rate $r_D*$. In equilibrium, a bank on the margin of exiting the industry will have a zero profit margin, $r_L* - r_D* - c = 0$. Active banks with lower operating cost ratios will earn positive profits.

FIGURE 11.1
**Equilibrium for a Bank in a Perfectly Competitive Industry**

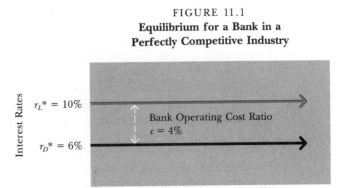

Quantity of Loans $L$ and Deposits $D$

The horizontal lines indicate that each bank can choose whatever quantity of loans and deposits it wishes, but that it cannot vary from the market interest rates for loans and deposits. Otherwise, if for example a bank tried to charge a higher loan rate than $r_L*$, borrowers would simply go to other banks; the same thing holds true for deposit rates lower than $r_D*$.

It is also important to understand the two factors that determine the equilibrium interest rates $r_L*$ and $r_D*$. The first factor is that the marginal bank has to earn zero profits, as indicated by equation (11.4). The second factor is that the supply of deposits and the demand for loans for the banking industry must be equal. We discussed this aspect in Chapter 6, where Figure 6.2 showed how the two rates are determined by the demand and supply of loanable funds.

### An Imperfectly Competitive Banking Industry

We can also consider what happens if the banking industry is **imperfectly competitive**. In this case, a bank that raises its loan rate above the competitive market level $r_L*$ will not lose all of its borrowers. Similarly, a bank that lowers it deposit rate below the competitive market level $r_D*$ will not lose all of its depositors. A bank in this situation can thus consider charging higher loan rates and lower deposit rates to maximize its profits. However, in doing so, the bank will have to take three additional factors into account:

1. The demand for loans will fall as its loan rate rises.

2. The supply of deposits will fall as its deposit rate falls.

3. The quantity of loans and deposits must be equal to satisfy the balance sheet constraint, equation (11.3).

A bank's managers consider these factors in determining the loan and deposit rates (or, equivalently, the quantities) that maximize profits.[1] A bank in an imperfectly competitive industry will normally adopt a rate spread, $r_L' - r_D'$, that is larger than the corresponding spread for a perfectly competitive industry, $r_L^* - r_D^*$. This is why banks prefer to operate in imperfectly competitive markets: they can earn higher profits. This is also why borrowers and depositors are worse off when there is imperfect competition: they pay higher loan rates and receive lower deposit rates. As a practical matter, a degree of imperfect competition is likely to be present in both deposit and loan markets.

Regarding *deposits*, imperfect competition will arise when consumers consider convenience in determining which bank to use. A bank with a particularly convenient location may then be able to attract deposits even though its deposit rate is below the rates paid by other banks. Consumers may also have *inertia*—they may consider it too much trouble to change banks just to gain a slightly higher deposit rate.

Regarding *loans*, imperfect competition will arise as a result of the *customer relationship* between a bank and a borrower, as we shall discuss in Chapter 12. Factors of convenience and inertia may also determine which bank a borrower uses.

The upshot is that a bank may be able to earn positive profits as the result of imperfect competition. Nevertheless, we will find it helpful to use the zero profit condition of a perfectly competitive industry as our standard of reference for studying how other factors affect a bank's profits.

## Bank Capital Requirements

Bank capital is usually evaluated in terms of **capital ratios**—the ratio of capital to assets. Figure 11.2 shows that the average capital ratio for commercial banks in the United States was falling until the early 1980s. Capital ratios also vary across banks, and the ratios for some banks became very low in the late 1970s—under 5%. As a result, banking regulators urged banks to raise their capital ratios, and set a 5.5% ratio as the minimum goal for all banks. Figure 11.2 indicates that the regulatory actions seem to have had an effect, although the ratios of some banks are still quite low.

Bank *regulators* want banks to maintain high capital ratios as a safety net to prevent insolvency. Regulators apply formulas based on the riskiness of bank assets to determine specific goals for capital ratios. The value of the safety net is particularly evident when a bank suffers a large loan loss. As we discussed in Box 1.6 in Chapter 1, banks reduce their capital when they write off loan losses. This process is illustrated in Table 11.1. If loan losses exceed capital, the bank becomes insolvent. Bank regulators encourage higher capital ratios in order to avoid this outcome.

Bank *managers* generally have mixed feelings about high capital ratios.

---

[1] Based on microeconomic theory, a bank will maximize its profits by setting the sum of the marginal cost of deposit interest and operating expenses equal to the marginal revenue on loans.

FIGURE 11.2
**Capital to Asset Ratios for All Commercial Banks**

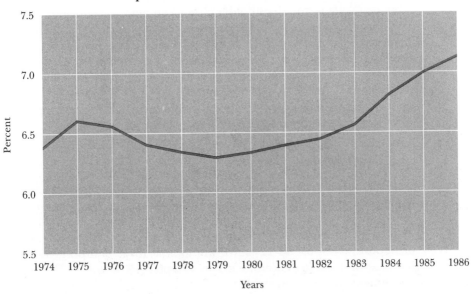

Bank capital ratios were falling during the late 1970s, reflecting faster growth in bank assets than in bank capital. Starting in the early 1980s, regulatory action reversed the trend. **Source:** Janice M. Moulton, "New Guidelines for Bank Capital," *Business Review*, Federal Reserve Bank of Philadelphia, July/August 1987.

Of course, they too want to avoid insolvency. However, the earnings on bank capital have only a minor influence on bank profits. So, generally speaking, the more capital a bank has, the lower will be its *return on capital*—profits divided by capital. Table 11.2 gives an example.

For this reason, it may be in the shareholders' interest to keep a bank's capital relatively low. Of course, the return on capital may be more

**TABLE 11.1**
**How Banks Write Off Bad Loans**

**Hypothetical Balance Sheet
Before Loan Losses Are Recognized**

| Assets | Liabilities and Capital |
|---|---|
| Loans $100 | Deposits $95 |
| | Capital  $5 |

**Same Balance Sheet
After Recognizing $5 Loan Loss**

| Assets | Liabilities and Capital |
|---|---|
| Loans $95 | Deposits $95 |
| | Capital  $0 |

**TABLE 11.2**
**Profits as a Function of Bank Capital Ratios**

**Hypothetical banks with profit rate of 1%
Capital**

| | Low | Moderate | High |
|---|---|---|---|
| Deposits | $950 | $950 | $950 |
| Capital | $10 | $50 | $100 |
| Total assets | $960 | $1,000 | $1,050 |
| Capital ratio (capital/assets) | 1.04% | 5% | 9.5% |
| Return on capital[a] (profits/capital) | 96% ($9.60) | 20% ($10.00) | 10.5% ($10.50) |

[a]Based on a profit ratio of 1% on assets.

volatile for a bank with a low capital ratio—small changes in profits will be reflected in large changes in the rate of return. But this should not be a major problem for shareholders: they can always balance this risk by holding other safe assets in their overall portfolio.

It may also be hard for some banks to raise additional capital. Banks raise capital either by retaining a higher percentage of profits or by issuing new capital stock. But this is difficult for a bank that has been suffering low profits. Also, it may not be able to sell new stock at prices that are acceptable to the existing shareholders. Of course, regulators must urgently want these sick banks to raise their capital.

## Bank Reserve Requirements

In addition to capital requirements, the Federal Reserve has **reserve requirements**—which require banks to hold specific percentages—**reserve ratios**—of their deposits in cash or in reserve accounts at the Federal Reserve. Reserve ratios currently vary, depending on the type of deposit, from 0% to 12%. We will look at these and other technical features of reserve requirements in Chapter 18 when we discuss the instruments of monetary policy.

However, one feature of required reserves must be considered here— that banks receive no interest on them. Cash, of course, pays no interest; and the Federal Reserve pays no interest on the money in reserve accounts. In this sense, reserve ratios represent an implicit tax on banks. Moreover, with perfect competition, the tax effects of reserve requirements are passed on to bank customers in the form of higher loan interest rates and lower deposit interest rates.

Suppose there is a single reserve ratio, $\theta$, which we will treat as 10% in numerical examples. The reserve requirement can then be expressed:

$$R_r = \theta D \qquad (11.5)$$

where $R_r$ = required reserves,
$\qquad \theta$ = required reserve ratio,
$\qquad D$ = deposits subject to the reserve requirement.

Without required reserves, a bank can apply all of its deposits to loans, $D = L$, as in equation (11.3). With required reserves, deposits have to cover the sum of loans $L$ and required reserves $R_r$:

$$D = L + R_r \qquad (11.6)$$

By substituting the amount of required reserves $R_r$ from equation (11.5) into equation (11.6) and solving for loans $L$, we have:

$$L = (1 - \theta)D \qquad (11.7)$$

And by substituting $(1 - \theta)D$ for loans $L$ into the bank profit equation (11.1), we have:

$$\begin{aligned} \pi &= (r_L\,L) - (r_D\,D) - (cD) \\ &= (r_L[1 - \theta]D) - (r_D\,D) - (cD) \\ &= (r_L - r_D - c - \theta r_L)\,D \qquad (11.8) \end{aligned}$$

Profits are still the product of the profit margin and deposits $D$, but the profit margin is now reduced by the term $(\theta r_L)$—the tax effect of reserve requirements.

The profit margin is still zero in a competitive equilibrium:

$$r_L{}^* - r_D{}^* - c - \theta r_L{}^* = 0 \qquad (11.9)$$

However, for this zero profit condition to be satisfied, in comparison with the situation without required reserves, the rate spread, $r_L{}^* - r_D{}^*$, must be large enough to cover the cost of the required reserves $(\theta r_L{}^*)$. Moreover, since all banks must satisfy the reserve requirement, the cost of doing so will be reflected in a larger rate spread for the whole industry. This means that a higher reserve ratio causes the market loan rate $r_L{}^*$ to rise and the market deposit rate $r_D{}^*$ to fall, the combined change in the two rates being equal to the cost of the reserve requirement $(\theta r_L{}^*)$.

Table 11.3 illustrates how higher required reserve ratios cause loan rates to rise and deposit rates to fall, given that the profit margin remains zero. However, in looking at this example, be aware that even when there are no reserve requirements, banks might still hold reserves for liquidity purposes—our next topic.

---

**TABLE 11.3**
**The Effect of Required Reserve Ratios ($\theta = 10\%$)**

**Bank Balance Sheets**

| Without Reserve Requirements | | With Reserve Requirements | |
|---|---|---|---|
| **Assets** | **Liabilities** | **Assets** | **Liabilities** |
| Loans $100 | Deposits $100 | Loans    $90 | Deposits $100 |
| | | Required reserves $10 | |

**Bank Profit Margins**

| Without Reserve Requirements | With Reserve Requirements |
|---|---|
| Loan rate $r_L{}^* = 10\%$ | Loan rate $r_L{}^* = 10.5\%$ |
| Deposit rate $r_D{}^* = 6\%$ | Deposit rate $r_D{}^* = 5.45\%$ |
| Operating cost ratio $c = 4\%$ | Operating cost ratio $c = 4\%$ |
| | Cost of reserve requirement $= \theta r_L{}^* =$ |
| | $(10\%)(10.5\%) = 1.05\%$. |
| Profit margin | Profit margin |
| $= r_L{}^* - r_D{}^* - c$ | $= r_L{}^* - r_D{}^* - c - \theta r_L{}^*$ |
| $= 10\% - 6\% - 4\%$ | $= 10.5\% - 5.45\% - 4\% - 1.05\%$ |
| $= 0\%$. | $= 0\%$. |

---

## Liquidity Management

A person can remove money from a bank account in basically two ways; by withdrawing cash or by writing a check. Banks hold vault cash to handle cash withdrawals, and they hold reserve deposits at the Federal Reserve to handle check withdrawals.

Banks need liquidity mainly because depositors can make withdrawals **without prior notice** from accounts that have no stated maturity—checking accounts and saving accounts. In contrast, time deposits (and other liabilities) that have a **fixed maturity** create only limited liquidity needs because money can be withdrawn from them only on a specified date. Time deposits mainly create *interest rate risk*, relating to the cost at which they can be replaced, as we discussed in Chapter 8. In this discussion, we will focus on the need for liquidity created by deposit accounts that require no prior notice for withdrawal.

## The Need for Bank Liquidity

The deposits that require no prior notice for withdrawal make up almost half of total bank deposits. Savings deposit accounts may have a formal requirement of prior notice, but banks rarely enforce it. Since withdrawals are more frequent and volatile from checking accounts than from savings accounts, checking accounts are the primary source of bank liquidity needs.

Checking account withdrawals can occur as either over-the-counter cash outflows or as reserve outflows to other banks. *Cash outflows* occur when customers withdraw cash from their accounts. *Reserve outflows* occur when a bank has to transfer some of its reserve deposits at the Federal Reserve to another bank because a customer's check has been deposited in that other bank.

All banks hold reserve deposits at the Federal Reserve to settle their check transfers. When a customer of bank A writes a check that is deposited in bank B, bank B presents the check at the Federal Reserve's check-clearing system for payment by bank A. This creates an **adverse check clearing** for bank A and a **favorable check clearing** for bank B. To settle the accounts, the Federal Reserve will transfer the amount of the check from the reserve account of bank A to the reserve account of bank B.

The daily **deposit outflows** of cash and reserves due to withdrawals are enormous for the typical bank. As discussed in Box 11.1, this is particularly true for large banks in financial centers. These banks would have to hold an enormous amount of liquidity—cash and reserve deposits—to meet their daily gross outflows.

However, banks benefit from the **banking principle**—each day, *deposit outflows* (including adverse check clearings) are balanced by **deposit inflows** (including favorable check clearings). This dramatically reduces the amount of liquidity most banks need. In fact, most banks, most of the time, have *net* deposit inflows—deposit inflows exceed deposit outflows.

A typical situation is illustrated in Figure 11.3, which shows the net flows of a bank's deposits over a four-week period. On most days, the bank receives a net inflow of deposits. But net outflows occur on some days. So even though the bank usually has little need for liquidity, it has to be prepared for the net outflows that occur occasionally.

FIGURE 11.3
**Net Flows of Deposits for a Typical Bank**

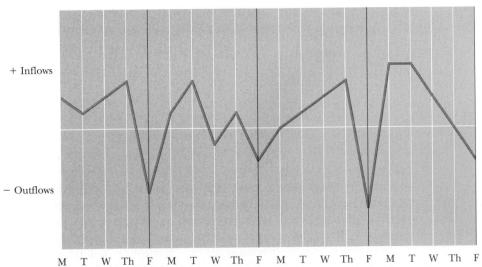

The bank usually receives a net inflow, but sometimes it has a net out-flow, especially on Fridays when people withdraw money for the weekend.

## BOX 11.1 BANKING BRIEFS

## Deposit Debit Rates

*Debit rates* measure the number of times a year the average balance in an account turns over. For example, if your average balance is $100 and during the year you withdraw $1,000 (redepositing this amount at other times), then your annual debit rate is 10 ($1,000/$100). As shown below, the debit rate for all commercial banks in the United States during 1987 was 612. Given that there are about 220 business days in a year, this means the average bank deposit is withdrawn (and deposited) more than twice each *day*. At New York City banks, the annual debit rate was 2,671 in 1987.

Several factors are at work here:

■ Most transaction accounts are held by businesses, which move their money around quite rapidly.

■ A good part of the deposits in New York City, and other financial centers, are used for financial transactions, where the same balances can be used many times a day.

■ The debit rates of consumers are rising, based on automated-teller machines and other methods they use to deposit and withdraw funds frequently.

**Deposit Debit Rates**

**Ratio of annual debits to average deposits**

|  | 1960 | 1970 | 1980 | 1987 |
|---|---|---|---|---|
| All commercial banks | 36 | 63 | 203 | 612 |
| New York City banks | 62 | 165 | 817 | 2,671 |
| Other banks | 26 | 47 | 135 | 357 |

**Source:** *Federal Reserve Bulletin*, Table 1.22, Board of Governors of the Federal Reserve System, 1988.

### Lines of Credit

**Lines of credit**—bank obligations to extend credit in the future—create a further need for liquidity. A firm may receive a line of credit either as a *loan commitment* (a promise by the bank to make a loan at a future date), or as a *standby letter of credit* (an obligation of a bank to make a specified payment on behalf of the firm). A consumer may receive a line of credit either as an *overdraft* (the value of checks the depositor can write in excess of his or her account balance), or as a *credit limit on a bank credit card* (the maximum amount of purchases that can be charged to the card).

Bank customers can generally use their credit lines at any time. When a credit line is used, a bank either makes a payment directly on the customer's behalf, or places money in the customer's account, from which the customer makes the payment. Either way, the bank needs liquidity to fulfill its obligation. Thus lines of credit and transaction deposits create a similar need for bank liquidity—in either case, money can be withdrawn from the bank without prior notice.

Banks do not expect that most of their credit lines will be used at the same time, but they must still hold some liquidity for that contingency. Indeed, as described in Box 11.2, the Federal Reserve now requires that each bank tabulate its credit lines as an aid in judging how much liquidity it needs.

## The Instruments of Liquidity Management

To provide liquidity, banks manage their assets and liabilities—the instruments of **liquidity management**. *Asset management* uses three categories of assets: (1) primary reserves, (2) secondary reserves, and (3) earning assets. *Liability management* uses time deposits and nondeposit liabilities.

A flow diagram of liquidity management is shown in Figure 11.4. The diagram can be referred to as we discuss the instruments of liquidity management, starting at the bottom of the figure with primary reserves, and then working our way upward through secondary reserves, liability management, federal funds, earning assets, and the Federal Reserve's discount facility.

### Primary Reserves

**Primary reserves** are the immediate source of liquidity for a bank facing a deposit outflow. Primary reserves include a number of components, as shown in Table 11.4.

**Vault cash**—cash in bank vaults—is used for over-the-counter cash outflows. Banks operate with a small average amount of vault cash—1% of total assets, on average. This amount is sufficient because banks can raise their cash positions temporarily when they anticipate cash outflows; such as on Fridays (illustrated in Figure 11.3) and on days before holidays. Banks also anticipate seasonal cash outflows, such as during Christmas and summer vacations.

## Loan Commitments: On and Off the Balance Sheet

The loans made by a bank are explicitly shown on its balance sheet, so their total amount is obvious. In contrast, credit lines are *off balance sheet* obligations—they are not explicitly shown on a bank's balance sheet. Some years ago the Fed began requiring banks to tabulate their credit line obligations to make sure they were not rising too rapidly. As shown in the table below, the results are remarkable: bank credit lines (the off balance sheet obligations) equal about half of the amount of loans actually made (the on balance sheet assets).

### Credit Lines and Loans of U.S. Commercial Banks

#### Dollars in billions

| Years | Lines of Credit | Loans |
|-------|-----------------|-------|
| 1984 | 635 | 1,271 |
| 1985 | 732 | 1,399 |
| 1986 | 755 | 1,536 |

**Source:** Reprinted by permission from the Federal Reserve Bank of Atlanta, from Sylvester Johnson and Amelia A. Murphy, "Going off the Balance Sheet." *Economic Review*, vol. LXXII, no. 5 (September/October 1987), p. 27.

Primary reserves, consisting of vault cash and reserve deposits at the Federal Reserve, are used directly to handle deposit outflows. If a bank starts to run short of primary reserves, then it has to replenish them using secondary reserves, liability management, earning assets, or the Federal Reserve discount facility.

FIGURE 11.4
**Alternative Instruments for Liquidity Management**

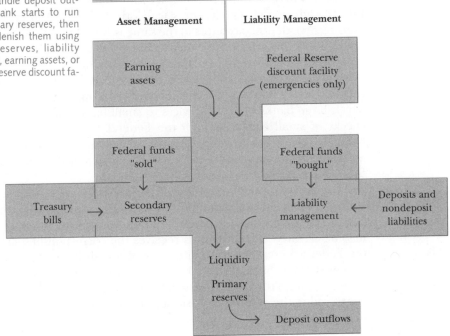

**TABLE 11.4**

**Commercial Bank Assets for Liquidity Management**

Year-end 1987
(For all commercial banks)

| Assets | Dollars in billions | Percentage of total assets |
|---|---|---|
| Primary reserves | | |
| Vault cash | $ 25 | 1 |
| Reserve deposits at the Federal Reserve | 37 | 1 |
| Cash due from other banks | 34 | 1 |
| Cash items in process of collection (CIPC) | 86 | 3 |
| Other cash assets | 43 | 2 |
| Secondary reserves | | |
| Securities | 479 | 19 |
| Federal funds sold | 128 | 5 |
| Earning assets loans | 1577 | 62 |
| Other assets | 155 | 6 |
| Total assets | $2564 | 100 |

**Source:** *Federal Reserve Bulletin,* Table 4.22, Board of Governors of the Federal Reserve System, April 1988.

The **reserve deposits** that banks keep at the Federal Reserve—also just called **reserves**—are the second component of primary reserves. A bank can make a withdrawal from its reserve account to obtain additional vault cash from the Federal Reserve. Similarly, a bank can deposit its excess cash in its Federal Reserve account. Banks also use their reserves to settle adverse check clearings with other banks. Overall, banks use their reserve deposit accounts in the same way that people use a checking account—in this sense, the Federal Reserve is the "bank for banks."

The third component of primary reserves is *cash due from other banks—* mainly the deposits that small banks keep at large banks as part of correspondent banking. **Correspondent banking** is an arrangement in which large banks provide services to small banks; such as clearing the checks of small banks through the Federal Reserve's system. A small bank therefore has to hold deposits at the large bank that settles its accounts, in the same way that reserves are held at the Federal Reserve for check clearing.

The last component of primary reserves is *cash items in process of collection—*also called **bank float.** When a check drawn on bank A is deposited in bank B for credit to the account of depositor B, depositor B's account may be credited before bank B receives the corresponding credit from the Federal Reserve. This is the basis of a cash item in process of collection (CIPC): bank B has a cash item—the check—in process of collection through the Federal Reserve's system. When the Federal Reserve later credits the reserve deposit account of bank B, the related CIPC becomes zero.

Bank float is not the only kind of float that arises out of the check-clearing system: Box 11.3 describes two other types of float—**Federal Reserve float** and **customer float**.

### Required Reserves and Excess Reserves

The use of primary reserves for liquidity management is affected by two other factors—required reserves and excess reserves. As we saw before, **required reserves** are held to satisfy the Fed's reserve requirement—equal to the reserve ratio times the amount of bank deposits subject to the requirement. **Excess reserves** equal total reserves minus required reserves.[2] Because required reserves *have* to be held, banks mainly use excess reserves to settle adverse check clearings and to pay for currency shipments received from the Fed.

Table 11.5 illustrates how a bank uses its excess reserves for liquidity purposes. In the initial position, the bank has deposits of $100, required reserves of $10 based on a reserve ratio of 10%, excess reserves of $9, and it invests the remaining $81 of assets in loans.

Now imagine that a depositor makes a cash withdrawal of $10. The bank obtains the $10 to meet the withdrawals from two sources. First, it gets $9 from its initial excess reserves. Second, it gets $1 from the required reserves that become excess reserves when deposits fall by $10. That is, if the required reserve ratio is 10% and deposits fall by $10, then required reserves fall by $1 (10% of $10). Thus $1 of required reserves becomes $1 of additional excess reserves.

### Determining the Amount of Excess Reserves

Cost considerations and the amount of expected withdrawals determine the exact amount of excess reserves each bank will want to hold. Since excess reserves pay no interest, they have an *opportunity cost*—measured by the rate of return the bank would have earned by investing that amount in interest-paying assets. So to determine its amount of excess reserves, a bank must evaluate the trade-off between the liquidity benefit and the opportunity cost.

**TABLE 11.5**

Using Required and Excess Reserves for Liquidity Purposes

| Initial Balance Sheet of Hypothetical Bank | | Balance Sheet After Cash Withdrawal of $10 | |
|---|---|---|---|
| Assets | Liabilities | Assets | Liabilities |
| Bank reserves $19 | Deposits $100 | Bank reserves $9 | Deposits $90 |
| Required $10 | | Required $9 | |
| Excess $9 | | Excess $0 | |
| Loans $81 | | Loans $81 | |

[2] Due to various accounting matters, the total reserves used to compute excess reserves are not exactly the same as the total primary reserves shown in Table 11.4. The precise computation of total reserves is shown in Chapter 18.

## BOX 11.3 BANKING BRIEFS

### Float

*Bank float* arises when a bank credits a customer's deposit account before the bank receives the corresponding credit from the Federal Reserve. Two other types of float—Federal Reserve float and customer float—also arise in the process of clearing checks.

Federal Reserve float is equal to the temporary difference between credits and debits given by the Federal Reserve in the process of clearing checks. Suppose the Federal Reserve is clearing a check written on bank A that has been deposited in bank B. If in clearing the check, the Federal Reserve gives a *credit to bank B* before it can give a *debit to bank A*, then Federal

Reserve float is created—the total reserves of the bank system rise temporarily. We will discuss this further, as part of monetary policy, in Part V.

*Customer float* arises if a bank delays crediting a deposit to a customer's account beyond the date on which the bank receives the corresponding credit from the Federal Reserve. In this case, the bank will be able to earn interest on the collected funds without paying interest to the customer on the corresponding deposit balance. Many states have now passed laws to reduce the amount of customer float by requiring banks to credit deposits promptly to customer accounts.

The process is illustrated in Figure 11.5, where the demand curve for excess reserves, $R_e$, is a negatively sloped function of the rate that the bank earns on interest-paying assets $r_A$. That is, other things being equal, a bank will want to hold less excess reserves, the greater the opportunity cost of holding them (the higher the rate $r_A$).

The location of the demand curve for excess reserves depends on the bank's need for liquidity and on the cost of obtaining liquidity in other ways. The exact amount of excess reserves is determined by the location of the demand curve and the level of the interest rate on assets. For example, for the demand curve in Figure 11.5, when the interest rate

The demand curve for excess reserves shifts to the right as the result of factors that raise the need for liquidity (such as anticipated net cash outflows), or that raise the cost of obtaining liquidity in other ways (such as a higher discount rate on loans from the Federal Reserve).

FIGURE 11.5
**The Demand for Excess Reserves**

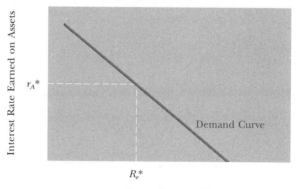

Interest Rate Earned on Assets

$r_A^*$

Demand Curve

$R_e^*$

Excess Reserves $R_e$

is $r_A{}^*$, the bank will hold excess reserves of $R_e{}^*$. Two factors that shift the demand curve for excess reserves to the right are:

- An anticipated net outflow of deposits.
- A higher interest rate on discount loans from the Federal Reserve (which makes excess reserves relatively more attractive as a source of liquidity).

Overall, excess reserves represent a necessary but high-cost solution for bank liquidity needs. The result is that banks use excess reserves to meet only those liquidity needs that are very likely to arise in the near future. Banks find less costly solutions for less likely liquidity needs and for those further in the future. We now consider some of these alternatives.

## Secondary Reserves

Banks sometimes use **secondary reserves**—usually short-term securities such as U.S. Treasury bills—to back up their primary reserves. A bank can then sell some of its Treasury bills when it needs to augment its vault cash or its reserve deposit account at the Federal Reserve. However, it takes several days to receive payment on a security sale, so the liquidity provided by secondary reserves is not immediately available, in contrast to primary reserves. On the other hand, banks earn interest on secondary reserve securities, if only at a modest rate, so their opportunity cost is less than that of primary reserves.

Treasury bills have very desirable features for a secondary reserve security. They are traded in active markets, so banks can sell large amounts on short notice without significantly affecting the market price. Also, because Treasury bills have short-term maturities (no more than one year), their price fluctuations are small, even when market interest rates change substantially. The effect is that Treasury bills can be liquidated rapidly and at low cost whenever a bank needs to augment its primary reserves. At the same time, Treasury bills provide at least a modest rate of return.

## Liability Management

**Liability management** is another way that banks can increase their primary reserves. To raise primary reserves with liability management, banks attract new deposits or issue nondeposit liabilities, holding the proceeds either as vault cash or in reserve deposit accounts. Table 11.6 shows the main liabilities that banks use for this purpose. Cost considerations determine whether a bank will use secondary reserves or liability management to manage its liquidity. In practice, liability management is now generally less expensive and has largely replaced secondary reserves (asset management).

An example that compares secondary reserves with liability management as methods of managing liquidity is shown in Table 11.7. For each case, the bank starts with $100 of deposits, and then $10 of the deposits are withdrawn.

**TABLE 11.6**

**Commercial Bank Liabilities for Liquidity Management**

<table>
<tr><td colspan="3" align="center">Year-end 1987<br>(For all commercial banks)</td></tr>
<tr><td>Liabilities</td><td align="center">Dollars in<br>billions</td><td align="center">Percentage<br>of total assets</td></tr>
<tr><td>Deposits</td><td></td><td></td></tr>
<tr><td>No prior notice accounts</td><td></td><td></td></tr>
<tr><td>  Transaction accounts</td><td align="center">$ 639</td><td align="center">25</td></tr>
<tr><td>  Savings accounts</td><td align="center">524</td><td align="center">20</td></tr>
<tr><td>Fixed maturity</td><td></td><td></td></tr>
<tr><td>  Time deposits</td><td align="center">493</td><td align="center">19</td></tr>
<tr><td>  CDs ($100,000 or more)</td><td align="center">298</td><td align="center">12</td></tr>
<tr><td>Liabilities</td><td></td><td></td></tr>
<tr><td>  Federal funds bought</td><td align="center">128</td><td align="center">5</td></tr>
<tr><td>  Discount borrowing</td><td></td><td></td></tr>
<tr><td>  from Federal Reserve</td><td align="center">1</td><td align="center">–</td></tr>
<tr><td>Other liabilities</td><td align="center">303</td><td align="center">12</td></tr>
<tr><td>Bank capital</td><td align="center">178</td><td align="center">7</td></tr>
<tr><td>  Total liabilities and capital</td><td align="center">$2564</td><td align="center">100</td></tr>
</table>

**Source:** *Federal Reserve Bulletin*, Table 4.22, Board of Governors of the Federal Reserve System, June 1988.

---

**TABLE 11.7**

**Liquidity Management with Secondary Reserves and Liability Management for a Hypothetical Bank**

**A. Secondary Reserves**

| Initial Position | | | Final Position<br>(After withdrawal of $10) | | |
|---|---|---|---|---|---|
| Assets | | Liabilities | Assets | | Liabilities |
| Required reserves | $10 | Deposits    $100 | Required reserves | $9 | Deposits       $90 |
| Secondary reserves | $9 | | Secondary reserves | $0 | |
| Loans | $81 | | Loans | $81 | |

**B. Liability Management**

| Initial Position | | | Final Position<br>(After withdrawal of $10) | | |
|---|---|---|---|---|---|
| Assets | | Liabilities | Assets | | Liabilities |
| Required reserves | $10 | Deposits    $100 | Required reserves | $10 | Deposits    $100<br>[old]    $90<br>[new]    $10 |
| Loans | $90 | | Loans | $90 | |

Panel A illustrates the use of *secondary reserves*. In the initial position, the bank has invested its $100 of deposits in $10 of required reserves, $9 of Treasury bills (as secondary reserves), and $81 of loans. After the deposit withdrawal of $10, the balance sheet is shown by the final position. To reach the final position, the bank sells $9 of Treasury bills and uses the $1 of required reserves that becomes excess reserves when deposits fall by $10.

Panel B illustrates *liability management*. In the initial position, the bank holds no secondary reserves, so it can invest $90 in earning assets. After the deposit withdrawal of $10, the balance sheet is again shown by the final position. To reach the final position with liability management, the bank raises the interest rate on deposits to attract $10 of new deposits to replace the deposits that were withdrawn.

The advantage of liability management is that a bank can make more loans given that it does not have to hold secondary reserves. In Table 11.7, with liability management, the bank holds an extra $9 of loans in the initial position ($90 versus $81). This is profitable because the interest rate on loans is generally higher than the rate on secondary reserve securities. Also, the cost of attracting new deposits may be less than the revenue lost in selling secondary reserve securities.

For a liability to be useful for liability management, banks must be able to attract additional amounts of it by offering to pay higher interest rates. In practice, time deposits work well in this respect. Transaction and savings deposits work less well because the demand for them also depends on the bank's reputation for good service, which usually cannot be changed rapidly.

Liability management based on deposits was hampered at one time by the Federal Reserve's Regulation Q ceilings—discussed in Chapter 10—which limited the interest rates banks could pay on deposits. During the 1960s and 1970s, market interest rates often reached or exceeded the Regulation Q ceiling level, at which point the banks were no longer able to offer higher deposit rates to attract additional deposits. This eliminated liability management of deposits as a tool for managing liquidity. However, now that deregulation has removed the ceilings, deposits are actively used for liability management.

## Federal Funds and Repurchase Agreements

Federal funds and repurchase agreements are two more instruments that banks use for liquidity management. In Part V, we will see that they also play a role in monetary policy.

### Federal Funds

**Federal funds** represent short-term loans of reserves between banks: banks with excess reserves lend them to other banks. *Federal funds sold*, shown in Table 11.4, is the asset that represents federal funds loaned by banks; this asset serves as a secondary reserve. *Federal funds bought*, shown in Table 11.6, is the liability that represents federal funds borrowed by banks as part of their liability management. Box 11.4 describes how the market for federal funds operates.

The trading of federal funds between banks allows the total amount of bank reserves to be efficiently distributed on the basis of the willingness of banks to pay for them. The interest rate on federal funds—*the federal*

BOX 11.4 BANKING BRIEFS

## The Market for Federal Funds

The market for federal funds is available to any bank or firm that maintains a deposit account at the Federal Reserve. Banks are the main participants, but some nonbank firms—such as dealers in U.S. Treasury securities—also keep deposits at the Fed and participate in the federal funds market. Transactions in federal funds are arranged by special brokers who are in constant contact with lenders and borrowers. When a transaction is completed, the Fed transfers the specified amount of reserve deposits from the lender to the borrower. Later, the transfer, including the amount of interest, is reversed.

Federal funds transactions are typically very large: $1 million is the minimum unit. The interest rate on these loans—the federal funds rate—is reported daily in the financial press (see Box 5.4 in Chapter 5). Federal funds transactions represent loans of very short maturities—often just one day, and rarely more than a week. The amount of interest on a one-day loan of course is very small: for example, when the federal funds rate is 8% on an annual basis, the daily interest on $1 million is just $200. So to keep operating costs low, the federal funds market uses *wire transfers* to notify the Fed when to transfer reserves from one bank to another.

*funds rate*—is determined at a level that balances the demand and supply of federal funds. By and large, large banks borrow, and small banks lend, federal funds. The basic reason is that most small banks are not known well enough to borrow in the federal funds market. Consequently, small banks can generally only lend federal funds as secondary reserve securities.

### Repurchase Agreements

**Repurchase agreements** are another instrument of liquidity management, serving a purpose similar to federal funds. Repurchase agreements are short-term borrowing and lending transactions that are collateralized with securities, usually U.S. Treasury bills or bonds.

A bank that needs to augment its primary reserves could just sell some Treasury bills it is holding. This would represent a standard use of secondary reserves. However, if the bank's need for liquidity is temporary, it could use a repurchase agreement—it would sell the Treasury bills, but also agree to *repurchase* them at a later date and at a specified price. The effect is that the bank obtains liquidity (from the sale of the Treasury bills), but only temporarily (it later repurchases the Treasury bills). Thus, repurchase agreements are tantamount to borrowing liquidity, somewhat like buying federal funds.

## Earning Assets

**Earning assets**—loans, U.S. Treasury bonds, and other long-term securities—are held by banks because of the high rates of return they offer. Earning assets can also provide banks with liquidity, but only to the extent that they can be sold in the same manner as secondary reserve securities. For this reason, U.S. Treasury bonds are usually *not* classified as secondary reserve securities: their prices can fluctuate substantially when interest rates change—on account of their long-term maturity— so their liquidity value is uncertain.

Loans also have not been used as secondary reserves, but for a different reason: it has been difficult to sell loans. Loans present two main problems in this regard: they have relatively high credit risk, and they are of relatively small size. An investor who otherwise might think of buying loans from a bank will find it costly to evaluate the credit risk of many individual loans, especially without access to the bank's information about the borrower. As a result, banks have usually just held their loans until maturity.

### Securitization: A New Way To Make Loans Liquid

A new process—**securitization**—is providing banks the opportunity to sell loans for liquidity purposes for the first time. Previously, if banks tried to sell their loans, buyers would require large discounts in the price as an inducement. With securitization, a large number of loans are collected in a single package, and the package is sold as if it were a security. Guarantees are also provided to reduce the credit risk of the total package. The result is that banks can now sell their loans for liquidity purposes, while investors obtain a relatively high-return/low-risk security.

Securitization raises the liquidity of bank loans much closer to secondary reserve securities, which is another reason that secondary reserve securities have become less important for liquidity management. However, securitization is still a time-consuming and cumbersome process. A number of investment banking firms are working to improve the process, so securitization is likely to expand in the future as a tool of liquidity management. Box 11.5 describes a related development—**loan-backed securities.**

---

**BOX 11.5 BANKING BRIEFS**

## Loan-Backed Securities

*Loan backed securities* are another innovation based on the securitization principle. Loan-backed securities are like other nondeposit liabilities that banks issue to raise money, except that they are backed—collateralized—by loan assets. The collateral is important because the securities are not deposits, and therefore they are not covered by federal deposit insurance.

Banks can achieve the same liquidity goal either by packaging loans and selling them—securitization—or by holding loans and using them to collateralize nondeposit liabilities—loan-backed securities. In either case, banks receive the cash proceeds from the sale of the security. The two techniques differ primarily in terms of the costs of creating the securities and the ease of providing investors the guarantee against default.

## Federal Reserve Discount Loans

Federal reserve discount loans are the last instrument of bank liquidity management we will consider; as we will see, discount loans are also the last instrument most banks use for liquidity management. Banks obtain **discount loans** at the **discount rate** through the Federal Reserve's *discount window*, introduced in Chapter 10. The normal maturity of the loans is two weeks. The Federal Reserve disburses a discount loan as a credit to the reserve account of the borrowing bank. This differs from borrowing federal funds only in that the Federal Reserve, not another bank, is the lender.

However, discount loans have a catch: the Federal Reserve considers discount borrowing "a privilege, not a right." That is, the Fed encourages banks to use the discount window only after all other sources of liquidity have been exhausted. In particular, banks do not receive discount loans if the Fed suspects them of borrowing for purposes of profit.

As a result, most large banks use the federal funds market, instead of the Fed's discount window, for their borrowing needs. Small banks— without access to the federal funds market—use the discount window more often, but again only if they have no other sources of liquidity. Of course, all banks use the discount window as their last resort when they are in trouble.

## Implementing Liquidity Management Policies

Having reviewed all of the instruments available to a bank for liquidity management, we can now summarize the steps a bank will use in implementing a liquidity management plan:

1. *Anticipate Liquidity Needs.* The bank will determine the likely level of its deposit outflows, both for the near term and for the future.

2. *Make Asset Decisions.* The bank will acquire adequate amounts of primary reserve and secondary reserve assets to handle expected deposit withdrawals.

3. *Use Primary Reserves.* When deposit outflows occur, the first response is always to use the primary reserves.

4. *Use Secondary Reserves and Liability Management.* If deposit outflows exceed primary reserves, then the bank will sell secondary reserve assets or issue new liabilities to replenish its primary reserves.

5. *Use the Discount Facility.* In a real emergency, the bank can borrow funds from the Federal Reserve.

---

## Chapter Summary

1. Bank profits equal the interest earned on loans and other assets, minus the interest paid on deposits, and minus bank operating expenses. Banking firms determine their interest rates, and deposit and loan quantities, to maximize profits.

2. With free entry and exit for the banking industry, bank profit margins will be zero in equilibrium. However, shareholders should still earn the minimum rate of return they require to keep the bank open, and additional profits may be earned if the bank has low operating costs or if it operates in imperfectly competitive markets.

3. Bank regulators prefer banks to have high capital ratios—the ratio of capital to assets—because capital provides a safety net to help prevent insolvency. A bank's managers and shareholders, in contrast, may have an incentive to keep the capital ratio low, so as to earn a high rate of return on the capital.

4. The Federal Reserve imposes required reserve ratios—required amounts of reserves relative to deposits. Reserve requirements are effectively a tax on banks. Moreover, with a competitive banking system, the tax is passed on to depositors as lower deposit interest rates and to borrowers as higher loan interest rates.

5. Banks need liquidity to deal with unexpected withdrawals of funds from accounts for which no prior notice of withdrawal is required, mainly transaction accounts. Withdrawals occur either as cash outflows or as adverse check clearings. Lines of credit also create a need for bank liquidity.

6. Banks can carry out liquidity management with either assets or liabilities. For asset management, assets are classified—beginning with the highest liquidity—as primary reserves, secondary reserves, and earning assets. For liability management, banks issue deposits or nondeposit liabilities to raise funds. Liability management is now more important than asset management for most banks.

7. Since required reserves are held by banks to satisfy Federal Reserve regulations, excess reserves—total reserves minus required reserves—are the main component of primary reserves used for liquidity management. Secondary reserves and liability management are both cases where securities are used to raise liquidity—in the case of the former by selling assets, and in the case of the latter by issuing liabilities (including new deposits).

## Key Terms

Adverse and favorable check clearings (between banks)

Balance sheet constraint

Bank, customer, and Federal Reserve Float

Banking principle

Capital ratio

Competitive banking industry

Correspondent banking

Deposit inflows and outflows

Deposits with no prior notice for withdrawal

Discount loans

Earning assets

Federal funds

Free entry and exit

Liability management

Lines of credit

Liquidity management

Loan-backed securities

Operating cost (ratio)

Perfect and imperfect competition

Primary and secondary reserves

Profit margin

Repurchase agreements

Required and excess reserves

Securitization

Vault cash

## Study Questions

1. Why does a zero profit condition hold for a competitive banking industry? Why does this not mean that all banks earn zero profits?

2. Why are bank profits higher under imperfect competition?

3. Why do bank regulators and bank managers often disagree about the level of bank capital ratios?

4. Why do reserve requirements result in higher loan rates and lower deposit rates with a competitive banking industry?

5. Why does the amount of the deposit outflow that a bank faces during a day overstate its liquidity needs?

6. Why are credit lines a source of bank liquidity needs?

7. How do banks use secondary reserves and liability management to supplement primary reserves for liquidity management?

8. What are the advantages of liability management over secondary reserves for liquidity management?

9. How can federal funds be used both as secondary reserve securities and as instruments of liability management?

10. How is the Federal Reserve's discount facility used for liquidity management? What is special about the circumstances under which it can be used?

## Recommended Reading

*The following books include texts, readings, and case studies on bank management, including liquidity management:*

Mona J. Gardner and Dixie L. Mills, *Managing Financial Institutions*, The Dryden Press, Hinsdale, Ill., 1988.

Benton E. Gup and Charles Meiburg, *Cases in Bank Management*, Macmillan, New York, 1986.

Thomas M. Havrilesky, Robert Schweitzer, and John T. Boorman, *Dynamics of Banking*, Harlan Davidson, Arlington Heights, Ill., 1985.

Timothy W. Koch, *Bank Management*, The Dryden Press, Hinsdale, Ill., 1988.

*The following articles discuss specific instruments of liquidity management:*

"The Economics of Securitization," *Quarterly Review*, Federal Reserve Bank of New York, Autumn 1987, pp. 11–23.

Marvin Goodfriend and William Whelpley, "Federal Funds: Instrument of Federal Reserve Policy," *Economic Review*, Federal Reserve Bank of Richmond, September/October 1986, pp. 3–11.

Sylvester Johnson and Amelia A. Murphy, "Going Off the Balance Sheet," *Economic Review*, Federal Reserve Bank of Atlanta, September/October 1987, pp. 23–35.

Stephen A. Lumpkin, "Repurchase and Reverse Repurchase Agreements," *Economic Review*, Federal Reserve Bank of Atlanta, January/February 1987, pp. 15–23.

*The following articles discuss bank capital regulations:*

Karlyn Mitchell, "Capital Adequacy at Commercial Banks," *Economic Review*, Federal Reserve Bank of Kansas City, September/October 1984, pp. 17–30.

Janice M. Moulton, "New Guidelines for Bank Capital," *Business Review*, Federal Reserve Bank of Philadelphia, July/August 1987, pp. 19–31.

# Risk Management
# by Banking Institutions

*"Creditors have better memories than debtors; they are a*

*superstitious sect, great observers of set days and times."*

**Benjamin Franklin**

**Large losses on loans made to foreign countries, to the farm sector, and to the oil industry have been responsible for many bank failures in recent years. Two of the largest banks in the country—Continental Illinois National Bank (Chicago) and First City Bancorp of Texas (Houston)—had to be rescued by the Federal Deposit Insurance Corporation (FDIC) as a result of their losses on loans to the oil industry. Many smaller banks failed on account of bad loans to the farm sector. And most of the major banks in the United States are holding large amounts of loans made to foreign countries that are likely to default.**

**When a bank fails, its top managers are likely to lose their jobs and the shareholders to lose most or all of their investment. (However, depositors, as we saw in Chapter 10, are usually safe because most accounts are insured up to $100,000 by federal deposit insurance.) This chapter describes the strategies and techniques bank managers use to avoid the risks that could cause their bank to fail—in spite of which, owing to bad luck or bad decisions, some banks still fail.**

Information is central to the process by which banks deal with **credit risk**—the risk that a borrower will default. We will first look at what this information is and then at how banks use it to evaluate and control credit risk. We will also see how banks take credit risk into account in setting loan interest rates. Last, we will consider credit rationing—where banks control credit risk by refusing to make loans to some borrowers.

# The Evaluation and Control of Credit Risk

The riskiness of a bank's assets ranges from the near-perfect safety of the cash in its vault to the high risk of unsecured consumer loans. Banks could, of course, avoid the problem of credit risk by investing only in safe assets. However, little interest is earned on such assets: vault cash pays no interest at all, and the interest earned on Treasury securities is too low to cover bank operating expenses and the interest paid on deposits.

Loans and other bank assets yield higher interest rates, but these assets also have credit risk. We will focus our attention on loans because they represent the majority of the earning assets held by banks and they can be especially risky. Banks invest in business, consumer, farm, international, and real estate loans.

## Loan Contracts and Credit Risk

A loan is a contract between a borrower and a lender in which the borrower receives the loan amount and agrees to a specified payment schedule. Simple schedules have a single lump-sum payment, whereas complex schedules have a sequence of payments. In either case, as we saw in discussing securities in Chapter 5, the implied interest rate on a loan can be computed from the loan amount and the schedule of payments. Here we will consider a simple one-year loan, with the loan amount $L$ and a lump-sum payment at the end of the year in the amount $A$. When the interest rate on the loan is $r$, then the payment amount $A$ equals $(1 + r)L$.

A loan becomes *delinquent* when the borrower is late in making a scheduled payment. Banks usually give borrowers a further opportunity to repay their loans. But then legal action begins. After a judge formally declares the loan to be in *default*, the borrower may be forced into **bankruptcy**. In bankruptcy, an accounting is made of the borrower's assets, which, except for some personal items, are distributed to the bank and other creditors.

Although a loan default is bad news for the lending bank, the consequences are usually worse for the borrower. If the borrower is a firm, the top managers will lose their jobs and the shareholders will lose their investments in the firm. If the borrower is an individual, the person will lose most of his or her assets, and will be denied loans until his or her credit worthiness is reestablished. (Some states have recently changed their bankruptcy laws, however, to allow bankrupt borrowers to keep more of their assets.)

Borrowers usually default on loans only when they do not have enough wealth—money or other assets—to make the required payments. This process is analyzed graphically in Figure 12.1. The three panels show various outcomes for the bank and the borrower depending on the amount of wealth $W$ the borrower has available for repaying the loan amount $A$. The borrower has ample wealth in panel A, just enough wealth in panel B, and inadequate wealth in panel C.

FIGURE 12.1
**Borrower Wealth and Loan Repayments**
A. Borrower with Ample Wealth $W$ To Make Loan Payment $A$

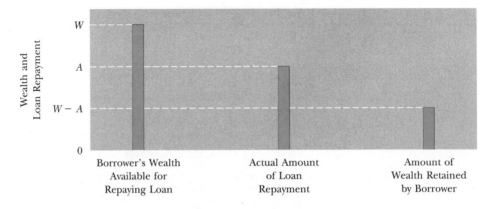

B. Borrower with Just Enough Wealth $W$ To Make Loan Payment $A$

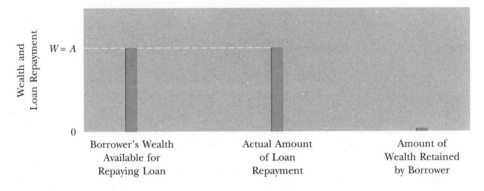

C. Borrower with Inadequate Wealth $W$ To Make Loan Payment $A$

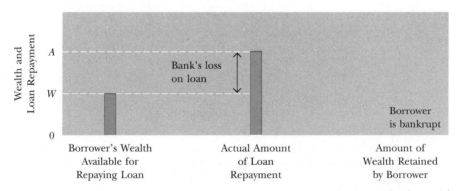

Panel A shows a borrower with an ample amount of wealth $W$ to make the loan payment $A$. The bank is paid in full and the borrower retains some wealth $(W - A)$.

Panel B shows another borrower who has just enough wealth $W$ to make the loan payment $A$. The bank is paid in full, but the borrower is left with no wealth $(W - A = 0)$.

Panel C shows a borrower who does not have enough wealth $W$ to make the loan payment $A$. The bank receives the available wealth $W$ as partial payment, while the borrower must deal with the consequences of bankruptcy.

The ability to make loan payments depends on the borrower's wealth at the time the payment is *due*. However, the borrower's wealth is evaluated by the bank at the time the loan is *made*, so the future wealth the borrower will have available for repaying the loan must be estimated. This process is illustrated in Figure 12.2. In each panel, the curve shown is a *probability distribution function*, showing the probability *p* that the borrower will have each amount of wealth *W* at the time the loan repayment is due. The amount of the loan payment *A* is shown on the horizontal axis. Panel A shows a safer borrower, panel B a riskier borrower.

FIGURE 12.2

**Probability Distributions of Wealth**

A. Safer Borrower

In panel A, the borrower is safer because there is a low likelihood (shown by the shaded area) that the wealth *W* will be less than the payment amount *A*.

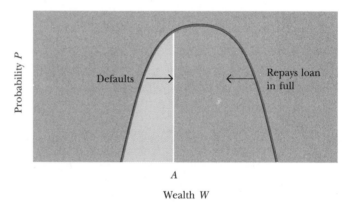

B. Riskier Borrower

In panel B, the borrower is riskier because there is a high likelihood that the wealth *W* will be less than the payment amount *A*.

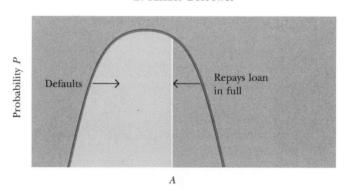

In principle, banks use such information regarding future wealth to make informed lending decisions. But in practice, accurate information of this type is usually not available. For example, just asking borrowers about their future wealth is generally not going to work—the answer surely is going to be too optimistic. Instead, banks have to obtain their own information about borrowers and they have to draw their own conclusions about the repayment prospects. We will now consider some of the procedures banks use for this purpose.

## Credit Risk for Various Types of Loans

The special skills of banks in obtaining information about credit risk enable them to dominate many loan markets. The techniques used depend on the particular kind of loan. We will now look at three main categories of bank loans—consumer loans, business loans, and international loans.

### Consumer Loans

For consumer loans, the borrower's future income is the key variable in determining credit risk. Banks and other lenders that operate in consumer loan markets use **credit scoring** procedures to evaluate repayment prospects. Potential borrowers fill out a loan application form that includes economic and demographic questions. The economic questions cover such factors as the loan applicant's current income, consecutive years on the job, assets owned, and debts owed. The demographic questions cover such factors as age, marital status, and the number of dependents.

Banks use statistical methods to translate this information into a single number—the *credit score*—that is supposed to predict the likelihood that the borrower will repay the loan. Credit scoring methods use the characteristics of people who have actually paid back loans as the standard of comparison. However, these methods have been challenged on the grounds that lenders may also use credit scores as an excuse to discriminate against particular groups of borrowers. As a result, banks must now document the statistical reliability of their methods for evaluating credit risk.

### Business Loans

The credit worthiness of a business is evaluated in a similar way, although different facts are relevant. Banks determine a firm's income record from its past profit and loss statements, and its financial condition from financial ratios based on its balance sheet. Most business loans are made to finance new capital investment or the production of goods, so the bank must also evaluate the firm's business prospects. For this reason, banks often specialize in making loans to particular industries.

### International Loans

International loans are made to foreign business and government borrowers. The credit worthiness of foreign borrowers and domestic borrowers depends on basically the same factors—how much income or wealth the borrower will have available to repay the loan. However, loans to a foreign government raise a special issue regarding the *willingness* of the country to repay the loan. A bank cannot take a sovereign government to bankruptcy court in order to obtain a claim on the country's assets. In fact, the main threat banks have over a defaulting foreign government is not to make future loans to that country. Although this is a substantial threat, countries still default—economic conditions deteriorate so much that there is no alternative, or a new government denies responsibility for past debts.

Because banks have very serious collection problems on delinquent loans to foreign governments, these loans are often just renegotiated with new repayment schedules. This is currently the situation for many international loans made by major American banks to Latin American governments. Although these loans may never be repaid, there is little reason to force a formal default. Box 12.1 further discusses the Latin American loan problems of American banks.

**BOX 12.1 BANKING BRIEFS**

## The Latin American Loans of U.S. Banks

Large U.S. banks made close to $200 billion of loans to Latin American countries—mainly Brazil, Mexico, and Argentina—during the 1970s. At the time, the countries seemed poised for dramatic economic growth, they were willing to pay high interest rates, and U.S. banks had lots of loanable funds.

During the early 1980s it became ever more clear that some of these countries would not be able to pay off their loans. The main problem was that the world economy was growing more slowly than anticipated. As the demand for Latin American exports fell, these countries were unable to earn the foreign exchange they needed to repay their loans.

When the problems first surfaced, there was hope they were temporary. However, it now appears that many of these loans will never be repaid. Brazil, for example, declared a "moratorium" on all loan payments in 1987, pending further renegotiation of its payment schedule. The U.S. banks then began to write off the loans—following the procedures described in Chapter 6.

## Customer Relationships

Banks obtain important information about borrowers from **customer relationships** that develop over time. For example, a lot of the information contained in the deposit and loan repayment record of a customer can be used when making new loans.

### Compensating Balance Requirements

**Compensating balances**—deposits that banks often require business borrowers to maintain as a condition for obtaining a loan—are part of the customer relationship. If a firm is taking out a $100,000 loan, for example, it might be required to maintain an average deposit of $10,000 in the bank—a 10% compensating balance requirement. Banks use compensating balance requirements as a form of collateral—this money is available if the borrower defaults—and to reinforce the customer relationship—the firm may use the compensating balance deposits to write checks as long as the required balance is maintained on average.

Compensating balances are also often required of borrowers who maintain lines of credit. **Lines of credit**, as we saw in Chapter 11, are bank commitments to make loans up to a specified amount available to borrowers for a certain period of time. In granting lines of credit, banks evaluate credit risk in much the same way they do when making loans.

### Competition for Bank Customers

It is difficult for new banks to enter a loan market because they do not have the backlog of information about borrowers that banks with established customer relationships possess. Also, new lenders may be wary of firms that require loans but have no current banking relationship—this may mean that their prior bank found the credit risk to be too high. The accumulation of information that results from a customer relationship may even lead to imperfect competition, with a bank charging an established customer a higher loan rate as a result of its privileged position.

Borrowers of course have an incentive to release favorable information about themselves so as to create competition among banks for their business. However, lenders recognize that borrowers may also wish to conceal unfavorable information, so they interpret the information provided by borrowers with caution. Information obtained through direct experience over time, as occurs in an established customer relationship, is generally considered more dependable.

### Prime Borrowers

Customer relationships and imperfect competition are less relevant for large, financially sound, corporations. Such firms are called **prime borrowers**—the highest credit rating available for a bank borrower. Prime borrowers can obtain loans from many banks, and they may also issue debt directly in the capital markets (selling bonds). Bank lending to these corporations is thus highly competitive.

A number of banks will frequently cooperate in making a loan to a prime borrower. *Loan participations* involve a consortium of lenders, with the "lead" bank taking responsibility for loan administration, and with each participating bank receiving a designated percentage of the loan. A consortium is often necessary on very large loans because banks are forbidden from lending more than 15% of their capital to any single borrower. In addition, since most information about prime borrowers is publicly available, banks are less reluctant to share their evaluations of prime borrowers with other banks.

## Collateral

Information allows banks to evaluate credit risk, but not to control it. Collateral is the main device used to control, and even to eliminate, credit risk. **Collateral** consists of assets owned by a borrower that are pledged as security that a loan will be repaid. If the borrower defaults on the loan, the lender takes title to the assets and sells them, using the proceeds to offset its losses on the loan.

### Real Estate Collateral on Mortgage Loans

*Mortgage loans*—on which real estate serves as the primary collateral—provide an example of how collateral works in a loan market. The old silent movie scene, showing bankers in black suits foreclosing on the homestead and sternly evicting the weeping family, represents real estate collateral in action.

Mortgage loans are usually granted in amounts that represent a specified percentage of the estimated market value—called the *appraised value*—of the real estate that will serve as the collateral. The ratio of the loan amount to the appraised value is called the **loan-to-value ratio**. Everything else being equal, low loan-to-value ratios (small loans relative to ample collateral) reduce the lender's potential loss from default.

As illustrated in Figure 12.3, lenders offer mortgage loans with alternative loan-to-value ratios, higher mortgage interest rates being charged on loans with higher loan-to-value ratios (higher risk loans).

Loan-to-value ratios for mortgage loans represent the ratio of the amount borrowed—the "loan"—to the appraised value—the "value"—of the property. Loans with lower loan-to-value ratios are safer because the loan is smaller relative to the collateral value of the property. Consequently, low loan-to-value ratios are associated with low mortgage interest rates, the low rates reflecting the low credit risk on these loans.

FIGURE 12.3

**The Risk Structure of Mortgage Interest Rates**

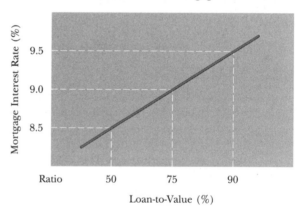

Loan-to-value ratios of about 75% are standard, with ratios near 50% considered very safe, and ratios near 90% considered fairly risky. Mortgages on commercial real estate operate in the same fashion, but even loans with 50% loan-to-value ratios can be risky because of the wider fluctuations that occur in the value of commercial real estate.

Homeowners can sometimes also use mortgages for other purposes—to pay for a college education or to consolidate a series of small debts into one large loan. Box 12.2 describes how **second mortgage loans**—or **home equity loans** as they are popularly called—are used for this purpose.

### Collateral for Business Loans

In the case of uncollateralized business loans, loan contracts usually grant lenders general access to the firm's assets in the case of default. However, this has limited value because the proceeds from the sale of these assets

BOX 12.2 CREDIT CHECK

## Using Home Equity Loans for Consumer Borrowing

Real estate collateral can be used to borrow money to purchase a house—called *the first mortgage*—and to borrow to buy consumption goods—called *the second mortgage* or *home equity* loan. The first mortgage has priority if there is a loan default. But given that loan-to-value ratios are much less than 100%, there can be extra *equity value*—the value of the house minus the amount of the first mortgage—to provide collateral for a second mortgage. This is why second mortgages are called home "equity" loans.

Consumer loans are usually risky because most consumers have very limited collateral. (They do have human capital—the value of their training and education—but lenders cannot sell human capital if a borrower defaults.) Home equity loans solve this problem by using the equity value of a home as collateral. Consequently, home equity loans are a rapidly growing part of the consumer loan market.

Because a home equity loan has a lower priority than the first mortgage loan if default occurs, interest rates on second mortgage loans are higher. When first mortgage interest rates are 9%, for example, home equity loan interest rates might be 12%. But under these circumstances, unsecured consumer loan interest rates might be 15% or higher, so home equity loans still represent a benefit to consumer borrowers.

---

are assigned to all creditors on a *pro rata* basis. In contrast, collateral agreements differentiate the priority of claims among the various creditors of a bankrupt firm. For example, a lender can immediately sell assets—factories, equipment, and inventories—that are specifically assigned as collateral in a loan agreement.

Collateral is the most common device used to control credit risk, but banks can also restrict firms—not to pay dividends to shareholders, or not to spend funds in other ways—so they will not jeopardize their loan repayments. Banks also frequently require installment payments such as monthly loan payments—instead of a single lump-sum payment at the end of the loan period—to limit the possible losses from loan default. **Leasing**—described in Box 12.3—is also used by banks to achieve much the same effect as collateral.

In summary, collateral and similar devices serve several key purposes in helping banks and other lenders control credit risk:

- Collateral reduces the lender's need to evaluate credit risk (the collateral will cover at least part of a loss due to default).

- Collateral limits the lender's involvement in bankruptcy proceedings arising from a loan default. Otherwise, a lender may find it is easier to write off a loan than to pay the legal fees of trying to collect it.

- Because collateralized loans are less risky, borrowers are charged lower interest rates.

---

## Leasing

*Leasing* is a growing type of bank lending that serves the same purpose as collateral. To create a lease, a bank buys assets and rents them to a firm on a long-term basis. For example, if an airline wants to buy new airplanes using a *bank loan*, the *airline* buys the airplanes and uses them as collateral for the loan. In contrast, with a *lease*, the *bank buys (and owns) the airplanes*, but leases (rents) them to the airline which uses the planes as if it owned them.

Leases have advantages over collateralized loans for both the bank and the firm. The advantage of a lease for the bank is that it can obtain the property back immediately if the firm fails to make the required payments. On a collateralized loan, in contrast, time-consuming and expensive bankruptcy proceedings may first be required. The advantage for the firm is that lease obligations do not appear as debts on the firm's balance sheet as do bank loans. (However, leases are now being recognized as "off balance sheet" debts.)

Individuals also use leases to buy automobiles and other consumer durables. Although the bank (or other lender) literally owns the item, this does not affect how the consumer uses it. At the end of the lease period, the consumer can either purchase the item at a reduced price or return it to the bank.

---

Unfortunately, collateralized loans can only be used when borrowers own assets that can be pledged as collateral. Also, the value of collateral may change over time, creating the risk that it will not cover a loan loss. Thus, even collateralized lending is a risky activity. Thus a bank must also set the loan interest rate at a level that is commensurate with the level of risk. We will now examine how this is done.

## Interest Rates and Credit Risk

We saw in Chapter 7 that investment decisions depend on whether the investor is risk neutral or risk averse. Similar considerations apply to bank lending decisions. Risk-neutral bank managers will focus on the *expected loan repayment*. Risk-averse bank managers will consider the *range of possible outcomes* as well as the expected loan repayment.

### Expected Returns on Risky Loans

When a loan is repaid in full, the bank earns the **contractual interest rate**—the interest rate set in the loan contract. When a borrower defaults, the bank's return depends on how much of the scheduled payment is actually made. The **expected rate of return** on a loan is thus a function of the contractual interest rate, the likelihood of default, and the probable amount of repayment when there is default.

We have already looked, in Figures 12.1 and 12.2, at the information that banks examine when evaluating the credit risk of a loan—the various amounts that the borrower may have available to repay the loan and the associated probabilities. Let us now consider a slightly simpler case with just two possible outcomes: either the borrower repays the loan in full, or the borrower defaults, repaying the bank a smaller amount.

The equation for computing the expected rate of return on a loan, $r_e$, is then:

$$r_e = p_c\, r_c + p_d\, r_d, \tag{12.1}$$

where $r_e$ = the expected rate of return on the loan,
$\quad p_c$ = the probability of repayment in full,
$\quad r_c$ = the contractual loan interest rate,
$\quad p_d$ = the probability of default,
$\quad r_d$ = the bank's likely rate of return when there is default.

The probabilities $p_c$ and $p_d$ must sum to 1.0 because they cover the only two possibilities.

The first term in equation (12.1) represents the bank's expected return when the loan is repaid in full (the contractual loan rate $r_c$ times the probability $p_c$).

The second term represents the bank's expected return when the borrower defaults (the rate of return $r_d$ times the probability $p_d$). The rate of return $r_d$ is computed as $r_d = (D - L)/L$, where $D$ is the amount received by the bank when there is a default and $L$ is the amount of the loan. The rate of return in the case of default is always less than the contractual rate of return $r_c$ and it is often negative (representing the loss of principal as well as interest).

Banks often use a **target rate of return** $r_t$ to determine the desired level of the expected rate of return $r_e$ on a loan. A target rate of return depends on the interest the bank pays on deposits, its operating expenses, and its desired profits, each specified as a percentage of the loan amount $L$:

$$r_t = i + c + g, \tag{12.2}$$

where $r_t$ = the target interest rate for the loan,
$\quad i$ = the interest rate paid on deposits,
$\quad c$ = the average operating cost ratio,
$\quad g$ = the profit margin.

These costs of providing intermediation services were discussed in Chapter 6. Equation (12.2) assumes that the bank obtains all of its funds from deposits and uses all of its deposits to make loans. Comparable, but more complex, equations apply if the bank has nondeposit sources of funds or invests in assets other than loans. A numerical example is given in Box 12.4.

A bank sets the contractual interest rate $r_c$ on a loan so that the expected return $r_e$ equals the target rate $r_t$. We can first see how this works for a borrower with no credit risk. In this case, because the probability of repayment in full $p_c$ is 1.0, the expected rate of return $r_e$ equals the

BOX 12.4 IN DEPTH

## Computing the Contractual Interest Rate on a Risky Loan

**Computing the Target Rate $r_t$**

Assumptions for computing the target rate $r_t$:

The interest rate on deposits $i$ is 5%.

The average operating cost ratio $c$ is 3%.

The desired profit margin $\pi$ is 2%.

Result: Using equation (12.2) for the target rate $r_t$:

$$r_t = i + c + \pi = 5\% + 3\% + 2\% = 10\%.$$

**Computing the Contractual Rate $r_c$**

Assumptions for computing the contractual rate $r_c$:

The probability of repayment in full $p_c$ is 80%.

The probability of default $p_d$ is 20%.

The rate of return when default occurs $r_d$ is $-10\%$.

Result: Using equation (12.1), the expected return $r_e$ is:

$$r_e = p_c r_c + p_d r_d.$$

Setting the target rate $r_t$ equal to the expected return:

$$r_t = p_c r_c + p_d r_d.$$

Then solving for the contractual loan rate $r_c$:

$$r_c = \frac{r_t - p_d r_d}{p_c} = \frac{0.10 - (0.20)(-0.10)}{0.80} = 0.15 \text{ or } 15\%.$$

contractual interest rate $r_c$ (see equation [12.1]). So the bank would just set the contractual rate $r_c$ equal to its target rate $r_t$, $r_c = r_t$.

For risky borrowers, the contractual rate $r_c$ must be set above the target rate $r_t$ to account for the possibility that the borrower will default. The additional interest charge equals the **expected loss due to default**— the probability that the borrower will default times the amount of the loss (the contractual rate $r_c$ minus the return when there is default $r_d$). This is illustrated in Box 12.4.

### The Prime Rate

The interest rate that banks charge their most secure business customers is called the **prime rate**. The prime rate and the three-month Treasury bill rate are compared in Figure 12.4. The pattern of the two rates is very similar, but the prime rate is higher because it has to cover the bank's operating costs and its profit margin.

FIGURE 12.4
**The Prime Rate and the Treasury Bill Rate**

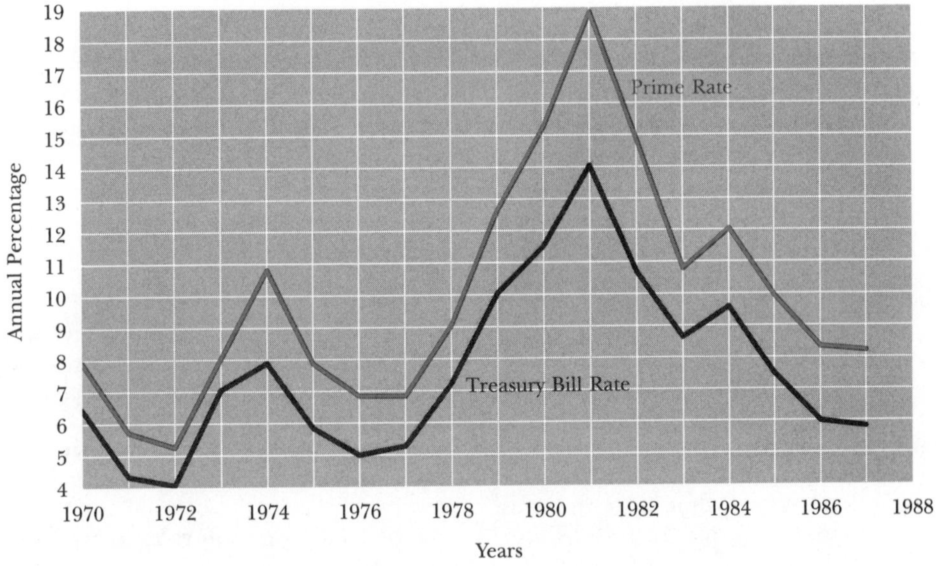

The prime rate is the interest rate that banks charge their safest borrowers. Riskier borrowers are charged a rate above the prime rate. Variations in the prime rate over time mainly represent changes in the general level of interest rates in the economy. This is represented in the figure by the similar patterns for the prime rate and the three-month Treasury bill rate. Source: *Economic Report of the President, February 1988.*

Interest rates on riskier loans are determined as a *markup*—an interest rate premium—over the prime rate. For example, a bank might set the interest rate on a risky loan at "three over prime," meaning the interest rate charged is 3 percentage points above the prime rate. The 3 percentage points correspond to the expected loss due to default that is included in the contractual rate for a risky loan.

In practice, the markup over the prime rate charged a risky borrower may also depend on the degree of competition in the loan market. When the market is highly competitive, the markup represents only the expected loss due to default. If a bank tried to charge more, competitors would offer a lower interest rate and take away the customer. With imperfectly competitive markets, however, banks may be able to charge risky borrowers a markup over the prime rate that represents more than the expected loss due to default.

The amount of competition in loan markets is different for prime and risky borrowers. For prime borrowers and for highly collateralized loans, the loan markets tend to be highly competitive. Whereas for risky borrowers, banks must determine the degree of risk, so considerations of customer relationships and information come into play. The result is that banks may be able to charge interest rate markups that represent more than the expected loss due to default. Box 12.5 describes how a bank attempted to deceive its risky customers by redefining the meaning of the prime rate.

BOX 12.5 BANKING BRIEFS

## A Bank Is Caught Cheating on Its Prime Rate

The prime rate plays a pivotal role in bank loan markets because it is both the rate charged to prime borrowers and the basis of the rates charged to risky borrowers. Since the market for prime borrowers is highly competitive, banks generally set their prime rate at the same level that other banks charge. The markup over the prime rate then reflects the additional interest charged to risky borrowers.

A bank in Atlanta, Georgia, recently tried to charge its risky borrowers a higher interest rate by adopting a novel interpretation of the prime rate. The bank announced a "prime" rate that was higher than the prime rates of other banks, and then used this "prime" rate to determine the interest rates for its risky borrowers. At the same time, it actually charged its prime borrowers a rate that was equal to the prime rate of other banks—an amount below its own "prime" rate.

One of its risky borrowers figured out the scheme, brought a law suit, and won the case. The court found that a bank's prime rate must be the rate that it charges its best business borrowers. Since the Atlanta bank was charging these borrowers a lower rate than its "prime" rate, this lower rate also had to be used as the basis for the bank's rates on risky loans.

## The Diversification of Loan Portfolios

**Diversification** plays a key role in how risk-averse banks deal with risky loans. As we discussed in Chapter 7, diversification requires that two conditions be satisfied:

1. The portfolio consists of a *large number of relatively small loans.*
2. The loans tend to have *independent risks*—the probability of default on a given loan is uncorrelated with the probability of default on other loans.

Diversification serves to reduce the overall risk of a portfolio of risky loans. The credit risk on individual loans remains, but the actual return for the portfolio can equal the expected return with virtual certainty. Figure 12.5 illustrates how this works.

Panel A shows the distribution of the rates of return a bank might earn on a single loan. The highest possible return is the contractual return, $r_c$. The expected rate of return is $r_e$, reflecting the expected loss due to default.

Panel B shows the distribution of the rates of return for a diversified portfolio, consisting of many individual loans with independent risks of the type illustrated in panel A. The expected rate of return for the portfolio is $r_e$, the same value as the expected return for each individual loan. The benefit of a diversified portfolio is that the bank will actually earn $r_e$, or a return close to it, most of the time, unlike the case of an individual loan.

Panel A shows the distribution of possible rates of return earned on an individual loan. The contractual rate is $r_c$ and the expected rate of return is $r_e$.

FIGURE 12.5

**The Gain from Diversification**

A. The Rate of Return on a Single Loan

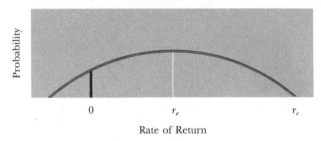

Rate of Return

Panel B shows the possible rates of return earned on a diversified portfolio consisting of many loans of the type illustrated in panel A, with independent risks. The expected rate of return on the portfolio is still $r_e$, but the distribution is more concentrated near this rate of return.

B. The Rate of Return on a Diversified Portfolio

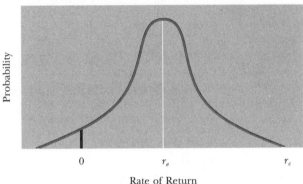

Rate of Return

Risk-averse bank managers will refer to the *range of possible outcomes*, as well as to the *expected return*, on a loan. The contractual interest rate they charge will therefore include a *risk premium*—an additional component to compensate the bank for the possibility that it may earn a low rate of return. However, such banks are at a competitive disadvantage relative to banks with risk-neutral managers who do not include such risk premiums in their loan rates.

Diversification allows risk-averse bank managers to reduce and possibly even eliminate the risk premiums in their loan rates. This happens because, as shown in Figure 12.5, the range of possible rates of return for a diversified portfolio is concentrated at the expected rate of return on each loan, $r_e$. This means that the bank faces less risk overall. Indeed, with perfect diversification, the rate of return for the portfolio will exactly equal the expected rate of return $r_e$.

It is relatively easy for banks to create diversified loan portfolios. The first condition for diversification—many small loans—is usually satisfied. The second condition—that the credit risk of individual loans be independent—can be satisfied by making loans to different types of borrowers (consumers, business firms, and international borrowers), by lending in different geographic regions (cities, states, and countries), and by making business loans to many different industries.

### Diversification Versus Specialization

Although diversification is useful for reducing the range of possible outcomes, other factors cause banks to *specialize in particular categories of loans*—just the opposite of diversification. Most importantly, banks that specialize are likely to achieve economies of scale in gathering and evaluating credit risk information. This creates a trade-off between diversification and specialization, and banks will vary in the particular choice they make.

Most of the major bank problems of recent years have been the result of too much specialization in lending, and therefore too little diversification. For example, some banks were so concentrated in making loans to the oil industry that, when the price of oil plummeted in the early 1980s and oil industry firms subsequently defaulted on their loans, these banks failed. The oil loan losses of other banks that had maintained diversified portfolios did not have such a disastrous effect. By and large, *lack of diversification turns "problem loans" into "problem banks."*

### Summary of the Factors That Determine Loan Interest Rates

Banks consider a wide range of factors in determining the interest rate to charge on a particular loan:

- The *target interest rate* determines the *expected rate of return* a bank requires on a loan. The target rate covers the bank's operating expenses, the interest it pays on deposits, and its profits.

- The *contractual interest rate*—the rate actually charged the borrower— includes an additional amount to cover the likelihood of loss due to default on risky loans.

- The contractual interest rate may also include a *risk premium* as compensation for the risk created by a range of outcomes. However, there is less need for such a premium if a bank maintains a diversified portfolio of loans.

## Credit Rationing

In all markets, the quantity of the goods that suppliers want to sell is limited. Suppliers normally use *price rationing* to limit the quantity sold— they set their price high enough so that the amount demanded equals the amount they want to sell. Price rationing also occurs in loan markets, where the interest rate plays the role of the price.

In this section, we will look at a different type of rationing—called **credit rationing**—which banks sometimes use to limit the amount of loans they supply to borrowers. With credit rationing, banks simply *refuse to make loans to certain borrowers* (even if these borrowers offer to pay higher interest rates). We will look at the various reasons why banks ration credit in this way and at how credit rationing affects the operation of loan markets.

## Usury Ceilings

**Usury ceilings** are maximum interest rates that lenders may legally charge on particular categories of loans. Most usury ceilings originated as laws passed by states after the Civil War to protect consumers from unscrupulous lenders. (Usury laws have generally not been applied to business loans.)

The connection between usury ceilings and credit rationing is illustrated in Figure 12.6. The figure shows the normal relationship—called the **risk structure of interest rates**—that exists between a borrower's credit risk and the interest rate the borrower is charged on a loan. The greater the risk, the higher the rate. This normal relationship is distorted by a usury ceiling—the horizontal line at the rate level $r_u$—for borrowers with a level of credit risk that exceeds $\sigma_u$, the level where the usury line intersects the ascending risk structure line. On account of the usury ceiling, banks cannot charge these borrowers an interest rate that is commensurate with their credit risk, so the bank simply denies them loans.

The positively sloped lines show the risk structure of interest rates—the interest rates that banks charge on loans as a function of a borrower's credit risk. The horizontal line at the level $r_u$ shows the legislated usury ceiling, prohibiting banks from charging interest rates above $r_u$.

For the initial risk structure line, borrowers with a credit risk above $\sigma_u$ will be denied loans. If market interest rates rise—the risk structure line shifts upward—while the usury ceiling remains unchanged, then credit rationing increases to include all borrowers with a risk level above $\sigma_u{}'$.

FIGURE 12.6
**The Risk Structure of Interest Rates and Usury Ceilings**

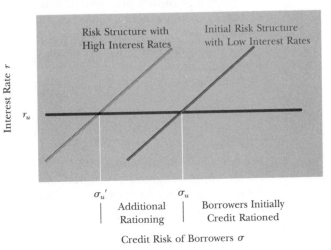

If market interest rates rise and the usury ceiling is unchanged, then the amount of credit rationing increases. This is illustrated in Figure 12.6, where the upward shift in the ascending risk structure line reflects an increase in market interest rates. The new risk structure line then intersects the usury line at a lower credit risk, $\sigma_u{}'$. As a result, loans are denied to more borrowers.

Economists have become increasingly skeptical about whether usury ceilings serve any useful purpose. In an earlier era, the ceilings did provide a measure of protection for poorly informed borrowers, but nowadays advertising ensures that most borrowers are well informed. The pitfall of usury ceilings—that certain borrowers are denied loans—

became particularly evident in the United States during the late 1970s. During that period, market interest rates rose rapidly, but state legislatures were slow to raise the usury ceilings correspondingly, so the amount of credit rationing escalated. This was especially true in mortgage markets where many people could not obtain loans to buy homes.

Congress finally interceded in 1980 and eliminated the state usury ceilings on mortgage loans. Also, although usury ceilings for consumer loans still exist in many states, state legislatures are now more prompt in raising these ceilings when market interest rates rise, so less credit rationing is created.

## Redlining

Banks will always refuse credit, of course, to would-be borrowers for whom there is no prospect of loan repayment. In panel C of Figure 12.1, for example, we considered a borrower for whom the amount of the loan repayment $A$ exceeded the wealth $W$ that was available for paying back the loan. Had the bank known that this was going to be the case, it would not have made the loan. And because higher interest rates are of no value to the lender when default occurs, it would not have helped for this borrower to have offered to pay a higher interest rate.

This brings us to a principle of bank lending policy called **redlining.** Redlining occurs when a bank refuses to make loans to a particular group of borrowers. The term had its origins in the refusal of many mortgage lenders to make loans on real estate properties in specific geographic regions, particularly decaying central city areas. These lenders used maps with red lines to indicate the prohibited lending areas.

The banks claimed that the redlined neighborhoods were decaying so rapidly that there was no hope that mortgage loans would be repaid. In contrast, the critics of redlining claimed that these neighborhoods were being destroyed by the very act of redlining. They argued that home improvements and property sales could not occur in neighborhoods where redlining precluded lending. Thus redlining and neighborhood decay might operate together in a vicious circle. One outcome of this controversy was community development legislation that requires banks to disclose their redlining policies.

Redlining controversies occur because lenders see things one way— that credit risk is very high—while borrowers see things another way— that mortgage loans are essential to preserve their neighborhood. More generally, divergent information between borrowers and lenders often leads to credit rationing. We will now examine two further cases of divergent information—moral hazard and adverse selection.

## Asymmetric Information Between Borrowers and Lenders

Divergent sets of information for borrowers and lenders—called **asymmetric information**—play a fundamental role in loan markets. Asymmetric information does not mean that banks are always too pessimistic in their appraisal of the prospects for loan repayment. Were that the case, lenders with neutral views would dominate the market by offering loans to borrowers whose credit risk had been judged too harshly. Rather, asymmetric information means that lenders misjudge credit risk in both directions—sometimes overestimating, but at other times underestimating it—because they are not as well informed as borrowers.

Two problems created by asymmetric information in insurance markets were introduced in Chapter 7: **moral hazard**—where individuals change their behavior after they are insured, and **adverse selection**—where bad risks tend to buy insurance and good risks do not. Borrowers in loan markets act in similar ways.

### Moral Hazard

Moral hazard arises in loan markets when borrowers, after receiving their loans, take actions that increase the likelihood of loan default. For example, consumers may buy goods and services—go on a consumption binge—with money that was budgeted for loan repayments. Moral hazard is thus likely to be greater on larger loans: the benefit of default is greater—the consumption binge is greater—the larger the loan. Of course, there are also costs to borrowers if they default—the forced sale of assets and the inconvenience of not obtaining further credit.

Given that there are both costs and benefits to defaulting on a loan, we can expect more borrowers to repay their loans, the smaller the size of the loans. Lenders may therefore be able to control the amount of loan defaults by reducing the size of the loans they offer. This is why moral hazard is a possible source of credit rationing.

The relationship between loan size and the percentage of borrowers who repay is illustrated in Figure 12.7. It is assumed that there is a loan size $L_0$ so small that all borrowers repay, and that there is a loan size $L_1$ so large that all borrowers default. Moral hazard is represented in this graphic model because individual borrowers know whether they intend to default, whereas a bank may only know the percentage of all borrowers

This figure shows that the larger the loan, the lower the percentage of borrowers who will repay it. There is a minimum loan size—labeled $L_0$—at which 100% of the borrowers will repay. There is also a maximum loan size—labeled $L_1$—at which none of the borrowers will repay. When the maximum size of the loan for all borrowers is $L^*$, the percentage of the borrowers who repay is $N^*$.

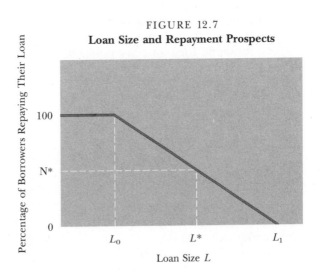

FIGURE 12.7
**Loan Size and Repayment Prospects**

who will default. A bank can then maintain the percentage of borrowers that repay ($N^*$ in the figure) by setting a maximum loan size ($L^*$ in the figure) for all borrowers.

### Adverse Selection

Banks may not only face a pool of loan applicants with greater credit risk than the average borrower in the economy, they may also find that when they raise the loan interest rate, an even riskier pool of loan applicants appears. This happens because higher loan rates have little effect on borrowers who anticipate that they will not repay their loans. Since risky borrowers recognize this fact, they dominate the pool of borrowers as the loan rate rises. Banks that face such adverse selection may therefore have to use credit rationing, rather than higher loan rates, to balance the demand and supply of loans.

## The Implications of Credit Rationing

Our discussion has shown how credit rationing arises as the result of loan market conditions such as usury ceilings, redlining, moral hazard, and adverse selection. These are all cases where the loan market fails to operate well.

At the *microeconomic* level, credit rationing distorts the distribution of loans in the economy. Because they are denied loans, some consumers have to reduce their consumption purchases, and some business firms cannot carry out their desired investment projects. Credit rationing can be reduced if the asymmetry in information between borrowers and lenders is reduced. Credit rationing may also be reduced through public policy. For example, special government agencies make loans to small businesses, farmers, and mortgage borrowers for whom credit rationing appears especially severe. Some legislative actions—such as removing usury ceilings—also reduce credit rationing.

At the *macroeconomic* level, the *availability* of loans becomes a potential instrument for monetary policy because of credit rationing. That is, the Federal Reserve may be able to slow down the economy by forcing banks to make fewer loans. We will look further at the implications of credit rationing for monetary policy in Part V of the book.

## Chapter Summary

1. Credit risk refers to the possibility that borrowers will fail to make the agreed upon loan payments for interest and principal. Banks have been able to dominate many loan markets because they specialize in dealing with such credit risk.

2. Banks invest substantial resources to obtain information to evaluate the credit risk of individual borrowers. Credit scoring methods are commonly used for consumer loans. Profit and loss statements and balance sheets are similarly analyzed for busi-

ness loans. Banks also use their relationships with established customers to obtain information.

3. Collateral represents assets that are pledged by borrowers as security that loans will be repaid. If a default does occur, the bank sells the collateral and uses the proceeds to reduce the amount of its loss. Mortgage loans—which use real estate for collateral—illustrate how collateral expedites the operation of a loan market.

4. Banks take credit risk into account when they set the contractual interest rate on a loan. A bank first determines its target rate of return for the loan, then sets the contractual interest rate so that it exceeds the target rate by an amount that compensates for the expected loss due to default.

5. With a diversified loan portfolio, a bank obtains an overall rate of return for its portfolio that is close to its expected rate of return for individual loans. Banks achieve the benefit of diversification by making relatively small loans to a large number of borrowers with credit risks that are independent of each other.

6. Credit rationing occurs when banks limit the amount of loans they supply simply by refusing to make loans to certain borrowers (even though these borrowers may offer to pay higher interest rates). Credit risk is the primary reason that credit rationing occurs in loan markets. Credit rationing operates through a variety of mechanisms, including usury ceilings and asymmetric information (redlining, moral hazard, and adverse selection).

7. At the microeconomic level, credit rationing affects which borrowers receive loans. Government policy can offset credit rationing by making loans available to rationed borrowers. Credit rationing can also be reduced if lenders obtain better information. At the macroeconomic level, credit rationing affects how monetary policy operates, as we will see in Part V of the book.

## Key Terms

Adverse selection

Asymmetric information

Bankruptcy

Collateral

Compensating balances

Credit rationing

Credit risk

Credit scoring

Customer relationship

Diversification

Expected loss due to default

Leasing

Line of credit

Loan interest rates:

    Contractual rate

    Expected rate of return

    Target rate

Loan-to-value ratio

Moral hazard

Prime rate

Redlining

Risk structure of interest rates

Second mortgage (home equity) loans

Usury ceilings

## Study Questions

1. Why do banks consider demographic factors such as age, marital status, and the number of dependents in computing credit scores for consumer borrowers?

2. Why is the customer relationship so important in bank lending?

3. Why are automobile loans collateralized loans?

4. Based on the following information, first compute the bank's target interest rate, then the prime rate it would charge a risk-free borrower, and last the contractual rate it would charge the risky borrower shown:

   Interest rate paid on deposits = 6%.
   Average operating cost ratio = 3%.
   Desired profit margin = 2%.

   For the *risky borrower:*

   Rate of return earned if borrower defaults = −5%.
   Probability of default = 20%.

5. In comparison with Question 4, what other factor might a bank include in computing its contractual interest rate if it were averse to risk? What alternative portfolio strategy could be used by the bank?

6. Banks suffer loan losses whether or not they are diversified. Why do loan losses due to default represent an ordinary cost of doing business for a diversified bank?

7. Why do usury ceilings lead to the credit rationing of risky borrowers? What happens if market interest rates rise while a usury ceiling is left unchanged?

8. In a consumer loan market with moral hazard, why are honest borrowers subsidizing dishonest borrowers?

9. Why does collateral control the problem of moral hazard in a consumer loan market?

10. Why does collateral control the problem of adverse selection in a business loan market?

## Recommended Reading

*There are many textbooks and books of readings on bank management. Some good ones include:*

Mona J. Gardner and Dixie L. Mills, *Managing Financial Institutions,* The Dryden Press, Hinsdale, Ill., 1988.

Benton E. Gup and Charles Meiburg, *Cases in Bank Management,* Macmillan, New York, 1986.

Thomas Havrilesky, Robert Schweitzer, and John T. Boorman, *Dynamics of Banking,* Harlan Davidson, Arlington Heights, Ill., 1985.

Timothy W. Koch, *Bank Management,* The Dryden Press, Hinsdale, Ill., 1988.

*More popular books that discuss banking and recent bank problems with bad loans include:*

Martin Mayer, *The Bankers,* Weybright and Talley, New York, 1974.

Martin Mayer, *The Money Bazaars,* Dutton, New York, 1984.

Mark Singer, *Funny Money,* Knopf, New York, 1985.

Irvine H. Sprague, *Bailout,* Basic Books, New York, 1986.

# Nonbank Intermediaries

*"A penny saved is a penny earned."*

*Benjamin Franklin*

Commercial banks in the United States have been advertising themselves as "full-service" institutions for many years. This may sound good, but it is not really accurate. Other financial intermediaries now provide essentially the same range of services as commercial banks, and some offer more.

These advertisements were probably first designed to promote comparisons with thrift institutions—savings and loan associations, savings banks, and credit unions. At that time, only commercial banks could provide transfer services—checking accounts. As the result of banking deregulation in recent years, however, all depository intermediaries—commercial banks and thrift institutions—now have basically the same powers, including transfer services.

Commercial bank advertising is now more often directed at competition with nondepository intermediaries—pension funds, insurance companies, and mutual funds. The pension contracts, insurance policies, and "shares" in investment portfolios that these firms provide are not available from commercial banks. In fact, now when commercial banks lobby Congress for expanded powers, they argue that they are *not* full-service institutions but would like to become so—quite a different tune than their advertisements.

In Chapter 6, we looked at the intermediation and transfer services provided by commercial banks. In this chapter, we will examine the main services of nonbank intermediaries, both those that are depository— thrift institutions—and nondepository—mutual funds, pension funds, insurance companies, and finance companies. We begin with an overview of these intermediaries. Then we will look at the special features of each type of institution.

# The Types of Financial Intermediaries

*Financial intermediaries* are in the business of raising money and investing it. The money raised represents their *liabilities:* they have to pay it back in the future. The money invested represents their *assets:* it is to be returned to them in the future. Because the funds raised by issuing liabilities are used to purchase assets, total assets and total liabilities (including shareholder capital) are equal.

The types of financial intermediaries are distinguished by their liabilities, their assets, and the services they provide. These differences are summarized in Table 13.1. Figure 13.1 shows the total assets controlled by each type of intermediary. Note that commercial banks have the most assets, and that all depository intermediaries are larger by about one-third than all nondepository intermediaries.

## Specialization

Why are there so many types of financial intermediaries? The answer has to do with the preferences of consumers, government regulations, and the benefits of specialization.

**TABLE 13.1**

**The Main Liabilities, Assets, Services, and Regulators of Financial Intermediaries**

| | Liabilities | Assets | Services | Regulators |
|---|---|---|---|---|
| **Depository** | | | | |
| Commercial banks | Deposits | Business and other loans | Business loans and checking accounts | Federal and state banking regulators |
| Thrift institutions | | | | |
| Savings and loan associations | Deposits | Mortgage loans | Mortgage banking | Federal Home Loan Bank System |
| Savings banks | Deposits | Mortgage loans | Mortgage banking | Banking regulators and Federal Home Loan Bank System |
| Credit unions | Deposits | Consumer loans | Consumer loans | National Credit Union Administration |
| **Nondepository** | | | | |
| Mutual funds | Shares | All types of investment securities | Investment services | Securities and Exchange Commission |
| Insurance companies | Insurance policies | Long-term investment securities | Insurance | State insurance commissioners |
| Pension funds | Pension contracts | Long-term investment securities | Pensions | Federal regulations |
| Finance companies | Capital market debt | Short-term loans | High-risk loans | State regulations |

FIGURE 13.1
**Size of Financial Intermediaries by Total Assets**
At year-end 1987

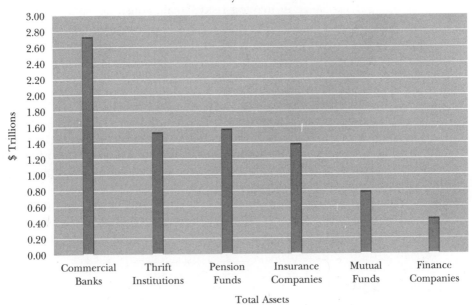

Commercial banks are the largest single type of financial intermediary. The total assets of all depository intermediaries (commercial banks and the thrift institutions) were about one-third greater than the total assets of all nondepository institutions at the end of 1987. **Source:** *Financial Assets and Liabilities,* Flow of Funds Accounts, Board of Governors of the Federal Reserve System; and *Sourcebook,* United States League of Savings Institutions, 1988.

We have seen in the preceding chapters that investment and borrowing decisions depend on a variety of factors:

- The expected rate of return on an investment.
- The investment's inherent risk.
- The maturity—when the invested money is returned.
- The liquidity—the ease of selling the investment.
- The transactions costs and overall convenience.
- The other services that are available, such as checking accounts.

Consumers weigh the factors in different ways. So it is not surprising that many types of financial intermediaries are needed to provide services to suit all the consumer demands.

The techniques intermediaries use to provide these services also lead to different types of institutions. There is often a benefit to specialization, as Adam Smith long ago observed with regard to the division of labor. The evaluation of information for making loans and buying securities—evaluating risk—is an important activity that benefits from specialization.

For example, both savings and loan associations and savings banks specialize in making mortgage loans, so much so that their business is sometimes called mortgage banking. Similarly, credit unions and finance companies specialize in making risky, small, consumer loans that have little collateral.

The assets an institution purchases, the liabilities it issues, and the special services it provides may also interact with each other, creating a distinctive combination. For example, life insurance companies tend to invest in long-term assets, issue life insurance policies as their liabilities, and provide insurance services.

Of course, financial intermediaries can still try to be all things to all people. Later in this chapter we will look at the current attempts of each type of institution to carry out the specialized activities of the others. A major problem they face in doing so is that government regulations often restrict them to specific activities.

Keeping these points in mind, we will now look at the distinguishing characteristics of each type of nonbank intermediary.

## Thrift Institutions

**Thrift institutions**—savings and loan associations, savings banks, and credit unions—are the major depository intermediaries in the United States besides commercial banks. Historically, commercial banks served business firms and relatively wealthy people, whereas thrift institutions provided services to the average consumer. As we will see, this distinction is rapidly disappearing.

### Thrift Institutions as Mutual Organizations

The form of ownership was one of the special features that traditionally distinguished thrift institutions from commercial banks. Commercial banks were, and are, almost all **shareholder-owned.** Thrift institutions were almost all **mutual organizations**—owned by their depositors and borrowers. However, regulations now allow savings banks and savings and loan associations to be shareholder-owned, and many have changed to shareholder ownership because it enables them to raise additional capital by issuing new stock.

The mutual form of organization has been and remains a hallmark of credit unions. In fact, it used to be required that credit unions be formed by so-called affinity groups—people who shared some common connection. Most credit unions were formed by the employees of a firm; many firms treat their credit union as a fringe benefit for employees, providing it facilities and other services without charge. Today, credit unions can be formed by groups of people without such a close common bond, but they still are all mutual organizations.

**TABLE 13.2**

Depository Intermediaries: Assets and Number of Institutions

| | At year-end 1987 | | |
| --- | --- | --- | --- |
| | Total Assets ($ Billions) | Number of Institutions | Assets/Institution ($ Millions) |
| Credit unions | $ 184 | 15,144 | $ 12 |
| Commercial banks | 2,721 | 13,789 | 197 |
| Savings and loan associations | 1,262 | 2,648 | 477 |
| Savings banks | 259 | 485 | 534 |

**Source:** *Financial Assets and Liabilities*, Flow of Funds Accounts, Board of Governors of the Federal Reserve System; and *Sourcebook*, United States League of Savings Institutions (thrift institutions).

## The Size and Number of Thrift Institutions

Thrift institutions vary substantially in their number and average size, as shown in Table 13.2. The average credit union had at the end of 1987 only $12 million in assets, but they were the most numerous type of depository intermediary, numbering over 15,000. Savings banks—which until recently could operate only in certain states—were the least numerous, 485 institutions nationally, but they had a large average size, $534 million in assets. The over 2,500 savings and loan associations fall between these extremes, with an average size of $477 million in assets. (In comparison, there were over 13,500 commercial banks, with an average size of $197 million, including huge banks with billions of dollars of assets.)

## Deposit Liabilities

Thrift institutions raise money by attracting insured deposits, just like commercial banks. In fact, following the major deregulation of the early 1980s, the deposit liabilities of all depository intermediaries are virtually identical, although the names of some of the accounts differ, and they are insured by different federal agencies. Credit union deposits, for example, are called shares and transaction accounts at credit unions are called share drafts. But from the consumer's standpoint, the deposit accounts of thrift institutions are basically indistinguishable, both from one another and from comparable accounts at commercial banks.

## Lending Activities

The feature that most distinguishes the investment activities of thrift institutions is the type of loans they specialize in making. Figure 13.2 shows how the three types of thrift institutions have distributed their total assets among mortgage loans, consumer loans, and other assets.

FIGURE 13.2
**The Distribution of Assets for Thrift Institutions**
Percentage at year-end 1987

A. Savings and Loan Associations

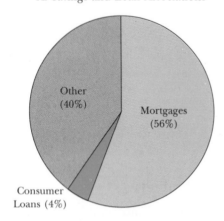

B. Savings Banks

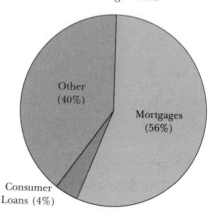

Savings and loan associations and savings banks both invest about half of their total assets in mortgage loans, and under 10% in consumer loans. Credit unions do basically the opposite. **Source:** *Financial Assets and Liabilities*, Flow of Funds Accounts, Board of Governors of the Federal Reserve System; and *Sourcebook*, United States League of Savings Institutions.

C. Credit Unions

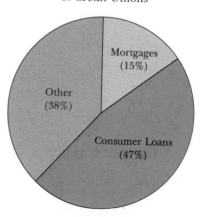

**Credit unions** specialize in small consumer loans. They operate efficiently in this market because they are mutual organizations in which individuals are generally well known to each other. Credit unions can thus make consumer loans on the basis of information concerning the borrower that would not be available to more autonomous lenders. The largest component of "other" credit union assets is deposits at commercial banks and other thrift institutions.

Both **savings and loan associations** and **savings banks** have traditionally specialized in mortgage lending. Historically, savings and loan associations were "building societies"—small cooperative groups of people who pooled their resources to build their own homes, one after another. Approximately 50% of all mortgage loans in the United States are made and held by savings and loan associations and savings banks. Securities issued by the U.S. Treasury and other government agencies are the largest component of "other" assets held by savings and loan associations and savings banks.

The specialization of **savings institutions**—referring to savings banks and savings and loan associations—in mortgages has been declining since the disaster of the early 1980s (discussed in Chapter 8) when interest rates rose so dramatically. We saw that savings institutions faced extreme interest rate risk because they held mainly long-term mortgages and attracted mainly short-term deposits. As a result, when interest rates spurted up, their profits tumbled. Since that time, the savings institutions have used adjustable-rate mortgages as one solution to interest rate risk and they have used futures and options contracts (discussed in Chapter 9) as another solution.

A third solution for savings institutions is to balance their long-term mortgage loans with other short-term loans. Short-term business and consumer loans are an obvious choice. These loans have been the specialty of commercial banks, so such a change increases competition between the two types of institutions. Since savings institutions already deal with consumers for deposits and mortgages, consumer loans are a natural addition—indeed, regulations (now mainly removed) were the main reason they did not make these loans earlier. Commercial loans are more problematic for savings institutions, because they have not dealt with business customers previously, and so they must first learn to evaluate the credit risk of such loans.

## Nondepository Intermediaries

As their name indicates, the distinguishing feature of **nondepository intermediaries** is that they do not issue deposits as their liabilities. As a result, their liabilities may have one or more of the following features:

- Their value may vary according to changes in security prices and interest rates.
- They are generally not federally insured.
- Often they cannot be redeemed at a local office or institution.
- They may be closely related to other services.

In addition, relative to depository intermediaries, nondepository intermediaries may invest in a wider range of assets (including common stocks) and some of them offer unique services.

Since the liabilities of mutual funds represent a particularly important contrast with bank deposits, we will first examine mutual funds in more detail. Then we will look at pension funds, insurance companies, and finance companies.

## Mutual Funds

**Mutual funds** are corporations that raise money by selling shares to shareholders, who then own the mutual fund. As with any corporation, a person's ownership interest is represented by the number of shares he or she owns relative to the total number outstanding. However, in other respects mutual funds are a very special type of organization. Formally, they are called *investment companies,* because their main activity is to invest the money they raise in a portfolio of financial securities. Each shareholder in a mutual fund then owns a proportional "share" of the fund's portfolio. The shareholders own the portfolio in this mutual or shared fashion; they do not own individual shares of the stocks (or other securities) that make up the portfolio.

Mutual funds were first authorized as investment companies by the Investment Company Act of 1940. Under this and related legislation, the funds must meet reporting requirements and other rules administered by the Securities and Exchange Commission (SEC). However, the SEC does not regulate mutual funds as closely as banking regulators do depository intermediaries. Legislation also allows mutual funds to be treated as *conduits* for federal income tax purposes—their tax liabilities are passed on to their shareholders based on the dividends paid by the fund. They must distribute at least 90% of their investment income to qualify for this "conduit" tax treatment.

### Buying and Selling Mutual Fund Shares

Because they represent ownership, shares in mutual funds have no specified maturity date. Therefore investors must originate and terminate their investments in mutual funds by buying and selling shares. Two types of mutual funds—*opened-end* and *closed-end*—can be distinguished on the basis of how shareholders buy and sell shares.

#### Opened-End Mutual Funds

For **opened-end** mutual funds, the shares are bought from, and sold to, the mutual fund itself. As a result, the size of an opened-end fund expands as people buy more of the shares and contracts as people sell (redeem) their shares—thus the name "opened-end." The price per share equals the **net asset value** per share, determined at the end of each day by dividing the value of the fund's total portfolio by the number of shares outstanding. This is the price used for purchases and sales of shares each day. Figure 13.3 shows the pattern of sales and redemptions of shares by opened-end mutual funds since 1970.

Many opened-end mutual funds have developed a convenient check-writing system that allows shareholders to redeem their shares immediately, in almost any amount, simply by writing a check. From the shareholder's standpoint, mutual fund checks are almost indistinguishable from bank checks. As a shareholder writes checks, the mutual fund

FIGURE 13.3
**Opened-End Mutual Fund Sales and Redemptions**

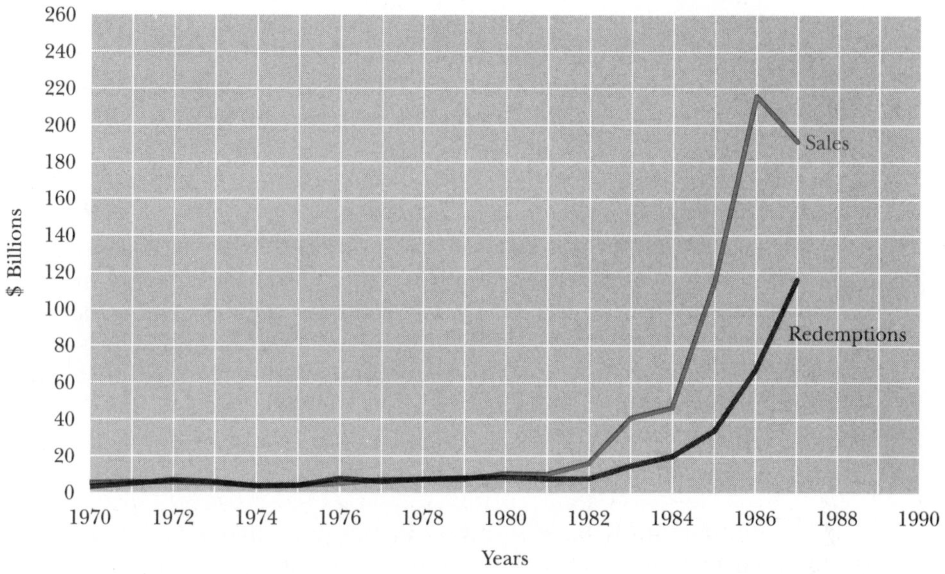

The ease of buying and selling mutual fund shares is a key benefit for investors. With opened-end funds, investors buy new shares from the mutual fund itself, and they redeem the shares by selling them back to the fund. In most years, sales of new shares exceed redemptions, so the total size of the funds is generally rising. **Source:** *Mutual Fund Factbook,* Investment Company Institute, 1988. The data exclude money market funds that invest in money market instruments.

provides the bank with money to cover them, while it simultaneously redeems the equivalent value of the customer's mutual fund shares.

To operate such a system, the mutual fund opens a transaction account (checking account) at a bank and provides its shareholders with checks that draw on the balances the mutual fund keeps in this account. Since mutual funds are not part of the Federal Reserve's check-clearing system, they must arrange for a bank to handle the large number of checks that shareholders write on the account. As an example, Merrill Lynch manages many mutual funds, and it uses Bank One of Ohio to clear all of its shareholder checks.

Opened-end mutual funds use different methods for distributing shares to new investors. **Load funds** charge new investors a fee when they buy shares (a "front-end" load) or, less commonly, when they sell the shares (a "back-end" load). **No-load funds** do not charge such fees. Therefore, load funds must maintain a reputation for exceptional investment performance to compete with no-load funds. However, there is no significant difference in performance between the two types of funds—some of each type perform very well, and others very poorly. One reason that so many load funds have survived is that stockbrokers are usually paid commissions for directing their customers to buy load funds.

### Closed-End Mutual Funds

For **closed-end** mutual funds, the number of shares equals the number originally issued when the fund started (unless the fund buys back some of its own shares)—hence the name "closed-end." Investors buy and sell shares of closed-end funds on a stock exchange—usually the New York Stock Exchange—and this trading determines the market price of the shares. The market price is generally related to the net asset value of a share, but unlike an opened-end fund, it need not equal the net asset value exactly.

In fact, shares in some closed-end mutual funds sell at a premium (the market price exceeds the net asset value), but, more commonly, they sell at a discount (the market price is less than the net asset value). Box 13.1 looks at some reasons why closed-end mutual fund shares sell at premiums and at discounts, and why funds selling at discounts might be good investments.

## Investment Portfolios

Most mutual funds have to invest in the particular class of securities specified in their bylaws. The major classes of funds and investments include:

- **Money market funds,** which invest in short-term securities such as Treasury bills.
- **Stock funds,** also called equity funds, which invest in common stocks.
- **Bond funds,** which invest in taxable and tax-exempt bonds.

There are also many specific categories within these general classes. Figure 13.4 shows how the total assets of stock and bond mutual funds are distributed among the particular types of stocks and bonds in which they invest. Figure 13.5 shows how money market, bond, and stock mutual funds have grown since 1970.

As of year-end 1987, investments in long-term mutual funds—funds investing in stocks and bonds—were distributed one-third in stocks and two-thirds in bonds. Investments in bond mutual funds include U.S. Treasury bonds, municipal bonds, and corporate bonds. Long-term mutual funds also invest small amounts in preferred stocks and other assets. **Source:** *Mutual Fund Factbook,* Investment Company Institute, 1988. The data exclude money market funds that invest in money market instruments.

FIGURE 13.4

**The Distribution of Investments by Bond and Equity Mutual Funds**

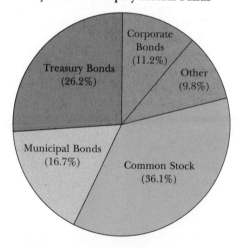

Corporate Bonds (11.2%)

Treasury Bonds (26.2%)

Other (9.8%)

Municipal Bonds (16.7%)

Common Stock (36.1%)

## BOX 13.1 CREDIT CHECK

## Premiums and Discounts on Closed-End Mutual Funds

Most closed-end mutual funds invest in portfolios of common stocks; so their net asset value per share is determined by dividing the value of their stock portfolio by their total number of shares. However, the price of a share of a closed-end mutual fund is determined by stock market trading. The market price of a share might differ from the net asset value for a number of reasons.

For example, the shares of closed-end funds that invest in portfolios of stocks of foreign companies traded only on foreign stock markets—so-called "country" funds—often sell at a substantial premium to their net asset value. This is because there is no easy way for investors to buy the stocks of foreign companies directly, so they are willing to pay a premium to obtain shares of a "country" fund.

It is more difficult to understand why the shares of many closed-end mutual funds sell at a discount from their net asset value. Although tax considerations and fund expenses are factors, they are not sufficient to explain the discounts of 20% or more that are sometimes observed. Such discounts led Burton Malkiel, in his book *A Random Walk Down Wall Street*, to recommend closed-end mutual funds selling at discounts as good investments; he noted that investors could in effect buy a portfolio of stocks at a below-market price. Possibly as the result of investors acting on Malkiel's advice, the discounts on many closed-end mutual funds then disappeared. More recently, however, they seem to be returning.

### FIGURE 13.5
### Total Assets of Money Market, Stock, and Bond Mutual Funds

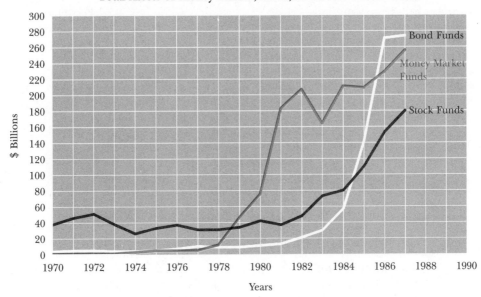

Stock mutual funds were the largest type of mutual funds until 1979, when money market funds surpassed them. More recently, both bond and stock mutual funds have been growing rapidly, and bond mutual funds are the largest type. **Source:** Mutual Fund Factbook, Investment Company Institute, 1988.

Mutual fund shareholders receive dividend payments based on the interest and dividends that their fund earns on its investment portfolio. In addition, when shareholders buy or sell a mutual fund share, they may receive a *capital gain*—if the net asset value of the fund has appreciated in value during the time of ownership—or a *capital loss*—if the net asset value has fallen. As a result, shareholders receive a *total rate of return*—the sum of dividend payments and capital gains or losses—that closely follows what they would have received had they owned the mutual fund's portfolio directly.

So deciding whether to invest in a particular mutual fund is tantamount to deciding whether to invest in its investment portfolio. For this reason, it is no more surprising that there are so many types of mutual funds than it is that there are so many types of securities. This also means that when investors in the stock market are generally selling their shares, investors in mutual fund shares are also likely to be selling. As discussed in Box 13.2, this was illustrated vividly during the stock market crash of October 1987.

---

**BOX 13.2 CREDIT CHECK**

## Mutual Funds and the Stock Market Crash of 1987

When the stock market plunges, many nervous investors want to sell their stocks. This applies equally to the owners of mutual fund shares. In the stock market crash of October 19, 1987, opened-end mutual funds were hit by massive amounts of share redemptions.

Redemptions create a problem if they are so extensive that they force the fund to sell securities from its portfolio to raise cash. Normally, this does not occur because redemptions are more than balanced by new share purchases, and a small amount of cash is maintained to cover an occasional imbalance. But when everyone wants to redeem shares, the funds have to sell stocks to raise cash.

This problem was anticipated by the manager of the large Fidelity group of mutual funds before stock market trading started on the day of the crash. Fidelity tried, with some success, to sell part of its portfolio on the London stock market, where trading begins earlier than in New York. As soon as trading started in New York, Fidelity sold more stock, making it one of the largest early sellers. The fund's shareholders benefited from this prompt action, although Fidelity's massive selling may have also contributed to the general panic that followed.

---

## The Advantages of Mutual Fund Investments

Since mutual funds invest in securities that are traded in the financial markets, why do investors buy mutual fund shares instead of buying the same securities directly? The answer is that mutual funds offer investors three key advantages: greater diversification, more liquidity, and lower transactions costs. All of these advantages are related to the large size of mutual fund portfolios.

The *diversification* advantage arises because each mutual fund share represents a prorated part of the fund's portfolio of many individual securities. The high transactions costs of buying small amounts of a large number of stocks would make it too expensive for most individual investors to purchase such a diversified portfolio directly.

The *liquidity* advantage is particularly strong for opened-end mutual funds. With an opened-end fund, investors just sell shares to the fund at the net asset value; they can even sell shares by just writing a check on their fund account. Closed-end mutual funds do not offer these services, but, nevertheless, it is easier to sell the shares of a closed-end fund than it would be to sell all the individual securities represented in its portfolio.

The *transactions cost* advantage of mutual fund shares arise from several considerations:

- The cost of managing a mutual fund is spread across a large portfolio, so the cost per share is low.

- Mutual funds do not have to pay for branch offices and other services that depository intermediaries provide.

- Mutual funds primarily hold capital market securities as their investments, so they do not face the costs of evaluating loan applications. (However, the rate of return may also be lower for this reason.)

These savings are passed on to shareholders in the form of higher dividend payments.

### Mutual Funds Versus Bank Deposits

In comparing mutual fund shares with bank and thrift institution deposits, investors face a trade-off between the generally higher expected returns provided by mutual funds and the generally higher levels of safety and service provided by depository intermediaries.

This distinction is particularly clear in the case of *long-term* mutual funds—stock and bond mutual funds. Unlike bank and thrift deposits, shareholders in these funds receive capital gains and losses on their shares. However, unlike the mutual funds, banks and thrifts guarantee to pay a specified interest rate and to return the principal amount. Also, federal insurance stands behind bank deposits.

Investments in *money market funds*—mutual funds that invest in money market securities—are more comparable to bank deposits. Capital gains and losses on money market funds are small because their investment assets are short-term; so the prices of these assets change little even when there are major swings in interest rates. And the possibility of losses on money market funds due to credit risk—bad investments—is minimized because these funds invest in diversified portfolios of high-quality securities.

So, even though money market funds lack interest rate guarantees, federal insurance, and local offices (most investments are made by mail), in practice many investors consider money market funds and bank deposits to be close substitutes. However, money market funds still generally have to pay slightly higher rates of interest to attract investors.

Figure 13.6 illustrates the competition that has occurred between money market funds and bank transaction deposits in recent years. Although small amounts had been invested in money market funds before 1979, the funds started to be actively marketed to investors only when interest rates began to rise dramatically at that time. They continued to grow dramatically through 1982, because depository intermediaries were limited in the interest rates they were allowed to pay on transaction deposits. After 1982, interest rates in the economy fell, banks were allowed to pay higher interest rates, and a competitive balance was reached. In fact, bank transaction deposits started rising rapidly again, and, as we saw in Figure 13.5, stock and bond funds grew rapidly.

FIGURE 13.6
**Money Market Funds and Transaction Deposit Accounts**

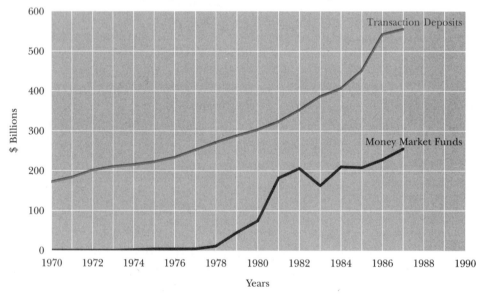

Money market funds began to grow rapidly in 1979 when interest rates in the economy rose dramatically. After 1982, interest rates fell and banks were allowed to compete by paying higher interest rates on transaction deposits, so the competitive balance returned. **Source:** *Mutual Fund Factbook*, Investment Company Institute, 1988.

## Pension Funds and Insurance Companies

Pension funds help people to accumulate money for their retirement; and insurance companies provide policies against various risks and hazards. Both are still financial intermediaries, however; in the course of providing their services, they raise money and invest it.

## Pension Fund Services

People make use of several types of **pension funds** to accumulate money for retirement: **business pension plans, Social Security,** and **Individual Retirement Accounts** (IRAs). We will focus on business pension funds as our example of financial intermediation. However, Social Security and individual retirement accounts are covered in Boxes 13.3 and 13.4.

---

**BOX 13.3 CREDIT CHECK**

## Social Security

Social Security—the Old Age and Survivors Insurance Fund—is a pension fund maintained by the federal government. Contributions—in the form of Social Security taxes—are paid to the fund by both the employee and his or her firm. The contributions are based on the employee's salary up to an established maximum (which rises over time). The government invests these payments in a portfolio, consisting of—what else?—government securities. As people reach retirement age, they receive monthly payments based on a schedule set and periodically revised by Congress. Social security benefits also include Medicare and aid to the disabled.

When Social Security was started in 1935, it was thought it would operate under the principle of a private plan—that is, over time the contributions collected and the benefits paid would balance. However, Congress kept raising the benefits without raising the required contributions by a corresponding amount, so the fund became seriously underfunded. In effect, the system operated on a "pay as you go basis"—the current contributions were only adequate to pay the current benefits, not the higher future benefits. However, Congress has recently started to recognize that higher benefits require higher contributions.

---

### Business Pension Funds

Contributions to business pension funds are made by the companies that sponsor these funds, by the employees, or by both. There are two main types of business pension funds: defined contribution and defined benefit plans.

With **defined contribution** pension funds, each employee owns a part of the fund's assets—as with a mutual fund—based on the contributions made by the employee or on his or her behalf by the company. The employee's retirement benefit then depends on the asset value of the fund at the date of retirement. However, unlike mutual funds, pension fund balances often can only be redeemed upon retirement.

With **defined benefit** pension funds—the more common type of pension fund—the pension holder is guaranteed a specific level of retirement income, separate from the actual performance of the pension fund. Commonly, retirement benefits are tied to a person's salary level just before retirement. The firm sponsoring the pension plan is then responsible for making sure that contributions made to the plan are adequate.

## BOX 13.4 CREDIT CHECK

### Individual Retirement Accounts

Individuals can, of course, save money on their own behalf for retirement. Individual Retirement Accounts (IRAs) (and similar Keogh accounts) encourage this by providing special tax-deferral privileges. Income taxes are paid on contributed funds only at retirement as money is withdrawn from the account, although recent tax law changes have reduced these benefits. Most of the IRA funds are placed in accounts at financial intermediaries, as shown in the table. It is also possible to retain discretionary control over one's IRA investments by setting up IRA accounts at brokerage firms.

**Individual Retirement Account Assets**
**At year-end 1987**
**(Dollars in billions)**

| | |
|---|---|
| Thrift institutions | $154 |
| Commercial banks | 72 |
| Mutual funds | 59 |
| Brokerage industry (self-directed) | 26 |
| Life insurance companies | 23 |
| Total IRA assets | $334 |

**Source:** *Sourcebook*, United States League of Savings Institutions, 1988

Contributions to a defined benefit pension plan are computed with *actuarial* methods—comparing the expected rate of return on the fund's investment assets with the benefits that have been promised. However, errors are made: the actual investment experience can be better or worse than expected; or the number of people retiring, or their salary levels, can turn out to be higher or lower than expected.

As a result, defined benefit pension plans can be *overfunded* (investment assets exceed promised benefits), or *underfunded* (investment assets are less than promised benefits). Firms with overfunded plans sometimes become the targets of hostile takeovers where the acquirer hopes to obtain some of the excess investment assets. Firms with underfunded plans create the risk for their employees that the pension fund may default on promised benefit payments.

In fact, during the early 1970s, some large firms with underfunded pension funds became bankrupt, threatening the benefits of retiring employees. As a result, in 1974, Congress passed the first of a series of Employee Retirement Income Security Acts (ERISA) that set requirements for how such pension plans are to be funded and administered. The Pension Benefits Guarantee Corporation was also created as a federal insurance plan to guarantee pension benefits.

### Insurance Services

**Insurance companies** are nondepository intermediaries chartered and regulated by the states in which they operate. Insurance policies are the liabilities of insurance companies. Insurance companies have funds to invest because there is a lag between the time that premium payments are received and the time insurance claims are settled. During the interim, the companies invest the money they hold. Insurance companies are properly treated as financial intermediaries because of these investment activities.

An insurance company sets its premiums on the basis of actuarial calculations incorporating two considerations: the expected underwriting experience and the expected investment experience. The **underwriting experience** refers to the insurance claims the company expects on its policies. The **investment experience** measures the interest, dividends, and capital gains that the company expects to earn on its investment portfolio.

Of course, actual experience may differ from what was expected. With *shareholder-owned insurance companies,* the profits (or losses) accrue to the shareholders. With *mutual insurance companies*—companies owned by the people they insure—the policyholders participate in the company's profits by receiving dividends or lower future premiums—these are called *participating policies.*

Holders of *casualty insurance*—fire, theft, and liability policies—rarely have participating policies. For these types of insurance, the period between the premium payment and the average claim settlement is usually short enough that the company can set its premiums with reasonable accuracy. However, policyholders still participate indirectly as the company revises its future premiums to reflect its actual experience.

Life insurance policies come in two main forms—term and "ordinary" life. *Term life insurance* provides coverage one year at a time. *Ordinary life insurance,* in contrast, represents a long-term contract between the insured and the insurance company. Some ordinary life insurance policies—such as *whole life* and *universal life*—combine a savings plan and a life insurance contract in one policy. The accumulated values are also sheltered to a degree from income taxation.

## Intermediation

In addition to the services provided by pension funds and insurance companies, both allow for **intermediation** services—they raise and invest funds. Table 13.3 shows how they invest their funds. They hold mainly long-term assets because their commitments—to pay pension benefits and insurance claims—are mostly long-term. This is a good example of how a nondepository intermediary also tries to match the maturity of its assets and its liabilities—a topic we discussed regarding depository intermediaries in Chapter 8.

Common stocks are the single largest asset group for pension funds, because common stocks are thought to provide protection against unexpected inflation—if the price level and benefits rise, then stock prices are also likely to rise in the long run. Most of the obligations of insurance companies are fixed in value, so they need less protection from unexpected inflation and, accordingly, buy smaller amounts of common stocks.

| TABLE 13.3 | | |
| --- | --- | --- |
| Assets of Pension Funds and Insurance Companies | | |
| At year-end 1987 (Dollars in billions) | | |
| | Pension Funds | Insurance Companies |
| U.S government securities | $ 294 | $ 235 |
| Corporate bonds | 289 | 429 |
| Common stocks | 638 | 166 |
| Mortgage loans | 23 | 215 |
| Other | 315 | 349 |
| Total assets | $1,559 | $1,394 |

Source: *Flow of Funds Accounts*, Board of Governors of the Federal Reserve System, 1988.

## Finance Companies

**Finance companies** are nondepository intermediaries that specialize in making short-term, high-risk loans, which most other intermediaries avoid. Finance companies are state-chartered, shareholder-owned institutions. They raise funds through capital invested by shareholders and by issuing debt in the capital markets. The interest rates they charge on their loans must be high enough to offset the high costs of evaluating such loan applications and the high incidence of default. There are three main types of finance companies—consumer, sales, and commercial.

**Consumer finance companies** specialize in *signature only* loans to individuals, on which no collateral is provided. They develop special expertise in evaluating such loans and in collecting from delinquent borrowers. Because they charge high interest rates, consumer finance companies frequently confront *usury ceilings*—state-regulated limits on the interest rates that can be charged on consumer loans. Although these ceilings are supposed to protect consumers, the effect in many cases, as discussed in Chapter 12, is credit rationing—lenders will not make loans.

**Sales finance companies** are owned by large manufacturing firms; they provide loans to consumers who buy the firm's products. For example, each of the major American auto manufacturers has a sales finance company—such as General Motors Acceptance Corporation (GMAC)—to make auto loans.

**Commercial finance companies** provide short-run financing to companies by purchasing their accounts receivable (at a discount from the face value). *Accounts receivable* represent the short-term credit, or loans made by a firm to its customers in the course of wholesale trade. A firm may sell its accounts receivable if it needs to raise cash for other purposes (such as paying its bills).

## Some Current Developments

The level of competition seems to be rising between commercial banks, thrift institutions, nondepository intermediaries, and other nonfinancial firms. A good indicator of this is the degree to which these types of companies are each trying to enter some part of the business of the others. For example:

■ Thrift institutions have obtained expanded powers that enable them to carry out most of the activities of commercial banks.

■ The depository intermediaries have been lobbying for expanded powers to provide some of the services of nondepository intermediaries, such as selling insurance and mutual funds.

■ Nondepository intermediaries and other nonfinancial firms (including large retailers like Sears) are trying to enter the banking business. They want to be able to accept deposits and make loans.

All such changes require the approval of regulatory agencies. In fact, the trend toward *deregulation* has allowed some of these changes to occur. However, many basic issues are still to be resolved, as we discussed in Chapter 10.

## Chapter Summary

1. Financial intermediaries operate by issuing liabilities and by investing the money they raise in assets. Depository intermediaries—commercial banks and thrift institutions—raise money by issuing federally issued deposits as their main liabilities. Nondepository intermediaries—mutual funds, pension funds, insurance companies, and finance companies—raise money by issuing different types of liabilities.

2. Thrift institutions—savings and loan associations, savings banks, and credit unions—now have the same basic powers as commercial banks to provide intermediation and transfer (checking account) services. Thrift institutions are thus increasingly identified only by the types of loans they specialize in making. Savings and loan associations and savings banks specialize in mortgage loans, while credit unions specialize in consumer loans.

3. Mutual funds invest in portfolios of securities—stocks, bonds, and money market instruments—and sell shares in these portfolios to investors. Each investor in a mutual fund owns a prorated share of the mutual fund's investment portfolio. The advantages of mutual fund investments over buying bonds and shares of stock directly include greater diversification, greater liquidity, and lower transactions costs.

4. Pension funds and insurance companies provide special services. People use pension contracts to save money for their retirement and insurance policies to obtain financial protection against various risks and hazards. Both pension funds and insurance companies are financial intermediaries because, in providing these services, they obtain money—when firms and individuals make contributions to pension plans and when people buy insurance policies—that they then invest.

5. There are three types of finance companies—consumer, sales, and commercial, each specializing in making a particular type of short-term, high-risk loan. They raise money through the invested capital of their shareholders and by borrowing on the capital markets.

## Key Terms

Depository intermediaries:
    Commercial banks
    Credit unions
    Savings and loan associations
    Savings banks
Finance companies:
    Commercial
    Consumer
    Sales
Forms of ownership:
    Mutual organizations
    Shareholder owned
Insurance companies:
    Investment experience
    Underwriting experience
Intermediation services:
    Insurance companies

Pension funds
Mutual funds:
    Bond, money market, and stock
    Closed-end and opened-end
    Load and no-load
    Net asset value
Nondepository intermediaries:
    Finance companies
    Insurance companies
    Mutual funds
    Pension funds
Pension funds:
    Defined benefit plans
    Defined contribution plans
Savings institutions
Thrift institutions

## Study Questions

1. Commercial banks advertise that they are "full-service" institutions. Briefly describe the two main services that commercial banks provide. To what extent are these services provided by other financial intermediaries?

2. Why do credit unions specialize in making small consumer loans?

3. Why do nondepository intermediaries often invest in long-term assets like stocks, while depository intermediaries mainly invest in short-term assets like loans?

4. What is the difference between *opened-end* and *closed-end* mutual funds? What factors distinguish money market and stock mutual funds?

5. Why does it represent an investment opportunity when the *market price* of a closed-end mutual fund is below its *net asset values*? Could this also happen with the shares of an opened-end mutual fund?

6. Why are stock mutual funds more advantageous for small investors than for large investors?

7. What are the differences between the rate of return paid on a stock mutual fund and

on a bank time deposit? Between a money market mutual fund and a bank transaction account?

8. Why are pension funds and insurance companies considered to be financial intermediaries, even though their main activities involve selling pension contracts and life insurance policies?

9. What important features do defined con-

tribution pension funds and mutual funds share? What important features do defined benefit pension funds and bank time deposits share?

10. Why do poor underwriting experience and poor investment experience both cause insurance companies to raise their premiums?

---

## Recommended Reading

*The trade associations of the nonbank intermediaries provide annual "fact books" that contain data as well as information about their industries:*

American Council of Life Insurance, *Life Insurance Fact Book*, Washington, D.C.

American Council of Life Insurance, *Pension Facts*, Washington, D.C.

Investment Company Institute, *Mutual Fund Fact Book*, Washington, D.C.

United States League of Savings Institutions, *Sourcebook*, Chicago.

*Some lighter, but informative, reading on insurance companies and pension funds includes:*

Peter F. Drucker, *The Unseen Revolution: How Pension Fund Socialism Came to America*, Harper and Row, New York, 1976.

Ronald Kessler, *The Life Insurance Game*, Holt, Rinehart & Winston, New York, 1985.

*The following discusses how savings institutions have shifted some lending activity away from mortgages:*

Frederick T. Furlong, "Savings and Loan Asset Composition and the Mortgage Market," *Economic Review*, Federal Reserve Bank of San Francisco, Summer 1985, pp. 14–24.

*The investment book mentioned with regard to closed-end funds is:*

Burton G. Malkiel, *A Random Walk Down Wall Street*, 4th edition, Norton, New York, 1985.

# Money Supply and
# Money Demand

So far, we have looked closely at the main functions of money—how it expedites the exchange of goods and services as a medium of exchange, and how it is used to hold wealth over time as a store of value. Now we will look at money itself, its supply, its demand, and its equilibrium (when money demand equals money supply).

In Chapter 14, we examine the process that determines the money supply in the United States. This process involves three main groups: the Federal Reserve, which determines the monetary base; the public (basically everyone in the economy except for banks), which holds part of the monetary base as currency; and banks, which create most of the money supply based on their part of the monetary base—bank reserves. The result of this process is that the money supply is determined to be a substantial multiple—the money supply multiplier—of the monetary base provided by the Federal Reserve.

Following the discussion of money supply, we look at money demand. People demand money primarily for its two main services: as a medium of exchange (for making payments) and as a store of value (for holding wealth). Consequently, in Chapter 15, we will look at two types of theories of the demand for money: transaction theories—based on money as a medium of exchange, and asset theories—based on money as a store of wealth. Using these theories, we will focus on three key variables that determine the demand for money: income, interest rates, and payments system factors (how payments are made in the economy).

This part concludes in Chapter 16 examines equilibrium between money demand and money supply. Since there is nothing intrinsic in the nature of the supply of money or the demand for money to make them equal, one or more variables in the economy have to adjust to establish equilibrium in the market for money. Interest rates and income are two variables that generally play this role. The analysis of how this works provides an introduction to monetary policy. That is, monetary policy can change the money supply—creating an imbalance between the supply of money and the demand for money—so that either interest rates or income have to adjust in order to reestablish equilibrium in the market for money. Once we understand this process, we will be ready to examine monetary policy in Part V.

# The Money Supply and Its Determinants

**14**

*"Money begets money."*

**Old English proverb**

Who determines the money supply? It is probably not surprising to learn that banks are important in the process. Bankers may be unaware of their role, however, because it is mainly the interaction of banks that affects the money supply.

The Federal Reserve and the "public"—the latter referring to everybody in the economy other than banks and the Fed—also affect the money supply. The Fed determines the monetary base, which equals the sum of currency and bank reserves, while the public determines the amount of currency.

So who really determines the money supply? Each of the three groups—the banks, the public, and the Federal Reserve—has an important role. However, only the Federal Reserve specifically *tries* to control the money supply—for the purpose of monetary policy. To set the money supply at the desired level, the Federal Reserve may anticipate, and therefore offset, the actions of the banks and the public.

In this chapter, we look at the process that determines the U.S. money supply.

---

We focus in this chapter on two definitions of the *money supply:* the M1 money supply—which equals the sum of currency held by the public and transaction deposits—and the M2 money supply—which equals the sum of the M1 money supply and time deposits. The details of these money supply definitions are pointed out later in this chapter.

In discussing the money supply, we will make use of the ideas of *liquidity management* that we studied in Chapter 11, especially the concept of bank reserves. We will see that the quantity of bank deposits is determined to be a large multiple of bank reserves—called the *reserve multiplier*—and that the money supply is determined to be a multiple of the monetary base—called the *money supply multiplier*.

Most of our discussion will apply to all *depository institutions*—banks and thrift institutions. For example, the relevant quantities of bank deposits, vault cash, and reserve deposits at the Federal Reserve are the totals for all depository institutions. For brevity, we will use the term "banks" in the text to refer to all of these institutions; but in tables and figures we will specify "depository institutions."

Our analysis of the money supply will proceed in a series of three steps:

1. We will look at how the Federal Reserve determines the *monetary base* and at how the banks and the public divide the monetary base between currency and bank reserves.

2. We next analyze how the *reserve multiplier* works to determine bank deposits as a function of bank reserves and at how the *money supply multiplier* works to determine the money supply as a function of the monetary base.

3. And finally, we study how *interest rates* and other factors influence bank deposits and the money supply.

## The Monetary Base

The **monetary base** is the sum of currency held by the public and total bank reserves. **Currency held by the public** includes dollar bills of all denominations and coins—hereafter simply called *currency*. **Bank reserves** consist of *vault cash* (currency held in bank vaults) and *reserve deposit accounts* at the Federal Reserve—hereafter simply called *reserve deposits*. So the *monetary base* can be expressed as:

$$B = C + R_t. \tag{14.1}$$

where  $B$ = monetary base,

$\quad C$ = currency (held by the public),

$\quad R_t$ = total bank reserves (equal to the sum of vault cash and reserve deposits).

Figure 14.1 shows the two components of the monetary base, indicating that currency is much larger than bank reserves. Figure 14.2 shows that the reserve deposit component of bank reserves is slightly larger than the vault cash component.

### How the Federal Reserve Increases the Monetary Base

The Federal Reserve increases the monetary base by buying assets and paying for them either by issuing currency or by crediting bank reserve deposits—each being a component of the monetary base. In principle, the Federal Reserve could increase the monetary base by buying *any* asset—even a refrigerator or a textbook. However, the Federal Reserve is legally restricted to certain assets—U.S. government securities are the largest group—as shown in Table 14.1.

FIGURE 14.1
**The Monetary Base and Its Components**

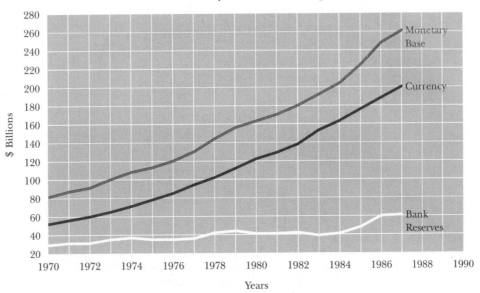

The monetary base equals the sum of currency held by the public and
the total reserves of depository institutions. The currency component of
the monetary base is about four times larger than total reserves. **Source:**
*Economic Report of the President,* February, 1988.

FIGURE 14.2
**Bank Reserves and Its Components**

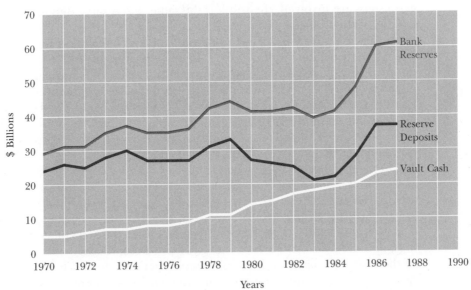

The total reserves of depository institutions equal the sum of their vault
cash and their reserve deposits at the Federal Reserve. Reserve deposits
tend to be slightly larger than vault cash. **Source:** *Economic Report of the
President,* 1988.

**TABLE 14.1**

**Federal Reserve Assets**

### At year-end 1987 (Dollars in billions)

| | |
|---|---:|
| U.S. government securities and federal agency obligations | $228 |
| Gold stock, foreign currencies, and related assets | 24 |
| Discount loans to depository institutions | 1 |
| Federal Reserve float[a] | 2 |
| Federal Reserve premises (office buildings, etc.) | 1 |
| Other assets | 8 |
| Total assets | $264 |

[a]As discussed in Chapter 11, Federal Reserve float is the temporary difference between the credits and the debits the Federal Reserve gives to banks in the process of clearing checks.

**Source:** *Federal Reserve Bulletin,* Table 1.11, Board of Governors of the Federal Reserve system, 1988.

The flow diagram in Figure 14.3 indicates more precisely what happens when the Federal Reserve buys government securities, either from a bank or from the public. When the Federal Reserve buys government securities from a bank, it credits the payment to that bank's reserve deposits. So this is a very direct route for increasing the monetary base.

In contrast, when the Federal Reserve buys securities from the public—individuals or firms—it often pays for them by check; only a few members of the public have deposit accounts at the Federal Reserve. The check will then be deposited in a bank, which sends it to the Fed, which, in turn, credits the bank's reserve deposit account. So although extra steps are involved, the result is the same: the reserve deposit component of the monetary base will rise.

By the same token, if the Federal Reserve *sells* securities, the payments it *receives* reduce the monetary base. If the securities are sold to *a bank*, the Fed directly reduces the bank's reserve deposit, thus reducing the monetary base. If the securities are sold to the *public*, payment may be made to the Federal Reserve with a check drawn on a bank. The Federal Reserve cashes the check by reducing the reserve deposit account of the bank. So, either way, the net effect is that the reserve deposit component of the monetary base is reduced.

The same concepts apply when the Federal Reserve buys or sells any of the other assets shown in Table 14.1. Assets related to international activities of the Federal Reserve—gold, foreign currencies, and similar assets—are the largest group after U.S. government securities. Then come discount loans to depository institutions, float, the Fed's office buildings, and other assets. Each of these Federal Reserve assets is a source of the monetary base, and we will discuss them further in Part V. For now, we will concentrate on government securities—the main asset the Fed buys or sells to control the size of the monetary base.

FIGURE 14.3
**How the Federal Reserve Increases the Monetary Base**

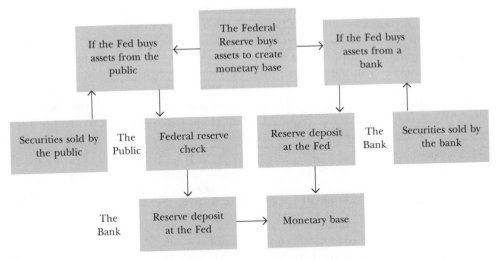

The Federal Reserve buys securities from either the public or from a bank to increase the monetary base. When the Fed buys a security from a bank, payment is made to the bank's reserve deposit account, which is counted as part of the monetary base. When the Federal Reserve buys a security from the public, the route is more circuitous, but the result is the same.

## How the Components of the Monetary Base Are Determined

The public has the main role in dividing the monetary base into its two components. That is, the public determines how much of the monetary base it wishes to hold as currency, and the rest is then deposited with banks, where it counts as bank reserves. The public demands currency for small transactions, such as buying the morning newspaper and paying taxi cab drivers, for transactions in the underground economy, and for *hoarding* (the latter two were discussed in Chapter 1).

Even though the public decides on the amount of the monetary base it wants to hold as currency (depositing the rest in banks), banks can influence this decision. They can raise their deposit rates, creating an incentive for people to place more of their currency in bank deposits, thus lowering the currency component of the monetary base and raising the bank reserve component. Nevertheless, it is useful to think of bank reserves $R_t$ as the residual in the process whereby the Federal Reserve determines the monetary base $B$ and the public determines the amount of currency $C$:

$$R_t = B - C. \qquad (14.2)$$

(Of course, this is just a restatement of equation [14.1], $B = C + R_t$.)

# The Multiple Expansion of Bank Deposits

We have now seen that the Federal Reserve determines the size of the monetary base and that the public determines how it is divided between currency and bank reserves. The next step in the process of determining the money supply considers how bank deposits are determined by the reserve multiplier. This process is called **deposit expansion.**

Recall that **required reserves** are held by banks to satisfy the Federal Reserve's reserve requirements, and **excess reserves** are the bank reserves that are not required. Thus, **total bank reserves** $R_t$ are the sum of required reserves $R_r$ and excess reserves $R_e$:

$$R_t = R_r + R_e. \tag{14.3}$$

## Deposit Expansion in the Bare-Bones System

We will now analyze the process of deposit expansion under a set of simplifying assumptions—the *bare-bones system:*

1. *The public holds no currency:* $C = 0$. The monetary base thus consists only of bank reserves. If members of the public temporarily receive currency, they deposit it immediately in a bank.

2. *There is only one class of deposits, D.* The required reserve ratio on deposits is $\theta$, so required reserves $R_r$ are equal to $\theta D$. We will use the numerical value $\theta = 10\%$ in examples. (Transaction deposits $D_1$ and time deposits $D_2$ are separated later.)

3. *Banks hold no excess reserves:* $R_e = 0$. Banks may temporarily receive excess reserves, but the funds are immediately invested in earning assets.

4. *The banking system consists of a single, monopoly, bank.* We will see later in the chapter that the same results hold for a system with many banks.

5. *The Federal Reserve supplies a monetary base B of $100.* It does not matter whether the monetary base is supplied initially as currency or as bank reserves, since the Fed will always exchange one for the other.

Our example of deposit expansion begins with the Fed creating a monetary base of $100 by purchasing $100 of Treasury bills from the public and paying for them by issuing $100 of currency. The $100 of currency received by the public is the monetary base. However, since individuals do not hold currency in the bare-bones system, they immediately deposit it in the bank. The monetary base is then in the form of bank reserves, but it is still $100 and will remain so during the entire process. Depositing the monetary base of $100 into the bank initiates deposit expansion. We will see how this works by examining a series of bank balance sheets (or T-accounts), beginning with the following stage 1.

**Stage 1: The Public Deposits Currency in the Bank**

| Assets | | Liabilities | |
|---|---|---|---|
| Bank reserves | $100 | Deposits | $100 |
| Required $10 | | | |
| Excess $90 | | | |

*Stage 1* is the point at which the public deposits $100 of currency in the bank; this deposit initially counts as bank reserves of $100, as reflected in the T-account. The T-account also shows how total reserves are split between required reserves of $10 (determined by multiplying the total amount of deposits by the required reserve ratio of 10%) and excess reserves of $90 (determined by subtracting required reserves from total bank reserves). However, under the assumptions of the bare-bones system, the bank should not hold any excess reserves. This leads to *stage 2* where the bank takes action—makes loans or buys securities—to use its excess reserves. We assume the bank makes loans.

**Stage 2: The Bank Lends Its Excess Reserves**

| Assets | | Liabilities | |
|---|---|---|---|
| Bank reserves | $10 | Deposits | $100 |
| Required $10 | | | |
| Excess $0 | | | |
| Bank Loans | $90 | | |

At *stage 2*, the balance sheet shows total bank reserves of $10 (all of which are required) and bank loans of $90. The public receives the bank loans in the form of currency. However, in the bare-bones system, the public's demand for currency is zero; this leads to stage 3, where the public deposits all of its currency back in the bank.

**Stage 3: The Public Deposits Currency in the Bank**

| Assets | | Liabilities | |
|---|---|---|---|
| Bank reserves | $100 | Deposits | $190 |
| Required $19 | | Stage 1 $100 | |
| Excess $81 | | Stage 3 $90 | |
| Bank Loans | $90 | | |

At *stage 3*, the public deposits the $90 of currency in the bank, so the bank's total deposits reach $190, the sum of the $100 deposited at stage 1 and the new deposits. Bank reserves now equal $100, representing the $10 of reserves the bank was holding at stage 2 and the $90 of currency deposited at stage 3. Required reserves are $19 (10% of $190), so excess reserves are $81. Bank loans are still $90. The bank is thus holding excess reserves at the end of stage 3, just as it did at the end of stage 1.

This leads to stage 4, where the bank makes more loans with its excess reserves.

### Stage 4: The Bank Lends its Excess Reserves

| Assets | | | Liabilities | | |
|---|---|---|---|---|---|
| Bank reserves | | $19 | Deposits | | $190 |
| Required | $19 | | Stage 1 | $100 | |
| Excess | $0 | | Stage 3 | $90 | |
| Bank Loans | | $171 | | | |
| Stage 2 | $90 | | | | |
| Stage 4 | $81 | | | | |

At *stage 4,* the bank uses its $81 of excess reserves from stage 3 to make loans. The process is just a repeat, with new numbers, of stage 2. Total loans then equal $171, the sum of the $90 of loans made at stage 2 and the $81 of new loans. This leaves the public holding the $81 of loans it just received as currency. Following the earlier pattern, the public will deposit this currency back in the bank.

The process of deposit expansion will thus continue through pairs of stages, with the bank lending its excess reserves to the public at one stage, and the public depositing its currency in the bank at the subsequent stage. The process ends only when the bank and the public reach an *equilibrium*—in the bare-bones system this means that *the public is holding no currency* and *the bank is holding no excess reserves.* The balance sheet of the bank in equilibrium is referred to as stage E.

### Stage E: The Equilibrium Stage

| Assets | | | Liabilities | |
|---|---|---|---|---|
| Bank reserves | | $100 | Deposits | $1,000 |
| Required | $100 | | | |
| Excess | $90 | | | |
| Bank Loans | | $900 | | |

At *stage E,* the bank has deposits of $1,000, reserves of $100 (all of which are required reserves), and loans of $900. This is an equilibrium because the public cannot make any further deposits (it has no currency) and the bank cannot make any further loans (it has no excess reserves). The equilibrium illustrates the power of deposit expansion by the banking system: an initial monetary base of $100 has grown to a total of $1,000 of deposits. In other words, the **reserve multiplier**—the ratio of deposits to the monetary base is 10 ($1,000/$100).

Table 14.2 tabulates the T-account information beyond stage 4, to stage 20, to show more details of how deposits, required reserves, and bank loans approach the equilibrium stage. However, even the last stages in Table 14.2 only approach stage E, because each successive stage represents a smaller change. We will now look at more direct ways to determine and compute the equilibrium of stage E.

**TABLE 14.2**
**The Stages of Bank Deposit Expansion**

| Stage | New Deposits | Total Deposits | Dollars Required Reserves | Excess Reserves | Bank Loans |
|-------|--------------|----------------|---------------------------|-----------------|------------|
| 1 | 100 | 100 | 10 | 90 | 0 |
| 2 | – | 100 | 10 | 0 | 90 |
| 3 | 90 | 190 | 19 | 81 | 90 |
| 4 | – | 190 | 19 | 0 | 171 |
| 5 | 81 | 271 | 27 | 73 | 171 |
| 6 | – | 271 | 27 | 0 | 244 |
| 7 | 73 | 344 | 34 | 66 | 244 |
| 8 | – | 344 | 34 | 0 | 310 |
| 9 | 66 | 410 | 41 | 59 | 310 |
| 10 | – | 410 | 41 | 0 | 369 |
| 11 | 59 | 469 | 47 | 53 | 369 |
| 12 | – | 469 | 47 | 0 | 422 |
| 13 | 53 | 522 | 52 | 48 | 422 |
| 14 | – | 522 | 52 | 0 | 470 |
| 15 | 48 | 570 | 57 | 43 | 470 |
| 16 | – | 570 | 57 | 0 | 513 |
| 17 | 43 | 613 | 61 | 39 | 513 |
| 18 | – | 613 | 61 | 0 | 552 |
| 19 | 39 | 652 | 65 | 35 | 552 |
| 20 | – | 652 | 65 | 0 | 587 |
| – | – | – | – | – | – |
| – | – | – | – | – | – |
| E | – | 1,000 | 100 | 0 | 900 |

## Alternative Views of Deposit Expansion

The deposit expansion process just described relies on a circular flow of currency and excess reserves: the public depositing currency in the bank at one stage, and the bank lending its excess reserves to the public at the next stage. In practice, however, instead of making loans in currency, banks normally credit the amount to the borrower's deposit balance.

### Deposit Expansion When Loans Are Credited as Deposits

Again assume that a monetary base of $100 is initially deposited in the bank at stage 1. But now assume that the bank immediately decides that it wants to use the entire $100 as required reserves. To do so, the bank first computes that $100 of required reserves will support $1,000 of deposits, given that the required reserve ratio is 10% ($100 = 10% of $1,000). To create $1,000 of deposits, the bank makes $900 of loans, creating $900 of additional deposits as it credits the loans to deposits. Total deposits—the sum of the initial deposits of $100 and the created deposits of $900—are thus immediately $1,000.

Notice that the same equilibrium is reached whichever way the bank works: by making incremental loans at each stage, or by immediately making loans in the full amount of $900. The system the bank uses to make loans affects only the number of intermediate stages between the initial deposit of the monetary base at stage 1 and the final equilibrium at stage E.

### An Algebraic View of Deposit Expansion

The equilibrium of the deposit expansion process can be derived even more rapidly with simple algebra. First combine the definition of the monetary base $B$ (equation [14.1]), $B = C + R_t$, and the definition of total reserves $R_t$ (equation [14.3]), $R_t = R_r + R_e$:

$$B = C + R_e + R_r, \qquad (14.4)$$

where $B$ = the monetary base,
$C$ = currency,
$R_r$ = required reserves,
$R_e$ = excess reserves.

In the bare-bones system, currency $C$ and excess reserves $R_e$ are both zero, and required reserves $R_r$ equal $\theta D$ (the required reserve ratio $\theta$ times the amount of deposits $D$), so equation (14.4) reduces to:

$$B = \theta D.$$

Then solving for the amount of deposits $D$, we have:

$$D = \frac{B}{\theta}. \qquad (14.5)$$

When the monetary base $B$ is $100 and the reserve ratio $\theta$ is 0.10, deposits $D$ equal $1,000 ($100/0.10). This, of course, is the same result we obtained using the other techniques. The algebraic approach also shows that the reserve multiplier is just the inverse of the required reserve ratio—$1/\theta$. Thus when the reserve ratio is 0.10, the reserve multiplier is 10 (1/0.10).

## Multiple Contraction of Deposits

We will now consider a deposit contraction in which the Federal Reserve *reduces* the amount of the monetary base. We will assume that the Federal Reserve reduces the monetary base from $100 to $50. What is the new equilibrium value of deposits? Using the algebraic approach, we find that $D = B/\theta = \$50/0.10 = (\$50)(10) = \$500$ is the new equilibrium value.

Table 14.3 illustrates the process, starting with the *initial position,* which is the same as Stage E in Table 14.2. The Federal Reserve then reduces the monetary base by $50 by selling $50 of securities to the public. The public sends a bank check to the Federal Reserve, and the Federal Reserve reduces the reserve deposits of the bank—so bank reserves fall to $50.

The bank balance sheet at this point is shown by the *intermediate position* in Table 14.3. Most importantly, bank excess reserves are now −$45: the bank has required reserves of $95 (10% of $950 of deposits), but its total reserves are only $50. This means the bank is deficient in required reserves—which can also happen to banks in practice, as we will see in Chapter 18 when we discuss monetary policy. In any case, the bank must rectify the situation.

**TABLE 14.3**
**The Process of Deposit Contraction**

**Initial Position**

| Assets | | Liabilities | |
|---|---|---|---|
| Bank reserves | $100 | Deposits | $1,000 |
| Required | $100 | | |
| Excess | $0 | | |
| Bank loans | $900 | | |

**Intermediate Position**
(After depositors withdraw $50)

| Assets | | Liabilities | |
|---|---|---|---|
| Bank reserves | $50 | Deposits | $950 |
| Required | $95 | | |
| Excess | −$45 | | |
| Bank loans | $900 | | |

**The Final Position**
(After bank reduces loans and deposits by $450)

| Assets | | Liabilities | |
|---|---|---|---|
| Bank reserves | $50 | Deposits | $500 |
| Required | $50 | | |
| Excess | $0 | | |
| Bank loans | $450 | | |

As one option, the bank can try to obtain additional reserves. However, nobody in the bare-bones system will provide them: the Federal Reserve wants the monetary base to be $50, so it will not supply more reserves; and the public is satisfied with its amount of currency (which also happens to be zero).

The bank's only solution then is to reduce the level of deposits, thus reducing the amount of required reserves and eliminating the reserve deficiency. A bank reduces its deposits by selling securities or calling in—not renewing—loans. People usually pay for securities purchased from a bank by reducing their deposit balances. Similarly, borrowers usually repay loans by reducing their deposit balances.

In the specific situation of Table 14.3, the bank calls in $450 of loans, deposits therefore fall by $450, and required reserves fall by $45 (10% of $450). In the *final position*, deposits are $500, bank reserves and required reserves are both $50, and loans are $450. So the bank is back in equilibrium.

## A Banking System Versus a Monopoly Bank

So far we have been looking at a monopoly bank, but the U.S. banking system consists of about 14,000 banks. Fortunately, deposit expansion occurs in the same way for the entire banking system as for a monopoly bank. In fact, with a slight trick, the T-account analysis is readily adapted to illustrate the process. The trick is to interpret each stage of new deposits as if it were a separate bank.

**TABLE 14.4**
**Deposit Expansion for a Banking System**

**Bank 1**

| Assets | | Liabilities | |
|---|---|---|---|
| Bank reserves | $10 | Deposits | $100 |
|   Required  $10 | | | |
|   Excess     $0 | | | |
| Bank loans | $90 | | |

**Bank 2**

| Assets | | Liabilities | |
|---|---|---|---|
| Bank reserves | $90 | Deposits | $90 |
|   Required  $9 | | | |
|   Excess     $0 | | | |
| Bank loans | $81 | | |

**The Banking System**
(Total for all banks)

| Assets | | Liabilities | |
|---|---|---|---|
| Bank reserves | $100 | Deposits | $1,000 |
|   Required $100 | | | |
|   Excess     $0 | | | |
| Bank loans | $900 | | |

Deposit expansion for a banking system is illustrated in Table 14.4. In the first T-account, bank 1 receives the initial deposit of $100 and it lends out $90, just as the monopoly bank did by its stage 2. This ends the story for bank 1, and its T-account in Table 14.4 is its final balance sheet. Under the terms of the bare-bones system, however, the $90 of currency dispensed by bank 1 must be redeposited in the banking system, and we now assume that these deposits are placed in bank 2.

Bank 2 receives $90 of deposits, holds required reserves of $9, and invests $81 in earning assets, just as the monopoly bank did in stages 3 and 4 of Table 14.2. However, the T-account shown for bank 2 in Table 14.4 is also its final stage. The process continues in this manner, with each bank receiving the deposits created by the loans made by the preceding bank.

The successive rounds of deposit creation become smaller and smaller, and the banking system ultimately approaches an equilibrium. The quantity of deposits for the banking system as a whole, shown in the bottom T-account of Table 14.4, is the same amount shown for the monopoly bank in stage E of Table 14.2.

## Do Banks Know They Create Deposits?

A long-standing issue concerns whether bankers are aware of their role in deposit expansion. To answer this, it is helpful to distinguish between a monopoly bank and an individual bank in a banking system. A monopoly bank is likely to recognize its role because each time it makes a loan, the funds are soon redeposited in the bank. But an individual bank in a banking system may be unaware of its role to the extent that the loans it makes are redeposited in other banks.

For example, in Table 14.4, bank 1 receives $100 of deposits and makes $90 of loans. The multiple expansion of deposits is then initiated when the loans made by bank 1 are redeposited in the banking system, but bank 1 does not participate in this process. Instead, the loan funds are deposited in bank 2, which then makes further loans on the basis of its excess reserves. Furthermore, the loans made by bank 2 are redeposited in still another bank, so bank 2 is also unaware of its role in the deposit expansion process.

In practice, how aware banks are of their role in deposit expansion depends on the percentage of each bank's loans that are redeposited in the bank—called a bank's **reflux ratio.** A monopoly bank will have a reflux ratio close to 1.0 (so it should be highly aware of its role in deposit expansion) whereas a single bank in a banking system usually has a small, but positive, reflux ratio. Reflux ratios determine the distribution of deposits among banks in a banking system—banks with high ratios will tend to have more deposits—but total deposits for the banking system are independent of the reflux ratios. Bankers and economists were confused about this point until C. A. Phillips clarified it in 1921 (see Box 14.1).

BOX 14.1 MONEY MATTERS

## The History of Deposit Expansion Equations

The process of money supply determination has been fully understood only since Chester Arthur Phillips set matters straight in his 1921 book, *Bank Credit.* During the nineteenth and early twentieth centuries, it was common for bankers to think they had *no role* in money supply creation: they thought that banks just accepted deposits and made a corresponding amount of loans, period. Economists, on the other hand, often analyzed individual banks as if they were monopoly banks.[1]

Phillips put all the pieces together. For one thing, he understood that the reflux ratios of individual banks limited how much they could expand their loans. For another thing, he understood that loans made by one bank were likely to be redeposited in *some* other bank, so deposit expansion could still proceed. Finally, he put these considerations together in an algebraic framework—very much like the one we are using.

[1] A useful introduction to the history of money supply analysis is provided by Thomas M. Humphrey, "The Theory of Multiple Expansion of Deposits: What It Is and Whence It Came," *Economic Review*, Federal Reserve Bank of Richmond, March/April 1987, pp. 3–11.

## Deposit Expansion Beyond the Bare-Bones System

So far, we have analyzed deposit expansion only under the assumptions of the bare-bones system. That is, we have been assuming that currency $C$ and excess reserve $R_e$ are zero and that required reserves $R_r$ refer to only one category of deposits.

We will now consider cases where currency $C$ and excess reserves $R_e$ are positive numbers, and where there are two classes of deposits, which we will refer to as transaction deposits $D_1$ (checking accounts) and time deposits $D_2$ (nontransaction accounts). The required reserve ratios are $\theta_1$ and $\theta_2$, respectively, with $\theta_1$ greater than $\theta_2$. Required reserves $R_r$ are therefore:

$$R_r = \theta_1 D_1 + \theta_2 D_2. \tag{14.6}$$

Substituting this expression for $R_r$ into the monetary base equation (14.4), $B = C + R_e + R_r$, we have:

$$B = C + R_e + \theta_1 D_1 + \theta_2 D_2. \tag{14.7}$$

Equation (14.7) is called the *sources equals uses condition for the monetary base*. The left side is the monetary base $B$ supplied by the Federal Reserve. The right side accounts for the uses of the monetary base by the public and banks—currency $C$, excess reserves $R_e$, required reserves on transaction deposits $\theta_1 D_1$, and required reserves on time deposits $\theta_2 D_2$. An important result is derived by solving equation (14.7) for transaction deposits $D_1$:

$$D_1 = \left[\frac{1}{\theta_1}\right] [B - C - R_e - \theta_2 D_2]. \tag{14.8}$$

This equation is an expanded version of equation (14.5), $D = B/\theta$, which applies in the bare-bones system. The first term in equation (14.8), $1/\theta_1$, shows that the reserve multiplier is now the inverse of the reserve ratio for transaction deposits.

The second term in equation (14.8), $[B - C - R_e - \theta_2 D_2]$, represents **reserves available to support transaction deposits.** This is the amount of the monetary base $B$ that is left after subtracting currency held by the public $C$, excess reserves held by the banking system $R_e$, and required reserves for time deposits $\theta_2 D_2$. (In contrast, in the bare-bones system, the entire monetary base $B$ is available to support transaction deposits since currency $C$, excess reserves $R_e$, and time deposits $D_2$ are all zero.)

Equation (14.8) shows how to compute transaction deposits $D_1$ as the product of the reserve multiplier and the reserves available to support transaction deposits. However, it is often more convenient to compute the *change* in transaction deposits as a function of *changes* in the variables that determine available reserves. The "change" form of equation (14.8) (the symbol $\triangle$ meaning "the change in") is:

$$\triangle D_1 = \left(\frac{1}{\theta_1}\right) (\triangle B - \triangle C - \triangle R_e - \theta_2 \triangle D_2). \tag{14.9}$$

Equation (14.9) is usually applied by leaving only one nonzero change term on the right-hand side to be multiplied by $1/\theta_1$. For example, the effect of a change in the monetary base, with everything else unchanged, is $\Delta D_1 = (1/\theta_1)\Delta B$.

Applications of equation (14.9) are shown in Table 14.5 (the columns for the M1 and M2 money supplies are discussed in the next section). For comparison, the assumptions of the bare-bones system are shown as Case 1. Each of the following cases then alters one assumption—all other variables retaining the value they have in the bare-bones system.

In case 2, the monetary base is raised by $20. Since the reserve multiplier is 10 ($= 1/\theta_1 = 1/0.10$), transaction deposits rise by $200 (10 $\times$ $20) to $1,200.

**TABLE 14.5**

**The Factors That Determine the Money Supply**

| | Change in Transaction Deposits $D_1$ (Relative to Case 1) $\Delta D_1$ | Level of Transaction Deposits $D_1$ | Money Supply | |
|---|---|---|---|---|
| | | | M1 | M2 |
| Case 1: (*Bare-bones System*)[a] | | 1,000 | 1,000 | 1,000 |
| Case 2: (The monetary base rises by 20) $\Delta B = 20$ | 200 | 1,200 | 1,200 | 1,200 |
| Case 3: (Currency rises by 20) $\Delta C = 20$ | −200 | 800 | 820 | 820 |
| Case 4: (Excess reserves rise by 20) $\Delta R_e = 20$ | −200 | 800 | 800 | 800 |
| Case 5: (Required reserves on time deposits rise by 20) $\Delta D_2 = 400$ and $\theta_2 = 0.05$ | −200 | 800 | 800 | 1,200 |
| Case 6: (Reserve ratio $\theta_1$ rises to 0.20) $\theta_1 = 0.20$ | −500 | 500 | 500 | 500 |
| Case 7: (Reserve ratio $\theta_2$ rises to 0.08) $\theta_2 = 0.08$ and $D_2 = 400$ | −320 | 680 | 680 | 1,080 |

[a]The monetary base: $B = 100$; reserve ratio for $D_1$: $\theta_1 = 0.10$; currency: $C = 0$; excess reserves: $R_e = 0$; time deposits: $D_2 = 0$; and the reserve ratio for $D_2$: $\theta_2 = 0$.

Cases 3, 4, and 5 show the effects of raising currency, $\Delta C$, excess reserves, $\Delta R_e$, and required reserves against time deposits, $\theta_2 \Delta D_2$, respectively. An increase in any of these variables is referred to as a **reserve drain**—a use of the monetary base that reduces the bank reserves that would otherwise be available to support transaction deposits. Consequently, transaction deposits will fall by an amount equal to the reserve multiplier times the amount of the reserve drain.

For example, if people decide to hold more currency—$\Delta C$ is the reserve drain—then bank deposits fall by an amount that equals the change in currency times the reserve multiplier. So, in case 3, when currency rises by 20, transaction deposits fall by 200, given that the reserve multiplier is 10. Similar considerations apply when excess reserves and required reserves on time deposits rise. In each case, the reserve drain—$\Delta C$, $\Delta R_e$, and $\theta_2 \Delta D_2$—causes deposits to fall by the amount of the drain times the reserve multiplier, as indicated in equation (14.9).

If either of the required reserve ratios—$\theta_1$ for transaction deposits or $\theta_2$ for time deposits—rises, then bank deposits fall, although for different reasons. The two possibilities are illustrated in cases 6 and 7 in Table 14.5.

In case 6, $\theta_1$ rises from 0.10 to 0.20, reducing the reserve multiplier from 10 (= 1/0.10) to 5 (= 1/0.20). Since the monetary base $B$ is $100, the new value of transaction deposits is $500 (5 × $100), a decline of $500 from the initial value. This demonstrates the powerful effect of the reserve ratio on transaction deposits.

In case 7, $\theta_2$ rises from 0 to 0.08, also representing a reserve drain. Since this change has an effect only if there are time deposits $D_2$, we also assume that $D_2$ is equal to $400. Thus, required reserves for time deposits rise from $0 to $32 (0.08 × $400), and given a reserve multiplier of 10, transaction deposits decline by $320 (10 × $32).

The same basic principle is at work in all the cases in Table 14.5: the amount of transaction deposits equals the product of two terms, the reserve multiplier ($1/\theta_1$) and the amount of reserves available to support transaction deposits ($B - C - R_e - \theta_2 D_2$). The quantity of transaction deposits is therefore affected, and only affected, by a change in one of these two terms.

## Money Supply Determination

We can now apply the principle of deposit expansion to money supply determination. Recall that the **M1 money supply** is the sum of transaction deposits $D_1$ and currency $C$, and the **M2 money supply** is the sum of the M1 money supply and time deposits $D_2$. Box 14.2 provides more detailed definitions.

### The M1 Money Supply

The M1 money supply can be expressed as:

$$M1 = C + D_1. \tag{14.10}$$

Based on this equation, M1 is computed by first determining transaction deposits $D_1$ (with results like those shown in Table 14.5) and then adding the amount of currency $C$. Computing the M1 money supply is this simple.

Currency is zero in all but one of the cases in Table 14.5, so M1 just equals transaction deposits $D_1$. Case 3 is the exception: since currency is $20 and transaction deposits $D_1$ are $800, M1 is $820 ($C + D_1$ = $20 + $800). In contrast, in case 1 currency is $0 and M1 is $1,000.

This result may be surprising: even though currency $C$ is one component of M1 (M1 = $C + D_1$), *the M1 money supply falls when currency C rises*. This happens because currency is also a reserve drain: an *increase* in currency creates a multiple *contraction* of transaction deposits $D_1$, and the contraction is the dominant effect on M1.

BOX 14.2 MONEY MATTERS

## Formal Definitions of the M1 and M2 Money Supplies

The definitions of the M1 and M2 money supplies currently used by the Federal Reserve are as follows:

The *M1 money supply* consists of:

1. Currency outside the Treasury, Federal Reserve, and the vaults of depository institutions;
2. Travelers checks of nonbank issuers;
3. All demand deposits of commercial banks other than those due to other domestic banks, the U.S. government, and foreign banks and official institutions, less float items; and
4. Other checkable deposits (OCDs)—the sum of NOW and automatic transfer accounts at depository institutions, credit union share draft accounts, and thrift institution demand deposits.

The *M2 money supply* consists of:

1. The M1 money supply plus overnight repurchase agreements issued by all commercial banks and overnight Eurodollars issued to U.S. residents by foreign branches of U.S. banks;
2. Money market deposit accounts, savings and small-denomination time deposits; and
3. Balances in both taxable and tax-exempt general purpose and broker/dealer money market mutual funds.

### The M2 Money Supply

The M2 money supply can be expressed in a similar fashion:

$$M2 = M1 + D_2. \qquad (14.11)$$

Based on this equation, M2 is also computed in two steps. The first step is to compute M1 (with the results shown in Table 14.5) and the second step is to add the quantity of time deposits $D_2$. Computing the M2 money supply is also this simple.

In most of the cases in Table 14.5, times deposits $D_2$ equal zero, so M2 equals M1. However, in case 5, time deposits equal $400, while M1 equals $800, so M2 equals $1,200 (M1 + $D_2$ = $800 + $400). Similarly, in case 7, $D_2$ equals $400 and M1 equals $680, so M2 equals $1,080 ($680 + $400).

Cases 5 and 7 reveal another surprising result: *higher values of time deposits $D_2$ reduce M1 but raise M2.* There are two forces at work here: (1) higher time deposits reduce M1 because the required reserves on time deposits are a reserve drain, as we saw in the last section; (2) higher time deposits increase M2, because they are a component of M2. The positive direct effect of higher time deposits on M2 dominates the negative effect of higher time deposits on the M1 component of M2.[2]

---

[2] This result requires that the reserve ratio for transaction deposits $\theta_1$ be greater than the reserve ratio for time deposits $\theta_2$, which is true for the actual ratios.

## A Complete Example of Money Supply Determination

So far, we have been considering the effects of the three variables—currency, excess reserves, and time deposits—on the money supply, one at a time. Box 14.3 presents a complete example of money supply determination where these variables all operate together. The assumptions are provided at the top of the table. Values of the M1 and M2 money supplies are then computed using the equations shown. The list of equations is also a handy reference.

The only new consideration in Box 14.3 concerns earning assets $E$—loans and securities. Given the amount of bank deposits and bank reserves, earning assets $E$ can be computed using the bank balance sheet constraint, which requires that total assets—the sum of required reserves $R_r$, excess reserves $R_e$, and earning assets $E$—equal total liabilities—transaction deposits $D_1$ and time deposits $D_2$:

$$R_r + R_e + E = D_1 + D_2.$$

---

BOX 14.3 IN DEPTH

## A Complete Example of Money Supply Determination

### Assumptions

| | |
|---|---|
| Monetary base $B$: | 200 |
| Reserve ratio for transaction deposits $\theta_1$: | 10% (=0.10) |
| Reserve ratio for time deposits $\theta_2$: | 5% (=0.05) |
| Currency $C$: | 40 |
| Excess reserves $R_e$: | 30 |
| Time deposits $D_2$: | 100 |

### Solutions

Transaction deposits:

$$\begin{aligned} D_1 &= (1/\theta_1)(B - C - R_e - \theta_2 D_2) \\ &= (10)(200 - 40 - 30 - 5) = 1{,}250 \end{aligned}$$

M1 money supply:

$$M1 = C + D_1 = 40 + 1{,}250 = 1{,}290$$

M2 money supply:

$$M2 = M1 + D_2 = 1{,}290 + 100 = 1{,}390$$

Earning assets:

$$\begin{aligned} E &= (1 - \theta_1)D_1 + (1 - \theta_2)D_2 - R_e \\ &= (0.9)(1{,}250) + (0.95)(100) - 30 \\ &= 1{,}190. \end{aligned}$$

Using equation [14.6] for required reserves, $R_r = \theta_1 D_1 + \theta_2 D_2$, this equation can be solved for earning assets $E$:

$$E = (D_1 + D_2) - (R_r + R_e),$$
$$= (D_1 + D_2) - (\theta_1 D_1 + \theta_2 D_2 + R_e),$$
$$= (1 - \theta_1)D_1 + (1 - \theta_2)D_2 - R_e. \qquad (14.12)$$

Equation (14.12) is used to compute the amount of earning assets that banks hold, as shown in Table 14.6. Note that the distribution of earning assets between loans and securities has no impact on the deposit expansion process. Indeed, once the amount of excess reserves is given, the amount of earning assets is a *result* of the deposit expansion process, not a *cause* of it.

## Nondeposit Liabilities and Deposit Expansion

Our analysis has not yet considered nondeposit liabilities—Federal funds, capital market securities, and discount loans from the Federal Reserve. Each of these was discussed in the context of bank liquidity management in Chapter 11. We will now see that nondeposit liabilities are usually *not directly* related to deposit expansion, although they may be *indirectly* related.

Recall that banks use *federal funds* to borrow and lend reserve deposits at the Federal Reserve. Federal funds have no direct effect on the money supply because they have no effect on the *total amount of bank reserves*. However, federal funds may reduce the banking system's *excess reserves*, and thereby indirectly raise the money supply. That is, banks with excess reserves may lend them as federal funds to other banks that are deficient in reserves, thus causing excess reserves for the banking system to fall. The money supply will then rise.

*Securities* issued as nondeposit liabilities by banks do not create reserves for the banking system either, so they have no direct effect on the money supply. Banks issue securities to raise funds so they can buy additional assets. But the *net* amount of additional assets—*earning assets* minus the nondeposit *security liabilities*—will be the same as give by equation (14.12), so no direct effect is implied for the money supply. However, securities issued by banks may have indirect links with excess reserves, and possibly even with currency and time deposits held by the public. Perhaps the most relevant case is when a bank holds fewer excess reserves because it plans on issuing nondeposit liabilities if it requires additional liquidity.

*Discount loans* obtained by banks from the Federal Reserve are a special case where nondeposit liabilities may directly affect deposit expansion, depending on how the Fed manages the process. As discussed in Chapter 11, discount loans are credited to a bank's reserve account at the Federal Reserve, where they count as part of the monetary base. Indeed, as Table 14.1 showed, discount loans are included among the Federal Reserve assets that create the monetary base.

So, when banks take out discount loans, the monetary base rises, and so does the money supply, given that everything else is unchanged.

Although the Federal Reserve sometimes lets this happen, it usually takes action—such as selling government securities—so everything else is not unchanged. The fall in the monetary base created by sales of government securities can eliminate the increase in the monetary base created by bank borrowing. The Federal Reserve often operates in this manner, in which case discount borrowing has no net effect on the money supply.

## The Money Supply Multiplier

So far, we have treated currency, excess reserves, and time deposits as if they were *constant amounts*. Now we will look at one final method for determining the money supply—the **money supply multiplier**—in which these variables are treated as if they were *constant proportions* of M1.

Specifically, we will assume the following:

$$C = c \, \text{M1},$$

$$R_e = e \, \text{M1},$$

$$D_2 = t \, \text{M1}.$$

where $c$ = currency ratio, the proportion of M1 the public holds as currency,

$e$ = excess reserve ratio, the proportion of M1 held by banks as excess reserves,

$t$ = time deposit ratio, the proportion of M1 held by investors as time deposits.

Each of the three ratios—$c$, $e$, and $t$—is treated as constant (as long as underlying economic conditions do not change).

Substituting these assumptions in the transaction deposit equation (14.8), and the results of that into the M1 and M2 equations (14.10) and (14.11):

$$\text{M1} = \frac{B}{\theta_1 + c(1 - \theta_1) + e + t\theta_2} = (m1)\,(B) \qquad (14.13)$$

and

$$\text{M2} = \frac{(1 + t)B}{\theta_1 + c(1 - \theta_1) + e + t\theta_2} = (m2)\,(B). \qquad (14.14)$$

where $m1$ = the M1 money supply multiplier =

$$\frac{1}{\theta_1 + c(1 - \theta_1) + e + t\theta_2},$$

and

$m2$ = the M2 money supply multiplier =

$$\frac{(1 + t)}{\theta_1 + c(1 - \theta_1) + e + t\theta_2}.$$

The only difference between these equations and the money supply equations (14.10) and (14.11) is that they are stated in terms of the ratios $c$, $e$, and $t$. The new equations (14.13) and (14.14) do *not* represent new results; they just make it possible to express each money supply—M1 or M2—as the product of the monetary base $B$ and its multiplier—$m1$ or $m2$. (Do not confuse the money supply multiplier, which relates each money supply to the monetary base, with the reserve multiplier, which relates the amount of transaction deposits to bank reserves.) A graph of the $m1$ and $m2$ money supply multipliers is given in Figure 14.4.

FIGURE 14.4
**The Money Supply Multipliers**

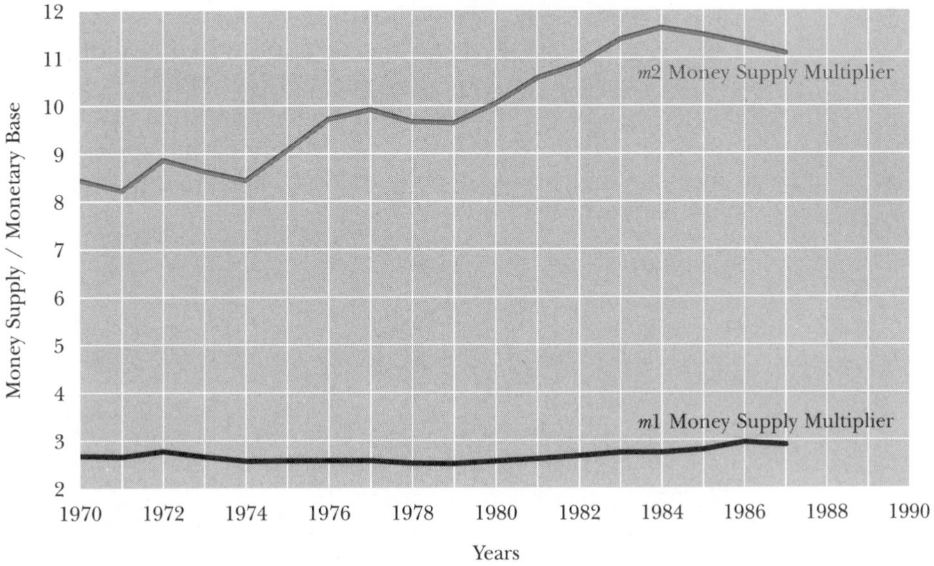

The graph shows the $m1$ and $m2$ money supply multipliers, which relate the respective money supplies (M1 and M2) to the monetary base. The $m2$ multiplier is much larger than the $m1$ because the M2 money supply is much larger than the M1 money supply. **Source:** *Economic Report of the President,* February, 1988.

In summary, the key relationships implied by the money supply multiplier equations (14.13) and (14.14) are:

- As the currency ratio $c$ rises, M1 and M2 both fall.
- As the excess reserve ratio $e$ rises, M1 and M2 both fall.
- As the time deposit ratio $t$ rises, M1 falls, but M2 rises (given that $\theta_1 > \theta_2$).
- As either of the reserve ratios—$\theta_1$ for transaction deposits and $\theta_2$ for time deposits—rise, M1 and M2 fall.
- When the monetary base $B$ rises, the M1 and M2 money supplies rise, each in the proportion indicated by its money supply multiplier, $m1$ and $m2$, respectively.

We will now apply the money supply multiplier approach to examine the factors, such as interest rates, that might cause the currency, excess reserve, and time deposit ratios to change.

## The Money Supply, Interest Rates, and Related Factors

We will look at the effects of three specific interest rates on the three ratios:

- The Federal Reserve discount rate $r_F$—the rate charged when banks borrow from the Federal Reserve.
- The interest rate banks pay on time deposits $r_{TD}$.
- The interest rate on investment securities $r_S$.

The effects on the ratios of raising the interest rates are shown in Table 14.6. We will examine the results by looking at each of the three ratios in turn. Since, as we have just seen, M1 and M2 both change in the *opposite direction* from the ratios (with the one exception that a higher time deposit ratio $t$ raises M2), knowing the connections between the interest rates and the ratios is tantamount to knowing the connections between the interest rates and the money supplies.

| TABLE 14.6 | | | |
|------------|---|---|---|
| **Interest Rates and the Money Supply Ratios** | | | |
| | Currency Ratio | Excess Reserve Ratio | Time Deposit Ratio |
| **Interest Rate Raised:** | | | |
| Federal Reserve discount rate: $r_F$ | – | rises | – |
| Time deposit interest rate: $r_{TD}$ | falls | rises | rises |
| Investment security interest rate: $r_S$ | falls | falls | falls |

### The Currency Ratio

We had mentioned that people demand currency for small transactions, for activity in the underground economy, and for hoarding (safety). If these categories of transactions rise as a percentage of total income, then currency may rise as a proportion of M1. With regard to interest rates, since currency pays no interest, if the interest rates payable on securities $r_S$ or time deposits $r_{TD}$ rise, then people may reduce their currency, so as to invest in the securities or time deposits, as indicated in Table 14.6. The Federal Reserve's discount rate is of no consequence to the currency ratio, since people cannot borrow from the Federal Reserve.

### The Excess Reserve Ratio

As indicated in Chapter 11, factors that increase the need for liquidity—such as larger anticipated deposit outflows or greater uncertainty about them—will increase the demand for excess reserves. Interest rates also play a role. Higher interest rates on bank liabilities (represented in Table

14.6 by the Federal Reserve discount rate and by the interest rate on bank time deposits), which make liabilities more expensive for liquidity management, generally raise the demand for excess reserves. Higher interest rates on bank assets (represented in Table 14.6 by the interest rate on investment securities), which cause banks to shift their funds to these assets, generally reduce the demand for excess reserves.

### The Time Deposit Ratio

Investors decide to hold time deposits as part of the general process in which they select assets for their portfolio. As portfolios grow larger, the demand for time deposits rises. The demand for time deposits may also be affected by relative interest rate levels—as shown in Table 14.6—with a higher interest rate on time deposits positively affecting the demand, and higher interest rates on investment securities negatively affecting it.

### A Summary of Interest Rates and the Money Supply

We can now look at the effects of the interest rates on the money supply. As Table 14.6 indicates, when the interest rate on investment securities rises, each of the three ratios falls, so the money supply will rise. However, when the discount rate and the time deposit interest rates rise, some of the ratios rise, so the money supply may fall.

For now, the key point is that interest rates can affect the money supply. Consequently, even though the Federal Reserve controls the monetary base, it has to take into account the additional effects that interest rates—and other factors—may have on the money supply. We will see the importance of this when we look at monetary policy in Part V.

## Chapter Summary

1. The monetary base equals the sum of currency held by the public (that is everyone in the economy except depository institutions) and bank reserves (vault cash plus bank reserve deposits at the Federal Reserve). The monetary base rises as the Fed purchases assets—mainly government securities—since it pays for its purchases by issuing currency or increasing reserve deposits.

2. The public holds its part of the monetary base as currency. The public determines its demand for currency, and then deposits the rest of the monetary base in banks where it counts as bank reserves.

3. Bank deposits, transaction and time deposits, are determined through the process of deposit expansion, based on the reserve multiplier—the ratio of deposits to bank reserves. Deposit expansion is analyzed with T-accounts or with simple algebra. The analysis applies to either a monopoly bank or a banking system.

4. In a bare-bones system—where currency held by the public, excess reserves, and time deposits are all assumed to be zero—deposits equal the monetary base divided by the required reserve ratio. The inverse of the deposit reserve ratio is the reserve multiplier.

5. Currency, excess reserves, and required reserves on time deposits all represent reserve drains—they reduce the amount of the monetary base that is available for required reserves on transaction accounts. An increase in any reserve drain item causes a decline in transaction deposits. Higher reserve ratios on deposits also reduce transaction deposits.

6. The M1 money supply equals the sum of transaction deposits and currency. Factors that raise transaction deposits thus tend to raise M1. Currency counts directly as a positive component of M1, but currency is also a reserve drain, reducing M1 with a multiplier effect.

7. The M2 money supply equals the sum of M1 and time deposits $D_2$. Factors that raise

M1 thus generally raise M2 as well. However, higher time deposits have two effects on M2: (1) higher time deposits reduce the M1 component of the M2 money supply; and (2) higher time deposits increase the time deposit component of M2.

8. The M1 and M2 money supplies can also be stated as the monetary base times the respective money supply multipliers. The money supply multipliers incorporate the reserve drains as ratios to the M1 money supply.

9. Changes in interest rates and related factors cause the ratios of currency, excess reserve, and time deposits to M1 to change. For example, a higher interest on investment securities reduces all three ratios. The lower ratios cause both M1 and M2 to rise.

## Key Terms

Bank Reserves:
  Available to support transaction deposits
  Excess
  Required
  Total
Currency
Deposit:
  Contraction
  Expansion

Monetary base
Money supply:
  M1
  M2
Money supply multiplier
Reflux ratio
Reserve deposit accounts (at the Fed)
Reserve drains
Reserve multiplier

## Study Questions

1. Why does the monetary base rise when the Federal Reserve buys Treasury securities from a bank? What additional steps are involved if the Federal Reserve buys the Treasury securities from the public?

2. Suppose the monetary base $B$ is 1,000 and the required reserve ratio on deposits $\theta$ is 0.10. Suppose also that currency held by

the public $C$, bank excess reserves $R_e$, and time deposits $D_2$ are all zero. What is the equilibrium amount of deposits $D$?

3. Compare a monopoly bank and a multibank banking system in terms of (1) the size of the deposit multiplier and (2) whether each bank is aware of its role in the deposit expansion process.

Questions 4 to 8 use the following values:

Monetary base $B = 1,000$.

Currency held by the public $C = 300$.

Bank excess reserves $R_e = 100$.

Bank time deposits $D_2 = 200$.

Required reserve ratio on transaction deposits $\theta_1 = 0.10$.

Required reserve ratio on time deposits $\theta_2 = 0.05$.

4. Compute the value of transaction deposits $D_2$.

5. Compute the values of the M1 and M2 money supplies.

6. Compute the amount of earning assets $E$.

7. What is the value of the *reserve multiplier* for this money supply system? Based on this reserve multiplier, how does the amount of transaction deposits $D_1$ change when:

a. Currency $C$ rises by 10.

b. Excess reserves $R_e$ rise by 10.

c. Time deposits $D_2$ rise by 100.

8. For each of the three cases in Question 7, what is the change in M1? In M2?

9. If a bank makes business loans by reducing its excess reserves, the money supply rises. But if a bank makes business loans by reducing its Treasury bills, the money supply is unchanged. Explain why there is a difference between the two cases.

10. In each of the following, does the indicated interest rate have to rise or fall so that M1 rises:

a. The Federal Reserve discount rate affects excess reserves.

b. The interest rate on time deposits affects time deposits.

c. The interest rate on investment securities affects currency.

## Recommended Reading

*The following three books—in increasing order of detail and difficulty—review the money supply process:*

Dorothy M. Nichols, *Modern Money Mechanics: A Workbook on Deposits, Currency, and Bank Reserves*, Federal Reserve Bank of Chicago, Chicago, 1982.

John T. Boorman and Thomas M. Havrilesky, *Money Supply, Money Demand, and Macroeconomic Models*, AHM, 1982.

Albert E. Burger, *The Money Supply Process*, Wadsworth, Belmont, Calif., 1971.

*This is a classic treatment of the factors that determine the money supply multiplier and the money supply:*

Phillip Cagan, "Determinants and Effects of Changes in the Stock of Money, 1875–1960," Columbia University Press, New York, 1965.

*These two articles look at the question of whether bankers are aware of how they participate in creating the money supply:*

Thomas M. Humphrey, "The Theory of Multiple Expansion of Deposits: What It Is and Whence It Came," *Economic Review*, Federal Reserve Bank of Richmond, March/April 1987, pp. 3–11.

James Tobin, "Commercial Banks as Creators of Money," in Deane Carson, editor, *Banking and Monetary Studies*, Irwin, Homewood, Ill., 1963.

# Theories of Money Demand

*"Money is always there, but the pockets change."*

*Gertrude Stein*

The decision makers who determine what the money supply of the United States should be must bear in mind that an overissue of money can cause inflation, while too little money might cause a recession. But how much money—defined either as the M1 money supply or the M2 money supply—is the right amount? To answer that, they must know how much money will be demanded under different conditions.

A key step is to identify the factors that determine the demand for money. The services of money as a medium of exchange and as a store of value explain *why* people hold money. But more precise and quantitative information is needed to predict *how much* money they will hold. In particular, we will see in this chapter that the demand for money depends on variables such as income and interest rates, as well as on features of the payments system.

---

The demand for money reflects the use of money both as a medium of exchange and as a store of value. Theories of money demand can be based on either concept: *transaction demand* theories are based on the role of money as a medium of exchange, and *asset demand* theories are based on its role as a store of value. We will examine both types of theories.

---

## Some Basic Concepts

Income, interest rates, and features of the payments system are important factors in most theories of the demand for money. We begin by introducing the tools needed to analyze the effects of these factors on money demand.

## Income and Interest Rate Elasticities of Money Demand

Income is generally considered the most significant variable affecting the demand for money. As their income rises, people demand more goods and services and they need more money to carry out transactions. However, the extent of the sensitivity of money demand to income differs from one theory to another. This sensitivity is measured by the **income elasticity of the demand for money:**

$$\text{income elasticity of money demand} = \frac{\text{percentage change in money demand}}{\text{percentage change in income}}.$$

For example, if income rises by 10 percent and money demand also rises by 10 percent, then the income elasticity is 1.0. We will use an income elasticity of 1.0 as a benchmark for comparing alternative theories of money demand.

In many theories, the demand for money is also negatively related to the level of interest rates. This occurs because investment securities such as bonds pay higher interest rates than the rates paid on money (on bank deposits, for example). Forgone interest is therefore a cost of holding money: as the interest rates payable on investment securities rise, people reduce their demand for money.

The sensitivity of money demand to interest rates is measured by the **interest elasticity of money demand:**

$$\text{interest elasticity of money demand} = \frac{\text{percentage change in money demand}}{\text{percentage change in interest rates}}.$$

This elasticity is usually negative because the demand for money *falls* when interest rates rise. For example, if interest rates rise by 10 percent— say from 10% to 11%—and money demand falls by 5%—say from $700 billion to $665 billion—then the interest elasticity of money demand is −0.5.

## Payments System Factors and Money Demand

Features of the payments system also influence money demand. The type of money people use for making payments—currency, checks, and so forth—is one payments system factor. The frequency with which people are paid (weekly, monthly, and so forth) is another.

The effects of payments system factors can be illustrated by a college student's demand for money. Consider a student who spends $10 a day and looks one week ahead in managing her money. She might therefore withdraw $70 from the bank each Monday morning to cover the expenses of the coming week. Starting at $70 on Monday morning, her money balance declines steadily during the week, reaching zero by Sunday night. The pattern for seven days is represented in Figure 15.1.

The student begins Monday morning with an initial money balance of $70, spends $10 each day, and runs out of money on Sunday night. The average money balance held can be calculated as the average of the beginning and ending balances: (70 + 0)/2 = $35.

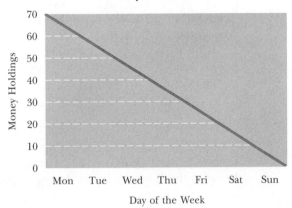

FIGURE 15.1
**A Weekly Money Balance, or Money Demand, Schedule**

Because the student's money holdings vary depending on the day of the week, her demand for money is defined as the *average money balance* held during the week. Given that the money balance declines steadily, adding the balance at the beginning of the week ($70) to the balance at the end of the week ($0) and dividing by 2 gives the average balance of $35 (= ($70 + $0)/2). You get the same answer, if you sum the average balances for each day and divide by seven.[1]

The frequency with which the money balance is replenished affects the demand for money. If the student withdraws money from the bank every 4 weeks instead of every week, but still spends $70 a week, her money balance at the beginning of each four week period will be $280 (= 4 × $70) and her demand for money (or the average money balance) will be $140 (the opening amount of $280 plus the closing amount of $0 divided by 2). Thus the demand for money rises when the money balance is replenished less frequently.

The demand for money also depends, of course, on how much money is spent each week. For example, if another student replenishes his money balance weekly and spends $140 each week ($20 per day)—twice the amount of the first student—then his money balance at the beginning of the week should be $140 and his demand for money will be $70 ($140 + $0 divided by 2)—also twice the amount of the first student. Thus, the demand for money is proportional to the weekly expenditures— which means that the income (or expenditure) elasticity of money demand equals 1.0.

---

[1] The sum of the 7 daily balances—65, 55, 45, 35, 25, 15, and 5—is 245, so the average is 35 (245/7).

## Transaction Theories of Money Demand

**Transaction theories** of the demand for money are based on money's role as the medium of exchange in the economy. Transaction theories focus on three types of variables that influence the quantity of money people hold for payments purposes:

1. The volume of transactions (or income).
2. Various payments system factors.
3. Interest rates.

The volume of transactions and payments system factors are emphasized in the Classical Quantity theory, while the effect of interest rates is the focus of the Baumol-Tobin theory of money demand.

## The Classical Quantity (CQ) Theory of Money Demand

The **classical quantity (CQ) theory** is the oldest theory of money demand. It was *the* theory well into this century, and it remains a basic tool for analyzing how much money people want to hold.

### The Quantity Equation of Exchange

A good place to begin examining the CQ theory is with the work of Irving Fisher, whose 1911 book, *The Purchasing Power of Money*, continues to influence modern theories of money demand. Fisher based his analysis on the *quantity equation of exchange*, which uses income as a measure of transactions as we studied in Chapter 1:

$$MV = Py = Y, \tag{15.1}$$

where $M$ = the stock of money,
$\quad\;\; V$ = the income velocity of money,
$\quad\;\; P$ = the price level,
$\quad\;\; y$ = the level of real income,
$\quad\;\; Y$ = the level of nominal income.

The *stock of money* $M$ can refer to either the supply of money or the demand for money. If we interpret it here as the demand for money, we can then solve equation (15.1) in terms of money demand $M^d$:

$$M^d = \left(\frac{1}{V}\right) Y. \tag{15.2}$$

Since the quantity equation of exchange is an identity—based on the definition of velocity, $V = Y/M$—equation (15.2) *by itself* does not represent a theory of money demand. A *theory* of money demand must refer to the amount of money people *desire* to hold. This means that the theory must identify the factors that determine the *desired velocity of money*.

For the CQ theory, we will see that the velocity of money depends mainly on payments system factors. Since payments system factors usually do not change much in the short run, the CQ theory treats velocity as if it were a constant. In this case, based on equation (15.2), money demand is proportional to the level of income $Y$, with $1/V$ being a constant that reflects payments system factors.

Two further aspects of the effect of income $Y$ on the demand for money in equation (15.2) deserve notice. First, obviously transactions must be measured as accurately as possible; nominal income is not a perfect measure of transactions, but as discussed in Box 15.1, it is a good choice among the variables for which data are available. Second, as shown in equation (15.1), both the *price level P* and *real income y* are variables that determine the demand for money, since these are the two components of nominal income $Y$.

---

### BOX 15.1 MONEY MATTERS

## Measures of Transactions and the Demand for Money

The amount of transactions carried out in the economy is a basic variable determining the demand for money, but it is not easy to measure. In practice, we generally have to use *proxy* variables—*income* or *gross national product* (GNP) being the common choices. However, income and GNP are likely to understate the actual amount of transactions.

For one thing, exchanges of assets are excluded from income and GNP, because they represent neither income nor the production of goods and services. For example, security transactions may create a

demand for money, but they are excluded from income and GNP. The same is true for most credit transactions.

For another thing, transactions between business firms that involve intermediate steps in production—such as when a grocery store buys food items from a producer—create a demand for money, but they are excluded from GNP. The GNP includes only the "value added" part of the transactions—such as the value the grocery store adds to the food items when it sells them at retail.

---

### The Basic CQ Theory

We begin our study of the CQ theory by analyzing the money demand of people who have a simple pattern of income receipts and consumption expenditures—similar to our earlier example of a student's money management. In this **basic CQ theory,** people receive all of their income in money, do not save any of it, and thus spend all of it on consumption. Also, the basic CQ theory focuses on the narrow M1 definition of money—the sum of currency and checking deposits.

The pattern over time of income receipts and consumption payments that apply in the basic CQ theory is illustrated in Figure 15.2. The flow of periodic income receipts is shown in the top panel. The individual earns *annual income Y;* the *income frequency f* is the number of income periods in a year (such as 52 weeks or 12 months); and *periodic income* $Y^*(= Y/f)$ is the amount of income received each income period. For example, if the annual income is \$12,000 and the income period is monthly, then the annual income frequency $f$ is 12 and the periodic (monthly) income $Y^*$ is \$1,000.

Consumption payments, shown in the middle panel, occur at a continuing daily rate of $Y/365$. The annual income $Y$ is therefore fully spent over the course of the year. The individual thus saves no income.[2]

---

[2] It is easiest to think of people being paid at the beginning of each income period, although, in practice, employees are normally paid at the end of income periods. As is apparent in Figure 15.2, each income payment can be interpreted as coming either at the beginning of a period or at the end of the previous period.

FIGURE 15.2
**Income, Consumption, and Money Demand
in the Basic CQ Theory**

A. Income Receipts

In panel A, the individual receives income $Y^*$ each income period. Based on $f$ income periods in a year, the annual income $Y$ is equal to $fY^*$.

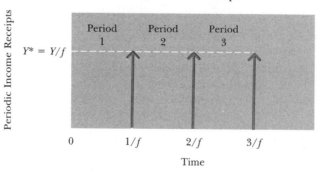

B. Consumption Payments

In panel B, the individual consumes at the daily rate of $Y/365$. Over a year, the individual consumes all of the income $Y$, so there is no saving.

C. Money Demand

In panel C, the money balance is filled at the beginning of each income period to $Y^*$, declines steadily as payments are made for consumption purchases, and reaches zero at the end of the income period. It is then refilled with the income receipt that arrives at that time.

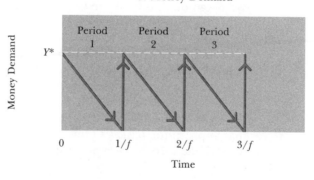

The money holdings that result from this pattern of income receipts and consumption payments are shown in the bottom panel of Figure 15.2. The money holdings start at $Y*$ at the beginning of each income period, then decline steadily, and are depleted by the end of the income period. The individual then receives another income flow of $Y*$, which is used for consumption during the next income period, and the pattern repeats itself.

The demand for money is defined in this context as the average money balance held. This amount is easily computed for the regular sawtooth pattern of money holdings illustrated in Figure 15.2. The average balance for each income period is just the sum of the initial and final values divided by 2:

$$\text{Average money balance} = \frac{Y* + 0}{2} = \frac{Y*}{2}.$$

This amount also equals the average money balance for the full year, since all income periods are identical. The demand for money $M^d$ can then be expressed as a function of either the periodic income $Y*$ or of the annual income $Y$:

$$M^d = \frac{Y*}{2} = \frac{Y}{2f}, \text{ where } Y* = \frac{Y}{f}. \tag{15.3}$$

Equation (15.3) is a special case—based on the specific assumptions of income receipts and consumption payments in Figure 15.2—of the general CQ theory equation (15.2). The equation illustrates that any change in annual income $Y$ produces a proportionate change in money demand $M^d$. That is, the *income elasticity of money demand for the CQ theory is equal to 1.0.*

Equation (15.3) also illustrates how the frequency of income receipts $f$ affects the demand for money. It is apparent from the equation that *money demand falls as the income frequency $f$ rises.* This happens because a given annual income $Y$ translates into a smaller periodic income $Y*$ ($= Y/f$), the higher the frequency of periodic income payments. Consequently, people have less money available at the start of each income period and hold less on average during the period.

## Velocity of Money

We can also look at the implications of the CQ theory of money demand for the velocity of money. To convert the demand for money equation into a velocity of money equation, substitute the demand for money $M^d$ from equation (15.3) into the definition of velocity ($V = Y/M^d$):[3]

$$V = \frac{Y}{M^d} = \frac{Y}{(Y/2f)} = 2f. \tag{15.4}$$

The velocity of money $V$ thus equals twice the income frequency $f$.

[3] In Chapter 1, the income velocity of money was defined as the ratio of income to money *supply.* However, it is now more convenient to interpret the velocity of money as the ratio of income to money *demand*—consistent with our earlier interpretation of the quantity equation of exchange.

For example, if people are paid 12 times a year, the velocity of money is 24; if they are paid 52 times a year, the velocity is 104. Velocity rises when income frequency rises because people hold a smaller amount of money, and therefore their money must turn over more rapidly to pay for a given amount of consumption.

The relationship of income frequency to velocity clarifies why adherents of the CQ theory of money demand, notably Irving Fisher, thought the velocity of money would be constant in the short run. They assumed that payments system factors such as income frequency were constant in the short run, which implied, according to the theory, that velocity would be constant.

### Summary of the Basic CQ Theory

These are the key results of the basic CQ theory:

- The demand for money is determined by two main factors: income $Y$ (a measure of transactions) and payments system factors (such as the frequency of income receipts $f$).

- The demand for money is proportional to annual income and is inversely related to the frequency of income receipts.

- The velocity of money is equal to twice the frequency of income receipts.

## An Expanded Version of the CQ Theory

The frequency of income receipts is only one of many payments system factors identified by Irving Fisher. Some of the others are shown in Box 15.2. Fisher showed that some factors—such as more densely populated areas and faster mail service—reduce the demand for money because less money is tied up during transit. We will now look at two other factors—the degree of synchronization and precautionary money holdings (and hoarding)—which have interesting implications for the demand for money.

---

BOX 15.2 IN DEPTH

### Payments System Factors Studied by Irving Fisher

#### Factors Decreasing the Demand for Money
- The density of population.
- The speed of mail service (and transportation).
- The synchronization of income receipts and consumption payments.

#### Factors Increasing the Demand for Money
- Precautionary money holdings.
- Money hoarding.

### Synchronization

**Synchronization** refers to a correspondence in timing between income receipts and consumption payments. There is no synchronization in the basic CQ theory represented in Figure 15.2, because income is received at specific points in time, whereas consumption payments are made smoothly over time. However, people can sometimes arrange their consumption payments to coincide with their income receipts, thus increasing the degree of synchronization.

*Credit cards* are particularly useful for raising the degree of synchronization. With credit cards, people still consume at a constant rate during a period, but they consolidate their consumption payments into a single credit card payment at the end of the period. As the date of the credit card payment more closely coincides with the date of the income receipt, the degree of synchronization rises.

An example in which credit cards are used to create *perfect synchronization* is shown in Figure 15.3. The income receipts shown in panel A are identical to those in Figure 15.2. The payments shown in panel B reflect the use of credit cards. That is, although consumption *expenditures* are made continuously as before, a single credit card payment of $Y^*$ is now made at the end of each income period. This creates perfect synchronization, because the date for the income receipt and the date for the credit card payment coincide perfectly.

**FIGURE 15.3**
**Credit Cards and Synchronization**
A. Income Receipts

Panel A shows the pattern of income receipts $Y^*$, just as in Figure 15.2.

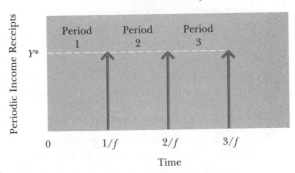

B. Credit Card Payments

Panel B shows the credit card payments of $Y^*$ at the end of each income period. Since the credit card payments and income receipts occur at the same time, this is an example of perfect synchronization.

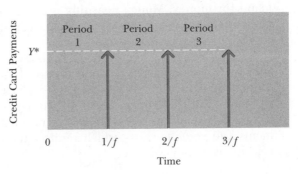

Panel C of Figure 15.3 shows the resulting pattern of money holdings: *with perfect synchronization, the demand for money is zero.* Money holdings are zero because an income receipt arrives just as each credit card bill is due for payment. (You can imagine a person receiving income with one hand, while paying the credit card bill with the other, so the money is held only for an instant.) Since all consumption purchases during the period are charged to the credit card, there is also no need to hold money at any other time.

FIGURE 15.3 (continued)
C. Money Demand

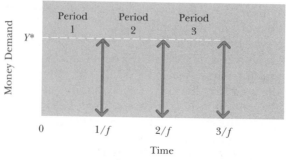

In panel C, the vertical double-headed arrows at the end of each income period indicate the simultaneous receipts of income and payment of the credit card bill. Since the income is immediately used to pay the bill, the average money balance is zero.

In practice, of course, people cannot perfectly synchronize all of their consumption payments and income receipts. People generally have to use money—currency or checking deposits—instead of credit cards for some of their consumption purchases. It is also difficult to achieve *perfect* synchronization even with credit cards because the dates for credit card payments may not coincide with the dates of income receipts.

### Precautionary Money Holdings and Money Hoarding

**Precautionary money holdings** are a special case of the transaction demand for money, where people hold money as a contingency for unexpected situations such as emergencies. These holdings are added to the money held for transaction purposes in determining the total demand for money. **Money hoarding** is a specific form of precautionary money holdings, such as when people keep money in a mattress or a shoebox.

Because velocity is the inverse of money demand, payments factors that cause the demand for money to rise—such as an increase in precautionary money holdings—cause the velocity of money to fall. That is, money will circulate more slowly on average when more money is being held. Similarly, when the degree of synchronization between payments and receipts rises—which reduces the demand for money—the velocity of money will rise.

### Summary

The key points of the classical quantity theory follow. *The demand for money is:*

- Proportional to the level of annual income $Y$; the income elasticity is therefore 1.0.
- Inversely related to the frequency of income payments $f$.
- Inversely related to the degree of synchronization between consumption payments and income receipts.
- Positively related to the amount of precautionary money holdings.

*The velocity of money is:*

- Proportional to the frequency of income payments $f$.
- Positively related to the degree of synchronization between consumption payments and income receipts.
- Inversely related to the amount of precautionary money holdings.

# The Baumol-Tobin (BT) Theory of Money Demand

The **Baumol-Tobin (BT) theory of money demand**[4] shares with the CQ theory the central feature that people demand money to carry out transactions. The BT theory, however, is more general because it recognizes that people may temporarily invest the funds they are holding. (In contrast, the CQ theory rules out the investment option.) The result, according to the BT theory, is that the demand for money falls when interest rates rise.

## Cash Management Decisions

The choice between holding money and investing it is a **cash management** decision. Business firms often use complex cash management policies because large amounts of money are involved. Individuals, in contrast, generally use relatively simple cash management policies because they are usually dealing with relatively small sums of money. The BT theory is based on a simplified set of cash management policies that are mainly relevant for individuals.

At any point in time, people will be holding funds for upcoming consumption purchases. The BT theory assumes, in effect, that people allocate these funds between two separate accounts: a **transaction account** containing the funds being held as money—checking accounts and currency; and a (financial) **investment account** containing the funds that are invested in securities—including bank time deposits and bonds.

---

[4] See William Baumol, "The Transactions Demand for Cash: An Inventory Theoretic Approach," *Quarterly Journal of Economics*, November 1952, pp. 545–556, and James Tobin, "The Interest Elasticity of the Transactions Demand for Cash," *Review of Economics and Statistics*, August 1956, pp. 241–247.

Of course, people may not literally set up two separate accounts, but it is useful to think of it this way.

The cash management policy determines how the funds are allocated between the transaction account and the investment account. Three factors influence this decision:

1. A market interest rate is earned on the funds placed in the investment account, but a lower interest rate or no interest is received on transaction account balances.

2. Only the transaction account balances—currency and checking deposits—can be used to pay for consumption purchases. Consequently, when funds in the investment account are needed for transactions, they have to be transferred to the transaction account.

3. Time, energy, and cash expenses are associated with transferring funds from the investment account to the transaction account.

Based on these considerations, Figure 15.4 illustrates a set of cash management decisions that people might make, assuming that they receive income and make consumption payments following the same pattern we used for the basic CQ theory in Figure 15.2. The new feature

FIGURE 15.4

**The Baumol-Tobin (BT) Theory of Cash Management**

A. Investment Account

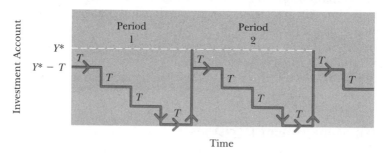

Time

B. Transaction Account

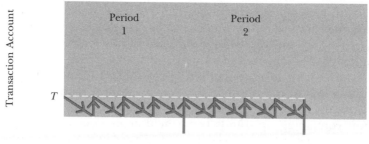

Time

In panel A, each income receipt of $Y^*$ is initially split into two parts: the amount $T$ going to the transaction account and the amount $Y^* - T$ going to the investment account. In panel B, the funds in the transaction account are used to pay for consumption purchases.

is that each receipt of periodic income $Y*$ is immediately split into two parts: the amount $T$ is placed in the transaction account, and the remainder, $Y* - T$, is placed in the investment account. In a moment, we will examine the factors that determine $T$.

Consumption payments are assumed to be made daily, as in the basic CQ theory (we are now putting aside the synchronization effects of credit cards). The first payment is due on the first day of the period, so the person immediately starts drawing down the transaction account balance, and this continues over the following days until the transaction account balance reaches zero.

The transaction balance is then refilled by another transfer of $T$ dollars from the investment account, and consumption payments continued until the transaction account is again depleted. This pattern is repeated as often as necessary, with the investment account declining in a series of steps, each step representing the withdrawal of $T$ dollars, while, correspondingly, the transaction balance is refilled and depleted in a sawtooth pattern.

At the end of the first income period, the investment account and the transaction account are both depleted because total consumption payments of $Y*$ have been made. The process is then repeated for income period 2 and all subsequent periods.

## Money Demand in the BT Theory

In the BT theory, the demand for money equals the average balance in the transaction account. As shown in Figure 15.4, the transaction account balance declines steadily and repeatedly from $T$ to 0. The average balance thus equals $T/2$:

$$M^d = \frac{T}{2}. \tag{15.5}$$

People determine the size of the transfers $T$ from the investment account to the transaction account as part of their cash management policy. Consequently, to use equation (15.5), we must know what factors people consider in determining the best value for $T$. As we will now see, these factors include income, interest rates, and the costs of making the transfers.

Two basic considerations enter into the decision that determines the best value for $T$:

1. *Making T smaller increases interest earnings for the investment account.* Interest earnings primarily depend on the average balance in the investment account. As shown in Figure 15.4, this balance varies between $Y* - T$ and 0, so the average balance is $(Y* - T)/2$. Thus, if smaller values of $T$ are adopted, the average balance in the investment account rises, and interest earnings rise.

2. *Making T smaller also increases the costs of transfers.* These costs include service fees and the time and inconvenience involved in transferring funds. Total transfer costs equal the cost of each transfer times the

number of transfers per income period. The number of transfers equals $Y^*/T$, since $Y^*$ is the total amount transferred each period and each transfer is of size $T$.[5] Thus, as $T$ falls, the number of transfers rise, and transfer costs rise.

Figure 15.5 shows the cash management profits that arise from the trade-off between interest earnings and transfer costs. Cash management profits are defined as the interest earnings minus the transfer costs. The goal is to set the size of the transfer $T$ so that profits are maximized.

Low values of $T$ imply many transfers and thus high costs, so the profits from cash management are low. High values of $T$ imply that little interest is earned, so again profits are low. Profits are thus maximized at an intermediate value for $T$, $T^*$ (also see Appendix 15.1).

FIGURE 15.5
**The Profits (Interest Minus Costs)
of Cash Management**

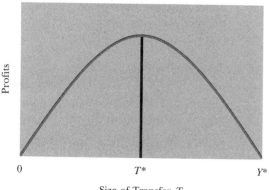

Size of Transfer $T$

Two factors are responsible for the shape of the profit function in Figure 15.5. First, when the value of $T$ is low, the number of transfers $(Y^*/T)$, and therefore the transfer costs, are high, so profits are low. Second, when the value of $T$ is high, investment account balances are low and relatively little interest is earned, so again profits are low. Between these extremes, the profit function rises, reaches a maximum at $T^*$, and then falls. The optimal size to transfer is thus $T^*$, the value that maximizes profits.

A precise formula can be derived for the optimal size of transfers $T^*$, as a function of the amount of income, the transfer cost, and the **opportunity cost of money**—the interest rate earned on investment account balances minus the interest rate earned on transaction account balances. Moreover, since the demand for money in the BT theory is $T/2$, we can derive the detailed money demand equation for the BT theory from the formula for $T^*$ (Appendix 15.1 formally derives the BT formula for $T^*$):

$$M^d = \frac{T^*}{2} = \sqrt{\frac{CfY^*}{2r_0}} = \sqrt{\frac{CY}{2r_0}},\qquad (15.6)$$

[5] The initial transaction, in which $T$ is deposited in the transaction account and $Y^* - T$ is deposited in the investment account, is counted as one of these transfers. It is also assumed that the cost of each transfer is independent of the size of the transfer.

where $T^*$ = the optimal size for the transfer $T$,
  $C$ = the cost of each transfer,
  $Y$ = the annual income,
  $Y^*$ = the periodic income $(Y/f)$,
  $f$ = the frequency of payments,
  $r_0$ = the opportunity cost of money $(r_I - r_T)$,
  $r_I$ = the rate of interest on investment accounts,
  $r_T$ = the rate of interest on transaction accounts.

## The Features of Money Demand

We will now look at a number of features of the BT theory based on equation (15.6). Figure 15.6 illustrates these points.

1. *The demand for money is positively related to income with an income elasticity of 1/2.* The income elasticity in equation (15.6) is 1/2 because money demand is a function of the square root of income $Y$, as proved in Appendix 15.1.[6] Thus, money demand rises with income, but less than proportionately, as shown by the BT curve in Figure 15.6. In contrast, in the CQ theory, the income elasticity of money demand is 1.0, as shown in Figure 15.6 by the straight line CQ.

2. *The demand for money depends positively on the transfer cost $C$.* As the cost per transfer $C$ rises, people increase the size of each transfer $T$, in order to reduce the number of transfers $(Y^*/T)$. Thus the demand for money—$T/2$—rises. This also means that the BT money demand curve in Figure 15.6 shifts upward as the cost per transfer $C$ rises.

3. *The demand for money in the BT theory is generally less than the demand in the CQ theory.* The largest possible value for money demand in the BT theory occurs when $T^*$ equals $Y^*$ in equation (15.6). In this case, there

[6] For example, the demand for money $M^d$ doubles when income $Y^*$ quadruples (2 is the square root of 4). Since the percentage change in money demand is one-half of the percentage change in income, the income elasticity of the demand for money is 1/2.

BT is the Baumol-Tobin theory demand curve for money based on equation (15.6). CQ is the classical quantity theory demand curve for money based on equation (15.3). The demand for money is generally greater under the CQ theory; however, the BT curve will shift upward as the transfer cost $C$ rises and the opportunity cost of money $r_0$ falls.

FIGURE 15.6

**Comparison of the BT and CQ Demand Curves for Money**

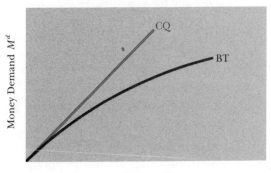

is just one transfer, so all funds are held as transaction balances, and money demand is $Y^*/2$. This is precisely the money demand of the basic CQ theory expressed by equation (15.3). However, the optimal size of the transfer $T^*$ in the BT theory is generally less than $Y^*$. Smaller values for $T^*$ shift the money demand curve BT down, so, as represented in Figure 15.6, the BT demand curve is generally lower than the CQ demand curve.

4. *The demand for money is negatively related to the opportunity cost of money $r_0$.* The opportunity cost $r_0$ equals the interest rate earned on investment accounts $r_I$ minus the interest rate earned on transaction accounts $r_T$. As the opportunity cost rises, more funds are allocated to the investment account (with less therefore allocated to the transaction account), so the demand for money falls. The money demand curve BT in Figure 15.6 thus shifts down as the opportunity cost $r_0$ rises. In fact, as a result of the square root of equation (15.6), the interest rate elasticity of money demand is $-0.5$ for the BT theory.

5. *The level of money demand in the BT theory is not affected by the frequency of income payments (for a given annual income Y).* For a given annual income $Y$, if the frequency of income payments $f$ changes, the periodic income $Y^*$ ($= Y/f$) changes in just the opposite direction. Consequently, since the term ($fY^*$) appears in the numerator of equation (15.6), any change in the frequency $f$ is cancelled by a corresponding change in periodic income $Y^*$. In contrast, in the CQ theory, the demand for money is inversely related to the frequency $f$.

6. *The BT demand for money is strictly proportional to the price level P but varies only with the square root of annual real income y.* In discussing the quantity equation of exchange (15.1) earlier, we saw that annual nominal income $Y$ equals the product of the price level $P$ and real expenditures $y$: $Y = Py$. Similarly, the (nominal) transfer cost $C$ can be separated into a price level factor $P$ and a real component $c$: $C = Pc$. Thus, by replacing $Y$ with $Py$, and by replacing $C$ with $Pc$, in the money demand equation (15.6), we obtain:

$$M^d = \frac{T^*}{2} = P\sqrt{\frac{cy}{2r_0}}.$$

7. *The velocity of money in the BT theory depends on the same factors as the demand for money, but in the opposite direction.* This is readily established by substituting the money demand equation (15.6) into the definition of velocity ($V = Y/M^d$). There are two key results: (1) the velocity of money depends positively on the opportunity cost of money $r_0$; and (2) the velocity of money rises as annual income $Y$ rises.

## Concluding Comments on the Baumol-Tobin Theory

The Baumol-Tobin cash management theory of money demand analyzes the transaction demand for money of people who have the option to invest funds that are not required immediately for payment purposes.

Therefore, the BT theory is more general than the classical quantity theory. The key result of the BT theory is that the demand for money is negatively related, and thus the velocity of money is positively related, to the opportunity cost of money $r_O$.

Although the Baumol-Tobin model applies mainly to the money demand of *individuals*, similar models have been developed for *business firms*. The main difference is that the income receipts of business firms (from goods sold) tend to arrive on a more continuous basis than the income receipts of individuals. Nevertheless, the demand for money of business firms and that of individuals share the same general properties, including the point that the demand for money is negatively related to its opportunity cost.

## Asset Theories of Money Demand

**Asset theories** of money demand are based on the role of money as a store of value—when it is used to hold wealth over time. We will examine the asset theories of the demand for money developed by John Maynard Keynes, James Tobin, and Milton Friedman. These theories all agree that the demand for money falls when interest rates rise. However, each theory has its own distinctive features.

## The Keynesian Theory of Liquidity Preference

John Maynard Keynes studied both transaction and asset theories of the demand for money. His 1930 study, *A Treatise on Money*, examined the transaction demand for money from a classical quantity theory viewpoint. His 1936 work, *The General Theory of Employment, Interest, and Money*, incorporated asset theory considerations as well.

Keynes called his overall theory of money demand the **liquidity preference (LP)** theory. As we saw in Chapter 5, the *liquidity* of an asset reflects how readily it can be exchanged for money. Most tangible capital assets, such as manufacturing equipment, have poor liquidity because they cannot be readily sold. Financial instruments, such as stocks and bonds, are usually more liquid. Money has the ultimate degree of liquidity since it is a medium of exchange.

Keynes's LP theory distinguishes three motives for money demand: a **transaction motive**, a **precautionary motive**, and a **speculative motive**. The Keynesian transaction and precautionary motives mainly reflect the CQ theory. The concept of speculative demand is Keynes's special contribution to money demand theory. The primary result of the Keynesian speculative theory is that the demand for money falls when interest rates rise—comparable to the result of the Baumol-Tobin theory.

## The Speculative Demand for Money

The speculative demand for money reflects how people invest their wealth among different assets, such as tangible capital assets, bonds, and money. However, Keynes analyzed only the choice between bonds and money as an issue of liquidity preference. Keynes felt that capital investment decisions would be made on a different basis because capital assets—such as manufacturing equipment—involve a substantial degree of risk. Looking only at the total wealth to be allocated between money and bonds—referred to as $W_L$—the speculative demand for money determines whether $W_L$ is to be kept in money or invested in bonds.

According to Keynes, people compare money and bonds in terms of two attributes: liquidity and the rate of interest. People generally prefer both more liquidity and more interest. Money offers more liquidity, but bonds pay more interest. The choice between money and bonds thus involves a trade-off.

This trade-off is represented in Figure 15.7 for someone deciding whether to put his "allocatable" wealth $W_L$ into bonds or money (such as a bank deposit). The decision can be described in terms of the *reservation interest rate r\* for bonds*—the minimum interest rate on bonds the investor requires before he will buy them. Otherwise, wealth $W_L$ is invested entirely in money. Thus, the speculative demand for money has an "all or nothing" form, depending on the market interest rate $r$ and the reservation interest rate $r^*$ for bonds:

$$M^d = \begin{cases} 0 & \text{if } r > r^*, \\ W_L & \text{if } r \le r^*, \end{cases} \tag{15.7}$$

where $r$ = the market interest rate on bonds,
   $r^*$ = the investor's reservation rate for bonds,
   $W_L$ = the total wealth allocated between money and bonds.

Each person determines a reservation rate $r^*$ based on three considerations:

1. *The reservation rate r\* will be higher when the person's liquidity preference is higher.* People with a high preference for the liquidity of money will have a high reservation rate for bonds.

Having set aside a portion, $W_L$, of their wealth to be invested in bonds or in money (such as a bank deposit), investors set a reservation rate, $r^*$. If the market interest rate on bonds, $r$, exceeds $r^*$, $W_L$ will be totally invested in bonds, and the speculative demand for money, $M^d$, will be zero. If $r$ equals or is less than $r^*$, $M^d$ will equal $W_L$.

FIGURE 15.7
**The Keynesian Speculative Demand for Money**

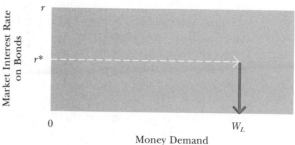

Money Demand

2. *The reservation rate r\* will be higher when the interest rate paid on money is higher.* Money is more attractive when its interest rate is higher, and this makes the reservation rate $r^*$ for bonds higher.

3. *The reservation rate r\* will be higher when the expectations of capital losses from holding bonds are higher.* Recall from Chapter 5 that investors receive capital losses because bond prices fall, which they do when interest rates rise. Since the prospect of capital losses on bonds deters investors from buying them, higher expected capital losses create a higher reservation rate for bonds.

The Keynesian Speculative theory explains why higher market interest rates have a negative effect on money demand. However, the theory has the disturbing feature that the wealth to be allocated is invested entirely in money, or entirely in bonds, but never split between them. In fact, as we saw in Chapter 7, investors should generally hold *diversified portfolios*, allocating their overall portfolio to many different assets. James Tobin subsequently extended the Keynesian speculative theory to solve this problem.

## Tobin's Theory of Liquidity Preference

We have already noted James Tobin's contribution to the transaction theory of money demand in the Baumol-Tobin model. Now we will look at his contribution to the Keynesian speculative (asset) theory of money demand. In reworking the Keynesian theory, Tobin combined two of his major interests: the demand for money and the principle of portfolio diversification, the latter being the basis for his Nobel Prize in economics.

The starting point of Tobin's theory, which he refers to as a theory of **liquidity preference (LP)** following Keynes's terminology, is an investor who is allocating a given amount of wealth among money, debt securities such as bonds, and equity investments such as common stocks.[7] Like Keynes' LP theory, Tobin's recognizes that a security's interest rate, or expected rate of return, will be a major factor determining the demand for the security. However, unlike Keynes' theory, Tobin's focuses on *risk* as another fundamental factor that investors should consider when selecting assets.

In the discussion of how decisions are made under uncertainty, in Chapter 7, we pointed out that *risk-averse investors* would consider both the *expected rate of return* and *risk* in evaluating investments. As a result, they would try to hold *diversified portfolios*. Tobin's liquidity preference theory of money demand applies the concept of diversification to portfolios of assets that include money, bonds, and common stocks. Tobin obtained two main results by applying portfolio selection theory in this way, one pertaining to diversification, and the other pertaining to the interest elasticity of money demand.

---

[7] See James Tobin, "Liquidity Preference as Behavior Towards Risk," *Review of Economic Studies*, February 1958, pp. 65–86.

Tobin's approach solved the problem that the Keynesian speculative theory did not provide for diversification. Once the risk of investments is recognized, and given that most investors are risk averse, it follows that most investors will hold diversified portfolios that include money. Moreover, since money has no credit risk, it may play a particularly important role in portfolio diversification.

Tobin's liquidity preference theory implies a negative interest rate elasticity of the same general form we saw in the Baumol-Tobin and Keynesian speculative models. In Tobin's LP theory, the negative interest rate elasticity is the result of investors reducing the percentage of their portfolios allocated to money when the rate of return on investment assets rises.

The two main conclusions of Tobin's liquidity preference theory are illustrated in Figure 15.8. The curve shows the demand for money of an investor who is allocating a total wealth $W_T$ between money and other investments (including bonds and stocks). The vertical axis is the opportunity cost of holding money $r_0$—the interest rate on investment assets minus the interest rate on money balances. The demand for money is measured as the horizontal distance rightward from the vertical axis to the money demand curve. The amount of total wealth allocated to investment assets is measured as the horizontal distance leftward from the vertical line $W_T$ to the money demand curve.

The figure shows the portfolio decision made by an investor allocating total wealth $W_T$ between money and investment assets. The amount of money is measured from the vertical axis rightward to the money demand curve. The amount of other investment assets is measured from the line $W_T$ leftward to the money demand curve. The demand for money falls as the opportunity cost rises because investors allocate a larger part of their portfolios to investment assets.

FIGURE 15.8
**Tobin's Liquidity Preference Theory of the Demand for Money**

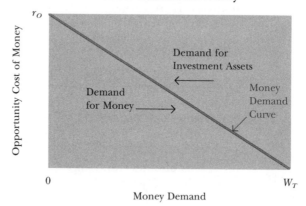

The investor generally holds a diversified portfolio with both money and investment assets. A negative interest rate elasticity is represented in the figure because the demand for money falls as the opportunity interest rate of money rises. Although Tobin's model provides a neat extension of the Keynesian speculative demand for money, it requires that money be an important component of diversified portfolios. However, there are two problems with this attribute of money, one concerning other risk-free assets, the other concerning inflation.

The problem raised by *other risk-free assets*, such as Treasury bills, is that they may displace money from portfolios. That is, money and Treasury bills are both risk-free assets, but Treasury bills pay higher interest. Thus other factors—such as transactions costs—have to be added to Tobin's theory to explain why people hold money as a store of value when they could hold Treasury bills instead.

The problem regarding *inflation* is that in its presence the *real rate of return* on money is not risk free. Recall from Chapter 4 that inflation imposes an implicit tax on money by depreciating its purchasing power. This places money at a disadvantage with respect to assets such as common stocks and real estate, which may have real rates of return that are not adversely affected by inflation.

# Milton Friedman's Modern Quantity (MQ) Theory

Milton Friedman, like Keynes and Tobin, analyzed how people allocate their wealth among investment alternatives (including money) on the basis of rates of return. Friedman went beyond Keynes and Tobin, however, because he considered all possible investments, not just money, bonds, and stocks. Friedman's theory even considers *human capital*—the valuable skills people acquire from training and education.

Friedman viewed money as *abstract purchasing power*, meaning that people hold money with the intention of using it for upcoming purchases of goods and services. In this sense, Friedman's theory integrates an asset theory and a transaction theory of the demand for money. Since Friedman derived his theory from the classical quantity theory, he described his approach as the **modern quantity theory.** Many aspects of Friedman's theory are summarized in the 1956 book he edited, *Studies in the Quantity Theory of Money.*

## The Permanent Income Theory of Money Demand

Friedman felt that people rely more on long-term factors—such as wealth—than on short-term factors—such as current income—in determining their demand for money. He used the concept of **permanent income** to clarify this point. Permanent income $Y_p$ corresponds to the part of current income that is *expected* to continue in the future. In particular, it does not include transitory components of current income that result from short-run factors. For example, a person's permanent income would include salary bonuses only if such bonuses are expected to continue in the future.

Friedman's permanent income theory of money demand is represented in the form of the basic CQ theory equation (15.3), but with permanent income $Y_p$ replacing current annual income $Y$:

$$M^d = kY_p, \tag{15.8}$$

where $k$ = a constant representing payments system factors.

The implications of Friedman's theory are readily seen after converting the money demand equation to the corresponding velocity of money equation:

$$V = \frac{Y}{M^d} = \frac{Y}{kY_p}. \tag{15.9}$$

The velocity of money thus depends on the level of current income $Y$ relative to permanent income $Y_p$. During economic booms, $Y$ rises relative to $Y_p$, and velocity should rise. In recessions, $Y$ falls relative to $Y_p$, and velocity should fall.

## The Role of Interest Rates in Friedman's Theory

Although interest rates have a negative effect on money demand in Friedman's theory, Friedman expected the interest rate effects to be small. His view stems primarily from the broad, M2, definition of money he uses—not from a new theoretical finding. He uses the M2 definition because he believes that money should be defined to cover a broad range of assets.

To appreciate the significance of using the M2 definition, consider a situation in which the interest rate paid on time deposits rises, and all other interest rates in the economy remain unchanged. There are two offsetting effects on the demand for M2 when the time deposit rate rises. First, the demand for time deposits rises, thus directly increasing this component of the demand for M2. Second, the demand for currency and transaction deposits falls, decreasing the demand for the M1 component of M2. As a result, the time deposit rate may have a modest effect—and in the extreme case a zero effect—on the total demand for M2. In this sense, Friedman's theory indicates a lower interest rate elasticity of the demand for money than most other theories.

## Money Demand When Money Is a Luxury Good

A **luxury good** is a good for which demand increases more than proportionately as income rises. Diamonds and furs are examples. Friedman argues that the liquidity value of money makes it a luxury good. (Poor people usually cannot afford the luxury of keeping spare money around, whereas rich people can.) Thus, as a person's income rises, his or her demand for money will rise more than proportionately. Friedman concluded on this basis that it would not be surprising to find that the income elasticity of money demand exceeded 1.0. Correspondingly, given that money demand rises faster than income, the velocity of money would fall as income rises.

We have now completed our analysis of the four major theories of money demand: the classical quantity theory, the Baumol-Tobin theory, the Keynesian speculative theory (including the extension by James Tobin), and Milton Friedman's modern quantity theory. Each theory has distinctive predictions for the effects of income, interest rates, and payments system factors on the demand for money.

A summary and synthesis of these theories, along with an examination of the empirical evidence regarding money demand, is provided in Chapter 16. We will also develop the money demand/supply theory of interest rates—which combines the demand and supply of money—in that chapter.

## Chapter Summary

1. Transaction theories of the demand for money—such as the classical quantity (CQ) theory and the Baumol-Tobin (BT) theory—are based on the role of money as a medium of exchange. Asset theories of the demand for money—such as the Keynesian speculative demand theory and Milton Friedman's modern quantity theory—are based on its role as a store of value.

2. The classical quantity theory derives the demand for money from the features of the payments system used in the economy. Relevant payments system factors include the frequency of income receipts, the use of credit cards to synchronize income and consumption, and the precautionary demand for money. Key results of the CQ theory include:

   a. The income elasticity of money demand is 1.0.

   b. The demand for money and the velocity of money depend on payments system factors.

   c. The velocity of money may be constant in the short run.

3. The Baumol-Tobin theory of money demand analyzes how people use cash management policies to allocate their wealth between a transaction account (currency and checking deposits) and an investment account (securities and bank time deposits). The key results of the BT theory are:

   a. The demand for money varies with the square root of income (the income elasticity of money demand is 1/2).

   b. The demand for money is inversely related to the opportunity interest cost of transaction accounts.

   c. The demand for money depends positively on the cost of making transfers.

4. The Keynesian theory of liquidity preference distinguishes three components of money demand: transaction, precautionary, and speculative demands. The speculative demand for money—the special part of the theory—is based on how people allocate their wealth between money and bonds. The main result of the theory is that the demand for money is inversely related to market interest rates.

5. James Tobin later extended the Keynesian speculative theory by incorporating considerations of risk. In Tobin's version, the speculative demand for money is still inversely related to market interest rates, but people hold diversified portfolios consisting of money, bonds, and stocks.

6. The modern quantity theory of Milton Friedman is also based on how people allocate wealth among alternative assets. Although Friedman's theory is based on the classical quantity theory, it has many distinctive features, including:

   a. Money demand is based on the M2 definition of money.

   b. Money demand depends on permanent income.

   c. Money is treated as a luxury good.

## Key Terms

Asset and transaction theories of money demand

Cash management

Elasticity of money demand:

   Income

   Interest rate

Investment and transaction accounts

Money demand theories:

   Baumol-Tobin (BT) theory

   Classical quantity (CQ) theory

   Liquidity preference (LP) theory (John Maynard Keynes)

Liquidity preference (LP) theory (James Tobin)

Modern quantity theory (Milton Friedman)

Money as a luxury good

Money hoarding

Opportunity cost of money (transaction accounts)

Permanent income

Precautionary money holdings

Synchronization of income receipts and consumption payments

## Study Questions

1. Define the income elasticity of money demand and indicate the specific value associated with the following theories of money demand: the classical quantity (CQ) theory, the Baumol-Tobin (BT) theory, and Milton Friedman's modern quantity (MQ) theory of money as a luxury good.

2. Define the interest rate elasticity of money demand and indicate whether this elasticity is positive, negative, or zero for the CQ, BT, MQ, and liquidity preference (LP) theories of money demand.

3. Define the GNP velocity of M1 money. Why might the velocity of money associated with the CQ theory be considered constant in the short run, but not in the long run?

4. Using the CQ theory of money demand, determine the demand for money based on the following facts: Annual income is $24,000 and the individual is paid monthly. Saving and precautionary money holdings are zero, and there is no synchronization of income receipts and consumption payments.

5. How does your answer to Question 4 change if precautionary money holdings equal 10% of the annual income. How does your answer to Question 4 change if 40% of consumption payments and income receipts are perfectly synchronized?

6. In the Baumol-Tobin theory of money demand, what is the incentive of people to keep funds in the transaction account? In the investment account?

7. Why is the demand for money less in the Baumol-Tobin theory than in the classical quantity theory?

8. Suppose an economy consists of ten people, each with total wealth equal to $1,000. Following the Keynesian speculative demand for money, suppose that the reservation rates for bond purchases are such that individual 1 has a 1% rate, individual 2 has a 2% rate, and so on up to individual 10 with a 10% reservation rate. How much money is demanded when the market rate for bonds equals 7%?

9. Based on Milton Friedman's two theories of money demand, (1) money demand

depending on permanent income and (2) money as a luxury good, would you expect the velocity of money to rise, fall, or remain unchanged when current income rises?

10. What is the significance of Milton Friedman's use of a broad definition of money for the interest elasticity of money demand?

## Recommended Reading

*The following is a classic statement of the Classical Quantity theory of money demand which we used as the basis of our discussion of that topic:*

Irving Fisher, *The Purchasing Power of Money,* MacMillan, New York, 1911.

*The following are the two original papers of the Baumol-Tobin transaction theory of money demand:*

William Baumol, "The Transactions Demand for Cash: An Inventory Theoretic Approach," *Quarterly Journal of Economics,* November 1952, pp. 545–556.

James Tobin, "The Interest Elasticity of the Transactions Demand for Cash," *Review of Economics and Statistics,* August 1956, pp. 241–247.

*The following present Keynes's original discussion of the speculative demand for money and James Tobin's extension of it:*

John Maynard Keynes, *The General Theory of Employment, Interest, and Money,* New York, Harcourt, Brace, 1936.

James Tobin, "Liquidity Preference as Behavior Towards Risk," *Review of Economic Studies,* February 1958, pp. 65–86.

*This is a collection of studies that illustrate Milton Friedman's Modern Quantity theory of money:*

Milton Friedman, editor, *Studies in the Quantity Theory,* Chicago, University of Chicago Press, 1956.

## Appendix 15.1: Money Demand and the Baumol-Tobin Theory

According to the cash management policy of the Baumol-Tobin (BT) theory of money demand, individuals periodically transfer the amount $T$ from their investment account to their transaction account. Here we derive the formula for the optimal size of the transfer $T^*$.

The profits earned from cash management equal the interest earned on the transaction and investment accounts, minus the costs of making the transfer between the accounts. The interest earned on each account equals the average balances maintained in the account multiplied by the rate of interest. Interest earnings per income period are thus:

$$\text{Interest earnings} = \left(\frac{r_T}{f}\right)\left(\frac{T}{2}\right) + \left(\frac{r_I}{f}\right)\left(\frac{Y^* - T}{2}\right)$$

where $f$ = the income frequency,
$\quad T$ = the transfer size,
$\quad r_T$ = the annual interest rate on transaction funds,
$\quad r_I$ = the annual interest rate on investment funds.

For the transaction account, $T/2$ is the average balance and $r_T/f$ is the interest earned during one income period. For the investment account, $(Y^* - T)/2$ is the average balance and $r_I/f$ is the interest earned during one income period.

Total transfer costs equal the number of transfers times the cost of each transfer. The number of transfers during an income period is $Y^*/T$ and the cost of each transfer is $C$. Thus, per income period:

$$\text{Total transfer costs} = C\left(\frac{Y^*}{T}\right).$$

The profits per income period from cash management equal the interest earnings minus the transfer costs:

$$\text{Profits} = \left(\frac{r_T}{f}\right)\left(\frac{T}{2}\right) + \left(\frac{r_I}{f}\right)\left(\frac{Y^* - T}{2}\right) - C\left(\frac{Y^*}{T}\right).$$

Individuals select the value for $T$ that maximizes these profits. Using calculus to determine this maximum, the profit function is differentiated with respect to $T$:

$$\frac{d\,\text{Profits}}{d\,T} = \frac{r_T}{2f} - \frac{r_I}{2f} + \frac{CY^*}{T^2}.$$

Setting this derivative equal to zero and solving for $T$ yields the optimal value $T^*$:

$$T^* = \sqrt{\frac{2CfY^*}{(r_I - r_T)}} = \sqrt{\frac{2\,CY}{r_O}}$$

where $Y = fY^* = $ the annual income,

$\quad r_O = $ the opportunity interest rate for transaction account balances

$\quad\quad (= r_I - r_T)$.

This is the value of $T^*$ used in the text equation (15.6) to determine the demand for money.

Two technical features of this solution for the demand for money were not covered in the text discussion:

*Integer solutions*: The number of transfers equals $Y^*/T$, the periodic income divided by the size of each transfer. Realistically, this must be an integer since it makes no sense to make a fractional trip to the bank. This integer aspect of the problem should be considered in a complete, rigorous, solution.

*Corner solutions*: The solution for $T^*$ guarantees that profits are maximized, but it does not guarantee that profits are positive. It is possible, in other words, that the cash management policy results in negative profits even when the optimal value $T^*$ is chosen. In this case, the person is at a "corner solution" and would do better to operate without cash management—holding only money—as under the classical quantity theory.

# Money Demand and Money Supply

**16**

*"Lack of money is the root of all evil."*

*George Bernard Shaw*

Soon after Paul A. Volcker took over as chairman of the board of the governors of the Federal Reserve system in 1979, he announced major changes in the way monetary policy was going to be carried out. At the time, inflation rates in the country were rising rapidly, and Volcker attributed part of this problem to lax control of the money supply. His new program specified a lower target for the annual increase in the money supply, including plans to monitor the actual increase closely.

Controlling the money supply turned out to be difficult. In his frequent testimony before Congress, Volcker excelled at explaining why the actual increase in the money supply turned out to be higher than the target the Fed had set. For one thing, since each definition of the money supply had its own target, at each session he would confine his testimony to the definition that was closest to meeting its target.

Volcker also testified that the Fed kept missing its money supply targets because the *demand for money was shifting*. Referring to the financial deregulation legislation of 1980 and related events, he argued that the major changes occurring in the financial markets were causing people to vary the amount of money they wanted to hold. At one Congressional hearing Volcker would point out that higher *checking account* interest rates explained the rapid growth of M1; while at another he would demonstrate that higher time deposit interest rates explained the rapid growth of M2. Volcker retired from the Fed in 1987, with a fine record both as an inflation fighter and as an expositor of why the demand for money shifts.

In this chapter, we will summarize and apply our results concerning the supply of money from Chapter 14 and the demand for money from Chapter 15.

The equilibrium that occurs when the demand and supply of money are equal will be the main focus of this chapter. We will pay particular attention to interest rates and nominal income as variables that can adjust to establish this equilibrium. Also, because the effect of changing the money supply depends on the properties of the demand for money—such as its interest rate elasticity—we will look at empirical features of the demand for money in the second part of the chapter.

## A Summary of the Demand and Supply of Money

We will start our study of equilibrium in the market for money by specifying equations for the demand for and the supply of money that summarize the theories developed in the preceding two chapters. We begin with the demand for money, using the narrow M1 definition of money unless indicated otherwise.

### The Demand for Money

We saw in Chapter 15 that the demand for money is determined basically by three variables:

- The value of transactions, measured by **nominal income** Y.

- The **opportunity cost of money** $r_0$—the market interest rate on securities $r_S$ minus the interest rate on money $r_M$. (In Chapter 15, we referred to the opportunity cost as the interest rate on the investment account minus the interest rate on the transaction account.)

- Various **payments system factors,** such as the frequency and synchronization of payments, which we will denote with the general symbol S.

The money demand relationship can be expressed as:

$$M^d = M^d[\overset{-}{r_0}, \overset{+}{Y}, S],\qquad (16.1)$$

where $M^d$ = the demand for money,
$r_0$ = the opportunity cost of money,
$Y$ = nominal income,
$S$ = payments system factors.

The signs above the equation indicate that the demand for money responds negatively to $r_0$ and positively to $Y$. No sign is shown above $S$ because, depending on the specific payments system factors comprising $S$, the effect on money demand can be either positive or negative.

The opportunity cost of money $r_0$—the market interest rate on securities $r_S$ minus the interest rate paid on money $r_M$—deserves further comment. Until the early 1980s, the market interest rate on securities $r_S$, by itself, was a proper measure of the opportunity cost of money, since little or no interest was paid on money (currency and checking accounts). However, competitive interest rates can now be paid on all bank deposits, so currency is the only component of the money supply that still does not pay interest. Therefore, the opportunity cost of money is now properly specified as the market interest rate on securities minus the interest rate on money. When we refer simply to the interest rate in this chapter, we mean this opportunity cost of money $r_0$.

Figure 16.1 is a graph of the demand for money as a function of the opportunity cost of money $r_0$. Changes in the opportunity cost of money are reflected as movements along the negatively sloped demand curve. Changes in the other factors that determine money demand—nominal income $Y$ and payments system factors $S$—are reflected as shifts of the curve. Specifically, when income rises, the demand curve shifts to the right.

### The Interest Rate and Income Elasticities of Money Demand

We saw in Chapter 15 that the elasticities with respect to interest rates and income are key features of money demand: the **interest rate elasticity of money demand** equals the percentage change in money demand relative to a given change in the opportunity cost of money. Similarly, the **income elasticity of money demand** equals the percentage change in money demand relative to a given change in income.

Money demand falls when the opportunity cost of money rises. Changes in other factors that determine the demand for money—nominal income and payments system factors—are represented as shifts in the demand curve for money. The income elasticity of money demand is represented here by the amount that the money demand curve shifts when nominal income changes.

FIGURE 16.1
**The Demand for Money in Terms of the Opportunity Cost**

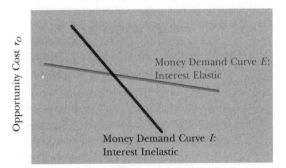

Figure 16.1 shows two demand curves, representing two interest rate elasticities. The relatively flat curve $E$ is *interest elastic:* a given change in the opportunity cost $r_0$ results in a relatively large change in the demand for money. The relatively steep curve $I$ is *interest inelastic:* a given change in $r_0$ results in a relatively small change in money demand. A perfectly vertical curve represents the extreme case of zero interest inelasticity because the demand for money then does not depend at all on the interest rate. The extent to which the demand curve for money in Figure 16.1 shifts when nominal income changes represents the *income* elasticity of money demand.

### The Demand for Money in Terms of Nominal Income

Figure 16.2 is also based on equation (16.1), but the graph is shown as a function of nominal income $Y$. Changes in nominal income are reflected as movements along the positively sloped demand curve. Changes in the opportunity cost of money $r_0$ and payments system factors $S$ are reflected as shifts of the money demand curve. Specifically, when the opportunity cost of money rises, the demand curve shifts to the left.

The income elasticity of money demand is the proportional amount that money demand rises when income rises. The income elastic money demand curve $E$ is relatively flat, since this means that money demand rises more when income rises. The interest rate elasticity of money demand is represented here by the amount that the money demand curve shifts when the interest rate changes.

FIGURE 16.2

**The Demand for Money in Terms of Nominal Income**

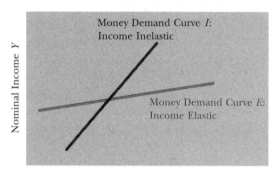

Money Demand

## The Supply of Money

As we saw in Chapter 14, the money supply is determined in a series of steps:

1. The Federal Reserve determines the size of the *monetary base* by buying and selling assets such as securities.

2. The public—everyone in the economy other than banks and the Federal Reserve—determines the amount of *currency* it wants to hold, depositing the rest of the monetary base in banks, where it counts as *bank reserves*.

3. *Transaction deposits* are determined through the process of deposit expansion. The quantity of deposits depends positively on the *monetary base*, negatively on the *reserve drains*—currency, excess reserves, and required reserves on time deposits—and negatively on the *required reserve ratios* for transaction and time deposits.

We also saw that the money supply $M^s$ can be stated in a simpler form as the product of the monetary base $B$ and a *money supply multiplier m:*

$$M^s = m B.$$

where $M^s$ = the $M1$ money supply,

$\qquad m$ = the corresponding money supply multiplier,

$\qquad B$ = the monetary base.

The money supply multiplier $m$ incorporates the factors that determine the money supply relative to the **monetary base.** As discussed in Chapter 14, $m$ is *greater,* the *smaller* the amount of:

- Currency held by the public.
- Excess reserves held by banks.
- Time deposits held by the public.
- The required reserve ratio on transaction deposits.
- The required reserve ratio on time deposits.

Changes in the first three of these variables—the *reserve drains*—can be created by changes in interest rates. Generally speaking, an increase in the opportunity cost $r_0$ will reduce the amount of the reserve drains, so $m$ will rise. For example, people will hold less currency when its opportunity cost is higher, so $m$ will rise. Here we will focus only on the **opportunity cost of money,** putting aside the other interest rates—with various effects on the money supply—we mentioned in Chapter 14.

The effect of the opportunity cost $r_0$ on the multiplier $m$ can be expressed in a money supply equation:

$$M^s = m[\overset{+}{r_0}]B, \qquad (16.2)$$

where $M^s$ = the money supply,
$m$ = the money supply multiplier,
$r_0$ = the opportunity cost of holding money,
$B$ = the monetary base.

The positive relationship between the multiplier and the opportunity cost is indicated by the plus sign above $r_0$.

The money supply $M^s$ of equation (16.2) is represented in Figure 16.3 as a positively sloped curve. Changes in the opportunity cost $r_0$ are thus reflected as movements *along* the money supply curve, while changes in the monetary base $B$ *shift* the curve.

Based on its control of the monetary base, the Federal Reserve can shift the money supply curve, either rightward—easy monetary policy—or leftward—tight monetary policy. The money supply can also be interpreted as a vertical line at the value—$M^*$ in the figure—the Federal Reserve has chosen as its target.

**FIGURE 16.3**
**The Supply of Money**

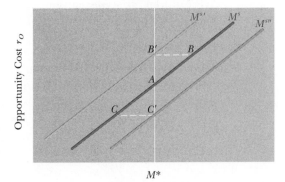

Money Supply

The monetary policy of the Fed is generally the source of the changes in the monetary base that cause the money supply curve to shift. When the Fed increases the money supply, this is called *easy* monetary policy; when it decreases the money supply—or causes it to grow less rapidly—this is called *tight* monetary policy. Thus, easy monetary policy creates a rightward shift in the money supply curve in Figure 16.3; and tight monetary policy a leftward shift.

Because the Federal Reserve can determine the size of the money supply through its control of the monetary base, it is also possible to interpret the money supply curve as a vertical line—in Figure 16.3, the line $M^*$. Starting at point A, suppose the opportunity cost $r_0$ changes—up or down—so there is a movement along the money supply curve to point B or C if the Federal Reserve takes no further action. However, the Federal Reserve can restore the original money supply, $M^*$, by changing the monetary base, so that the money supply curve shifts either to point $B'$ on curve $M^{s'}$, or to point $C'$ on curve $M^{s''}$.

Based on such Federal Reserve actions, the actual money supply will trace out a vertical line, $A$-$B'$-$C'$. In this chapter, our graphical analysis of the effects of changing the money supply will be based on such a vertical supply curve.

## The Equilibrium of Money Demand and Money Supply

Having summarized the theories of the demand and supply of money, we will now look at the characteristics of an equilibrium in which money demand and money supply are equal. Although we will focus on the market for money, we also have to be aware of the markets for goods (and services) and for financial securities, because there are important interactions between these markets and the market for money.

We will treat all the goods in the economy as if they were traded in one aggregate market. The price in this market represents the economy's price level $P$, and the income produced in this market represents aggregate nominal income $Y$. In a similar fashion, we will represent all financial securities in the economy as if they were traded in one aggregate financial market, with the opportunity cost of money $r_0$ representing the interest rate in this market relative to the interest rate on money.

We will look at a special type of equilibrium—called a **partial equilibrium**—in which *only* the market for money is assured to be in equilibrium. As a result, the prices and quantities in other markets—for goods and securities—will be treated as given values. This will simplify our analysis of equilibrium in the market for money. For example, when we evaluate what happens to the interest rate in the context of an easy monetary policy, we need not consider that nominal income may also change, creating further shifts in the demand and supply curves for money.

Partial equilibrium facilitates our analysis because we do not have to consider these more complicated interactions. However, it also means that our analysis is incomplete. Our answers will not be "wrong," but they may be oversimplified. The alternative to partial equilibrium analysis is **general equilibrium** analysis—which looks at equilibrium simultaneously in all markets, taking all interactions into account. We will use general equilibrium analysis in Part VII when we study monetary theory.

The equilibrium condition in the market for money can be expressed simply, based on equation (16.1) for money demand and equation (16.2) for money supply, as:

$$M^d = M^s$$

or

$$M^d[r_0, Y, S] = m[r_0]B. \tag{16.3}$$

The left side of equation (16.3) represents money demand and the right side represents money supply. Since there is nothing intrinsic in the nature of money demand or money supply to make them equal, $r_0$, $Y$, $S$, or $B$ has to change to establish equilibrium.

However, two of these variables can be ruled out of consideration—payments system factors $S$ and the monetary base $B$. Payments system factors—such as the frequency of income receipts—generally do not vary enough to establish equilibrium in the market for money on a short-run basis. The monetary base also cannot adjust to establish equilibrium, because it is normally controlled by Federal Reserve for purposes of monetary policy. Indeed, the Fed uses the monetary base to shift the money supply curve.

So this leaves us with two variables—**the opportunity cost of money $r_0$ and nominal income Y**—either one of which can steer the supply and demand of money toward equilibrium. We will now look at each one in turn.

## The Interest Rate as the Source of Money Market Equilibrium

We will focus first on how the opportunity cost of money $r_0$ adjusts to reestablish equilibrium in the market for money. To do so, we will assume—as part of the partial equilibrium analysis—that nominal income is a fixed value. More precisely, we will assume that each of the components of nominal income—real income and the price level—are constant. Thus, given an imbalance between money demand and money supply, $r_0$ will adjust to restore the equilibrium. We will refer to this as the **MD/MS (money demand/money supply) theory of interest rates.**

Equilibrium in the market for money is illustrated in Figure 16.4 at the point $M$, where the money supply curve $M^*$ and the money demand curve $M^d$ intersect. The money demand curve is negatively sloped as a function of the interest rate, as we illustrated in Figure 16.1. The money supply curve is a vertical line, as we illustrated in Figure 16.3. The intersection of these curves determines the equilibrium interest rate $r_0^*$.

The initial equilibrium occurs at the point $M$ where the money demand curve $M^d$ intersects the vertical money supply line $M^*$. If the Federal Reserve adopts an easier monetary policy—shifting the money supply line to the right to $M'$—then the equilibrium interest rate falls to $r_0'$.

FIGURE 16.4

**Interest Rate Determination and Money Demand**

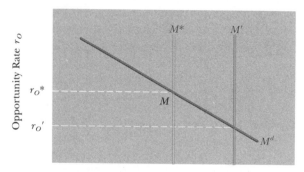

Money Supply and Demand

From this starting point, consider how a change in monetary policy—a change in the monetary base, which causes the money supply curve to shift—affects the equilibrium interest rate. For example, if the Federal Reserve institutes an easier monetary policy—increases the monetary base—the money supply curve shifts to the right, which reduces the interest rate. In a similar manner, a tighter monetary policy shifts the money supply curve to the left, which raises the interest rate.

A larger money supply causes the opportunity cost of money to fall because people have to be provided with incentive to hold the larger supply. Thus, if the Federal Reserve shifts the money supply to line $M'$ in Figure 16.4, the interest rate falls to $r_0'$, the level at which demand intersects with supply. If the interest rate were to remain at $r_0^*$, supply would exceed demand—that is, people would have excess money.

There are basically two things people can do with excess money: spend it, or lend it. We will focus first on what happens when they lend it. We will refer to this as the **LF (loanable funds) theory of interest rates.** Lending excess money increases the supply of loanable funds in the economy. As discussed in Chapter 3, an increase in the supply of loanable funds causes the interest rate to fall. So, whichever way you look at it—as an increase in the supply of money, or as an increase in the supply of loanable funds—the interest rate will fall.

## The Money Demand/Supply and Loanable Funds Theories of Interest Rates

In fact, the money demand/money supply (MD/MS) and loanable funds (LF) theories of interest rates are logically equivalent. This equivalence can be seen in terms of the aggregate market for financial assets, in which equilibrium occurs when the demand for financial assets $A^d$ equals the supply of financial assets $A^s$:

$$A^d = A^s.$$

It is helpful to divide all the financial assets in the economy into two categories: money $M$ and all other financial assets $F$. Thus, the total demand for financial assets $A^d$ equals the demand for money $M^d$ plus the demand for all other financial assets $F^d$; and the total supply of financial assets $A^s$ equals the supply of money $M^s$ plus the supply of all other financial assets $F^s$. Therefore, in equilibrium:

$$A^d = A^s$$

or

$$M^d + F^d = M^s + F^s. \tag{16.4}$$

The logical equivalence of the LF and MD/MS theories is illustrated by equation (16.4). The equilibrium condition for the MD/MS theory is: $M^d = M^s$. The equilibrium condition for the LF theory is $F^d = F^s$. Referring to equation (16.4), we can see that each theory implies the other: if $M^d = M^s$, then $F^d = F^s$. And if $F^d = F^s$, then $M^d = M^s$.

This equivalence means that if the MD/MS theory predicts the interest rate will have a specific equilibrium value, then the LF theory must predict the same value, and vice versa. Similarly, if one of the theories predicts that a change in some factor, such as monetary policy, has a specific effect on the interest rate, then so will the other theory.

Which theory to use for analyzing interest rates is a matter of convenience. People working in the securities markets, who deal directly with the demand and supply of loanable funds, tend to think in terms of the LF theory. This is why, at the end of each year, many Wall Street firms provide a forecast of interest rates for the following year based on the expected demand and supply of loanable funds. Box 16.1 provides an example from one of these forecasts.

In contrast, people trying to interpret monetary policy—in terms of Federal Reserve control of the money supply—tend to think in terms of the MD/MS theory. For example, the Federal Reserve announces a current estimate of the money supply each week. Interest rates often change based on these announcements, reflecting new interpretations of monetary policy. Box 16.2 describes how this works.

## Predicting Interest Rates With the Loanable Funds Theory

The following is reprinted from *Prospects for Financial Markets in 1988*, Salomon Brothers Inc.

### Demand For Credit Remains Light

Private credit demands will be constrained in 1988 by the periodic bouts of financial unrest and economic uncertainty that we expect. Households will, in many cases, voluntarily pull back, and some business and state and local borrowers will encounter increased risk avoidance and liquidity preferences on the part of lenders and investors.

As a result, credit growth will again slow relative to economic activity. Because Government borrowing is expected to increase next year, we anticipate virtually no change in the dollar level of total demands. Higher interest rates, the overhang of existing debt and the mood of uncertainty will discourage mortgage and installment borrowing.

The bond market will remain volatile and will likely witness another major setback. The push toward higher interest rates will intensify as foreign investors grow wary of new international policy frictions and evidence of higher U.S. inflation. Long-term Treasuries will rise to 11% or higher, perhaps as early as the summer.

Yields in Japan and West Germany will also trend higher, rising by 50–100 basis points from their lows. The much faster increase in U.S. yields implies a widening of spreads versus these markets.

(Bond Market Research Department of Salomon Brothers, *Prospects for Financial Markets in 1988*, 1987, p. 2; © 1987 by Salomon Brothers, Inc.)

## The Effect of Money Supply Announcements on Interest Rates

Speculators in the financial markets recognize that a change in the money supply may have a predictable effect on interest rates. Therefore, they attempt to profit from the announcement of such a change. If speculators expect market interest rates to decline as the result of an announced increase in the money supply, for example, they might purchase debt securities before the interest rates fall and the security prices rise.

Naturally, there are pitfalls to this strategy. For one thing, other speculators may also have anticipated the announcement and already purchased the securities, so their prices may already be high. For another, an announced increase in the money supply may also indicate that the Fed will pursue a *tighter monetary policy in the near future* in order to stabilize the money supply. In this case, after the announcement is made, security prices may actually *fall*. Thus to earn a profit on money supply announcements, it is critical to know what other speculators are *already expecting* and to know how the announcement is likely to affect *expectations of future monetary policy*.

## The Role of the Interest Elasticity of Money Demand

Given that an increase in the money supply reduces the interest rate, the interest elasticity of money demand is a factor in determining *how much* the interest rate will fall. Figure 16.5 shows how the interest rate responds for two alternative money demand curves, when the money supply increases from the line $M^*$ to the line $M'$. The money demand curve $E$ is the interest elastic curve and curve $I$ is the interest inelastic curve, both shown earlier in Figure 16.1.

We have arranged the demand curves so that the opportunity cost $r_0^*$ is the initial equilibrium rate for both, given the initial money supply line $M^*$. After the money supply shifts to $M'$, the equilibrium interest rate is $r_E'$ or $r_I'$, for curve $E$ or curve $I$, respectively.

FIGURE 16.5

**Interest Rate Changes and the Interest Elasticity of Money Demand**

When the money supply curve shifts to the right, the interest rate falls more with the inelastic demand curve *I* than with the elastic curve *E*.

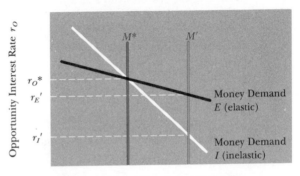

Money Supply and Demand

As shown in the figure, the equilibrium rate falls more when the demand curve is *inelastic*—$r_I'$ is lower than $r_E'$. This occurs because an inelastic demand curve means that people are less responsive to interest rates, so the interest rate has to fall substantially before people will hold the additional supply of money. In contrast, if the money demand curve is interest elastic, then even a small decline in interest rates may be adequate to cause people to hold the additional supply of money.

## Summary of Money Supply Shifts and Interest Rate Changes

We have seen that when the money supply curve shifts, the interest rate—the opportunity cost of money—can adjust to reestablish equilibrium between money demand and money supply. Specifically:

1. When the money supply rises, the interest rate must fall, to induce people to hold the larger money supply.
2. The interest rate falls more when the interest rate elasticity of the demand for money is low.

However, the interest rate is not the only variable that may change to establish equilibrium. Nominal income is another.

## Nominal Income as the Source of Money Market Equilibrium

When the money supply increases, people can either spend the additional money or lend it. Having seen that interest rates fall when people lend the extra money, we will now see that nominal income—that is, either real income or the price level—can rise when people spend it.

The effect of an increase in the money supply on nominal income is illustrated in Figure 16.6. In this analysis, the opportunity cost of money $r_0$ is treated as a fixed value. The positively sloped demand curve represents the positive relationship between the demand for money and nominal income. The vertical supply curve assumes that the Fed is maintaining the money supply at the level it desires.

The initial equilibrium for money demand and supply occurs at point $M$ in Figure 16.6, where nominal income is $Y^*$. An easier monetary policy shifts the money supply curve to the right, from $M^*$ to $M'$, in the same manner we have seen in the previous diagrams. Here the result is that the equilibrium value of nominal income rises from $Y^*$ to $Y'$.

At point $M$, where money demand equals money supply, the equilibrium value of nominal income is $Y^*$. An increase in the money supply from $M^*$ to $M'$— easier monetary policy—causes nominal income to rise to $Y'$.

FIGURE 16.6
**Nominal Income Determination and Money Demand**

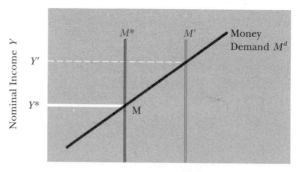

Money Supply and Demand

The amount by which nominal income rises when the money supply rises depends on the income elasticity of money demand. In particular, for a given change in the money supply, the lower the income elasticity of money demand, the more income will rise, as illustrated in Figure 16.7. In other words, if the demand for money is inelastic with respect to nominal income, then a given increase in nominal income will cause people to hold relatively little additional money; so for a given increase in the money supply, nominal income must rise substantially to reestablish equilibrium.

In the case of the income elastic money demand curve E, a relatively small increase in income creates a large increase in money demand. So a small increase in income can reestablish equilibrium in the market for money. In the case of the income inelastic money demand curve I, a larger increase in income is necessary to increase money demand and reestablish equilibrium.

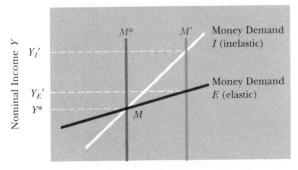

FIGURE 16.7

**Nominal Income Changes and the Income Elasticity of Money Demand**

Money Supply and Demand

## Changes in the Money Supply: Interest Rates and Income

We have now seen that there are two possible effects of an increase in the money supply: (1) the interest rate falls, and (2) nominal income rises. Why two results? The reason is that we are using partial equilibrium analysis: nominal income is fixed in the first case, and the interest rate is fixed in the second case. In Part VII, we will consider more general cases, based on general equilibrium analysis, in which interest rates and nominal income may adjust together.

## Inflation, Interest Rates, and the Money Supply

Since nominal income is the product of real income and the price level, if monetary policy affects nominal income, it must thereby also affect the price level or real income. For example, if the economy is initially near full employment, so that real income cannot rise immediately, then an increase in the money supply may have its predominant effect on the price level. Whereas if the economy is below full employment, both real income and the price level may rise. Generally speaking, a continuing increase in the money supply will cause the price level to rise at some point, because real income will reach the full-employment level.

Since *inflation* involves an increase in the price level, an increase of the money supply can cause inflation. Because of the connection between nominal interest rates, real interest rates, and inflation, inflation is an additional channel through which the money supply can influence interest rates. Recall from Chapter 4 that:

nominal interest rate = real interest rate + inflation rate.

From this relationship, we can see that a change in the nominal interest rate can be attributed to changes in either the real interest rate or the inflation rate. To the extent that an increase in the money supply raises the inflation rate, the inflation component of the nominal interest rate will rise. This is called the **inflation effect.**

However, we have also seen that an increase in the money supply can cause the nominal interest rate to fall. So it follows that an increase in the money supply can cause the real interest rate to fall. This is called the *liquidity effect*—the effect of increased liquidity (an increase in the money supply) on real and nominal interest rates.

The relative magnitude and timing of the inflation and liquidity effects of an increase in the money supply are a matter of uncertainty and sometimes controversy in economics. One view is that the liquidity effect tends to come first, followed later by the inflation effect. After all, nominal interest rates change minute by minute in the financial markets, while it generally takes time for the prices of goods and services to change. So, there may be a short run in which an increase in the money supply causes the nominal interest rate to fall—the liquidity effect—and a long run in which the nominal interest rate falls less or rises—the inflation effect.

The inflation effect can depend on *expected* inflation or on *actual* inflation. This corresponds to the distinction between *ex post* real interest rates (which depend on actual inflation) and *ex ante* real interest rates (which depend on expected inflation), as discussed in Chapter 4. If an increase in the money supply immediately causes higher inflationary expectations, then the inflation effect could immediately create upward pressure on nominal interest rates.

Distinctions can also be made between a one-time increase in the money supply and a continuing increase (the Federal Reserve raises the growth rate of the money supply). With a one-time increase, the price level will eventually adjust to the new level of the money supply, after which the inflation effect will stop. So the inflation effect on the nominal interest rate would be temporary. In contrast, with a continuing increase in the money supply, inflation may continue, causing nominal interest rates to remain higher.

*Summary.* An increase in the money supply has both liquidity and inflation effects on interest rates. An increase in the money supply may cause real interest rates to fall in the short run due to the liquidity effect, but nominal interest rates may rise in the long run due to the inflation effect.

## Empirical Evidence on the Demand for Money

We have discussed a variety of effects that depend on the interest rate and income elasticities of the demand for money. In this section, we will look at the empirical evidence regarding these elasticities. This discussion will also demonstrate something about how economists evaluate theories against real world observations, data, and evidence.

## Estimating Money Demand Elasticities

The first step in evaluating money demand theories is to look at the available data. We will start by looking at the data for income and the stock of money (M1 money supply) as a step toward evaluating the income elasticity of money demand. Figure 16.8 shows a standard tool—a *scatter diagram*—used for this purpose. Each point marked as • in this diagram is an *observation*, meaning that it represents a pair of values—one for annual income $Y$ and the other for the stock of money $M$—which were observed on a specific date. A complete scatter diagram represents a full set of observations, such as one for the last day of each year.

FIGURE 16.8

**A Scatter Diagram of Income Y and the Stock of Money M**
Dollars in billions

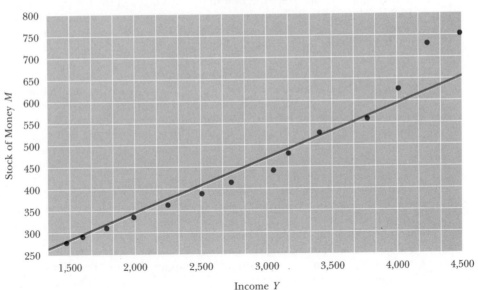

The • marks represent data observations of nominal income $Y$ and the stock of money $M$ at different dates. Estimated income and interest rate elasticities are based on the equation for the demand for money that the regression line, the straight line that most closely fits the data, represents. **Source:** *Economic Report of the President,* February, 1988.

The information in a scatter diagram can be summarized by sketching a line that closely *fits* the observations, as shown in Figure 16.8. A fitted line is technically called a **regression line,** referring to the statistical method that is used to determine it. Box 16.3 describes how regression analysis works.

BOX 16.3 IN DEPTH

## Fitting Regression Lines to a Scatter Diagram

Based on the observation points in Figure 16.8, your eye can probably pick out the broad outline of the positive relationship that should exist between income and the demand for money. The purpose of regression analysis is to identify the specific line, and the equation for that line, that provides the closest fit to the observations.

The first step is to draw a trial line, such as the one shown in Figure 16.8. The vertical distance between this line and each observation is a *residual*. Each residual measures how closely the trial line fits (or approximates) the corresponding observation. By squaring each of the residuals and summing them for all the observations, we obtain a summary measure of how well the trial line fits the observations.

This technique can be repeated for alternative trial lines to judge which one provides the best fit to the observations. In practice, formulas are used to determine, in one step, the best line. The equation for the line in Figure 16.8 is: $M = 0.2Y$. Because the demand for money is determined by more than one variable—including the price level, real income, and the opportunity cost of money—an expanded version of the technique—*multivariate regression analysis*—is often used.

There are also a number of *econometric issues*—econometrics being the application of statistical techniques in economics—in estimating money demand equations. One of these issues—*simultaneous equation bias*—comes into play in estimating the effect of nominal income on money demand, because the causation may also run in the other direction—the amount of money may affect income. The result is that an estimate of the effect of income on money demand may overstate the truth (although there are additional statistical methods that deal with this problem).

Another problem is that money demand functions may not be *stable*— that is, the equation determining money demand may change over time. A particularly important example is that the amount of money people want to hold may depend on the rule they think (or know) the Federal Reserve is following in determining the money supply. As a result of problems such as these, specific numerical estimates of money demand equations have to be interpreted with caution.

An *estimate* of the income elasticity of money demand is obtained when a regression line is fitted to the actual data. This estimate can be used to evaluate alternative theories of money demand. The same technique is also used to obtain estimates of the interest rate elasticity of money demand. Together, these provide the main information that is available to evaluate the alternative theories.

Estimates based on empirical evidence for the income and interest rate elasticities of money demand are shown in Table 16.1. Separate

**TABLE 16.1**
**Income and Interest Rate Elasticities of the Demand for Money**[a]

|  | Income Elasticity | Interest Rate Elasticity |
|---|---|---|
| Overall economy | 0.6 | −0.2 |
| Households | 1.1 | −0.4 |
| Business | 0.5 | −0.3 |

[a]Derived from the estimates of Stephen M. Goldfeld, "The Case of the Missing Money," *Brookings Papers on Economic Activity*, 1976, 3 pp. 683–740. The equation was estimated using data from 1952 to 1973.

estimates are shown for the money demand of the overall economy, of households alone, and of business firms alone. In all cases, the income elasticity is positive and the interest rate elasticity is negative, as predicted by all theories of money demand. The income elasticities range from a low value of 0.5 for the business sector to a high value of 1.1 for the household sector. The interest rate elasticities are estimated (based on the U.S. Treasury bill rate) to be in a narrower range, between −0.2 and −0.4. These can be compared with the theoretical values, summarized in Box 16.4, of the theories we studied in Chapter 15.

BOX 16.4 IN DEPTH

# Income and Interest Rate Elasticities of Money Demand

### The Classical Quantity Theory

The income elasticity of money demand is 1.0 (money demand is proportional to income). The interest rate elasticity is 0 (the theory does not consider interest rates to be a factor affecting money demand).

### The Baumol-Tobin Theory

The income elasticity of money demand is 0.5, and the interest rate elasticity is −0.5.

### The Keynesian Liquidity Preference Theory of Money Demand

The income elasticity is 1.0, since the theory is essentially the same as the Classical Quantity theory in this respect. However, the interest rate elasticity is based on the speculative demand for money, which predicts a significant (negative value) for this elasticity.

### Milton Friedman's Modern Quantity Theory

The income elasticity of money exceeds 1.0 (money is a luxury good) and money demand depends on permanent income. The interest rate elasticity may be small, given Friedman's use of a broad definition of money.

## Instability in Money Demand Equations: The Case of the Missing Money

For many years, money demand equations based on the estimated elasticities of Table 16.1 fitted closely with the new data for money, income, and interest rates that became available each year. This meant that policy makers could rely on these estimated money demand equations as a guide for determining how much money to provide each year.

However, the accuracy of the equations started to deteriorate in the mid-1970s: people were holding less money than the amount predicted by the equations. This became known as **the case of the missing money.** Later, the process reversed itself, so there was also **the case of the surplus money.**

The situation is illustrated in Figure 16.9, which is the same as Figure 16.8, except that the year of each observation is labeled. The four observation points for the years 1978 to 1981 represent the amount of money people were actually holding in these years. In contrast, the regression line shows the amount of money demand predicted by an estimated equation for money demand. The fact that the observation points lie below the regression line indicates that people were holding less money in those years than the amounts predicted by the equation.

FIGURE 16.9
**The Case of the Missing Money**
Dollars in billions

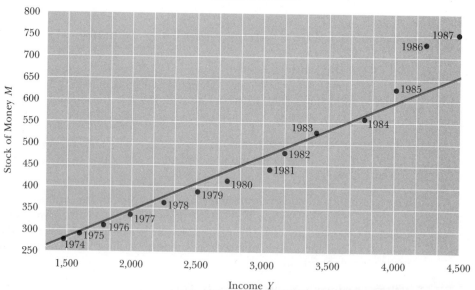

For the years 1978 to 1981, the amount of money held (the ● marks) was less than the demand for money predicted by the equation from the fitted regression line. This is the "case of the missing money."

After 1982, we see the opposite case: the amount of money held generally exceeds the demand for money predicted by the equation from the fitted regression line. This is the "return" of the missing money. **Source:** *Economic Report of the President,* February, 1988.

The mystery would be solved if some factor not included in the estimated money demand equation had caused people to hold less money. A solution to the mystery thus required identifying the factor or factors that might have caused such a downward shift in money demand. Payments system factors were the main suspects because they had not been included in the estimated equations. We will now look at four payments system factors, each of which provides a plausible explanation for why the money demand equation shifted down.

1. **Credit Cards**
   As discussed in Chapter 15, credit cards decrease the demand for money because they increase the degree of synchronization between consumption payments and income receipts. Credit card use was expanding rapidly during the late 1970s, and this could explain why people were suddenly holding less money than was predicted by the money demand equation.

2. **Money Substitutes**
   Money substitutes are financial instruments that are used to substitute for money, either as a medium of exchange or as a store of value. Money market funds, discussed in Chapter 13, are a money substitute that serve both these functions. Money market funds were expanding rapidly during the late 1970s, and this could be the reason that people held less money than expected.

3. **Higher Rates Paid on Bank Time Deposits**
   Bank time deposits are not included in the M1 definition of money, although they are included in the broader M2 definition. Banks began to pay higher interest rates on time deposits in the late 1970s when Regulation Q interest rate ceilings on these deposits were lifted. Higher rates on time deposits, of course, give people an incentive to shift money from currency and checking deposits to time deposits, so this could explain why people were holding less M1 money.

4. **High Inflation**
   The "tax" effect of inflation causes people to reduce their money holdings: inflation depreciates the value of money and therefore imposes a high cost on holding it. High inflation could thus explain why the demand for money suddenly fell. Inflation had been relatively low in the United States until the time of the missing money.

As it happened, the case of the missing money disappeared as an issue almost as quickly as it had arrived. In fact, moving into the 1980s, a surplus of money appeared. The surplus situation is illustrated in Figure 16.9 by the points after 1982 (except 1984), which indicate that people were holding more money than the amount predicted by the estimated money demand equation.

The banking deregulation of the early 1980s is the likely reason that a surplus of money developed. We just saw that lifting the Regulation Q ceilings on bank time deposits was a possible explanation for the earlier case of the missing money. However, the ceilings were also lifted on checking accounts, and this provided incentive for people to reverse their earlier transfers out of checking accounts. Money becomes more attractive when it pays more interest. So this payments system factor may explain why people were holding so much money in the early 1980s.

Unexpected shifts in money demand are still occurring as evidenced by the data in Figure 16.9 for 1986 and 1987. Such instability, or potential instability, makes the task of monetary policy—determining the right amount of money to supply—more complicated.

## Instability in Money Demand Equations: The Velocity of Money

Figure 16.10 shows a detailed version of the graph of the GNP velocity of the $M1$ money supply—GNP/$M1$—first presented in Chapter 1. Here we will focus on recent trends in the velocity of money. Between 1974 and 1981, the long-standing upward trend in velocity continued. After 1981, the trend suddenly reversed and became negative. Interest rates and payments system factors are both possible sources of this reversal.

Regarding *interest rates*, their changes paralleled those of the velocity of money over the period of the graph, rising before 1981 and falling afterward. Since the GNP velocity of money equals GNP divided by the

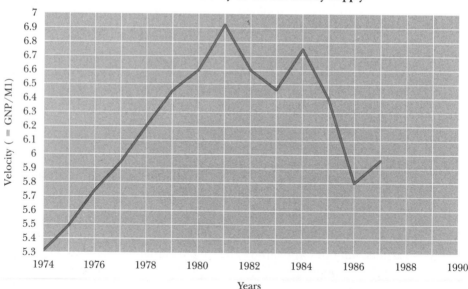

FIGURE 16.10
**The GNP Velocity of the M1 Money Supply**

Two major trends are evident in this graph of the velocity of money: a rising trend from 1974 until 1981, and a falling trend—with the exception of 1984—from 1981–1986. Interest rates and payments system factors may explain these trends. **Source:** *Economic Report of the President,* February 1988.

stock of money, $V = \text{GNP}/M1$, and since the demand for money falls when interest rates rise, the velocity of money should move in step with interest rates. So the observed trends in velocity are consistent with the pattern of interest rates.

Regarding *payments system factors*, the same factors that were culprits in the cases of the missing and surplus money could also be responsible for the trends in velocity. That is, the payments system factors that reduced the demand for money until 1981 would have also increased the velocity of money; and the factors that increased the demand for money after 1981 would have decreased the velocity of money. So the trends in velocity are also consistent with the changes in payments system factors.

Fluctuations in the velocity of money make it more difficult for the Federal Reserve to manage monetary policy. As can be seen from the quantity equation of exchange, $MV = Py$, variations in the velocity of money $V$ make it more difficult for the Fed to use the money supply $M$ to reach a desired goal for the price level $P$ or real income $y$. This and other issues regarding monetary policy are addressed in Part V.

## Chapter Summary

1. The demand for money is determined by three sets of factors: the opportunity cost of money (the interest rate on securities minus the interest rate paid on money), nominal income, and payments system factors.

2. The supply of money is determined by two basic factors: the monetary base and the opportunity cost of money. The opportunity cost of money influences the money supply because it affects the reserve drains—currency, excess reserves, and time deposits—which determine the money supply multiplier.

3. Two main variables—the opportunity cost of money and nominal income—can adjust to establish equilibrium between the demand and supply of money. For example, as the result of a larger money supply, the interest rate falls or nominal income rises. In each case, the change is generally larger if the demand for money is more inelastic.

4. Since nominal income is the product of the price level and real income, an increase in the money supply will also generally raise prices—that is, create inflation. When the money supply increases, the nominal interest rate (the sum of the real interest and the inflation rate) may fall due to the larger money supply (the liquidity effect) or may rise because of the higher inflation rate (the inflation effect).

5. Historical data are used to estimate the actual income and interest rate elasticities of money demand. The "case of the missing money" in the late 1970s and the "case of the surplus money" in the early 1980s are particular episodes that illustrate the impact of payments system factors on the demand for money.

6. The properties of money demand functions can also be studied by analyzing the velocity of money. Between 1974 and 1981, the velocity of money rose; but it has been falling in recent years. These trends in velocity can be explained by the same payments factors used in the case of the missing money.

## Key Terms

Cases of the missing money and the surplus money

Elasticity of money demand with respect to:

Income

Interest-rate

Interest rate theories:

LF (loanable funds)

MD/MS (money demand/money supply)

General and partial equilibrium

Money supply effects on nominal interest rates:

Inflation effects

Liquidity effects

Regression line

Variables affecting money demand:

Nominal income

Opportunity cost of money

Payments system factors

Variables affecting money supply:

Monetary base

Opportunity cost of money

## Study Questions

1. Why is the demand for money negatively related to the opportunity cost of holding money, but positively related to nominal income?

2. Why is the supply of money positively related to the monetary base and to the opportunity cost of holding money?

3. Define the interest rate and income elasticities of money demand. According to the Baumol-Tobin theory, what are the values for each of these?

4. How can the Federal Reserve create a vertical money supply curve, even though the money supply depends on the opportunity cost of money?

5. How does the interest rate elasticity of money demand affect how much the interest rate falls when the money supply rises?

6. How does the income elasticity of money demand affect how much income rises when the money supply rises?

7. Why can the Federal Reserve operate with smaller changes in the monetary base when money demand is inelastic with respect to the interest rate and to income?

8. How can an increase in the money supply cause the real rate of interest to fall while the nominal rate of interest rises?

9. Why are payments system factors probably responsible for the "case of the missing money" and the "case of the surplus money"?

10. Why are trends in the velocity of money consistent with recent trends in interest rates?

## Recommended Reading

*In addition to the references given in Chapter 15, this book provides a thorough description of the evidence used to evaluate alternative theories of money demand:*

David Laidler, *The Demand for Money: Theories and Evidence,* 3rd edition, 1985.

*A recent survey of the many issues involved in estimated demand functions for money:*

John Judd and John Scadding, "The Search for a Stable Money Demand Function," *Journal of Economic Literature,* September 1982, pp. 993–1023.

*A description of the case of the missing money and the source of the estimates of the income and interest rate elasticities in Table 16.1:*

Stephen Goldfeld, "The Case of the Missing Money," *Brookings Papers on Economic Activity,* 1976, pp. 683–740.

Stephen Goldfeld, "The Demand for Money Revisited," *Brookings Papers on Economic Activity,* 1973, pp. 577–646.

# Monetary Policy and the Federal Reserve System

The Federal Reserve's most important task as the central bank of the United States is to implement monetary policy. As we study monetary policy and the Fed in this part, we will be making use of many of the things we studied earlier, including: how the money supply is determined and money market equilibrium is established; how banks and the banking system operate, and how interest rates are determined in the financial markets.

We will also combine three different aspects of money, banking, and credit: *theory* (how things work in principle); *institutions* (how they work in practice), and *policy* (how they might work better). For example, in Chapter 16, we studied the money demand/money supply *theory* of interest rates, showing that an increase in the money supply should cause interest rates to fall, other things being equal. Now we will look at why and when the Federal Reserve increases the money supply to try to reduce interest rates.

We will look at the organization of the Federal Reserve System and at the goals of monetary policy in Chapter 17. Within the Federal Reserve System, monetary policy is determined by the Board of Governors, and specifically by a powerful committee called the Federal Open Market Committee. Because people—in-

cluding Congress and the presidential administration—have different views about monetary policy, the Federal Reserve works hard to maintain its right to formulate an independent monetary policy. The result is that Congress and the administration determine the overall *goals* of monetary policy—such as low rates of inflation and unemployment—while the Federal Reserve implements monetary policy to meet the goals.

The Federal Reserve uses the *instruments* of monetary policy to try to reach these goals. In Chapter 18, we will look at the instruments the Federal Reserve uses—open market operations, the discount window, and reserve requirements. Open market operations—buying and selling government securities—are the main instrument the Fed uses to determine monetary aggregates (bank reserves, the monetary base, and the money supply) and interest rates. The discount window is the facility through which the Federal Reserve can directly lend money to banks. Reserve requirements are ratios that banks must maintain between the amount of their deposits and the amount of their reserves.

In a simple world, the Federal Reserve could use its instruments like the volume dial on a stereo, turning the power up if the economy needs a boost, and turning it down if the economy is too strong. Unfortunately, the real world is more complex—and so is managing monetary policy. For one thing, after the Federal Reserve changes an instrument—turns the dial—the effects on the policy goals often occur with long time lags. For another thing, the magnitude of the effects is uncertain—it is even possible that nothing at all will happen. In Chapter 19, we will look at the Fed's techniques for tuning the economy.

Learning often comes through experience, and the Fed is not an exception. In Chapter 20, we will look at the Fed's practical experiences in coping with a diverse range of economic conditions under the leadership of different chairmen of the Board of Governors.

Equilibrium for international trade and finance is one other factor that plays a role in monetary policy. We will look at this topic in Part VI.

# The Federal Reserve System and the Goals of Monetary Policy

*"A feast is made for laughter, and wine maketh merry, but money answereth all things."*

*Ecclesiastes*

How would you feel if your every action was being watched by highly trained observers? Every time you go to a meeting, they study the minutes, every time you miss a meeting, they try to guess why. Whenever you say something, they work so hard at interpreting it that you consider not saying anything at all.

Such is the life of the chairman of the Federal Reserve System, the main spokesman for the central bank of the United States. The people who watch his actions so closely are "Fed Watchers;" they are employed by Wall Street firms that want to know about Federal Reserve actions as promptly as possible—preferably before anyone else.

In his book, *Fed Watching and Interest Rate Projections: A Practical Guide,* David Jones—a highly successful Fed watcher himself—provides some basic rules for interpreting Federal Reserve actions:

- Watch what the Fed watches—not what you think it should watch.
- View potential Fed policy shifts as a reaction to—rather than a cause of—undesired economic or monetary fluctuations.
- Try to anticipate the next Fed policy shift—not to explain the last one.
- Pay attention to what the Fed does—not to what it says.

This should give you a basis for doing some Fed watching of your own.

In this chapter we will look systematically at the structure, activities, and goals of the Federal Reserve System.

The Federal Reserve System—the U.S. *central bank*—is the federal agency with responsibility for *monetary policy*. We begin this chapter by describing the structure of the Federal Reserve System and how it operates. We will then discuss the relationship of the Fed to the major branches of the federal government, particularly how the Federal Reserve tries to remain independent of them. Lastly, we will look at the goals of Federal Reserve monetary policy.

## The Structure of the Federal Reserve System

Since it was created by Congress in 1913, the **Federal Reserve System** has changed relatively little—testimony to a good design—although some changes were made during the 1930s. The system has three main components: the Board of Governors, which sets system policy; the twelve regional Federal Reserve banks, which carry out the system's banking business; and the member banks, which are the commercial banks that belong to the system. More than 25,000 people are employed in the Federal Reserve System. A flow diagram of its organizational structure is shown in Figure 17.1.

### The Board of Governors

The seven members of the **Board of Governors** are the chief executives of the Federal Reserve. Governors are appointed by the president with the advice and consent of the Senate for fourteen-year terms of office. The terms are staggered so that a new governor starts every two years; thus, a president who serves for eight years can select four of the seven members. In addition, most presidents have the opportunity to fill the terms of resigning governors.

The president also designates one governor as the **Chairman** of the Board of Governors, for a four-year term. The chairman presides at meetings of the Board, assigns each governor specific tasks, and is the main spokesman for the Federal Reserve. However, Board decisions are made by majority vote, so the Board can overrule the chairman.

Influential chairmen usually have specific programs, strong personalities, and strong support from Congress, the president, and the financial markets. Paul Volcker, a recent chairman, had extraordinary influence on this account, as we will see throughout this part of the book. Box 17.1 describes what Volcker did after he was not reappointed for a third term by President Reagan in 1987.

### The Regional Federal Reserve Banks

The twelve **regional Federal Reserve banks** manage a variety of important tasks for the Federal Reserve System, such as check clearing and

## FIGURE 17.1
### The Organizational Structure of the Federal Reserve System

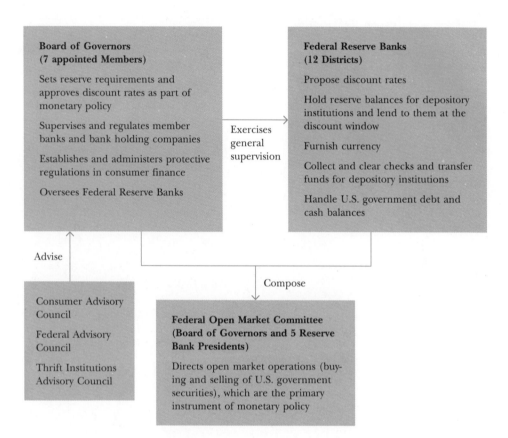

**Board of Governors (7 appointed Members)**

Sets reserve requirements and approves discount rates as part of monetary policy

Supervises and regulates member banks and bank holding companies

Establishes and administers protective regulations in consumer finance

Oversees Federal Reserve Banks

Exercises general supervision

**Federal Reserve Banks (12 Districts)**

Propose discount rates

Hold reserve balances for depository institutions and lend to them at the discount window

Furnish currency

Collect and clear checks and transfer funds for depository institutions

Handle U.S. government debt and cash balances

Advise

Consumer Advisory Council

Federal Advisory Council

Thrift Institutions Advisory Council

Compose

**Federal Open Market Committee (Board of Governors and 5 Reserve Bank Presidents)**

Directs open market operations (buying and selling of U.S. government securities), which are the primary instrument of monetary policy

Source: *The Federal Reserve System: Purposes and Functions,* Board of Governors of the Federal Reserve System, Washington D.C., 1984.

other business with member banks in their region. The *Federal Reserve districts* and the branch offices of the twelve Reserve banks are shown in the map in Figure 17.2. Each Reserve bank has a board of directors consisting of six members elected by the member banks of the district and three members appointed by the Board of Governors. Nominations for the president and vice-president of each reserve bank must be approved by the Board of Governors. So, in practice, the governors dominate the selection process.

Each Reserve bank carries out the daily business of the Federal Reserve System in its district. One key task is to operate the discount loan window for depository institutions that have their home offices in the district. The Reserve banks decide which loan requests to honor and they initiate changes in the discount rate. However, the Board of Governors has the final say on all discount rate changes.

BOX 17.1 MONEY MATTERS

## What's Next After Being Fed Chairman?

Since World War II, Chairmen of the Board of Governors of the Federal Reserve System have had varied backgrounds: Wall Street (William McChesney Martin), academia (Arthur Burns), business (G. William Miller), public service (Paul Volcker), and economic forecasting (Alan Greenspan).

The following excerpt from the *Wall Street Journal* of March 3, 1988, tells what Paul Volcker decided to do after being chairman of the Federal Reserve System for eight years.

The great Volcker sweepstakes is over.

Former Federal Reserve Board Chairman Paul A. Volcker ended months of deliberation by announcing that he will become the chairman of James D. Wolfensohn Inc., a New York investment banking firm, and teach part time at Princeton University.

The choice of a small firm by the 60-year-old Mr. Volcker came as surprise to many on Wall Street, where big investment banks had been vying energetically for his services. . . .

Mr. Wolfensohn beamed as he sat with Mr. Volcker yesterday at the firm. "We've never had a former chairman of the Federal Reserve Board here before," Mr. Wolfensohn said. Both he and Mr. Volcker declined to discuss what Mr. Volcker would be paid as chairman of the investment bank. "I'm making more than as chairman of the

Fed," Mr. Volcker said. At the Fed, Mr. Volcker's annual salary was $89,500. . . .

During his eight years as chairman of the Fed, Mr. Volcker won worldwide respect for conducting a monetary policy that helped bring the U.S. inflation rate from 11.3% in 1979, the year he was appointed, to 3.7% last year. . . .

Because of his success as an inflation fighter, as a crisis manager and as someone who helped rebuild confidence in the U.S. economy, Mr. Volcker received a wide range of job offers. But he moved slowly, telling friends that he was reluctant to take a job where he would be "a door opener" or where he might be put in a position in which he felt he had to give advice that might run counter to national policy.

Before announcing his decision to join Wolfensohn, Mr. Volcker appeared yesterday at Princeton, which announced that he will become a professor there. He will teach half time at Princeton, serving on the faculty of the Woodrow Wilson School of Public and International Affairs. . . .

Mr. Volcker also will continue as an adviser to the World Bank in Washington.

(Kenneth H. Bacon and Peter Truell, *"Volcker Plans to Join Wolfensohn Firm As Chairman and to Teach at Princeton," Wall Street Journal*, 3 March, 1988.)

FIGURE 17.2
**Regional Federal Reserve Banks and Federal Reserve Districts**

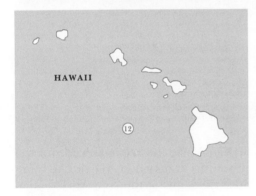

—— Boundaries of Federal Reserve Districts

—— Boundaries of Federal Reserve Branch
Territories

⊗ Board of Governors of the Federal
Reserve System

⊚ Federal Reserve Bank Cities

▵ Federal Reserve Branch Cities

• Federal Reserve Bank Facility

The United States is divided up into twelve Federal
Reserve districts, each of which has a regional Federal Reserve bank. **Source:** *The Federal Reserve Bulletin*,
1988.

## The Distribution of Power Within the Federal Reserve System

As envisioned in the original Federal Reserve Act of 1913, power in the Federal Reserve System was to be balanced between the Board of Governors in Washington and the regional Reserve banks. This reflected a compromise, following a Congressional battle, between those wishing to centralize power in the Board and those wishing to decentralize power in the Reserve banks. The governors have now come to dominate the System on most matters, particularly those relating to monetary policy.

An interesting insider's view of the Federal Reserve System is provided by Sherman Maisel, who was an economics professor at the University of California at Berkeley before becoming a Federal Reserve governor between 1965 and 1972. Based on his experiences as a member of the Board of Governors, Maisel estimated the relative power of various groups within the Federal Reserve System in determining monetary policy. As shown in Table 17.1, he attributes most of the power to the chairman, the other governors, and their staffs, leaving only 10% with the Reserve banks.

| TABLE 17.1 | |
|---|---|
| **The Balance of Power Within the Federal Reserve System** | |
| The chairman | 45% |
| The staff of the Board and FOMC[a] | 25% |
| The other governors | 20% |
| Federal Reserve banks | 10% |

[a]Federal Open Market Committee to be described in the text.

**Source:** Adapted from *Managing the Dollar* by Sherman J. Maisel, by permission of W. W. Norton & Company, Inc., Copyright © 1973, by Sherman J. Maisel.

The Federal Reserve Bank of New York, the regional bank for the New York district, carries out all security transactions relating to monetary policy for the Board of Governors, giving the New York bank a predominant position in the Federal Reserve System. At times, the president of the New York bank has even challenged the Board of Governors for influence. Benjamin Strong, the first head of the Federal Reserve Bank of New York, is a good example. However, cases like Strong's are infrequent exceptions to the dominant power of the Board of Governors.

The Reserve banks are treated like private banks in many respects (such as relatively high salary scales), whereas the Board of Governors is generally treated as a public agency (with salaries based on standard government scales). The difference was illustrated in July 1979 when Paul Volcker left the presidency of the Federal Reserve Bank of New York to become the chairman of the Board of Governors: his salary was cut from $116,000 to $60,000; by 1987, the chairman's salary had risen to $89,500. Such is the cost of public service, or power.

## The Federal Open Market Committee

**The Federal Open Market Committee (FOMC)** determines most aspects of Federal Reserve monetary policy. Most importantly, the FOMC decides on purchases and sales of securities—called *open market operations*—through which the Federal Reserve controls the *monetary base* (as we discussed in Chapter 14). The FOMC also controls Federal Reserve operations in foreign exchange markets. Accordingly, the FOMC is the most important policy arm within the Federal Reserve System.

The FOMC consists of twelve members: seven governors, the president of the Federal Reserve Bank of New York, and the presidents of four other Reserve banks who serve on a rotating basis. However, all of the Reserve bank presidents attend meetings and participate in the discussions. The FOMC meets approximately once a month, and additional meetings are held as required.

The FOMC provides *policy directives* to the Domestic Manager, System Open Market Account, at the Federal Reserve Bank of New York, who implements them. This part of the New York bank is called the *Trading Desk*—it carries out the main transactions of buying and selling securities for the Federal Reserve System. Box 17.2 shows a sample of an FOMC policy directive. Fed watchers meticulously study these directives to keep current with Federal Reserve policy.

---

BOX 17.2 MONEY MATTERS

### An FOMC Policy Directive

The following is an excerpt from the FOMC meeting of February 10–11, 1987, as reported in the *Federal Reserve Bulletin* of June 1987. (The Fed always delays the release of the minutes from FOMC meetings to maintain their secrecy.)

At its meeting on February 10–11, 1987 the Committee established monetary growth ranges for 1987 of 5 1/2 to 8 1/2 percent for both M2 and M3. The associated range for growth in total domestic nonfinancial debt was set at 8 to 11 percent. The Committee anticipated that growth in M1 would slow in 1987 from its very rapid pace in 1986, but the members decided not to establish a precise target for the year; instead, the appropriateness of M1 changes would be evaluated during the year in the light of the behavior of M1 velocity, developments in the economy and financial markets, and the nature of emerging price pressures. . . . The members agreed that the intermeeting range for the federal funds rate. . . should be left unchanged at 4 to 8%.

## The Member Banks

The commercial banks that belong to the Federal Reserve constitute another tier of the System—the **member banks.** All federally chartered commercial banks are automatically members; state-chartered banks may choose to belong. Member banks "own" the regional Reserve banks in the sense that: (1) they own the common stock of the Reserve banks; (2) they elect six people to each Reserve bank's Board of Directors; and (3) they are paid a fixed 6% dividend rate on the Reserve bank common stock they own. Nevertheless, the member banks do not control the policies of the Reserve banks—this power resides with the Board of Governors.

Member banks receive various Federal Reserve services, but they must abide by the Fed's regulations, most importantly, the reserve requirements. As discussed in Chapter 10, the Depository Institutions Deregulation and Monetary Control Act of 1980 provided *all depository institutions* with access to Federal Reserve services, but it also imposed reserve requirements on them.

## Profits of the Federal Reserve System

The Federal Reserve System earns immense profits—about $20 billion annually in recent years—representing primarily interest earnings on its portfolio of U.S. Treasury securities. As we saw in Chapter 14, the Federal Reserve pays for securities by issuing Federal Reserve notes—currency printed for the Fed by the Bureau of Engraving and Printing—or even more simply, by crediting the seller's reserve deposit account at the Federal Reserve. Neither form of payment represents much of a cost to the Federal Reserve: there is no cost to creating a reserve deposit and the cost of printing money is almost trivial. (Box 17.3 looks at the Federal Reserve's actual cost of printing its notes.) The Federal Reserve's profit potential from purchasing a portfolio of securities was first recognized in the 1920s by Benjamin Strong.

However, the Federal Reserve's large profits do not mean it has luxurious facilities: Congress controls Fed expenses, just as it does the expenses of other Federal agencies, through budget oversight. Moreover, the Federal Reserve is required to return most of its profits each year to the Treasury Department. Indeed, this has caused the Treasury to lobby against the Fed's paying interest on member bank reserve deposits, because this would reduce the amount to be turned over to the Treasury.

## The Tasks of the Federal Reserve System

The most important function of the Federal Reserve is monetary policy, as determined by the FOMC and the Board of Governors. However, as shown by the 1987 Federal Reserve budget in Table 17.2, monetary policy accounts for just a small part of the Fed's total expenses. We will now look at the other **Federal Reserve tasks** reflected in its expense budget.

BOX 17.3 MONEY MATTERS

## The Fed's Cost of Printing Money

The Federal Reserve Act requires the Fed to bear the costs of printing, maintaining, and retiring its currency. The Fed pays the Bureau of Engraving and Printing to produce Federal Reserve notes. The demand for notes, and the wear and tear on them, has increased in recent years due to the growth in automated teller and cash-dispensing machines. The Fed's 1987 budget for maintaining Federal Reserve notes is shown below. Given that the total cost of maintaining the currency during 1987 was $191 *million*, while about $200 *billion* of currency was outstanding

at year-end 1987, the annual cost per each $1,000 of currency outstanding was about $1.

### 1987 Federal Reserve Budget for New Currency

**Dollars in millions**

| | |
|---|---|
| Printing | $184 |
| Shipping | 5 |
| Reimbursements to the Treasury for issuance and retirement | 2 |
| Total cost to Federal Reserve | $191 |

**Source:** *Annual Report: Budget Review 1986–1988,* Board of Governors of the Federal Reserve System.

### Services to Financial Institutions

Services provided to member banks and other depository institutions represent a large part of the Federal Reserve's budget—$802 million in 1987. These services include the check-clearing system and related facilities to transfer funds electronically and to deliver currency and coins to banks.

Before 1980, these services were provided by the Federal Reserve either without charge or at artificially low prices, as an inducement for banks to become Fed members. However, the 1980 banking legislation required the Fed to set prices for its services in line with its costs. The objective was to make the Fed compete fairly with private companies that supply the same services, such as shipping currency and coins.

TABLE 17.2

Federal Reserve Expense Budget for 1987

**Dollars in millions**

| | |
|---|---|
| Monetary and economic policy | $ 147 |
| Services to financial institutions and the public | 802 |
| Supervision and regulation | 199 |
| Services to U.S. Treasury and government agencies | 136 |
| Total | $1,284 |

**Source:** *Annual Report: Budget Review 1986–1987,* Table 1.2, Board of Governors of the Federal Reserve System.

## Supervision and Regulation

Together with state and other federal banking regulators, the Federal Reserve System is responsible for supervising and examining banks and bank holding companies. The Fed also regulates bank mergers. Staff members at the Board of Governors and at the Reserve banks gather the relevant information on each matter, and then the policy decision is made by the Board of Governors.

The Fed shares the task of supervising member state-chartered banks with state banking regulators, and of supervising federally chartered banks with the Comptroller of the Currency. The supervisors look at a bank's soundness and solvency, analyze its lending policies, and determine whether it is in compliance with banking laws. When a problem is found, the supervisors normally recommend a solution to the bank; if the problem is serious or the bank is not cooperative, cease and desist court orders can also be issued.

The Federal Reserve is also required by Congress to oversee consumer protection regulations for different types of financial transactions. Examples include: truth in lending, which requires disclosure of credit and loan terms; fair credit billing, which provides remedies for errors on credit cards and credit accounts; and electronic funds transfer, which delineates the rights of those using electronic transfer mechanisms.

## Fiscal Agent for the Federal Government

The Federal Reserve System performs a number of tasks as the primary bank for the federal government. One such task is to manage the Treasury Department's checking account. Federal government receipts from taxes and fees are usually first deposited in local banks—in special *Treasury tax and loan accounts*. The Treasury prefers to keep its deposits in local banks because it receives interest on the balances. But when the Treasury needs the funds for writing checks, it transfers the money to its account at the Federal Reserve. Most federal government checks are written on the Treasury Department's account at the Federal Reserve.

The Federal Reserve System is also the main agent for the Treasury Department in managing the federal debt. When the federal government runs a budget deficit, the Treasury must issue securities to cover the shortfall. Most of the securities are sold to investors through an auction process managed by the Federal Reserve. The cash proceeds of these sales are deposited in the Treasury's account at the Fed. Although the Federal Reserve normally does not purchase Treasury securities at the auctions, it does buy (and sell) outstanding Treasury securities, following the directives of the FOMC.

## Economic Research and Statistics

Both the Board of Governors in Washington and the Reserve banks maintain large staffs of economists who carry out research having to do with monetary, banking, and financial market developments with potential applications to Federal Reserve System policy. Some of the regional Reserve banks are well known for their specific style or "school" of economic research. The Federal Reserve System also publishes a diverse set of statistics, data bases, and reports, regarding money, banking, and credit. The list of Federal Reserve statistical releases in Box 17.4 shows the range of data available.

## Independence of the Federal Reserve System

**Federal Reserve independence** has been a major issue right from its founding in 1913, because of its unusual status as a *quasi-agency*, or *independent agency*. This means that the Fed is not part of either the Executive or the Legislative branch of the government. So, unlike agencies such as the Treasury Department, the Federal Reserve is not responsible on matters of policy to the president or any other branch of the government.

Independence in this context mainly concerns the right of the Fed to determine monetary policy, even if its views are contrary to those of Congress or the president. Nevertheless, the Fed is still part of the government—it was created by Congress, and therefore it could be dissolved by Congress—so its independence remains a matter of degree and circumstances.

Federal Reserve independence depends on the extent to which the Administration or Congress attempt to influence policy decisions. Table 17.3 shows how Sherman Maisel, whose views we looked at earlier regarding power *within* the Fed, evaluates the various *outside influences* on the Federal Reserve. Most would agree with Maisel in ranking the Administration first and Congress second in terms of influence, but there may be disagreement with the specific rankings of the other groups. In any case, it is clear that even with its quasi agency status, the Federal Reserve can be affected by the Administration and Congress.

---

**TABLE 17.3**
**Outside Influences on the Federal Reserve**

| | |
|---|---|
| The Administration (35%) | The Public Directly (20%) |
|   The President |   Unorganized |
|   The Treasury |   The press, economists |
|   The Council of Economic Advisers |   Lobbyists |
|   The Office of Management and Budget | The Financial Interests (10%) |
| The Congress (25%) |   Banks |
|   House and Senate Committees on Banking |   Savings and loan associations |
|   Joint Economic Committee |   Stockbrokers |
|   Senate Finance Committee | Foreign Interests (5%) |
|   House Ways and Means Committee | Other Regulatory Agencies (5%) |

**Source:** Sherman J. Maisel, *Managing the Dollar*, W. W. Norton, 1973, p. 110.

BOX 17.4 FINANCIAL NEWS

## Federal Reserve Statistical Releases

| | Date or Period To Which Data Refer |
|---|---|
| **Weekly Releases** | |
| Aggregate Reserves of Depository Institutions and the Monetary Base. | Week ended previous Wednesday |
| Actions of the Board: Applications and Reports Received | Week ended previous Saturday |
| Assets and Liabilities of Insured Domestically Chartered and Foreign Related Banking Institutions | Wednesday, 3 weeks earlier |
| Changes in State Member Banks | Week ended previous Saturday |
| Factors Affecting Reserves of Depository Institutions and Condition Statement of Federal Reserve Banks | Week ended previous Wednesday |
| Foreign Exchange Rates | Week ended previous Friday |
| Money Stock, Liquid Assets, and Debt Measures | Week ended Monday of previous week |
| Selected Borrowings in Immediately Available Funds of Large Member Banks | Week ended Thursday of previous week |
| Selected Interest Rates. | Week ended previous Saturday |
| Weekly Consolidated Condition Report of Large Commercial Banks, and Domestic Subsidiaries. | Wednesday, 1 week earlier |
| **Monthly Releases** | |
| Capacity Utilization: Manufacturing, Mining, Utilities and Industrial Materials. | Previous month |
| Changes in Status of Banks and Branches. | Previous month |
| Consumer Installment Credit. | 2nd month previous |
| Debits and Deposit Turnover at Commercial Banks. | Previous month |
| Finance Companies. | 2nd month previous |
| Foreign Exchange Rates. | Previous month |
| Industrial Production. | Previous month |
| Loans and Securities at all Commercial Banks. | Previous month |
| Major Nondeposit Funds of Commercial Banks. | Previous month |
| Monthly Report of Assets and Liabilities of International Banking Facilities. | Wednesday, 2 weeks earlier |
| Research Library—Recent Acquisitions. | Previous month |
| Selected Interest Rates. | Previous month |
| **Quarterly Releases** | |
| Agricultural Finance Databook. | January, April, July, and October |
| Country Exposure Lending Survey. | Previous 3 months |
| Domestic Offices, Commercial Bank Assets and Liabilities Consolidated Report of Condition. | Previous 6 months |
| Flow of Funds: Seasonally Adjusted and Unadjusted. | Previous quarter |
| Flow of Funds Summary Statistics. | Previous quarter |
| Geographical Distribution of Assets and Liabilities of Major Foreign Branches of U.S. Banks. E.11 | Previous quarter |
| Survey of Terms of Bank Lending. | February, May, August, and November |
| List of OTC Margin Stocks. | February, May, August, and November |
| **Semiannual Releases** | |
| Balance Sheets of the U.S. Economy. | Previous year |
| **Annual Releases** | |
| Aggregate Summaries of Annual Surveys of Securities Credit Extension. | End of previous June |

**Source:** *Federal Reserve Bulletin*, 1988.

## The Federal Reserve and the Administration

The relationship between the Federal Reserve and the administration regarding monetary policy has evolved over the years, reflecting both actual events and how observers view the relationship. One key event was the 1951 *Treasury/Federal Accord*, which granted *explicit independence* to the Federal Reserve. However, some careful observers have recently argued that the Federal Reserve is *implicitly controlled* by the administration. We will now look at the Accord and at current views of the relationship.

### The Treasury/Federal Reserve Accord of 1951

The original Federal Reserve Act in 1913 created only one formal link between the administration and the Federal Reserve—the secretary of the Treasury and the Comptroller of the Currency, both Presidential appointees, were *ex officio* members of the Board of Governors. Although this link was removed by the Banking Act of 1935, the emergency conditions of World War II allowed the Administration to reassert its control of the Federal Reserve.

In particular, the Fed had to support the Treasury in selling large issues of securities to finance the government deficits created by the war. The Treasury adopted a *pegging policy*—setting interest rates on Treasury securities from 3/8 of 1% on short-term debt to 2.5% on long-term debt. The Treasury could peg the interest rates because the Fed would buy any bonds that were not purchased by private investors, and, in fact, the Fed bought substantial amounts of Treasury securities during World War II under this policy.

Following the war, the pegging policy was the focus of a dispute between the Federal Reserve and the Treasury. Not surprisingly, the Treasury liked the low interest rates created by the pegging policy and wanted them to continue. However, the Federal Reserve was concerned that continuing purchases of Treasury securities would expand the money supply and create inflation. Inflation had been held in check during World War II by price controls.

Marriner Eccles was the Chairman of the Board of Governors at the time, having been appointed by President Roosevelt in 1934—the same Eccles who earlier succeeded in defending his Utah bank against a bank run, as we saw in Box 10.3. Eccles was a highly influential Fed chairman and was strongly opposed to continuing the pegging policy. As a result, he was not reappointed chairman by President Truman in 1948. However, Eccles completed his term as a member of the Board of Governors and used this position to fight hard for the Fed's independence.

By early 1951, the pegging dispute had become heated and public, with angry press releases flowing from both sides. However, cooler heads finally prevailed and the **Treasury/Federal Reserve Accord** was announced on March 4, 1951. The Accord recognized the independence of the Federal Reserve, and the wartime policy of pegging Treasury security interest rates was abandoned. The Accord also set the tone for future Federal Reserve/administration relations, eliminating most explicit attempts by the administration to control Federal Reserve monetary policy.

Presidential administrations may, of course, still criticize Federal Reserve monetary policy, and they do so frequently. But the Fed is free to answer back. Box 17.5 illustrates how this worked in a sharp exchange between a Treasury Department official and Fed chairman Alan Greenspan.

This case also illustrates the need for *coordination* between the monetary policy of the Federal Reserve and the fiscal (tax and expenditure) policy of the administration and Congress. The need to coordinate policies potentially limits the Fed's independence, but the Fed can retain an independent "vote" in setting the overall direction of macroeconomic policy, both monetary and fiscal.

## BOX 17.5 MONEY MATTERS

## The Treasury Department and the Fed Still Fight

The following excerpt from an article in the *Wall Street Journal* of February 25, 1988, shows the Treasury and Fed still fighting, almost forty years after their 1951 Accord:

Chairman Alan Greenspan of the Federal Reserve Board harshly criticized a top Treasury official's attempt to influence Fed policy and warned that further attempts could be dangerously counterproductive.

At a Senate Banking Committee hearing, Mr. Greenspan said, "I objected quite strongly" after learning of a letter sent to Reserve Board members and district reserve bank presidents by Assistant Treasury Secretary Michael Darby. In the letter, sent shortly before the latest meeting of the Fed's policy-setting Federal Open Market Committee, Mr. Darby argued that weak money growth posed a risk to the economy.

"All I can say is as best I can judge he was not aware of the implications of what he was doing just prior to an FOMC meeting," said Mr. Greenspan. "I am reasonably certain that such actions will not occur in the future." Mr.

Darby couldn't be reached for comment. . . .

Mr. Greenspan's statements seemed aimed at countering any suggestion that the Fed may be susceptible to undue influence from the Reagan administration. Mr. Greenspan, a Republican, heads a board that has been appointed entirely by President Reagan.

The Fed chief said he worries that efforts to influence the Reserve could backfire. He said he hopes the Fed's concern about political pressure doesn't get so "extraordinary we will feel the necessity to do precisely the opposite and . . . could very well be taking actions which would be counter to our best judgment."

At the same time, Mr. Greenspan said it's important that the Fed not shut itself off from all advice, adding: "I, myself, am not particularly concerned that we will be unduly influenced by the administration. I'm not certain that they really are intent upon pressuring us.

(Rose Gutfeld, "Greenspan Criticizes Top Treasury Aid for Attempting to Influence Fed's Policy," *Wall Street Journal*, 25 Feb. 1988.)

### The Political Business Cycle and Related Views

Although there has been little *explicit control* of Federal Reserve monetary policy by the administration, many economists now feel there might be substantial *implicit control*. According to one theory—called the **political business cycle**—the Fed has managed monetary policy to help incumbent presidents be reelected, reflecting implicit presidential control of monetary policy.[1] The idea is that a president may manipulate the economy to maximize the likelihood of reelection—such as by encouraging an easy monetary policy to stimulate the economy just before an election. Since this policy may later create inflation, tight monetary policy may be necessary after the election. Thus, the PBC theory predicts that easy monetary policy and a strong economy might be observed just before presidential elections, with the opposite after the election. Although certain episodes are consistent with the PBC theory, others are not. The period of Richard Nixon's reelection in 1972 fits the PBC theory; the period of Jimmy Carter's loss in 1980 does not. Overall, a strict PBC theory does not hold, but there might still be something to it.

Administrations make their wishes known to the Federal Reserve, presumably because they feel it has an effect. To measure this relationship for the period from 1979 to 1984, Thomas Havrilesky compared changes in monetary policy with the number of articles appearing in the *Wall Street Journal* that he considered to be signals of desired policy from the Administration. He found that changes in monetary policy and the number of signals matched quite closely.[2]

## The Federal Reserve and Congress

Although in principle the Federal Reserve is less independent of Congress than it is of the administration, in practice just the opposite seems to be true. As we have seen, the Federal Reserve was created by Congress, so Congress potentially has the power to dictate policy, even to dissolve the Fed. However, congressional attempts to dictate monetary policy have been infrequent—perhaps because Congress itself rarely reaches a consensus on the matter. However, this is subject to change.

In fact, during the 1970s, Congress began structured dialogues with the Fed concerning monetary policy. Later, the Humphrey-Hawkins Full Employment and Balanced Growth Act of 1978, required the Fed to testify at congressional hearings and to provide detailed reports regarding its monetary policy. Such hearings could subject the Fed to control, since monetary policies are discussed even before they have been implemented; but, so far, Fed independence has not been compromised.

---

[1] The theory of the political business cycle (PBC) was developed by William Nordhaus, "The Political Business Cycle," *Review of Economic Studies*, April 1975, pp. 169–190; and by Edward Tufte, *Political Control of the Economy*, Princeton University Press, Princeton, N.J., 1978.

[2] See Thomas Havrilesky, "Monetary Policy Signaling from the Administration to the Federal Reserve," *Journal of Money, Credit, and Banking*, February 1988, pp. 83–101. Other evidence of political influence is given in John Wooley, *Monetary Politics: The Federal Reserve and the Politics of Monetary Policy*, Cambridge University Press, Cambridge, Mass., 1984.

Former chairman Paul Volcker was adept at testifying and satisfying the reporting requirements, while protecting the Fed's options and independence. Alan Greenspan seems to have the same skill.

## Should the Federal Reserve Be Independent?

Beyond political battles among the Fed, the administration, and Congress, a more basic question is whether the Federal Reserve *should* be independent. Although there is no "right" answer to this question, the main arguments on each side are quite clear.

### The Case Against Federal Reserve Independence

The main case against independence is that a major government institution should be run by elected officials in a democratic society. The Federal Reserve does not meet this criterion—its officials are not elected, and their terms extend well beyond the terms of the elected officials who appoint them. Box 17.6 describes a recent lawsuit claiming that the makeup of the FOMC is unconstitutional.

### The Case for Federal Reserve Independence

The main case for Federal Reserve independence is that the effects of monetary policy, such as on inflation, can extend over a long time, so it is essential that the policies are made from a long-term perspective. Many politicians, in contrast, have short-run horizons, looking mainly to their next election. These office holders might use monetary policy for political ends, as suggested by the theory of the political business cycle. Box 17.7 shows that a well-known economic columnist has a similar view.

### And a Compromise

Our actual system can be interpreted as a compromise between these positions—elected officials may properly determine *the goals of monetary policy*, while the Fed *implements them*. In this view, Federal Reserve independence means that it can interpret the stated goals and decide how best to implement monetary policy to reach them. With this in mind, we will now turn to the macroeconomic goals of monetary policy.

---

# The Macroeconomic Goals of Monetary Policy

The concepts of **monetary policy** and its **macroeconomic goals** are relatively recent developments. As we saw in Chapter 10, the original goal of the Federal Reserve Act, in 1913, was to make the banking system safe and the currency elastic to the seasonal and regional needs of trade. These objectives remain today, but monetary policy now focuses on macroeconomic goals. Indeed, the modern concept of monetary policy originated only in the 1920s. Macroeconomic goals for monetary policy evolved even later, primarily as an aftermath of the Great Depression and World War II.

BOX 17.6 IN DEPTH

## The Case Against Federal Reserve Independence

The following article by Stephen Wermiel appeared in the *Wall Street Journal* on December 12, 1987.

A federal appeals court ruled that legislators who doubt the constitutionality of the Federal Reserve's policy-making committee should take their case to Congress, not the courts.

A three-judge panel of the appeals court in the District of Columbia dismissed a lawsuit filed by Sen. John Melcher (D., Mont.) challenging the composition of the Federal Open Market Committee. The committee sets monetary policy by expanding or restricting bank reserves.

In an opinion written by Judge Kenneth Starr, the court said Congress may change the membership of the Open Market Committee if there is a constitutional problem. Espousing a limited role for the courts, Judge Starr wrote, "If a legislator could obtain substantial relief from his fellow legislators through the legislative process itself, then it is an abuse of discretion for a court to entertain the legislator's action."

**Five Seats at Issue**

The suit by Sen. Melcher claimed that five of the 12 members of the Open Market Committee are chosen in an unconstitutional manner. Seven seats are held by the Federal Reserve Board members, who are appointed by the president and confirmed by the Senate. But five other seats are occupied by presidents of regional banks in the Federal Reserve System, who aren't picked by the president or reviewed by the Senate.

The lawsuit asserted that the five regional Fed bank presidents shouldn't be allowed to vote because the Constitution requires that those exercising executive-branch authority be presidential appointees who have been confirmed by the Senate.

A federal district court ruled last year that the five aren't the kind of "officers of the United States" that the Constitution says must be nominated by the president and approved by the Senate. The district court said the Open Market Committee "represents an exquisitely balanced approach" to public and private interests in the banking system.

But the appeals court ruled Friday that the district court was wrong to rule on the constitutionality of the Open Market Committee. The appeals court said judges should exercise their discretion to refrain from deciding disputes that may interfere with the legislative process.

(Stephen Wermiel, "Suit Over Makeup of Fed Committee Loses on Appeal, *Wall Street Journal*, 12 Dec. 1987.)

BOX 17.7 IN DEPTH

## The Case for Federal Reserve Independence

Leonard Silk wrote the following column, which appeared in the *New York Times* on February 26, 1988.

The conflict between the Federal Reserve and the Reagan Administration over what monetary policy should be and whose monetary policy is it, anyway, can easily be turned into a morality play.

Cast in the role of hero would be Alan Greenspan, named by President Reagan in August to succeed Paul A. Volcker as Fed chairman. In this role, Mr. Greenspan is upholding the independence of the central bank against the Administration's efforts to push the Fed into what might be too stimulative a monetary policy. The Administration wants a vigorous economy, which would help the Republican Presidential nominee in November.

And cast in the role of villains would be Beryl W. Sprinkel, chairman of the President's Council of Economic Advisers; Michael R. Darby, chief economist of the Treasury, and various unnamed Administration heavy hitters. All worry that the Greenspan policy may do to their candidate's chances in 1988 what the restrictive Volcker

policy did to Jimmy Carter's re-election effort in 1980. . . .

Apparently no one had told Mr. Reagan that his Council of Economic Advisers, in its annual Economic Report, criticized the Fed for monetary policies that sent interest rates up and the stock market into the October crash. The report did praise the Fed for supplying "ample liquidity" to the financial system right after the Dow's 508-point drop, but it also said that, once the immediate danger was past, the Fed "underestimated the risks to adequate economic growth." More recently, however, the Fed, according to the President's economic advisers, "has been more supportive of economic growth." . . .

Mr. Greenspan told Congress this week that he "objected quite strongly" to Administration interference and would resist any election-year pressure on the Fed's monetary policy.

Only the most politically naive could be shocked by news of pressure for economic expansion in an election year. Scholarly studies have found that, since World War II, the growth of real income after taxes accelerated in 83 percent of the election years (both four-

---

Macroeconomic goals were legislated by Congress in the *Employment Act of 1946* and the *Humphrey-Hawkins Act of 1978*. The 1946 Act called on government agencies "to promote maximum employment, production, and purchasing power." The Humphrey-Hawkins Act reaffirmed

year Presidential and two-year Congressional elections), compared with 40 percent in the off years. Prof. Edward R. Tufte of Yale found a "four-year cycle in unemployment, with downturns in the jobless rate during the months before a Presidential election and rises in unemployment starting a year to a year and a half after the election."

But there are two major issues in Administration-Fed relations that go beyond election-year politics. The first issue is the need for closer intergration of fiscal and monetary policy. Those who favor coordination of economic policy of the United States and its major allies cannot treat the need for domestic coordination of fiscal and monetary policy as a simple morality play.

At a time when the Administration's decisions to support the dollar or let it decline are crucial to interest rates, monetary growth, financial markets and economic expansion, monetary policy cannot be ceded as a monopoly of the Fed. . . .

The second major issue, not contained in the simple morality-play format, is whether the Fed's monetary policy is too loose or too tight, not just this year but over the long run. Not every critic who says the Fed is too restrictive can be dismissed as a political hack. Some of the harshest critics of Mr. Volcker's tight-money regime during the Reagan years were Democratic liberals, who would be just as critical of Mr. Greenspan if the Fed should thrust the economy into a recession and send unemployment soaring.

Some critics of the Fed even argue that electoral politics may be a fortunate thing, required to jar the central bank away from too heavy a "sound money" slant that worries unduly about inflation at the cost of excess unemployment and sluggish growth. That may be as true of the Bundesbank in West Germany as the Fed in the United States.

Nevertheless, undue monetary stimulus, stemming from electoral politics, could generate inflationary pressures and send interest rates soaring and the markets and the economy plunging, as Mr. Greenspan argued.

these goals, and added a high rate of capital investment, a balanced budget, and international trade equilibrium to the priorities. The Federal Reserve may also refer to the soundness of the financial system and bank safety when implementing monetary policy.

## Maximum Employment

**Maximum employment** is generally recognized as the priority item among the macroeconomic goals. Employment goals are most commonly measured in terms of the *unemployment rate*—the percentage of the labor force that is unemployed. As shown in Figure 17.3, the unemployment rate has varied between 5% and 9.5% since 1970. Serious losses occur in the economy when the unemployment rate is high—unemployed individuals and their families suffer, often harshly, from loss of income; and the output level of the economy as a whole is reduced because labor resources are wasted.

FIGURE 17.3
**The Unemployment Rate and the Inflation Rate**

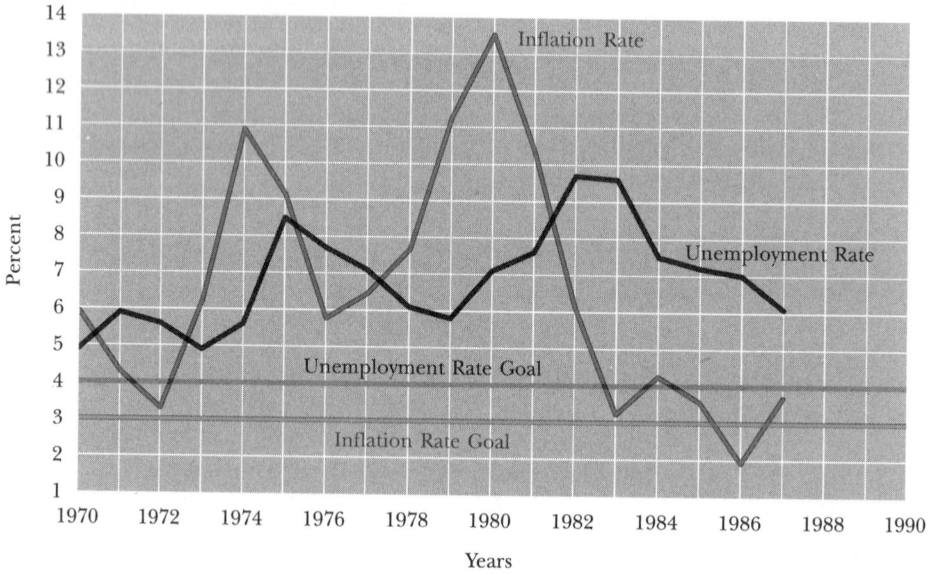

The unemployment rate has ranged from 5% to 9.5% since 1970, often well above the Humphrey-Hawkins Act goal of 4%. The inflation rate has fluctuated through a wider range, from about 2% to 14%, reaching the Humphrey-Hawkins Act goal of 3% in 1986. **Source:** *Economic Report of the President,* 1988.

The Humphrey-Hawkins Act set a goal of 4% unemployment, which was interpreted as *full employment*. The goal could not be *zero unemployment* because there is always some *frictional unemployment*—people counted as unemployed because they have quit their jobs and are searching for better ones. (Economists refer to the time and effort of switching jobs as a "friction.") The objective of the employment goal is thus to eliminate *unintended unemployment*. As shown in Figure 17.3, 4% unemployment has proven to be an elusive goal. (In Part VII, we will see that labor market performance can also be judged in terms of the *natural rate of unemployment*—the unemployment rate at which the demand and supply of labor balance.)

## Price Stability

Inflation imposes a variety of costs on the economy, making **price stability**—the absence of inflation—another key goal of macroeconomic policy. Inflation has costs because people use *nominal prices* and *nominal contracts*—contracts stated in terms of money and current prices—while most transactions refer to *real activity*, such as the consumption of real goods and services. The problem is that nominal prices and contracts may distort real activity when unexpected inflation occurs.

Financial markets, labor markets, and the holding of money all provide good examples where inflation distorts decisions:

- Most *financial contracts*—loans and securities—specify the amount to be repaid in dollars. Unexpected inflation reduces the real value of the amount repaid, creating a loss for lenders and a gain for borrowers.

- Most *labor contracts* are stated in nominal terms, based on the nominal wage rate. Unexpected inflation lowers the resulting real wage rate, creating a loss for workers and a gain for employers.

- Decisions to *hold money for transactions purposes* are made in nominal terms based on nominal prices. Unexpected inflation imposes a cost on money holdings—the "inflation tax" we discussed in Box 4.4.

Inflation imposes the least burden when it is *anticipated*—its effects can be taken into account in specifying nominal prices and contracts. Nominal interest rates on loan contracts, for example, implicitly include a component for expected inflation, and the same is true for the nominal wage rate in a labor contract. Inflation, however, generally cannot be *perfectly* anticipated, making the adjustments for expected inflation necessarily imperfect. The problem is particularly severe when inflation rates are volatile, because it then becomes especially hard to predict the inflation rate accurately.

People respond to the problem of *unexpected inflation*—the deviation of actual inflation from the anticipated level—in a variety of ways. Commonly, they just carry on as they were, accepting the fact that inflation may sometimes distort their real plans. Alternatively, people can try to limit those activities that are most adversely effected by unexpected inflation. For example, they may hold less money in order to avoid the inflation tax.

*Price-indexed contracts* are a particularly interesting solution for unexpected inflation. With price-indexed contracts, nominal values are automatically revised as the price level changes. For example, many wage contracts include price escalator clauses that automatically adjust nominal wage rates as inflation occurs. This reduces—or even eliminates—the unintended changes in real wage rates that would otherwise result from unexpected inflation. Indexed contracts can be costly to arrange, however, especially when some sectors of the economy use them and others do not. For example, a firm may be reluctant to offer an indexed wage contract to its employees given that the prices for the goods it sells are not indexed to the overall inflation rate in the economy.

In view of inflation's costs, a zero rate of inflation might seem the proper goal for monetary policy. However, a moderate inflation rate has beneficial effects, especially in markets for goods with falling demand. When a good's demand is falling, its *relative price*—the nominal price relative to the overall price level—should also fall. However, producers are often reluctant to reduce nominal prices. But if there is some inflation, then the relative price of the good can fall, even if the nominal price is unchanged or rises (at a rate below the overall inflation rate).

The Humphrey-Hawkins Act specified a goal of 3% inflation by 1983. (It also stated a goal of no inflation by 1988, but this has never been taken seriously.) As shown in Figure 17.3, the 3% goal was reached in 1986. As we will see in Chapter 20, the Federal Reserve may be credited with carrying out the monetary policies that achieved this goal, reflecting the high priority the Fed places on inflation fighting.

## Capital Investment and Real Economic Growth

The Humphrey-Hawkins Act explicitly introduced high rates of **capital investment** in the economy as another goal of macroeconomic policy. Capital investment refers to the accumulation of real assets such as manufacturing plants and equipment. It is also includes technological research and development. Capital investment is stimulated by low real interest rates, tax incentives, and a strong overall economy.

In the long term, capital investment increases the economy's capacity and thus is a *source* of **real economic growth**. In the short term, high capital investment is also a *result* of real economic growth: rising demand for goods causes firms to increase their capacity for producing goods. Capital investment and real economic growth thus reinforce one another. Figure 17.4 shows how this has been reflected in the growth rates of real GNP and real capital investment in recent years.

There are two main reasons that the Fed makes a strong effort to encourage investment:

- Among federal agencies, the Fed has an especially long-term perspective on economic policy.
- Capital investment may depend on interest rates, which the Fed helps to determine.

## International Trade and Finance

Economic policies for international trade and finance are divided into two components—trade policies and exchange rate policies. The Federal Reserve carries out *exchange rate policies* by buying or selling foreign exchange as directed by the Board of Governors and the Treasury Department, with the Treasury Department having overall responsibility. A stable foreign exchange value for the dollar, which encourages international trade, is the main continuing goal of U.S. international financial policy. In Chapter 22, we will look at this goal in detail, as a function of alternative international monetary arrangements.

FIGURE 17.4
**Growth Rates in Real GNP and Capital Investment**

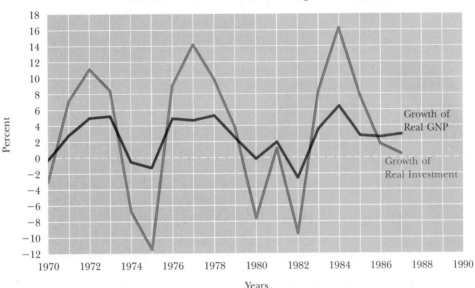

The figure shows that periods of high growth for real GNP generally coincide with periods of high growth for real capital investment, but the growth of capital investment tends to be more volatile than the growth of GNP. **Source:** *Economic Report of the President*, February, 1988.

## A Sound Financial System

The Federal Reserve refers to its objective of a sound financial system as maintaining *an even keel* in the financial markets. After the stock market crash of October 19, 1987, for example, the Fed rushed to reassure the financial markets. Otherwise, their instability might have had negative repercussions for the level of real economic activity. A sound financial system is also useful for encouraging bank safety and helping the Treasury Department to issue new securities.

Nevertheless, the Fed has been concerned that, in the name of financial soundness, it might be called on to bail out individual companies or agencies that are in financial distress. The Federal Reserve Act provides for the Fed to buy securities issued by specific firms under special conditions, but the Fed has attempted to avoid this responsibility, reasoning that Congress and the administration can deal better with the political ramifications that inevitably arise.

The Federal Reserve also has potential powers regarding *selective credit controls*—such as determining the terms of lending for different sectors of the economy. Here, too, the Fed has been reluctant to accept this responsibility, although from time to time it has had to do so. For example, the Fed was required by Congress and the administration to enforce a variety of selective credit controls during World War II to ensure that particular resources were available for the war effort. Since then, the Fed has been generally successful in avoiding the use of selective credit control policies.

## Conflicts Among the Macroeconomic Goals

Since the macroeconomic goals all must be considered together, conflicts may arise between them. For example:

- Maximum employment and price stability may conflict, since expansionary policies (which stimulate the economy and increase employment) may also create inflation.

- Capital investment and a strong international exchange value for the dollar may conflict, because the former is aided by low U.S. interest rates, while the latter is helped by high interest rates.

- Policies directed toward soundness of the financial system—such as increasing the money supply after a stock market crash—may conflict with the goal of price stability.

Such conflicts may be resolved in theory if enough policy instruments are available. For example, if there are two goals (such as maximum employment and price stability), then two instruments (such as monetary policy and fiscal policy) may be adequate for reaching each of the goals. Each instrument could be assigned to manage one goal, fiscal policy to manage employment and monetary policy to manage price stability.

If the matching of instruments to goals is to work, however, each instrument must produce an independent effect on its goal. Also, since there is always uncertainty concerning the precise effect of any instrument, it may be hard to gauge how much to use it.

Consequently, even when coordinated policies are used, the conflict between goals is often resolved by giving one goal priority. For example, if the unemployment rate is very high while the inflation rate is low, then the policy may be to reduce the unemployment rate, even though higher inflation may result. However, at other times the unemployment and inflation rates may both be high, creating a policy dilemma. The combination of high unemployment and high inflation actually was a serious problem for the United States during the late 1970s. Box 17.8 discusses how an **economic discomfort index** was developed to measure the problem.

In the following chapters of Part V, we will look at how monetary policy is operated in the United States to meet the Federal Reserve's goals. We will first examine the specific instruments available to the Fed for managing monetary policy and then at issues that arise in implementing policy.

## An Economic Discomfort Index

It is relatively easy to grade policymakers on how well they have managed policy when there is one economic goal. However, when there are at least two goals, the evaluation becomes more complicated. In order to evaluate policy in such situations, priorities must be established.

Arthur Okun, an economist at the Brookings Institution with an active interest in policy matters, devised a simple but instructive method for evaluating the conflict between unemployment rate and inflation rate goals: his economic discom-

fort index (also known as the "misery index") just adds the two rates together. Since low unemployment rates and low inflation rates are always preferred, the higher the index value, the greater the economic discomfort.

The Discomfort Index shown in Figure 17.5 is the sum of the unemployment and inflation rates shown in Figure 17.3. It can be seen that the economic discomfort was intense during the late 1970s, but it became much more comfortable by the mid-1980s.

FIGURE 17.5
**The Discomfort Index**

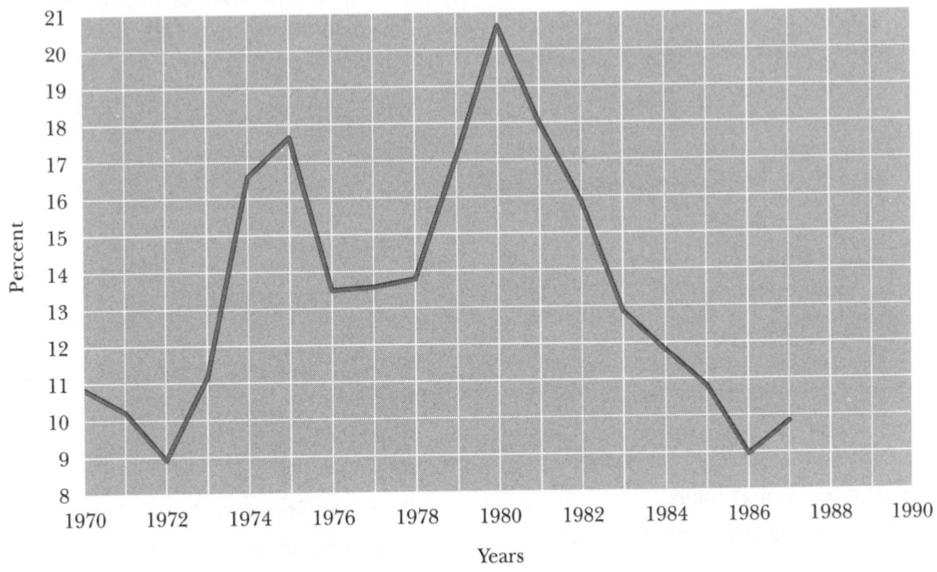

The discomfort index is the sum of the inflation and unemployment rates. The index declined sharply and remained low during the 1980s. **Source:** *Economic Report of the President*, February, 1988.

## Chapter Summary

1. The Board of Governors is the most important body within the Federal Reserve System; the chairman and other members of the board are the Fed's chief executives. The twelve regional Federal Reserve banks, operating under the Board of Governors, carry out the Fed's banking business. The Federal Open Market Committee (FOMC), consisting of the Board of Governors and a rotating set of Reserve bank presidents, determines monetary policy. Member banks are commercial banks that belong to the Federal Reserve System.

2. Besides the primary activity of determining monetary policy, the Federal Reserve System has a variety of other tasks. These include the services it provides to all depository intermediaries, its responsibilities for bank supervision and regulation, and its role as the federal government's fiscal agent.

3. Federal Reserve independence refers to the Fed's ability to determine monetary policy separately from Congress or the Administration. The Treasury/Federal Reserve Accord of 1951 explicitly provided

for Federal Reserve independence from the Administration, although some Administration influence is probably unavoidable. The Fed now regularly attends Congressional hearings and provides monetary policy reports each year, but these procedures have not jeopardized its independence.

4. Macroeconomic goals for monetary policy have been stated in two major legislative acts, the Employment Act of 1946 and the Humphrey-Hawkins Act of 1978. These acts emphasize maximum employment and price stability, and also refer to real economic growth, capital investment, and international trade balance. The Federal Reserve also considers the soundness of the financial system to be important.

5. Conflicts may arise between the macroeconomic goals of monetary policy, such as between lower unemployment rates and lower inflation rates. Although in principle such conflicts may be resolved by using more than one policy instrument, in practice it is often necessary to determine which goal has priority.

## Key Terms

Board of Governors of the Federal Reserve System
Chairman of the Board of Governors
Economic Discomfort Index
Federal Open Market Committee (FOMC)
Federal Reserve independence
Federal Reserve System
Federal Reserve tasks
Macroeconomic goals of monetary policy:
   Capital investment

International trade and finance
Maximum employment
Price stability
Real economic growth
Soundness of the financial system
Member banks
Political business cycle (PBC)
Regional Reserve banks
Treasury/Federal Reserve Accord of 1951

## Study Questions

1. What are the three main components of the Federal Reserve System? What is the main responsibility of each?

2. Why is there an issue of the balance of power within the Federal Reserve System?

3. Why is the Federal Reserve System so profitable? What does it do with the profits?

4. What are the Federal Reserve's responsibilities as the fiscal agent for the federal government?

5. What is meant by Federal Reserve independence?

6. In what sense is the Federal Reserve explicitly independent of the presidential administration, yet is probably still influenced by it?

7. In what sense is the Federal Reserve *not* explicitly independent of Congress, yet is probably *not* influenced by it?

8. What variable measures the goal of maximum employment? Currently, what is the specific target?

9. What variable measures the goal of a stable price level? Currently, what is the specific target?

10. Give an example of a conflict between two policy goals. How could it be resolved?

## Recommended Reading

Many Federal Reserve System publications are available without charge by writing to the Federal Reserve, Publications Services, Washington, D.C. 20551. The *Federal Reserve Bulletin* lists current publications, including: *The Federal Reserve System, Purposes and Functions*, the *Annual Report* (issued each year), and the *Budget Review* (first issued for the period 1985–1986)

*This is an excellent biography and description of the Federal Reserve System in its early years:*

Lester Chandler, *Benjamin Strong, Central Banker*, The Brookings Institution, Darlington, D.C., 1958.

*This is a key guide for potential Fed watchers:*

David M. Jones, *Fed Watching and Interest Rate Projections: A Practical Guide*, New York Institute of Finance, New York, 1986.

*The first is an outsider's report, and the second is an insider's report, of what goes on in the Federal Reserve:*

William Greider, *Secrets of the Temple*, Simon & Schuster, New York, 1987.

Sherman J. Maisel, *Managing the Dollar*, W. W. Norton, New York, 1973.

*The following discuss the political business cycle:*

Thomas Havrilesky, "Monetary Policy Signaling from the Administration to the Federal Reserve," *Journal of Money, Credit*, and *Banking*, February 1988, pp. 83–101.

William Nordhaus, "The Political Business Cycle," *Review of Economic Studies*, April 1975, pp. 169–190.

Edward Tufte, *Political Control of the Economy*, Princeton University Press, Princeton, N.J., 1978.

John Wooley, *Monetary Politics: The Federal Reserve and the Politics of Monetary Policy*, Cambridge University Press, Cambridge, Mass., 1984.

# 18

# The Instruments of Monetary Policy

*"Any government that robs Peter to pay Paul can count on support from Paul."*

*George Bernard Shaw*

The day following a meeting of the Federal Open Market Committee (FOMC) is always busy for the manager for domestic operations at the New York Federal Reserve Bank. He runs the Fed's Trading Desk for open market operations, buying and selling securities to keep bank reserves, the monetary base, and the money supply in line with FOMC policy directives. When an FOMC directive indicates a change in monetary policy, he carries out the appropriate open market operations. When the directive leaves monetary policy unchanged—which is the normal case—he tries to let Fed watchers know that nothing new is happening.

The manager follows a standard routine each day:

- Review his staff's projections for the amount of security purchases or sales needed.
- Check the financial markets for last minute developments that might require revised projections.
- Call the Treasury Department to learn its plans for the day regarding its deposit account at the Federal Reserve.
- Formulate a specific plan for the day's transactions.
- Receive confirmation from the FOMC that the day's plan is acceptable.
- Obtain bids from dealers for the intended purchases or sales of government securities.

If the manager makes a mistake, he could end up buying $1 billion in Treasury bills when he meant to sell them, or vice versa. Then, to make matters even more uncomfortable, he would have to explain the mistake to the Fed watchers who would be busy interpreting the unexpected action as an abrupt change in monetary policy.

In this chapter, we will look at open market operations and the other instruments the Federal Reserve uses to execute monetary policy.

The three main instruments of Federal Reserve monetary policy—open market operations, discount loans, and reserve requirements—are called *general instruments* because they all affect the money supply. After looking at these instruments, we will briefly consider other selective instruments that the Fed sometimes uses.

## Open Market Operations

**Open market operations**—purchases and sales of securities—are the most important, flexible, and commonly used of the Federal Reserve's instruments. The impact of such transactions on the money supply was first recognized by Benjamin Strong in the 1920s. Open market operations are carried out at the trading desk of the New York Federal Reserve Bank by the manager for domestic operations. They are used to control the **monetary aggregates**—bank reserves, the monetary base, and the money supply—following the directives of the Federal Open Market Committee.

### The Effect on Monetary Aggregates

Recall the process—which we introduced in Chapter 14—through which open market operations change the monetary aggregates. This can be expressed in three equations:

$$M1 = m_1B, \tag{18.1}$$

$$M2 = m_2B, \tag{18.2}$$

$$B = C + R_t, \tag{18.3}$$

where M1 = the M1 money supply,
$m_1$ = the M1 money supply multiplier,
M2 = the M2 money supply,
$m_2$ = the M2 money supply multiplier,
$B$ = the monetary base,
$C$ = currency held by the public,
$R_t$ = total bank reserves.

Given the money supply multipliers—$m_1$ for the M1 money supply and $m_2$ for the M2 money supply—the Fed tries to control M1 or M2 by controlling the monetary base $B$. And given the currency held by the public $C$, the Fed controls the monetary base by controlling total bank reserves $R_t$.

### The Effect on Bank Reserves and the Monetary Base

Table 18.1 shows the factors that determine bank reserves and the monetary base. The organization of the table is similar to a financial accounting statement in which the sources and uses of funds for an activity or enterprise are compared. *Part A* of the table lists the *sources* of funds for bank reserves and the monetary base:

- *Domestic credit* covers the funds issued by the Federal Reserve to purchase government securities, discount loans, float, and other assets.
- *International reserves* cover the funds issued to buy gold, foreign currencies, and special drawing rights (see Chapter 22).
- *Treasury currency* is the amount of currency previously issued by the Treasury that is still outstanding.[1]

*Part B* of the table represents the *uses* of funds for purposes other than bank reserves:

- *Currency held by the public* equals currency outstanding minus vault cash held for bank reserve requirements.
- *Treasury cash holdings* represent currency held by the Treasury Department.
- *Other deposits at Reserve banks* are deposits at the Fed other than the reserve deposits of depository intermediaries.
- *Miscellaneous accounts* include other Federal Reserve liabilities and Fed capital.

*Part C* of the table shows that **total bank reserves** equal the *sources* (part A) minus the *uses* (part B). Total bank reserves can also be separated into two parts:

- **Borrowed reserves** equal the discount borrowing of banks.
- **Nonborrowed reserves** equal the remaining part of total bank reserves.

The *monetary base* equals the sum of total bank reserves and currency held by the public.

Open market operations consist of changes in item (1.a) in Table 18.1—*security holdings*. Bank reserves and the monetary base rise as the Federal Reserve credits bank reserve accounts to pay for its security purchases. The seller of the securities can be either a bank or someone else who deposits the Fed's check in a bank. The process is reversed for open market *sales*.

### The Effect on the Money Supply

Given that open market operations change the monetary base, it follows that:

1. The money supply multipliers will determine the M1 and M2 money supplies, based on equations (18.2) and (18.3). (Figure 14.4 in Chapter 14 is a graph of the two multipliers.)
2. Interest rates and income will be determined in part by the equilibrium between money supply and money demand.

In this chapter, we will focus on the direct effects of open market operations and the other instruments of Federal Reserve policy on the monetary base. In the following chapters, we will focus on the effects on the money supply, interest rates, and income.

---

[1] This is currency that was issued earlier directly by the U.S. Treasury. Treasury currency is similar in appearance to the currency now issued by the Federal Reserve, but it is marked "United States Treasury."

**TABLE 18.1**

**The Funds Available for Bank Reserves**

### At year-end 1987 (Dollars in billions)

**Part A: Sources for Bank Reserves and the Monetary Base**

| | | |
|---|---:|---:|
| 1. Domestic credit | | |
|    a. Security holdings | $227.9 | |
|    b. Loans | 0.8 | |
|    c. Float | 1.6 | |
|    d. Other assets | 8.0 | |
| | | 238.3 |
| 2. International Reserves | | |
|    a. Gold stock | 11.1 | |
|    b. Special drawing rights | 5.0 | |
|    c. Foreign currencies | 7.8 | |
| | | 23.9 |
| 3. Treasury Currency Outstanding | 18.2 | 18.2 |
| | | **280.4** |

*LESS:*

**Part B: Uses Other Than Bank Reserves**

| | | |
|---|---:|---:|
| 4. Currency held by the public | 203.6 | 203.6 |
| 5. Treasury cash holdings | 0.5 | 0.5 |
| 6. Other deposits at Reserve banks | | |
|    a. Treasury deposits | 4.2 | |
|    b. Foreign deposits | 0.2 | |
|    c. Other deposits | 2.5 | |
| | | 6.9 |
| 7. Miscellaneous accounts | 12.0 | 12.0 |
| | | **223.0** |

*EQUALS:*

| | |
|---|---:|
| **Total Bank Reserves** | **57.4** |

**Part C: Bank Reserves and the Monetary Base**

| | | |
|---|---:|---:|
| 8a. Borrowed Reserves | 0.8 | |
| 8b. Nonborrowed Reserves | 56.6 | |
|    **Total Bank Reserves** | | **57.4** |

*PLUS:*

| | |
|---|---:|
| **Currency Held by the Public** | **203.6** |

*EQUALS:*

| | |
|---|---:|
| **The Monetary Base** | **261.0** |

**Source:** *Federal Reserve Bulletin,* Tables 1.11, 1.12, and 1.20, Board of Governors of the Federal Reserve System, 1988.

## Types of Open Market Operations

Two types of open market operations—*defensive* and *dynamic* (or policy-initiated)—are distinguishable, depending on what factors motivate the Federal Reserve's action.

**Defensive open market operations** are used to offset a change in bank reserves or the monetary base that is created by outside factors. For example, the large amount of currency held by the public (item 4 in Table 18.1) during the Christmas shopping season will cause bank reserves to fall unless the Fed carries out defensive open market purchases. Federal Reserve float (item 1.c in Table 18.1)—described in Appendix 18.1—is also a common source of defensive open market operations.

**Dynamic (policy-initiated) open market operations** are carried out following the policy directives of the Federal Open Market Committee to change the monetary base (or bank reserves). Dynamic open market operations are less common than defensive operations because FOMC policy directives only occasionally change monetary policy, while outside factors have a continuous impact on the monetary base.

Open market operations are carried out in two ways: outright purchases and sales are often used for dynamic operations; repurchase agreements and matched sale-purchase transactions are generally used for defensive operations.

**Outright purchases and sales** are normal security transactions: the seller delivers the security, and the buyer pays for it and keeps it. The Fed uses outright purchases or sales to create a permanent change in the monetary base, which is why they are used mainly for dynamic open market operations. In contrast, most defensive operations are based on temporary factors, so outright purchases and sales are generally not appropriate for them.

**Repurchase agreements**—which we discussed as a tool of bank liquidity management in Chapter 11—are used by the Fed to create a temporary increase in the monetary base. For example, the monetary base might be temporarily depressed because the Treasury department is holding an unusually large amount of currency (item 5 in Table 18.1) in anticipation of issuing tax refund checks; the Fed could then use a repurchase agreement to increase the monetary base temporarily, until people receive their tax refund checks.

To carry out repurchase agreements, the Fed purchases Treasury securities from dealers who agree to repurchase the securities at a specified price at a later date. The initial purchase by the Federal Reserve increases the monetary base, while the later repurchase by the dealers cancels the increase. Most repurchase agreements cover about one week, although they can be as short as one day and as long as two weeks.

**Matched sales and purchases** use the same principle as repurchase agreements, but they work in the opposite direction—they are also called reverse repurchase agreements ("reverse repos," for short). The Federal Reserve uses matched sales and purchases to extinguish a temporary increase in the monetary base, such as might result from bank borrowing at the discount window (item 1.b in Table 18.1). Given that the monetary

## TABLE 18.2
### Federal Reserve Open Market Operations by Type

**At year-end 1987 (Dollars in billions)**

| | |
|---|---|
| Outright Purchase and Sales | |
| Gross purchases | $ 37.2 |
| Gross sales and redemptions | 16.9 |
| Repurchase Agreements | |
| Gross purchases | 314.6 |
| Gross sales | 324.7 |
| Matched Sale-Purchase Transactions | |
| Gross sales | 950.9 |
| Gross purchases | 950.9 |

**Source:** *Federal Reserve Bulletin*, Table 1.17, Board of Governors of the Federal Reserve System, 1988.

base increase is temporary, the Fed will only want to sell securities temporarily.

Table 18.2 shows the open market operations carried out by the Federal Reserve during 1987 based on the three techniques. Outright purchases and sales are always the smallest category, because they are used mainly for dynamic open market operations, which occur much less frequently than defensive operations.

For repurchase agreements or matched transactions, a complete transaction involves an initial purchase or sale, followed by a second transaction that cancels it, so the totals for purchases and sales should be equal. However, as shown in Table 18.2, gross purchases and sales for repurchase agreements during the calendar year were not exactly equal—because transactions initiated in late December were not completed until early January of the next year. This effect is not trivial because open market operations are actively used at the end of the year to provide currency for the Christmas shopping season.

## Special Features of Open Market Operations

Because open market operations are flexible and general, they are the only instrument of monetary policy used daily by the Federal Reserve. Open market operations are *flexible* because:

- They can be executed in almost any amount.
- They can be easily reversed (using repurchase agreements).
- They generally do not draw a lot of public attention.

Open market operations are *general* because:

- They affect the monetary aggregates—bank reserves, the monetary base, and the money supply.
- They are usually carried out in Treasury securities—not securities issued by specific firms or banks.

In contrast, we will see later that selective instruments of monetary policy affect specific industries, firms, or banks.

# The Discount Window

The **discount window,** the popular name for the Federal Reserve's facility for making loans to banks, was considered to be the main instrument of central banking in the original Regulation A of the Federal Reserve Act of 1913. Discount loans remained the only actively used instrument of monetary policy until they were displaced by open market operations starting in the 1920s. Today, the discount window is mainly used—as we described in Chapter 11—by banks that need liquidity. Changes in the discount rate—the interest rate the Fed charges on discount loans—may also be interpreted by Fed watchers as a broad indicator of changes in monetary policy. Separate discount windows are managed by each of the twelve regional reserve banks for institutions in their region. The term discount "window" derives from the special tellers' windows that existed at each of the banks. The Monetary Control Act of 1980 provided all depository institutions in the United States with access to the discount window.

## The Effect of Discount Loans on Bank Reserves

Discount loans directly increase bank reserves (and the monetary base) because banks receive these loans as credits to their reserve accounts at the Fed. The effect on bank reserves is thus the same whether the Fed makes discount loans or carries out open market purchases of securities.

However, as shown in lines 8a and 8b of Table 18.1, an increase in reserves that results from discount loans is counted as *borrowed reserves,* whereas an increase that results from open market purchases is counted as *nonborrowed reserves.* Borrowed reserves satisfy reserve requirements in the same manner as nonborrowed reserves, but they have two distinguishing features:

1. They are a *temporary* source of bank reserves, since discount loans eventually have to be repaid. To repay its loans, a bank will have to attract more deposits, make fewer loans, or sell securities.
2. They are created on the *initiative of banks,* not of the Federal Reserve. As a result, the Fed may have to use defensive open market sales (reducing the monetary base) to cancel an undesired increase in the monetary base due to borrowed reserves.

## Types of Discount Loans

The word "discount" in the name "discount window" originally referred to transactions between banks and the Federal Reserve in which the Fed *bought* business loans that a bank had made earlier. As the new owner of the loans, the Fed would receive the loan payments made by the business borrowers. To earn a return on these loans, the Fed would "discount" them—pay a lower price than the amount of the scheduled payments. The discount rate was the percentage by which the purchase price fell below the amount of scheduled payments.

This type of discounting has not been actively used since the 1930s. Today, almost all discount window transactions are *loans*—technically called *advances*—that the Federal Reserve makes to banks. However, they are still called *discount* loans—indeed, banks still have to provide securities or business loans as collateral when they borrow from the Fed. Currently, the Fed makes discount loans under three main programs: adjustment credit, seasonal credit, and extended credit.

**Adjustment credit** refers to short-term loans (no more than fourteen days) that banks use if they need temporary liquidity as the result of unexpected deposit withdrawals or loan requests based on lines of credit. Also, malfunctions in electronic transfers or computers are an increasingly common reason why banks need adjustment credit—it may be some comfort to know that banks also suffer from such calamities.

**Seasonal credit** refers to discount loans that allow banks to adjust their liquidity in response to seasonal factors. Seasonal credit is available for a longer time than adjustment credit. For example, banks in farming regions use seasonal credit to extend loans to farmers at the time of spring planting, with repayment occurring at the time of the fall harvest.

**Extended credit** is provided for either of two purposes:

1. In response to a major problem, such as a failing bank.

2. As a remedy for a problem facing a group of institutions, such as a natural disaster in an area.

Figure 18.1 shows the amounts of discount loans in the adjustment, seasonal, and extended credit categories since 1970. The total is usually less than $1 billion—a tiny amount for a banking system with about $2.5

FIGURE 18.1
**Discount Lending of the Federal Reserve**

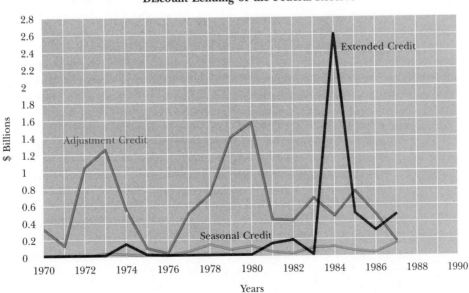

Federal Reserve discount loans include adjustment credit for temporary liquidity needs, seasonal credit for seasonal liquidity needs, and extended credit for longer-lasting problems. The large jump in extended credit in 1984 represented loans made to bail out the Continental Illinois Bank. **Source:** *Economic Report of the President,* February, 1988.

trillion of total assets. This is because the Fed lends only to banks that have no other source of liquidity. For example, the large jump in extended credit in 1984 represents the discount loans used to save the Continental Illinois Bank—discussed in Chapter 10.

## The Procedures for Borrowing

The main steps banks use to obtain discount loans are:

1. The bank's directors make the decision to borrow.
2. A lending agreement is drawn up between the bank and the Fed.
3. The bank applies to the Fed for a specific loan, indicating the amount, length of time, and purpose.
4. The Federal Reserve verifies that the loan represents an appropriate use of the discount window.
5. After approval by the Fed's lending officer, the loan is credited to the bank's reserve account.

## The Discount Rate

In the original Federal Reserve Act, each regional Reserve bank was to set its own discount rate, reflecting the economic conditions in its region. But as we saw in Chapter 17, the Board of Governors now determines the discount rate. The discount rate applies to most adjustment and seasonal loans, but surcharges are added on extended credit loans and on some loans to heavy and frequent borrowers.

The Federal Reserve sets the discount rate keeping in mind the **federal funds rate**—the interest rate on overnight loans between banks—since banks can choose between federal funds and discount loans to satisfy their liquidity needs. As shown in Figure 18.2, the discount rate is usually below the federal funds rate, but the two rates tend to move together. The discount rate is usually lower because the Fed does *not* want to penalize banks that are in trouble—it would be counterproductive to maintain an emergency facility, then to charge a penalty rate when it has to be used.

However, liquid and healthy banks that are making loans to customers may also want to use the discount window as a low-cost source of funds. To rule out **discount borrowing as a source of profit,** the Fed has adopted the dictum that *discount borrowing is a privilege, not a right*—meaning that the purpose of discount loan applications is carefully scrutinized. Among other things, the lending officer will look at how frequently the bank has borrowed in the past, at how long each of its loans has remained outstanding, and at other activities of the bank. Applications for discount loans are likely to be accepted when:

FIGURE 18.2
**The Discount Rate and the Federal Funds Rate**

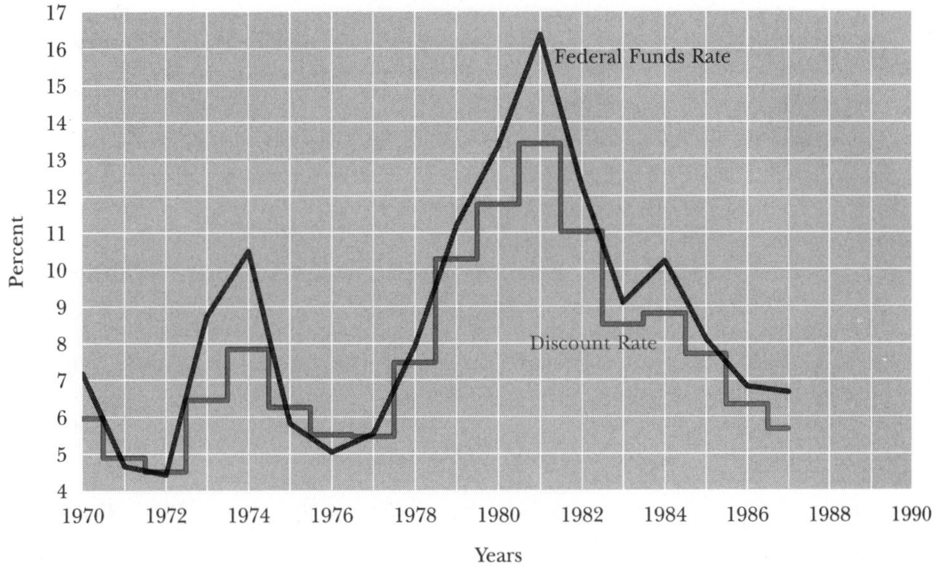

Since the discount rate is generally below the federal funds rate, banks have a profit incentive to borrow from the Federal Reserve. However, the Fed will only make discount loans for approved purposes. Source: *Economic Report of the President*, February, 1988.

- The bank cannot borrow more federal funds because it is already borrowing large amounts.
- The bank needs liquidity because one of its borrowers has just failed to make a large expected loan payment.

Of course, the Fed's screening out of banks that try to borrow for profit is not perfect. Indeed, as shown in Figure 18.3, discount borrowing tends to rise when the federal funds rate is high relative to the discount rate, which is evidence that at least some discount borrowing is motivated by profits. Nevertheless, the Fed's scrutiny certainly reduces the amount of such borrowing.

## Credit Rationing of Discount Loans

Another way of looking at the Fed's discount procedures is based on the concept of *credit rationing*. That is, because the discount rate is low, loan demand is high, so the Fed has to ration the amount of loans it makes. This gives the Fed leverage—*moral suasion*—to get banks to do things it wants. As a result, banks may feel that the cost of using the discount window is higher than the explicit discount rate.

FIGURE 18.3
**Discount Borrowing and the Cost of Borrowing**

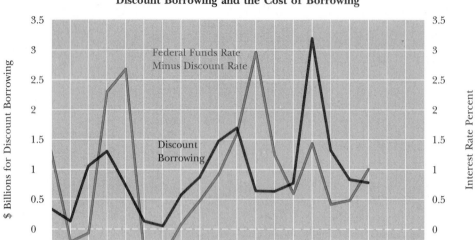

When the spread between the federal funds rate and the discount rate is high, the cost of borrowing from other banks (federal funds) is high compared to borrowing from the Fed (discount loans). The positive relationship between the amount of discount borrowing and this cost spread indicates that profit may be a motive in some discount borrowing.
**Source:** *Economic Report of the President*, February, 1988.

An example—using the credit rationing theory we developed in Chapter 12—is shown in Figure 18.4. If the discount rate is $r_0$, the bank would want a loan of size $L_0$, based on its demand curve for discount loans. However, the Fed may ration the bank to a smaller loan, the size $L_1$.

When the discount rate is $r_0$, the bank asks for a loan of size $L_0$. However, the Fed may ration the bank to a smaller loan of size $L_1$. In this case, the rate $r_1$ is the shadow price of the discount loan, the difference between $r_1$ and $r_0$ being the implicit cost introduced by credit rationing.

FIGURE 18.4
**Credit Rationing at the Discount Window**

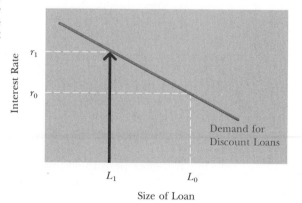

When the borrower receives a smaller loan than desired, it is *as if* the Federal Reserve had charged the borrower a discount rate of $r_1$, the so-called "shadow rate"—the rate the bank would be willing to pay for a loan of size $L_1$.

## The Announcement Effect of Changing the Discount Rate

Changes in the Federal Reserve discount rate can be either defensive or dynamic, based on the same principle we applied to open market operations.

**Defensive changes in the discount rate** occur when the Fed revises the rate to match changes in market interest rates. For example, if the Fed sets the discount rate a fixed amount below the federal funds rate and the federal funds rate rises by 1/2%, then the Fed will raise the discount rate by 1/2% as a defensive measure.

**Dynamic changes in the discount rate** occur when the Fed changes the rate to initiate a new monetary policy. For example, to initiate a tighter monetary policy, the Fed might raise the discount rate relative to the federal funds rate, thus altering the previous pattern.

The Federal Reserve changes the discount rate infrequently—not at all like its daily use of open market operations. For example, from 1970 to 1986, the discount rate was changed 57 times, an average of about 3.5 times a year. Partly because the rate is changed so infrequently, the changes that do occur are usually headline news in the financial press and are closely analyzed by Fed watchers. Is the change dynamic, meaning that it represents a new monetary policy? The Federal Reserve sometimes gives Fed watchers information in this respect, and sometimes not.

The financial markets may react strongly—with higher interest rates— if an increase in the discount rate is thought to be dynamic. That is, if investors expect a tighter monetary policy is being initiated, they may immediately respond by selling securities—before interest rates rise and security prices fall. These sales may themselves cause prices to fall, however, thereby causing interest rates to rise. When this happens, changes in the discount rate are said to have an **announcement effect.** An announcement effect can be helpful to the Fed when it is initiating a change in monetary policy—the investors' actions help the policy work. If, for example, the Fed initiates a tightening of monetary policy by announcing an increase in the discount rate and if investors respond by selling securities, the Fed may not need to make as many open market sales of securities as otherwise to achieve its desired effect.

Announcement effects can become a problem when investors misinterpret the policy. For example, suppose the Fed raises the discount rate as a defensive measure—just to bring it back into line with the federal funds rate. If the public misinterprets the action as a signal of tighter monetary policy, market interest rates, including the Federal funds rate, might rise. The Fed will have then failed to bring the discount rate back into line with the federal funds rate.

To avoid such situations, the Federal Reserve generally issues a short explanation when the discount rate is changed. But misunderstandings still occur. To illustrate the subtle differences involved, Box 18.1 shows the Federal Reserve's explanation for a 1986 discount rate change, while Box 18.2 shows some of the opinions quoted in the *Wall Street Journal* the next day.

---

BOX 18.1 BANKING BRIEFS

## The Fed Announces a Discount Rate Change

Fed watchers are experienced in interpreting the Federal Reserve statements that announce a change in the discount rate, but sometimes even they have trouble determining whether a change is dynamic or defensive. What would you think about the following Fed statement that accompanied a reduction in the discount rate?

**Change in the Discount Rate**

The Federal Reserve announced a reduction in the discount rate from 6 1/2 percent to 6 percent, effective on Friday, July 11, 1986.

The action, conforming in part to recent declines in a number of market interest rates, was taken within the framework of the generally accommodative stance of monetary policy that has prevailed for some time. More specifically, the action appeared appropriate in the context of a pattern of relatively slow growth, comfortably within capacity constraints, in the United States and in the industrialized world generally. That pattern has been accompanied by relatively low prices of a number of important commodities and greater stability in prices of goods generally. Measures of the broader monetary aggregates—M2 and M3—are near the midpoints of the target ranges set at the start of the year. In making the change, the Board voted on requests submitted by the Boards of Directors of the 12 Federal Reserve Banks. The discount rate is the interest rate that is charged depository institutions when they borrow from their District Federal Reserve Banks.

*(Wall Street Journal, 11 July, 1986.)*

---

## Proposals for Reforming the Discount Rate

Most proposals to reform the discount window have either the goal of eliminating the need for defensive changes in the discount rate or the goal of reducing the need for credit rationing. One proposal would have the discount rate change automatically each week based on the change in the federal funds rate, thus eliminating the most common reason for defensive changes. A second proposal would keep the discount rate at or above the federal funds rate, thus eliminating the incentive that banks have to borrow for profit.

## Wall Street Journal Interprets a Discount Rate Change

The following excerpts are from the *Wall Street Journal* report of the July 11, 1986, discount rate cut.

### Fed Cuts Discount Rate Half Point to 6%

The Federal Reserve System, concerned about the economy's sluggishness, cut its discount rate to 6% from 6 1/2%, bringing it to the lowest level since October 1977.

The move had been widely expected although some economists were disappointed that the Fed didn't reduce the rate a full percentage point.... Bond traders reacted cautiously to the move. Prices of actively traded Treasury bonds edged higher after the news was announced late yesterday afternoon, but later drifted lower, ending up with small gains for the day.... The Fed move is likely to persuade banks to cut their prime lending rates to 8% soon, several analysts predicted.

The wording of the Fed statement "does suggest they have some concerns about the economy, which remains extremely sluggish," said Robert A. Brusca, chief economist and senior vice president at Nikko Securities Co. International in New York.

"I think Fed officials will wait for quite some time for third-quarter data before they cut the discount rate below 6%," said James L. Cochrane, chief economist of Texas Commerce Bancshares Inc. in Houston. He expects interest rates to be "stable" in coming months.

"I expect at least two more half percentage point cuts in the discount rate within the next two months," said H. Erich Heinemann, chief economist of Ladenburg, Thalmann and Co. "The pressure from the Reagan administration to force rates lower to provide stimulus to the economy is absolutely overwhelming."

Senate Majority Leader Bob Dole (R. Kan.), who in a series of recent statements had urged Chairman Volcker to cut the discount rate, praised the Fed action. "I'm pleased the Fed has taken action to lower interest rates. It's the first step in stabilizing, and hopefully stimulating, today's sluggish economy," Sen. Dole said.

(*Wall Street Journal*, 12 July, 1986.)

Although the Federal Reserve carried out a major study of these and similar proposals in 1980, no major changes were made. Thus, it seems the Fed is not prepared to give up its discretionary power to set the discount rate and to decide which banks receive loans.

## The Lender of Last Resort

From the standpoint of monetary policy, the discount rate creates more problems than it solves, because the Fed:

1. Must decide whether loan applications represent borrowing for profit.

2. Must take care not to mislead Fed watchers when it changes the discount rate.

3. May need to neutralize with defensive open market operations the changes in the monetary base that are created by discount borrowing.

However, the Federal Reserve puts up with these problems because, through the discount window, the Fed is the **lender of last resort**—when all else fails, banks come to the discount window to obtain emergency funds.

If a large bank or firm suffers a serious setback threatening its solvency, the existence of a lender of last resort prevents a domino effect—with sound banks and firms also failing—from spreading through the financial system. Often, just the knowledge that the Federal Reserve is available to act as the lender of last resort is sufficient to solve the problem. The reassurance the Fed can offer was manifested in October 1987 following the stock market crash; Box 18.3 shows the Fed's official announcement at that time and the corresponding report in the *Wall Street Journal*.

## Reserve Requirements

The Federal Reserve has always required that member banks maintain **reserve ratios**—specified amounts of bank reserves relative to bank deposits. The 1980 Monetary Control Act extended **reserve requirements** to all depository institutions (including nonmember commercial banks and thrift institutions) in the United States. The Act also required that reserve ratios be imposed uniformly on all institutions, although the ratios could vary by the type of deposit and by the size of the institution.

### The Structure of Reserve Requirements

*Reserve requirements* are imposed on the following categories of "reservable liabilities":

- On *net transaction deposits*, the required ratio is 3% of an institution's first $40.5 million of deposits, and between 8% and 14% (12% in 1988) of deposits above this amount.

- On *nonpersonal time deposits* (time deposits held by partnerships and firms), the required ratio is 3% on deposits with original maturity of less than 1 1/2 years, and between 0% and 9% (0% in 1988) on longer-term deposits.

- On *Eurocurrency liabilities* (dollars transferred to U.S. banks from their foreign subsidiaries), the Fed can set any required ratio (3% in 1988).

- On *personal time deposits*, the reserve ratio is normally 0%, but the Federal Reserve has emergency authority to impose reserve requirements.

BOX 18.3 FINANCIAL NEWS

## Fed Lending After the Stock Market Crash of 1987

Sometimes, the shorter the Fed announcement, the more powerful it is. The following is the complete statement of Chairman Alan Greenspan on October 20, 1987, the day after the crash:

> The Federal Reserve, consistent with its responsibilities as the Nation's central bank, affirmed today its readiness to serve as a source of liquidity to support the economic and financial system.

The following excerpts from the *Wall Street Journal* of October 21, 1987, indicate how this reassured the financial markets:

### Stock Market's Frenzy Puts Fed's Greenspan in a Crucial Position

The stock market's Monday collapse has put Federal Reserve chairman Alan Greenspan on the front line in the fight to prevent a market panic from turning into a general economic slump.

"I think Greenspan is the only candidate for restoring the confidence of the markets," said Jerry Jordan, the chief economist at First Interstate Bank Corp. "It's the Chairman of the Fed, when it comes down to it, who pulls the levers."

Whether Mr. Greenspan is up to that task remains to be seen. He tried to calm markets yesterday with a one-sentence statement signaling the Fed's switch from an anti-inflation to an anti-recession policy.

The Federal Reserve quickly backed up its statement with action, driving the federal funds rate down to about 6 3/4% late in the day from more than 7 1/2% Monday.

The central bank's response seemed to soothe the worst fears troubling the markets. . . . The Fed's statement "was the most calming thing that was said yesterday," said James E. Annable, the chief economist of the First National Bank of Chicago. "The Fed is aggressively creating liquidity in the market, and that's what you want now."

*(Wall Street Journal, 21 October, 1987.)*

Box 18.4 reproduces an official statement of the reserve requirements in effect as of December 31, 1987, including a variety of details given in the footnotes.

Two principles underlie the structure of reserve requirements:

1. *Shorter-term deposits generally have higher reserve ratios.* Transaction deposits, for example, have the highest ratio because unexpected withdrawals may create a need for liquidity. However, since the reserve ratio is only 12%, institutions must still provide 88 cents from their own liquidity for every $1 that is withdrawn.

2. *Smaller institutions bear lower reserve ratios.* Smaller institutions receive this benefit in part for providing special services to their local community.

BOX 18.4 BANKING BRIEFS

## Reserve Requirements

The following table is an official statement of reserve requirements published in the January 1988 *Federal Reserve Bulletin*. The details of how required reserves are held, the special exemptions for small institutions, and the precise definitions of "reservable liabilities" are shown in the notes.

Reserve Requirements of Depository Institutions[1]
Percent of deposits

| Type of deposit, and deposit interval[2] | Depository institution requirements after implementation of the Monetary Control Act | |
|---|---|---|
| | Percent of deposits | Effective date |
| *Net transaction accounts*[3,4] | | |
| $0 million–$40.5 million | 3 | 12/30/86 |
| More than $40.5 million | 12 | 12/30/86 |
| *Nonpersonal time deposits*[5] | | |
| By original maturity | | |
| Less than 1½ years | 3 | 10/6/86 |
| 1½ years or more | 0 | 10/6/83 |
| *Eurocurrency liabilities* | | |
| All types | 3 | 11/13/80 |

1. Reserve requirements in effect on Dec. 31, 1987. Required reserves must be held in the form of deposits with Federal Reserve Banks or vault cash. Nonmembers may maintain reserve balances with a Federal Reserve Bank indirectly on a pass-through basis with certain approved institutions. For previous reserve requirements, see earlier editions of the *Annual Report* and of the FEDERAL RESERVE BULLETIN. Under provisions of the Monetary Control Act, depository institutions include commercial banks, mutual savings banks, savings and loan associations, credit unions, agencies and branches of foreign banks, and Edge corporations.

2. The Garn-St. Germain Depository Institutions Act of 1982 (Public Law 97–320) requires that $2 million of reservable liabilities (transaction accounts, nonpersonal time deposits, and Eurocurrency liabilities) of each depository institution be subject to a zero percent reserve requirement. The Board is to adjust the amount of reservable liabilities subject to this zero percent reserve requirement each year for the succeeding calendar year by 80 percent of the percentage increase in the total reservable liabilities of all depository institutions, measured on an annual basis as of June 30. No corresponding adjustment is to be made in the event of a decrease. On Dec. 29, 1987, the exemption was raised from $2.9 million to $3.2 million. In determining the reserve requirements of depository institutions, the exemption shall apply in the following order: (1) net NOW accounts (NOW accounts less allowable deductions); (2) net other transaction accounts; and (3) nonpersonal time deposits or Eurocurrency liabilities starting with those with the highest reserve ratio. With respect to NOW accounts and other transaction accounts, the exemption applies only to such accounts that would be subject to a 3 percent reserve requirement.

3. Transaction accounts include all deposits on which the account holder is permitted to make withdrawals by negotiable or transferable instruments, payment orders of withdrawal, and telephone and preauthorized transfers in excess of three per month for the purpose of making payments to third persons or others. However, MMDAs and similar accounts subject to the rules that permit no more than six preauthorized, automatic, or other transfers per month, of which no more than three can be checks, are not transaction accounts (such accounts are savings deposits subject to time deposit reserve requirements).

4. The Monetary Control Act of 1980 requires that the amount of transaction accounts against which the 3 percent reserve requirement applies be modified annually by 80 percent of the percentage increase in transaction accounts held by all depository institutions, determined as of June 30 each year. Effective Dec. 29, 1987, the amount was increased from $36.7 million to $40.5 million.

5. In general, nonpersonal time deposits are time deposits, including savings deposits, that are not transaction accounts and in which a beneficial interest is held by a depositor that is not a natural person. Also included are certain transferable time deposits held by natural persons and certain obligations issued to depository institution offices located outside the United States. For details, see section 204.2 of Regulation D.

(*Federal Reserve Bulletin*, January 1988.)

## The Timing of Reserve Requirements

Banks generally try to minimize their reserves in excess of the required amount, because they receive no interest on them. However, it would be hard for a bank to keep its excess reserves close to zero if it were required to hold the right amount of required reserves each day. Large changes in deposits late in the day could upset its plans. The Federal Reserve has devised two timing rules for reserve requirements—reserve periods and carry forward options—that help banks to deal with this problem.

### Reserve Periods

The Federal Reserve currently allows banks a 14-day **reserve period**—ending every other Wednesday—to meet their reserve requirements. With this system, banks use their *average reserves* over the period to meet reserve requirements based on their *average deposits* over basically the same period. Thus a bank with insufficient reserves during the first part of a 14-day period can rectify the deficiency with excess reserves during the last part of the period. This also means that there is a lot of borrowing and lending of reserves in the federal funds market every other Wednesday as each reserve period ends.

The reserve period system uses *contemporaneous* periods to compute the average reserves and the average deposits. For *nontransaction deposits*, the two periods coincide. For *transaction deposits*, the period used to calculate average deposits is two days ahead of the one used to calculate average reserves. This means that banks can defer adjusting their reserves for changes in transaction deposits that occur on a Tuesday or Wednesday at the end of a reserve period. (In Chapter 20, we will discuss the problems that the banks and the Fed had before 1984, when reserve requirements were not contemporaneous.)

### Carry Forward Options

*Carry forward options* are another timing feature of reserve requirements:

- A bank may carry forward *excess reserves* (up to 2% of required reserves) from one reserve period to the next.
- A bank may also carry forward *a reserve deficiency* (up to 2% of required reserves) from one reserve period to the next.

If a bank still violates the reserve requirements after taking these carry forward options into account, it is charged a penalty equal to the reserve deficiency times the discount rate plus 2 percentage points for the duration of the deficiency.

## The Effect of Changing Reserve Requirements on Bank Reserves

In meeting their reserve requirements, banks sometimes have to contend with situations in which the total *available reserves* provided by the Fed are less than the total required reserves. When this happens, some banks will have reserve deficiencies. A bank with a reserve deficiency must take immediate action, either by borrowing reserves from banks with excess reserves or by reducing its deposits—selling securities or calling in (not renewing) loans (as discussed in Chapter 11).

For the banking system, an unexpected increase in reserve requirements has a particularly shocking effect because *all* banks may find they have a reserve deficiency, in which case they all have to contract their deposits. For this reason, reserve requirements are potentially the most powerful of the Federal Reserve's instruments.

This is illustrated by recalling equation (14.5) from Chapter 14 for bank deposits in the "barebones" system (where currency held by the public, excess reserves, and time deposits all equal zero):

$$D = \left(\frac{1}{\theta}\right)(B), \tag{18.4}$$

where $D$ = deposits,
   $\theta$ = the required reserve ratio for deposits,
   $B$ = the monetary base.

When the reserve ratio on deposits rises, the amount of deposits falls substantially. For example, if the monetary base is $100 and the reserve ratio on deposits is initially 10%, then deposits will initially equal $1,000 (that is, $100/0.10). If the reserve ratio on deposits is then raised to 15%, deposits will fall to $666 ($100/0.15), a reduction of 33%.

## Reserve Requirements and Monetary Policy

Because reserve requirements have such dramatic effects on bank deposits, they are rarely changed for monetary policy purposes. In fact, most changes in reserve requirements are "defensive" adjustments to new regulations or developments in the banking industry. For example, the most recent change in reserve requirements—created by the Monetary Control Act of 1980—reflected a structural change in the overall system of managing monetary policy rather than a shift in policy.

Moreover, when the Fed does raise reserve requirements (for either monetary policy or structural reasons), it usually gives the banking system substantial warning. Otherwise, it might be impossible for banks to adjust to the new requirements within a single 14-day reserve period. Indeed, the new reserve requirements imposed by the Monetary Control Act of 1980 were instituted over a *series of years*, so all institutions had ample time to prepare.

Even though the Fed rarely changes reserve requirements as part of a specific monetary policy, this does *not* mean that reserve requirements are unimportant for monetary policy. In fact, reserve requirements represent a fulcrum that provides open market operations leverage for affecting deposits and the money supply.

In an extreme case without reserve requirements, the required reserve ratio would be zero. Banks could then decide on any amount of deposits and the amount would not be directly affected by open market operations. Of course, even without reserve requirements, banks would want to hold some reserves—to meet cash withdrawals and adverse check clearings. So open market operations would still have an impact on deposits, but higher reserve ratios tend to improve the extent and dependability of the Fed control.

## Proposals for Reforming Reserve Requirements

Given that reserve requirements make the Fed's open market operations more effective, a long-standing proposal is to maximize this benefit by requiring banks to maintain 100% reserves for all deposits (or at least all transaction deposits). The reserve ratio $\theta$ in equation (18.4) would then equal 1.0:

$$D = B. \tag{18.5}$$

A 100% reserve ratio thus means that deposits $D$ equal the monetary base $B$, obviously a dependable basis for controlling deposits. Remember, however, that this is based on our barebones system. In more realistic situations, the reserve drain variables—currency held by the public, excess reserves, and required reserves on time deposits—also affect bank deposits. But equation (18.5) shows the principle that underlies proposals for 100% reserve ratios.

These proposals have not been enacted for two main reasons:

1. They would sharply reduce bank profits—banks earn no interest on required reserves.

2. They would sharply reduce bank lending—banks would have to call in loans (or sell securities) to meet the higher reserve ratios.

A second long-standing proposal for reforming reserve requirements is for the Fed to *pay interest on bank reserve account balances* in order to stabilize the amount of reserves that banks hold. Having the Fed pay interest on *total reserves*, of course, would constitute a major profit windfall for banks, something unlikely to generate much congressional support. There is also no incentive for the Fed to pay interest on *required* reserves. So it would be more practical for the Fed to pay interest only on *excess* reserves. Bank excess reserves would then fluctuate less, since the interest rate paid on them would change in line with market interest rates. This would make it easier for the Fed to determine the money supply accurately.

An excellent opportunity for instituting interest on excess reserves was available when the Monetary Control Act of 1980 restructured reserve requirements.[2] However, this opportunity was passed up, one reason being that the Treasury Department opposed any change that would reduce the Fed's profits—remember from Chapter 17 that the Fed returns its profits to the Treasury. Given this is the situation, it seems unlikely that changes will be enacted any time soon.

---

[2] The Act did provide the Fed with the power to pay interest on supplemental reserve requirements, but only under special conditions.

## Other Instruments of Monetary Policy

We have now surveyed the Fed's three main instruments for monetary policy—open market operations, the discount window, and reserve requirements. The Fed has two additional instruments that it sometimes uses for monetary policy—**foreign exchange operations** and **selective credit controls**. We will now take a brief look at selective credit controls, deferring the discussion of foreign exchange operations to Chapter 22, where we will study the international monetary system.

The Fed generally discourages the use of selective control instruments—instruments that could be directed at specific credit or debt markets—as we noted in Chapter 17. There are, nevertheless, a few points to make:

- The Federal Reserve was relieved of its most important selective control power—**Regulation Q ceilings** on deposit interest rates—by the 1980 banking regulation.

- The Fed used its power under the Credit Control Act of 1969 to restrict credit card lending during 1980, but this was unsuccessful and the Act expired in 1982. (We will examine the 1980 experience in Chapter 20 when we look at monetary policy in practice.)

- **Margin requirements** on common stocks—the amount of cash investors must provide when buying stocks on credit—are the Fed's only current selective control power. Margin requirements are briefly described in Box 18.5.

---

**BOX 18.5 CREDIT CHECK**

### Stock Margin Requirements

Stock margin requirements are stated in terms of the percentage of a stock purchase that must be paid in cash. For example, the 1988 margin requirement of 50% means that an investor buying $1,000 of stock has to pay at least $500 in cash—this cash payment is the *margin*. The other 50% can be borrowed from a stockbroker (under Regulation T of the Federal Reserve Act) or from a bank (under Regulation U).

Higher margins require investors to pay cash for a larger percentage of their purchase, a factor that could reduce the overall demand for stocks. In the past, the Federal Reserve occasionally used higher margins to reduce the demand for stocks when it felt there was unwarranted speculation in the stock market. Today, the Fed seems less confident that it can identify periods of unwarranted speculation or that higher margin requirements are the appropriate solution. In fact, the margin requirements on stocks were last changed on January 3, 1974 (from 65% to 50%).

## Chapter Summary

1. The Federal Reserve uses three main instruments for monetary policy: open market operations, the discount window, and reserve requirements. It can also carry out foreign exchange operations and use selective credit controls.

2. Open market operations are the main instrument the Fed uses to influence bank reserves, the monetary base, and the money supply. Open market purchases increase these variables, while open market sales decrease them. Open market operations are carried out by the Manager for Domestic Operations at the New York Federal Reserve Bank under directives he receives from the Federal Open Market Committee. Open market operations are generally carried out in Treasury securities, specifically Treasury bills.

3. The discount window is the Federal Reserve's facility for making loans to dep-

ository institutions. Discount loans increase bank reserves because the Fed directly credits the loan amount to the institution's reserve account. The discount rate—the rate charged on discount loans—is generally maintained below the federal funds rate, but the Fed restricts banks from borrowing for profit.

4. Reserve requirements determine the percentage of a bank's deposits that it has to maintain as bank reserves. Currently, reserve requirements are imposed on transaction accounts, nonpersonal time deposits, and Eurocurrency funds. All depository institutions in the United States are subject to the Fed's reserve requirements. Because changes in required reserve ratios force banks to make substantial adjustments in their reserves and other assets, this instrument is rarely used for monetary policy.

## Key Terms

Bank reserves:
  Borrowed
  Nonborrowed
Discount rate:
  Announcement effect
  Defensive
  Dynamic
Discount window:
  Adjustment credit
  Borrowing for profit
  Extended credit
  Lender of last resort
  Seasonal credit
Federal funds rate
Foreign exchange operations
Open market operations:
  Defensive
  Dynamic (policy-initiated)

Matched purchase-sales
Outright purchases and sales
Repurchase agreements
Reserve requirements:
  Required reserves
  Reserve period
  Reserve ratios
Selective credit controls:
  Regulation Q ceilings
  Margin requirements

## Study Questions

1. Suppose the Manager for Domestic Operations at the New York Federal Reserve Bank receives an FOMC directive to carry out a tighter monetary policy. What actions would he take, and what would be the effect on the monetary base?

2. What factor determines whether open market operations are defensive or dynamic?

3. What factor determines whether open market operations are carried out with outright purchases and sales, repurchase agreements, or matched sale-purchase transactions?

4. Why do market interest rates sometimes rise immediately when the Federal Reserve announces an increase in its discount rate?

5. Why does the Federal Reserve often have to undertake defensive open market operations because of discount window borrowing by banks?

6. Why does the Federal Reserve consider discount borrowing "a privilege, not a right" of banks? How does the Federal Reserve decide which banks receive the "privilege"?

7. Box 18.1 reproduces the statement that accompanied the Federal Reserve's reduction in the discount rate on July 11, 1986. If you were a Fed watcher, how would you have interpreted this statement?

8. Why would 100% reserve ratios on bank transaction deposits allow the Federal Reserve to determine bank deposits more accurately with open market operations?

9. Given that small banks have lower reserve requirements than large banks, what would happen to the total amount of bank deposits if there were a switch in deposits from large banks to small ones? What might the Federal Reserve do about this?

10. Why are stock margin requirements considered a selective credit control instrument of the Federal Reserve?

## Recommended Reading

*A single source on Federal Reserve instruments for monetary policy is the publication:*

*The Federal Reserve System: Purposes and Functions,* 7th edition, Board of Governors of the Federal Reserve System, Washington, D.C., 1984.

*Other sources on the specific instruments include:*

*Open Market Operations*

Neil G. Berkman, "Open Market Operations Under the New Monetary Policy," *New England Economic Review,* Federal Reserve Bank of Boston, March/April 1981, pp. 5–20.

Paul Meek, *U.S. Monetary Policy and Financial Markets,* Federal Reserve Bank of New York, 1982.

William Melton, *Inside the Fed: Making Monetary Policy,* Dow-Jones Irwin, Homewood, IL, 1985.

Howard L. Roth, "Federal Reserve Open Market Techniques," *Economic Review,* Federal Reserve Bank of Kansas City, March 1986, pp. 3–15.

*Discount Window*

Thomas M. Humphrey, "The Real Bills Doctrine," *Economic Review,* Federal Reserve Bank of Richmond 68, September/October 1982, pp. 3–13.

Thomas M. Humphrey and Robert E. Keleher, "The Lender of Last Resort," *Cato Journal* 4, Spring/Summer 1984, pp. 275–318.

David L. Mengle, "The Discount Window," in Timothy Q. Cook and Timothy D. Rowe, editors, *Instruments of the Money Market,* 6th edition, Federal Reserve Bank of Richmond, Richmond, VA, 1986.

*Reserve Requirements*

Marvin Goodfriend and Monica Hargrave, "A Historical Assessment of the Rationales and Functions of Reserve Requirements," reprinted in Donald S. Fraser and Peter S. Rose, editors, *Financial Institutions and Markets in a Changing World,* 2nd edition, Business Publications, Plano, TX, 1984.

## Appendix 18.1: Federal Reserve Float

Federal Reserve float is an accounting balance that may temporarily arise as the Fed clears checks. When customer B deposits a check in her bank B that was written by customer A on his account at bank A, bank B will use the Fed's check-clearing system to collect the funds from bank A. The Fed will eventually credit the reserve account of bank B and will debit the reserve account of bank A—thus leaving total bank reserves unchanged. However, positive Federal Reserve float is created if the Fed credits bank B's reserve account before it debits bank A's account, and negative float is created in the opposite case. Federal Reserve float thus represents a temporary change in reserves for the banking system. The following chronology, illustrated in Figure 18.5, describes more precisely how this works.

*On day 1*, bank B presents the check to the Federal Reserve for collection from bank A. The Fed does not immediately make entries in the banks' reserve accounts because it takes time to deliver the check to bank A, and the Fed will debit bank A's account only after bank A has received the check and verified that it is valid. Comparably, the Fed will credit the account of bank B on the specified day—day 3 in this example—determined by the average time it takes the Fed to clear such checks.

Although the Federal Reserve does not change the banks' reserve accounts on day 1, it does create two accounting balances on its own books: a cash item in the process of collection (CIPC)—representing the amount that will be later debited from the account of bank A—and a deferred availability cash item (DACI)—representing the amount that will later be credited to the account of bank B. Since these two items are equal on day 1, Federal Reserve float—which equals CIPC minus DACI—is zero.

*On day 2*, the check in transit to bank A is delayed by bad weather. This means that the check will arrive at bank A on day 4 instead of the scheduled day 3. Federal Reserve float is still zero, there being no change in CIPC or DACI.

*On day 3*, the Federal Reserve credits the reserve account of bank B per the original schedule. It also eliminates the DACI, since the credit to bank B is no longer being deferred. Consequently, Federal Reserve float—CIPC minus DACI—becomes positive at this time.

*On day 4*, bank A indicates that the check is valid, so the Fed can debit its reserve deposit. The Fed also eliminates the CIPC, since the cash item has been collected. The transaction has then been completed and the related Federal Reserve float is again zero.

FIGURE 18.5

**Float and the Chronology of Check Clearing**

Day 1

Bank B presents $100 check to Federal Reserve for collection.

Federal Reserve immediately sends check to bank A.

Federal Reserve will credit bank B on day 3.

Federal Reserve will debit bank A after check is verified.

Cash items in process of collection (CIPC) = $100.

Deferred availability cash items (DACI) = $100.

Federal Reserve float (CIPC − DACI) = $0.

Day 2

Bad weather delays check on way to bank A.

CIPC = $100. DACI = $100.

Federal Reserve float = $0.

Day 3

Bank B receives $100 reserve credit from Federal Reserve.

CIPC = $100. DACI = $0.

Federal Reserve float  = $100.

Day 4

Bank A receives and verifies check.

Bank A receives $100 reserve debit from Federal Reserve.

CIPC = $0. DACI = $0.

Federal Reserve float = $0.

# 19

# Techniques for Implementing Monetary Policy

*"A penny saved is a penny earned."*

*Benjamin Franklin*

Most of us find it tedious to balance our checking accounts each month, but we have to do it to be sure that our checks do not bounce. The task is simplified by monthly bank statements that credit deposits to the account and debit checks as their amounts are withdrawn.

If, instead, a bank were to record deposits and checks at random, anywhere from three to nine months after the transactions were made, customers would have far greater difficulty managing their accounts. To avoid overdrawing, they would have to recognize that their current transactions will determine their account balance six months later on average. Also, because of the uncertainty in the lag time—anywhere from three to nine months—they would have to keep a larger average balance.

In a similar way, the effects of Federal Reserve monetary policy usually occur with long and uncertain lags. So the Fed also has to look ahead to anticipate the future effects of its current policies, and it has to proceed with caution because of the uncertainty of these effects. In this chapter we will examine the specific techniques the Fed uses in implementing monetary policy.

---

We will now study how the Federal Reserve uses its **instruments of monetary policy (open market operations, discount loans,** and **reserve requirements)** to achieve its policy goals (such as lower inflation and unemployment rates). We will begin by looking at the *channels of monetary policy*—the paths through which Fed instruments have their impact. The Federal Reserve faces two main difficulties in gauging the effects of monetary policy. First, there tend to be *long and variable lag times* between the origin of a problem and the effect on it of the Fed's actions. Second, there is *uncertainty* concerning the amount of the effect. We will study the main technique—*the target approach*—used by the Fed to deal with these difficulties. We will also examine the role of expectations in conducting monetary policy.

## The Channels of Monetary Policy

The Federal Reserve's macroeconomic goals for monetary policy were discussed in Chapter 17: low inflation and unemployment rates are the two main goals, along with a high rate of capital investment, equilibrium in foreign exchange markets, and financial market stability. However, the Fed's instruments of monetary policy do not have a direct effect on these policy goals. For example, open market operations—buying and selling Treasury securities—have a direct and immediate impact on the prices and interest rates for Treasury securities and on the monetary base, but not on the inflation and unemployment rates. The same is true for the discount window and reserve requirement instruments of monetary policy.

Nevertheless, the Fed can ultimately achieve its policy goals, at least to some extent, through the **channels of monetary policy,** which are identified in Figure 19.1: the money supply, interest rates, wealth, credit availability, and liquidity. To understand how these channels work, think of an economy where people hold portfolios of assets consisting of money, securities, and real capital (manufacturing equipment or durable consumer items)—as we did in Chapter 4. Now imagine that the Federal Reserve carries out easy monetary policy by increasing the money supply. Given that people were initially satisfied with their portfolios, the monetary policy creates an excess supply of money.

FIGURE 19.1
**The Channels of Monetary Policy**

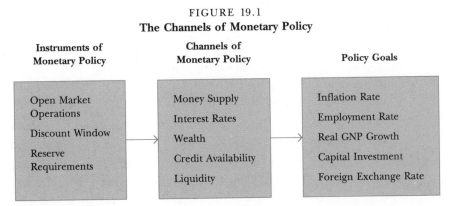

The channels of monetary policy constitute the economic relationships that link the instruments of monetary policy with the Federal Reserve's policy goals. The monetary policy instruments operate through various channels—the money supply, interest rates, wealth, credit availability, and liquidity—to realize the policy goals.

As we discussed in Chapter 16, people can do two basic things with an excess supply of money—they can spend it or lend it. The first channel in Figure 19.1—the **money supply channel**—comes into effect when people spend their excess money directly on goods and services. The specific link between the money supply and the policy goal depends on exactly how people spend their money—on consumption goods, capital goods, or foreign goods. But whatever the specifics, higher spending is a desired result of easy monetary policy.

The **interest rate channel** in Figure 19.1 comes into effect when people lend their excess money. We saw in Chapter 16 that the money demand/money supply theory and the loanable funds theory of interest rates both indicate that an increase in the money supply will cause interest rates to fall. Lower interest rates then stimulate the demand for capital investment, another desired result of easy monetary policy. Higher capital investment may in turn also influence the other policy goals.

The **wealth channel** is closely related to the interest rate channel. When interest rates fall, the prices of assets like stocks and bonds will rise (other things being the same). People holding these assets therefore feel wealthier and they may increase their demand for goods and services. Thus an easy monetary policy can be promoted by Federal Reserve actions that increase the market value of wealth in the economy.

The **credit availability channel** operates if Fed policy has an impact on the amount of credit available to borrowers. When the Fed's actions increase credit availability—allowing people to borrow more and thereby spend more—this represents easy monetary policy.

The **liquidity channel** is related to both the credit availability and money supply channels. It refers specifically to the possibility that people and firms will spend more on goods and services when they hold more liquid assets—assets that can be easily exchanged for money. The Fed can increase the amount of liquidity in the economy by increasing the money supply, again a case of easy monetary policy.

We will now look at two characteristics that are shared by all of the channels of monetary policy. One concerns the lag between the time the Fed acts on an instrument—such as open market operations—and the time the effect occurs—such as a lower inflation rate. The other concerns uncertainty in the magnitude of the effect (including the possibility that nothing may happen). In Part VII, we will look in more detail at how these channels operate and at the factors that determine how powerful each one is.

## Lags in Monetary Policy

Managing monetary policy would not be a good occupation for an impatient person. Picture the person in charge of monetary policy sitting at a control panel with a series of dials—one for each of the instruments of monetary policy—and with a series of gauges measuring the impact of the instruments on the policy goals. The person turns a control dial to a new setting, looks at the gauges expectantly, but nothing happens.

Six months later, still very little may have happened. But nothing is wrong. It is just that *there are long lags in the effects of monetary policy instruments.*

Three specific lags can be identified—the recognition lag, the implementation lag, and the impact lag. The recognition and implementation lags are also called the **inside lags** of monetary policy—they constitute the time needed to recognize problems and make decisions inside the Federal Reserve. The impact lag is called the **outside lag**—it is the time it takes the instruments to work in the economy (outside of the Federal Reserve). Taken together, these lags delay the effects of monetary policy, sometimes for a year or longer, as illustrated in Figure 19.2.

FIGURE 19.2

**Lags in Monetary Policy**

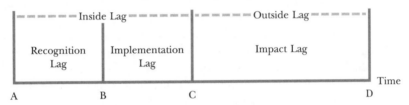

At time A, a problem arises in the economy that can be solved with monetary policy. At time B, the Federal Reserve recognizes that the problem exists. The elapsed time between A and B is the recognition lag.

At time C, the Fed makes use of monetary policy instruments to deal with the problem. The elapsed time between B and C is the implementation lag.

The recognition and implementation lags taken together equal the inside lag.

At time D, the monetary policy instruments, acting through the channels of monetary policy, have their effect. The elapsed time between C and D is the impact—or outside—lag in the effects of monetary policy.

The **recognition lag** is the time it takes the policy makers—the Board of Governors of the Federal Reserve and the Federal Open Market Committee—to learn that a problem exists in the economy. The recognition lag arises because it takes time to collect, tabulate, and analyze economic statistics. For example, suppose that the economy's inflation rate is suddenly higher. The Department of Commerce collects statistics on prices in the economy every day, but it takes the Department about a month to organize the data, and the numbers are released only on a monthly basis. So, practically speaking, the Fed may not learn about the problem until two months after it has started.

One blip in the inflation rate, moreover, is not necessarily going to convince the Board of Governors that there is a problem. Several additional months may have to pass, as more monthly data are received and other related indicators are observed, before the policymakers reach a consensus that a problem exists. Similar considerations apply to data relating to the other policy goals of the Federal Reserve.

Once a problem is recognized, the Fed has to decide how to implement its policy; this gives rise to the **implementation lag.** In part, the implementation lag arises because the FOMC meets only about once a month. (In an emergency the FOMC can meet by telephone and make rapid decisions.) In addition, since monetary policy decisions are made cautiously, action is often deferred until the next meeting. Other practical matters—such as the need for defensive open market operations or new auctions of Treasury securities—may also cause action to be delayed, adding to the implementation lag.

Finally, the longest lag—the **impact lag**—comes after the policy instruments have been employed. It usually takes time for the channels of monetary policy to operate—for individuals and firms to react to a change in policy.

As an example, consider how easy monetary policy, operating through lower interest rates, might affect the decision of a firm to build a new manufacturing plant. Generally, lower interest rates induce firms to increase their capital investment in plants and equipment. But if a shift to an easier monetary policy causes the Treasury bill rate to fall by 1% one morning, there is little likelihood of an immediate response in the amount of the firm's capital investment. This is because the firm's board of directors will probably require a series of meetings to decide whether to go ahead with as major an undertaking as a new plant.

If the board does eventually decide to order a new plant, its decision still does not represent capital investment, which is recorded only when the builder begins digging the foundation. Thus, months, or even a year or more, may pass between the time the Fed initiates its policy and the time the firm's capital investment begins.

## Long and Variable Impact Lags

The impact lags of monetary policy are **variable** and **long** because of many factors. For one thing, the response to a tightening of monetary policy depends on the status of *investment projects already in process.* For example, if the plant we just described is 75% completed when a tight monetary policy is initiated, the firm will probably decide to complete it anyway—so the effect of the new policy in this case will have a longer lag. But if the plant is only 10% completed, the firm may immediately cancel it—so the effect will be quicker.

For another thing, the response to a tight monetary policy may depend on the *expectations people hold* regarding its intensity and duration. Obviously, people will respond more promptly and definitively if they expect interest rates to rise rapidly and to remain high—the implementation lag will then be shorter. On the other hand, people may ignore what they expect to be a slight or temporary increase in interest rates—making the implementation lag far longer.

Lags in the effects of monetary policy create a risk that the Fed will make a mistake in implementation. Figure 19.3 shows in panel A an economy experiencing successive booms and recessions in real GNP, each lasting two years. The goal of a tight monetary policy in this situation is to stop the economy from overheating during its boom phase—due to inflationary pressures—in order to avoid the following recession.

*Panel A* shows how the economy performs in the absence of monetary policy. The boom phase creates inflationary pressure through date 1, leading to the recession between dates 1 and 3.

FIGURE 19.3

**Managing Monetary Policy When There Are Lags in Its Effects**

A. The Economy Without Monetary Policy

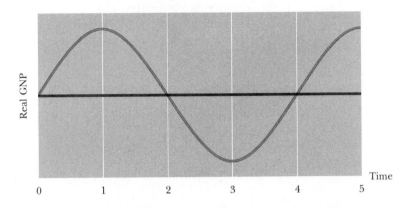

B. Monetary Policy Extends the Boom

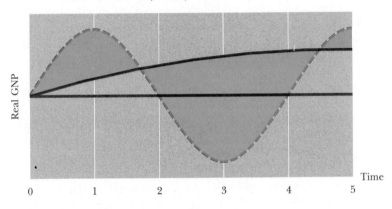

C. Monetary Policy Extends the Recession

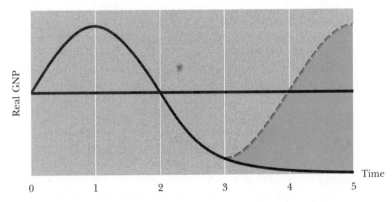

In panel A, the economy has a boom through date 1 and a recession between dates 1 and 3. In panel B, monetary policy works with a short lag to extend the boom, the net impact of monetary policy being shown by the shaded area. In panel C, monetary policy works with a longer lag and inadvertently extends the recession. Again, the shaded area shows the net impact of monetary policy.

*Panel B* shows what happens when tight monetary policy—implemented at date 0—*promptly impacts the economy.* Because the policy stops the economy from overheating at date 1, the economic boom is extended, and the subsequent recession is eliminated. The shaded area represents the change in real GNP caused by monetary policy.

*Panel C* shows the effect of exactly the same tight monetary policy, but for a case in which it *impacts the economy only at date 2.* As a result of the longer lag, its impact is too late to stop the economy from overheating at date 1. Instead, the policy has its impact only after the economy is already in recession, making the recession worse.

## Implementing Policy in the Face of Uncertainty

We have looked so far only at the uncertainty concerning the timing of the effects of monetary policy. The magnitude of the effects is also likely to be quite uncertain. To get a sense of this, again assume that the Fed tries to stimulate capital investment by reducing interest rates through open market purchases of Treasury bills. To executive this monetary policy, the Trading Desk at the New York Federal Reserve Bank must know the proper amount of Treasury bills to buy.

If the Fed is thinking in terms of the interest rate channel, then it might break the process down into two steps. First, it would determine how much interest rates must fall in order to cause capital investment to rise by the desired amount. Then, it would determine the amount of open market purchases needed to cause interest rates to fall by that much.

These two steps are illustrated in Figure 19.4. In panel A, investment demand $I^D$ rises as the interest rate $r$ falls, because more investment projects are profitable when the cost of financing is lower. In the case illustrated, the initial amount of investment is $I_0$ (when the interest rate is $r_0$), and the desired amount is $I^*$. Therefore, the Fed can gauge that the interest rate must fall from $r_0$ to $r^*$ to achieve the desired effect.

Panel B shows how the interest rate is determined by the equilibrium between money demand and money supply, as we discussed in Chapter 16. The initial equilibrium occurs where the money demand curve $M^D$ intersects the vertical money supply line $M_0$—that is, where the interest rate is $r_0$. Open market purchases that increase the money supply from $M_0$ to $M^*$ will then decrease the interest rate from $r_0$ to $r^*$.

Figure 19.4 illustrates the important point that the change in *monetary policy can be gauged either by the change in the interest rate or by the change in the money supply.* FOMC policy directives that (1) reduce the interest rate from $r_0$ to $r^*$, or (2) that increase the money supply from $M_0$ to $M^*$ are equivalent ways of measuring monetary policy, as long as a one-to-one relationship exists between the interest rate and the money supply along the money demand curve $M^D$ (as in panel B of Figure 19.4). However, we will now see that the situation is more complicated when uncertainty is reflected in either the money demand or investment demand curves.

In panel A, the interest rate is initially $r_0$ and investment is $I_0$. Therefore, the Fed must reduce the interest rate to $r^*$ to reach the investment goal of $I^*$.

FIGURE 19.4

**Monetary Policy: The Interest Rate and the Money Supply**

A. Gauging the Desired Change in Interest Rates

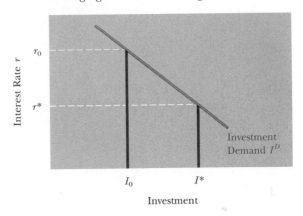

In panel B, the money supply is initially $M_0$ and the interest rate is $r_0$. The money supply is then increased to $M^*$ to lower the interest rate to $r^*$.

B. Increasing the Money Supply

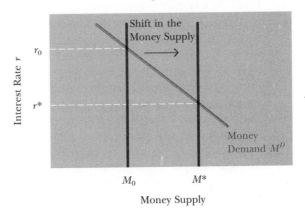

## Monetary Policy When Money Demand Is Uncertain

The analysis in Figure 19.4 assumes that the Fed knows the exact location of the money demand and investment demand curves. In practice, it may be uncertain about the location of either of these curves. The best way to carry out monetary policy then depends on which curve is the main source of the uncertainty. We will now look at the two possibilities, starting with the money demand curve.

We saw in Chapter 16, in the case of the missing money, that the Fed may be uncertain about the exact location of the money demand curve. It may still be able to estimate the normal relationship between money demand and the interest rate, but at any given time the demand curve may unexpectedly shift rightward or leftward.

Figure 19.5 illustrates such a situation, based on the same investment, money demand, and money supply curves as Figure 19.4, but with a band of uncertainty around the money demand curve. The Fed *expects*

Uncertainty about the location of the money demand curve is indicated by the shaded area around the curve. With this type of uncertainty, the FOMC should give instructions to the trading disk to carry out open market purchases of securities until the interest rate falls from $r_0$ to $r^*$.

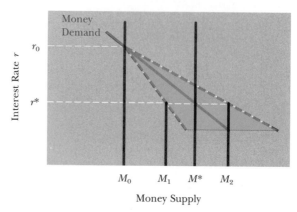

FIGURE 19.5

**Uncertainty in Money Demand**

that an interest rate of $r^*$ will result in money demand of $M^*$ (as in Figure 19.4), but it recognizes that $r^*$ may *actually* result in money demand anywhere between the values $M_1$ and $M_2$.

When the location of the money demand curve is uncertain, it is better for the FOMC to specify directives to the Trading Desk at the New York Reserve Bank in terms of the *interest rate, not the money supply*. That is, the FOMC should tell the trading desk to carry out open market purchases of securities until the interest rate falls from $r_0$ to $r^*$, the level that causes investment to be $I^*$.

Giving policy directives in terms of the interest rate ensures that the interest rate will be $r^*$ and that investment will be $I^*$. At the same time, the open market purchases that cause the interest rate to reach $r^*$ will also cause the money supply to equal the demand for money—$M_1$, $M^*$, or $M_2$—whichever is the actual case.

However, the process will not work in reverse: that is, the Fed cannot specify its instructions directly in terms of the money supply when money demand is uncertain. The problem is that the Fed does not know the proper money supply because it does not know ahead of time which will be the relevant money demand curve. This is why monetary policy should be stated in terms of *the interest rate* under these circumstances.

## Monetary Policy When Investment Demand Is Uncertain

Figure 19.6 shows the case where the source of uncertainty is the location of the investment demand curve. This uncertainty is illustrated by the shaded band around the investment demand curve $EA$ in panel A. The Fed may be able to estimate the normal relationship between investment demand and the interest rate, but at a given time the investment demand curve may unexpectedly shift rightward or leftward. The result is that the Fed may expect that an interest rate or $r^*$ will result in investment demand of $I^*$ (the case used in Figure 19.4), but it also knows that if the investment curve shifts, an interest rate as low as $r_b$ or as high as $r_c$ will be required to reach investment of $I^*$.

In panel A, the investment demand curve is expected to be *EA*, but it may turn out to be *EB* or *EC*. To reach the investment goal of *I\**, the interest rates would be *r\**, $r_b$, and $r_c$ for the respective cases. If the FOMC's policy directive specifies the interest rate *r\**, it will result in the wrong amount of investment if the investment curve shifts.

FIGURE 19.6

**Uncertainty in Investment Demand**

A. Gauging the Desired Change in Interest Rates

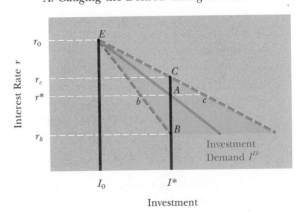

In panel B, the money demand curve is expected to be *E'A'*, but it will shift to *E'B'* or *E'C'* if there is a similar shift in investment demand. If the Fed specifies the money supply to be *M\**, the equilibrium interest rate will be *r\**, $r_b$, or $r_c$, depending on the location of the money demand curve. Whichever is the case, investment demand is *I\**, as represented in panel A by the points *A*, *B*, and *C*.

B. Increasing the Money Supply

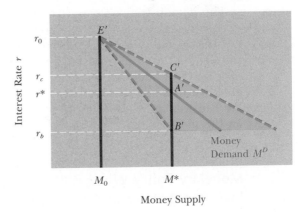

With uncertainty regarding investment demand, the FOMC should *not* give its monetary policy directive to the Trading Desk in terms of the interest rate. The problem is that for investment to be *I\**, the interest rate may have to be $r_b$, *r\**, or $r_c$, depending on the location of the investment demand curve; and the FOMC does not know ahead of time which case will apply.

There is a better way to implement monetary policy if it can be assumed that a shift in the investment demand curve is matched one-for-one by a shift in the money demand curve. This may happen, for example, if an increase in investment demand raises the level of income, thereby increasing the demand for money by the same amount.[1] This case is illustrated in Figure 19.6: if the investment demand curve *EA* shifts to *EB* or *EC*, the money demand curve *E'A'* shifts to *E'B'* or *E'C'*.

---

[1] In contrast, in Figure 19.5, a shift in the money demand curve does not create a corresponding shift in the investment demand curve, given that investment demand depends on the interest rate but not on income.

The result is that the FOMC can reach its investment goal of $I^*$ with a directive to maintain a money supply of $M^*$, even though it is uncertain whether the investment demand curve will shift or in which direction. Three outcomes are possible, depending on how the investment curve shifts:

1. When investment demand is $EA$, as expected, then money demand is $E'A'$, so the money supply of $M^*$ determines the interest rate $r^*$ and investment $I^*$.

2. If investment demand shifts left to $EB$, then money demand shifts left to $E'B'$, so the money supply of $M^*$ determines the interest rate $r_b$. Because $r_b$ is less than $r^*$, there is a movement down the investment curve $EB$ from point $b$ to point $B$, resulting in the desired investment $I^*$.

3. If investment demand shifts right, to $EC$, then money demand shifts right to $E'C'$, so the money supply of $M^*$ determines the interest rate $r_c$. Because $r_c$ is greater than $r^*$, there is a movement up the investment curve $EC$ from point $c$ to point $C$, again resulting in investment $I^*$.

This demonstration assumes that the money demand curve shifts by exactly the same amount as the investment demand curve. In practice, it is reasonable to expect that the two curves will shift in the same direction, but not necessarily by the same amount. As a result, the money supply $M^*$ will not determine an amount of investment precisely equal to $I^*$. Nevertheless, as long as the two curves shift in the same direction, the Fed will come closer to its goal of $I^*$ with a policy directive based on the money supply $M^*$ rather than with one based on the interest rate $r^*$.

## Monetary Policy When Both Money Demand and Investment Demand Are Uncertain

The preceding analysis leads to a simple set of rules for implementing monetary policy when there is uncertainty:

- If the source of the uncertainty is the money demand curve, then FOMC policy directives should be given in terms of the interest rate $r^*$.

- If the source of the uncertainty is the investment demand curve, the FOMC policy directives should be given in terms of the money supply $M^*$.

As a practical matter, the Fed is likely to face uncertainty in *both* the money and investment demand curves. The FOMC directive might then be stated in terms of *both* the interest rate $r^*$ and the money supply $M^*$. However, the Trading Desk can act on such a directive only when the money demand curve turns out to be the expected curve. For example, the Trading Desk could reach both $r^*$ and $M^*$ for the money demand curve $E'A'$ in Figure 19.6, but it could not do so for the money demand curves $E'B'$ or $E'C'$, because the point $\{r^*, M^*\}$ does not lie on these curves.

---

BOX 19.1 MONEY MATTERS

## Proviso Clauses in FOMC Directives

The Federal Reserve has used proviso clauses in its policy directives since 1966. The following two examples show how the proviso clause (identified by italics) has evolved:

> *FOMC meeting of June 7, 1966.* To implement this policy, System open market operations until the next meeting of the Committee shall be conducted with a view to maintaining net reserve availability and related money market conditions in about their recent ranges; *provided, however, that if required reserves expand considerably more than that seasonally expected, operations shall be conditioned with a view to attaining some further grad-*

> *ual reduction in net reserve availability and firming of money market conditions.*

> *FOMC meeting of September 22, 1987.* This approach is expected to be consistent with growth in M2 and M3 over the period from August through December at annual rates of around 4 percent and around 6 percent, respectively. M1 is expected to continue to grow relatively slowly. *The Chairman may call for Committee consultation if it appears to the Manager for Domestic Operations that reserve conditions during the period before the next meeting are likely to be associated with a federal funds rate persistently outside a range of 5 to 9 percent.*

> (*FOMC Directives*, June 1966 and September 1987.)

---

The Federal Open Market Committee has a clever solution to this problem—called a **proviso clause**—in which the Trading Desk is told which variable (the interest rate or the money supply) should have priority. For example, the FOMC directive might give priority to the money supply $M^*$, *provided* that the interest rate does not exceed a given limit. While this is not a perfect solution, it is practical. Box 19.1 illustrates proviso clauses in two FOMC policy directives.

## Monetary Policy Targets

The specific method generally used by the Fed in dealing with the lags and uncertainty of monetary policy is the target approach—using both operating and intermediate targets:

**Operating targets** are variables like the federal funds rate and the monetary base that are closely related to the Fed's instruments, such as open market operations. Operating targets are used to aim the instruments.

**Intermediate targets** are variables like the money supply and bond interest rates that are closely related to the Fed's policy goals. Intermediate targets are used to gauge the impact of monetary policy in achieving the Fed's goals.

## Using Operating and Intermediate Targets

The Fed initiates a new monetary policy by using one of its instruments, such as open market operations. This starts the flow of effects. In turn, the change in the instrument variable affects an operating target variable, the change in the operating target variable affects an intermediate target variable, and the change in the intermediate target varible affects a policy goal variable. This is illustrated in Figure 19.7, moving from the top of the figure to the bottom.

However, in *planning* monetary policy, the Fed works in just the opposite direction—from the bottom of Figure 19.7 to the top. That is, given the lags and uncertainty in the effects of monetary policy, the Fed has to work backward starting with the policy goal.

Given the policy goal, the first step is to determine the change in the *intermediate target* needed to reach the goal. The Fed refers to the channels of monetary policy to determine the necessary change in the intermediate target. (In Part VII, we will discuss how the Fed uses models of the economy for this purpose.)

Once an intermediate target is selected, the Fed then works backward to the second step, which is the *operating target*. The value selected for the operating target is based on the desired change in the intermediate target. Instructions are given by the FOMC to the Trading Desk at the New York Federal Reserve Bank regarding the operating target. Then at planning step 3, the Manager of the Trading Desk uses the operating target to gauge how much to change the appropriate monetary *instrument,* such as open market operations.

## The Properties of Targets

To be effective, operating and intermediate targets should have certain properties: they should be controllable, have predictable impacts on the policy goals, and be measurable. The importance of these properties depends on how the instruments, targets, and policy goals interact:

- Since *operating targets* are linked with the Fed's instruments, they should be **controllable** by the instruments. This way, operating targets can be used to monitor monetary policy.

- Since *intermediate targets* are linked with the policy goals, they should have a **predictable impact** on the goals. This way, intermediate targets can be used to gauge monetary policy.

- Since the operating and intermediate targets are used to monitor and gauge monetary policy, they both should be **measurable.**

## Operating Targets

Based on these properties, the Federal Reserve has settled on two basic classes of *operating targets:* **reserves** and **interest rates.** Reserves used as operating targets include nonborrowed reserves, borrowed reserves, and the monetary base. Interest rates used as operating targets include the federal funds rate and the Treasury bill rate.

FIGURE 19.7
**Planning Monetary Policy with Operating and Intermediate Targets**

| Instruments of Monetary Policy | Open Market Operations<br>Discount Window<br>Reserve Requirements |
|---|---|

Implementation Step 1 ↓ | ↑ Planning Step 3

| Operating Targets | Reserves | Nonborrowed Reserves<br>Borrowed Reserves<br>Monetary Base |
|---|---|---|
| | Interest Rates | Federal Funds Rate<br>Treasury Bill Rate |

Implementation Step 2 ↓ | ↑ Planning Step 2

| Intermediate Targets | Money Supply | M1, M2, or M3 |
|---|---|---|
| | Interest Rates | Corporate or<br>Treasury Bonds |

Implementation Step 3 ↓ | ↑ Planning Step 1

| Policy Goals | Inflation Rate<br>Unemployment Rate<br>Real GNP Growth<br>Capital Investment<br>Foreign Exchange |
|---|---|

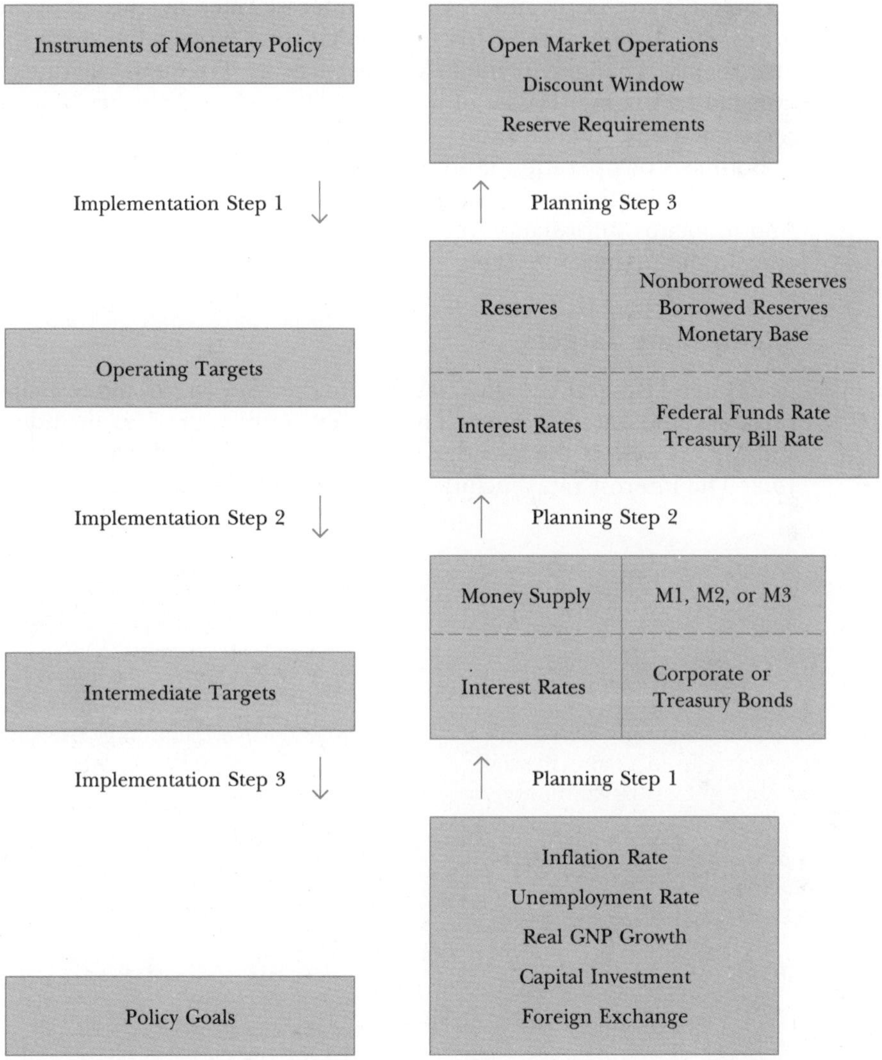

The diagram shows schematically how the Fed uses operating and intermediate targets to plan monetary policy. Initially, as shown at the bottom of the diagram, the Fed has to determine its policy goals. It then plans backward, first to the intermediate targets, and then to the operating targets, to determine how much to change the instruments of monetary policy. The implementation of monetary policy works in the opposite direction, starting with the instruments.

Both sets of operating targets can be controlled with open market operations. Open market purchases of securities directly raise the reserve variables. They also reduce security interest rates by raising security prices. Furthermore, as we discussed in Chapter 8 regarding term structure theory, changes in interest rates such as Treasury bill rates are transmitted to other classes of interest rates, such as Treasury bond and corporate bond interest rates.

Both sets of operating targets are also measurable. The Fed obtains information on the reserve targets from the reports made to it by banks. And it obtains information on the interest rate targets from the quotations in the financial markets.

## Intermediate Targets

The Federal Reserve uses two classes of *intermediate targets:* **money supply variables** and **interest rates.** The money supply variables include M1 and M2, as well as the broader monetary aggregates described in Box 19.2. The interest rates include corporate and Treasury bond rates.

---

BOX 19.2 FINANCIAL NEWS

## Monetary Aggregates Used as Intermediate Targets

Various money supplies and related monetary aggregates are used as intermediate targets. This table shows the components that make up five frequently used monetary aggregates—M1, M2, M3, L (liquid assets), and D (debt).

**Measures of the Monetary Aggregates
At year-end 1987
(Dollars in billions)**

| M1 | |
|---|---:|
| Currency | 197 |
| Travelers checks | 7 |
| Demand deposits | 288 |
| Other checkable deposits | 259 |
| Total | $751 |

| M2 | |
|---|---:|
| M1 | 751 |
| Savings deposits | 414 |
| Small time deposits | 913 |
| Money market deposit accounts | 525 |
| Money market mutual funds (noninstitutional) | 222 |
| Overnight repurchase agreements and Eurodollars | 77 |
| Total | $2,902 |

| M3 | |
|---|---:|
| M2 | 2,902 |
| Large time deposits | 483 |
| Term repurchase agreements and Eurodollars | 191 |
| Money market mutual funds (institutional) | 89 |
| Total | $3,662 |

| L (Liquid assets) | |
|---|---:|
| M3 | 3,662 |
| Savings bonds | 100 |
| Short-term Treasury securities | 268 |
| Bankers' acceptances | 46 |
| Commercial paper | 259 |
| Total | $4,334 |

| | |
|---|---:|
| D (Debt of nonfinancial sectors) | $8,299 |

**Source:** Federal Reserve *Statistical Release* H.6 (506). Totals may not equal the sum of the components due to seasonal adjustment.

A key issue has been whether the money supply or an interest rate is a better intermediate target. Since the answer may depend on the particular policy goal, we will discuss the issue with two examples, one where a money supply target is used to reduce the inflation rate, and another where an interest rate target is used to stimulate investment. An example for each intermediate target is given in Boxes 19.3 and 19.4.

BOX 19.3 MONEY MATTERS

## The Money Supply Used as the Intermediate Target

The following excerpt is from Paul Volcker's testimony before Congress on February 25, 1981, as reported in the *Federal Reserve Bulletin*. At that time, the Federal Reserve was carrying out a very determined effort to control inflation with money supply targets.

The basic premise of the System's policy is the broadly accepted notion that inflation can persist over appreciable spans of time only if it is accommodated by monetary expansion. The strategy to which the System has committed itself is to hold monetary growth to rates that fall short of such accommodation and thus encourage adjustments consistent with a return to

price stability over time. To be sure, the relationships between the growth of money and the behavior of the economic variables of ultimate concern—such as production, employment, and inflation—are not in practice absolutely stable or predictable, especially in the short run. But the crucial fact is that rates of monetary expansion in the vicinity of those specified by the Federal Open Market Committee (FOMC) last February implied a substantial degree of restraint on the growth of nominal growth national product—that is, the combined result of inflation and real growth.

(*Federal Reserve Bulletin*, February, 1981.)

### The Money Supply as the Intermediate Target

The money supply is a natural intermediate target for lowering the inflation rate because the growth rate in the money supply readily translates into a corresponding inflation rate. This can be seen by recalling the quantity equation of exchange first introduced in Chapter 1, $MV = Py$, which can be rewritten as:

$$P = \frac{MV}{y},$$ (19.1)

where $M$ = the money supply,
$V$ = the velocity of money,
$P$ = the price level,
$y$ = the level of real income.

BOX 19.4 MONEY MATTERS

## Interest Rates Used as the Intermediate Target

The following *Wall Street Journal* article by Alan Murray of February 24, 1988, suggests that interest rate targets may be the focus of monetary policy under Fed chairman Alan Greenspan, in contrast to Paul Volcker's testimony in Box 19.3.

**Greenspan Confirms Fed Allowed Interest Rates To Decline Recently. But Chairman Is Optimistic On Economy, Indicating More Easing Isn't Likely**

WASHINGTON—Federal Reserve Board Chairman Alan Greenspan confirmed that the Fed recently eased its grip on credit, allowing interest rates to fall.

In his semiannual testimony to Congress on monetary policy, Mr. Greenspan said that signs of weakness in the economy, as well as the recent stability of the dollar, "led us to take a further small easing step a few weeks ago." . . .

Like his predecessor, Paul Volcker, Mr. Greenspan demonstrated considerable skill in avoiding direct answers to questions about interest rates or the future direction of policy. . . .

In his testimony yesterday, Mr. Greenspan made it clear that current Fed members have little confidence in the various measures of money supply as a guide to policy. For the second year in a row, the central bank refused to set a target range for the basic money supply measure, M1, which includes currency and checking accounts. It also widened its target ranges for growth in the broader measures, M2 and M3, which include various types of savings accounts and time deposits as well as currency and checking accounts. . . .

Mr. Greenspan said the relationship between the money measures and economic growth and inflation "appear to have changed considerably in the 1980s," and as a result they are less reliable as a guide to policy than in the past.

(Alan Murray, "Greenspan Confirms Fed Allowed Interest Rates to Decline Recently, *Wall Street Journal*, 24 February, 1988.)

Thus, the inflation rate—the growth rate of the price level—will equal the growth rate of the money supply, unless the velocity of money $V$ or real income $y$ also changes.

For example, suppose the inflation rate and the growth rate of the money supply are both initially 10%, and that the Federal Reserve wishes to reduce the inflation rate to 5%. A 5% growth rate in the money supply might then be a reasonable target. However, the Fed also has to factor in the possibility that real income $y$ or the velocity of money may change. Since the growth rate in real income is itself a policy goal, the Fed often just adds the desired growth rate for real income to the growth rate target for the money supply. Since the Fed generally just wants the change in velocity to be small (or at least predictable), it often chooses as its intermediate target the money supply aggregate that provides the most stable value for the velocity of money.

The patterns for the velocity of money for the main money supply aggregates are illustrated in Figure 19.8. Other things being the same, the Federal Reserve will use the money supply that leads to the most stable (or predictable) velocity. On this basis, the Fed shifted in 1987 from M1 to the broader definitions, as we will discuss further in Chapter 20.

FIGURE 19.8
**The Velocity of the Main Money Supply Aggregates**

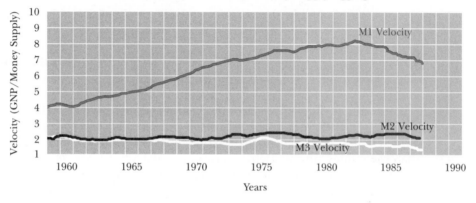

Although M1 was commonly used as an intermediate target of monetary policy, large fluctuations in its velocity caused the Federal Reserve to switch in 1987 to broader measures, such as M2 and M3. Box 19.2 describes the various monetary aggregates.

### Interest Rates as Intermediate Targets

When capital investment is the policy goal, interest rates are natural intermediate targets because there is a predictable relationship between the target and the goal: when interest rates fall, capital investment rises. The Fed would refer to the relationship between capital investment and the bond rate—as illustrated in Figure 19.4—in determining the desired value for the bond interest rate.

*Real interest rates* are generally more appropriate than *nominal interest rates* as intermediate targets. Recall from Chapter 4 that ex ante real interest rates are defined as:

Ex Ante Real Rate = Nominal Interest Rate − Expected Inflation.

A *real* interest rate is generally a better intermediate target because firm managers look at the *real* cost of borrowing money when making their *real* investment decisions. *Real* capital investment is the relevant policy goal because the Fed is not going to be pleased if high inflation results in a high *nominal value* of investment, while *real* investment remains low.

However, ex ante real interest rate targets are not easily measured, unlike nominal interest rates. This is because ex ante real interest rates are based on *expected inflation,* and the expected inflation rate is not directly observable in the economy. Even if members of the Federal Open Market Committee know what *they* expect inflation to be, firm managers may have quite a different view. They may doubt, for example, that the Fed will succeed in meeting its inflation rate goal, in which case their expected inflation rate will be higher than that of the FOMC.

## Other Intermediate Targets

Because it is often difficult to manage monetary policy using either monetary aggregates or real interest rates as intermediate targets, alternative variables are also considered. However, these alternative intermediate targets generally involve an unfortunate trade-off: the targets that are *most controllable* tend to have *less predictable* effects on the policy goals; and vice versa.

For example, Benjamin Friedman has recommended that the Federal Reserve use the outstanding *debt* of all nonfinancial borrowers in the United States as an intermediate target, a broader monetary aggregate than the money supply. Debt has two potential advantages: (1) it tends to be affected less than the money supply by changes in the financial system such as deregulation; (2) it may have a more predictable effect than the money supply on the Fed's policy goals. However, compared to the money supply, debt has the clear drawback that it is much further removed from Fed control.

As another example, Karl Brunner and Allen Meltzer have recommended the *monetary base* as an intermediate target for money policy. The monetary base has the virtue of being highly controllable by the Federal Reserve—indeed, we saw earlier that it is used as an operating target. However, it is problematic whether the impact of the monetary base on monetary policy goals is sufficiently predictable to use it as an *intermediate target.*

There have even been proposals to use either *nominal GNP* or *real GNP* as intermediate targets for monetary policy. These variables, however, have just the opposite problem of the monetary base: although they should have predictable impacts on the policy goals—indeed, they *are* the goals—they are probably not sufficiently controllable to function as intermediate targets.

It is on the basis of such trade-offs that the Fed has chosen the money supply and interest rates as practical compromises for its intermediate targets.

## The Role of Expectations for Monetary Policy

We have emphasized that the Federal Reserve has to adopt a forward-looking approach in conducting monetary policy because of the long and variable lags in the effects of its actions. The result is that *expectations* play a fundamental role in the Fed's conduct of monetary policy. These *expectations* refer to where the economy will be at a future date, and to the future relationships between its instruments, operating targets, intermediate targets, and policy goals.

Another role for expectations arises in terms of the economy's response to monetary policy. This response is based to an important extent on the expectations that people form regarding monetary policy and how the economy will react to it. This creates a complicated situation in which the economy responds to monetary policy on the basis of the expectations that have been formed, while the expectations are formed on the basis of how the economy responds to monetary policy. We will examine this interaction in detail as part of the theory of *rational expectations* in Chapter 26.

However, we can immediately illustrate a key implication of the interaction, namely that monetary policy can lose much of its effectiveness as a result of expectations. If Federal Reserve policy is to be effective, it has to be *credible*—people have to believe that the Federal Reserve will carry out its stated policy. For example, if firms are to build new plants on the basis of a stated easy monetary policy, they have to expect that lower interest rates will actually occur.

To be credible, the Federal Reserve certainly should be *honest* in stating its monetary policy—a useful trait in any case. However, even honest policies have a potential problem—what economists call **time inconsistency.** Time inconsistency refers to the possibility that, if people in the economy change their behavior after a monetary policy is announced, then the Fed may honestly change its mind about the proper policy. In this circumstance, the Fed may fail to carry through with its stated policy.

Using a tight monetary policy to fight inflation illustrates how time inconsistency can develop. Suppose that inflation is initially very high and that the Fed announces a tight monetary policy to solve the problem. Based on this policy, people will make plans, assuming that inflation will soon be lower. In fact, their behavior—such as postponing consumption expenditures—is likely to help reduce inflation. So a year or two later, the Fed may find that inflation has vanished as a problem—but the economy may then be in the midst of a recession. It would then be sensible for the Fed to switch to an easier monetary policy, even if this means creating some inflation in the process and causing losses for people who have made plans based on low inflation.

In this scenario, the Federal Reserve had the best of intentions, but it was time inconsistent—it announced one policy, then changed its policy after people responded. The result could be that people would not respond the next time the Fed tried such a policy, and thus the policy would not be effective. There are no simple solutions to this problem of time inconsistency. In the case just described, for example, it would probably be worse for the Fed to be *time consistent*—that is, to adhere to its tight monetary policy—even when the economy was entering into a recession. Time consistency is something we will look into as we turn to the practice of monetary policy in Chapter 20.

## Chapter Summary

1. The Federal Reserve carries out monetary policy using its policy instruments—open market operations, the discount window, and reserve requirements—to achieve its policy goals, such as the unemployment and inflation rates. The channels of monetary policy are the mechanisms through which changes in the Fed's policy instruments bring about its policy goals. The channels include the money supply, interest rates, wealth, credit availability, and liquidity.

2. Lags in the effects of monetary policy force the Federal Reserve to look ahead in conducting monetary policy. The variability of the lags and the uncertainty in the extent of the policy's effects cause the Fed to carry out monetary policy cautiously, to avoid doing more harm than good.

3. To deal with these problems, the Fed uses operating targets and intermediate targets to conduct monetary policy. Operating targets include various reserve variables and interest rates that are closely related to the Fed's instruments. Intermediate targets include various definitions of the money supply and various interest rates that are closely related to the Fed's policy goals.

4. It is important that operating and intermediate targets be measurable, controllable, and have predictable impacts on the Federal Reserve's policy goals. Controllability is particularly important for operating targets, while predictability of impact is particularly important for intermediate targets.

5. There is a major debate over whether monetary aggregates or interest rates are the better intermediate target. Which intermediate target works best in a particular circumstance may depend on the particular policy goal and on the main source of uncertainty in the economy at the time. When there is uncertainty regarding money demand, for example, interest rate targets are generally preferred, whereas when there is uncertainty regarding investment demand, money supply targets generally work better.

6. Expectations play an important role both in how the Federal Reserve conducts monetary policy and in how the economy responds to it. Because of the lags and uncertainty in the effects of monetary policy, the Fed has to form expectations about economic conditions and the likely effect of its policies. At the same time, the economy's response to monetary policy will depend on how people expect monetary policy to be carried out.

## Key Terms

Channels of monetary policy:
Credit availability
Interest rates
Liquidity
Money supply
Wealth
Instruments of monetary policy:
Discount window
Open market operations
Reserve requirements
Intermediate targets:
Interest rates
Monetary aggregates
Lags in the effects of monetary policy:

Inside (recognition and implementation)
Long and variable
Outside (impact)
Operating targets:
Reserves
Interest rates
Proviso clause
Properties of targets:
Controllable
Measurable
Predictable (impact on policy goals)
Time inconsistency
Uncertainty in the extent of the effects of monetary policy

## Study Questions

1. Suppose the Federal Reserve is using open market sales as the policy instrument to curtail inflation in the economy. Briefly describe how monetary policy activates each of the following channels:

   a. The money supply

   b. Interest rates

   c. Wealth

   d. Credit availability

   e. Liquidity.

2. Based on Question 1, how could each of the channels help the Federal Reserve reach its policy goal of curtailing inflation?

3. For the interest rate channel in Question 1, describe the impact lag and the uncertainty in the effect of the policy.

4. Suppose the Federal Reserve is using open market purchases to increase the amount of capital investment in the economy. How does uncertainty about the location

of the *investment demand curve* make monetary policy more difficult? How does uncertainty about the location of the *money demand curve* make monetary policy more difficult?

5. Based on Question 4, when is the Federal Reserve better off using an interest rate as its intermediate target? And when is it better off using the money supply?

6. What is the key feature of a good operating target? Of a good intermediate target?

7. Why are nonborrowed reserves a good *operating target,* while the M1 money supply is a good *intermediate target*?

8. What features of interest rates make them useful *both* as good operating targets and as good intermediate targets? What problem is there with interest rates serving both roles?

9. Evaluate the use of the *monetary base* versus real GNP as an intermediate target.

10. Suppose the Federal Reserve announces a tight monetary policy that is designed to eliminate inflation in two years. If people believe the policy will work, how might they change their behavior so that the policy becomes more effective?

---

## Recommended Reading

*A classic article indicating how the Federal Reserve should conduct monetary policy when there is uncertainty.*

William C. Brainard, "Uncertainty and the Effectiveness of Policy," *American Economic Review* 57, May 1967, pp. 411–425.

*An analysis of monetary indicators by authors who prefer the monetary base as an intermediate target and have been critical of the Federal Reserve:*

Karl Brunner and Allan Meltzer, "The Meaning of Monetary Indicators," in G. Horwich, editor, *Monetary Process and Policy,* Richard D. Irwin, Homewood, Ill., 1967.

*The following set of articles provides a critique of Federal Reserve use of its targets and suggests some alternatives:*

Benjamin Friedman, "The Inefficiency of Short-Run Monetary Targets for Monetary Policy," *Brookings Papers on Economic Activity* 2, 1977, pp. 293–335.

Benjamin Friedman, "The Roles of Money and Credit in Macroeconomic Analysis," in James Tobin, editor, *Macroeconomic Price and Quantities: Essays in Memory of Arthur M. Okun,* The Brookings Institution, Washington, D.C., 1983.

Benjamin Friedman, "The Value of Intermediate Targets in Implementing Monetary Policy," in Federal Reserve Bank of Kansas City, editor, *Price Stability and Public Policy,* Federal Reserve Bank of Kansas City, Kansas City, Mo., 1984.

*This classic study analyzes the circumstances under which the money supply or interest rates might be the better intermediate target for monetary policy:*

William Poole, "Optimal Choice of Monetary Policy Instruments in a Simple Stochastic Macro Model," *Quarterly Journal of Economics* 84, May 1970, pp. 197–216.

*An accessible description of the problems the Federal Reserve faces when people worry that its policies will be inconsistent over time:*

Herb Taylor, "Time Inconsistency: A Potential Problem for Policymakers," *Business Review,* Federal Reserve Bank of Philadelphia, March/April 1985, pp. 3–12.

# The Recent Practice of Monetary Policy

**20**

*"To lean against the winds of deflation or inflation, whichever way they are blowing."*

*William McChesney Martin*

Due in part to the economic conditions with which he had to contend, and also to his own unique blend of experience and personality, the chairman of the Board of Governors of the Federal Reserve System is often remembered for a distinctive way of conducting monetary policy. Since World War II, three chairmen—William McChesney Martin, Arthur Burns, and Paul Volcker—have been particularly influential.

### Recent Chairmen of the Board of Governors

| | |
|---|---|
| William McChesney Martin | April 1, 1951–January 31, 1970 |
| Arthur F. Burns | February 1, 1970–January 31, 1978 |
| G. William Miller | March 8, 1978–August 6, 1979 |
| Paul A. Volcker | August 6, 1979–August 11, 1987 |
| Alan Greenspan | August 11, 1987– |

William McChesney Martin was appointed chairman by President Truman in April 1951, following a Wall Street career that included the presidency of the New York Stock Exchange. Martin's tenure was twice as long as that of any other Chairman, lasting through 5 presidential elections. Owing to his financial market experience, Martin tended to gauge monetary policy in terms of money market factors. Over his term, the average annual inflation rate was 2.68% and the growth rate of real GNP was 3.40%.

Arthur Burns, a well-known academic economist appointed by President Nixon, used both the money supply and the federal funds rate as key targets of monetary policy. Some suggested—but others denied—that Burns adopted easy monetary policy to benefit the incumbent during Presidential elections. Over his term, the average annual inflation rate was 6.96% and the growth rate of real GNP was 2.53%.

Paul Volcker was appointed Chairman by President Carter in 1979, replacing G. William Miller who became secretary of the Treasury after a brief stint as Chairman. Volcker was already known for his public service, first in the Treasury department and later as President of the New York Federal Reserve bank. Arriving in a period of rapidly escalating inflation, Volcker immediately used tight control of the money supply to fight inflation. He resigned at the end of his second term, having dramatically reduced the rate of inflation. During his term, the average annual inflation rate was 5.0% and the growth rate of real GNP was 2.58%.

In this chapter, we will look at the Federal Reserve's experience in carrying out monetary policy under these Chairmen.

---

This chapter will proceed in chronological order, starting with a brief review of Federal Reserve policy before World War II, then looking more closely at recent developments.

---

## Monetary Policy Through World War II

As we discussed in Chapter 17, the Federal Reserve Act of 1913 was designed to make the discount window the Fed's main instrument of monetary policy. The concept of *stabilization policy*—using monetary policy to offset current developments in the economy—did not appear until the 1950s. In contrast, before World War II the discount window was administered in a *procyclical fashion*—the opposite of stabilization policy—using the *real bills doctrine*.

### The Real Bills Doctrine

Under the **real bills doctrine,** the Federal Reserve discounted as many loans as member banks requested, the only restriction being that the banks had to sell "real bills"—the old term for sound business loans. Remember that during this period the Fed literally "discounted" loans—purchased them from banks at a discount from their face value. The operation of the discount window was thus guided by two main principles:

1. The Fed would discount only sound loans, a sensible rule since it was purchasing the loans.
2. In "meeting the needs of trade," the Fed would discount as many sound loans as the banks requested.

   As it evolved, the system also had two main drawbacks:

1. Because discounting was initiated by the banks, the Fed was simply responding; it wasn't managing monetary policy.
2. Banks used the discount window actively during business booms when they needed to obtain funds to make more loans, but not very much during recessions when they had ample funds.

This created a *procyclical* pattern to the supply of bank reserves. During a business boom, bank reserves would rise sharply as the Fed discounted a large volume of loans, even though too many reserves might overheat the economy. During a recession, bank reserves would fall, because the banks had no need for discounting, possibly prolonging the recession. This is not a good way to manage the discount window, but it was the state of the art for central banking at the time.[1]

## The Great Depression of the 1930s

Open market operations were developed as an instrument of monetary policy during the 1920s, but the Great Depression began before the Fed had gained much experience in using them. As a result, the discount window—managed under the real bills doctrine—remained the Fed's main instrument as the economy entered the 1930s.

The Federal Reserve's performance during the Great Depression only served to make things worse. It faithfully operated the discount window under the real bills doctrine, which is to say it hardly used it at all: under the Depression conditions, the banks had few sound business loans to discount. In fact, the banks badly needed to discount loans to augment their *liquidity,* but the Fed would not use the discount window for this purpose; so it sat idly by as thousands of banks failed. Adding insult to injury, required reserve ratios were actually increased in 1936 and 1937 in an attempt to "mop up" the excess reserves that banks were holding at the time. This further reduced the banking system's potential to expand loans, just as economic activity was starting to recover.

## World War II Interest Rate Pegging

World War II's *pegging policy*—keeping interest rates on Treasury securities low to reduce the Treasury's cost of financing the war effort—placed still another constraint on monetary policy. The Treasury wanted to continue the pegging policy after the war, but the Federal Reserve was wary of its inflationary consequences. As we saw in Chapter 17, the Fed's view dominated: the Treasury/Federal Reserve Accord in 1951 officially ended the pegging policy and established the Fed's right to determine monetary policy.

---

[1] Although the real bills doctrine was discredited as a practical policy after the Depression, it might still compare favorably with other forms of monetary policy under specific conditions, as discussed by Thomas Sargent and Neil Wallace, "The Real Bills Doctrine versus the Quantity Theory: A Reconsideration," *Journal of Political Economy*, December 1982, pp. 1212–1236.

## Monetary Policy During the 1950s and 1960s: The Martin Years

The Federal Reserve entered the 1950s with its independence intact and all of its instruments ready to use. William McChesney Martin was designated chairman in 1951 and remained in that office until 1970. Three main developments occurred during Martin's tenure:

- Stabilization policy developed as a principle of monetary policy.

- The "availability doctrine" provided a means of managing monetary policy with low interest rates. (Figure 20.1 shows that low and stable interest rates characterized the U.S. economy well into the 1960s.)

- "Free" reserves and the federal funds interest rate were used as the Fed's operating targets.

FIGURE 20.1
**The Treasury Bond Interest Rate**

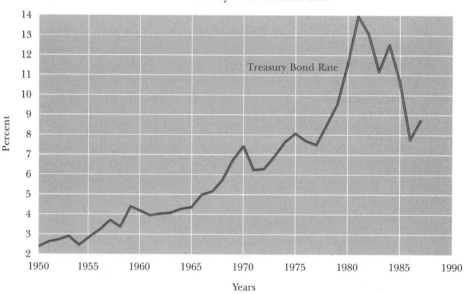

The Federal Reserve continued to treat low and stable interest rates as a goal of monetary policy even after the World War II pegging policy ended. This was generally achieved throughout the 1950s and most of the 1960s. **Source:** *Economic Report of the President,* February, 1988.

## Stabilization Policy: Leaning Against the Wind

In general, the pace of economic activity varies over time, cycling between recessions and booms. Such fluctuations are generally undesirable: inflation rates may rise if the pace of activity is too fast, and unemployment rates may rise if the pace is too slow.

With this in mind, after William McChesney Martin became chairman of the Fed in 1951, he adopted a strategy of *stabilizing the economy*—slowing it down when it was growing too fast, and speeding it up when it was growing too slowly—just the opposite of the real bills doctrine. In his words, Martin's strategy was "to lean against the winds of deflation or inflation, whichever way they are blowing." He recognized, of course, that people would be unhappy with a tight monetary policy that would **lean against the winds** of inflation because it would "take away the punch bowl just when the party gets going." Nevertheless, from a long-term perspective, he felt it was essential to keep inflation in check.

An **accommodating monetary policy** is the opposite of a stabilizing policy. With an accommodating policy, the Fed provides the economy with an adequate supply of money to carry out all planned expenditures; this is the natural policy if the economy is in equilibrium, growing neither too fast nor too slow. However, an accommodating monetary policy can be harmful if the economy shows signs of inflation. In this case, an accommodating policy may *validate the inflation*—provide enough money to carry out the economy's transactions at *rising prices*.

Why would the Fed ever validate inflation with an accommodating monetary policy? To see why, suppose there is a large, onetime, unexpected, increase in an important price—what economists call a *price shock*—such as an increase in oil prices by OPEC. Given that in such a situation oil prices will rise no matter what else happens, the Fed must choose either to keep the overall price level constant by forcing other prices to fall (tight monetary policy), or to let all prices rise (accommodating policy).

The problem with the tight policy option is that it may create higher unemployment. This is the reason that the Fed might decide to accommodate a price shock. Still, the accommodating policy creates the risk of perpetuating the inflation, either because a series of price shocks occurs or because the inflationary process continues on its own. In these cases, the Federal Reserve will end up accommodating *continuing inflation*. We will see how monetary policy responded to just such a problem later in this chapter. (We will also study the theory of price shocks and inflation in Part VII.)

## The Availability Doctrine

Although the policy of pegging interest rates ended in 1951, the Federal reserve felt constrained for some time after that to try to avoid large interest rate fluctuations. For one thing, the Fed wanted to help the Treasury minimize the interest cost of financing the public debt. For another, the Fed did not want to risk disrupting the financial system.

In this setting, a group of economists at the Federal Reserve emphasized *credit availability*—in contrast to interest rates—as a channel through which to achieve the Fed's policy goals. This approach was known as the **availability doctrine.** According to it, even relatively small open market sales of securities, with only a limited impact on interest rates and bank reserves, could have a significant influence in realizing the Fed's policy goals.

The operation of the availability doctrine is illustrated in Figure 20.2, showing the loan supply curve of banks $L^S$ and the loan demand curve of borrowers $L^D$, each as a function of the loan interest rate $r$. The supply curve is positively sloped because banks generally allocate a larger share of their portfolio to loans as the loan rate rises. The demand curve is negatively sloped because borrowers generally demand more loans as the loan rate falls. Equilibrium in the loan market is represented by the loan quantity $L_0$ and the loan rate $r_0$.

In the initial equilibrium, the loan supply of banks, $L^S$, and the loan demand of borrowers, $L^D$, are equal at the loan rate $r_0$ and the loan quantity $L_0$. A Federal Reserve open market sale of securities causes bank reserves to fall and the loan supply curve of banks to shift leftward to $L^{S*}$. According to the availability doctrine, loan rates are "sticky", so instead of interest rates rising to $r^*$ they might remain at $r_0$. Accordingly, banks would make loans of $L_1$ at the unchanged interest rate $r_0$ (on the supply curve $L^{S*}$), while borrowers would demand loans of $L_0$ (on the demand curve $L^D$). Credit rationing then equals $L_0 - L_1$.

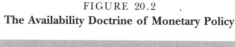

FIGURE 20.2
**The Availability Doctrine of Monetary Policy**

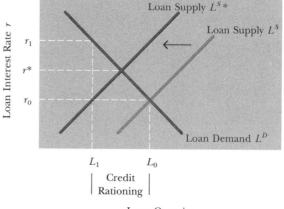

Now suppose the Federal Reserve carries out a small open market sale of Treasury bills. The resulting increase in the Treasury bill rate and decrease in bank reserves cause the supply curve of loans to shift leftward, to $L^{S*}$. Loan market equilibrium then occurs at the loan rate $r^*$. However, according to the availability doctrine, loan rates are "sticky," so the loan rate may not rise to $r^*$.

Indeed, in an extreme case, the loan rate might just remain at $r_0$. If this happens, despite the supply curve shifting leftward to $L^{S*}$, banks will supply loans of $L_1$, while borrowers will demand loans of $L_0$. The result is credit rationing in the amount $L_0 - L_1$, the difference between loans demanded and loans supplied.

According to the availability doctrine, such credit rationing is a main channel for monetary policy: borrowers have to reduce their expenditures for goods and investment when they cannot obtain loans. When borrowers are limited to the loan quantity $L_1$, it is *as if* they are charged the interest rate $r_1$ for loans—$r_1$ is the **shadow price of loans.** The implication is that if tight monetary policy does not affect the actual loan rate $r_0$, it may still raise the shadow price of loans to $r_1$—a level above even the equilibrium rate $r^*$. This is why, according to the availability doctrine, monetary policy can generate the *effects* of higher interest rates—even when the quoted interest rate changes little or not at all.

## The Federal Funds Rate and Free Reserves as Operating Targets

As chairman of the Federal Reserve, William McChesney Martin conducted monetary policy on the basis of money market conditions. Specifically, he used the **federal funds rate** (the rate banks pay when borrowing reserves from other banks) and **free reserves** (excess reserves minus borrowed reserves) **as the operating targets for monetary policy.** To shift to easier monetary policy, the Federal Open Market Committee would direct the Trading Desk at the New York Federal Reserve Bank to carry out open market purchases, which would both reduce the federal funds rate and increase free reserves.

*Free reserves* measure the amount of reserves that banks have available for lending:

$$R_f = R_t - R_r - R_b,$$

where $R_f$ = free reserves,

$\quad R_t$ = total reserves,

$\quad R_r$ = required reserves,

$\quad R_b$ = borrowed reserves (through discount loans).

Equivalently, since excess reserves $R_e$ equal total reserves $R_t$ minus required reserves $R_r$, free reserves also equal excess reserves minus borrowed reserves:

$$R_f = R_e - R_b.$$

A high level of free reserves indicates easy monetary policy because banks can use free reserves to make additional loans. Table 20.1 shows the amount of reserves in two contrasting cases, one when a tight monetary policy was in effect and therefore the amount of free reserves was small (actually negative), and the other when the monetary policy was easy. If free reserves were to fall below the desired level, the Fed would use open market purchases of securities to increase the amount of total reserves, thus raising free reserves. Box 20.1 shows an FOMC directive from the Martin era based on free reserves and the federal funds rate.

**TABLE 20.1**

**Computing Free Reserves**

| | (Dollars in millions) | |
| --- | --- | --- |
| | Tight Policy (Dec. 1959) | Easy Policy (Dec. 1960) |
| Total reserves ($R_t$) | $13,654 | $13,823 |
| Required reserves ($R_r$) | − 13,148 | − 13,080 |
| Excess reserves ($R_e$) | 506 | 743 |
| Borrowed reserves ($R_b$) | − 941 | − 74 |
| Free reserves ($R_f$) | −435 | 669 |

BOX 20.1 MONEY MATTERS

## FOMC Policy Directive from the Martin Years

During 1966 the Federal Reserve was concerned that the economy was too strong, based on various factors including the buildup from the money being spent on the Vietnam War. The following summary is from the FOMC meeting of May 10, 1966.

The economic and financial developments reviewed at this meeting indicate that the domestic economy is expanding vigorously, with industrial prices continuing to rise and credit demands remaining strong. Our international payments continue in deficit. In this situation, it is the Federal Open Market Committee's policy to resist inflation-

ary pressure and to strengthen efforts to restore reasonable equilibrium in the country's balance of payments, by restricting the growth in bank reserves, bank credit, and the money supply.

To implement this policy, while taking into account the current Treasury financing, System open market operations until the next meeting of the Committee shall be conducted with a view to attaining some further gradual reduction in net reserve availability, and a greater reduction if growth in required reserves does not moderate substantially.

Figure 20.3 shows the pattern that developed for the federal funds rate and for free reserves over the years of Martin's tenure. Since higher federal funds rates generally corresponded to lower levels of free reserves, either of these variables could serve as an operating target for tighter monetary policy.

However, the Fed had difficulty using free reserves as an operating target because banks played a key role in determining their level. For example, suppose that the Federal Reserve is satisfied with the level of free reserves, but the banks, facing increased loan demand, make additional loans, causing free reserves to fall. To maintain the target value of free reserves, the Fed would have to carry out defensive open market purchases, increasing total reserves. The problem here is that by accommodating the increase in loan demand, the Fed will have unwittingly shifted to an easier monetary policy. To be sure, most operating targets are affected by the economy and bank behavior, but free reserves are particularly sensitive to this, because banks control the two components—excess reserves and borrowed reserves. Put another way, free reserves tended to create a procyclical monetary policy—akin to the effect of the real bills doctrine.

FIGURE 20.3
**The Federal Funds Rate and Free Reserves: 1955 to 1969**

The federal funds rate and free reserves were the Fed's operating targets during the 1950s and 60s. The tightening of monetary policy is indicated by higher federal funds rates or by lower free reserves.
**Source:** *Federal Reserve Bulletin*

# Monetary Policy During the 1970s: The Burns Years

When Arthur Burns became chairman of the Board of Governors in 1970, the money supply replaced free reserves as the Fed's target for monetary policy. Burns was a well-known economist associated with the "monetarist" theory of central banking, which held that the Fed should use the money supply as its intermediate target. (We will look at monetarist theory in Part VII.)

The Federal Open Market Committee continued to use the federal funds rate as its interest rate target. FOMC policy directives referred to target ranges for both the federal funds rate and the money supply growth rate. In addition, the directives often used a *proviso clause*—the money supply growth target was to be met, *provided* that the federal funds rate did not exceed a target range, or vice versa.

Box 20.2 shows a typical FOMC policy directive during the Burns years. The Trading Desk at the New York Federal Reserve Bank was to focus on M1 and M2 money supply targets as long as the federal funds rate remained within its target range. If the federal funds rate moved

## BOX 20.2 MONEY MATTERS

## FOMC Policy Directive from the Burns Years

In early 1975, the economy was in the midst of a severe recession. The following excerpts are from the FOMC policy directive of February 19, 1975.

> The Committee decided that the economic situation and outlook called for more rapid growth in monetary aggregates over the months ahead than had occurred in recent months . . . .
>
> The Committee concluded that growth in M1 and M2 over the February-March period at annual rates within ranges of tolerance of 5 1/2 to 7 1/2 percent and 6 1/2 to 8 1/2 percent,

respectively, would be consistent with longer-run objectives for the monetary aggregates. . . . The members agreed that in the period until the next meeting the weekly average Federal funds rate might be expected to vary in an orderly fashion in a range of 5 1/4 to 6 1/4 percent, if necessary in the course of seeking monetary growth rates within the ranges specified. The members also agreed that in the conduct of operations, account should be taken of developments in domestic and international financial markets.

outside of this range, the money supply targets would be changed. This happened frequently, leading some to conclude that Burns targeted the money supply more in words than in deeds.

The results are shown in Figure 20.4, in terms of the federal funds rate, the growth rate of M1, and the inflation rate. Between 1970 and 1975, the patterns for both of the operating targets and for the inflation rate were erratic. Following the recession of 1969–1970, an easy monetary policy was adopted, with M1 rising rapidly and the federal funds rate falling. As a result, the inflation rate began to rise sharply in 1972. So monetary policy was tightened—with M1 growth slowing and the federal funds rate rising rapidly—leading in part to the severe recession of 1974–1975.

From 1976 until the end of Arthur Burns' tenure as chairman in early 1978, the inflation rate rose steadily. Although this condition clearly called for tighter monetary policy—leaning against the winds of inflation—the policy response was modest at best. In fact, the growth rate of M1 continued to increase, validating the inflationary pressure that was building in the economy. The federal funds rate did rise steadily, but this mainly reflected the effect of rising inflation on nominal interest rates. Indeed, the *real* Federal funds rate was actually falling, since the inflation rate was rising faster than the (nominal) federal funds rate.

FIGURE 20.4
**Monetary Policy Targets and Inflation Rates: 1970 to 1979**

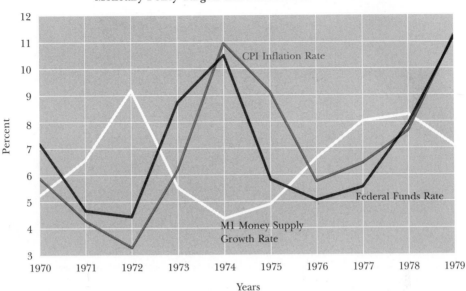

During Arthur Burns' tenure as chairman, the federal funds rate was the main target, the M1 money supply being a target more in name than in fact. As a result, monetary policy was erratic until 1975 and then was accommodating toward inflation through 1978. The increase in the (nominal) federal funds rate from 1976 to 1978 was more the result of rising inflation than an instrument of inflation fighting.

## Credit Crunches

A **credit crunch** occurs when the Fed combines tight monetary policy with actions to restrict bank lending. This occurred during 1966, and again during 1969–1970, 1974–1975, and 1980. In all of these cases, the Fed told banks not to expand the net amount of their loans. This was done mainly through *jaw-boning* and *moral suasion*—the causal communications the Federal Reserve uses to let banks know what it wants. Banks usually respond promptly.

In some regards, a credit crunch looks just like tight monetary policy—both involve higher interest rates and slower growth rates of the money supply. In a credit crunch, however, borrowers also find that the *availability* of loans is limited—at any price. The result is that credit crunches affect the economy more rapidly than does tight monetary policy alone, so the Fed tends to use credit crunches if matters seem to be getting out of control or if normal policy is not working.

In Figure 20.5, the four credit crunch episodes are represented by the pink shaded areas. The growth rate of real GNP slowed in every case, and, except in 1966, actually became negative. The 1982 period of negative real growth was the only one without a credit crunch; we will see in a moment that this period was exceptional for other reasons.

FIGURE 20.5
**The Impact of Credit Crunches on Real GNP**

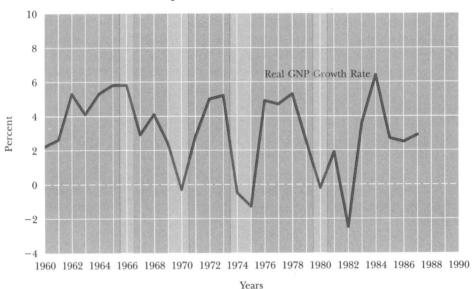

Major credit crunches occurred in 1966, 1969–1970, 1974–1975, and 1980, as shown by the pink shaded areas. In each case, the Federal Reserve told banks to limit their new loan extensions; real GNP fell dramatically as a result.

FIGURE 20.6
**Housing Starts and Mortgage Interest Rates**

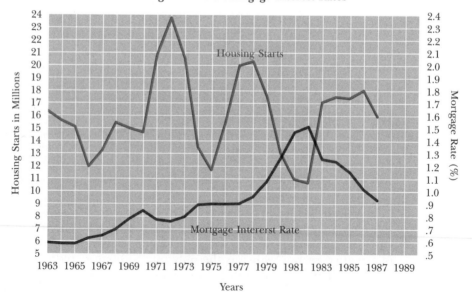

Housing starts fell substantially in 1966, and 1974–1975, even though mortgage rates rose only slightly during those periods. This reflects the powerful effect credit crunches have on housing construction.

A credit crunch also occurs if banks stop lending because loan interest rates are constrained from rising. As we saw in Chapter 12, usury ceilings on mortgage interest rates worked this way. For example, when tight monetary policy caused market interest rates to rise above the usury ceilings for mortgages in 1974 and 1975, lenders stopped making mortgage loans in the affected states, sharply curtailing home purchases. The result was that the number of new housing units started—called *housing starts*—fell sharply, even though mortgage interest rates rose only modestly, as shown in Figure 20.6.

However, credit crunches have drawbacks, so the Fed uses them only in an emergency. For one thing, credit crunches are perceived as unwarranted and unfair by the affected sectors, including home buyers, small business borrowers, and credit card users. For another thing, credit crunches may get out of control, because they are such powerful instruments. Nevertheless, some economists favor more frequent use of credit crunches, arguing that they are the only way that monetary policy can really have an impact on the economy.[2]

There is no extreme form of *easy* monetary policy that corresponds to a credit crunch. That is, tight monetary policy—particularly a credit crunch—can generally slow the pace of economic activity, but easy monetary policy cannot always stimulate the economy. This is sometimes described as *trying to push on a string*—monetary policy pushes the economy, but nothing happens.

## Disintermediation

Starting in the 1960s and continuing throughout the 1970s, the Federal Reserve took advantage of Regulation Q ceilings—the maximum interest rates banks were allowed to pay on deposits—to create a controlled version of a credit crunch. The process was called **disintermediation**—meaning that deposits were withdrawn from *intermediaries* (banking institutions) when, because of the Regulation Q ceilings, investors could obtain higher interest rates on other investments. The banks then had to reduce their loans to the extent that they could not replace the lost deposits, which is why disintermediation is a type of credit crunch.

In practice, commercial banks often could replace some of their lost deposits with nondeposit funds, so bank lending would slow, but it would not stop. In contrast, thrift institutions had few alternatives to deposits, so they had to stop lending when there was disintermediation. This particularly affected potential home buyers, since thrift institutions were the major mortgage lenders. The effect of disintermediation on housing starts in 1966 and 1974–1975 is illustrated in Figure 20.6.

Regulation Q ceilings unfairly affected small savers who had limited opportunities to invest outside of banks. For this and the other reasons discussed in Chapter 10, the 1980 Depository Institutions Decontrol Act eliminated the Regulation Q ceilings. While this is generally considered an improvement for the financial system, the Fed did lose a powerful tool of monetary policy.

[2] See Albert N. Wojnilower, "The Central Role of Credit Crunches in Recent Financial History," *Brookings Papers on Economic Activity 2*, 1980, pp. 277–340.

BOX 20.3 CREDIT CHECK

## Monetary Policy and the Stock Market

An unexpected shift to tight monetary policy generally causes stock market prices to fall, and an unexpected shift to easy monetary policy generally causes the stock market to rally. Although many factors may connect stock prices to monetary policy, the main link is that investors compare stocks to other securities in terms of their rates of return. If tight monetary policy raises the interest rate on bonds, for example, then investors will not buy stocks unless they offer higher returns as well. One standard measure of the rate of return on stocks is the earnings-price ratio—the ratio of a firm's earnings (its profits) per share to its stock price. (The inverse of the earnings-price ratio, the price-earnings ratio, is also commonly used in stock analysis.) Given earnings, if interest rates rise, the stock's price must fall to provide investors a higher earn-

ings-price ratio (a higher rate of return).

The actual relationship between interest rates and earnings-price ratios is illustrated in Figure 20.7, where the interest rate is the rate for Treasury bills and the earnings-price ratio is the ratio for the Standard and Poor's 500 stock index. There is generally a positive relationship between the earnings-price ratio and the interest rate, meaning that stock prices fall when interest rates rise.

However, this relationship does not represent an easy way to make money on the stock market. First, many shifts in monetary policy are *already expected*, so stock prices already reflect the new monetary policy. Second, many *other factors* affect the stock market, so you may be right about monetary policy but still lose money on the stock market.

FIGURE 20.7
**The Treasury Bill Rate and the Earnings-Price Ratio on Stocks**

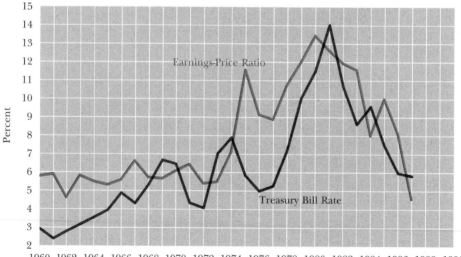

## The Differential Effects of Monetary Policy

**Differential effects** refer to the especially harsh effects that tight monetary policy can have on certain sectors of the economy, such as the effects of credit crunches and disintermediation on the housing sector and to a lesser extent on small businesses and local government agencies. The stock market can also be sensitive to monetary policy, although for different reasons, as explained in Box 20.3.

The housing market illustrates two key factors that make a sector of the economy sensitive to monetary policy:

- The commodity—a house—is large and durable, so people or firms usually borrow money in order to purchase it.

- The borrowers have one main source of funds—mortgage loans—so purchases must stop when there is disintermediation or a credit crunch.

Differential effects on certain sectors of the economy are really an inevitable aspect of monetary policy. High interest rates mean that some expenditures must be postponed. Expenditures based on borrowed money, such as new home purchases, are usually the ones most easily postponed. In this sense, differential effects constitute an efficient—if not always fair—way of distributing the burden of tight monetary policy.

Poorly functioning loan markets can make monetary policy *inefficient* as well as *unfair*. For example, usury ceilings on mortgages and Regulation Q ceilings on deposits caused mortgage lending to be sharply curtailed when market interest rates rose above the ceilings. As a result, housing construction declined because the *supply* of credit declined, not because of a reduced demand for housing. The mortgage and housing markets went through recurrent cycles of this type until the 1980 deregulation legislation eliminated the usury ceilings on mortgages and the Regulation Q ceilings.

# Monetary Policy During the 1980s: The Volcker Era

During G. William Miller's brief term (1978–1979) as Fed chairman, inflation rates escalated to double-digit levels, the federal funds rate rose in tandem, and the growth rate of the money supply remained high. By the summer of 1979, the economic system was out of control. In this setting, Paul Volcker arrived as chairman, with the urgent task of doing something quickly about inflation. On October 6, 1979, following an unusual Saturday meeting of the Board of Governors—sometimes called the *Saturday massacre*—a radical new monetary policy was announced (see Box 20.4). In addition, the Federal Reserve imposed temporary selective controls in March 1980 (see Box 20.5).

BOX 20.4 MONEY MATTERS

## Volcker's New Monetary Policy of October 6, 1979

The following is the summary announcement in the *Federal Reserve Bulletin* following the "Saturday massacre":

> The Federal Reserve on October 6, 1979, announced a series of complementary actions that should assure better control over the expansion of money and bank credit, help curb speculative excesses in financial, foreign exchange, and commodity markets, and thereby serve to dampen inflationary forces.
>
> Actions taken are as follows:
>
> 1. A 1 percent increase in the discount rate, approved unanimously by the Board, from 11 percent to 12 percent.
>
> 2. Establishment of an 8 percent marginal reserve requirement on increases in "managed liabilities"—liabilities that have been actively used to finance rapid expansion in bank credit.

> This action was also approved unanimously by the Board.
>
> 3. A change in the method used to conduct monetary policy to support the objective of containing growth in the monetary aggregates over the remainder of this year within the ranges previously adopted by the Federal Reserve. These ranges are consistent with moderate growth in the aggregates over the months ahead. This action involves placing greater emphasis in day-to-day operations on the supply of bank reserves and less emphasis on confining short-term fluctuations in the federal funds rate. It was approved unanimously by the Federal Open Market Committee, which comprises all members of the Board of Governors and five of the twelve Presidents of the Federal Reserve Banks. (*Federal Reserve Bulletin,* October 1979.)

BOX 20.5 CREDIT CHECK

## The Emergency Credit Controls of March 1980

On March 14, 1980, President Jimmy Carter and the Federal Reserve announced an emergency credit control program—limiting consumer credit, credit card loans, and other bank loans—under the Credit Control Act of 1969. William Greider, in *Secrets of the Temple,* tells how the Federal Reserve was pressured into the program:

> The idea of controls had first been raised in the President's councils four months earlier, right after the Fed's dramatic policy initiative [of October 6, 1979]. . . .
>
> Volcker was ambivalent. He thought controls on credit cards and retail

> credit seemed particularly pointless since consumer borrowing was already subsiding. The President insisted that the controls cover credit cards, Volcker was told, because that was something average citizens could understand. . . . [But] "I wasn't entirely allergic to some sort of way of telling the banks to slow down their lending, some sort of moral suasion," Volcker said.

The program proved to be a disaster, with the economy falling so rapidly that the controls were all rescinded by July of 1980. The experience no doubt added to the Fed's overall mistrust of selective control programs. (William Greider, *Secrets of the Temple,* 1987, pp. 182–183.)

## The New Monetary Policy: 1979 to 1982

The focus of the new monetary policy was a strict adherence to tight **money supply growth targets.** Money supply targets, of course, were not entirely novel: they had been the proclaimed policy during the Arthur Burns years as well. But, as we saw, the money supply actually played a relatively small role in monetary policy under Burns. In contrast, the October 6, 1979, policy directive indicated that Paul Volcker planned to enforce the targets.

Volcker succeeded in delivering a tight monetary policy between 1979 and 1982. Three key indicators of this tight policy are evident in Figures 20.4 and 20.8:

1. Money supply growth rates were much lower than the corresponding inflation rates.

2. The Federal funds rate reached extremely high levels after 1980, far exceeding the inflation rate.

3. The most severe recession since the 1930s occurred between 1980 and 1982.

The policy worked extremely well in the sense that inflation and inflationary expectations were controlled by 1982. However, the policy had large costs in the form of extremely high interest rates and a very deep recession.

FIGURE 20.8
**Monetary Policy Targets and Inflation Rates: 1979 to 1987**

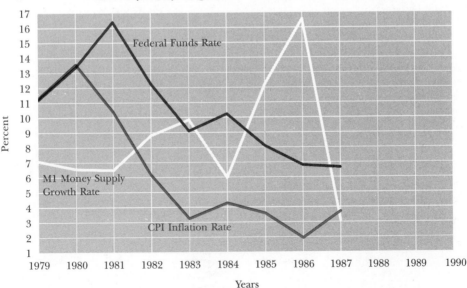

Between 1979 and 1982, the Federal Reserve enforced strict limits on the growth rate of M1, causing inflation rates to fall dramatically. Real GNP also fell (see Figure 20.5) and the federal funds rate rose sharply. Until easier policies were adopted in 1982, the Fed ignored these costs of its tight monetary policy. **Source:** Economic Report of the President, February, 1988.

## Tight Monetary Policy Based on the Money Supply

The experience of using a money supply target between 1979 and 1982 illustrates two basic points, one relating to the Fed's ability to fight inflation, and the other relating to the difficulty of using a money supply target.

*Regarding inflation,* the experience showed that the Fed could apply strict money supply growth targets to control inflation. But to do so, the Federal Reserve had to withstand pressure from two sources. First, given that money demand initially continues to grow faster than money supply, interest rates are likely to escalate sharply. Second, as the result of the slow money supply growth and high interest rates, the economy is likely to fall into a recession, possibly a severe one.

*Regarding the money supply,* the Fed found that it was more difficult to meet the targets than had been anticipated. The result was that Chairman Volcker had to reassure the Fed watchers, who studied the Fed's weekly money supply announcements for indications of a change in policy, that the policy was unchanged. Box 20.6 describes how the markets reacted to the weekly money supply announcements.

---

BOX 20.6 FINANCIAL NEWS

## The Weekly Money Supply Announcements

Each week, the Fed announces current money supply values, illustrated here with the report for the week ending August 22, 1988. During the period 1979 to 1982, the weekly announced money supply was more often than not higher than the Fed's targets: this could mean to Fed watchers either that the Fed had adopted an easier policy or that it was about to reinforce the tight policy to reach its target.

According to the money demand/money supply theory of interest rates, a higher than expected level for the money supply should cause interest rates to fall. However, the Fed watchers often interpreted high money supply numbers to mean that monetary policy would soon be tighter, to bring the money supply back into line with the targets. As a result, market interest rates often *rose* when the announced money supply was unexpectedly high.

### FEDERAL RESERVE DATA

MONETARY AGGREGATES
(daily average in billions)

| | One week ended: | |
| --- | --- | --- |
| | Aug. 22 | Aug. 15 |
| Money supply (M1) sa | 783.4 | 780.1 |
| Money supply (M1) nsa | 777.8 | 786.7 |
| Money supply (M2) sa | 3033.6 | 3027.8 |
| Money supply (M2) nsa | 3028.6 | 3036.5 |
| Money supply (M3) sa | 3830.8 | 3824.7 |
| Money supply (M3) nsa | 3823.7 | 3831.3 |
| | Four weeks ended: | |
| | Aug. 22 | Jly 25 |
| Money supply (M1) sa | 782.5 | 781.4 |
| Money supply (M1) nsa | 783.6 | 787.2 |
| Money supply (M2) sa | 3029.9 | 3023.8 |
| Money supply (M2) nsa | 3032.5 | 3030.3 |
| Money supply (M3) sa | 3826.2 | 3813.8 |
| Money supply (M3) nsa | 3825.6 | 3822.8 |
| | Month | |
| | July | June |
| Money supply (M1) sa | 792.4 | 776.5 |
| Money supply (M2) sa | 3025.4 | 3016.4 |
| Money supply (M3) sa | 3816.8 | 3799.3 |

nsa-Not seasonally adjusted. sa-Seasonally adjusted.

**Source:** *Wall Street Journal,* 22 August, 1988.

## The Federal Reserve's Procedures for Controlling the Money Supply

To understand the Fed's difficulty in controlling the money supply, we should look first at the procedures it used. The basic idea was simple: toward the end of each year, the Fed would set a target range for the growth rate of the money supply during the following year. It would then use open market operations during that year to try to keep the money supply within the target range. Box 20.7 discusses how the procedures were implemented and gives an example.

## Monetary Policy After 1982

The inflation that greeted Paul Volcker in 1979 had virtually vanished by 1982. Indeed a recession had become the main economic problem. However, this too passed by 1983, and the remainder of Volcker's term as chairman, through 1987, was characterized by low inflation rates and moderate to good real economic growth. As a result, the Fed reverted to a more traditional mixture of the federal funds rate and monetary aggregates as targets. The renewed attention to the federal funds rate is reflected in Figure 20.8, which shows the federal funds rate falling after 1984, even when the M1 money supply was rising rapidly.

## Monetary Policy Since 1987

The economy had been expanding steadily for five years when Alan Greenspan arrived as chairman of the Board of Governors in 1987. So one of Greenspan's main goals was to avoid actions that would disturb this period of exceptional economic performance. This was not easy, as a number of problems required Greenspan's attention.

*A Fragile Financial System.* Shortly after taking office, Greenspan had to deal with the stock market crash of October, 1987. As described in Box 18.3, he responded promptly to the crash, assuring the financial markets that the Fed would support the system.

In addition, two other factors in the financial system may require future action by Greenspan. First, the effects of the recent deregulation may still create unexpected problems. Second, corporations were becoming highly leveraged—issuing large amounts of debt relative to the amount of their equity capital—which increases the potential for bankruptcies, especially if the economy starts to grow more slowly.

*Failing Banks and Thrift Institutions.* Record numbers of commercial banks and thrift institutions were bailed out by the federal deposit insurance agencies in 1987 and 1988, and this is likely to continue. Although the Federal Reserve is not directly responsible for dealing with the failure of banking institutions, such events may threaten the overall financial system, forcing the Fed to provide additional discount loans.

*Inflation.* Inflation rates often start to rise after a long period of economic growth, calling for a shift to tighter monetary policy. Given the problems that were faced during the late 1970s in stopping inflation

BOX 20.7 MONEY MATTERS

## Target Cones and Target Tunnels for the Money Supply

Based on the actual targets and results for 1986, Figure 20.9 shows how the Federal Reserve controls the money supply:

1. About December 1, 1985, the Fed set the 1986 growth rate target at 3% to 8% for M1 and at 6% to 9% for M2. Based on the initial money supply values ($620 billion for M1 and $2,550 billion for M2), growth lines were drawn to represent the acceptable range for each money supply during the coming year. Because the space between each pair of lines is cone shaped, it is called a **target cone.**

2. Since the target cone is narrow in the early part of each year, the Federal Reserve has little margin for error. To provide more room for maneuver, the Fed also uses a **target tunnel,** with its width for the entire year equal to the width of the target cone at the end of the year. The target tunnels for 1986 are illustrated in Figure 20.9 by the parallel dashed lines. The money supply is con-sidered on target if it is *inside the target tunnel,* even if it is *outside the target cone.*

3. During the year, as the Fed receives actual money supply data, it uses open market operations to try to keep each money supply aggregate within its target range. However, the situation illustrated in Figure 20.9 was common: *the M1 money supply exceeded its target range,* while *the M2 money supply stayed within its range.*

4. At the end of the year, the procedure is repeated for the following year, using the most recent money supply data as the starting point. With this method, if the money supply exceeds its target one year, then the new cones and tunnels will represent higher target levels the next year. This problem is called **base drift,** meaning that past errors tend to accumulate. Of course, the Fed can offset this effect with lower growth rate targets for the following year.

once it became established, Greenspan announced that he intended to stop inflation promptly this time. To reinforce his policy and make it credible, he raised the Fed's discount rate in August 1988, following some signs of impending inflation. On the other hand, Greenspan must use the tight monetary policy with care, to avoid stopping the economic expansion prematurely.

*The Budget Deficit.* Although Congress and the president are directly responsible for dealing with the continuing deficits of the federal government—expenditures exceeding tax receipts—the Federal Reserve has to deal with any current problems that arise from it. Some economists expect that higher interest rates and inflation rates are a likely result of the deficits, but others disagree (as we will discuss more fully in Part VII).

*The Trade Deficit.* The international trade deficit—imports exceeding exports—is another continuing problem facing Greenspan and the Federal Reserve. Many economists feel that the *trade* deficit is a result of the *budget* deficit, in the sense that the high rate of government spending is being financed directly or indirectly by importing foreign goods or borrowing from foreign lenders. We will see in the following Chapters 21 and 22 how Federal Reserve monetary policy may be used to deal with a trade deficit.

FIGURE 20.9
**Money Supply Targets in Terms of Cones and Tunnels**

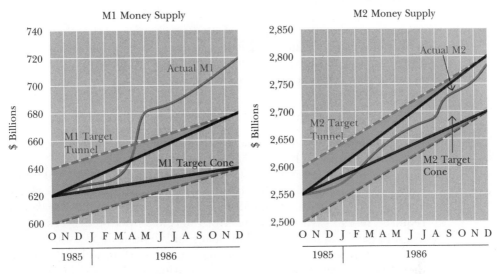

The M1 money supply has repeatedly exceeded the Federal Reserve's targets, both in 1986 as shown above, and at other times. This is illustrated for the period from 1976 to 1985 in Figure 20.10. The dashed lines represent the money supply target cones for each year ; the solid line shows the actual money supply. In 1976 and 1984, the money supply was within the target cone at the end of the year, so the target was met; but these years were exceptions.

FIGURE 20.10
**The M1 Money Supply and Its Target Ranges: 1976 to 1985**

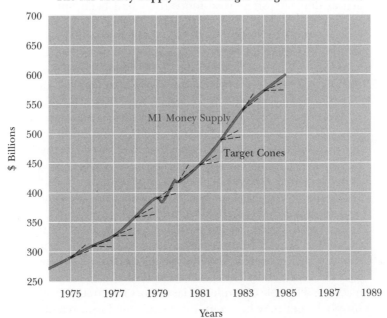

# Can the Federal Reserve Control the Money Supply?

In reviewing monetary policy since 1970, we have seen that the Federal Reserve had a continuing problem in meeting its money supply targets. Since the Fed's business, in a sense, *is* to control the money supply, and it also gets to set the targets, how can this happen?

## Problems with Controlling the M1 Money Supply

Here are some of the factors that made it difficult for the Fed to control the money supply with precision.

*Lagged Reserve Requirements.* Prior to 1984, the Fed used a system of *lagged reserve requirements* that hampered money supply control. Bank loans and deposits in an initial week (week 1) determined the bank's required reserves two weeks later (for the reserve period of week 3). As a result, banks could expand their loans and deposits in week 1, even if they did not possess the corresponding reserves. If an individual bank then found it was deficient in reserves during week 3, it could borrow reserves from other banks. But it was also possible for the *banking system* to be deficient in reserves, in which case only the Fed could provide the additional reserves. The result was that the Fed would have to accommodate the bank actions, thus unintentionally making monetary policy easier. As we described in Chapter 18, a system of *contemporaneous* reserve requirements has been used since 1984, so this is no longer a problem.

*Deregulation.* In implementing the Depository Institutions Deregulation and Monetary Control Act of 1980, interest rate ceilings on bank deposits were raised in steps from 1980 to 1986. As the ceilings rose, depositors shifted their funds between accounts, searching for the account paying the highest interest rate at the time. Consequently, transaction deposits often rose more than had been anticipated in the M1 targets.

*Aggressive Competition for Deposits.* Early in the period, aggressive competition from money market mutual funds caused banks to lose deposits, resulting in unexpected declines in M1. Later, after the removal of Regulation Q, banks recovered some of the lost deposits, causing M1 to rise unexpectedly.

*Expectations Created by Money Supply Announcements.* As described in Box 20.6, the Fed's weekly money supply announcements created large interest rate swings when Fed watchers incorrectly concluded that there had been a change in the direction of monetary policy. As with the announcement effects of discount rate changes (discussed in Chapter 18), monetary policy can become more difficult to manage when Fed watchers misinterpret the situation.

*The Fed as the Lender of Last Resort.* The Fed can be forced to expand the money supply when it acts as the lender of last resort. For example, it may have to provide discount loans to bail out a bank or it may have to carry out open market purchases of securities to reassure the financial markets. The role of lender of last resort has first priority, but the money supply target may be temporarily exceeded as a result.

*The Sources and Uses of Reserves.* The Federal Reserve had trouble anticipating changes in outside factors that caused changes in the sources of reserves (such as discount borrowing and float) and in the uses of reserves (such as currency held by the public) during this period. The money supply would change unexpectedly as a result.

*The Velocity of Money.* We saw in Chapter 19 that the velocity of money—especially the velocity of M1—fluctuated substantially during this period. If the velocity of money fell while the Fed was trying to reduce money supply growth, the Fed might accept above-target growth for the money supply, because velocity and the money supply have comparable effects on nominal income (as is clear from the quantity equation of exchange, $MV = Y$).

## New Money Supply Target: M2

Can the Federal Reserve control the M1 money supply? In principle, by steadfastly offsetting changes in outside factors that affect the money supply, the answer is yes, at least *eventually*. But over a period of weeks or months, and possibly even over a year, the Fed may continue to be surprised by unexpected changes in the money supply. And this seems to keep happening to M1. So as a practical policy, the Fed switched in 1987 to M2 and other broader targets.

Were the 1980s an exceptionally difficult period for controlling M1? Given the major events that occurred, including deregulation and increased competition, the recent past may have been exceptional. However, some of the changes in the financial markets will create continuing problems for M1 targets.

Probably the most important lasting change is that banks can now pay interest on transaction deposits. The result is that the amount of these deposits changes as banks change the interest rate they pay. This problem did not exist, of course, when banks were prohibited from paying interest on transaction deposits. In principle, the Federal Reserve can account for the influence of bank deposit rates on the money supply, just as it can account for any other outside factor. However, banks have not yet adopted predictable patterns in setting interest rates on transaction deposits, so it will be some time before the Fed can anticipate their effect on M1.

As shown in Figure 20.9, the Fed has often done better at meeting its M2 target than its M1 target. This reflects a general principle: when money is being shifted between different types of deposits, the Fed will do better with targets based on broader monetary aggregates. Suppose that the Fed has determined targets for the M1 and M2 growth rates, for example, but then people unexpectedly shift funds from time deposits (counted only in M2) to transaction deposits (counted in both M1 and M2). Even though M1 will exceed its target, M2 will remain on target: the *M1 component of M2 will exceed its target,* but *the time deposit component of M2 will be below its target* by the same amount.

But there are also problems with M2 as a target. First, changes in the sources and uses of bank reserves also have an influence on an M2 target. Second, M2 consists mainly of *time deposits that people hold for savings purposes*, so M2 may not be connected as closely as M1 to current economic activity. Nevertheless, an M2 target has the key advantage that the Fed seems to control it better.

## Chapter Summary

1. Prior to World War II, Federal Reserve monetary policy was usually based on the real bills doctrine—discounting sound bank loans whenever banks requested it. This was a key reason the Fed did so little during the Great Depression of the 1930s. By the early 1950s, the Federal Reserve could carry out an independent monetary policy, but it still tried to keep interest rates as low and stable as possible. This was reflected in the availability doctrine, a theory that monetary policy could affect the economy by limiting the availability of loans, even if interest rates were quite stable.

2. During the 1950s, under William McChesney Martin as chairman, the Federal Reserve adopted stabilization policy—"leaning against the wind"—by managing monetary policy to slow down a fast-growing economy before it overheats, and to speed up a slow-growing economy before it sinks into a recession. Martin also focused monetary policy on money market conditions, using the federal funds rate and free reserves as operating targets.

3. When Arthur Burns became chairman of the Federal Reserve in 1970, the M1 money

supply replaced free reserves as an operating target. However, the federal funds rate remained the primary target, M1 being used more in name than in fact. This became a serious problem after 1975, as inflation rates in the United States rose steadily. Inflation also continued to rise after G. William Miller replaced Arthur Burns as chairman in 1978.

4. When Paul Volcker became chairman of the Federal Reserve in 1979, he faced the immediate task of controlling inflation. He responded by enforcing strict growth rate targets for M1. The policy worked in that by 1982 inflation was again under control. However, there was a high cost in terms of a severe recession and extremely high interest rates.

5. Even when it was successfully fighting inflation, the Fed always found it difficult to meet its money supply targets. Factors such as lagged reserve requirements, deregulation, and competition for bank deposits contributed to this problem. As a result, M2 emerged as the Federal Reserve's money supply target under Chairman Alan Greenspan.

## Key Terms

Accommodating monetary policy

Availability doctrine

Controlling the money supply:

   Base drift

   Target cones and tunnels

   Target growth rates

Credit crunch

Differential effects of monetary policy

Disintermediation

Leaning against the wind

Operating targets:

   Federal funds rate

   Free reserves

   M1 money supply

   M2 money supply

Real bills doctrine

Shadow price of loans

## Study Questions

1. Why is stabilization policy referred to as "leaning against the wind"?

2. Why is an *accommodating* monetary policy the opposite of "leaning against the wind"? How can an accommodating policy end up *validating a continuing inflation?*

3. According to the *availability doctrine,* how can tight monetary policy reduce the expenditures on goods, even if interest rates remain relatively low and stable?

4. What is the problem with *free reserves* as an operating target for monetary policy?

5. In what ways are credit crunches the same as very tight monetary policy? In what ways are they different?

6. How is *disintermediation* a controlled form of a credit crunch? How did the 1980 Depository Deregulation Act eliminate most disintermediation?

7. What are the differential effects of monetary policy? Why are they an *efficient* feature of monetary policy, even though the affected sectors may consider them *unfair?*

8. How does monetary policy affect the stock market? Why is it hard to make money in the stock market on the basis of this relationship?

9. How did control of the M1 money supply growth rate target under Arthur Burns during the 1970s differ from its control under Paul Volcker between 1979 and 1982? As a result, what happened to inflation, the federal funds rate, and the growth rate of real GNP under Volcker?

10. Why did the Fed switch from M1 to M2 as a money supply target in 1987?

## Recommended Reading

*The* Federal Reserve Bulletin *of the Federal Reserve System and the* Quarterly Review *of the Federal Reserve Bank of New York both provide excellent annual reviews of the monetary policy of the preceding year. More specific aspects of monetary policy are covered in the following items.*

John Y. Campbell, "Money Announcements, The Demand for Bank Reserves, and the Behavior of the Federal Funds Rate Within the Statement Week," *Journal of Money, Credit, and Banking,* February 1987 pp. 57–67.

Thomas F. Cosimano, "Reserve Accounting and Variability in the Federal Funds Market," *Journal of Money, Credit, and Banking,* May 1987, pp. 198–209.

William Greider, *Secrets of the Temple,* Simon & Schuster, New York, 1987.

John P. Judd and Bharat Trehan, "Portfolio Substitution and the Reliability of M1, M2, and M3 Indicators," *Economic Review,* Summer 1987, Federal Reserve Bank of San Francisco, pp. 5–30.

William R. Keeton, "Deposit Deregulation, Credit Availability, and Monetary Policy," *Economic Review,* June 1986, Federal Reserve Bank of Kansas City, pp. 26–42.

Brian Motley and Robert H. Rasche, "Predicting the Money Stock: A Comparison of Alternative Approaches," *Economic Review* Spring 1986, Federal Reserve Bank of San Francisco, pp. 38–54.

Robert V. Roosa, "Interest Rates and the Central Bank", in *Money, Trade, and Economic Growth. Essays in Honor of John Henry Williams,* Macmillan, New York, 1951.

Howard L. Roth, "Has Deregulation Ruined M1 as a Policy Guide?" *Economic Review,* June 1987, Federal Reserve Bank of Kansas City, pp. 24–37.

Thomas Sargent and Neil Wallace, "The Real Bills Doctrine versus the Quantity Theory: A Reconsideration," *Journal of Political Economy,* December 1982, pp. 1212–1236.

Carl Walsh, "Monetary Targeting and Inflation: 1976–1984," *Economic Review,* Winter 1987, Federal Reserve Bank of San Francisco, pp. 5–16.

Albert N. Wojnilower, "The Central Role of Credit Crunches in Recent Financial History," *Brookings Papers on Economic Activity,* 1980, pp. 277–340.

# International Trade
# and Finance

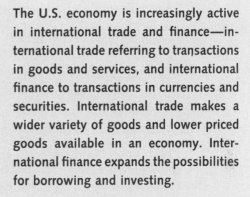

The U.S. economy is increasingly active in international trade and finance—international trade referring to transactions in goods and services, and international finance to transactions in currencies and securities. International trade makes a wider variety of goods and lower priced goods available in an economy. International finance expands the possibilities for borrowing and investing.

In Chapter 21, we will examine the specific factors of demand and supply that determine exchange rates—the price of one currency in terms of another—under the current system of flexible exchange rates. We will also look at the expanding activities of banks in international trade and finance.

Through exchange rates, trade flows, and capital flows, world economic conditions have an impact on the United States, and vice versa. In Chapter 22, we study the implications of these interactions for monetary policy. We will focus on the Fed's responsibilities and policy options under alternative exchange rate systems—fixed exchange rates, flexible exchange rates, and various combinations of the two.

# 21

# International Finance and Banking

*"The chief value of money lies in the fact that one lives in a world in which it is overestimated."*

*H. L. Mencken*

Press reports of the foreign exchange value of the dollar and the U.S. trade deficit reflect the growing extent to which the U.S. economy is *open*—open to foreign influences through international trade and finance. Because of an improved flow of information, U.S. consumers can readily learn about lower-cost foreign goods and U.S. producers can learn about foreign markets. Changes toward freer trade—lower tariffs and other reductions in trade restrictions—are also helping, although there is some concern that free trade is not fairly balanced, especially between the United States and Japan.

Banks play an integral part in international transactions. The number of U.S. banks with foreign offices and foreign banks with U.S. offices has grown dramatically. The activities of these banks include buying and selling foreign currencies and helping firms to import or export goods.

This chapter analyzes U.S. participation in the world economy, emphasizing matters of international finance, foreign exchange markets, and international banking.

We begin by looking at how the United States participates in the world economy. Next, we will study how exchange rates are determined. Lastly, we will consider the special role of banks in international transactions.

In looking at exchange rates between the dollar and foreign currencies, we will focus on the basic exchange rate system now in use—*flexible exchange rates*—based on the market demand for and supply of each foreign currency. Later, in Chapter 22, we will look at alternative ways of organizing the international monetary system and at the role of government policy in determining exchange rates.

# The United States in the World Economy

**International trade**—the *exporting* and *importing* of goods and services—and **international finance**—the trading of financial instruments—are the two main types of international transactions. The **foreign exchange market**, in which foreign currencies are traded, is at the center of most international transactions.

## International Trade of the United States

Imported goods, such as Japanese cars and electronic goods, are now as basic to everyday life in the United States as are such domestic products as Coke and pizza (actually, the idea of pizza was imported too). At the same time, many U.S. firms export goods ranging from computers to soft drinks, sometimes dominating their respective world markets.

Between 1950 and 1980, U.S. imports and exports almost tripled as a share of GNP, as shown in Figure 21.1. The difference between exports and imports is the **trade balance.** For many years the United States had a *trade surplus*—a positive trade balance—with the value of exports exceeding the value of imports. After 1976, however, we have had each year a *trade deficit*—a negative trade balance—with the value of imports exceeding the value of exports.

FIGURE 21.1
**Exports, Imports, and the U.S. Trade Balance**

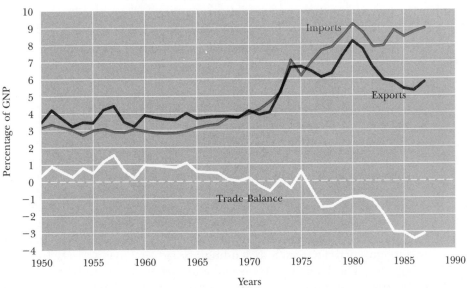

U.S. exports and imports were fairly steady as a percentage of GNP until about 1970, with exports regularly exceeding imports—a trade surplus. During the first half of the 1970s, the trade position was about balanced as the amount of international trade rose as a percentage of GNP. During the 1980s, exports fell sharply as a percentage of GNP, and for the first time in many years the United States had a continuing trade deficit. **Source:** *Economic Report of the President,* February 1988.

## How To Pay for a Trade Deficit

The U.S. trade deficit means that larger quantities of imported goods are available to U.S. consumers and firms for domestic consumption and capital investment. The United States obtains the foreign currency to pay for these goods in four main ways:

1. *Exporting U.S. goods:* Since overseas buyers need dollars to pay for U.S. goods, they will want to exchange their own currency for dollars. In fact, when international trade is balanced—exports equal imports—this part of the U.S. demand for foreign currency and the supply of foreign currency are equal. But when there is a U.S. trade deficit, the United States will need additional sources of foreign currency.

2. *Borrowing foreign currency:* We can borrow foreign currency directly in international debt markets, or we can borrow dollars from foreigners through U.S. debt markets. In the latter case, foreigners exchange their currency for dollars, then lend us the dollars, so it comes to the same thing. Borrowed foreign currency can be used to finance a *temporary* trade deficit, but not a *continuing* one, since loans have to be repaid.

3. *Selling assets to foreigners:* The assets that are sold may have been held in the United States—such as common stocks in American companies—or owned by Americans abroad. In either case, foreign purchasers will supply foreign currency to buy them. However, as with borrowing, there are limits both to the amount of assets we want to sell and to the amount that foreigners want to buy.

4. *Foreign currency reserves:* These are foreign currencies held by a country's central bank. In the U.S. case, the reserves are small relative to the size of recent trade deficits, so they will be rapidly depleted if used to pay for a continuing trade deficit.

*Summary.* Since the last three sources of foreign currency become depleted, the U.S. trade deficit cannot continue indefinitely. Eventually, the country must have balanced trade, which means more exports or fewer imports. Actually it will need a trade surplus, so it can repay its foreign debts.

## International Capital Flows

International purchases and sales of capital assets and international borrowing and lending are called **capital flows**. Specifically, capital *inflows* are transactions that increase the supply of foreign currency to a country—such as borrowing abroad or selling assets to foreigners—and capital *outflows* are transactions that increase the domestic demand for foreign currency—such as lending abroad or buying assets from foreigners. The United States is currently selling assets to foreigners and borrowing abroad on net—so we have a *net capital inflow*.

Figure 21.2 shows U.S. ownership of foreign assets and foreign ownership of U.S. assets (including loans), and the difference between them—the **net international investment position** of the United States. U.S. ownership of foreign assets and foreign ownership of U.S. assets have been rising steadily, and each now exceeds $1 trillion. But since 1985, the United States has been a net debtor.

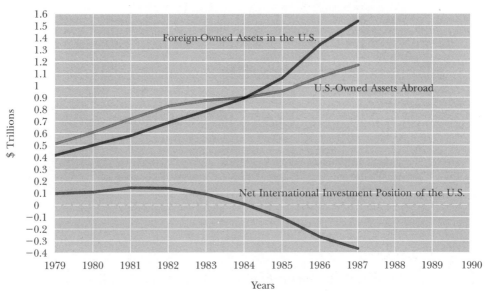

FIGURE 21.2
**The International Investment Position of the United States**

The net U.S. international investment position—U.S. ownership of foreign assets minus foreign ownership of U.S. assets—was positive and steady until about 1982. It then fell sharply and became negative. **Source:** *Survey of Current Business*, U.S. Department of Commerce, June 1988.

This was a shocking development for the United States. Countries, like individuals, typically pass through stages of borrowing and lending. Young, developing, countries are often debtors, and this was the case for the United States during the eighteenth and nineteenth centuries. Mature, productive economies, in contrast, generally have positive net international investment positions. The United States reached this mature stage long ago. That is why it was so shocking to return to net debtor status. But we know the reason: we have had to pay for a continuing trade deficit.

## The Balance of Payments Accounts

A country's **balance of payments** consists of three main components: the current account, the capital account, and the statistical discrepancy:

The **current account** consists of the *trade balance*, together with smaller items such as net government grants and private gifts sent abroad. Transactions that create payments *to U.S. residents*—U.S. exports—count as *positive* items, and transactions that create payments *by U.S. residents*—U.S. imports—count as *negative* items. The U.S. current account was positive until 1980, but then turned sharply negative, as shown in part A of Table 21.1.

The **capital account** covers international financial transactions—buying and selling assets and borrowing and lending money. Again, transactions that create payments *to U.S. residents*—capital inflows, such as borrowing foreign currency—count as *positive* items, while transactions

| TABLE 21.1 | | | | |
| --- | --- | --- | --- | --- |
| **The Balance of Payments of the United States** | | | | |
| **Dollars in billions** | | | | |
| | **1970** | **1975** | **1980** | **1987** |
| A: Current Account Items | | | | |
| Net exports (trade balance) | 2.6 | 8.9 | −25.5 | −160.3 |
| Other current account | −0.3 | 9.2 | 27.4 | −0.4 |
| Current account balance | 2.3 | 18.1 | 1.9 | −160.7 |
| B: Capital Account Items[a] | | | | |
| Change in U.S. assets abroad | −9.3 | −39.7 | −86.1 | −63.8 |
| Change in foreign assets in U.S. | 6.4 | 15.7 | 58.1 | 202.6 |
| Capital account balance | −2.9 | −24.0 | −28.0 | 138.8 |
| C: Statistical Discrepancy | 0.6 | 5.9 | 26.1 | 21.9 |

[a]Capital outflow is indicated as a negative number; capital inflow is indicated as a positive number.

**Source:** *Federal Reserve Bulletin*, Table 3.10, Board of Governors of the Federal Reserve System, 1988.

which create payments *by U.S. residents*—capital outflows, such as U.S. purchases of foreign assets—count as *negative* items. Part B of Table 21.1 shows that the capital account was negative until 1980, but then turned positive. The accumulated amount of capital flows determine the international investment position, as shown in Figure 21.2.

Part C of Table 21.1 represents the **statistical discrepancy**—reporting errors in either the current or capital accounts. For example, smuggling creates a current account error, and "money laundering"—discussed in Chapter 1—creates a capital account error.

### The Balance of Payments Must Balance

The balance of payments is based on the double-entry system of accounting: each transaction gives rise to two entries, one positive and one negative. For example, the export of goods creates a positive entry in the current account (when the goods are shipped) and a negative item in the capital account (when payment is made for the goods).

If we ignore the statistical discrepancy, the current account and capital account balances must therefore be of equal magnitude and of opposite algebraic sign. Thus, for many years the U.S. balance of payments consisted of a positive current account (exports exceeding imports) and a negative capital account (a capital outflow). After 1980, these accounts flip-flopped—a negative current account is balanced by capital inflows. Thus U.S. trade deficits and capital inflows are intrinsically related.

## Foreign Exchange Rates

A *foreign exchange rate* is the exchange ratio—the relative price—between two currencies. If $D$ dollars exchange for $F$ units of foreign currency, then the exchange rate—the dollar price of foreign currency—is $D/F$. For example, if 1 dollar exchanges for 4 French francs, then the exchange rate is $1.00 per 4 French francs or $.25 per French franc.

A currency **appreciates** when it commands more units of foreign currency, and **depreciates** when it commands fewer units. Thus, when the dollar *appreciates*, the exchange rate *falls*—from say $.25 per franc to $.20 per franc (or, equivalently, from 4 francs for 1 dollar to 5 francs for a dollar).

Exchange rates can also be written in the inverse form—as $F/D$—representing the foreign currency price of a dollar. Box 21.1 shows how exchange rates are reported in the financial press in both forms. We will use the $D/F$ form. But remember, when we say the *dollar appreciates*, this means that the *exchange rate $D/F$ falls*—a dollar translates to more foreign currency.

BOX 21.1 FINANCIAL NEWS

## Foreign Exchange Rate Reports

This table shows how exchange rates were reported for a specific date, June 13, 1988.

The first numerical column shows exchange rates as the dollar price of each foreign currency—that is, dollars per unit of foreign currency. The French franc cost $.1720 on this date.

The second numerical column shows exchange rates as the foreign currency price of the dollar—foreign currency per dollar. The dollar was worth 5.8155 French francs on this date.

### FOREIGN EXCHANGE

Monday, June 13, 1988

The New York foreign exchange selling rates below apply to trading among banks in amounts of $1 million and more, as quoted at 3 p.m. Eastern time by Bankers Trust Co. Retail transactions provide fewer units of foreign currency per dollar.

| Country | U.S. $ equiv. | Currency per U.S. $ | Country | U.S. $ equiv. | Currency per U.S. $ |
|---|---|---|---|---|---|
| Argentine (Austral) | .1350 | 7.405 | Malaysia (Ringgit) | .3885 | 2.5740 |
| Australia (Dollar) | .8028 | 1.2456 | Malta (Lira) | 3.0994 | .3226 |
| Austria (Schilling) | .08251 | 12.12 | Mexico (Peso) | | |
| | | | Floating rate | .0004405 | 2270.00 |
| Bahrain (Dinar) | 2.6525 | .377 | Netherland (Guilder) | .5173 | 1.9330 |
| Belgium (Franc) | .02775 | 36.04 | New Zealand (Dollar) | .7050 | 1.4184 |
| Commercial rate | | | | | |
| Financial rate | .02763 | 36.19 | Norway (Krone) | .1586 | 6.3050 |
| Brazil (Cruzado) | .005736 | 174.34 | Pakistan (Rubee) | .05621 | 17.79 |
| Britain (Pound) | 1.8168 | .5504 | Peru (Inti) | .03030 | 33.00 |
| Canada (Dollar) | .8192 | 1.2207 | Phillippines (Peso) | .04757 | 21.02 |
| Chile (Official rate) | .004057 | 246.47 | Portugal (Escudo) | .007107 | 140.70 |
| China (Yuan) | .2687 | 3.7220 | Saudi Arabia (Rival) | .2663 | 3.7555 |
| Colombia (Peso) | .003404 | 293.79 | Singapore (Dollar) | .4958 | 2.0175 |
| | | | South Africa (Rand) | | |
| Denmark (Krone) | .1526 | 6.5530 | Commercial rate | .4462 | 2.211 |
| Ecuador (Sucre) | | | Financial rate | .3355 | 2.9800 |
| Official rate | .004008 | 249.50 | South Korea (Won) | .001364 | 733.20 |
| Floating rate | .002099 | 476.50 | Spain (Peseta) | .008776 | 113.95 |
| Finland (Markka) | .2443 | 4.0930 | Sweden (Krona) | .1663 | 6.0150 |
| France (Franc) | .1720 | 5.8155 | Switzerland (Franc) | .6942 | 1.4405 |
| Greece (Drachma) | .007236 | 138.20 | Taiwan (Dollar) | .03500 | 28.57 |
| Hong Kong (Dollar) | .1281 | 7.8085 | Thailand (Baht) | .03968 | 25.20 |
| India (Rubee) | .07321 | 13.66 | Turkey (Lira) | .0007520 | 1329.81 |
| Indonesia (Rupiah) | .0005970 | 1675.00 | United Arab (Dirham) | .2724 | 3.671 |
| Ireland (Punt) | 1.5510 | .6447 | Uruguay (New Peso) | | |
| Israel (Shekel) | .6309 | 1.5850 | Financial | .002941 | 340.00 |
| Italy (Lira) | .0007813 | 1280.00 | Venezuela (Bolivar) | | |
| Japan (Yen) | .007994 | 125.10 | Official rate | .1333 | 7.50 |
| Jordan (Dinar) | 2.7739 | .3605 | Floating rate | .03183 | 31.42 |
| Kuwait (Dinar) | 3.6284 | .2756 | W. Germany (Mark) | .5807 | 1.7221 |
| Lebanon (Pound) | .002755 | 363.00 | | | |

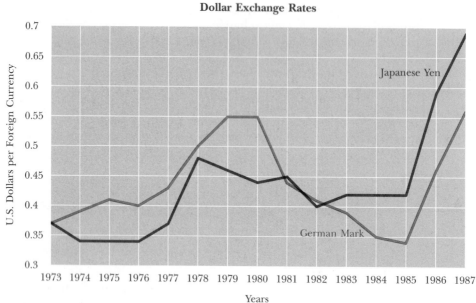

FIGURE 21.3
**Dollar Exchange Rates**

Exchange rates between the dollar and most major foreign currencies were stable until 1973 because a system of fixed rates was used. After that, the shift to flexible exchange rates allowed the rates to fluctuate. **Source:** *Economic Report of the President*, February 1988.

Dollar exchange rates for the Japanese yen and the German mark are shown in Figure 21.3. Prior to 1973, the rates were stable because a **fixed exchange rate system** was used—that is, the governments maintained each exchange rate at a specific value. After that, a **flexible exchange rate system** was used—meaning that the market forces of demand and supply determined the rates.

Since 1980, exchange rates have often been highly volatile. Volatility is a drawback to the extent that it hampers international trade. In Chapter 22, in discussing international monetary policy, we will compare alternative systems for managing exchange rates.

## The Determinants of Flexible Exchange Rates

Flexible exchange rates are determined in foreign exchange markets by the demand and supply of foreign currency in terms of the domestic currency. Two main groups of variables determine demand and supply: price levels and related long-run factors, and interest rates and related short-run factors.

## Price Levels and Related Long-Term Factors

Americans often have a choice between purchasing a good produced in the United States or buying a nearly equivalent imported version. For example, people have a choice between California and French wines. When the quality and related factors are similar, the choice might be made simply on the basis of price. This is easy to do in American wine stores because the merchant or importer has *converted* the French price to U.S. dollars. Otherwise, not many customers could tell whether an $8 California wine or a 40 franc French wine is the less expensive one.

### Converting Foreign Prices to Dollar Prices

The exchange rate $E$ is used to convert a *foreign price* $p^F$—the price of a foreign good quoted in terms of a foreign currency—to a *converted price*:

$$\text{Converted price} = (\text{Foreign price}) \times (\text{Exchange Rate})$$
$$= (p^F) \times (E)$$

So, if the French price $p^F$ of wine is 40 francs and the exchange rate $E$ is $.25 per franc, then the converted price of the French wine is $10 (= 40 francs × $.25 per franc). The $8 California wine is therefore less expensive.

The decision whether to buy a U.S.-produced good or the foreign equivalent can be made by comparing the price of the U.S. good ($p^{US}$) with the converted price of the foreign good:

**Buy the foreign good if $\dfrac{(p^F)(E)}{p^{US}}$ is less than 1.**

When the ratio is less than 1, the foreign good is less expensive. Otherwise, the U.S. good is purchased. In practice, of course, factors other than price may enter the decision whether or not to buy any product— some people may prefer to buy French wine even if it is more expensive. Nevertheless, as the foreign good becomes less expensive—as the price ratio falls—the overall demand for it should rise.

### Converting Foreign Price Levels

Similar considerations apply when the *price levels* of countries are compared. For example, U.S. tourists traveling abroad know that goods and services are more expensive in some countries than in others. Basically, these tourists are comparing the cost of living in foreign countries with a comparable price index for the United States. Box 21.2 shows that a similar situation arises when the U.S. Department of State assigns employees abroad.

Price levels in different countries are compared in the same way that the U.S. and foreign prices of an individual good are compared. Specifically, if the exchange rate is $E$ and the foreign price level is $P^F$, then

---

BOX 21.2 MONEY MATTERS

## Salary Adjustments for Employees Assigned Overseas

When employees are assigned abroad, their salaries are usually adjusted for the higher costs of living in certain countries. The U.S. Department of State makes these computations in a systematic way. The table below shows the State Department's salary adjustments for some foreign cities as of October 1987. The *local index* is the cost of living in the foreign city relative to Washington, D.C. The cost of living in Tokyo, for example, is nearly twice as high as Washington, D.C.

**State Department Cost of Living Adjustments**

| Foreign City | Local Index (Percent of Washington, D.C.) |
|---|---|
| Ottawa | 101% |
| Copenhagen | 167 |
| Paris | 146 |
| Berlin | 145 |
| Athens | 102 |
| Tokyo | 197 |
| Geneva | 147 |
| Taipei | 119 |
| London | 118 |

**Source:** *U.S. Department of State Indexes of Living Costs Abroad*, U.S. Department of Labor, October 1987.

---

the *converted price level* is $(P^F)(E)$. (Notice that the symbol for price *levels* has an uppercase $P$, while the symbol for the price of an individual good has a lowercase $p$.)

Thus, when people say it is more expensive to travel abroad, they mean the converted foreign price level—$(P^F)(E)$—is high relative to the U.S. price level—$P^{US}$. A higher converted foreign price level—or a lower U.S. price level—reduces the overall demand for foreign goods in the same manner that the foreign and U.S. prices for a specific good affect the demand for the foreign version of that good.

### Price Level Variables and the Demand for Foreign Currency

Since a higher relative foreign price level—$(P^F)(E)/P^{US}$—reduces the U.S. demand for foreign goods, it also reduces the U.S. demand for foreign currency to purchase the goods. Thus, other things being equal, as the converted foreign price level rises relative to the U.S. price level, the demand for foreign currency falls.

Relative price levels, of course, are not the only variables that determine the imports and exports of a country. Other variables that influence the demand for a foreign currency include:

- Higher *tariffs and quotas* make imported goods more expensive, thus reducing the demand for foreign currency.

- Shifts in *preferences away from imported goods* reduce the demand for foreign currency.

- Technological changes that create *new imported goods* may raise the demand for foreign currency.

A common feature of price levels and the other variables mentioned is that they mainly affect the demand for imports in the *long run*. For example, tariffs and quotas, preferences for foreign goods, and technology usually do not fluctuate in the short term. And even after these variables have changed, it may take people time to adjust their established buying patterns.

## The Purchasing Power Parity Theory

According to the **purchasing power parity (PPP) theory,** the exchange rate $E$ between two currencies—say the U.S. dollar and a foreign currency—is such that the U.S. price level, $P^{US}$, and the converted foreign price level, $(P^F)(E)$, are equal:

$$P^{US} = P^F E.$$

This means that the "purchasing power" of a dollar—how many goods it will buy—is the same whether applied to U.S. goods or to foreign goods. In other words, if an item costs $10 in the United States and the exchange rate for Canadian dollars is $0.80, then the same item should cost about 10/0.8, or $12.50 in Canadian dollars. Thus, the PPP value of the exchange rate $E^{(p)}$ equals the ratio of the U.S. price level $P^{US}$ to the foreign price level $P^F$:

$$E^{(P)} = \frac{P^{US}}{P^F}. \tag{21.1}$$

In other words, according to the PPP theory, the relative price level is the only variable that determines the exchange rate.

### The Law of One Price

The basis of the PPP theory is what economists call the **law of one price:** when the same good is for sale at different locations, the same price will be charged at each one. For example, if wine is for sale at several stores in the same neighborhood, we would expect to find the same price at each store, putting aside differences between types of stores and things like that. Even if this were not so initially, the fact that people would tend to buy wine only at the low-priced stores would cause all the prices to gravitate toward the same level.

**International commodity arbitrage** works in much the same way. We have looked at arbitrage in Chapter 8 with regard to securities of different maturities and in Chapter 9 with regard to spot and futures markets. Here the idea is that arbitrage traders will buy a commodity in the country (and currency) where its price is low, and they will sell it in the country (and currency) where its price is high. As a result of this activity, the U.S. price for the good, $p^{US}$, and the converted foreign price, $(p^F)(E)$, will be equal: $p^{US} = (p^F)(E)$.

According to the PPP theory the same process applies to the price levels for all the goods in the two countries. Thus we have, $P^{US} = (P^F)(E)$, which is equivalent to equation (21.1) of the PPP theory.

### The Role of Nontraded Goods

The PPP theory has one serious drawback: not all goods enter into international trade—there are *nontraded* goods. Nontraded goods arise when trading costs are too high to warrant international trade. For example, it may be too costly to transport certain goods over long distances; and other goods have a fixed location. Housing in an obvious case. Even if the converted price of a house in Paris is less than the price of a similar house in Chicago, the Paris house cannot be sold as if it were a Chicago house. The result is that variations between the prices of traded and nontraded goods limit the accuracy of the PPP theory in predicting exchange rates.

### Purchasing Power Parity: The Evidence

The accuracy of the PPP theory has been an issue in economics for centuries. Compare, for example, the *trade-weighted* exchange rate—an index of dollar exchange rates based on the amount of the U.S. trade with different countries—with the price level parity—the ratio of the U.S. price level to the foreign price level—as shown in Figure 21.4. The more accurate the PPP theory, the more closely the two curves should coincide.

FIGURE 21.4

**Purchasing Power Parity Theory as a Predictor of Exchange Rates**

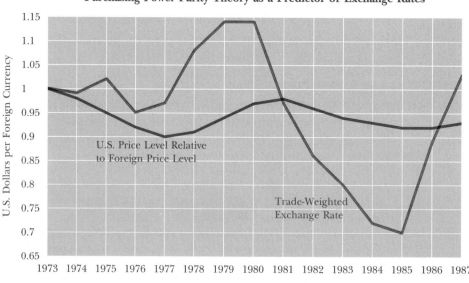

According to the PPP theory, the line representing the *trade-weighted* dollar exchange rate and the line representing the price level ratios should fit together closely. The theory is evidently not accurate on a year-to-year basis. But there may be more to it over longer periods of time. **Source:** *Economic Report of the President,* February 1988.

## MacCurrencies

The *Economist*, a British weekly business magazine, has tabulated the price of a Big Mac hamburger in various countries to see whether the exchange rates reflect purchasing power parity. If they do, the converted price from a foreign currency for a Big Mac should be close to the U.S. dollar price, $2.39. The following table shows that the results are mixed: based on the actual exchange rate, a Big Mac is too expensive in Sweden, too cheap in Hong Kong, and about right in West Germany. Of course, such price differences are possible because hamburgers are perishable—Big Macs produced in one country are *nontraded* goods for consumption in another country.

### Big Mac Prices in Local Currencies and U.S. Dollars

| Country | Price in Local Currency | Converted Price in U.S. Dollars |
|---|---|---|
| Australia | A$ 1.95 | $2.65 |
| Belgium | BFr 90 | 1.43 |
| Britain | £ 1.19 | 2.20 |
| Canada | C$ 2.05 | 1.65 |
| Denmark | DKr 22.75 | 3.57 |
| France | FFr 17.30 | 3.07 |
| Holland | FL 4.85 | 2.60 |
| Hong Kong | HK$ 7.60 | 0.97 |
| Ireland | IRL 1.22 | 1.97 |
| Italy | Lire 3,300 | 2.69 |
| Japan | Y 370 | 2.98 |
| Singapore | S$ 2.80 | 1.40 |
| Spain | Ptas 285 | 2.57 |
| Sweden | SKr 18.50 | 3.14 |
| W. Germany | DM 4.10 | 2.47 |
| Yugoslavia | Dinar 2,300 | 1.64 |
| U.S. | $ 2.39 | $2.39 |

Source: *The Economist*, April 2, 1988, p. 66.
Reprinted with permission from *The Economist*.

The theory is evidently far from perfect when examined at specific time intervals, such as annually. But based on the two endpoints—1973 and 1987—there seems to be *something* to it in the long run. Given that the demand for foreign goods will eventually respond to price differences, the exchange rate will gravitate toward the PPP level. So relative price levels do play a role in determining exchange rates between currencies, even if the PPP theory does not hold perfectly.

Box 21.3 provides more casual evidence regarding PPP—how the cost of a Big Mac compares in various currencies.

## Interest Rates and Related Short-Term Factors

The relative levels of interest rates in the United States and another country will influence the demand for that country's currency because interest rates are important in determining where people invest their money. If foreign interest rates are high relative to U.S. interest rates, for example, Americans will have an incentive to buy foreign securities, raising the U.S. demand for foreign currency to pay for them.

Suppose an American investor is going to invest $1,000 for a year and must decide between (1) investing it in the United States at the annual interest rate $r^{US}$ and (2) investing it in a foreign country at the annual foreign interest rate $r^F$. The decision will depend on which investment provides the largest accumulated amount in U.S. dollars after one year:

1. If the *investment is made in U.S. securities*, then the amount accumulated after one year will be:

$$(\$1,000)(1 + r^{US}).$$

2. If *the investment is made abroad*, the amount accumulated (in dollars) after one year will be:

$$\left(\frac{\$1,000}{E}\right)(1 + r^F)(E^e),$$

where $r^F$ = the foreign interest rate,
$\quad\quad E$ = the exchange rate at the time the investment is made,
$\quad\quad E^e$ = the expected exchange rate at the end of the year.

The formula in (2) is more complicated because the investor first has to buy foreign currency and then later has to sell it. The steps in this process are:

2.1. The investor first exchanges $1,000 at the exchange rate $E$ to obtain $\$1,000/E$ units of foreign currency. (Since the exchange rate $E$ represents the number of dollars per unit of foreign currency, $\$1,000/E$ is the equivalent number of units of foreign currency.)

2.2. The $\$1,000/E$ units of foreign currency are invested for one year at the foreign interest rate $r^F$, so $(\$1,000/E)(1 + r^F)$ units of foreign currency are accumulated.

2.3. The accumulated amount of foreign currency is converted to dollars at the end of the year. If we denote the expected exchange rate for the end of the year as $E^e$, then the expected accumulation of dollars is $(\$1,000/E)(1 + r^F)(E^e)$. (When the exchange rate is $E^e$, you multiply by $E^e$ to determine the number of dollars received for a given amount of foreign currency.) Box 21.4 provides a numerical example based on these steps.

The decision whether to invest in the U.S. or in the foreign country is made by comparing the amounts that are expected to be accumulated. The decision criterion can be stated in terms of the ratio of the two accumulated amounts—the *interest rate parity (IRP) ratio*:

$$\text{IRP} = \frac{(\$1,000)(1 + r^{US})}{\left(\dfrac{\$1,000}{E}\right)(1 + r^F)(E^e)} = \left[\frac{(1 + r^{US})}{(1 + r^F)}\right]\left[\frac{E}{E^e}\right] \quad\quad (21.2)$$

The investment decision can thus be expressed as:

**When IRP > 1.0:**    **Invest in the United States;**
**When IRP < 1.0:**    **Invest abroad;**
**When IRP = 1.0:**    **Investor is indifferent.**

BOX 21.4 IN DEPTH

## Comparing Returns from U.S. and Foreign Investments

The following facts are available to an American investor who is deciding where to invest $1,000.

Annual U.S. interest rate $r^{US}$ = 10%.

Annual French interest rate $r^{F}$ = 8%.

Initial exchange rate $E$ = $.20 per French franc.

Expected exchange rate (one year later) $E^{e}$ = $.25 per Franch franc.

1.  The amount accumulated from a U.S. investment is:

    ($1,000)$(1 + r^{US})$ = ($1,000)(1.1) = $1,100.

2.  The amount accumulated from a foreign investment is:

2.1. French francs that can be invested =

    $1,000/E$ = $1,000/$.20 = 5,000 francs.

2.2. Accumulated amount of French francs =

    ($1,000/E$)$(1 + r^{F})$ = (5,000 francs)(1.08) = 5,400 francs.

2.3. Dollars received at year-end after currency conversion =

    ($1,000/E$)$(1 + r^{F})(E^{e})$ = (5,400 francs)($.25) = $1,350.

Even though the U.S. interest rate is higher, the expected appreciation of the French franc—from $.20 per franc to $.25 per franc—makes the French investment the better choice.

This rule is easily interpreted on the basis of the two ratio terms in the second part of equation (21.2): the interest rate ratio $(1 + r^{US})/(1 + r^{F})$ and the exchange rate ratio $E/E^{e}$.

The *interest rate ratio* indicates that U.S. investment is favored when the U.S. interest rate $r^{US}$ is high relative to the foreign interest rate $r^{F}$.

The *exchange rate ratio* indicates that U.S. investment is favored when the dollar is expected to appreciate in value. To see this, notice that when the dollar is expected to appreciate in value, the ratio $E/E^{e}$ is greater than 1—the expected exchange rate is less than the current exchange rate. We will look further at expected exchange rates in a moment.

### Interest Rate Variables and the Demand for Foreign Currency

IRP ratios greater than 1 have a negative effect on the demand for foreign investments, and thus on the demand for foreign currency. Conversely, when the IRP ratio is less than 1.0, foreign investments are preferred, so the demand for foreign currency—to make foreign investments—is high. Of course, the IRP ratio is not the only variable taken into account in investment decisions. Other factors include:

- *Risk.* Investing abroad is often *considered* risky—many people are more confident investing in their own country. The higher the perceived risk of foreign investment, or the more risk averse the investor, the lower the demand for foreign currency.

- *Domestic income.* Higher U.S. income may increase the demand for foreign currency because people may invest some of their greater income abroad (or otherwise spend some of it on imported goods).

- *Government action.* The government may intervene in foreign exchange markets, buying or selling foreign currency.

All of these variables—the IRP ratio (interest rates and expected exchange rate appreciation), risk, income, and government action—affect the exchange rate in the short run. That is, these variables may change suddenly, causing people to adjust their investment decisions promptly.

## The Interest Rate Parity Theory

The **interest rate parity (IRP) theory** states that the exchange rate is determined by the level of interest and expected exchange rates at which investors are just indifferent between investing in the United States or in a foreign country; that is, when the IRP equals 1. Therefore the IRP value of the exchange rate, $E^{(r)}$, is expressed as:

$$\text{IRP} = \left[\frac{(1 + r^{US})}{(1 + r^F)}\right]\left[\frac{E^{(r)}}{E^e}\right] = 1, \text{ or that}$$

$$E^{(r)} = \frac{E^e(1 + r^F)}{(1 + r^{US})}. \tag{21.3}$$

The IRP theory is thus based only on relative interest rates and the expected exchange rate, just as the purchasing power parity (PPP) theory is based only on relative price levels.

The IRP theory also depends on **international financial arbitrage,** just as the PPP theory depends on international commodity arbitrage. International financial arbitrage occurs when investors lend their money in the country—or currency—that offers the highest interest rate, and correspondingly borrow money in the country with the lowest interest rate. Such arbitrage activity would cause the IRP ratio to gravitate toward 1.0.

However, the IRP theory has the problem that investors often consider international financial arbitrage to be risky. In addition to the general risk of investing abroad, there is the particular risk that the rate of return on foreign investment involves the **expected exchange rate.** These factors may limit the amount of international arbitrage, as discussed further in Box 21.5.

Due to these problems, the interest rate parity theory, like the purchasing power parity theory, may not accurately predict the level of the exchange rate. Nevertheless, the IRP theory offers a convenient way of

## Expected Exchange Rates and Futures Markets

Decisions in international trade and finance often involve expected exchange rates. For international finance, the interest rate parity (IRP) ratio depends on the expected appreciation of the dollar. For international trade, expected exchange rates often matter because it takes time to ship goods. In either case, traders may want to specify ahead of time the exchange rate that will apply to their transactions.

This is the purpose of futures contracts and forward contracts in the markets for foreign currency. *Futures contracts* for foreign currencies are traded on public futures exchanges, whereas *forward contracts* for foreign currencies are traded by commercial banks (the term "forward" refers to the "forward securities" discussed in Chapter 8). Otherwise, the two types of contracts serve the same function.

Banks that operate forward markets are also involved in international financial arbitrage. An IRP ratio close to 1.0 can be assured if the **forward rate**—the exchange rate on a forward contract—is substituted for the expected exchange rate $E^e$ in equation (21.3). However, this does not mean the expected exchange rate has to equal the forward rate: each trader may still form his own expectations.

analyzing the effect of interest rates on exchange rates. Appendix 21.1 also demonstrates that *real* interest rates will be equal across countries if both the PPP and IRP theories hold.

## The Equilibrium Exchange Rate

The *equilibrium exchange rate* is the exchange rate at which the demand for and the supply of foreign currency are equal. The *U.S. demand for foreign currency* comes from Americans who need to pay for their purchases of foreign goods and foreign investments. The demand for foreign currency (by Americans) $F^d$ can be expressed as:

$$F^d = F^d\left[\frac{(\overline{P^F})(E)}{P^{US}}, \frac{(1 + \overline{r^{US}})E}{(1 + r^F)E^e}, \cdots\right]. \qquad (21.4)$$

The minus signs above the PPP and IRP variables indicate that they are both negatively related to the U.S. demand for foreign currency. The dots at the end of the function are a reminder that other factors may also influence demand.

Equation (21.4) can be used to illustrate the important result that the demand for foreign currency is negatively related to the exchange rate $E$: as the exchange rate $E$ rises (the dollar depreciates), the demand for foreign currency falls. This is true for both the PPP and IRP variables in equation (21.4):

- A higher exchange rate $E$ raises the converted foreign price level, $(P^F)(E)$, which shifts demand toward U.S. goods. This reduces the demand for foreign currency to import foreign goods.
- A higher exchange rate ratio $E/E^e$ indicates the dollar is more likely to appreciate, which raises the IRP ratio and makes foreign investment less attractive. This reduces the demand for foreign currency to purchase foreign assets.

The *supply of foreign currency* comes from traders abroad who exchange foreign currency for dollars in order to pay for their purchases of U.S. goods and U.S. investments. The foreign supply of foreign currency, $F^s$, is expressed as:

$$F^s = F^s \left[ \overset{+}{\frac{(P^F)(E)}{P^{US}}}, \overset{+}{\frac{(1 + r^{US})E}{(1 + r^F)E^e}}, \cdots \right]. \tag{21.5}$$

The supply of foreign currency depends on exactly the same PPP and IRP variables as the demand for foreign currency, but with the algebraic signs reversed. Two points clarify this:

First, the same variables determine the demand for and the supply of foreign currency because the variables are specified as ratios of foreign variables to U.S. variables—such as the price level ratio, $P^F/P^{US}$.

Second, it is sensible to assume that Americans and foreigners will respond in exactly the opposite way to changes in these variables: if the American demand for foreign currency is negatively related to a price level ratio, then the supply of foreign currency will be positively related to the same ratio. This is even true for the exchange rate: as the exchange rate $E$ rises—the dollar depreciates, and equivalently, the foreign currency appreciates. Figure 21.5 shows how the demand for and supply of foreign currency determine the equilibrium exchange rate $E^*$.

FIGURE 21.5
**The Equilibrium Exchange Rate**

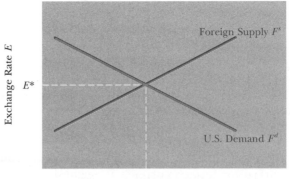

Foreign Currency

A variety of factors may shift the demand and supply curves, as indicated in Table 21.2. Factors that raise the demand for foreign currency cause the demand curve to shift to the right and the supply curve to shift to the left. As a result, the equilibrium exchange rate $E^*$ will rise, which means the dollar depreciates in value.

## Factors That Change the Equilibrium Exchange Rate

Table 21.2 summarizes the factors that may cause the demand curve for foreign currency to shift. For example, if the U.S. price level $P^{US}$ rises, then consumers will shift their purchases toward foreign goods, so the demand for imports and for foreign currency will rise. As a result the exchange rate for those currencies will rise—the dollar will depreciate—to reestablish equilibrium. That is, in Figure 21.5, factors that shift the demand curve to the right cause the equilibrium exchange rate to rise.

| TABLE 21.2 Factors That May Shift the U.S. Demand for Foreign Currency | |
|---|---|
| **Long-Term Factors** | **U.S. Demand for Foreign Currency** |
| U.S. price level $P^{US}$ rises | Rises |
| Foreign price level $P^F$ rises | Falls |
| Tariffs and quotas rise | Falls |
| Preferences shift toward U.S. goods | Falls |
| New foreign goods introduced | Rises |
| **Short-Term Factors** | |
| U.S. interest rates $r^{US}$ rise | Falls |
| Foreign interest rates $r^F$ rise | Rises |
| Expected future exchange rate $E^e$ rises | Rises |
| Foreign investment is more risky | Falls |
| U.S. income rises | Rises |
| U.S. government buys foreign currency | Rises |

Factors that change demand in one direction must change supply in the opposite direction. For example, when the U.S. price level $P^{US}$ rises, the supply curve of foreign currency will shift to the left, as foreigners shift their purchases away from U.S. goods. This also causes the equilibrium exchange to rise—the dollar to depreciate. In other words, the effect on the exchange rate of a shift in the supply curve of foreign currency reinforces the effect of a shift in the demand curve—so if you know the demand curve effects, you know the whole story.

## The Exchange Rate for the Dollar Since 1980

In principle, we can change the variables in Table 21.2 one at a time to evaluate their effect on the equilibrium exchange rate. In practice, however, the factors may be related to one another, and several may change at the same time. We will now look at some factors that may have affected dollar exchange rates from 1980 to 1987. Figure 21.3 on page 513 shows that this was a turbulent period in which the dollar first appreciated dramatically against all currencies (the exchange rate $E$ fell), and then reversed the process.

Changes in *real* interest rates—the real interest rate is defined as the nominal interest rate minus the expected inflation rate—are a key to what happened. When real interest rates in the United States rise relative to real rates in other countries, we expect the dollar to appreciate (as it did between 1980 and 1985). The reason is that a rise in real interest rates reflects either a rise in nominal interest rates or a decrease in expected inflation, both of which decrease the demand for foreign currency.

In fact, between 1980 and 1985, nominal interest rates rose and expected inflation fell. Rising nominal interest rates and falling expected inflation—rising real interest rates—are a sound recipe for appreciating a currency.

Since 1985, the opposite seems to have been happening: real interest rates in the United States have been falling relative to those in other countries as the result of rising expectations of inflation in the United States. The result is that the dollar has depreciated, almost back to its 1980 level for the mark, and well beyond it for the yen. (The relationships between exchange rates and real interest rates are discussed further in Appendix 21.1.)

# International Banking

As the U.S. economy has become open to international trade and finance during the last 25 years, a comparable trend has occurred in international banking. In 1960, only a handful of U.S. banks had offices abroad. By the end of 1987, close to 200 U.S. banks maintained over 1,000 offices—branches or subsidiaries—around the world, with about $400 billion of assets. Similarly, more than 200 foreign banks maintained over 600 offices in the United States, representing about 15% of total U.S. banking assets.

## International Banking Services

**International banks** carry out three main activities.

- They provide services—such as foreign currency services—to customers engaged in international trade.
- They raise deposits through their foreign offices.
- They make loans to foreign borrowers.

### Information and International Banking

Imagine that a medium-sized U.S. manufacturing firm, hearing of the success of other firms' sales overseas, decides to try to export some of its own products. Although the executives of such a company may know very little about selling abroad, they can ask their banker for advice. Large U.S. banks with international offices can be very helpful in gathering, evaluating, and distributing international trade information. They carry this out through a network of offices in different countries.

Based on the information received from its foreign offices, for example, the bank might recommend which country to target first. Additionally, once the company starts selling its products abroad, it may use the bank's foreign offices to deal with other problems that arise.

### International Payment Services

International trade and finance tend to be more complicated than their domestic counterparts. For example, international receipts of money and shipments of goods may take a substantial amount of time, and it is sometimes hard to determine the credit standing of foreign customers. International banks often take care of these matters, especially with regard to foreign currency.

When an importer and an exporter make a deal, each side is likely to want to set the price of the trade in his or her own currency. Since both traders cannot have it their own way, one or the other must deal in foreign currency. International banks provide a variety of services that help simplify this arrangement. First and foremost, the banks act as dealers in foreign exchange, standing ready to buy or to sell foreign currency at posted exchange rates. As a related matter, the banks help firms transfer money from country to country, a process that is necessarily more complicated than making payments within one country.

A special problem of *timing* often arises in international transactions. For example, a U.S. importer may have agreed to pay in French francs for a wine order. However, the importer probably does not want to pay the French exporter until the wine actually arrives in the United States. Meanwhile, the dollar could depreciate against the franc, forcing the importer to spend more dollars to pay the bill in francs.

There are basically two ways of dealing with this problem. One way is to buy the francs immediately, then invest them in French securities or in an interest-paying deposit account at the bank's Paris branch until the payment is made. The other way is to buy francs on a forward contract. As discussed in Box 21.5, the exchange rate—the forward exchange rate—is guaranteed, allowing the U.S. firm to keep its money invested in dollars until it is needed. In practice, the two approaches usually work out to about the same thing.

## The Structure of International Banking

The structure of international banking has three components: (1) U.S. international banks in the United States; (2) foreign banks in the United States; and (3) U.S. international banks abroad.

### U.S. International Banks in the United States

The special needs of U.S. international banks have long been recognized in U.S. banking laws and regulations. The 1919 Edge Act provided that U.S. international banks could operate subsidiaries in the United States—called *Edge Act banks*—with privileges, such as interstate banking, that were not available to other banks. The privileges allowed these banks to serve customers who were active in international trade and to compete with foreign banks in the U.S. that provided similar services. However, Edge Act banks could *not* carry out a domestic banking business.

*International Banking Facilities* (*IBFs*) have now extended the concept of Edge Act banks. IBFs are exempt from most U.S. banking regulations—including reserve requirements, interest ceilings on bank deposits, and even some U.S. taxes. However, IBFs are not allowed to carry out a domestic banking business.

### Foreign Banks in the United States

Foreign banks operate in the United States in a variety of forms. Some foreign banks just maintain offices in the United States to gather information and to help their customers. At the other extreme, foreign banks can maintain full-service facilities—accepting deposits and making loans—either as a branch of their parent bank or as a separate subsidiary. Moreover, until 1978, foreign banks in the United States were largely unregulated—they operated in much the same manner as the IBFs we just described. However, the International Banking Act of 1978 balanced the situation, making foreign banks subject to basically the same rules as U.S. banks.

### U.S. Banks Abroad

U.S. banks operate abroad in the same way that foreign banks operate in the United States, with facilities that range from information offices to full-scale branches. Table 21.3 provides some additional information about the foreign branches of U.S. banks.

About a third of the assets of the foreign branches of U.S. banks are in the United Kingdom. This is not surprising since London is a center, along with New York City, of international banking. More surprising is the large percentage of the assets of the foreign branches of U.S. banks that are in the Bahamas and Cayman Islands. This represents more than the desire of international bankers to take a Caribbean vacation. But to see why, we first have to go to Europe; after all, this *is* international banking.

## The Market for Eurodollars

U.S. banks originally set up many of their branches in Europe—particularly in London—so they could participate in the **Eurodollar market**—which is located in Europe but deals in deposits denominated in dollars. Normally, the funds are initially deposited in dollars but, in principle, foreign currency could be deposited if it is then converted to dollars by the bank. A main factor in the early development of the Eurodollar market was that U.S. banks were trying to avoid U.S. interest rate ceilings which limited their ability to attract deposits.

**TABLE 21.3**
**Foreign Branches of U.S. Federal Reserve Member Banks**

| Item | Unit | At year-end | | | | | | | |
|------|------|------|------|------|------|------|------|------|------|
| | | 1970 | 1975 | 1980 | 1981 | 1982 | 1983 | 1984 | 1985 |
| Member banks operating foreign branches | Number | 79 | 126 | 159 | 159 | 162 | 166 | 163 | 164 |
| Foreign branches | Number | 532 | 762 | 787 | 841 | 900 | 892 | 905 | 1,001 |
| Assets of foreign branches[a,b] | Bil. dol. | 50.0 | 145.3 | 310.5 | 343.3 | 341.3 | 333.1 | 291.3 | [c]294.0 |
| Assets of branches in United Kingdom[a] | Bil. dol. | 24.0 | 66.7 | 107.4 | 111.9 | 110.8 | 132.4 | 86.7 | [c]100.0 |
| Assets of branches in The Bahamas and Cayman Islands[a] | Bil. dol. | 4.0 | 36.6 | 93.3 | 104.8 | 100.5 | 116.7 | 85.5 | [c]78.0 |

[a] Data exclude claims on other foreign branches of the same bank. [b] Includes assets of foreign branches in countries other than those shown separately. [c]Estimated.

**Source:** *Statistical Abstract of the United States*, 1987, Table 813.

Once the foreign branch had attracted Eurodollar deposits, the funds could be transferred to the main office in the United States and used to make loans and to buy securities in the normal way. Eurodollar deposits were not subject to U.S. reserve requirements and similar regulations, because the transfer of funds from a European branch to the U.S. main office was not treated as a deposit.

### The Current Structure of the Eurodollar Market

The original factors that created the Eurodollar market have largely disappeared: banking deregulation in 1980 eliminated the interest rate ceilings, while reserve requirements were imposed on Eurodollar transfers. Nevertheless, the Eurodollar market now has a life of its own because it meets a need.

An international market is needed for dollars because the dollar is an **international reserve currency**—it is used even in international trades that do not involve Americans. Prime examples are oil and coal transactions, which are priced in dollars even though neither the buyer nor the seller is American. This makes both traders responsible for exchanging their own currency for dollars, or vice versa. These transactions create a demand for Eurodollar deposits and Eurodollar loans.

The Eurodollar market functions primarily for firms—the smallest trade is usually $1 million. The market now also includes other securities, such as Eurodollar bonds—bonds denominated in dollars and traded in Europe. The overall size of the market is about $1 trillion.

### Offshore Markets

The Eurodollar market reflects the international demand for deposits and loans that are stated in terms of dollars, but it is not essential for the market to be located in Europe. Indeed, the key factor is that banking operations be relatively *unregulated*. This is the basis of **offshore banking**—meaning that banking operations are not subject to standard regulations. Two Caribbean countries—the Bahamas and the Cayman Islands—have encouraged this activity with tax benefits and the like. This is why, as shown in Table 21.3, U.S. banks maintain a substantial part of their foreign assets on these islands.

However, these offshore banking facilities are "shells"—entities that exist only for the record. The firms that actually deposit and borrow money through these facilities probably are located in New York City or London, and deal in standard fashion with bankers located there. This is why International Banking Facilities (IBFs)—described earlier—are now allowed to operate within the United States. Since the business is really being done in the United States, it makes sense to acknowledge this.

## Foreign Lending of U.S. Banks

The last component of international banking is foreign lending by U.S. banks. In the course of financing international trade, these banks of course make loans to many U.S. and foreign firms. The loans to less developed countries (LDCs), particularly in Latin America, have attracted attention because—as we mentioned in Chapter 12—it is now doubtful that many of them will be repaid.

The amount of the loans to developing countries is shown in the first column of Table 21.4. In each region, most of the loans are held by nine money-center banks—nine of the largest banks in the United States.

### TABLE 21.4
### U.S. Bank Loans to Developing Countries

| Region | Total U.S. Banks | 9 Money-Center Banks $ billion | % of Capital |
|---|---|---|---|
| Latin America | 67.4 | 42.6 | 94.3 |
| Asia | 19.6 | 12.9 | 28.6 |
| Africa | 3.3 | 2.5 | 5.6 |
| OPEC | 18.9 | 14.0 | 31.0 |
| Total | 109.2 | 72.0 | 159.5 |

**Source:** *Country Exposure Lending Survey*, February 1987.

For these banks, Latin American loans alone are about equal to their bank capital. Table 21.5 provides more details.

| TABLE 21.5 | | |
| --- | --- | --- |
| Latin American Loans of Nine Money-Center Banks | | |

### Claims at March 31, 1987

| | $ billion | % of Capital |
| --- | --- | --- |
| Bank of America | 7.1 | 94 |
| Bankers Trust | 3.1 | 78 |
| Chemical | 1.1 | 45 |
| Citibank | 10.5 | 75 |
| Chase Manhattan | 7.2 | 106 |
| Continental Illinois | 4.4 | 98 |
| 1st National Chicago | 2.4 | 72 |
| Manufacturers Hanover | 7.6 | 136 |
| Morgan Guaranty | 4.3 | 65 |

**Source:** *Investment Research*, Goldman Sachs, June 1987.

## Chapter Summary

1. International trade involves transactions in goods and services between countries. International finance involves transactions in financial instruments. International transactions generally involve foreign currencies which are traded in foreign exchange markets.

2. The balance of payments, the summary of a country's international transactions, has three components: (1) the current account—consisting primarily of the country's trade balance; (2) the capital account—covering the country's international financial transactions; and (3) the statistical discrepancy—arising from reporting errors in the current and capital accounts.

3. A foreign exchange rate is the exchange ratio between the currencies of two countries. If $D$ dollars exchange for $F$ units of a foreign currency, then the exchange rate $E$—the dollar price of foreign currency— is calculated as $E = D/F$. The dollar is said to appreciate when it commands more units of foreign currency; the exchange rate $E$ falls in this case.

4. With a flexible exchange rate system, exchange rates are determined by the demand and supply for foreign currencies.

The demand and supply depend, in turn, on relative price levels, interest rates, and related variables for the two countries. The dollar appreciates (the exchange rate falls) as U.S. prices fall or U.S. interest rates rise.

5. According to the purchasing power parity theory, the exchange rate between two currencies is equal to the ratio of the price levels of the two countries. According to the interest rate parity theory, the exchange rate depends on the ratio of interest rates, at home and abroad, and on the expected exchange rate. Both theories rely on arbitrage transactions that force the exchange rate to the specified level.

6. International banking provides special services to firms that engage in international trade and finance. The two main services are: access to pertinent information, and foreign exchange facilities. In addition, U.S. banks helped to develop the Eurodollar market, a large and active market for dollar denominated deposits that was originally located in Europe. U.S. banks also make loans to foreign borrowers— including the large loans made to less developed countries, some of which will probably not be repaid.

## Key Terms

Balance of payments accounts:
    Capital account
    Current account
    Statistical discrepancy
Capital flows
Eurodollar market
Exchange rates:
    Appreciation
    Depreciation
    Expected
    Fixed
    Flexible
    Forward

International:
    Banking
    Commodity arbitrage
    Financial arbitrage
    Investment position
    Reserve currency
    Trade and finance
Law of one price
Offshore banking
Parity:
    Purchasing power (PPP)
    Interest rate (IRP)
Trade balance

## Study Questions

1. Under a flexible exchange rate system, why must a country receive capital *inflows* if it is running a trade *deficit*?

2. Why has the United States become a net debtor nation?

3. What condition would cause the *law of one price* to fail to hold for a good that is traded in several markets?

4. What is the purchasing power parity (PPP) theory of exchange rates? Why might it fail to hold?

5. Why does a higher expected appreciation of the dollar cause U.S. investors to direct their investments toward the United States? What about foreign investors?

6. What is the interest rate parity (IRP) theory of exchange rates? Why might it fail to hold?

7. Describe the type of transactions a U.S. arbitrage trader would carry out if the interest rate parity ratio (equation 21.2) were greater than 1.0. What risk is involved?

8. Considering the effects on both the demand for and the supply of foreign currency, describe what happens to the equilibrium exchange rate when the U.S. price level rises, other things being equal.

9. Considering the effects on both the demand for and the supply of foreign currency, describe what happens to the equilibrium exchange rate when U.S. interest rates rise, other things being equal.

10. Why is it useful for the United States that the dollar is an *international reserve currency*?

## Recommended Reading

*The growing openness of the U.S. economy and the particular current problems of capital inflows and a trade deficit are discussed in these three publications:*

Martin Feldstein, editor, *The United States in the World Economy*, NBER Summary Report, National Bureau of Economic Research, Cambridge, Mass., 1987.

Banjamin M. Friedman, "Implications of the U.S. Net Capital Inflow," in R. W. Hafer, editor, *How Open is the U.S. Economy?* D.C. Heath, Lexington, Mass., 1986.

Owen F. Humpage, "Requirements for Eliminating the Trade Deficit," *Economic Commentary* Federal Reserve Bank of Cleveland, April 1, 1987.

*The following two articles provide excellent introductions to the operations of foreign exchange markets:*

K. Alec Chrystal, "A Guide to Foreign Exchange Markets," *Review*, Federal Reserve Bank of St. Louis, March 1984, pp. 5–18.

Roger M. Kubarych, *Foreign Exchange Markets in the United States*, revised edition, Federal Reserve Bank of New York, 1983.

*A standard reference on the PPP theory of exchange rates:*

Lawrence H. Officer, "The Purchasing Power Parity Theory of Exchange Rates: A Review Article," *Staff Papers* 23, International Monetary Fund, March 1976, pp. 1–60.

*Two different aspects of international banking, the Eurodollar market and U.S. bank loans to developing countries, are discussed in these two articles:*

Jack M. Guttentag and Richard J. Herring, "Disaster Myopia in International Banking," *Essays in International Finance*, no. 164, International Finance Section, Princeton University, Princeton, N.J., September 1986.

Ramon Moreno, "The Eurodollar Market and U.S. Resident," *Economic Review*, Federal Reserve Bank of San Francisco, Summer 1987, pp. 43–59.

# Appendix 21.1: Combining Purchasing Power Parity and Interest Rate Parity

The theory of purchasing power parity states that exchange rates are a function of price levels; the theory of interest rate parity states that exchange rates are a function of interest rates. This appendix shows that when both theories hold, real interest rates are equal across countries.

Based on equation (21.1) for purchasing power parity, an exchange rate $E$ is determined by the ratio of the U.S. price level $P^{US}$ to the foreign price level $P^F$:

$$E = \frac{P^{US}}{P^F}.$$

If inflation occurs in the United States at the annual rate $\pi^{US}$ and in the foreign country at the annual rate $\pi^F$, then a year later the price level in the United States will be $P^{US}(1 + \pi^{US})$ and in the foreign country it will be $P^F(1 + \pi^F)$. If the expected exchange rate $E^e$ is based on these price levels, then we have:

$$E^e = \frac{P^{US}(1 + \pi^{US})}{P^F(1 + \pi^F)}.$$

These values for the exchange rate and the expected exchange rate can be substituted into the interest rate parity relationship, equation (21.3):

$$\left( \frac{P^{US} (1 + \pi^{US}) P^F}{P^F(1 + \pi^F) P^{US}} \right) = \frac{(1 + r^{US})}{(1 + r^F)}, \tag{21.6}$$

which simplifies to:

$$\frac{(1 + r^{US})}{(1 + \pi^{US})} = \frac{(1 + r^F)}{(1 + \pi^F)} \tag{21.7}$$

with $\pi^{US}$ the U.S. inflation rate during the year,
   $\pi^F$ the foreign inflation rate during the year.

In Chapter 4, we established that the expressions on each side of equation (21.7) represent *real* interest rates, for the United States and the foreign country, respectively. The combination of purchasing power parity and interest rate parity thus implies that real rates of interest are equal across currencies. When real rates of interest are not equal across currencies, then there must remain opportunities to carry out either commodity or financial arbitrage. The condition of equal real rates of interest thus represents the most complete form of international economic integration.

# The International Monetary System and Monetary Policy

**22**

*"Put not your trust in money, but put your money in trust."*

*Oliver Wendell Holmes*

In August 1971, President Nixon announced that foreign central banks could no longer convert dollars into gold at the established price of $35 per ounce. He had ended an era—known as fixed exchange rates, or the Bretton Woods period.

About twenty-seven years earlier, with the end of World War II imminent, statesman and economic advisers had assembled in the small town of Bretton Woods, New Hampshire, to plan a new international monetary system. The system they adopted featured fixed exchange ratios between the major currencies, centered on the dollar and gold. For a quarter of a century, the Bretton Woods system worked well: with exchange rate uncertainties virtually eliminated, world trade flourished.

To be sure, there were occasional imbalances, particularly regarding the British pound. In 1949 and again in 1967, the pound had to be devalued in order to end a British trade deficit—a situation familiar to Americans today. The United States was having trouble of its own in maintaining the Bretton Woods Agreement (as we will see later in the chapter). In 1971 the dollar was separated from gold, and finally, in 1973 the leading trading countries agreed to substitute flexible exchange rates for fixed ones.

Not that the debate is over yet. Even now, there are proposals to return to the gold standard, which would require all of the nations' central banks to maintain their money supply in strict ratio to gold reserves. It is argued that this discipline would eliminate the discretionary aspects of monetary policy and reduce inflation on a worldwide basis.

The fact is that both fixed and flexible exchange rate systems have costs and benefits. In this chapter, we will examine the issues and problems that are raised by exchange rates, and related aspects of the international monetary system.

In this chapter, we will study monetary policy issues that arise for the United States due to international finance and trade. First we will look at alternative exchange rate systems and at how the international monetary system evolved; then we will examine the current policy decisions that face the United States.

# Alternative Exchange Rate Systems

Each country has to decide—explicitly or implicitly—which exchange rate system to use to determine the foreign exchange value of its currency. Three main systems are available: *flexible exchange rates*, *fixed exchange rates*, and *managed floats* (various combinations of the first two).

## Flexible Exchange Rates

We examined the operation of a **flexible exchange rate system** in Chapter 21. Here we will again refer to the dollar exchange rate $E$ as the *dollar price of foreign exchange*—the number of dollars paid for a unit of foreign currency. We will use the British pound as our specific example of a foreign currency. The **equilibrium exchange rate** is the exchange rate at which the demand and supply for a foreign currency are equal under a flexible exchange rate system. This is shown as $2 per pound in Figure 22.1.

The demand and supply of foreign currency are initially equal at the equilibrium exchange rate $E^*$ ($2 per pound) for a flexible exchange rate system. Factors that shift the demand curve for foreign currency rightward generally shift the supply curve of foreign currency leftward. In the figure, these shifts cause the exchange rate to rise to $3 per pound—which means the dollar depreciates.

FIGURE 22.1
**A Flexible Exchange Rate System**

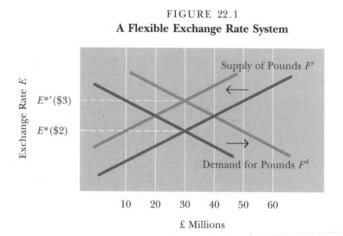

The *demand curve for foreign currency* (by Americans), $F^d$, is negatively sloped as a function of the exchange rate $E$—as the exchange rate falls (and the dollar appreciates), the demand for foreign currency rises, because U.S. purchases of foreign goods and assets rise. We saw in Table 21.2 on page 525 that, among other factors, the demand curve for foreign currency shifts *rightward* as:

1. U.S. prices rise relative to the foreign prices.
2. U.S. income rises relative to foreign income.
3. U.S. interest rates fall relative to foreign rates.

The *supply curve of foreign currency* (from foreigners), $F^s$ in Figure 22.1, is positively sloped as a function of the exchange rate $E$—as the exchange rate $E$ rises (and the dollar depreciates), foreign purchases of U.S. goods rise. The location of the supply curve generally depends on the same variables as the demand curve, but with just the opposite effects. The supply curve thus shifts *leftward* for the three factors listed.

Starting at the equilibrium exchange rate of $2 per pound in Figure 22.1, factors that shift the demand and supply curves cause the equilibrium rate to change. Higher U.S. prices, for example, cause the demand curve to shift rightward and the supply curve to shift leftward. The result is that the dollar depreciates (the exchange rate $E^*$ rises) from $2 to $3 per pound.

## Fixed Exchange Rates

The key feature of a **fixed exchange rate system** is that the exchange rate is *pegged* at a specific value $E^f$, which is not necessarily equal to the equilibrium exchange rate $E^*$. In Figure 22.2, the fixed rate $E^f$ is $2, while the equilibrium rate $E^*$ is $2.50.

Under a fixed exchange rate system, central banks buy or sell foreign currency to keep the exchange rate "fixed" at the desired level. The dollar is overvalued at the fixed rate $E^f$ ($2 per pound) relative to the equilibrium rate $E^*$ ($2.50 per pound). To "fix" the exchange rate at $E^f$, the central banks have to sell (supply) 40 million pounds to balance the excess demand for pounds in the market. At the fixed rate $E^{f'}$ ($3 per pound), the dollar is undervalued, and the central banks would have to buy pounds to maintain the fixed rate.

FIGURE 22.2
**A Fixed Exchange Rate System**

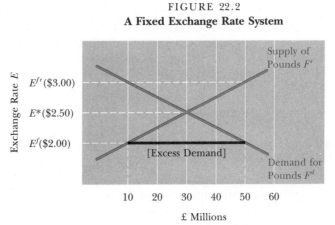

In this situation, the dollar is **overvalued** at the fixed exchange rate $E^f$; this means that it takes fewer dollars to buy one pound at the fixed rate $E^f$ ($2 per pound) than it would at the equilibrium rate $E^*$ ($2.50 per pound). Put another way, an overvalued dollar means that there is an excess market demand for pounds. For the $2 per pound fixed exchange rate to be maintained, the central banks of the two countries must be willing to sell (supply) enough foreign currency (pounds) to balance the market's excess demand. In Figure 22.2, the central banks would have to sell 40 million pounds to maintain the fixed exchange rate $E^f$ at $2 per pound. The central bank supply plus the market supply would then equal the market demand.

In contrast, the dollar would be **undervalued** if the fixed exchange rate were at $E^{f'}$, \$3 per pound. Here the market supply of pounds would exceed the demand, so the central banks would have to buy (demand) pounds to maintain the fixed rate.

## A Managed Float

Flexible and fixed exchange rate systems represent the two extreme ways to organize the international monetary system. There are also intermediate cases, known as **managed floats.** Under a managed float, the exchange rate is usually determined by market demand and supply, but the central bank sometimes intervenes in the exchange market to alter the exchange rate. Two examples:

With a **crawling peg,** a central bank maintains a fixed rate most of the time, but the rate is changed periodically to keep it from becoming significantly overvalued or undervalued. A crawling peg is often used by countries with high rates of inflation—such as Brazil—to keep their fixed exchange rates in line with the equilibrium exchange rates.

With a **dirty float,** the exchange rate is flexible and equals the equilibrium rate most of the time, but the central bank occasionally, and usually surreptitiously, intervenes to alter the exchange rate. (The greater the intervention of the central bank, the "dirtier" the float is considered to be.) Dirty floats allow the central bank to influence the exchange rate, but without the need to maintain a fixed rate.

Since 1973, the flexible exchange rate system for the dollar has usually been a dirty float, although the extent of Fed intervention has varied over time. Box 22.2 on page 540 shows two press discussions of exchange market activity by the Fed, one reflecting a relatively "clean" and the other a relatively "dirty" float.

## A Fixed Exchange Rate System

The main purpose of a fixed exchange rate system is to eliminate temporary and unexpected fluctuations in currency values. Changes in exchange rates can disrupt international trade because importers and exporters will be uncertain about the specific rate to use for their transactions.

The benefit of a fixed exchange rate system is illustrated in Figure 22.3. In the initial case, the equilibrium exchange rate $E^*$ and the fixed rate are equal at \$2.50 per pound. Now suppose that the demand curve shifts leftward and the supply curve rightward, as illustrated in the figure. Under a *flexible* system, the market exchange rate equals the equilibrium rate $E^*$, so the market rate would fall to \$2 per pound. (Box 22.1 describes how firms deal with such changes in flexible exchange rates.)

BOX 22.1 IN DEPTH

## How Firms Deal with Exchange Rate Risk

Let us suppose that IBM is negotiating a large computer sale to a British firm, with the shipment to be made in six months. The British company is prepared to pay IBM's listed dollar price but wants to make payment after it receives the computers *in pounds*—based on the then-current exchange rate between pounds and dollars.

This requires IBM to deal with the possibility that, if the dollar depreciates between the order and the delivery, it will receive fewer dollars after converting the pounds into dollars. As a first step, IBM determines how much it *expects* the dollar to depreciate, incorporating this amount, if possible, into its dollar price. In addition, it must decide how to deal with the *exchange rate risk*—the possibility that the dollar will depreciate more than expected. IBM can just accept this risk, but its profits will then be lower if the dollar depreciates more than expected. Alternatively, IBM can use the forward market in foreign exchange—described in Box 21.5 in Chapter 21—to set the exchange rate that will be used later to exchange pounds for dollars.

In contrast, if the same shifts in the demand and supply curves occur under a fixed exchange rate system, the central bank would buy (demand) whatever amount of foreign currency was needed to match the market's excess supply. So the exchange rate would remain at $2.50 per pound. The result is that firms would confidently carry out international trade based on the fixed exchange rate.

Initially the equilibrium exchange rate and the fixed exchange rate $E^f$ are equal at $2.50 per pound. Then the demand curve for foreign currency shifts leftward and the supply curve shifts rightward, causing the equilibrium exchange rate $E^*$ to fall to $2 per pound. With flexible exchange rates, the market rate would also fall to $2 per pound. To maintain a fixed rate at $2.50 per pound, the central banks would have to buy 40 million pounds to offset the excess supply.

FIGURE 22.3

**Central Bank Support of a Fixed Exchange Rate**

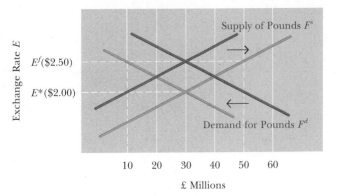

BOX 22.2 FINANCIAL NEWS

## The Dirty Float for the Dollar Varies Over Time

Federal Reserve interventions in the foreign exchange market have varied over time. The subtleties of such interventions are illustrated in the following excerpts from press reports.

On June 4, 1981, the *Wall Street Journal* reported that U.S. foreign exchange intervention had fallen to a five-year low. This report was made at the end of the April 30 quarter and reflected the then "new" Reagan administration policy:

> The U.S. sharply reduced its intervention in foreign-exchange markets during the three months ended April 30, reflecting a new Reagan administration policy.

> Scott E. Pardee, a senior vice president of the Federal Reserve Bank of New York, which runs the nation's foreign-exchange operations, said the $852.8 million in intervention transactions was the least for any quarter in more than five years.

> Mr. Pardee said at a news conference that the Fed intervened in the market on only 10 days in the quarter. Between Feb. 2 and Feb. 23, when the mark was under heavy selling pressure, the Fed purchased $610 million of the German currency in the market and an additional $168.4 million from other central banks.

> Further market intervention didn't come until the day President Reagan was shot, when the New York Fed purchased dollars by unloading marks into the New York foreign-exchange market. That action, Mr. Pardee said, "helped to calm" the market, because participants saw that "the Fed was there" to support the U.S. currency. The dollar rebounded the next day. . . .

> After that dollar-support operation, Mr. Pardee said, there wasn't any further U.S. intervention in foreign-exchange markets.

> The Reagan administration's policy of restraint in market operations has been articulated by Treasury Under Secretary Beryl W. Sprinkel, who told Congress on May 5 that the government would intervene "only when necessary to counter conditions of disorder in the market." . . .

> Asked if the Fed would intervene to support the dollar if it eventually weakens, he [Mr. Pardee] replied: "I can't forecast policy. This is worked out on a day-to-day, week-by-week, month-by-month basis." . . .

> Mr. Pardee, who must implement intervention policy, said the Reagan administration's approach represented a "free-market philosophy, which I'm comfortable with." He added, "I think we'll have more of an emphasis on letting the market clear itself."

(*Wall Street Journal*, 4 June, 1981.)

In a January, 1988, article entitled, "Intervention: Simple but Secret," Robert D. Hershey, Jr., gave a different account of government intervention in the currency markets:

> The process by which governments intervene in the currency markets—these days in vigorous support of the dollar—is procedurally straightforward but typically veiled in secrecy.
>
> The United States pays for the dollars it buys in the market by drawing from its inventory of yen, marks and other foreign currencies—a stockpile that totaled $8 billion at the end of September. When Japan, West Germany or any other foreign country wants to buy dollars, it simply creates quantities of its own money and uses this to acquire the American currency in the open market. . . .
>
> While foreign central banks can buy dollars merely by printing whatever money they need to pay for them, the United States—or any country defending its own currency—is a bit more constrained.

### Reciprocal Currency Plan

> If its holdings of marks or yen run low, the United States will then borrow the foreign currency it needs for further purchases of dollars. This would mean tapping a reciprocal currency arrangment, otherwise known as a "swap line."
>
> The Federal Reserve has agreements with 14 other central banks and the Bank for International Settlements, the central bankers' "central bank," under which the countries can borrow each other's currencies. A total of $30.1 billion of these swap lines are now in effect, with none drawn upon at last report. . . .
>
> Currency intervention, while easy to accomplish, can involve risks to economic policy. Countries that create money to buy dollars are thereby expanding their money supply. If carried to excess, this could lead to an overheated economy and undersireably high inflation.
>
> The risk, however, can be eliminated if the intervention is "sterilized." This is done by selling a similar amount of bills or other government securities in the market, a process that extinguishes money as the buyers of the securities pay the central bank for them.

### Monetary Targets Issued

> The United States, which publishes monetary targets, generally sterilizes its interventions almost automatically. But other countries, including West Germany, are less likely to do so for various reasons. . . .
>
> Although some countries never disclose much about their currency-market operations, the United States does make quarterly reports on them well after the fact. Its most recent data show that it intervened three times in the May–July 1987 period.

## Foreign Exchange Operations and the Monetary Base

Under either a fixed exchange rate or a managed float, the Fed intervenes in markets by buying or selling foreign currencies. The policy directives of the Federal Open Market Committee (FOMC) determine the transactions, following the overall directions of the Treasury Department. Box 22.3 shows a typical FOMC directive issued prior to 1973 when the United States was operating under a fixed exchange rate system.

Foreign exchange operations affect the monetary base and other monetary aggregates in basically the same way as open market operations. The only difference is that foreign exchange operations involve buying or selling foreign currencies, whereas open market operations involve buying or selling securities, such as Treasury bills. Thus, a purchase (or sale) of a foreign currency increases (or decreases) bank reserves, the monetary base, and the money supply in the same way as an open market purchase (or sale) of Treasury bills:

1. The Federal Reserve purchases foreign currency.
2. If the seller is a U.S. bank, the Federal Reserve pays for the currency by crediting the bank's reserve account. This raises the monetary base directly.
3. If the seller is not a U.S. bank, the Fed pays for the currency with a check, which eventually will be presented by a U.S. bank for credit to its reserve account. So the monetary base still rises.

---

BOX 22.3 MONEY MATTERS

## The Federal Reserve Under Fixed Exchange Rates

Between World War II and 1973, the United States was on a fixed exchange rate system. The following is a policy directive issued during this period by the Federal Open Market Committee to the Manager for Foreign Operations at the New York Federal Reserve Bank:

**Foreign Currency Directive**
**(In effect January 1, 1964)**

The basic purposes of System operations in and holdings of foreign currencies are:

1. To help safeguard the value of the dollar in international exchange markets;

2. To aid in making the system of international payments more efficient and in avoiding disorderly conditions in exchange markets. . . .

The transactions shall be conducted with a view to the following specific aims:

1. To offset or compensate . . . disequilibrating fluctuations in the international flow of payments to or from the United States.

2. To temper and smooth out abrupt changes in spot exchange rates . . .

(Federal Open Market Committee, January 1, 1964.)

### Sterilized Interventions

For foreign exchange operations that are designed to influence the exchange rate, changes in the monetary base may be an undesired side effect. To eliminate the changes in the monetary base, the Fed can use a **sterilized intervention**—undertake open market operations to offset the effect on the monetary base of the foreign exchange operations[1].

For example, suppose that the Fed sells Japanese yen to stabilize the dollar/yen exchange rate and wants to sterilize the associated reduction in the monetary base. To do so, it must carry out an open market purchase of Treasury bills at the same time. The Treasury bill purchase increases the monetary base by the amount that the yen sale decreases it, so the net change in the monetary base is zero.

## Maintaining a Fixed Exchange Rate System

Let us now suppose that the Fed alone is responsible for maintaining a fixed exchange rate, such as $E^F$ in Figure 22.3. This means that the Fed will have to sell foreign currency whenever the dollar becomes *overvalued*—the foreign exchange market has an excess demand for foreign currency—and to do the opposite whenever the dollar becomes *undervalued*.

The degree of the dollar's over- or undervaluation determines how much support the fixed exchange rate will require, and the Fed's foreign currency reserves determine how long the support can be provided. If the equilibrium exchange rate remains relatively close to the fixed rate, then the Fed can perform its role with a modest amount of foreign currency reserves. In contrast, if the dollar becomes overvalued by a large amount and for a long time, the Fed will have to supply larger quantities of foreign currency to the exchange market, and it may run out of foreign currency reserves.[2] At that point, the Fed has to allow the dollar's value to fall (the exchange rate to rise).

The Fed can reduce the dollar's value in two ways. First, it can replace the fixed exchange rate with a flexible exchange rate, allowing the currency to depreciate to the equilibrium level. Second, it can lower the fixed exchange rate closer to the equilibrium level.

A decrease in the value of the dollar is called a **devaluation**—comparable to a depreciation under a flexible exchange rate system. Similarly, an increase in the value of the dollar is called a **revaluation**—comparable to an appreciation under a flexible exchange rate system. Since a central bank can always buy foreign currency—paying for it with its domestic currency—to avert a revaluation, revaluations are less common than devaluations.

---

[1] However, sterilized interventions may reduce the impact on the exchange rate; see Warren E. Weber, "Do Sterilized Interventions Affect Exchange Rates?" *Quarterly Review*, Federal Reserve Bank of Minneapolis, Summer 1986, pp. 14–23.

[2] In practice, (as the newspaper article on page 541 explains) central banks cooperate by swapping currencies—lending one another foreign currency—to increase the amount of foreign exchange operations that each central bank can undertake. But the amounts of the swaps are limited.

FIGURE 22.4
**The Dollar/Pound Exchange Rate**

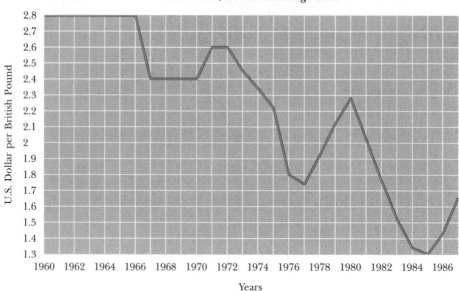

Prior to 1973, the pound had a fixed exchange rate with the dollar, which was devalued in 1967 and was revalued in 1971. After 1973, the pound appreciated and depreciated frequently under the flexible exchange rate system.

We can see these differences in Figure 22.4, which shows the exchange rate between the British pound and the U.S. dollar since 1960. Until 1973, the exchange rate was fixed, so the 1967 change from $2.80 to $2.40 is a devaluation of the pound and the 1971 change from $2.40 to $2.60 is a revaluation of the pound. After 1973, the exchange rate was flexible, so the changes shown are depreciations and appreciations of the pound.

## Monetary Policies To Deter a Devaluation

Devaluation of a currency under a fixed exchange rate system is often traumatic, both for importers and for the central bank. For importers, a devaluation means that the invoices that are payable in foreign currency after the devaluation must be converted into domestic currency at the new exchange rate, creating an additional cost. For the central bank, the problem is that speculators may anticipate that the country's currency is going to be devalued, leading them to sell the currency at the initial fixed exchange rate (while planning to buy it back at a lower price after the devaluation takes place). This increases the supply of the currency, making it more likely that devaluation will have to take place. Box 22.4 describes how this happened to the British pound in 1967.

BOX 22.4 MONEY MATTERS

## A Speculative Run on the British Pound

During 1967, the British pound was based on a fixed and overvalued exchange rate of $2.80 to one pound. To support that rate, the Bank of England—the British central bank—had to sell large amounts of its foreign currency reserves in exchange for pounds.

As speculators saw the Bank of England's foreign currency reserves falling, they became convinced that the Bank could not keep the pound at $2.80; so they sold large amounts of British pounds for dollars and other foreign currencies. This made it all the harder for the Bank of England to maintain the $2.80 rate. Finally, on November 18, 1967, the Bank devalued the pound, from $2.80 to $2.40. Speculators who had sold British pounds for $2.80 were thus able to buy them back at $2.40, a tidy profit for them and a comparable loss for the Bank of England.

Tight monetary policy is one way a central bank can try to avoid a devaluation. To illustrate this, again consider Figure 22.3 as a case where the Federal Reserve is trying to maintain an overvalued fixed exchange rate $E^f$ of $2 per pound relative to the equilibrium exchange rate of $2.50 per pound. To do this, the Fed could attempt to reduce the excess demand for foreign currency, thereby reducing the amount of foreign currency it has to sell. This means it wants to create a leftward shift in the demand curve for foreign currency and, correspondingly, a rightward shift in its supply curve. Tight monetary policy achieves these effects because it will:

1. Reduce the U.S. inflation rate relative to foreign inflation rates.

2. Raise the U.S. interest rate relative to foreign interest rates.

3. Reduce the growth rate of U.S. income relative to foreign growth rates.

However, the use of tight monetary policy to defend a fixed exchange rate may conflict with domestic economic goals, such as lower unemployment. Facing such conflicts, the central bank has a limited range of choices. It can:

1. Use a tight monetary policy to defend the exchange rate, thus giving up the domestic policy goal.

2. Use an easier monetary policy, but maintain the fixed exchange rate by reducing the demand for foreign currency through tariffs and quotas on imported goods, and similar restrictions on capital outflows.

3. Use an easier monetary policy and devalue the fixed exchange rate.

4. Use an easier monetary policy and switch to a flexible exchange rate system.

BOX 22.5 IN DEPTH

## Operation Twist

In the early 1960s, the Federal Reserve experimented with *operation twist*—a combination of easy and tight monetary policy. The easy monetary policy involved buying *Treasury bonds* to *lower* Treasury bond interest rates, thereby stimulating domestic investment. The tight monetary policy involved selling U.S. *Treasury bills* to *raise* Treasury bill interest rates, thereby reducing the demand for foreign currency and defending the exchange rate.

The Fed's ability to "twist" the relationship between short-term and long-term interest rates depends on whether it can change the factors that determine the yield curve. Under the pure expectations theory, the yield curve will "twist" only if expectations change.

As it happened, investors did not expect the Fed to succeed and thus did not change their expectations. However, the Fed may not have tried hard enough. Whatever the reason, the policy failed to work.

Box 22.5 describes an attempt by the Federal Reserve—called **operation twist**—to combine an easy monetary policy for domestic purposes with a tight monetary policy for exchange rate purposes.

## The Operation of a Managed Float

Since 1973 most of the world's major central banks have been operating under a flexible exchange rate system. However, this does not preclude individual central banks, among them the Fed, from intervening in foreign exchange markets—a "dirty" float. The Fed (and U.S. Treasury Department) try to manage the flexible exchange rate system for two basic reasons—to deal with disorderly markets, and to achieve policy goals.

*Disorderly foreign exchange markets* are usually the result of a dramatic event—such as a president being shot. As we saw in Box 22.2, even in the early years of the Reagan administration—when the policy was *not* to manage the flexible exchange rate—the Fed would still intervene in foreign exchange markets for this reason.

The *exchange rate is used as a policy tool* to alter the effects of the U.S. economy on the rest of the world, and vice versa. The exchange rate may influence how economic conditions in the rest of world are "imported" into the United States economy; or it may influence how economic conditions in the U.S. are "exported" abroad, as we will now see.

## Inflation Policies Under a Managed Float

The equilibrium exchange rate depends on, among other things, the ratio of U.S. prices to foreign prices, $P^{US}/P^F$. To focus on the connection between relative price levels and exchange rates, we will use the purchasing power parity (PPP) theory of exchange rates—discussed in Chapter 21—as a specific example. According to the PPP theory, the exchange rate $E$ will be at the level where the U.S. price level $P^{US}$ and the converted foreign price level $(P^F)(E)$ are equal:

$$P^{US} = P^F E. \tag{22.1}$$

Now suppose that the Fed initiates a tight monetary policy to reduce the U.S. inflation rate (as we saw in Chapter 20, it did precisely this between 1979 and 1982). Let us also suppose that this policy starts to succeed—that is, the price level $P^{US}$ is rising less than it would have without the tight policy. There are two main possibilities for how the exchange rate may respond to the lower U.S. inflation rate.

One is that the dollar would appreciate (the exchange rate $E$ would fall) by the same percent that the inflation rate falls, so that equation (22.1) would continue to hold. In this case, the exchange rate *responds* to the U.S. inflation rate, and has no independent influence on the inflation rate.

The other possibility is that the exchange rate would appreciate by a smaller amount than the reduction in the inflation rate. For example, other factors might influence the exchange rate, including expectations that *future* U.S. inflation rates will be higher. This means in equation (22.1) that the U.S. price level would be below the converted foreign price level. This in turn might cause the U.S. inflation rate to rise, contrary to the Fed's policy goal. The reason is that both United States and foreign consumers will shift their purchases toward U.S. goods, and the increased demand for U.S. goods will create upward pressure on U.S. prices.

Faced with this situation, the Fed can try to appreciate the dollar, so as to eliminate the extra demand for U.S. goods and the inflationary pressure it creates. In other words, *an appreciation in the exchange value of the dollar helps the Fed's anti-inflation policy.*

The same principle applies when foreign countries suffer from high inflation and the Fed is concerned that the foreign inflation will be "imported" into the United States—because purchases will be shifted to the less expensive U.S. goods. Here too, a policy of appreciating the dollar—lowering the exchange rate $E$—will cause the converted foreign prices to fall relative to U.S. prices, thus eliminating the undesired demand for U.S. goods.

## Trade Deficit Policies Under a Managed Float

The United States has had a continuing **trade deficit**—imports exceeding exports—since 1976. A trade deficit can continue as long as it is balanced by capital inflows. The negative effects of the trade deficit include the

BOX 22.6 MONEY MATTERS

## Recent Federal Reserve Exchange Rate Policy

In this article entitled, "Economic Scene: Policy on Dollar: A Puzzle to Solve." Leonard Silk reported on the policy of the Federal Reserve and the Reagan administration toward the dollar as 1988 began.

With the financial markets pursuing the dollar down, up and sideways, the big question remains: What is United States policy on the dollar?

When a Federal Reserve spokesman was asked that yesterday, the answer was: "No answer. You know there is no answer to that question."

Could the spokesman elaborate on that "no answer"? The answer was no, accompanied by a suggestion to talk to the Administration (which the Fed does not consider itself to be part of).

The Administration was more responsive. Although it chose not to say what United States policy on the dollar is, it did say the markets had been underestimating policy coordination since October.

Asked if that coordination would be continued to keep the dollar from declining below its recent record lows, the Administration suggested that the answer could be found in the Group of Seven's Dec. 23 communiqué, especially Paragraph 8. (The communiqué was issued although there was no meeting; instead the finance ministers and central bank governors of seven industrial nations had conferred for weeks over the telephone.)

Paragraph 8 said they agreed that "either excessive fluctuation of exchange rates, a further decline of the dollar or a rise in the dollar to an extent that becomes destabilizing to the adjustment process could be counter-productive by damaging growth prospects in the world economy."

Translation: Foreign governments, worried about a loss of markets, were eager for the dollar not to decline further. The United States, determined to shrink its trade deficit, did not want the dollar to rise too much. "Adjustment process" is jargon for the changes in different nations' fiscal, monetary and trade policies needed to reduce the

sale of U.S. assets to foreigners to finance it (the capital inflows), and the shift of employment from U.S. to foreign workers (who produce the imported goods). U.S. policy—including monetary policy—has been trying to eliminate the trade deficit.

Tight monetary policy is one way to reduce the trade deficit. First, tight policy will reduce the U.S. inflation rate relative to that in other countries. This will shift consumption purchases away from foreign goods and toward U.S. goods, thus reducing the deficit. Second, tight policy will reduce the real growth rate of the U.S. economy, reducing the demand for all goods, including imported goods. However, tight monetary policy has the serious drawback that it decreases the economy's real growth rate.

A depreciation of the dollar provides an alternative solution for the trade deficit. As the dollar depreciates (that is, the exchange rate $E$ rises), the converted prices of foreign goods rise relative to the prices of corresponding U.S. goods. Foreign and U.S. consumers thus have an in-huge American trade deficit and foreign surpluses.

Did the United States make a concession in agreeing to keep the dollar from falling further, provided that foreign governments agreed not to let the dollar rise too high? A senior Administration official said no. "Everybody wants stability," he said, "no less than the United States."

Indeed, in Paragraph 8, all stressed "their common interest in more stable exchange rates." They agreed "to continue to cooperate closely in monitoring and implementing policies to strengthen underlying economic fundamentals to foster stability of exchange rates. . . ."

The communiqué is not specific on interest-rate policy. The United States wants to hold its rates down and avoid pushing the economy into a recession. It wants foreign governments to help make lower United States rates possible, without forcing down the dollar, by reducing their own rates.

The Administration also rejects the counsel of those economists who say the trade deficit cannot be cut unless it lets the dollar decline further if that is where the market wants to take it. . . .

The ministers and governors resolved to carry forward their "economic policy coordination efforts" in 1988 in order to "accelerate progress towards the increased, more balanced growth and sustainable external positions necessary for greater exchange rate stability. . . ."

Market traders who can figure out what this recondite economic language means deserve to be richly rewarded. Immediately, it appears to mean that last week the dollar fell too far but that this week it has risen far enough. For the longer run, through this year, it means that a deal has been cut—but one that is pretty loose around the edges.

(*The New York Times*, 2 January, 1980. Copyright © 1980 by The New York Times Company. Reprinted by permission.)

centive to switch their purchases from foreign goods to U.S. goods, reducing U.S. imports and raising U.S. exports.

However, there are potential pitfalls to using depreciation of the dollar to improve the trade deficit:

1. The process may take time, as consumers learn about the new price relationships and adjust their buying patterns.

2. When the dollar depreciates, foreigners can purchase a given amount of U.S. goods with a *smaller* amount of foreign currency. This factor may actually cause the trade deficit to become worse initially.

3. Foreign exchange operations also affect the monetary base and the money supply unless the Fed can sterilize them with an offsetting open market operation.

4. The Fed will have to coordinate its policy with the central banks of other countries—exchange rates, after all, involve the currencies of two countries (see Box 22.6).

## Using Capital Inflows To Finance the U.S. Budget Deficit

Capital inflows—the other side of the trade deficit—played a major role in financing the U.S. federal government's *budget* deficits during the 1980s. Since budget deficits represent negative saving, either the amount of U.S. capital investment has to fall or another source of saving has to be found. International capital inflows provided an alternative source of saving. The capital inflows were achieved by maintaining high interest rates, so that foreign investors found U.S. investments attractive.

However, capital inflows are only temporary: sooner or later the U.S. will need a trade surplus to generate the foreign currency to repay foreign lenders. This is another reason for eliminating the trade deficit soon.

# The Development of the International Monetary System

In the last part of the nineteenth century, all major countries were on the gold standard, in which each currency is fully convertible into gold. During the first half of the twentieth century, countries were forced off the gold standard from time to time as a result of the two world wars and the Great Depression of the 1930s. In 1944, with the end of World War II in sight, the major trading countries agreed on a new fixed exchange rate system—the **Bretton Woods Agreement**. The Bretton Woods system lasted until the early 1970s, when the current flexible exchange rate system was adopted.

## The International Gold Standard

The **international gold standard** is a particular type of fixed exchange rate system, based on the conversion ratio of gold for currency in each country. In 1900, for example, $20 converted to an ounce of gold in the United States, and 4 pounds converted to an ounce of gold in England; thus, the fixed exchange rate between the dollar and pound was $5 per British pound.

To remain on the gold standard, a country had only to convert its currency into gold at the established ratio whenever requested to do so. This was not particularly hard as long as (1) the fixed exchange rate was about equal to the equilibrium exchange rate, and (2) the country had sufficient gold reserves to meet the requests for gold conversion. On any given day, some traders might want to convert currency into gold— leading to a gold outflow—but other traders would want to convert gold into currency—creating a gold inflow. A modest gold reserve was thus generally adequate to meet any temporary imbalances.

However, the task of maintaining a gold standard became more difficult when the fixed exchange rate was significantly overvalued relative to the equilibrium exchange rate. As under any fixed exchange rate system—recall Figure 22.2—the central bank had to support the exchange rate by selling foreign reserves or gold. Under a gold standard, this meant the central bank had to sell (or convert) gold for domestic currency. Eventually, of course, the country would run out of gold.

At that point, there were two possible courses of action. One was to discontinue the gold standard, adopting a flexible exchange rate system instead. The other was to adjust the domestic economy so as to bring the equilibrium exchange rate back toward the fixed exchange rate. The specific adjustment procedures were referred to as the *rules of the gold standard:*

1. A country facing gold outflows was to allow its money supply to fall, which was the natural outcome as long as it did not sterilize the gold outflows.

2. As its money supply fell, the country's interest rate would rise and its real economic growth would slow, reducing the inflation rate.

3. These adjustments in the domestic economy would reduce the demand for foreign currency, eventually bringing the equilibrium exchange rate back in line with the fixed rate and stopping the gold outflows.

The key problem with the gold standard was that, while it provided benefits for international trade, it also imposed costs—the rules of the gold standard—on the domestic economy. From time to time, when the costs seemed especially high, countries would drop out, returning to a flexible exchange rate system.

## The Bretton Woods Agreement

In 1944, the major trading countries met in Bretton Woods, New Hampshire, to map out a new international payments system for the postwar era. The gold standard had performed badly during the Great Depression of the 1930s, with one country after another leaving it. Moreover, it was evident that a major realignment of exchange rates would be necessary after the war, since the European countries needed time to reestablish their industrial production, whereas the United States was strong, both financially and economically.

### The International Monetary Fund

A key result of Bretton Woods was the establishment of the **International Monetary Fund** (the **IMF**), a new organization that was to monitor and maintain the new fixed exchange rate system. Some of the key features of the IMF system were:

- The value of the U.S. dollar was initially fixed in terms of gold at $35 an ounce.

- The exchange rates of other countries were fixed in terms of the dollar.

- Countries were to maintain their fixed exchange rates, selling gold or foreign currency reserves as needed.

- To help member countries, the IMF would lend them gold or foreign currencies. In 1970, this facility was expanded to include *special drawing rights (SDRs)*—assets created by the IMF that were treated as the equivalent of gold, sometimes referred to as *paper gold*.

- If a country faced a *fundamental disequilibrium* in its balance of payments—a continuing excess demand for foreign currency—then it could devalue its currency after obtaining IMF agreement.

An important feature was that the U.S. dollar was a **reserve currency**—other countries had to peg their fixed exchange rates in terms of the dollar. The dollar, in turn, was pegged against gold. This was a benefit for the United States because other countries had to demand and hold dollars for their currency reserves. As a result, when the United States ran a trade deficit, there was foreign demand to hold the additional supply of dollars. However, it also made it difficult to devalue the dollar. A devaluation of the dollar required that the dollar price of gold rise *and* that the other countries agree to revalue their currencies upward against the dollar.

### Other Aspects of the Bretton Woods System

The Bretton Woods Agreement included two other important components—the **World Bank** and the **General Agreement on Tariffs and Trade (GATT)**.

The World Bank (also called the International Bank for Reconstruction and Development) was initially established to foster the postwar redevelopment of Europe. After this was completed, the World Bank turned to helping developing countries. It continues to do so, raising money by issuing bonds, and then lending the money to these countries.

The *GATT* was designed to provide "reciprocal and mutually advantageous arrangements directed to the substantial reduction of tariffs and other barriers to trade and to elimination of discriminatory treatment in international commerce." In brief, members were supposed to lower their tariffs and to eliminate quotas (quantitative restrictions on imports). Much of the current tension between Japan and the United States on trade issues centers on whether Japan is fulfilling its GATT obligations.

## The Switch to Flexible Exchange Rates

The fixed exchange rate system worked well for a quarter of a century after World War II. When a country did have to devalue its currency, this was usually done in an orderly fashion to correct a fundamental problem. However, flaws in the system were evident by the later 1960s. For example, devaluation of the British pound in 1967 disrupted the system because the pound, along with the dollar, was a reserve currency.

The U.S. dollar came under international pressure in the early 1970s. The basic problem was that foreigners were holding as many dollars as they wanted, yet the United States continued to run trade deficits that supplied even more dollars to the market. The result was that foreigners were converting their dollars for gold, thus creating a threat to the U.S. gold reserves. To solve the problem, the U.S. wanted to devalue the dollar. But other countries would not cooperate by revaluing their currencies. So in August of 1971 the United States simply stopped converting dollars into gold for international trade purposes. Later in 1971, this led to the Smithsonian Agreement—which changed the dollar price of gold from $35 to $38 an ounce, an effective devaluation of the dollar by 12%. However, this attempt to reestablish the fixed exchange rate system soon also broke down. By 1973 the major currencies were on a flexible exchange rate system.

## The Choice Between Fixed and Flexible Exchange Rates

Fixed exchange rate systems encourage international trade by reducing or eliminating exchange rate fluctuations. Flexible exchange rate systems, however, provide more protection for the domestic economy from unwanted repercussions from international economic events. The choice between the two systems thus depends on international economic conditions and the relative importance of the two factors.

A continuing U.S. trade deficit was a major impetus for the change to flexible exchange rates, since it was easier to have the dollar depreciate under a flexible exchange rate system than it was to devalue it under a system of fixed exchange rates. The oil price shocks caused by the dramatic price increases announced by OPEC, the cartel of oil-producing countries, during the early 1970s also created strains in the international monetary system that could not be handled by a system of fixed exchange rates. In brief, economic conditions were simply changing too rapidly and unpredictably to maintain a fixed exchange rate system.

## Flexible Exchange Rates During the 1970s and 1980s

The flexible exchange rate system in effect since 1973 has dealt well with changing economic conditions. Although exchange rates have fluctuated substantially—as short-term factors shift the demand and supply curves for foreign currency—the volume of international trade has grown substantially.

We should also not lose sight of the fact that many of the world's currencies are still on a fixed exchange rate system, pegged to a major currency such as the dollar, the French franc, or the German mark. Also a group of European countries operate the **European Monetary System (EMS)** with a chain of fixed exchange rates—called the "snake"—to encourage intra-European trade. This system obliges members to restrict fluctuations of their currencies against each other, but allows them to float against the dollar. In practice, the "snake" is confined to a "tunnel," which means that these currencies cannot fluctuate against each other by more than a small amount.

## Current Issues for the International Monetary System

The international monetary system now faces three main issues: the U.S. trade deficit, the international debt crisis, and a future return to fixed exchange rates, possibly even to the gold standard.

### The U.S. Trade Deficit

The U.S. trade deficit is a serious problem. During the 1980s, it reached about $150 billion annually, or 3% of the U.S. gross national product. As we saw earlier, one remedy is to depreciate the dollar, making it more profitable for U.S. firms to export goods, and more costly for U.S. consumers to buy imports.

Although the dollar did depreciate substantially in 1985 and 1986, the improvement in the trade deficit was slow to arrive, as shown in Figure 22.5. Most economists remained confident, though, that depreciation of the dollar eventually will erase the trade deficit. It is also helpful that U.S. firms are becoming more adept at exporting, and that Japan has been willing to restrict some of its exports—such as autos—to the United States.

FIGURE 22.5
**The Trade Deficit as a Percentage of GNP**

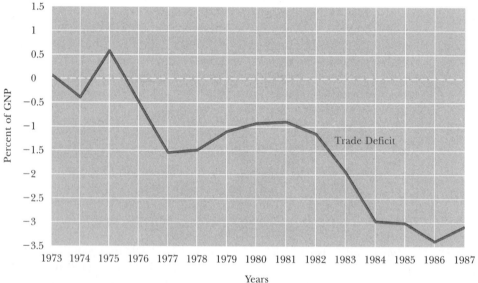

Although the dollar depreciated substantially between 1985 and 1987, the U.S. trade deficit has shown little improvement as a percentage of the gross national product. Nevertheless, most economists expect that, sooner or later, the depreciated value of the dollar will result in an improving trade picture.

### The International Debt Crisis

Foreign lending to developing countries illustrates how international finance can provide countries with the resources to solve some of their problems. The economic history of the United States is instructive. Until the second half of the nineteenth century, the United States was what would now be called a developing country. Part of the rapid growth of the U.S. economy was financed by European investment—in railroads, factories, plant and equipment, and bridges and tunnels.

In the 1970s, U.S. banks were the primary lenders to many developing countries. A developing country must generate a trade surplus to obtain the foreign currency to repay its loans. However, many developing countries are finding that hard to do, as we discussed in Chapter 21. The basic problem is that the world economy is growing relatively slowly, limiting the demand for the raw materials and commodities—oil, coffee, cocoa, tin, and lead—that the developing countries produce.

Many of the developing countries may have to default on their loans as a result. The lenders, of course, are not eager for this, and so they have "extended" the loans. The International Monetary Fund and the World Bank are also trying to help. Ultimately, however, the best hope is that a strong world economy will provide the developing countries with trade surpluses.

### A Return to Fixed Exchange Rates or the Gold Standard

Many firms, economists, and central banks look forward to the possibility that the international monetary system will return to fixed exchange rates. However, the Bretton Woods Agreement broke down in the early 1970s precisely because not all members were willing to meet the obligations of a fixed exchange rate system. A return to fixed rates would require countries to coordinate their monetary policies and to sacrifice their domestic policy goals. This seems unlikely to happen any time soon. Put another way, the conditions that would make exchange rates stable under a flexible rate system are basically the same conditions that would allow a return to fixed exchange rates.

A return to the gold standard is an even more extreme proposal. Proponents of this policy have at least two goals in mind. First, they want to return to fixed exchange rates. Second, they would like the money supply to be determined by the gold flows that occur as the result of a country's international payments position. Basically the money supply would grow less rapidly if it were determined by increases in the U.S. gold stock instead of discretionary Federal Reserve monetary policy. Moreover, if each country were subject to this "discipline," then inflation on a world-wide basis might be lower.

President Reagan appointed a commission to look into the gold standard matter in 1981. That commission confirmed the need for international cooperation in monetary policy, but did not recommend a return to the gold standard. Political factors also make it unlikely that the gold standard will soon be readopted: the major gold producers who would benefit from such a change are the Soviet Union and South Africa. More basically, the "rules" of the gold standard, which caused countries to leave it half a century ago, still work against it.

## Chapter Summary

1. Three exchange rate systems can be distinguished. Under *flexible exchange rates,* the market exchange rate reaches an equilibrium value where the demand for and the supply of foreign currency are equal. Under *fixed exchange rates* the central banks of each pair of countries peg the exchange rate between their currencies at a fixed value. Under a *managed float,* the exchange rate is usually flexible but central banks may intervene in the market from time to time to change the rate. Fixed exchange rates provide stability and encourage international trade. Flexible exchange rates provide more insulation for the domestic economy from foreign influences. Most major trading countries are now using managed floats.

2. Under a fixed exchange rate system, the central banks maintain the exchange rate at its fixed value, selling foreign currency reserves for domestic currency whenever an excess demand for foreign currency develops in the market. A fixed exchange rate system presents two potential problems: (1) As countries use their foreign currency reserves to support the fixed rate, their monetary base and money supply will fall, possibly an undesired result; (2) Sooner or later some countries will run out of foreign currency reserves. At this point, they have either to shift to a flexible exchange rate system or to devalue the currency.

3. Inflation, recession, and trade deficits are transmitted between countries by the international monetary system. Fixed exchange rate systems pass economic conditions directly from one country to another. Flexible exchange rates systems provide more insulation from international forces. A managed float provides countries with the possibility of managing their exchange rates for policy goals.

4. The borrowing of foreign funds is one of the most common and important uses of international finance. The United States used foreign borrowing to finance part of the federal government's deficits during the 1980s. Developing countries borrow to finance capital investment that aids their development. However, all such borrowing must eventually be repaid; this requires that countries generate a trade surplus to obtain foreign exchange.

## Key Terms

Bretton Woods Agreement

Equilibrium exchange rate

European Monetary System (EMS)

Exchange rate changes:

    Devaluation

    Revaluation

Exchange rate systems:

    Fixed

    Flexible

    Managed float

Fixed exchange rates:

    Overvalued

    Undervalued

General Agreement on Tariffs and Trade (GATT)

International gold standard

International Monetary Fund (IMF)

Managed floats:

    Crawling peg

    Dirty float

Reserve currency

Sterilized interventions

Trade deficit

World Bank

## Study Questions

1. Why would an increase in U.S. prices cause the dollar to depreciate under a flexible exchange rate system?

2. What would be the effects of an increase in U.S. prices under a fixed exchange rate system?

3. Why does a central bank sell foreign currency when it has an overvalued currency based on a fixed exchange rate system?

4. What is "dirty" about a dirty float?

5. When do speculative runs against a currency become a threat under a fixed exchange rate system?

6. What is the key advantage of a fixed exchange rate system? Of a flexible exchange rate system?

7. Why would a central bank use tight monetary policy to avert a devaluation under a fixed exchange rate system?

8. Why is a *sterilized* foreign currency purchase by the Federal Reserve the equivalent of the Fed buying foreign currency and paying for it with Treasury securities?

9. Under a managed float, why would an appreciation in the exchange rate reduce inflationary pressure in the country?

10. In what ways does the gold standard stand for more than just fixed exchange rates?

## Recommended Reading

*A number of official and Federal Reserve publications describe various aspects of the international monetary system:*

Anatol Balbach, "The Mechanics of Intervention in Foreign Exchange Markets," *Monthly Review*, Federal Reserve Bank of St. Louis, February 1978, pp. 2–7.

Board of Governors of the Federal Reserve System, *The Federal Reserve System: Purposes and Functions*, 7th edition, 1985.

Owen F. Humpage, "Exchange-Market Intervention: The Channels of Influence," *Economic Review*, Federal Reserve Bank of Cleveland, Quarter 3, 1986, pp. 2–13.

International Monetary Fund, *Annual Report*, Washington, D.C., 1987.

George A. Kahn, "Dollar Depreciation and Inflation," *Economic Review*, Federal Reserve Bank of Kansas City, November 1987, pp. 32–49.

Roger M. Kubarych, *Foreign Exchange Markets in the United States*, revised edition, Federal Reserve Bank of New York, 1983.

U.S. Government Printing Office, *Report to the Congress of the Commission on the Role of Gold in the Domestic and International Monetary Systems*, Washington, D.C., March 1982.

Warren E. Weber, "Do Sterilized Interventions Affect Exchange Rates," *Quarterly Review*, Federal Reserve Bank of Minneapolis, Summer 1986, pp. 14–23.

The World Bank, *World Development Report*, Oxford University Press, New York, 1986.

*Some texts on the structure and history of the international monetary system:*

Robert Solomon, *The International Monetary System: 1945–81*, Harper and Row, New York, 1982.

John Williamson, *The Open Economy and the World Economy*, Basic Books, New York, 1983.

# Monetary Theory

We will now consider how money affects such macroeconomic variables as the price level inflation rate, national income, aggregate output, and the unemployment rate. We have seen in Part V that these variables represent the main goals of monetary policy. So, although we will now study the *theory* of how money affects the economy, this is not merely a theoretical exercise. On the contrary, we will be looking at the primary channels through which real world monetary policy might influence the real world economy.

One measure of the importance of monetary theory is that it is the center of a major debate in economics. There are now four major approaches to monetary theory—Keynesian, monetarist, new classical, and nonclassical. These approaches disagree about such basic questions as whether monetary policy affects aggregate output. Nevertheless, they are in agreement on other issues.

Our discussion is organized around macroeconomic *models* of the economy—combinations of economic relationships that provide a distinctive set of conclusions. We will begin in Chapter 23 by developing the IS/LM model. Although this model presents the Keynesian framework for macroeconomics, you do not have to be a Keynesian to gain insights from it. In fact, various assumptions about the economy are readily incorporated into the IS/LM model, which is the reason we will study it first.

In Chapter 24, we will use the IS/LM model to study monetary policy and fiscal policy with regard to:

- The *effects* of the policies—the channels through which they operate and the sectors of the economy on which they have their largest effects.

- The *effectiveness* of the policies—how a specific change is likely to affect national income.

- The *interaction* of monetary policy and fiscal policy.

Many of the differences between Keynesians and monetarists are reflected in these results.

Since the IS/LM model assumes the price level is fixed at a constant value, it cannot deal directly with inflation. In Chapter 25, therefore, we will introduce the aggregate demand/aggregate supply model to study the sources of inflation. We will also use this model to evaluate the effects of monetary policy and fiscal policy on the price level and aggregate output.

A further limitation of both the IS/LM and aggregate supply/aggregate demand models is that people's expectations of economic variables are assumed to be fixed at constant values. In Chapter 26, therefore, we will study how people form expectations of economic variables. We will focus on the theory of *rational expectations*—the idea that people use all available and relevant information in forming their expectations. Based on rational expectations, we then use two macroeconomic models—the new classical model and the nonclassical model—to evaluate the effectiveness of monetary policy.

# The IS/LM Model

**23**

*"Annual income twenty pounds, annual expenditure nineteen nineteen six, result happiness. Annual income twenty pounds, annual expenditure twenty pounds ought and six, result misery."*

**Charles Dickens**

John Maynard Keynes was already a distinguished economist in 1936 when his macroeconomic theory of the economy was presented in his book *The General Theory of Employment, Interest, and Money*. Before writing this economic classic, Keynes was:

a Cambridge University professor,

a representative for England at the Versailles Peace Conference at the end of World War I,

a highly successful financial investor and speculator,

and a member of the Bloomsbury Group—a circle of well-known English writers and intellectuals.

His *General Theory*—as it is called for short—was written under the dismal economic conditions of the Great Depression, as depressing in England as they were in the United States. Consequently, the book analyzed how *pump priming*—increased government spending—might bring a depressed economy to life.

Keynes's classic stimulated the development of macroeconomic theories and models, which study how economic policy can affect real economic activity. Macroeconomic models are used to evaluate alternative economic policies, such as the effects of changing the money supply (monetary policy) or of changing government expenditures and taxes (fiscal policy). Macroeconomic models are also used to predict such variables as income, interest rates, consumption, and investment. We will examine a specific version of the Keynesian model—the IS/LM model, which was developed by John Hicks, another British economist.

In this chapter, we study the Keynesian macroeconomic theory of national income and interest rates and develop the IS/LM model. The

Keynesian model determines equilibrium values of income and the interest rate for a fixed price level; that is, it is assumed there is no inflation. Consequently, the nominal values of output, income, and expenditures used here can be interpreted as real values. We will study inflation in Chapter 25.

A key feature of the Keynesian approach is that it focuses on the equality between income and expenditures—which is why it is called the *income equals expenditures* approach. In fact, we will see that there are two relationships between income and expenditures. First, as a matter of accounting identities—how the terms are defined—*actual* expenditures equal income. Second, as an equilibrium condition for the economy—that people are satisfied with their expenditures relative to income—*desired* expenditures equal income. We will start with the accounting relationship.

## Aggregate Income, Expenditures, and Output

The Keynesian "income equals expenditures" approach is based on the relationships that exist in the economy between the aggregate concepts of output, income, and expenditures. To start, here are their definitions:

**Aggregate output** is the total value of goods *produced* in the economy. (Remember, when we say goods, we mean goods and services.)

**Aggregate income** is the total value of payments made to *factors of production*—wages to labor, interest to capital, rent to landowners—to produce the aggregate output.

**Aggregate expenditures** are the total value of goods *purchased*.

Income has to equal expenditures for the economy as a whole. Of course, some families may have positive saving—their income will exceed their expenditures—and others may have negative saving. But as we saw in Chapter 3, the net amount of saving is always equal to the amount of capital investment. For example, in an economy with positive net saving, income that is not allocated to consumption or government expenditures will be allocated to investment expenditures.

We can illustrate this accounting relationship between income and expenditures in two ways—as represented in the circular flow of income and expenditures, and as represented in the National Income Accounts.

### The Circular Flow of Income and Expenditures

The *circular flow* of income and expenditures is illustrated in Figure 23.1. *Income* represents payments made by business firms to the factors of production—mainly labor, capital, and land—to produce goods. Income is used by the factors of production to make *expenditures*—buying goods from the business sector. As a result of the circular flow, income and expenditures are equal in the aggregate.

Aggregate income (payments made by firms to factors of production) and aggregate expenditures (the value of goods purchased) are equal, and both are equal, as we will see, to aggregate output (the value of goods produced).

FIGURE 23.1
**The Circular Flow of Income and Expenditures**

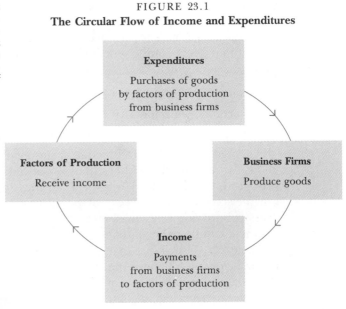

## The National Income Accounts

The **National Income Accounts,** which measure total output in terms of *gross national product* (GNP), illustrate more precisely that output, income, and expenditures are equal in the aggregate. Table 23.1 shows

| TABLE 23.1 |
| --- |
| Gross National Product as Expenditures and Income |

| Dollars in billions for 1987 | |
| --- | --- |
| Gross National Product, $Y$ | $4,486 |
| Expenditures | |
| Personal consumption expenditures, $C$ | 2,966 |
| Gross private domestic investment, $I$ | 716 |
| Government purchases of goods and services, $G$ | 924 |
| Net exports of goods and services, $X$ | − 120 |
| Total expenditures | $4,486 |
| Income | |
| Compensation of employees | 2,648 |
| Proprietor's income | 328 |
| Net interest | 337 |
| Rental income | 18 |
| Corporate profits[a] | 1,155 |
| Total income | $4,486 |

[a]Corporate profits are before capital depreciation and taxes paid, and include net losses of government enterprises.

**Source:** Federal Reserve *Bulletin*, Table 2.16, Board of Governors of the Federal Reserve System, 1988.

that aggregate output in the United States, measured by GNP, was $4,486 billion in 1987. It also shows the components and corresponding totals for aggregate expenditures and aggregate income.

The four main components of *aggregate expenditures* add up to GNP:

- Personal consumption expenditures, $C$;
- Gross private domestic investment, $I$;
- Government purchases of goods and services, $G$;
- Net exports of goods and services, $X$.

Aggregate output (GNP) equals aggregate expenditures because goods that are purchased have to be produced. Of course, goods can be produced, but not sold. However, even these goods are counted as aggregate expenditures as part of *inventory investment*—a component of gross private domestic investment $I$. In a moment, we will see that investment can be either intended or unintended.

Table 23.1 also shows that the sum of the components of aggregate income equals GNP, since the total value of production is accounted for by income payments to one or another of the factors of production. (We will refer to aggregate income from now on simply as *income* and denote it with the traditional symbol $Y$.) Since income and total expenditures are equal, income $Y$ equals the sum of the four components of expenditure:

$$Y = C + I + G + X.$$

## Equilibrium Between Income and Expenditures

The equality between income and expenditures discussed so far represents only an *accounting identity*. That is, if income exceeds expenditures, then firms will be accumulating undesired inventories of goods—unintended inventory investment. Or if expenditures exceed income, then firms will be unintentionally running down their inventories of goods. For an economy to be in *equilibrium,* firms have to be maintaining the desired level of inventories—there cannot be unintended inventory investment. For this to be the case, *desired expenditures have to equal income,* which is the *equilibrium condition* in the goods market of the Keynesian model. When this condition holds, changes in desired expenditures cause output and income to respond in the same direction. We will now look at how this works, starting with consumption demand—desired consumption expenditures.

## Consumption Demand and the Consumption Function

We looked at the *microeconomic* foundations of consumption demand when we developed the loanable funds theory of interest rates in Chapter 3. There we saw that consumption demand can depend on such variables as current and expected income, time preference (the tradeoff between current and future consumption), and interest rates. The Keynesian

**consumption function** represents a simplified *macroeconomic* theory of the desired amount of consumption $C^D$:

$$C^D = \overline{C} + c\,(Y - \overline{T}), \qquad (23.1a)$$

where $C^D$ = consumption demand (desired consumption expenditures),
$\quad\quad\; Y$ = income,
$\quad\quad\; \overline{T}$ = taxes,
$\quad\quad\; \overline{C}$ = the part of consumption determined by factors other than disposable income $(Y - T)$,
$\quad\quad\; c$ = marginal propensity to consume.

**Disposable income** $(Y - \overline{T})$ is the part of income $Y$ that people retain after paying their taxes $\overline{T}$. The *coefficient* $c$, the **marginal propensity to consume,** is the percentage of disposable income that is consumed (the other part is saved). The term $\overline{C}$ represents the part of consumption expenditures determined by factors other than disposable income; we will look at these factors shortly.

Equation (23.1a) is easily rearranged to separate consumption demand into two parts—autonomous expenditures and induced expenditures (these two categories of expenditures are described further in Box 23.1):

$$C^D = (\overline{C} - c\overline{T}) + (cY). \qquad (23.1b)$$

The term $(\overline{C} - c\overline{T})$ represents **autonomous expenditures**—the part of consumption demand determined by *factors other than current income Y.* Autonomous expenditures are determined by such factors as the desire for current consumption (time preference), expected future income (based on the degree of consumer optimism), and taxes. Variables that represent autonomous expenditures are identified by a bar above their symbol.

---

BOX 23.1 IN DEPTH

## Autonomous and Induced Expenditures

*Autonomous* literally means "functioning independently of other parts." In our usage, *autonomous expenditures* are expenditures that are *independent of current income.* For example, consumption expenditures for basic food and other necessities are independent of income—everyone must consume a minimum amount. Also, consumption expenditures that depend on the consumer's expectations regarding *future* income are autonomous expenditures.

*Induced* literally means "to bring about." In our usage, *induced expenditures* are expenditures that *depend on the level of current income.* For most people, induced consumption expenditures are a large part of their total consumption—income determines a large proportion of their consumption demand.

The term $(cY)$ in equation (23.1b) represents **induced expenditures**—the part of consumption demand determined by *current income Y*. The amount of induced consumption depends on the size of the marginal propensity to consume $c$, the percentage of current income that is consumed.

Figure 23.2 illustrates a specific consumption function, $C^D = 100 + 0.5\,Y$; in this case, autonomous expenditures are $100 billion and the marginal propensity to consume is 0.5. Moving along the consumption function, each $100 billion of incremental income $Y$ generates $50 billion of incremental consumption, since the marginal propensity to consume is 0.5. Box 23.2 discusses further the autonomous factors that may cause the consumption function to shift vertically.

FIGURE 23.2
**The Consumption Function**

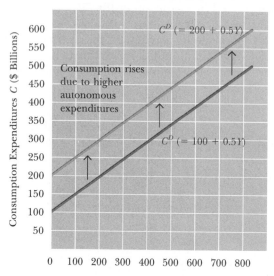

When the consumption function is $C^D = 100 + 0.5Y$, autonomous expenditures are 100 and induced expenditures are 0.5Y. This means that each additional $100 billion of income creates an additional $50 billion of consumption expenditures. When autonomous expenditures rise from $100 billion to $200 billion, the consumption function shifts upward by $100 billion at every level of income.

## Investment Demand

**Investment demand** represents desired expenditures for durable assets—that is, goods and materials that are not immediately consumed or used up in the course of production. There are three main categories of investment expenditures:

1. Manufacturing equipment.

2. Residential and nonresidential structures.

3. Inventories (goods produced for later sale).

As this list indicates, the term *investment* refers here specifically to *durable capital goods*, not to *financial investment*. In macroeconomics, "investment"

BOX 23.2 FINANCIAL NEWS

## Factors That Cause the Consumption Function To Shift

Economists keep close track of consumer spending trends because consumption represents the largest component of GNP. The following excerpts from a *Wall Street Journal* article (of March 7, 1988) by Pamela Sebastian discuss the wide range of variables that potentially can shift the consumption function.

Economists are carefully watching U.S. spenders to see whether they ante up to keep the economy in drive.

This week's report on overall February retail sales is expected to be lackluster, with many analysts expecting a gain of not much more than 0.5%—flat with or slightly better than January's 0.5% rise.

The estimates reflect the unexpectedly weak February sales reported last week by individual major retailers. Paine Webber's index of chain store sales for the month eked out a 0.5% gain from a year earlier, following a 3.7% jump the previous month.

Much of the thrust in the broad retail sector lately has come from auto sales. Late-February sales of North American-built cars jumped a surprising 24%, thanks partly to buyer incentive programs, according to figures out last week. That end-of-the-month spurt boosted total February sales to 889,301 cars—the highest total for any February since 1973.

Still, cars alone can't carry the economy.

"The major hole in consumer sales is in women's apparel," says David Hale, chief economist at Kemper Financial Services Inc., Chicago.

Mr. Hale and others say women don't seem to be responding to shorter skirts as retailers had hoped. "We need a hemline adjustment to the figures as well as a seasonal adjustment," he says.

Sluggish spending in the big retail sector is worrisome because it could cause stores to cut back on orders, forcing manufacturers to trim output and workers. Laid-off workers are hesitant to buy, so a downdraft in spending can feed on itself.

(Pamela Sebastian, "Economists Are Tracking Spending Trends," *Wall Street Journal*, 7 March, 1988.)

---

usually means only capital investment, and we will use the term in that sense in the rest of this book.

Recall from the microeconomic foundations studied in Chapter 3 that investment demand depends on the expected profitability of additional capital. The Keynesian theory of investment demand reflects two basic factors that affect expected profitability: (1) the value of the goods that can be produced with the new capital, and (2) the interest cost of financing the investment.

According to the Keynesian theory, high interest rates cause investment expenditures to fall, because the interest rate is the cost of financing. Even when the investment can be made without borrowed money, the interest rate represents the *opportunity cost*—the interest income forgone by making a capital investment instead of buying securities.

In addition to the interest rate, Keynes identified another determinant of autonomous investment, **animal spirits**—his colorful term for the willingness of entrepreneurs to take risks. According to Keynes, investment demand will be high when the animal spirits are high and vice versa. Since Keynes developed his theory during the Great Depression, he stressed that low animal spirits depress investment demand.

Investment demand $I^D$ can thus be expressed as a function of interest rates and other autonomous factors:

$$I^D = \bar{I} - br, \tag{23.2}$$

where $I^D$ = investment demand,

$\quad r$ = the interest rate,

$\quad b$ = the sensitivity of investment demand to the interest rate,

$\quad \bar{I}$ = the part of investment demand determined by other autonomous factors.

The coefficient $b$ measures how much investment demand responds to a change in interest rates: the larger the coefficient $b$, the more investment expenditures fall when interest rates rise. We will see later that monetary policy affects investment through this term. The term $\bar{I}$ ac-

---

BOX 23.3 IN DEPTH

## Factors That Cause the Investment Function To Shift

Economists keep close track of investment spending because it is a volatile component of GNP. Its volatility is due to the fact entrepreneurs determine their desired amount of investment spending on the basis of *expected* profits. This is why Keynes, who had a very practical feel for such matters, emphasized *animal spirits*—the extent to which entrepreneurs are optimistic or pessimistic regarding the economic outlook.

*Taxes* are another key factor that influences investment demand. Business managers are concerned with their *after-tax* profits, so lower tax rates encourage capital investment. In fact, as a way of raising the amount of investment in the United States, Congress has in the past provided special tax breaks—called *investment tax credits*—based on a company's investment spending.

To carry out its investment plans, a firm must, of course, have access to the required amount of funds. Thus investment spending generally falls when there is *credit rationing*—a reduction in the availability of credit from lenders (as we discussed in Chapter 12). By the same token, when firms are more *liquid*—they have accumulated more funds themselves—they are able to carry out more investment.

counts for other factors that determine autonomous investment—such as animal spirits and taxes that affect the expected profitability of capital investment. Keynes also believed that part of investment demand might be induced by current income—that is, higher current income might raise capital investment. Later, we will point out how we can also include this in our analysis.

An **investment demand function** based on equation (23.2) is illustrated in Figure 23.3. Investment demand is a negatively sloped function of the interest rate $r$, since investment falls when interest rates rise. Box 23.3 discusses some of the autonomous factors that may cause the investment demand function to shift horizontally.

FIGURE 23.3
**The Investment Demand Function**

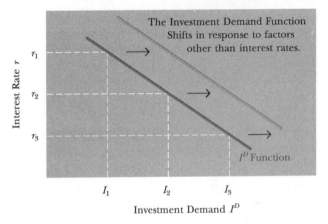

The Investment Demand Function
Shifts in response to factors
other than interest rates.

$I^D$ Function

Higher interest rates raise the financing cost or opportunity cost of investment, causing investment demand to fall. Changes in other autonomous factors cause the investment function to shift (see Box 23.3).

## Government Spending on Goods and Services

**Government spending** on goods and services includes such diverse expenditures as military spending, new government buildings, and the salaries of government employees. It covers all levels of government—federal, state, and local. Although government expenditures may vary depending on the state of the economy, they will be treated as autonomous spending, denoted as $\overline{G}$, because their amount is determined by government economic policy.

Figure 23.4 shows the pattern of federal government expenditures, tax receipts, and budget deficits from 1979 through 1987. After 1981 the budget deficit was large, approaching $200 billion in some years. Later, we will look at the impact of the government deficit on income.

FIGURE 23.4

**Federal Government Expenditures, Tax Receipts, and the Deficit**

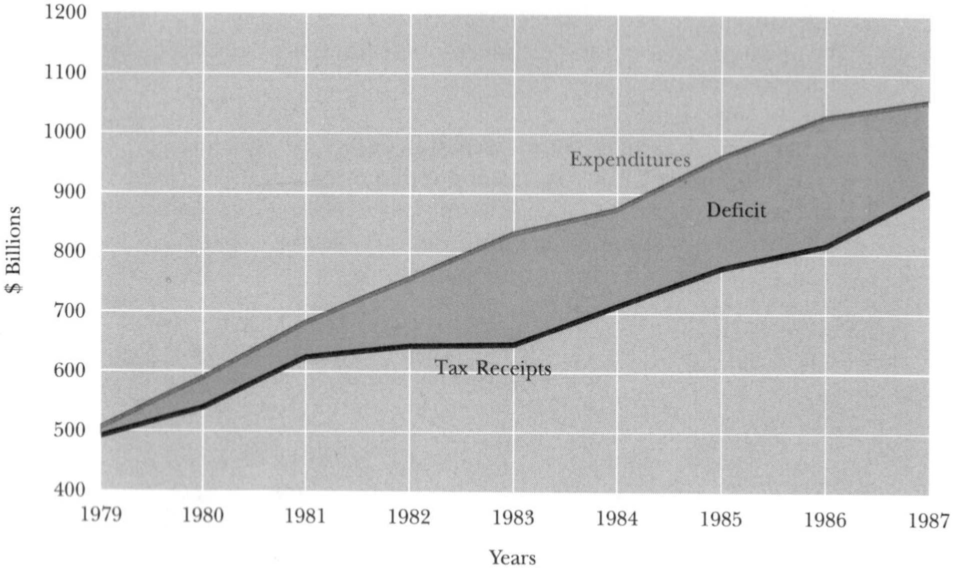

Government expenditures expanded more rapidly than tax receipts after 1979, leading to budget deficits that sometimes approached $200 billion. **Source:** Economic Report of the President, February 1988.

## Net Exports

Net exports—exports minus imports—represent the net amount of foreign expenditures made in the U.S. economy. The United States' *exports* are counted as a positive part of expenditures because the goods are produced by U.S. firms; in contrast, *imports* count as negative expenditures because they are not produced in the United States. (It might also be helpful to see this from another perspective. Imports are already counted as a positive component of GNP as part of total consumption. So they have to be subtracted as part of net exports in order not to be counted twice.)

As we noted when discussing international finance in Chapters 21 and 22, the United States generally had positive net exports until the early 1970s. But, as illustrated in Figure 23.5, net exports then became negative—imports exceeded exports. And after 1980, the trade deficit became very large, approaching $150 billion in some years.

We will assume that net exports are autonomous expenditures, denoted $\overline{X}$. The assumption is accurate regarding U.S. exports, since foreign demand for U.S. goods is mainly determined by foreign economic conditions. The assumption is less accurate regarding U.S. imports, since the demand for them may depend on the level of U.S. income. Shortly, we will see how an induced component of net exports can be included in our analysis.

FIGURE 23.5
**Net Exports**

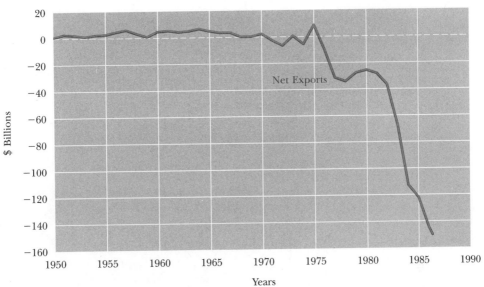

Years

U.S. net exports have been negative—imports exceeding exports—by as much as $150 billion during the 1980s, reflecting a trade deficit. **Source:** *Survey of* *Current Business*, U.S. Department on Commerce, June 1988.

## A Summary of Desired Aggregate Expenditures

We have now reviewed all of the components of desired expenditures—consumption, investment, government spending, and net exports. The sum of these desired expenditures is called *aggregate expenditures*, which we will denote $Y^E$. By combining consumption demand $C^D$ (equation [23.1]), investment demand $I^D$ (equation [23.2]), autonomous government spending $\overline{G}$, and autonomous net exports $\overline{X}$, we can express aggregate expenditures $Y^E$ in a summary equation:

$$Y^E = C^D + I^D + \overline{G} + \overline{X}$$
$$= (\overline{C} - c\overline{T} + cY) + (\overline{I} - br) + \overline{G} + \overline{X}.$$

It is also convenient to arrange the autonomous expenditures, including the interest rate variable $(-br)$, in a single term, $A_0$:

$$Y^E = A_0 + cY, \qquad (23.3)$$

where $A_0 = (\overline{C} - c\overline{T} + \overline{I} - br + \overline{G} + \overline{X})$.

Equation (23.3) thus represents aggregate expenditures as the sum of autonomous expenditures $(A_0)$ and consumption expenditures induced by income $(cY)$. We can also now see that income-induced expenditures for investment, government spending, or net exports can be incorporated into equation (23.3) by adding more terms of the same type as the induced consumption expenditures $(cY)$.

Figure 23.6 shows the *aggregate expenditure function,* a graph of equation (23.3). When income $Y$ is zero, aggregate expenditures just equal autonomous expenditures $A_0$. As income rises, the induced component of aggregate expenditures rises, increasing the total expenditures. If the amount of autonomous expenditures increases, then the aggregate expenditure function shifts upward by the same amount.

The aggregate expenditure function, $Y^E = A_0 + cY$, is a positively sloped function of income $Y$. It intersects the vertical axis (where income is zero) at $A_0$, the amount of autonomous expenditures. When the amount of autonomous expenditures increases from $A_0$ to $A_1$, the aggregate expenditure function shifts upward by the same amount.

FIGURE 23.6
**The Aggregate Expenditure Function**

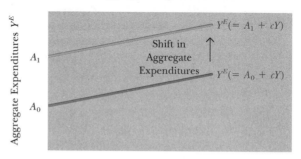

Income (Output) $Y$

## Equilibrium Income

The aggregate expenditure function indicates that higher income creates higher aggregate expenditures. However, not all combinations of income and aggregate expenditures represent *equilibrium.* In equilibrium, aggregate output, income, and expenditures must be equal. Otherwise, firms will tend either to accumulate undesired inventories, or to deplete their desired inventories, neither of which represents an equilibrium. The *equilibrium condition* is thus expressed:

$$Y = Y^E, \tag{23.4}$$

where $Y$ = aggregate output (or income),
$Y^E$ = aggregate expenditures.

When this condition holds, the market for goods is in equilibrium.

### The Keynesian Cross Diagram

The equilibrium condition is illustrated in Figure 23.7 by the Keynesian cross—a graphical method of determining equilibrium income. The aggregate expenditure function represents $Y^E$ as a function of income $Y$,

Equilibrium occurs at point $E_0$, where the aggregate expenditure function ($Y^E = A_0 + cY$) intersects the 45° line ($Y = Y^E$). In contrast, at point $F$ aggregate expenditures exceed production (and income), and at point $G$ aggregate expenditures are less than production, so neither of these two points represents an equilibrium.

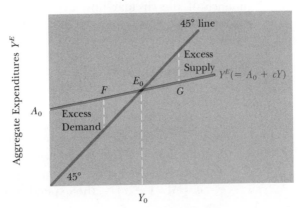

FIGURE 23.7
**The Keynesian Cross Equilibrium**

Income (Output) $Y$

as in Figure 23.6. The 45° line represents the equilibrium condition, $Y = Y^E$. That is, $Y$ and $Y^E$ are equal at each point on the line.

Equilibrium income $Y_0$ is determined at point $E_0$, where the aggregate expenditure function intersects the 45° line. At point $E_0$, $Y^E$ is determined by the aggregate expenditure function (equation [23.3]), and $Y^E$ equals $Y$ (the equilibrium condition). Since output equals income, point $E_0$ also determines equilibrium output.

The significance of point $E_0$ can be clarified by looking at other points on the aggregate expenditure function, such as point $F$ in Figure 23.7. Since point $F$ is above the 45° line, aggregate expenditures exceed current income (there is an excess demand for goods); hence point $F$ is not an equilibrium.

When firms face such an excess demand, they first sell off goods from their inventory. Then, as their inventories are depleted, they step up production. Since aggregate expenditures rise as income payments to the factors of production rise, this results in a movement along the aggregate expenditure function from point $F$ toward the equilibrium point $E_0$. (Firms may also raise prices when there is excess demand. However, the basic Keynesian model focuses on output changes by assuming that prices are constant.)

The process also works in reverse for points such as $G$ in Figure 23.7, where aggregate expenditures are less than production. As firms accumulate unintended inventories, they reduce production, which decreases income, until equilibrium is restored at point $E_0$.

## The Keynesian Expenditure Multiplier

By substituting aggregate expenditures from equation (23.3), $Y^E = A_0 + cY$, into the equilibrium condition (23.4), $Y = Y^E$, the equilibrium condition can also be expressed as:

$$Y = A_0 + cY. \qquad (23.5)$$

This means that income $Y$ on the right side of this equation determines income $Y$ on the left side of the equation. This is an important consequence of the circular flow of income: income determines aggregate expenditures, which in turn determine income. This relationship is the basis of the Keynesian expenditure multiplier, to which we now turn.

By solving equation (23.5) for income $Y$, we can derive a formula for the equilibrium value of income, $Y_0$:

$$Y_0 = \frac{1}{1 - c} A_0 = \mu A_0, \tag{23.6}$$

where $Y_0$ = equilibrium income (and output),

$A_0$ = autonomous expenditures,

$c$ = marginal propensity to consume,

$\mu = 1/(1 - c)$ = the expenditure multiplier.

Equation (23.6) demonstrates that equilibrium income $Y_0$ is a precise *multiple* of autonomous expenditures. The term $\mu$ $(= 1/[1 - c])$ is the Keynesian **expenditure multiplier.** For example, if the marginal propensity to consume $c$ is 0.5 (that is, $1/2$), then the multiplier $\mu$ is 2, (that is, $1/[1 - c] = 1/0.5 = 2$). Equilibrium income $Y_0$ is then 2 times autonomous expenditures $A_0$.

Equation (23.6) can also be stated in a form where a *change* in autonomous expenditures, $\Delta A$, results in a multiplier *change* in equilibrium income, $\Delta Y$:

$$\Delta Y = \mu \Delta A. \tag{23.7}$$

If the multiplier $\mu$ is 2, and autonomous expenditures rise by \$10 billion, then equilibrium income will rise by \$20 billion. It may be obvious that equilibrium income will rise when autonomous expenditures rise, but it is not so obvious that equilibrium income will rise by a *multiple* of the increase in autonomous expenditures—this is the significance of the expenditure multiplier.

The expenditure multiplier is illustrated in Figure 23.8 by combining the Keynesian cross diagram of Figure 23.7 with an increase in autonomous expenditures $\Delta A$. When autonomous expenditures rise by $\Delta A$, the aggregate expenditure function shifts upward by this amount and the equilibrium value of income rises by $\Delta Y$ $(= \mu A)$.

Figure 23.9 provides a magnified version of Figure 23.8, which illustrates the steps of the expenditure multiplier:

1. The aggregate expenditure function shifts up by $\Delta A$ when autonomous expenditures rise by this amount.

2. Income rises by $\Delta A$ as new production occurs to satisfy the increase in aggregate expenditures.

3. Aggregate expenditures rise further on the basis of the increase in income from step 2, representing expenditures induced by the higher income.

4. A cumulative process ensues, with higher expenditures raising income, and higher income inducing more expenditures.

The initial equilibrium based on autonomous expenditures $A_0$ occurs at point $E_0$, with total expenditures equal to equilibrium income $Y_0$. When autonomous expenditures rise by $\Delta A$, from $A_0$ to $A_1$, the equilibrium shifts to point $E_1$. Equilibrium income thus rises by $\Delta Y$, from $Y_0$ to $Y_1$. This reflects the Keynesian expenditure multiplier: $\Delta Y = \mu\Delta A$.

FIGURE 23.8

**The Keynesian Expenditure Multiplier**

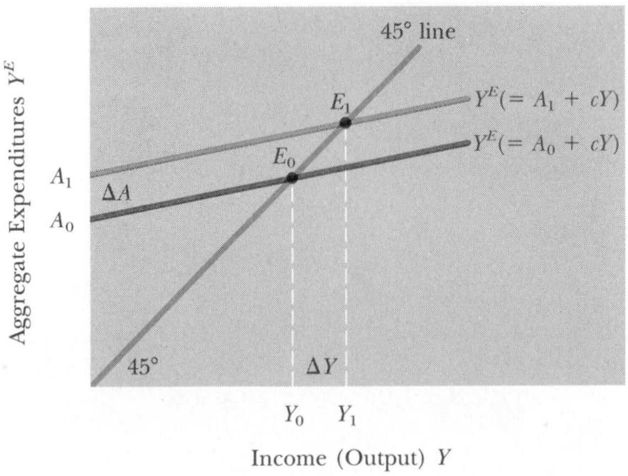

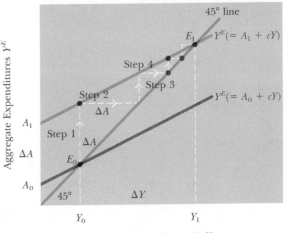

Income (Output) $Y$

The initial equilibrium is at point $E_0$. If autonomous expenditures rise by $\Delta A$, the following steps occur as part of the Keynesian multiplier:

1. Aggregate expenditures rise by $\Delta A$.

2. Income rises by $\Delta A$.

3. Higher income induces additional expenditures.

4. Income and aggregate expenditures continue to rise.

5. A new equilibrium is reached at point $E_1$.

FIGURE 23.9

**Steps in the Keynesian Expenditure Multiplier**

Income (Output) $Y$

5. A new equilibrium is reached because only $c$ percent (the marginal propensity to consume) of each round of new income is reflected in higher aggregate expenditures.

## Fiscal Policy, Monetary Policy, and the Expenditure Multiplier

The expenditure multiplier applies to any change in autonomous expenditures, including fiscal policy or monetary policy.

With *fiscal policy*, the expenditure multiplier is applied to a change in *government spending* or to a change in consumption created by a change in *taxes*. Box 23.4 discusses how U.S. fiscal policy during the early 1980s affected income.

BOX 23.4 MONEY MATTERS

## Fiscal Policy During the 1980s

The federal government in the United States has not been able to balance its budget during the 1980s. Indeed, as we saw in Figure 23.4, the government's annual budget deficit has sometimes approached $200 billion. The deficits started to escalate after 1981 when Congress, in support of President Reagan's policies, cut taxes by about $40 billion annually, but did not cut government spending by a comparable amount.

A tax cut of $40 billion represents expansionary fiscal policy—income will rise on this account. Specifically, if we assume the marginal propensity to consume $c$ is 0.6, then the multiplier $\mu$ is 2.5 (that is,

$1/[1 - c] = 2.5$). The tax cut then raises income by the multiplier times the increase in autonomous consumption created by the tax cut:

1. Recall from equation (23.1b) that taxes affect consumption demand by $(-c\overline{T})$. So, if the marginal propensity to consume $c$ is 0.6, and taxes fall by $40 billion, then autonomous consumption expenditures will rise by $24 billion (0.6 × $40 billion).

2. Given that the multiplier $\mu$ is 2.5 and autonomous expenditures rise by $24 billion, equilibrium income will rise by $60 billion (2.5 × $24 billion).

BOX 23.5 MONEY MATTERS

## Monetary Policy During the 1980s

We discussed in Chapter 20 how the Federal Reserve used tight monetary policy between 1979 and 1982 to reduce the inflation rate in the United States. The changes during this period for real investment expenditures and real GNP were:

### Change in Billions of 1982 Dollars

|                          | 1979 | 1980 | 1981 | 1982 |
|--------------------------|------|------|------|------|
| Investment expenditures  | -2   | -66  | +37  | -99  |
| Gross national product   | +77  | -5   | +62  | -83  |

Investment spending thus fell in three of the four years, for a total net decline

of $130 billion over the period. If this total decline is attributed to the tight monetary policy, and if the expenditure multiplier is 2.5, then the decline in GNP would be $325 billion (2.5 × $130 billion).

However, real GNP fell in only two of the four years, and it actually rose by the net amount of $51 billion over the four-year period. This is because other factors had a positive impact on GNP during this period, such as the expansionary fiscal policy discussed in Box 23.4. The overall change in GNP represents the sum of the multiplier effects of each of the changes in autonomous expenditures.

With *monetary policy,* the expenditure multiplier applies to the change in investment spending that is created by the policy. The steps in the process for the case of easy monetary policy are:

1. Easy monetary policy causes interest rates to fall, the result, for example, of open market purchases of Treasury bills by the Federal Reserve.

2. Lower interest rates cause investment spending to rise (equation [23.2] and Figure 23.3).

3. Higher investment spending has a multiplier effect on income. For example, if the multiplier is 2, and investment spending rises by $10 billion, then income will rise by $20 billion.

Box 23.5 discusses how Federal Reserve monetary policy during the early 1980s affected income.

## A Summary of the Factors Determining Equilibrium Income

When any category of autonomous expenditures increases, income rises by a multiple of that amount. Higher autonomous expenditures may arise from a variety of sources, including:

- *Consumption expenditures* may rise because people become more optimistic about the economic outlook.

- *Net exports* may rise due to improving economic conditions abroad.

- *Government spending* may rise as the result of expansionary fiscal policy.

- *Capital investment* may rise as the result of lower interest rates created by easy monetary policy.

# The IS/LM Model

The Keynesian "income equals expenditures" approach focuses on the equilibrium condition in the market for goods—aggregate expenditures equal aggregate output (or income). However, we know from our discussion in Chapter 16 that there is also an equilibrium condition in the market for money—money demand equals money supply. The two equilibrium conditions are treated together in a special version of the Keynesian model—the **IS/LM model.**

The IS/LM model handles the two equilibrium conditions in an explicit and symmetric fashion, basing the IS curve on the equilibrium condition in the market for goods and the LM curve on the equilibrium condition in the market for money. We will now analyze how the IS/LM model works, first developing the IS curve, then the LM curve, and finally the complete model.

## The IS Curve: Equilibrium in the Market for Goods

The **IS curve,** which represents equilibrium in the market for goods, is based on the same factors that we just discussed with regard to the Keynesian "income equals expenditure" approach and the expenditure multiplier. However, the IS curve also integrates the effect of interest rates on investment demand. In brief, as shown in panel C of Figure 23.10, the IS curve represents all combinations of income $Y$ and interest rates $r$ that are consistent with equilibrium in the market for goods. (Box 23.6 discusses the origins of the name *IS curve*.)

The IS curve in Figure 23.10 is derived by combining the investment demand function (in panel A) and the Keynesian cross diagram (in panel B). In panel A, each level of the interest rate ($r_0$, $r_1$, or $r_2$) determines an amount of investment demand ($I_0$, $I_1$, or $I_2$). In panel B, each amount of investment demand fixes the location of the aggregate expenditure function, which in turn determines the amount of equilibrium income ($Y_0$, $Y_1$, or $Y_2$). This information is combined in panel C, where the points $\{r_0, Y_0\}$, $\{r_1, Y_1\}$, and $\{r_2, Y_2\}$ represent the IS curve.

---

BOX 23.6 IN DEPTH

## The IS Curve in Terms of Investment and Saving

Since the IS curve represents equilibrium between income $Y$ and aggregate expenditures $Y^E$, it could be called the $Y/Y^E$ curve. Why is it called the "IS" curve?

The name "IS" stands for "investment equals saving," meaning that the curve can be derived from a relationship between desired investment and desired saving. Recall from the derivation of equation (23.3) that:

$$Y = C^D + I^D + \overline{G} + \overline{X}.$$

Now move the terms for consumption demand $C^D$ and government spending $\overline{G}$ to the left, and add and subtract taxes $\overline{T}$:

$$\underset{\substack{\text{Personal}\\\text{Saving}}}{(Y - C^D - \overline{T})} + \underset{\substack{\text{Government}\\\text{Saving}}}{(\overline{T} - \overline{G})} = \underset{\substack{\text{Domestic}\\\text{Investment}}}{I^D} + \underset{\substack{\text{Net Foreign}\\\text{Investment}[1]}}{\overline{X}}.$$

The left side of this equation represents *total saving,* and the right side represents *total investment.* This condition—total saving equals total investment—is the basis of the name "IS" curve.

[1] Based on the balance of payments discussion in Chapter 21, recall that net exports equal net capital inflows into the United States—net foreign investment.

## FIGURE 23.10
### Deriving the IS Curve
### A. The Investment Demand Function

Panel A shows how interest rates determine investment demand, as in Figure 23.3.

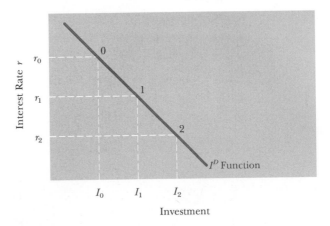

### B. The Keynesian Cross Diagram

Panel B shows that higher investment shifts the aggregate expenditure function upward, leading to higher equilibrium income, based on the Keynesian cross concept.

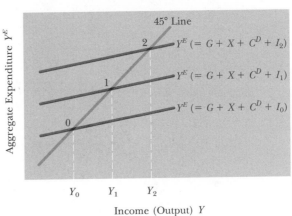

### C. The IS Curve

Panel C shows how the IS curve is derived by combining each interest rate $r$ in panel A with the corresponding equilibrium income $Y$ in panel B. The IS curve is thus a graph of the combinations $\{r_0, Y_0\}$, $\{r_1, Y_1\}$, and $\{r_2, Y_2\}$.

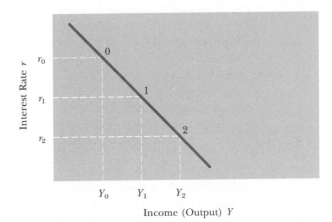

## Using the IS Curve

To make use of the IS curve, we have to understand several of its features:

- How the economy moves along the IS curve.
- What it means if the economy is off the IS curve.
- What factors cause the IS curve to shift.

We will now look at each of these features, using the IS curve illustrated in Figure 23.11.

At point $Q_1$, the interest rate is lower than at point 0, so investment demand and aggregate expenditures are higher than at point 0. This is why there is an excess demand for goods to the left of (or below) the IS curve. The opposite condition holds at points to the right (or above) the IS curve, such as $Q_2$.

A rightward shift in the IS curve occurs when one of the components of autonomous expenditures rises. Each point on the initial IS curve (such as 0, 1, or 2) then shifts to the right (to 0', 1', or 2').

FIGURE 23.11
**Using the IS Curve**

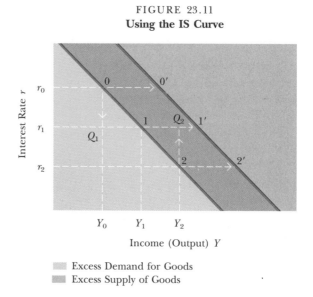

Excess Demand for Goods
Excess Supply of Goods

### Moving Along the IS Curve

Suppose the economy is initially at point 0 on the IS curve with the interest rate $r_0$ and income $Y_0$. Now suppose there is a change in the economy—such as easier monetary policy—that causes the interest rate to fall to $r_1$. If output is temporarily unchanged at $Y_0$, then the economy will move initially to point $Q_1$ in Figure 23.11. However, the lower interest rate $r_1$ stimulates investment demand, so income will rise until it reaches the equilibrium level $Y_1$ at point 1. This is why the IS curve represents *equilibrium in the market for goods:* each point on the IS curve represents an interest rate $r$ and income $Y$ combination for which aggregate expenditures and aggregate output (or income) are equal.

### When the Economy Is Off the IS Curve

In moving along the IS curve from point 0 to point 1, we saw that the economy might pause at point $Q_1$, a point off the IS curve. At $Q_1$, aggregate output equals $Y_0$ (the amount associated with point 0), but aggregate expenditures are higher than $Y_0$ (because investment demand rises as the interest rate falls). This illustrates that *there is an excess demand for goods to the left of (or below) the IS curve.* The excess demand causes income to rise and the economy to return to the IS curve.

The opposite occurs if the economy starts at point 2 on the IS curve, and then a change in the economy—such as tight monetary policy—causes the interest rate to rise from $r_2$ to $r_1$. If output is initially unchanged at $Y_2$, then the economy will pause at the point $Q_2$ above (or to the right of) the IS curve. Investment demand will be lower at this point because the interest rate is higher. Thus, *there is an excess supply of goods above (or to the right of) the IS curve.*

### Factors That Shift the IS Curve

Many applications of the IS/LM model also involve shifts in the IS curve. For a given interest rate, the IS curve will shift rightward as the amount of autonomous expenditures rises. That is, larger autonomous expenditures raise aggregate expenditures, which raise equilibrium income through the expenditure multiplier, causing the IS curve to shift rightward. A rightward shift in the IS curve in Figure 23.11 can result from any of the following changes:

*Autonomous Consumption*
Higher consumption demand based on such factors as consumer optimism.

*Autonomous Investment*
Higher investment demand based on such factors as entrepreneurial animal spirts.

*Autonomous Net Exports*
Higher net exports—an increase in exports or a decrease in imports.

*Expansionary Fiscal Policy*
Either higher government spending or higher consumption spending based on lower taxes.

## The LM Curve: Equilibrium in the Market for Money

The **LM curve** represents the equilibrium condition that money demand equals money supply. Its name is based on L for liquidity preference—Keynes' term for money demand—and M for the money supply. The LM curve works together with the IS curve to determine equilibrium values for income and the interest rate. The derivation of the LM curve is based on the money demand and money supply model developed in Chapter 16, which we will now briefly review.

We noted in Chapter 16 that *money demand* $M^d$ depends positively on income $Y$ and negatively on the interest rate $r$. Money demand rises when income rises because people need more money to carry out their larger consumption expenditures. Money demand falls when interest rates rise because people shift some of their money to investment securities.

The money demand curves in panel A of Figure 23.12 illustrate these relationships. The negative effect of interest rates on money demand is represented by the negative slope of each money demand curve. The positive effect of income on money demand is indicated by the location of the money demand curves: higher income shifts the money demand curves rightward (or upward).

In panel A, the negative relationship between money demand and the interest rate is shown by the negative slope of each money demand curve. The positive relationship between money demand and income is shown by the series of money demand curves, with higher income shifting the curve rightward (or upward). Equilibrium occurs in the market for money when money demand $M^d$ is equal to the money supply $\overline{M}$.

FIGURE 23.12
**Deriving the LM Curve**

A. The Demand for Money

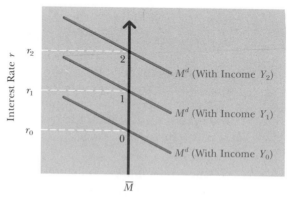

Money Demand $M^d$ and Supply $M^s$

Panel B shows the interest rate and income combinations—such as $\{r_0, Y_0\}$, $\{r_1, Y_1\}$, and $\{r_2, Y_2\}$—for which money demand and money supply are equal. These combinations represent the LM curve.

B. The LM Curve

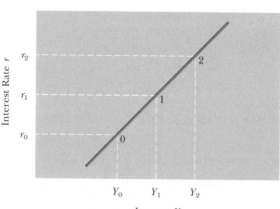

Income $Y$

We also saw in Chapter 16 that the *money supply* $M^s$ can be represented as the amount, $\overline{M}$, that the Federal Reserve desires. This will be the case as long as the Fed carries out defensive open market operations to keep the money supply fixed at $\overline{M}$. The money supply is thus illustrated in panel A as the vertical line at $\overline{M}$.

The *equilibrium condition* in the market for money is that money demand $M^d$ should equal the money supply $\overline{M}$. The equilibrium points in panel A (numbered 0, 1, and 2), represent the intersection of the vertical money supply line with a money demand curve, the position of each money demand curve being determined by the amount of income ($Y_0$, $Y_1$, or $Y_2$).

The LM curve is derived in panel B of Figure 23.12 by graphing the equilibrium combinations of the interest rate and income in panel A. That is, the LM curve in panel B consists of the combinations $\{r_0, Y_0\}$, $\{r_1, Y_1\}$, and $\{r_2, Y_2\}$.

## Using the LM Curve

To make use of the LM curve, we have to understand the same effects we studied for the IS curve: how the economy moves along the LM curve; what it means if the economy is off the LM curve; and what factors cause the LM curve to shift.

### Moving Along the LM Curve

Suppose the economy is initially in equilibrium at point 0 on the LM curve in Figure 23.13, with the interest rate $r_0$ and income $Y_0$. Now, suppose that an autonomous increase in expenditures, such as higher government spending, raises income to the level $Y_1$. If the interest rate were temporarily unchanged at $r_0$, then the economy will move initially to point $Q_1$. However, the higher income of $Y_1$ raises the money demand, so the interest rate will rise until it reaches the equilibrium level $r_1$. The new equilibrium is then illustrated on the LM curve at point 1, with the interest rate $r_1$ and income $Y_1$. This is why the LM curve represents *equilibrium in the market for money*—each point on the LM curve represents an interest rate $r$ and income $Y$ combination for which money demand and money supply are equal.

At point $Q_1$, income is higher than at point 0, so the demand for money is higher than at point 0. This is why there is an excess demand for money to the right of (or below) the LM curve. The opposite condition holds at points to the left of (or above) the LM curve, such as $Q_2$.

A rightward shift in the LM curve occurs when the money supply rises. Each point on the initial LM curve (such as 0, 1, and 2) then shifts to the right (to 0′, 1′, and 2′).

FIGURE 23.13
**Using the LM Curve**

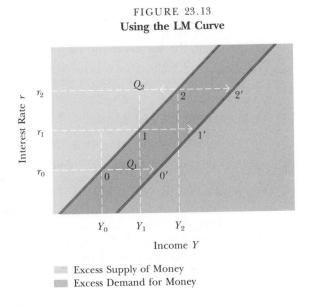

Income $Y$

░░ Excess Supply of Money
▓▓ Excess Demand for Money

### When the Economy Is Off the LM Curve

In moving along the LM curve from point 0 to point 1, we saw that the economy might pause at point $Q_1$, a point off the LM curve. At point $Q_1$, the money supply is unchanged, but higher income raises the demand for money. This illustrates that there is an *excess demand for money at points to the right of (or below) the LM curve*. As a result, the interest rate will rise, restoring the balance between money demand and money supply, and the economy will move to a point on the LM curve.

The opposite occurs if the economy starts at point 2 on the LM curve, but a change such as lower government spending causes income to fall. The economy might then pause at a point such as $Q_2$. Here, the lower income will reduce the demand for money, so *there will be an excess supply of money to the left of (or above) the LM curve*.

### Factors That Shift the LM Curve

In using the IS/LM model, we will be shifting the LM curve as well as the IS curve. We will now look at how changes in the money demand curve $M^d$ and in the amount of the money supply $\overline{M}$ cause the LM curve to shift.

If we are initially in equilibrium with money demand equal to money supply, an *increase in the money supply* will create a temporary excess supply of money at the initial interest rate and income. To reestablish equilibrium in the market for money, the demand for money must rise. A rightward (or downward) shift in the LM curve, as shown in Figure 23.13, reflects that either higher income or a lower interest rate will raise money demand in order to restore equilibrium after the money supply rises.

Alternatively, let us assume the economy is initially in equilibrium, but now suppose that *money demand decreases*, reflecting a change in a factor other than interest rates or income—for example, that increased use of credit cards reduces the demand for money. A decrease in money demand, like an increase in money supply, creates a temporary excess supply of money. Money demand must therefore rise to restore equilibrium in the market for money. Figure 23.13 again shows that a rightward (or downward) shift reflects that either higher income or a lower interest rate will raise money demand in order to restore equilibrium.

## Using the IS/LM Model

It is easy to combine the IS and LM curves to form the *IS/LM model*. With two equilibrium relationships (the IS curve and the LM curve), we can determine equilibrium values for income $Y$ and the interest rate $r$ simultaneously. This is the main point of the IS/LM model.

Figure 23.14 illustrates the IS/LM model. The equilibrium point is $E_0$ where the IS and LM curves intersect. Corresponding to point $E_0$, equilibrium income is $Y_0$ and the equilibrium interest rate is $r_0$. Now consider what happens if the economy moves temporarily away from point $E_0$. Points $a$, $b$, $c$, and $d$ in Figure 23.14 represent some possibilities

Equilibrium for the IS/LM model occurs at point $E_0$, where the IS and LM curves intersect. At any other points, such as $a$, $b$, $c$ and $d$, forces are created to push the economy back toward $E_0$.

FIGURE 23.14

**The IS/LM Model**

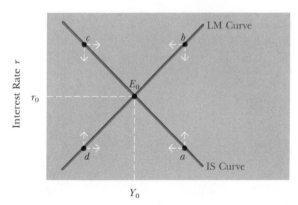

where the economy is on either the IS curve or the LM curve, but not on both at the same time. At each of these points, pressure is created to return the economy to the equilibrium point $E_0$.

For example, at point $a$, which is on the IS curve, but to the right of (or below) the LM curve, actual income is greater than equilibrium income $Y_0$, so actual money demand—which depends positively on income—is greater than equilibrium money demand. Thus to restore equilibrium, either income must fall or interest rates must rise, to reduce the demand for money. These changes direct the economy back toward equilibrium. Similar considerations apply at points $b$, $c$, and $d$. In each case, the interest rate and income will change to direct the economy back toward equilibrium at point $E_0$.

This completes our development of the IS/LM model. In Chapter 24, we will use the model to analyze monetary and fiscal policy.

## Chapter Summary

1. The determination of equilibrium income involves three related aggregate concepts: output, income, and expenditures. Aggregate output represents the production of goods in the economy. Aggregate income represents the payments made to *factors of production* to produce the output. Aggregate expenditures represent the *purchases* of goods by factors of production.

2. There are four components of aggregate expenditures: consumption, investment, government spending, and net exports.

Each of these has an autonomous component, representing expenditures that are determined without reference to income. Consumption expenditures also have an induced component that depends on income, as determined by the marginal propensity to consume. Investment demand has the special feature that it depends on interest rates and on what Keynes identified as entrepreneurial "animal spirits."

3. There are two macroeconomic equilibrium conditions, one for the aggregate market

for goods, the other for the market for money. The equilibrium condition for the market for goods is that aggregate expenditures—the sum of all desired expenditures—should equal income. This is represented by the IS curve. The equilibrium condition for the market for money is that money demand should equal money supply. This is represented by the LM curve. The IS/LM model combines the IS and LM curves. Equilibrium in the IS/LM model occurs where the IS curve intersects the LM curve, thus determining equilibrium values for the interest rate and income.

## Key Terms

Aggregate:
   Expenditures
   Income
   Output
Aggregate Expenditures:
   Consumption
   Investment
   Government
   Net exports
Animal spirits
Disposable income

Expenditure multiplier
Expenditures:
   Autonomous
   Induced
Functions:
   Consumption
   Investment
Marginal propensity to consume
The IS/LM model:
   The IS curve
   The LM curve

## Study Questions

1. Referring to Table 23.1, why does the sum of all expenditures equal the gross national product (GNP)? Why does the sum of all types of income equal GNP?

2. Suppose that the consumption function, relating consumption expenditures $C$ to income $Y$ (both in billions of dollars), were $C = 50 + 0.5Y$. What is the amount of *autonomous* consumption expenditures? If income were $800 billion, what is the amount of *induced* consumption expenditures? What is the total amount of consumption expenditures?

3. Referring to Question 2, if income were $900 billion, what would be the amount of total consumption expenditures?

When income rises from $800 billion to $900 billion, how does the change in consumption expenditures reflect the marginal propensity to consume?

4. Why does investment fall when interest rates rise?

5. Suppose that investment demand, government spending, and net exports each equal $100 billion (and taxes are $0). Based on the consumption function given in Question 2, what is the equilibrium condition determining equilibrium income? What is the equilibrium value of income?

6. Briefly explain why each of the following raises aggregate expenditures:

    *a.* Autonomous consumption expenditures rise.

    *b.* The interest rate falls.

    *c.* Government spending rises.

    *d.* Government taxes fall.

7. If the multiplier is 3, and government spending rises by $20 billion, how much will aggregate income rise? How much will aggregate output rise?

8. What are the steps through which easy monetary policy results in a multiplier increase in equilibrium income?

9. The IS curve has the feature that the aggregate expenditures for goods equal aggregate income (and output). What is the relationship between aggregate expenditures and income for a point to the *left* of the IS curve? What change in income is then needed to restore equilibrium in the market for goods?

10. The LM curve has the feature that money demand and money supply are equal. What is the relationship between money demand and money supply for a point to the *right* of the LM curve? What change in the interest rate is then needed to restore equilibrium in the market for money?

## Recommended Reading

*The classic that is the basis of Keynesian economics:*

John Maynard Keynes, *The General Theory of Employment, Interest, and Money,* Harcourt, Brace, New York, 1936.

*The paper that developed the IS / LM version of the Keynesian model:*

John R. Hicks, "Mr. Keynes and the 'Classics': A Suggested Reinterpretation," *Econometrica,* April 1937, pp. 147–159.

*The following are four standard macroeconomic textbooks or readings that discuss Keynesian macroeconomics and the IS / LM model:*

Ben Bernanke, *Readings and Cases in Macroeconomics,* McGraw-Hill, New York, 1987.

Stanley Fischer and Rudiger Dornbusch, *Macroeconomics,* 4th edition, McGraw-Hill, New York, 1987.

Robert J. Gordon, *Macroeconomics,* 4th edition, Little, Brown, Boston, 1988.

Robert E. Hall and John B. Taylor, *Macroeconomics,* 2nd edition, Norton, New York, 1988.

# 24

# Monetary Policy and Fiscal Policy Based on the IS/LM Model

*"A national debt, if it is not excessive, will be to us a national blessing."*

*Alexander Hamilton*

Macroeconomic policy in the United States is based on two main instruments—monetary policy and fiscal policy. Monetary policy reflects the control of the money supply by the Federal Reserve, while fiscal policy reflects the control of government spending and taxes by Congress and the administration. Both expansionary monetary policy (increasing the money supply) and expansionary fiscal policy (increasing government spending or cutting taxes) can raise the level of income.

When monetary and fiscal policy are used together, they must be coordinated. Otherwise, they can create undesired results: if both instruments are set in an expansionary mode, they might provide the economy with too much stimulus; or, if they are set in opposite directions, their effects on the economy might cancel each other out.

Coordinated use of monetary and fiscal policies can achieve macroeconomic goals beyond changing the level of income. For example, expansionary monetary policy tends to *lower* interest rates, which generally stimulates investment demand—a key reason that expansionary monetary policy raises income. In contrast, expansionary fiscal policy tends to *raise* interest rates, because it works without an increase in the money supply. Expansionary fiscal policy raises income through higher government spending or higher consumption spending (based on lower taxes), not through higher investment demand. As we will see in this chapter, policymakers can use coordinated monetary and fiscal policies to try to affect the mix of output—the allocation of total output among consumption, investment, government spending, and net exports.

In this chapter, we will study monetary policy and fiscal policy, based on the IS/LM model developed in Chapter 23. Specifically, we will study how the two policies affect the level and mix of output. The discussion continues to assume that the price level is fixed. The effects of monetary and fiscal policy on inflation will be examined in Chapter 25.

## The Slopes of the IS and LM Curves

The IS/LM model is particularly useful for evaluating monetary policy and fiscal policy because the model separates them—associating monetary policy with shifts in the LM curve, and fiscal policy with shifts in the IS curve.

Moreover, the effectiveness of the two policies—how much a given dose of policy affects income—is determined by the interest elasticities of money demand and investment demand, as reflected in the slopes of the IS and the LM curves. So, before we evaluate monetary policy and fiscal policy, it is helpful first to examine how the interest elasticities are reflected in the slopes of the curves. Box 24.1 reviews the definitions of the interest elasticities. (The slope of the IS curve is also affected by the size of the expenditure multiplier. However, in this chapter, we will assume that the size of the multiplier is fixed, so it will not be a factor when we compare the slopes of IS curves.)

---

BOX 24.1 IN DEPTH

### Interest Rate Elasticities

The following are the definitions of two interest rate elasticities that we will frequently use in this chapter.

The **interest elasticity of investment demand** is the percentage change in investment demand that occurs in response to a given percentage change in the interest rate. Since investment demand rises when the interest rate falls, a higher interest elasticity means that investment demand rises more for a given decline in the interest rate.

The **interest elasticity of money demand** refers to the percentage change in money demand that occurs in response to a given percentage change in the interest rate. Since money demand rises when the interest rate falls, a higher interest elasticity means that money demand rises more for a given decline in the interest rate.

## The Slope of the IS Curve

The slope of the IS curve is illustrated in Figure 24.1. In each panel, the economy is initially at the point $I$ on the IS curve. Then several steps cause the economy to move from point $I$ to point $S$:

1. The Federal Reserve uses easier monetary policy to reduce the interest rate by $\Delta r$ and then maintains the rate at the lower level. If income is unchanged, this causes the economy to move to point $T$.

2. The lower interest rate causes investment spending to rise, reflecting the interest elasticity of investment demand.

3. As investment spending rises, income rises (based on the expenditure multiplier), until equilibrium is restored at point $S$.

FIGURE 24.1
**The Slope of the IS Curve**

A. Flatter IS Curve                    B. Steeper IS Curve

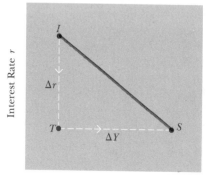

Income $Y$                             Income $Y$

C. Vertical IS Curve

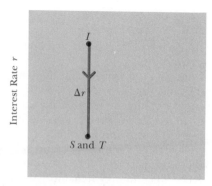

Income $Y$

The slope of the IS curve is flatter when income rises by a larger amount for a given reduction in the interest rate. A flatter IS curve (panel A) reflects a larger value for the interest elasticity of investment demand. A steeper IS curve (panel B) reflects just the opposite condition. A vertical IS curve (panel C) reflects a *zero* interest elasticity of investment demand.

## The Slopes of the IS and LM Curves

### The Slope of the IS Curve

1. The slope of the IS curve is *flatter*, the larger the interest elasticity of investment demand.
2. The slope of the IS curve is *steeper*, the smaller the interest elasticity of investment demand.
3. The slope of the IS curve is *vertical* when the interest elasticity of investment demand is zero.

### The Slope of the LM Curve

1. The slope of the LM curve is *flatter*, the larger the interest elasticity of money demand.
2. The slope of the LM curve is *steeper*, the smaller the interest elasticity of money demand.
3. The slope of the LM curve is *horizontal* when the interest elasticity of money demand is infinite.
4. The slope of the LM curve is *vertical* when the interest elasticity of money demand is zero.

The panels of the diagram differ only in the amount that income rises in response to the given decline in the interest rate. A relatively flat IS curve (panel A) results when the increase in income is relatively large, whereas a relatively steep IS curve (panel B) results when the increase in income is relatively small.

The increase in income will be larger, and the IS curve will be flatter, as the *interest elasticity of investment demand* is larger. The extreme case of a *vertical IS curve* (panel C) represents a *zero* interest elasticity of investment demand. In this case, because investment demand does not respond at all to the interest rate, there is no effect on aggregate expenditures when the interest rate falls.

The main results for the slope of the IS curve are summarized in Box 24.2. This box also summarizes the results for the slope of the LM curve, to which we now turn.

## The Slope of the LM Curve

The slope of the LM curve is illustrated in Figure 24.2. In each panel, the economy is initially at the point $L$ on the LM curve. Then several steps cause the economy to move from point $L$ to point $M$:

1. Expansionary fiscal policy causes income to rise by $\Delta Y$ (which includes the effect of the expenditure multiplier). If the interest rate is unchanged, this causes the economy to move to point $T$.

2. Higher income raises the demand for money, so that money demand exceeds the given money supply. The interest rate then has to rise to reduce money demand, so money demand and money supply will again be equal.

3. Equilibrium in the market for money occurs at point $M$, reflecting a higher interest rate (except in panel C) and larger income (except in panel D).

The panels of Figure 24.2 differ only in the amount the interest rate has to rise (in step 3) to restore equilibrium in the market for money. The less the interest rate has to rise, the flatter the LM curve will be. Panel A shows a relatively flat LM curve and panel B shows a relatively steep one.

FIGURE 24.2
**The Slope of the LM Curve**

A. Flatter LM Curve

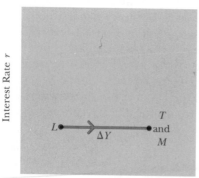

B. Steeper LM Curve

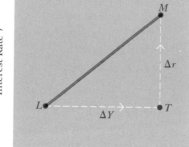

C. Horizontal LM Curve

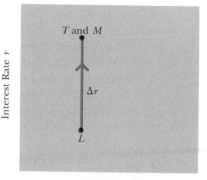

D. Vertical LM Curve

The slope of the LM curve is flatter the less the interest rate must rise to offset the increase in money demand that occurs when income rises. If money demand is highly interest elastic, then the interest rate must rise very little and the LM curve is flatter (panel A). If money demand is interest inelastic, then the interest rate must rise more and the LM curve is steeper (panel B). If the interest elasticity of money demand is infinite, then the LM curve is horizontal (panel C), and if the interest elasticity is zero, then the LM curve is vertical (panel D).

The interest rate elasticity of money demand—recall Box 24.1—determines how much the interest rate must rise to offset the increase in money demand created by the initial increase in income. The interest rate has to rise less the greater the interest elasticity of money demand. It follows that the LM curve is *flatter*, the higher the interest elasticity of money demand, and vice versa.

The extreme cases of horizontal (panel C) and vertical (panel D) LM curves are also illustrated in Figure 24.2. A horizontal LM curve occurs if the interest elasticity of money demand is infinite, so that a negligible increase in the interest rate is sufficient to restore equilibrium in the market for money. A vertical LM curve occurs if the interest elasticity of money demand is zero, so that the interest rate has no role in restoring equilibrium in the market for money.

# Monetary Policy in the IS/LM Model

We now turn to monetary policy as represented in the IS/LM model. First we will consider the shift in the LM curve that occurs when monetary policy—a change in the money supply—is initiated. Second we will evaluate the effectiveness of monetary policy—how much income changes in response to a given change in the money supply—in terms of the slopes of the IS and LM curves. We will use the case of easy monetary policy as our main example. The results of tight monetary policy are generally just the opposite, as can be seen in Box 24.3, which provides a summary of our main conclusions regarding monetary policy.

## Monetary Policy and the LM Curve

A rightward shift in the LM curve caused by an increase in the money supply is illustrated in Figure 24.3. The initial LM curve, $(LM)_0$, is based on the initial money supply, $M_0$. The resulting LM curve, $(LM)_1$, is based on a larger money supply, $M_1$. The resulting LM curve lies to the right of (or below) the initial curve because:

1. Each LM curve represents the interest rate and income combinations at which money demand and money supply are equal.
2. Since the money supply is larger along the resulting LM curve, money demand also has to be larger.
3. Money demand will be larger along the resulting curve if either the interest rate is lower or income is higher.
4. So, the resulting curve, $(LM)_1$, must either shift rightward (income is higher) or downward (the interest rate is lower) relative to $(LM)_0$.

Figure 24.3 also illustrates the impact that easy monetary policy has on the economy. Suppose that the economy starts at point $E_0$ and that the Fed then raises the money supply from $M_0$ to $M_1$, so that the LM curve shifts rightward to curve $(LM)_1$. The economy will then move to a point on the curve $(LM)_1$.

Starting at the point $E_0$ on the initial LM curve, $(LM)_0$, easy monetary policy shifts the LM curve rightward (or downward), so that either the interest rate falls (as at point A on $(LM)_1$), or income rises (as at point A' on $(LM)_1$), or a combination of these may occur (as at other points on $(LM)_1$).

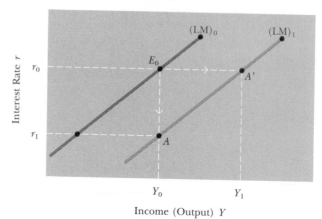

. FIGURE 24.3
**Monetary Policy and the LM Curve**

Income (Output) Y

However, curve $LM_1$ represents a series of interest rate and income combinations, so we still have to identify the specific point to which the economy heads. For example, at one extreme, only the interest rate might fall, so the economy would move from point $E_0$ to point A on $(LM)_1$. At the other extreme, only income might rise, so the economy would move from point $E_0$ to point A' on $(LM)_1$.

---

BOX 24.3 IN DEPTH

## Monetary Policy

The following are the main conclusions regarding monetary policy that we will establish in this section.

1. Easy monetary policy causes the LM curve to shift rightward (or downward).

2. Easy monetary policy causes the interest rate to fall and income to rise.

3. Easy monetary policy is more effective—income rises more for a given change in the money supply—as:

  a. The IS curve is flatter (investment demand is more interest elastic).

  b. The LM curve is steeper (money demand is less interest elastic).

The effects of tight monetary policy are just the opposite to those of easy monetary policy:

4. Tight monetary policy causes the LM curve to shift leftward (or upward).

5. Tight monetary policy causes the interest rate to rise and income to fall.

6. Tight monetary policy is more effective—income falls more for a given change in the money supply—as:

  a. The IS curve is flatter.

  b. The LM curve is steeper.

How can an increase in the money supply have these different effects? The answer is that any point on the resulting LM curve can establish equilibrium in the market for money. To determine where the actual point is, we must refer to the IS curve, which allows us to identify where an increase in the money supply actually leads the economy.

## The Effects of Monetary Policy

In Figure 24.4, we have added an IS curve to the LM curve of Figure 24.3, to determine where an increase in the money supply actually leads the economy. That is, after the LM curve shifts, the IS curve identifies the precise change in the economy from the initial equilibrium at point $E_0$ to the resulting equilibrium at point $E_1$. It is thus evident that *an increase in the money supply generally causes the interest rate to fall and income to rise.* The steps that bring about this result are illustrated by the arrows (a), (b), and (c) in Figure 24.4:

1. The Federal Reserve increases the money supply, shifting the LM curve to the right (arrow a).

2. The interest rate falls as an immediate effect of the increase in the money supply (arrow b).

3. The lower interest rate raises investment spending and the expenditure multiplier then raises income (arrow c).

The initial LM curve $(LM)_0$ is based on the initial monetary policy. For the given IS curve, $(IS)_0$, the economy is in equilibrium at $E_0$. Then an increase in the money supply shifts the LM curve rightward to $(LM)_1$ (arrow a). The resulting equilibrium occurs at point $E_1$, where the resulting LM curve, $(LM)_1$, and the initial IS curve, $(IS)_0$, intersect. The effect of easy monetary policy is thus to lower the interest rate (arrow b) and to raise income (arrow c).

FIGURE 24.4
**Monetary Policy and the IS/LM Model**

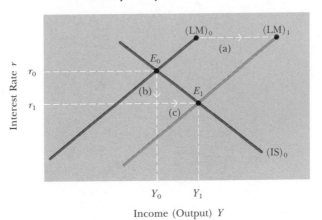

4. Equilibrium is reestablished when the fall in the interest rate and the increase in income place the economy at the intersection of the IS curve and the resulting LM curve. (The IS curve does not shift because its location is determined by fiscal policy—which we assume is unchanged for the time being.)

## The Effectiveness of Monetary Policy

We can now consider the *effectiveness* of monetary policy—how much income rises for a given change in the money supply. By establishing a measure of effectiveness, the Federal Reserve can determine *how much* to increase the money supply in order to raise income a desired amount. We will see that monetary policy is more effective, the flatter the slope of the IS curve or the steeper the slope of the LM curve.

### The Effectiveness of Monetary Policy and the Slope of the IS Curve

Both panels in Figure 24.5 illustrate easy monetary policy, based on the LM curves used in Figure 24.4. Panel A shows a relatively flat IS curve, and panel B a relatively steep one. We can see immediately that *monetary policy is more effective*—income rises more for the same shift in the LM curve—*the flatter the slope of the IS curve* (panel A).

Why does a flatter IS curve make monetary policy more effective? Recall that a flatter IS curve represents a relatively high interest elasticity for investment demand. So a given decline in the interest rate produces a larger increase in investment demand, and therefore in income.

FIGURE 24.5
**Monetary Policy with Alternative IS Curves**

A. Effective Monetary Policy with a Flat IS Curve

Easy monetary policy, which creates a rightward shift in the LM curve, is more effective the flatter the IS curve.

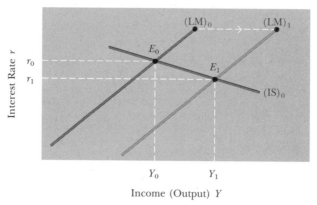

B. Ineffective Monetary Policy with a Steep IS Curve

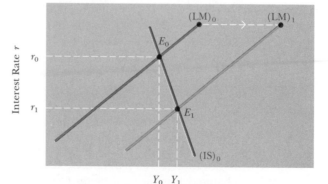

In the same fashion, as shown in panel B, a steeper IS curve produces a smaller increase in income for a given decline in the interest rate. In fact, in the extreme case of a *vertical IS curve*, monetary policy has *no effect at all on income*. Recall that a vertical IS curve means that the interest elasticity of investment demand is zero; thus, even though monetary policy reduces the interest rate, there will be no effect on income. Although most economists today would consider this an unrealistic extreme case, it is useful for remembering that monetary policy is less effective the steeper the slope of the IS curve.

### The Effectiveness of Monetary Policy and the Slope of the LM Curve

Figure 24.6 shows how the slope of the LM curve also determines the effectiveness of monetary policy. The IS curve is the same one that we used in Figure 24.4. Panel A shows a relatively steep LM curve, and panel B a relatively flat one. Clearly, monetary policy is more effective—the increase in income is greater—the steeper the slope of the LM curve.

Easy monetary policy is more effective—income rises more for a given rightward shift in the LM curve—the steeper the LM curve.

FIGURE 24.6

**Monetary Policy with Alternative LM Curves**

A. Effective Monetary Policy with a Steep LM Curve

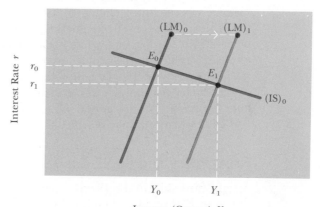

Income (Output) $Y$

B. Ineffective Monetary Policy with a Flat LM Curve

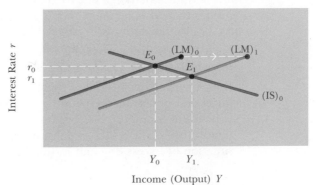

Income (Output) $Y$

Why does a steeper LM curve make monetary policy more effective? Recall that a steeper LM curve represents a lower interest elasticity for money demand. So to restore equilibrium after the money supply rises, the interest rate must fall substantially. And a larger fall in the interest rate causes a larger increase in investment and income.

Indeed, *monetary policy is most effective in the extreme case of a vertical LM curve.* A vertical LM curve means that the interest rate does not affect money demand at all, so income must rise enough by itself to raise money demand to the level of the higher money supply.

In contrast, *monetary policy is ineffective in the extreme case of a horizontal LM curve.* A horizontal LM curve means that money demand is highly interest elastic, so a decline in the interest rate raises money demand a great deal, even without an increase in income.

Even if these extreme cases for the LM curve are not realistic, they are useful for remembering that monetary policy is more effective with a steeply sloped LM curve.

## Fiscal Policy in the IS/LM Model

We now turn to fiscal policy—changes in government spending and taxes—which we will study, as we did monetary policy, in two stages. First we will see how a change in fiscal policy shifts the IS curve. Second we will evaluate the effectiveness of fiscal policy. It is particularly important to recognize that, while both expansionary fiscal policy and easy monetary policy raise income, expansionary fiscal policy *raises interest rates*, while easy monetary policy reduces them. We will use the case of expansionary fiscal policy as our main example. The results of contractionary fiscal policy are generally just the opposite, as can be seen from Box 24.4, which summarizes the main conclusions regarding fiscal policy.

### Fiscal Policy and the IS Curve

A rightward shift in the IS curve caused by expansionary fiscal policy is shown in Figure 24.7. The initial IS curve, $(IS)_0$, is based on the initial fiscal policy—government spending $G_0$ and taxes $T_0$. The resulting IS curve, $(IS)_1$, is based on a more expansionary fiscal policy—government spending $G_1$ and taxes $T_1$, with $G_1 > G_0$ and $T_1 < T_0$. The resulting IS curve lies to the right of (or above) the initial curve because:

1. Each IS curve represents the interest rate and income combinations for which the market for goods is in equilibrium.

2. Both types of expansionary fiscal policy increase aggregate expenditures: (a) government spending is itself a component of aggregate expenditures, and (b) lower taxes raise autonomous consumption expenditures. As a result, expansionary fiscal policy initially creates a situation of excess demand in the market for goods.

## Fiscal Policy

The following are the key conclusions regarding fiscal policy that we will establish in this section.

1. Expansionary fiscal policy—an increase in government spending or a decrease in taxes—causes the IS curve to shift rightward (or upward).

2. Expansionary fiscal policy causes the interest rates to *rise* and income to rise.

3. Expansionary fiscal policy is more effective—income rises more for a given dose of policy—as:

   *a.* The LM curve is flatter (money demand is more interest elastic).

   *b.* The IS curve is steeper (investment demand is less interest elastic).

   The effects of contractionary fiscal policy are just the opposite of those of expansionary fiscal policy:

4. Contractionary fiscal policy causes the IS curve to shift leftward (or downward).

5. Contractionary fiscal policy causes the interest rate to fall and income to fall.

6. Contractionary fiscal policy is more effective—income rises more for a given dose of policy—as:

   *a.* The LM curve is flatter.

   *b.* The IS curve is steeper.

Starting at the point $E_0$ on the initial IS curve, $(IS)_0$, expansionary fiscal policy shifts the IS curve rightward (or upward), so that either the interest rate may rise (as at point $A$ on $(IS)_1$), or income may rise (as at point $A'$ on $(IS)_1$), or a combination of these may occur (as at other points on $(IS)_1$).

FIGURE 24.7
**Fiscal Policy and the IS Curve**

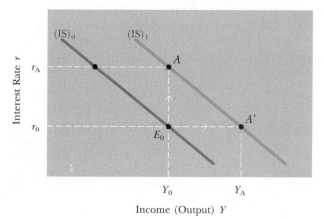

3. Equilibrium in the market for goods can be restored if either (a) a higher interest rate reduces investment demand, or (b) higher output increases the supply of goods.

4. So, the resulting IS curve, $(IS)_1$, must either shift upward (the interest rate is higher) or rightward (income is higher) relative to $(IS)_0$.

Figure 24.7 also illustrates the impact that expansionary fiscal policy has on the economy. Assume that the economy is initially at point $E_0$ and then fiscal policy becomes more expansionary, so that the IS curve shifts rightward to $(IS)_1$. The economy will then move to a point on $(IS)_1$.

However, we also want to identify the specific point on the resulting IS curve to which the economy might head. For example, at one extreme, only the interest rate might rise, so the economy would move from point $E_0$ to point $A$ on $(IS)_1$. At the other extreme, only income might rise, so the economy would move from point $E_0$ to point $A'$ on $(IS)_1$.

How can a change to expansionary fiscal policy have these different effects—raising only the interest rate at one extreme, and raising only income at the other extreme? The answer is that the IS curve determines a series of interest rate and income combinations, each of which is consistent with equilibrium in the market for goods. To determine which combination it is, we must also refer to the LM curve. The LM curve provides the additional information that identifies where a change in fiscal policy actually leads the economy.

## The Effects of Fiscal Policy

In Figure 24.8, we have added an LM curve to the IS curve of Figure 24.7, to determine where expansionary fiscal policy actually leads the economy. That is, after the IS curve shifts, the LM curve identifies the precise change in the economy from the initial equilibrium at point $E_0$ to the resulting equilibrium at point $E_1$. It is thus evident that *expansionary*

The initial IS curve is $(IS)_0$ based on the initial fiscal policy. For the given LM curve, $(LM)_0$, the economy is in equilibrium at $E_0$. Then a change to more expansionary fiscal policy shifts the IS curve to $(IS)_1$ (arrow a). The resulting equilibrium occurs at point $E_1$, where the resulting IS curve, $(IS)_1$, and the initial LM curve intersect. The effect of expansionary fiscal policy is thus to raise income (arrow b) and to raise the interest rate (arrow c).

FIGURE 24.8
**Fiscal Policy and the IS/LM Model**

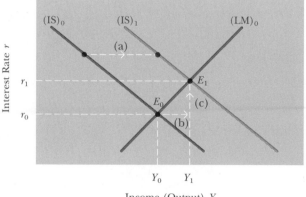

*fiscal policy causes the interest rate to rise and income to rise.* These steps that bring about this result are illustrated by the arrows (a), (b), and (c) in Figure 24.8:

1. Expansionary fiscal policy shifts the IS curve rightward (arrow a).

2. Aggregate expenditures immediately rise, reflecting either higher government spending or higher consumption (based on lower taxes). The expenditure multiplier then raises income (arrow b).

3. Since higher income raises money demand, to restore equilibrium in the market for money, interest rates must rise to reduce money demand (arrow c).

4. Equilibrium is reestablished when the increase in the interest rate and in income place the economy at the intersection of the LM curve and the resulting IS curve.

## The Effectiveness of Fiscal Policy

We can now consider the *effectiveness* of fiscal policy—how much income rises for a given dose of expansionary fiscal policy. By establishing a measure of effectiveness, policy makers can gauge *how much* expansionary policy is needed to raise income a desired amount. We will see that fiscal policy is more effective the flatter the slope of the LM curve and the steeper the slope of the IS curve.

### The Effectiveness of Fiscal Policy and the Slope of the LM Curve

Both panels in Figure 24.9 illustrate the use of expansionary fiscal policy, based on the IS curves used in Figure 24.8. Panel A shows a relatively flat LM curve, and panel B a relatively steep one. It is apparent that *fiscal policy is more effective*—income rises more for a given shift in the IS curve—*the flatter the slope of the LM curve* (panel A).

Expansionary fiscal policy, which creates a rightward shift in the IS curve, is more effective the flatter the LM curve.

FIGURE 24.9
**Fiscal Policy with Alternative LM Curves**

A. Effective Fiscal Policy with a Flat LM Curve

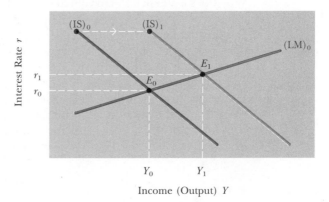

FIGURE 24.9
(continued)

B. Ineffective Fiscal Policy with a Steep LM Curve

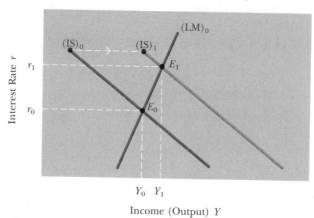

Income (Output) $Y$

Why does a flatter LM curve make fiscal policy more effective? Recall that a flatter LM curve represents a more interest elastic money demand curve. So, with a flatter LM curve, money demand falls more for a given increase in the interest rate, and thus income must rise more to restore money demand to its initial level (equal to the supply of money).

In the same fashion, as shown in panel B, for a steeper LM curve, income does not have to rise as much to restore the balance between money demand and money supply. In fact, for a *vertical LM curve*, fiscal policy would have *no effect at all on income*—because money demand is unaffected by the interest rate. Although this is an extreme case, it is useful for remembering that fiscal policy is less effective the steeper the slope of the LM curve.

### The Effectiveness of Fiscal Policy and the Slope of the IS Curve

Figure 24.10 shows how the slope of the IS curve also determines the effectiveness of fiscal policy. The LM curve is the same one that we used in Figure 24.8. Panel A shows a relatively steep IS curve, and panel B a relatively flat one. Clearly, *fiscal policy is more effective*—the increase in income is greater—*the steeper the slope of the IS curve.*

Why does a steeper IS curve make fiscal policy more effective? Recall that a steeper IS curve means that the interest elasticity of investment demand is smaller. So even though expansionary fiscal policy causes the interest rate to rise, investment demand falls by a relatively small amount. The situation is just the opposite for a flatter IS curve.

Indeed, fiscal policy is most effective in the extreme case of a vertical IS curve, because the interest elasticity for investment demand is zero, so there is no reduction at all in investment demand. Even though the case is not realistic, it is helpful for remembering that fiscal policy is more effective when the IS curve is more steeply sloped.

Expansionary fiscal policy is more effective the steeper the IS curve.

FIGURE 24.10
**Fiscal Policy with Alternative IS Curves**

A. Effective Fiscal Policy with a Steep IS Curve

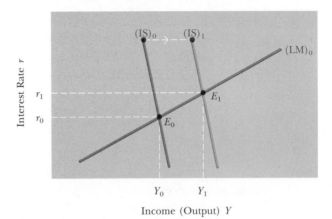

B. Ineffective Fiscal Policy with a Flat IS Curve

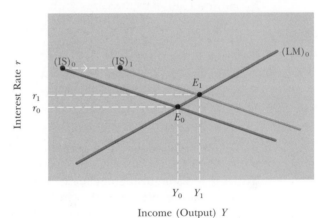

# Applications of Monetary Policy and Fiscal Policy

We will now apply the IS/LM model to see how monetary policy and fiscal policy interact when the policymakers—the Federal Reserve, Congress, and the president—agree to raise the level of income. We will first consider why one of the instruments—monetary policy or fiscal policy—might be preferred. We will then consider how the two policies could be combined in a coordinated policy action.

## The Effectiveness of Monetary Policy and Fiscal Policy

Three factors are potentially relevant in comparing the effectiveness of monetary policy and fiscal policy:

1. Both easy monetary policy (increasing the money supply) and expansionary fiscal policy (increasing government spending or reducing taxes) generally raise income.

2. Easy monetary policy lowers the interest rate, whereas expansionary fiscal policy raises the interest rate.

3. Depending on the slopes of the IS and LM curves, one or the other of the policies may be more effective—raise income more for a given dose of policy.

While one policy is likely to be more effective (point 3), this is usually not critical to the choice between them. Given a large enough policy dose, either monetary or fiscal policy can generally achieve a given goal for desired income. So, unless smaller policy actions are important for their own sake, effectiveness should not cause one policy to be preferred over the other.

However, in extreme cases, one or the other of the policies may be *ineffective*:

1. If the interest elasticity of money demand is zero (the LM curve is vertical), fiscal policy is ineffective.

2. If the interest elasticity of money demand is infinite (the LM curve is horizontal), monetary policy is ineffective.

3. If the interest elasticity of investment demand is zero (the IS curve is vertical), monetary policy is ineffective.

Few economists see these extremes as realistic situations in the economy. Nevertheless, they can be helpful in understanding some of the issues that distinguish monetarists from Keynesians. Monetarists tend to believe that the interest elasticity of money demand is low, which makes fiscal policy less effective. Monetary policy is then the main policy instrument that can dependably affect nominal income. Keynesians tend to believe that the interest elasticity of money demand is high, which makes monetary policy less effective. Fiscal policy is then the main instrument that can dependably affect income. Boxes 24.5 and 24.6 elaborate on monetary policy as viewed by these two schools.

## The Output Mix

We now turn from the issue of how monetary and fiscal policy affect the level of income, or output, to how they affect the **output mix**—the composition of total output among consumption, investment, government spending, and net exports. We will compare the policies in a situation where each is used to raise total output (and income) by the same amount. The two policies will have different effects on the output mix because:

## BOX 24.5 MONEY MATTERS

## Monetarist Monetary Policy

Monetarists believe that monetary policy is a powerful instrument, so they follow closely how monetary policy is managed. Many monetarists, such as Milton Friedman, propose that monetary policy should be based on a constant growth rate target for the money supply. They feel this would be the best way to minimize fluctuations in the economy caused by monetary actions.

Monetarists have generally been disappointed with the Federal Reserve's management of monetary policy. During the 1950s and 1960s, the Fed operated under a more Keynesian approach—focusing on interest rates more than on the money supply. During the 1970s, with Arthur Burns as chairman, the Fed's monetary policy was supposed to be based upon money supply growth rates, but it did not work out this way in practice.

Monetarists were delighted in 1979 when Paul Volcker, the new Fed chairman, introduced his new monetary policy based on strict money supply growth rate targets. However, even this did not work out well. For one thing, the Fed had a lot of trouble controlling the money supply—although monetarists might say it did not try hard enough. For another thing, the velocity of money was volatile, so there was not a dependable link between the growth rate of the money supply and the growth rate of nominal income.

## BOX 24.6 MONEY MATTERS

## Keynesian Monetary Policy

Keynes believed that monetary policy was likely to be ineffective in influencing the level of income because he thought that (1) the interest elasticity of money demand was very high, and (2) the interest elasticity of investment demand was very low. Most economists today would describe these as extreme cases that are unlikely to occur in practice. Why would Keynes—who in most respects was a highly pragmatic economist—emphasize extreme cases as a guide for practical policy.

The answer is that Keynes developed his *General Theory* under extreme economic conditions—during the Great Depression of the 1930s. Interest rates were extraordinarily low during the 1930s—sometimes less than 1%—so it was *realistic* to believe that easy monetary policy would be unable to make the interest rate fall very much. For another thing, investors were very pessimistic about the economy—their animal spirits were low—so it was also *realistic* to believe that investment demand might not rise, even if monetary policy did succeed in reducing interest rates. This is why Keynes believed that fiscal policy should be the principal instrument to revive the economy.

1. Easy monetary policy tends to lower interest rates, while expansionary fiscal policy tends to raise them.

2. Expansionary fiscal policy raises government spending or consumption spending by lowering taxes.

The effects of easy monetary policy and expansionary fiscal policy on the output mix are compared in Table 24.1. There are two key points. First, easy monetary policy tends to raise investment demand (reflecting lower interest rates) while expansionary fiscal policy tends to reduce investment demand (reflecting higher interest rates). Second, only expansionary fiscal policy can raise government expenditures or can raise consumption demand on the basis of lower taxes.

**TABLE 24.1**
**Monetary Policy, Fiscal Policy, and the Output Mix**

| | Effect[a] on Output Mix Resulting from | |
| --- | --- | --- |
| | Easy Monetary Policy | Expansionary Fiscal Policy |
| Consumption Demand | | |
| Effect of interest rates | rise | fall |
| Effect of autonomous factors | none | RISE |
| Overall (including income)[b] | RISE | RISE |
| Investment Demand | | |
| Effect of interest rates | RISE | FALL |
| Effect of autonomous factors | none | none |
| Overall (including income)[b] | RISE | fall |
| Government Expenditures | | |
| Effect of interest rates | none | none |
| Effect of autonomous factors | none | RISE |
| Overall (including income)[b] | none | RISE |
| Net Exports | | |
| Effect of interest rates | rise | fall |
| Effect of autonomous factors | none | none |
| Overall (including income)[b] | mixed | fall |

[a]Primary channels are shown in capitals: RISE or FALL; Secondary channels are shown in lowercase: rise or fall.
[b]The overall term combines the effect of higher income and of interest rates and autonomous factors.

To be more specific, the table identifies three channels through which each policy may affect the output mix—interest rates, autonomous factors, and an overall term (which includes the effect of higher income). The table also distinguishes *primary* and *secondary* channels for the effects of the policies. The primary channels refer to the main effects of the policies. The secondary channels refer to less important effects.

The primary effects of *easy monetary policy* are to raise both consumption and investment demand. The increase in consumption is mainly due to higher income, although the lower interest rates associated with easy monetary policy may also raise consumption spending. The increase in investment spending is mainly due to lower interest rates. The effect of easy monetary policy on net exports is mixed. Lower interest rates may raise net exports by causing the dollar to depreciate. However, higher income tends to raise the demand for imported goods, thus reducing net exports.

The primary effects of *expansionary fiscal policy* are to raise government expenditures, to raise consumption demand (due to lower taxes or higher income), and to reduce investment demand (due to higher interest rates). As secondary effects, expansionary fiscal policy may reduce investment demand or consumption demand through higher interest rates. Expansionary fiscal policy may also have the secondary effect of reducing net exports, because higher interest rates cause the dollar to appreciate and higher income increases the demand for imports.

Based on the primary effects shown in Table 24.1, the policies that should be carried out to achieve specific goals for the output mix are:

1. Use easy monetary policy to increase investment demand.
2. Use expansionary fiscal policy—that is, higher government spending—to increase autonomous government expenditures.
3. Use expansionary fiscal policy—that is, lower taxes—to increase consumption demand.

We can now look at two important applications of the effects of monetary policy and fiscal policy on the output mix. The first—called *crowding out*—refers mainly to the fact that expansionary fiscal policy may cause investment demand to fall. The second—called the *policy mix*—refers to the possibility that monetary policy and fiscal policy may be coordinated to achieve a desired outcome.

## Crowding Out

The term **crowding out** refers to the possibility that expansionary fiscal policy may cause one or more of the components of aggregate expenditures to fall. This is usually discussed in the context where increased government spending "crowds out" other components of aggregate expenditures.

Crowding out is a special feature of expansionary fiscal policy because that policy creates higher interest rates, which in turn crowd out investment demand. Expansionary fiscal policy may also have the secondary effect of crowding out net exports. Easy monetary policy does not have crowding out effects of this type because it does not cause any components of aggregate expenditures to fall. (However, we will see in Chapter 25 that easy monetary policy may cause another type of crowding out as the result of inflation.)

An obvious implication of crowding out is that expansionary fiscal policy will be a poor instrument when high investment spending is part of the policy goal. A more subtle implication is that expansionary fiscal policy may cause *complete crowding out*—the decline in investment demand may be so large as to nullify the expansionary effect of the policy on total output (and income). This will occur under the same circumstances that fiscal policy has no effect on aggregate output—a vertical LM curve. A vertical LM curve and complete crowding out are really the same thing in the IS/LM model.

## The Policy Mix and the Output Mix

Given that monetary policy and fiscal policy have different effects on the composition of output, it is possible to design combinations of the two policies—called a **policy mix**—to achieve a particular output mix.

To take a realistic example, suppose that policymakers feel the level of aggregate output is satisfactory, but they want to shift the output mix toward capital investment. Easy monetary policy alone will reduce interest rates and increase investment demand, but it will also increase aggregate output, an undesired result in this scenario.

However, easy monetary policy can be combined with contractionary fiscal policy to achieve the desired output mix, while keeping aggregate output unchanged. Both policies raise investment spending (remember we are talking about contractionary fiscal policy, which *reduces* the interest rate). In addition, easy monetary policy raises output while contractionary fiscal policy lowers output, so a mixture of the two can keep the net effect on aggregate output at zero.

Of course, if total output is unchanged while the investment component of aggregate expenditures rises, then some other component of aggregate expenditures must fall. As Table 24.1 indicates, there are two possibilities. If the contractionary fiscal policy reduces government spending, then the government expenditure component of aggregate expenditures will fall. While, if the contractionary fiscal policy represents increased taxes, then autonomous consumption will fall.

The mix of easy monetary policy and contractionary fiscal policy is illustrated by the IS/LM model in Figure 24.11. The initial equilibrium occurs at point $E_0$, where the curves $(LM)_0$ and $(IS)_0$ intersect. Easy monetary policy then shifts the initial LM curve to the right, to $(LM)_1$, and contractionary fiscal policy shifts the initial IS curve to the left, to $(IS)_1$. The equilibrium then occurs at point $E_1$, where the curves $(LM)_1$ and $(IS)_1$ intersect.

The initial equilibrium $E_0$ and the new equilibrium $E_1$ occur at the same level of output, $Y_0$; that is, the policy mix does not affect aggregate output. However, the equilibrium interest rate declines from $r_0$ to $r_1$. This decline in the interest rate causes investment spending to rise, the goal of the policy.

A policy mix of easy monetary policy and contractionary fiscal policy is represented by shifting the LM curve to the right to $(LM)_1$ and by shifting the IS curve to the left to $(IS)_1$. Since the equilibrium output is the same at the initial point $E_0$ and at the resulting point $E_1$, the policy mix does not affect aggregate output. However, the decline in the interest rate from $r_0$ to $r_1$ causes investment demand to rise.

FIGURE 24.11

**Easy Monetary Policy and Contractionary Fiscal Policy**

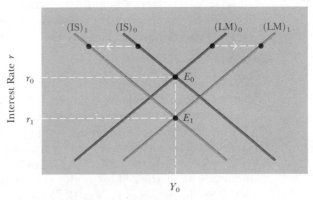

The Government Budget Constraint and Budget Deficits

The *government budget constraint* provides another connection between fiscal policy and monetary policy. The basis of the government budget constraint is that a *government deficit*—government spending in excess of tax receipts—has to be financed by issuing U.S. Treasury securities. This can occur in two ways. One possibility, **debt financing**, is that the Treasury sells securities to the public—anybody in the economy other than federal government agencies or the Federal Reserve. The other possibility, **monetizing the deficit**, is that the Federal Reserve buys Treasury securities.[1] These two ways of financing a government deficit can be expressed:

$$G - T = \Delta S_P + \Delta S_F, \tag{24.1}$$

where $G$ = federal government expenditures,

$T$ = federal tax receipts,

$\Delta S_P$ = U.S. Treasury securities sold to the public,

$\Delta S_F$ = U.S. Treasury securities sold to the Federal Reserve.

The left side of the equation shows the government deficit, and the right side shows the two ways of financing it.

When the Federal Reserve buys securities from the Treasury, it pays for them with a credit to the Treasury's deposit account at the Federal Reserve. The Treasury then uses these funds to pay for its expenditures.

---

[1] The Federal Reserve generally only buys outstanding securities, not new securities being issued by the Treasury. However, it comes basically to the same thing whether the Fed buys outstanding or new Treasury securities.

The securities purchased by the Federal Reserve thus represent an addition to the *monetary base*—the sum of deposit accounts at the Federal Reserve and currency held by the public. Therefore, in equation (24.1) for the government budget constraint, we can replace securities bought by the Federal Reserve, $\Delta S_F$, by the change in the monetary base, $\Delta B$:

$$G - T = \Delta S_P + \Delta B. \qquad (24.2)$$

This form of the government budget constraint indicates that the government's deficit must be financed either by selling Treasury securities to the public ($\Delta S_P$) or by increasing the monetary base ($\Delta B$).

This government budget constraint is related to monetary policy because the monetary base is a main factor determining the money supply, as we saw in Chapter 14. That is, the money supply rises when the monetary base rises. This is the reason that financing a government deficit by having the Federal Reserve purchase Treasury securities is called *monetizing the deficit*.

## The Relationship Between Monetary Policy and Fiscal Policy

A key result of the government budget constraint is that monetary policy and fiscal policy may be related. In particular, the following steps illustrate how an expansionary fiscal policy can create an easy monetary policy:

1. Expansionary fiscal policy creates or enlarges a government deficit.
2. The Federal Reserve purchases Treasury securities, thus monetizing the deficit.
3. The securities purchased by the Federal Reserve increase the monetary base, creating easy monetary policy.

The relationship between fiscal policy and monetary policy that arises from the government budget constraint is represented in Figure 24.12. The initial equilibrium occurs at $E_0$, at the intersection of $(IS)_0$ and $(LM)_0$. Now suppose that expansionary fiscal policy increases the deficit and causes the IS curve to shift rightward to $(IS)_1$. There are then two possibilities for the new equilibrium, depending on whether the Treasury uses debt financing or the deficit is monetized.

If the Treasury uses debt financing, then only the IS curve shifts in Figure 24.12; there is no change in the money supply or the LM curve. The resulting equilibrium then occurs at point $E_1$, where the curves $(IS)_1$ and $(LM)_0$ intersect. (This part of the diagram is the same as Figure 24.8, which represented expansionary fiscal policy without regard to the government budget constraint.) A debt-financed deficit is sometimes called *pure fiscal policy* for this reason.

In contrast, if the deficit is monetized, then, in addition to the shift in the IS curve, the money supply will increase and the LM curve will shift rightward, as represented by $(LM)_1$. The resulting equilibrium then occurs at point $E_2$, where the curves $(IS)_1$ and $(LM)_1$ intersect. Income

The initial equilibrium is represented at point $E_0$ where the curves $(IS)_0$ and $(LM)_0$ intersect. Two possibilities then result when expansionary fiscal policy causes the IS curve to shift to the right to $(IS)_1$. If the deficit is *debt financed*, then the resulting equilibrium is represented at point $E_1$, by the intersection of $(IS)_1$ and $(LM)_0$. If the deficit is *monetized*, then the LM curve also shifts to the right to $(LM)_1$, so the resulting equilibrium is represented at point $E_2$, where the curves $(IS)_1$ and $(LM)_1$ intersect.

FIGURE 24.12

**The Relationship Between Fiscal Policy and Monetary Policy**

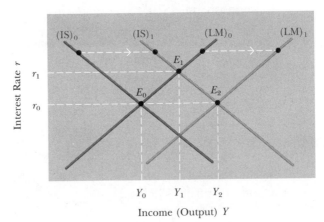

Income (Output) $Y$

rises more when the deficit is monetized because expansionary fiscal policy (increased government spending) and easy monetary policy (monetization of the deficit) are combined. (*Pure monetary policy* represents the change in the money supply when the Federal Reserve buys Treasury securities in the absence of any fiscal policy action.)

## The IS/LM Model as a Theory of Interest Rates

In earlier chapters, we introduced two theories of interest rate determination. In Chapter 3, we looked at the *loanable funds* theory based on the demand for loans by borrowers and the supply of loans by lenders. And in Chapter 16, we looked at the *money demand/money supply* theory based on the demand and supply of money. We also pointed out in Chapter 16 that these two theories were logically equivalent, the choice between them depending on which was easier to apply in the particular circumstances.

The **IS/LM model** provides **a third interest rate theory**, because an equilibrium interest rate is determined, along with equilibrium income, at the point where the IS and LM curves intersect. The IS/LM theory of interest rates can be interpreted as a combination of the loanable funds and money supply/money demand theories. Specifically, the LM curve represents equilibrium between money supply and money demand, which is the basis of the money supply/money demand theory, while the IS curve (recalling Box 23.6 in Chapter 23) represents the condition that saving equals investment, a version of the loanable funds theory.

The IS/LM theory of interest rates not only combines the other two theories, it also provides something extra—the determination of equilibrium income along with the equilibrium interest rate. This is because the loanable funds and money supply/money demand theories each represent *partial equilibrium*—they are based on a given value for income. In contrast, the IS/LM theory represents *general equilibrium*—equilibrium income is determined as part of the theory. As a consequence, the three theories of interest rate determination are logically consistent—applying the same value for income, they each determine the same equilibrium interest rate. However, only the IS/LM theory determines equilibrium income and the equilibrium interest rate together.

## Chapter Summary

1. A larger interest elasticity of investment demand is a source of a flatter IS curve. A larger interest rate elasticity of money demand is a source of a flatter LM curve. The slopes of the IS and LM curves are the main factors that determine the effectiveness of monetary and fiscal policy.

2. Easy monetary policy—an increase in the money supply—causes the LM curve to shift rightward (or downward). This causes income to rise and the interest rate to fall. Easy monetary policy is more effective—income rises more—the flatter the IS curve and the steeper the LM curve.

3. Expansionary fiscal policy—an increase in government spending or a decrease in taxes—causes the IS curve to shift rightward (or upward). This causes both income and the interest rate to rise. Expansionary fiscal policy is more effective—income rises more—the steeper the IS curve and the flatter the LM curve.

4. Monetary policy and fiscal policy also determine the output mix—the distribution of total output among the components of aggregate expenditures. Easy monetary policy shifts the output mix toward investment because lower interest rates stimulate investment demand. Expansionary fiscal policy shifts the output mix toward government spending (if the fiscal policy instrument is increased government spending) or consumption (if the fiscal policy instrument is lower taxes). As a result, expansionary fiscal policy can crowd out investment demand.

5. The government budget constraint reflects the fact that a government deficit must be financed either by debt financing (selling Treasury securities to the public) or by monetizing the deficit (having the Federal Reserve buy Treasury securities). Monetizing the deficit represents a combination of pure fiscal policy (increased government spending or reduced taxes) and pure monetary policy (the Fed increasing the monetary base as it buys Treasury securities).

6. The IS/LM model provides a general equilibrium theory of interest rates that combines the partial equilibrium loanable funds and money supply/money demand theories. This means that the IS/LM theory determines equilibrium income along with the equilibrium interest rate.

# Key Terms

Crowding out

Easy monetary policy:

Larger money supply

Role of the IS curve

Role of the LM curve

Expansionary fiscal policy:

Higher government spending

Lower taxes

Role of the IS curve

Role of the LM curve

Effectiveness of:

Fiscal policy

Monetary policy

Financing the deficit:

Debt financing

Monetizing the deficit

Interest elasticity of:

Investment demand

Money demand

IS/LM theory of interest rates

Output mix

Policy mix

# Study Questions

1. What factors create a steeply sloped IS curve?

2. What factors create a steeply sloped LM curve?

3. What IS curve and LM curve slopes—flatter or steeper—cause monetary policy to be most *effective*? In what special cases is monetary policy *ineffective*?

4. What IS curve and LM curve slopes—flatter or steeper—cause fiscal policy to be most *effective*? In what special case is fiscal policy *ineffective*?

5. What are the effects of monetary policy on income, the interest rate, and investment demand?

6. What are the effects of expansionary fiscal policy on income, the interest rate, and investment demand?

7. What policy mix of easy or tight monetary policy and expansionary or contractionary fiscal policy should policymakers use to increase investment spending and reduce consumption spending, while keeping income unchanged?

8. In terms of the IS/LM model, what is the difference between expansionary fiscal policy where the deficit is debt financed and expansionary fiscal policy where the deficit is monetized?

9. Referring to Question 8, which case of expansionary fiscal policy provides the greater stimulus to income?

10. In what sense does the IS/LM model theory of interest rates combine the loanable funds and money supply/money demand theories?

# Recommended Reading

*The references to macroeconomic textbooks given in Chapter 23 also apply here. In addition, the following provide further reading on specific topics of this chapter.*

*Crowding Out*

Alan S. Blinder and Robert M. Solow, "Does Fiscal Policy Matter?" *Journal of Public Economics*, 1973, pp. 319–337.

Keith M. Carlson and Roger W. Spencer, "Crowding Out and Its Critics," *Review*, Federal Reserve Bank of St. Louis, December 1975, pp. 2–17.

Federal Reserve Bank of Minneapolis, "The Unpleasant Arithmetic of Budget and Trade Deficits," *Annual Report*, 1986, pp. 3–17.

Benjamin Friedman, "Crowding Out and Crowding In," *Brookings Papers on Economic Activity*, 1978, pp. 593–641.

*Monetarism*

The October 1986 issue of the *Review* of the Federal Reserve Bank of St. Louis has collected a number of papers describing current and past monetarist thinking.

*Monetary Policy and Fiscal Policy*

Keith M. Carlson, "The Mix of Monetary and Fiscal Policies: Conventional Wisdom Vs. Empirical Reality," *Review*, Federal Reserve Bank of St. Louis, October 1982, pp. 7–21.

Aris Protopapadakis and Jeremy J. Siegel, "Are Government Deficits Monetized?" *Business Review*, Federal Reserve Bank of Philadelphia, November/December 1986, pp. 13–22.

# Aggregate Demand, Aggregate Supply, and Inflation

**25**

*"Inflation is repudiation."*

*Calvin Coolidge*

Demand and supply curves are used to study both microeconomic and macroeconomic activity in the economy. Microeconomic activity occurs in the market for an individual good, whereas macroeconomic activity occurs, at least conceptually, in the *aggregate market*—the market for all goods treated together. This is why macroeconomics is based on *aggregate* demand and supply curves—demand and supply curves for the aggregate market.

By analogy with demand and supply for a single good, the aggregate demand for goods is inversely related to the price level (the aggregate price for all goods), and the aggregate supply of goods is positively related to the price level. In equilibrium, aggregate demand and supply are equal, and this condition determines the equilibrium price level.

The analogy between the market for a single good and for the aggregate market is not as close when it comes to the factors that shift the aggregate demand and supply curves. For example, the market price for an individual good is likely to depend on the market prices for other goods that are *substitutes* for it. But the concept of substitute goods does not apply in the aggregate market because aggregate demand includes all goods, and the price level includes all prices.

Instead, aggregate demand and supply are affected by such macroeconomic variables as the money supply and government spending and taxes. Changes in these variables cause the aggregate demand and supply curves to shift, thus forcing the price level to adjust to restore equilibrium.

In this chapter, we will study the properties of aggregate demand and aggregate supply curves and how they determine such variables as aggregate output and the price level.

In the two preceding chapters, we saw how equilibrium interest rates and output are determined in the IS/LM model when the price level is fixed. In this chapter, we will study how the equilibrium price level and output are determined on the basis of aggregate demand and supply curves. We will look first at the factors that determine those curves. Then we will use the curves to determine aggregate output, the price level, and the inflation rate (the rate of change in the price level).

# The Aggregate Demand Curve

**Aggregate demand** is the total value of goods (and services) demanded in the economy for consumption, investment, government expenditures, and net exports. We used a related concept (which we called aggregate expenditures) in studying the IS/LM model in the last two chapters, but with the price level assumed to be constant. We will now look at how changes in the price level influence aggregate demand, starting with the effect of a changing price level in the IS/LM model.

## The IS/LM Approach to Aggregate Demand

When the price level is a variable, we have to analyze the IS and LM curves in *real terms*—as functions of *real income*. The IS curve then represents equilibrium between the real demand and real supply of goods, and the LM curve represents equilibrium between the real demand and real supply of money. We will now see that this does not create any basic changes for the IS curve, but it does for the LM curve.

### The IS Curve and Price Level Changes

The IS curve is unaffected when the price level changes as long as there is *no money illusion*—that is, as discussed in Chapter 4, when the real demand and supply of goods is not affected by the price level. Put another way, no money illusion means that the real demand and real supply of goods are unchanged if real income is unchanged. Therefore, given an initial price level $P_0$ and the equilibrium combinations of real income $y$ and interest rates $r$ that determine an IS curve (such as $(IS)_0$ in Figure 25.1), the same combinations and the same IS curve will represent equilibrium in the market for goods at any other price level (such as $P_1$).[1]

### The LM Curve and Price Level Changes

The *real demand for money*—the nominal demand for money deflated by the price level—will also be *unaffected* by price level changes, as long as there is no money illusion. That is, the nominal demand for money $M^d$ will rise in proportion as the price level $P$ rises, so the real demand for

---

[1] In more detailed versions of the IS/LM model, the IS curve may shift to the left when the price level rises because the amount of real wealth falls. That is, a fall in real wealth may cause a fall in the real demand for goods.

Panel A shows an IS/LM model based on real income, with an initial equilibrium at point $E_0$, based on the initial IS and LM curves, $(IS)_0$ and $(LM)_0$, and the initial price level $P_0$. A higher price level, $P_1$, does not affect the location of the IS curve, but it causes the LM curve to shift to the left—from $(LM)_0$ to $(LM)_1$. When the price level is $P_1$, the resulting equilibrium occurs at point $E_1$.

FIGURE 25.1

**The Aggregate Demand Curve: Based on the IS/LM Model**

A. The IS/LM Model with a Price Level Change

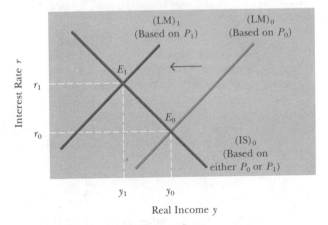

Real Income $y$

Panel B shows that the aggregate demand curve $D$ represents a graph of the equilibrium points, such as $E_0$ and $E_1$, of the IS/LM model in panel A. The aggregate demand curve is negatively sloped because the real money supply falls as the price level rises.

B. The Aggregate Demand Curve $(D)$

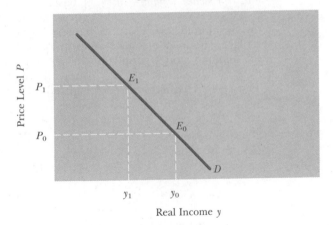

Real Income $y$

money—$M^d/P$—is unchanged. Thus, the demand for money is *not* the source of a shift in the LM curve as the price level changes.

Instead, the source of the shift is that the *real money supply*—the nominal money supply deflated by the price level—falls as the price level rises. The key point is that the Federal Reserve generally does *not* allow the *nominal money supply* $M^s$ to change in proportion as the price level rises. So, as the price level $P$ rises, the *real money supply*, $M^s/P$, falls, and the LM curve shifts to the left.

As illustrated in panel A of Figure 25.1, when the price level rises from $P_0$ to $P_1$, the curve $(LM)_0$—based on the initial price level $P_0$—shifts to the left to the resulting curve $(LM)_1$—based on the resulting price level $P_1$. The leftward shift of the LM curve due to a lower *real* money supply is analogous to the leftward shift in the LM curve due to a lower *nominal* money supply that was discussed in Chapter 24. Box 25.1 discusses this result for the real money supply further.

BOX 25.1 IN DEPTH

## The LM Curve and the Price Level

The steps that cause the LM curve to shift leftward when the price level rises can be expressed with basic algebra. Recall that the nominal LM curve represents the combinations of nominal income $Y$ and the interest rate $r$ for which nominal money supply $M^s$ and nominal money demand $M^d$ are equal:

$$M^s = M^d[Y, r]. \qquad (25.1)$$

If the Federal Reserve controls the nominal money supply and the real demand for money does not reflect money illusion, then there is an equivalent real LM curve:

$$\frac{M^s}{P} = M^d[y, r]. \qquad (25.2)$$

Equation (25.2) indicates that the LM curve represents the combinations of real income $y$ and the interest rate $r$ for which the *real money supply*—$M^s/P$— and *real money demand*—$M^d[y, r]$, based on real income $y$—are equal.

This real version of the LM curve has the same properties we discussed for the nominal version in Chapters 23 and 24, but with real income $y$ replacing nominal income $Y$ and with the real money supply $M^s/P$ replacing the nominal money supply $M^s$. In particular, since an increase in $P$ causes $M^s/P$ to fall, an increase in $P$ causes the real LM curve to shift to the left. This is reflected in panel A of Figure 25.1.

### The Aggregate Demand Curve

We can now use Figure 25.1 to generate the aggregate demand curve from the IS/LM model. In panel A of the figure, the initial price level $P_0$ corresponds to curves $(IS)_0$ and $(LM)_0$, the equilibrium point $E_0$, and real income $y_0$. The resulting price level $P_1$ corresponds to curve $(LM)_1$, the equilibrium point $E_1$, and real income $y_1$.

In panel B, the aggregate demand curve $D$ is determined by graphing each pair of equilibrium values for the price level $P$ and real income $y$ from panel A—such as $\{P_0, y_0\}$ and $\{P_1, y_1\}$. Indeed, in panel A, any given value for $P$ will determine an associated value for $y$, so we can generate the entire aggregate demand curve this way. And because a higher price level reduces the real money supply, the aggregate demand curve is negatively sloped.

Furthermore, since the aggregate demand curve is determined by the IS and LM curves, the aggregate demand curve will shift if any factor— other than the price level—shifts the IS curve or the LM curve. Most

BOX 25.2 MONEY MATTERS

## The Keynesian Approach to Aggregate Demand Management

Factors that shift the IS curve or the LM curve also shift the aggregate demand curve in the same direction. In particular, Keynes emphasized factors that would shift the IS curve to the right, such as consumer optimism (which raises consumption spending) or higher animal spirits for firm managers (which raise investment spending). These factors would cause the aggregate demand curve to shift rightward.

More generally, Keynesians assume that the aggregate demand curve tends to be *unstable*—that is, aggregate demand tends to fluctuate on the basis of shifts in the IS and LM curves. Consequently, Keynesians believe that monetary policy must be used flexibly to offset changes in aggregate demand. That is, when aggregate demand is low, the money supply growth rate should be high, and when aggregate demand is high, the money supply growth rate should be low. This contrasts with the constant money supply growth rate rule that some monetarists recommend (see Box 25.3).

importantly, we will now look at how easy monetary policy and expansionary fiscal policy shift the aggregate demand curve. Boxes 25.2 and 25.3 discuss how shifts in the aggregate demand curve are related to the Keynesian and monetarist approaches to monetary policy and aggregate demand management.

BOX 25.3 MONEY MATTERS

## The Monetarist Approach to Aggregate Demand Management

The monetarist approach to the aggregate demand curve is based on the *quantity theory of money demand* (discussed in Chapter 15). According to the monetarist approach, the money supply is the main variable that shifts the aggregate demand curve. This means that aggregate demand is relatively stable with respect to changes in factors other than the money supply and the price level. Monetarists also stress that the effects of changes in the money supply on aggregate demand may occur with long and variable lags (which we discussed with regard to monetary policy in Chapter 19).

Consequently, some monetarists—in particular Milton Friedman—offer the Federal Reserve a simple prescription for managing the level of aggregate demand: if the money supply grows at a constant rate, this will help stabilize aggregate demand. And as we will see later in this chapter, if aggregate demand grows at a constant rate, then so may the price level.

If the aggregate demand curve does shift due to other factors, then the Federal Reserve may want to change the growth rate of the money supply to offset these shifts. However, monetarists argue that, as a result of the long and variable lags in the effects of monetary policy, such policies may create more harm than good.

## Monetary Policy and Shifts in the Aggregate Demand Curve

We will first look at how easy monetary policy—which shifts the LM curve to the right—causes the aggregate demand curve to shift to the right. In panel A of Figure 25.2, the initial situation is represented by the curves $(IS)_0$ and $(LM)_0$ and the equilibrium point $E_0$. Easy monetary policy then shifts the LM curve to the right, to $(LM)_1$, causing the equilibrium point to shift to $E_1$. Throughout this process, the price level is fixed at $P_0$.

The corresponding shift in the aggregate demand curve is shown in panel B of Figure 25.2. The point $E_0$ is on the initial aggregate demand curve $D_0$ and the point $E_1$ is on the resulting aggregate demand curve $D_1$. Thus, easy monetary policy shifts the aggregate demand curve from $D_0$ to $D_1$.

This process can be repeated for another price level, $P_1$. The result, as shown in panel B, is a second pair of points—$F_0$ and $F_1$—on the aggregate demand curves $D_0$ and $D_1$. So, by repeating the procedure for all price levels, the aggregate demand curves $D_0$ and $D_1$ can be fully determined.

In panel A, easy monetary policy shifts the LM curve from $(LM)_0$ to $(LM)_1$, shifting the equilibrium point from $E_0$ to $E_1$.

FIGURE 25.2

**How Monetary Policy Shifts the Aggregate Demand Curve**

A. The IS/LM Model with Easy Monetary Policy
(With Both LM Curves Based on the Price Level $P_0$)

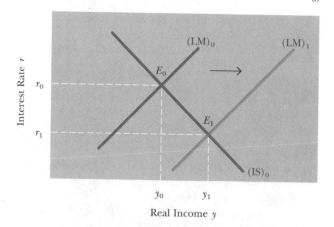

In panel B, points $F_0$ and $F_1$ are similar to $E_0$ and $E_1$, but they are based on the price level $P_1$.

B. The Aggregate Demand Curve

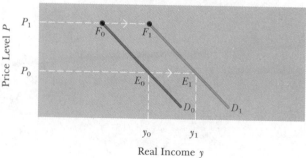

## Fiscal Policy and Shifts in the Aggregate Demand Curve

We will next see that expansionary fiscal policy—which shifts the IS curve to the right—also causes the aggregate demand curve to shift to the right. In panel A of Figure 25.3, the initial situation is represented by curves $(IS)_0$ and $(LM)_0$ and the equilibrium point $E_0$. Expansionary fiscal policy then shifts the IS curve to the right, causing the equilibrium point to shift from $E_0$ to $E_1$. Again, the price level is assumed to remain fixed at $P_0$ throughout the process.

In panel A, expansionary fiscal policy shifts the IS curve from $(IS)_0$ to $(IS)_1$, moving the equilibrium point from $E_0$ to $E_1$.

FIGURE 25.3

**How Fiscal Policy Shifts the Aggregate Demand Curve**

A. The IS/LM Model with Expansionary Fiscal Policy

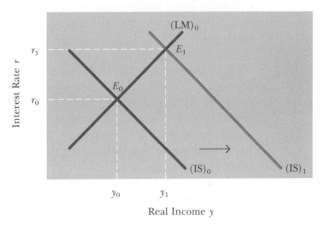

In panel B, points $F_0$ and $F_1$ are similar to $E_0$ and $E_1$, but they are based on the price level $P_1$.

B. The Aggregate Demand Curve

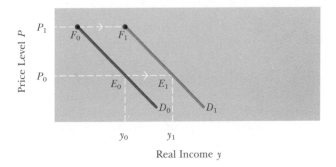

The corresponding shift in the aggregate demand curve is shown in panel B. The initial equilibrium point $E_0$ is on the initial aggregate demand curve $D_0$ and the resulting equilibrium point $E_1$ is on the resulting aggregate demand curve $D_1$. Thus, expansionary fiscal policy shifts the aggregate demand curve from $D_0$ to $D_1$. In a similar fashion, based on other price levels, such as $P_1$, other points—such as $F_0$ and $F_1$—can be determined for the demand curves $D_0$ and $D_1$. Comparing Figures 25.2 and 25.3, we see that easy monetary policy and expansionary fiscal policy both shift the aggregate demand curve to the right.

## Nonactivist and Activist Prescriptions for Monetary Policy

Most versions of the aggregate demand curve share three basic features:

1. The negative slope of the aggregate demand curve represents the negative effect of a higher price level on the real money supply.

2. Easy monetary policy—based on a larger money supply—shifts the aggregate demand curve to the right.

3. Any other factors that shift the IS curve or LM curve to the right—such as autonomous changes in consumption demand, investment demand, or fiscal policy—will also shift the aggregate demand curve to the right.

Nevertheless, economists have different views regarding the implications of these features for monetary policy. This is particularly evident in debates over whether the Fed should use nonactivist or activist monetary policy—also referred to as the issue of *rules versus discretion*.

**Nonactivist monetary policy** conforms to the monetarist money supply growth rate "rule" described in Box 25.3. The notion is that aggregate demand is basically *stable* with regard to changes in factors other than the price level and the money supply. Furthermore, given the lags in the effects of monetary policy, active monetary policies could end up destabilizing aggregate demand.

**Activist monetary policy,** on the other hand, advocates the use of changes in the money supply growth rate to offset shifts in the aggregate demand curve, as illustrated by the Keynesian view described in Box 25.2. The notion here is that aggregate demand tends to be *unstable*, so the Fed should use its *discretion* to intervene with activist monetary policy to offset fluctuations in aggregate demand.

# The Aggregate Supply Curve

The aggregate supply curve represents the quantity of goods that are supplied (or produced) in the economy as a function of the price level. Based on standard microeconomic principles, a firm's supply of a good should rise as the price of the good rises. However, this assumes that *input prices*—the prices paid for *factors of production*, such as labor, materials, and capital—do not also change. This assumption is reasonable for the supply of a single (small) firm, but matters are more complicated for the *aggregate* supply of all firms.

Aggregate supply is more complicated because an increase in the aggregate quantity of goods produced may significantly raise the demand for factors of production, thereby raising input prices. In our discussion, we will focus on labor as the main factor of production and on the wage rate as the corresponding input price.

## Short-Run Aggregate Supply Curves

First consider aggregate supply in a situation in which the nominal wage rate $W$ remains temporarily fixed at the value $W_0$ as firms expand aggregate output. This assumption is most reasonable in the *short run*, before an increase in labor demand is reflected in higher wage rates. The **short-run aggregate supply curve** $S_0$ in Figure 25.4 shows explicitly that it is based on the wage rate $W_0$. The curve is positively sloped as a function of the price level because—given the wage rate $W_0$—higher prices for goods create a larger supply of goods.

Along each short-run aggregate supply curve—with a given wage rate—firms will generally supply more goods when the price level rises. When the wage rate rises, from $W_0$ to $W_1$, the short-run aggregate supply curve shifts leftward (or upward), from $S_0$ to $S_1$, because firms earn lower profits on the goods that they sell.

FIGURE 25.4

**Short-Run Aggregate Supply Curves**

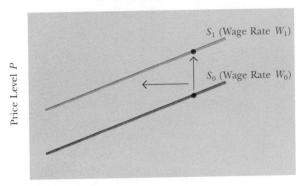

Aggregate Output $y$

Next suppose that the wage rate rises from $W_0$ to $W_1$, as shown also in Figure 25.4 If the price level $P$ is temporarily unchanged, the firms will want to supply fewer goods, because their profit margin (which depends on the difference between the price level and the wage rates) will be reduced. This reduction in the quantity supplied causes the short-run aggregate supply curve to shift leftward (or upward) to $S_1$. (Later, we will look at other factors that may shift supply curves.)

We will now look further at why wage rates change, in order to learn more about why and when short-run aggregate supply curves shift.

## Wage Rate Changes and Full Employment Output

How much and when wage rates rise is mainly determined by the demand/supply balance in the labor market. That is, wage rates will tend to rise more when the demand for labor is high relative to its supply. Since higher demand in the labor market results in *lower unemployment rates*, larger wage rate changes are associated with lower unemployment rates.

This relationship between wage rate changes and unemployment rates is illustrated in Figure 25.5. The negatively sloped curve is called a **Phillips curve**—named after Professor A. W. Phillips, who first documented the relationship. Box 25.4 provides more background on the Phillips curve. Three points are especially noteworthy:

■ Along the Phillips curve, a higher unemployment rate $U$ corresponds to a lower wage rate increase $\Delta W/W$.

■ There is a specific unemployment rate $U_N$—the natural rate of unemployment—at which the demand and supply of labor are in balance. Wage rates tend to remain unchanged at this unemployment rate.

■ For each unemployment rate $U$, there is a corresponding level of real aggregate output $y$. The natural rate of unemployment $U_N$ corresponds to full employment output $y_F$.

The Phillips curve indicates that wage rates rise less rapidly when the unemployment rate is higher. Each unemployment rate also corresponds to a level of aggregate output, higher unemployment rates implying lower levels of aggregate output. The natural rate of unemployment, $U_N$, is the unemployment rate at which the demand and supply of labor are in balance.

FIGURE 25.5
**The Phillips Curve**

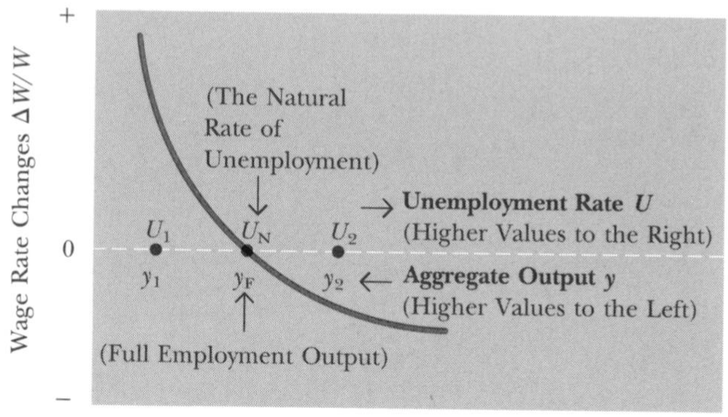

The **natural rate of unemployment** serves as a benchmark for determining whether wage rates are rising or falling, because only at this unemployment rate is there a balance between demand and supply in the labor market.[2] However, this balance includes *frictional unemployment*—people in the process of changing jobs—as described in Chapter 17. This means that the natural rate of unemployment will be a positive number, estimated in the late 1980s to be about 6%.

Each unemployment rate corresponds to a level of aggregate output. Higher levels of real output—which create a higher level of labor demand—correspond to *lower* unemployment rates. This is why, in Figure 25.5, the level of the unemployment rate rises when moving along the horizontal axis to the right, but the level of aggregate output rises when moving along the horizontal axis to the left.

---

[2] Of course, other factors, such as increased labor productivity and expected future inflation, also might affect how much the wage rate changes.

## The Phillips Curve

The *Phillips curve* (illustrated in Figure 25.5) is named after Professor A. W. Phillips, author of the 1958 article that discussed the negative relationship between wage rate changes and unemployment rates in England.

The negative slope of the Phillips curve indicates that at higher unemployment rates, wage rate changes tend to be smaller. The natural rate of unemployment $U_N$ serves as a benchmark for determining whether wage rates will be rising (the unemployment rate is less than $U_N$) or falling (the unemployment rate is greater than $U_N$).

Factors other than the unemployment rate may cause the Phillips curve to shift. For example, a change toward a *younger labor force* may shift the Phillips curve to the right, given that young workers tend to have higher unemployment rates. Also, a *higher expected rate of inflation* may shift the Phillips curve upward (or leftward), given that workers insist on larger wage increases when they expect higher inflation. We will return to these aspects of the Phillips curve later in this chapter and in Chapter 26.

**Full employment output** $y_F$ is the maximum level of output that can occur without wage rates rising. More generally, there is a direct relationship between wage rate changes and the level of output relative to $y_F$:

- Wage rates will be unchanged when actual output equals $y_F$.
- Wage rates will be falling when actual output is less than $y_F$.
- Wage rates will be rising when actual output exceeds $y_F$.

Full employment output thus serves as a benchmark for determining when and how wage rates will change.

### The Long-Run Aggregate Supply Curve

In the context of aggregate supply curves, *long-run equilibrium* refers to a situation in which there is no tendency for wage rates to change at a given price level.[3] Since we have just seen that wage rates will not change when actual output is at the full employment level $y_F$, it follows that the **long-run aggregate supply curve**—which determines long-run equilibrium—will correspond to full employment output.

Figure 25.6, shows the long-run aggregate supply curve together with the two short-run aggregate supply curves from Figure 25.4. The key

---

[3] As in the previous footnote, also other factors, such as expected inflation, might cause wage rates to change.

For the economy to be in long-run equilibrium, nominal wage rates must *not* be changing. This happens only when actual output in the economy equals full employment output. This is why the long-run aggregate supply curve is vertical at full employment output. Points such as $L_0$ and $L_1$ show that the economy can simultaneously lie on a short-run supply curve and on the long-run supply curve.

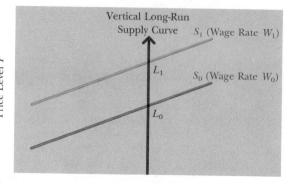

FIGURE 25.6
**The Long-Run Aggregate Supply Curve**

$y_F$ (Full Employment Output)

Aggregate Output

feature of the long-run supply curve is that it is *vertical*—whatever the value of the price level $P$, long-run supply is at the full employment level of output $y_F$. To see why this must be the case, consider the alternative. If long-run supply were more (or less) than full employment output, then wage rates would be rising (or falling), so the situation would not represent a long-run equilibrium.

# Equilibrium Between Aggregate Demand and Aggregate Supply

We will now look at how equilibrium between aggregate demand and aggregate supply develops. We will first consider an economy that starts at a high level of aggregate output, above full employment output $y_F$.

## Equilibrium Adjustment from a High Initial Output

Starting at a high initial output, the economy will pass through several different equilibrium stages:

- **Short-run equilibrium** represents the initial situation, based on the initial wage rate $W_0$, where the aggregate demand curve $D_0$, and the short-run supply curve $S_0$ intersect.

- **Medium-run equilibrium** occurs as the wage rate rises and the short-run supply curve shifts leftward (or upward).

- **Long-run equilibrium** occurs when aggregate demand and short-run supply are equal at $y_F$, so wage rates have no further tendency to change.

### Short-Run Equilibrium

A *short-run equilibrium* is illustrated in Figure 25.7 at point $E_0$, where the aggregate demand curve $D_0$ intersects the initial short-run supply curve $S_0$. The equilibrium price level is $P_0$ and aggregate output is $y_0$. Point $E_0$ is a *short-run* equilibrium because it is *temporary*—since $y_0$ exceeds $y_F$, wage rates will rise and the aggregate supply curve will shift leftward (or upward), so the location of the equilibrium will change.

The initial short-run equilibrium occurs at the intersection of the aggregate demand curve $D_0$ and the short-run supply curve $S_0$, based on the nominal wage rate $W_0$. Because the initial output $y_0$ exceeds full employment output $y_F$, the wage rate will rise. As the wage rate rises, the short-run supply curve shifts upward, leading first to the medium-run equilibrium at point $E_1$, and eventually to the long-run equilibrium at point $E_2$. Point $E_2$ represents long-run equilibrium because the short-run supply curve $S_2$ and the aggregate demand curve $D_0$ intersect on the vertical long-run supply curve.

FIGURE 25.7

**Equilibrium Based on an Initially High Output Level**

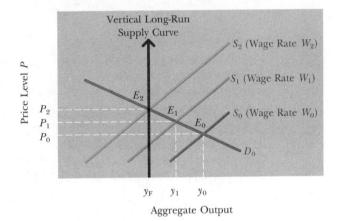

### Medium-Run Equilibrium

As the wage rate rises from $W_0$ to $W_1$, the short-run supply curve will shift leftward (or upward) from $S_0$ to $S_1$, as shown in Figure 25.7. The *medium-run* equilibrium then occurs at point $E_1$, where $S_1$ intersects $D_0$. The medium-run equilibrium is also temporary—since output $y_1$ still exceeds full employment output $y_F$, wage rates continue to rise.

### Long-Run Equilibrium

As the wage rate rises from $W_1$ to $W_2$, the short-run supply curve continues to shift leftward (or upward), eventually reaching curve $S_2$. The curve $S_2$ intersects $D_0$ at the point $E_2$, which corresponds to full employment output $y_F$. Since there is no further tendency for wage rates to change when aggregate output equals $y_F$, point $E_2$ represents the long-run equilibrium.

## Equilibrium Adjustment from a Low Initial Output

We will now look at another case of equilibrium adjustment, but starting with an initial output $y_0$ that is less than full employment output, as shown in Figure 25.8. Here, the wage rate falls and the short-run supply curve shifts rightward (or downward), just the opposite of the previous

The situation is the same as in Figure 25.7, except that the initial output, $y_0$, is less than full employment output, $y_F$. Consequently, wage rates fall, causing the short-run supply curve to shift downward (or rightward). However, the economy reaches the same long-run equilibrium point $E_2$ as in Figure 25.7, because the long-run supply curve is the same vertical line in both cases.

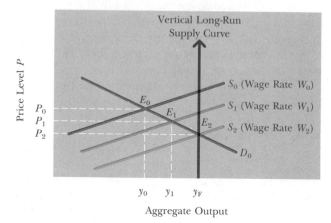

FIGURE 25.8
**Long-Run Adjustment from Low Output Levels**

case. Nevertheless, the long-run equilibrium still occurs at full employment output $y_F$, because the *long-run supply curve* is a *vertical line* at $y_F$.

# Shifts in Aggregate Demand and Aggregate Supply

Since the equilibrium price level and output are determined by the aggregate demand and supply curves, shifts in these curves will change the equilibrium values. We will now look at how this works.

## Shifts in Aggregate Demand

To illustrate the effects of a shift in aggregate demand, we will use easy monetary policy or expansionary fiscal policy, either of which—as we saw earlier—shifts the aggregate demand curve rightward. The effect of these policies is illustrated in Figure 25.9.

Initially, the aggregate demand curve $D_0$ intersects the short-run aggregate supply curve $S_0$ at point $E_0$. Point $E_0$ also represents a long-run equilibrium, because it lies on the long-run supply curve. The initial position is set up this way so that any deviations that occur from full employment output can be attributed to the effects of the monetary or fiscal policies.

Furthermore, we will not have to distinguish between easy monetary policy and expansionary fiscal policy, because each one shifts the aggregate demand curve to the right. However, we will distinguish the short-run effects of the shift in aggregate demand (during which wage rates do not change) from the long-run effects (after wage rates adjust).

### The Short-Run Effects of Increased Aggregate Demand

The short-run effects occur as soon as the policy change shifts the aggregate demand curve to the right, from $D_0$ to $D_1$. A short-run equilib-

The initial point $E_0$ represents both a short-run equilibrium (where the short-run supply curve $S_0$ and the aggregate demand curve $D_0$ intersect) and a long-run equilibrium (on the long-run supply curve). After easy monetary policy or expansionary fiscal policy shifts the aggregate demand curve to $D_1$, the short-run equilibrium occurs at point $E_1$, reflecting higher aggregate output and a higher price level. However, output $y_1$ exceeds full employment output $y_F$, so wage rates will rise and the short-run supply curve will shift upward, eventually reaching long-run equilibrium at point $E_2$.

FIGURE 25.9

**The Equilibrium Effects of Raising Aggregate Demand**

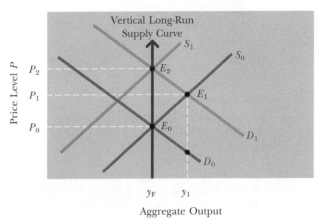

rium is then reached at point $E_1$, where $D_1$ and $S_0$ intersect. Thus, in the short run, easy monetary policy or expansionary fiscal policy raises both aggregate output (or real income) and the price level.

Similarly, in Chapter 24 based on the IS/LM model, we saw that easier monetary policy or expansionary fiscal policy raises *nominal* income $Y$. However, the IS/LM model does not indicate how much of the change in nominal income $Y$ occurs as a change in the price level $P$ and how much occurs as a change in real income $y$. The key advantage of the aggregate supply/aggregate demand model is that it provides separate results for the change in the price level and for the change in real income. On the other hand, only the IS/LM model shows explicitly that easy monetary policy lowers the interest rate while expansionary fiscal policy raises it.

## The Long-Run Effects of Increased Aggregate Demand

The long-run effects of monetary and fiscal policy are illustrated in Figure 25.9. Since aggregate output $y_1$ exceeds full employment output $y_F$ at the short-run equilibrium point $E_1$, wage rates will rise and the supply curve $S_0$ will shift upward. In due course, the long-run equilibrium is determined at point $E_2$, where the short-run supply curve $S_1$ intersects the aggregate demand curve $D_1$ at $y_F$.

We can see in Figure 25.9 that points $E_0$ and $E_2$ are both on the long-run vertical supply curve. Thus, the only long-run effect of easy monetary policy or expansionary fiscal policy is to raise the price level, from $P_0$ to $P_2$. In other words, *these policies have no effect on aggregate output in the long run.*

Since easier monetary policy and expansionary fiscal policy have no long-run effects on aggregate output, the policies must be *crowding out* other components of aggregate demand. Crowding out occurs in the aggregate supply/aggregate demand model because, starting at full employment output, an increase in aggregate demand in one sector of the economy must displace an equal amount of aggregate demand from another sector. Box 25.5 discusses how this occurred in the United States

BOX 25.5 IN DEPTH

## Crowding Out During the Vietnam War

Among its many effects, the Vietnam War raised the demand of the U.S. government for goods and labor (soldiers). Since monetary policy during this period generally tried to keep interest rates from rising, the government's demand for goods and labor could be satisfied only by letting a higher price level crowd out other components of aggregate demand.

Figure 25.10 shows how this developed between 1964 and 1970. The major part of the Vietnam buildup began in 1964, with the unemployment rate at 5.0%—about equal to the natural rate of unemployment at the time—and the inflation rate at the low level of 1.3%. Then, as rising government demand caused the aggregate demand curve to shift to the right between 1965 and 1969, the unemployment rate fell and the inflation rate rose.

By 1969–1970, the major buildup was over, so the unemployment rate rose rapidly (toward the natural rate of unemployment). Also, the inflation rate continued to rise, which became a continuing problem during the 1970s. We will look further at the process of inflation later in this chapter.

during the late 1960s as the Vietnam War escalated. (In comparison, in Chapter 24 based on the IS/LM model, we saw that crowding out occurs when increased government spending reduces investment expenditures due to the effect of higher interest rates.)

## Shifts in Aggregate Supply

Just as the aggregate demand curve may shift in response to monetary policy and fiscal policy, the aggregate supply curve may shift in response to various factors. In fact, we have already made extensive use of one such factor, the change in the wage rate that occurs when actual output differs from full employment output. We will now study how other factors cause the aggregate supply curve to shift. We will see that, generally speaking, aggregate output rises and the price level falls as the aggregate supply curve shifts rightward.

### Improved Productivity

We will first consider a case where **labor productivity**—the amount of goods produced by a given amount of labor—rises due to *better business management techniques*. The initial situation is illustrated at the equilibrium point $E_0$ in Figure 25.11, where the aggregate demand curve $D_0$ intersects the short-run supply curve $S_0$. Higher labor productivity then shifts the short-run supply curve to the right to $S_1$ and the long-run supply curve to the right to $y_F'$ (representing an increase in full employment output).

FIGURE 25.10
**Unemployment Rates and Inflation Rates During the Vietnam War**

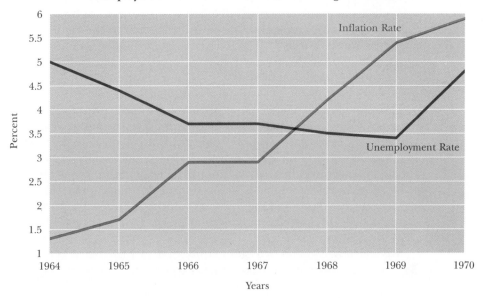

Source: *Economic Report of the President*, February 1988.

FIGURE 25.11
**The Equilibrium Effects of an Increase in Aggregate Supply**

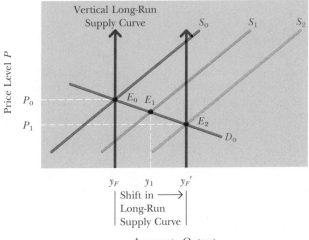

Aggregate Output

The initial equilibrium occurs at point $E_0$ where the curves $S_0$ and $D_0$ intersect. Improved labor productivity causes the short-run supply curve to shift rightward (or downward) to $S_1$, and the long-run supply curve to shift rightward, causing full employment output to rise to $y_F'$. A new short-run equilibrium occurs at point $E_1$ and a new long-run equilibrium occurs at point $E_2$. Thus, in both the short run and the long run, the effect of higher labor productivity is higher output and a lower price level.

In the short run, a new equilibrium is established at point $E_1$, where $D_0$ and $S_1$ intersect. Output thus rises from $y_F$ to $y_1$. However, the output $y_1$ is still less than the resulting full employment output $y_F'$. So wage rates fall, and the short-run supply curve shifts further to the right, eventually reaching the curve $S_2$. The long-run equilibrium is then established at point $E_2$, where $S_2$ intersects the aggregate demand curve $D_0$ at $y_F'$. The effects of higher labor productivity, in both the short and long run, are thus to *raise aggregate output and to reduce the price level*.

More generally, any factors that raise **input productivity**—the amount of aggregate output produced for a given amount of inputs—will shift the aggregate supply curves rightward. For example, technological advances will have the effect of raising the quantity or quality of the goods produced by a given amount of labor. Since higher productivity provides very tangible benefits—output rises and prices fall—policymakers are always looking for ways to raise productivity. In particular, Box 25.6 discusses how changes in productivity are related to **supply-side economic policies.**

We will now look at two other important factors that may shift the aggregate supply curve—labor market conditions and supply shocks.

### Labor Market Conditions

We have been using the natural rate of unemployment, corresponding to full employment output, as the benchmark that determines how and when wage rates change. However, changing conditions in the labor

---

**BOX 25.6 IN DEPTH**

## Supply-Side Economics

The term *supply-side economics* was used during the 1980 presidential campaign of Ronald Reagan to describe a set of policies that he recommended for simultaneously increasing output (and income) and decreasing inflation. As the term suggests, these policies involved shifting the aggregate supply curve in the economy.

Lower marginal tax rates were one of the main instruments recommended. The idea was that lower marginal tax rates would provide workers with an incentive to supply more labor and to work harder (because their after-tax income would be higher). Firms would also have an incentive to increase their capital investment (because their after-tax profits would be higher). Increases in the labor supply and in the stock of capital both cause the aggregate supply curve to shift to the right.

Unfortunately, it is hard to tell whether these policies actually worked. The problem is that other factors in the economy, including the government's budget deficit, the trade deficit, and monetary policy, also had large influences on the economy at the same time.

market can cause the natural rate of unemployment to change, which will cause the short-run and long-run supply curves to shift. Specifically, the long-run vertical supply curve shifts to the right when the natural rate of unemployment falls—because more of the labor supply is then available to produce output. The short-run supply curve shifts to the right under the same circumstances.

A change in the *demographic structure of the population* toward a younger population is a factor that *increases* the natural rate of unemployment. Since young people typically change jobs more frequently than older people, frictional unemployment increases, thus increasing the natural rate of unemployment. The result is that the supply curves shift leftward, aggregate output falls, and the price level rises.

Factors related to changes in the *power of trade unions* may alter the willingness of workers and firms to bear strikes, thus affecting the natural rate of unemployment. For example, the natural rate of unemployment will fall if the policy of trade unions changes so that strikes are called only when actual unemployment rates are very low.

In Box 25.4, we noted that *expected inflation* was a factor that could affect how much nominal wage rates change. That is, if workers (and firms) are expecting higher rates of inflation in the future, then they will negotiate higher increases in nominal wage rates as compensation for the expected loss in the *real wage rate*—the nominal wage rate deflated by the price level. A higher rate of expected inflation thus shifts the short-run supply curve leftward (or upward). It does not, however, affect the long-run supply curve.

### Supply Shocks

**Supply shocks**—changes in input costs other than labor costs—also shift the short-run supply curve. *Positive shocks*—reductions in input prices—shift the supply curve to the right; *negative shocks*—increases in input prices—shift it to the left. The OPEC oil price increases of the 1970s are a good example of negative supply shocks that raised input costs, shifting the short-run supply curve leftward. Bad harvest conditions, a depreciating foreign exchange value of the dollar, and tariffs on imported materials are other examples of negative supply shocks. In all these cases, aggregate output falls and the price level rises.

## Summary: Shifts in Aggregate Supply and Aggregate Demand

The following points compare the effects of an increase in aggregate demand (Figure 25.9) with the effects of an increase in aggregate supply (Figure 25.11):

- The *short-run* effect of an increase in either aggregate demand or aggregate supply is to raise output. However, an increase in aggregate demand tends to raise the price level, whereas an increase in aggregate supply tends to reduce the price level.

- The *long-run* effect of an increase in aggregate demand is that the price level remains permanently higher, while output returns to the full employment level.
- The *long-run* effect of an increase in aggregate supply is that the price level remains permanently lower, while output will be permanently higher (assuming that the long-run supply curve shifts).

# The Process of Inflation

Our analysis of the aggregate supply/aggregate demand model has shown that a higher price level may occur because:

- The aggregate demand curve shifts to the right—due to easy monetary policy, expansionary fiscal policy, or similar factors. In this case, the price level will be permanently higher.
- The short-run aggregate supply curve shifts to the left—due to higher input prices or similar factors. In this case, the price level is temporarily higher.
- The long-run vertical supply curve shifts to the left. The price level is then permanently higher.

If the shift in the aggregate demand curve or aggregate supply curve is a onetime event, then the change in the price level will also be a onetime event. A onetime increase in the price level is sometimes referred to as inflation. However, when economists use the term *inflation,* they generally mean a continuing increase in the price level. In this section, we will look at the factors that may create continuing inflation.

## Aggregate Demand Inflation

**Aggregate demand** inflation (or **demand pull** inflation) is created by rightward shifts in the aggregate demand curve. The old saying, "too much money chasing too few goods," reflects the basic notion of aggregate demand inflation. However, a onetime increase in aggregate demand causes only a onetime increase in the price level. Thus, a series of rightward shifts in aggregate demand is necessary to create continuing aggregate demand inflation.

Shifts in the aggregate demand curve that lead to continuing inflation are illustrated in Figure 25.12. The initial equilibrium is at point $E_0$, where the aggregate demand curve $D_0$ and the long-run vertical supply curve intersect at full employment output $y_F$. (Since we are looking only at continuing price level changes, we will ignore the short-run aggregate supply curves.) If the aggregate demand curve then shifts to the right to $D_1$, the price level will rise from $P_0$ to $P_1$. And if the aggregate demand curve continues to shift to the right, to $D_2$ and then to $D_3$, the price level will continue to rise, to $P_2$ and then to $P_3$. This is how a sequence of shifts in the aggregate demand curve creates continuing inflation.

The initial equilibrium occurs at point $E_0$ where the aggregate demand curve $D_0$ intersects the long-run vertical supply curve at full employment output $y_F$. As the aggregate demand shifts successively to $D_1$, $D_2$, and $D_3$, the price level rises successively to $P_1$, $P_2$, and $P_3$. A sequence of shifts in aggregate demand thus creates a rising price level—continuing inflation.

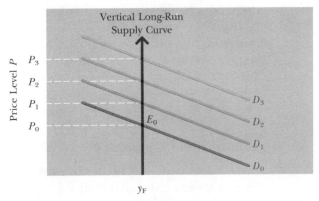

FIGURE 25.12
**Aggregate Demand Curve Shifts and Continuing Inflation**

## Monetary Policy as a Source of Inflation

To identify the possible sources of continuing inflation, we have to look for factors that create a series of shifts in the aggregate demand curve. *Monetary policy* is obviously one such factor. As we saw in Part V, monetary policy is often targeted to the money supply growth rate. So continuing easy monetary policy—higher money supply growth rates—could be the basis of continuing inflation. Indeed, **hyperinflation**—very high inflation rates that may reach several hundred percent per year—invariably involves high growth rates in the money supply. The German hyperinflation in the early 1920s is the most famous case. However, a number of Latin American and other countries have experienced hyperinflation in the 1980s. In all these cases, the money supply rises at about the same rapid rate as the price level.

Does this mean that a rising money supply is always the source of continuing inflation? Not necessarily. There is also the possibility that *inflation causes the money supply to rise,* so a rising money supply might actually be the *result* of inflation, not the *cause.* We will now look at other possible sources of inflation.

## Fiscal Policy as a Source of Inflation

We saw earlier that expansionary fiscal policy, like easy monetary policy, shifts the aggregate demand curve to the right. But only a series of expansionary fiscal policies—continuing increases in government spending or decreases in taxes—could create continuing inflation. In other words, deficits would have to rise continually—a constant deficit would not cause continuing inflation.

However, continuing expansionary fiscal policy means either that government spending continues to rise or that taxes continue to fall. As a consequence, *government spending* would start to encompass *all* aggregate output, or *taxes* would eventually become negative. Putting aside the theoretical question of whether such policies are even possible, politicians who pursued them would obviously not last long in office. Based on such considerations, the prevalent view of economists is that fiscal policy is unlikely to be the source of continuing inflation.

However, it is also possible for expansionary fiscal policy to be the source of a rising money supply, which in turn may create inflation, at least in the medium run. This can happen because, recalling the discussion in Chapter 24, monetary policy and fiscal policy may interact: a federal deficit (expansionary fiscal policy) may be monetized by the Federal Reserve, creating easy monetary policy.

## Supply-Side Influences on Inflation

Since a leftward shift in the aggregate supply curve raises the price level, a series of such leftward shifts could create continuing inflation. However, as with fiscal policy, *continuing* aggregate supply curve shifts are an unlikely scenario: negative supply shocks, such as a bad harvest, tend to be onetime events.

## Cost-Push Inflation

Another possibility for continuing inflation is to combine a leftward shift in the aggregate supply curve with an accommodating monetary policy—called **cost-push inflation.** For example, labor unions may initiate the process by demanding higher wage rates. Since a leftward shift in the aggregate supply curve reduces aggregate output, the Federal Reserve may try to balance this with an easier monetary policy, which then raises the price level. If the process repeats itself, continuing inflation will result.

Cost-push inflation is illustrated in Figure 25.13. The process is initiated by the leftward shift in the short-run supply curve, from curve $S_0$ to curve $S_1$, as unions raise the wage rate from $W_0$ to $W_1$. This causes the equilibrium point to move from $E_0$ to $E_0'$, so that aggregate output falls from $y_F$ to $y_1$ and the price level rises from $P_0$ to $P_0'$. To avert the decline in aggregate output, the Federal Reserve may adopt easier monetary policy, shifting the aggregate demand curve to the right, from $D_0$ to $D_1$. The economy then reaches equilibrium at point $E_1$, with full employment output $y_F$ and the price level $P_1$.

The higher price level at $P_1$ erodes the union's gain from the higher nominal wage rate $W_1$. Thus, to recover the higher *real* wage rate, the union has to try again, by demanding a still higher nominal wage rate, $W_2$. The process could then be repeated, with the short-run supply curve shifting to $S_2$, the aggregate demand curve shifting to $D_2$, and the economy heading to point $E_2$. If the process continues in this fashion, the price level will rise steadily—there is continuing cost-push inflation, which is also called **wage-push inflation.**

Cost-push inflation can be initiated by any factor that creates a leftward shift of the short-run supply curve. For example, firms might cut back on production in order to raise their prices and increase their profits (sometimes called profit-push inflation). Whatever its origins, cost-push

The initial equilibrium occurs at point $E_0$ where curves $S_0$ and $D_0$ intersect. Unions then raise the wage rate to $W_1$, which shifts the short-run supply curve to $S_1$, so the equilibrium moves temporarily to point $E_0'$. However, if the Federal Reserve adopts an easier monetary policy, then the aggregate demand curve shifts to $D_1$, so the equilibrium moves to point $E_1$. There could then be further rounds of wage rate hikes and accommodating monetary policy.

FIGURE 25.13

**Cost-Push Inflation**

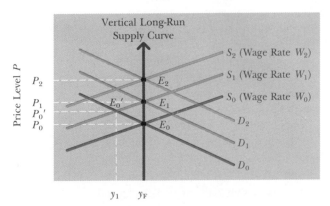

Aggregate Output

inflation continues only because the Federal Reserve adopts an accommodating easier monetary policy. Such policies usually present a costly trade-off: they may avert a temporary fall in aggregate output, but in the long run they create cost-push inflation.

## Summary of Inflation

We have seen that, in one way or another, easy monetary policy is the basic source of **continuing inflation.** As Milton Friedman has put it, "inflation is always and everywhere a monetary phenomenon." Inflation occurs when the Federal Reserve shifts the aggregate demand curve to the right, either to raise aggregate output above the full employment level (aggregate demand inflation) or to avert a temporary reduction in aggregate output (cost-push inflation). Other factors that shift the aggregate demand curve (such as fiscal policy) or shift the aggregate supply curve (such as supply shocks) tend to be onetime events, so they are unlikely to be a source of continuing inflation.

## Chapter Summary

1. Aggregate demand refers to the total amount of goods demanded in the economy. The aggregate demand curve is negatively sloped as a function of the price level, because a higher price level reduces the real money supply. Factors such as easy monetary policy and expansionary fiscal policy shift the aggregate demand curve to the right.

2. Aggregate supply refers to the total amount of goods produced in the economy. The short-run aggregate supply curve—based on a given wage rate for labor—is positively sloped as a function of the price level, because firms will produce more goods as the prices for those goods rise. The long-run aggregate supply curve—which applies in long-run equilib-

rium—is vertical at the level of full employment output.

3. Starting with an initial value for aggregate output that is above or below the full employment level, the economy will pass through a short-run equilibrium (where wage rates do not change), a medium-run equilibrium (where wages and prices start to adjust), and a long-run equilibrium (where there is no further tendency for wages and prices to adjust). In the long-run equilibrium, aggregate output is always equal to full employment output.

4. A rightward shift in the aggregate demand curve has different effects in the short run and the long run. In the short run, aggregate output and the price level both rise. In the long run, aggregate output returns to the full employment level, while the price level is permanently higher.

5. A rightward shift in the aggregate supply curve also has different effects in the short run and the long run. In the short run, aggregate output rises and the price level falls. In the long run, aggregate output returns to the full employment level (which itself may have shifted rightward) and the price level is permanently lower.

6. Continuing increases in the money supply are the main source of continuing inflation. Other factors that shift the aggregate demand curve to the right (such as expansionary fiscal policy) or that shift the aggregate supply curve to the left (such as supply shocks) create only a onetime increase in the price level. Cost-push inflation is a particular form of continuing inflation that arises when easy monetary policy accommodates leftward shifts in the short-run supply curve.

## Key Terms

Activist and nonactivist monetary policy

Aggregate demand curve

Aggregate supply curve:

    Long run

    Short run

Aggregate supply / aggregate demand equilibrium:

    Long run

    Medium run

    Short run

Full employment output

Inflation:

    Aggregate demand (demand pull)

    Continuing

    Cost-push

    Hyperinflation

    Wage-push

Natural rate of unemployment

Phillips curve

Productivity:

    Input

    Labor

Supply shocks

Supply-side economics

## Study Questions

1. What happens to the aggregate demand curve when the Federal Reserve initiates easier monetary policy?

2. What happens to the aggregate demand curve when government spending rises?

3. If labor unions demand (and receive) higher wage rates, what happens to:
   a. the short-run aggregate supply curve
   b. the long-run aggregate supply curve?

4. How are wage rate changes related to full employment output?

5. If the Federal Reserve initiates easier monetary policy, what happens to aggregate output and the price level in:
   a. the short run
   b. the long run?

6. If improved production technology raises the productivity of workers, what happens to aggregate output and the price level in:
   a. the short run
   b. the long run?

7. Is a shift in the aggregate demand curve or the aggregate supply curve the more likely reason why the price level might rise while aggregate output falls?

8. Why are increases in the money supply the primary source of continuing inflation?

9. If bad weather conditions reduce the farm harvest one year, what happens to:
   a. the price level
   b. the inflation rate?

10. How might cost-push inflation start with a supply shock, such as higher oil prices?

## Recommended Reading

*The aggregate demand/aggregate supply model is discussed in each of the standard macroeconomic texts listed at the end of Chapter 23.*

*The following provide an introduction to the large literature on the differences between Keynesians and monetarists:*

Alan S. Blinder, "The Rules-Versus-Discretion Debate in the Light of Recent Experience," *Weltwirtschaftliches Archive*, 1987, pp. 399–414.

Milton Friedman, "The Role of Monetary Policy," *American Economic Review*, March 1968, pp. 1–17.

Thomas Mayer, *The Structure of Monetarism*, Norton, New York, 1978.

Franco Modigliani, "The Monetarist Controversy, or Should We Forsake Stabilization Policy?" *American Economic Review*, March 1977, pp. 1–19.

James Tobin, "The Monetarist Counter-Revolution Today—An Appraisal," *Economic Journal*, March 1981, pp. 29–42.

*The following discuss various aspects of inflation:*

Federal Reserve Bank of Kansas City, *Price Stability and Public Policy*, 1984

Robert E. Hall, editor, *Inflation: Causes and Effects*, University of Chicago Press, Chicago, 1982.

Thomas M. Humphrey, "Changing Views of the Phillips Curve," *Monthly Review*, Federal Reserve Bank of Richmond, July 1973, pp. 2–10.

# 26

# Rational Expectations and Macroeconomic Policy

*"A man always has two reasons for doing anything—a good reason and the real reason."*

*J. P. Morgan*

We have studied many situations where economic decision makers are influenced by their expectations of the future values of economic variables. For example:

- *Expected income affects current consumption and saving.* People who expect higher future income will consume more and therefore save less currently.

- *Expected profits influence current capital investments.* When the expected profits on investments rise, entrepreneurs are encouraged to investment more.

- *Expected interest rates are relevant to security investments.* People who expect lower interest rates in the future may lock in temporarily higher interest rates by purchasing long-term securities.

- *Expected returns on common stocks affect stock purchases.* For a given risk level, higher expected returns—higher capital gains and dividends—raise the demand for common stocks.

- *Expected inflation affects many economic decisions.* One example is that people accelerate current purchases of goods when they expect inflation to raise prices. Another is that workers negotiate higher nominal wages if they expect higher prices in the near future.

In looking at these cases in earlier chapters, we treated each expectation as a given value. In this chapter, we will look at how people form expectations of economic variables and at how these expectations affect the economy's performance.

In this chapter, we will focus on the theory of *rational expectations*—based on the notion that people use all available and relevant information to form their expectations. We will see that the theory of rational expectations has powerful—and often surprising—implications for the effects of economic policy on aggregate output and the price level. In particular, if wages and prices change freely, then due to rational expectations, monetary policy may have no effect on aggregate output.

## Rational Expectations

Let us first consider the familiar situation of a person trying to determine his or her expected income for the following year. Many current economic decisions are based on next year's income, including how much of this year's income can be consumed and how elaborate a vacation can be planned for next year. An accurate estimate of expected income is clearly useful for making such decisions.

What factors do people consider when determining their expected income? The amount of this year's income is obviously one factor. However, this year's income may be unusually high—the person may have won a lottery—or unusually low—the person may have had bad luck. So it is better to compute expected income as an average of past and current income. Expectations computed as an average of the previous values of a variable are called **adaptive expectations**—meaning that the expectation is adapted to experience.

The accuracy of adaptive expectations is limited, however, because only information on previous values of the variable is included. As an alternative, someone may know, for example, that he has been performing exceptionally well on his job and should receive a large pay raise next year. Or another person may work for a firm that pays bonuses on the basis of the firm's profits, so she may expect a large bonus, given her firm is having a good year. These cases show that additional information can often be used to determine expected income more accurately.

**Rational expectations** are formed on the basis of *all available and relevant information*. That is, rational people will apply all useful information to form their expectations. Rational expectations also have two important, and perhaps surprising, features:

1. Rational expectations are *not biased*—the *average error is zero*. If a person tends to overestimate his income each year, for example, then, rationally, he would revise the way he forms his expectations to eliminate the bias.

2. Rational expectations depend on the structure of the economic system. For example, only a person working at a firm that pays profit-sharing bonuses would factor in the firm's profits in determining her expected income.

### Rational Expectations in a Microeconomic Model

Expectations of variables determine how people make decisions. This is particularly true when the outcome of a decision occurs at a later time—such as when a farmer plants a crop in the spring that will be harvested and sold in the fall. How much the farmer decides to plant in the spring will depend on what he expects the crop price to be in the fall.

Rational expectations have been used in models of economic behavior since 1961 when John Muth developed the technique.[1] We will first look at how rational expectations work in a microeconomic model, using an example of Muth's—the market for hogs.

We will suppose that the market price of hogs is determined in the standard fashion by the demand and supply of hogs. As illustrated in panel A of Figure 26.1, the demand for hogs (for pork and bacon) is negatively related to hog prices, and the supply of hogs is positively related to hog prices. In equilibrium, 100,000 hogs are supplied and consumed annually at a price of $5 (per pound).

However, the time it takes to raise hogs should also be considered.

_____

[1] See John Muth, "Rational Expectations and the Theory of Price Movements," *Econometrica* 29 July 1961, pp. 315–335.

Panel A illustrates the long-run equilibrium for the hog market, where demand and supply determine the equilibrium price of $5 per pound and the equilibrium quantity of 100,000 hogs.

FIGURE 26.1
**The Demand and Supply for Hogs**

A. Long-Run Equilibrium

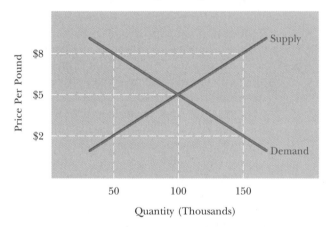

Panel B illustrates the short-run equilibrium after a supply shock—disease wipes out half of the young pigs before they reach the market—so only 50,000 hogs are supplied. The equilibrium price that year is $8 per pound.

B. Short-Run Equilibrium (After Supply Shock)

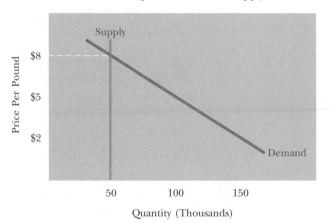

Assuming it takes one year to prepare a hog for market, the number of hogs supplied each year will equal the number of hogs raised the previous year. Therefore, rational farmers will refer to next year's *expected* hog price when deciding how many hogs to raise this year. For example, if the expected price is $5 (per pound), then 100,000 hogs will be brought to market the following year.

Now suppose there is a *supply shock*—disease wipes out half the young pigs—so that only 50,000 hogs can be supplied to the market the next year. This situation is illustrated in panel B of Figure 26.1, where the vertical supply curve indicates that the supply that year equals 50,000 hogs. As a result, the market price for hogs is $8 that year.

How do farmers adjust the number of hogs being raised for the next year's market when they observe the $8 market price for hogs? The answer depends on how farmers determine their expectations of hog prices. We will begin with a simple case of *adaptive expectations*, where the expected hog price for the following year is equal to the actual hog price in the current year. Based on such adaptive expectations, if a supply shock causes the market price to be $8 one year, then the expected price for the following year will also be $8. And given that farmers expect an $8 price, panel A of Figure 26.1 shows that they will step up production to supply 150,000 hogs.

The pattern of hog prices and quantities that evolves from such adaptive expectations is shown in panel A of Figure 26.2. Year 1 reflects the supply shock, so 50,000 hogs are brought to market and the price of hogs is $8. Using adaptive expectations, farmers then expect a price of $8 for year 2, so they raise 150,000 pigs during year 1 and they bring this amount to market in year 2. As a result of this large supply, the market price for hogs during year 2 is only $2.

The hog market continues to operate in this manner, with hog supply and hog prices varying between high and low values in successive years. This peculiar pattern of quantity and prices arises because adaptive expectations are not rational expectations. Indeed, in this simple example, farmers are always wrong about expected hog prices—when they expect a high price ($8), the actual price turns out low ($2), and vice versa. The problem, of course, is that the farmers are not taking into account the market's demand and supply structure.

In contrast, rational hog farmers would recognize that the price jump in year 1 was an unusual event, so they would (if the disease is not expected to be repeated) refer to the normal demand and supply conditions (shown in panel A of Figure 26.1) to form their *rational expectations* for the next year's hog price. The pattern of hog prices and quantities that evolves with rational expectations is shown in panel B of Figure 26.2.

Thus, price expectations determine how a market responds to a supply shock. With adaptive expectations, a supply shock is reflected in prices and quantities for an extended period. With rational expectations, a supply shock is recognized to be a onetime event, so the market quickly returns to its long-run equilibrium. Box 26.1 describes another context—the Phillips curve—in which price expectations play a key role in how a market operates.

Both panels show how quantity and price vary over time after a supply shock occurs in year 1. In panel A, the supply shock reduces the quantity to 50,000 (top) and raises the price to $8 in year 1 (bottom). The actual market price each year then determines the expected price for the following year—a simple form of adaptive expectations. So farmers expect the price in year 2 to remain at $8. Therefore, they raise 150,000 hogs during year 1, causing the hog price in year 2 to be $2. Output and prices then continue to fluctuate in the following years.

FIGURE 26.2

**The Price and Quantity of Hogs After a Supply Shock**

A. Adaptive Price Expectations

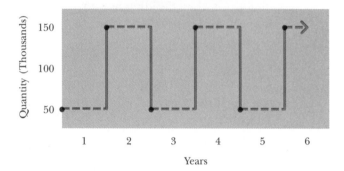

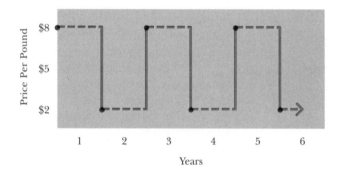

This panel shows how quantity (top) and price (bottom) vary over time based on rational expectations. With rational expectations, the expected price each year equals the market's equilibrium price, $5 (see panel A, Figure 26.1). Even though the supply shock in year 1 raises the price to $8 in year 1, the expected price for year 2 is still $5. Based on a $5 expected price, farmers will raise 100,000 hogs. As a result, $5 is the actual market price in year 2, and this continues for the remaining years.

B. Rational Price Expectations

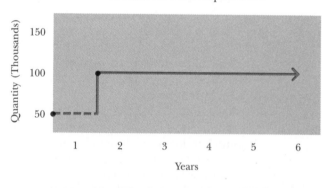

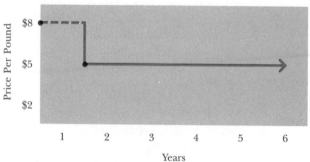

BOX 26.1 IN DEPTH

## Inflation Expectations and the Phillips Curve

Expected inflation can play a key role in the Phillips curve—the relationship between wage rate changes and unemployment rates—that we introduced in Box 25.4 in Chapter 25. Wage rate changes and unemployment rates for the U.S. economy from 1950 to 1987 are shown in Figure 26.3. The Phillips curve shown by the solid line approximates the pattern of points in the lower and lefthand area of the graph, but it does not fit well with the points at the upper right. The second Phillips curve, shown by the dashed line, seems to apply to this second group of points. What is happening?

FIGURE 26.3
**Wage Rate Changes and Unemployment Rates**

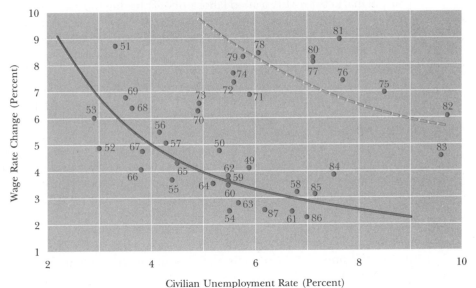

It is noteworthy that all of the points in the upper right part of the figure represent the years from 1970 to 1983, when inflation rates either were rising or were already high. This suggests that the Phillips curve may have shifted rightward (or upward) because workers and firms expected high rates of inflation. With rational expectations, expectations of higher inflation by workers and firms would result in larger increases in nominal wage rates. The name *expectations augmented* Phillips curve is applied to a Phillips curve that shifts in the short run on the basis of changes in the expected inflation rate.

**Source:** *Economic Report of the President*, February 1988.

## Evidence Regarding Rational Expectations

We will now look at whether people's expectations are actually rational in this way. Since people have to understand how the economy (or market) operates to form rational expectations, it is an open question whether they are used in practice.

Unfortunately, one cannot just ask people whether they use rational expectations, since most people will not know the term. Alternatively, we can use surveys to determine people's expectations and then compare the findings to rational expectations. Such tests are often based on expected inflation, because future inflation is relevant to many decisions (as noted in Box 26.1). Surveys of inflation expectations often indicate that the expectations are not rational ones. However, many economists question the accuracy of such tests, suspecting that people are careless, and even untruthful, in answering surveys.

Fortunately, financial market data offer more dependable evidence, which indicates that investors generally do use rational expectations. The financial markets provide a good laboratory for testing the use of rational expectations because new information and new security prices are available on a steady basis. If people are rationally revising their expectations on the basis of new information, then that information should be rapidly reflected in security prices.

The tests of rational expectations look specifically for instances in which relevant information is *not* rapidly reflected in security prices. When this occurs, there is a violation of rational expectations. Of course, millions of bits of new information are released daily in the financial markets, so the evaluation of rational expectations is not based on just occasional violations. Instead, economists look for *systematic violations* of rational expectations—situations in which people systematically ignore information that would have increased their investment profits.

As a result of this research, it is known that systematic violations of rational expectations are rare in financial markets—valuable information is almost always promptly reflected in security prices. But some cases—such as the one described in Box 26.2—still puzzle economists. Many economists suspect that investors will even be found to be rational in these cases—once all the relevant factors have been considered.

# The New Classical Model and Rational Expectations

Based on this encouraging view of rational expectations, we will now look at what happens when rational expectations are included in a macroeconomic model of the economy. In our discussion, we will focus on the price level as the macroeconomic variable for which people might form rational expectations, because the price level is a key determinant of aggregate demand, as shown in Chapter 25.

We will start with a macroeconomic model developed by Robert Lucas and Thomas Sargent, which was among the first to include rational

## Exceptions to Rational Expectations in Security Prices

Economists find few instances in which readily available information about securities can be used to increase investment profits. This is consistent with the use of rational expectations by investors. However, there are a few puzzling patterns in stock prices that may imply untapped profit opportunities.

The best known example is called the **January effect:** common stock prices often rise by an unusually large amount between mid-December and mid-January each year. Although this does not occur every year, it occurs frequently enough that investors could earn extra profits on average by purchasing a portfolio of

stocks every December and selling it every January.

In principle, investors with rational expectations would buy stocks and drive prices up in December, and would sell stocks and drive prices down in January. If investors did this, the January effect would disappear. The fact that the January effect is still observed is thus inconsistent with rational expectations. Of course, it is possible that investors have other good—rational—reasons for not buying stocks in December or selling them in January. It may just be that economists have not yet discovered them.

expectations. It is called the **new classical model** because it shares a key assumption—that wages and prices are free to change—with the standard classical model. The distinctive result of the new classical model is that monetary policy may have no effect in changing aggregate output.

To develop this analysis, we will apply the aggregate demand/aggregate supply model of Chapter 25, shown here in Figure 26.4. We will first summarize our earlier results regarding monetary policy, which did not take rational expectations into account.

The initial equilibrium at point $E_0$ is based on the aggregate demand curve $D_0$ and the short-run aggregate supply curve $S_0$. Easy monetary policy shifts the aggregate demand curve rightward to $D_1$, causing the long-run equilibrium to move to point $E_2$. Without rational expectations, the economy makes intermediate stops at points such as $E_1$ before it reaches the new long-run equilibrium at point $E_2$. With rational expectations, people immediately recognize that monetary policy will raise the price level to $P_2$, so they take actions that cause the economy to jump to the equilibrium point $E_2$.

FIGURE 26.4
**Monetary Policy with Rational Expectations**

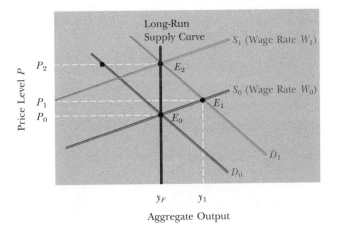

Aggregate Output

The initial equilibrium in Figure 26.4 occurs at point $E_0$, based on the aggregate demand curve $D_0$ and the short-run aggregate supply curve $S_0$. Easy monetary policy causes the aggregate demand curve to shift to the right, from $D_0$ to $D_1$, so a new short-run equilibrium is determined at point $E_1$. At point $E_1$, aggregate output $y_1$ exceeds full employment output $y_F$, so wage rates will rise, causing the short-run supply curve to shift upward (or leftward) toward $S_1$. The long-run equilibrium then occurs at point $E_2$, reflecting a higher price level and full employment output $y_F$.

## Monetary Policy in the New Classical Model

We now consider how monetary policy works in the new classical model. Initially, the expected price level would equal the actual price level $P_0$, given that there is no information indicating that the price level will change. But once it is known that the money supply will increase as a result of easy monetary policy, people will rationally raise their expectation of the future price level to $P_2$—the price level that will actually result from the monetary policy.

With rational expectations, the economy moves rapidly, possibly even instantaneously, to point $E_2$. The reason is that people will take two main actions when they expect a higher price level:

- Workers will try to raise their nominal wage rates in line with the expected rise in the price level from $P_0$ to $P_2$. (Otherwise they will suffer a decline in their real wage rate.) As a result, the short-run supply curve shifts upward from the initial position $S_0$ to the final position $S_1$, and the price level rises from $P_0$ to $P_2$.

- Firms and consumers in the economy who were planning on purchasing goods at a later date will accelerate their purchases when they expect the price level to rise. That is, they will try to buy the goods at the lower initial price level $P_0$. This creates an increase in aggregate demand until the price level reaches $P_2$.

## Anticipated and Unanticipated Monetary Policy

The special effects of monetary policy in the new classical model arise because people revise their rational expectations of the price level on the basis of the expected monetary policy. In practice, of course, people may find that it is difficult to determine whether the Federal Reserve has initiated a new monetary policy. Among other things, the Fed is usually highly secretive about its policy. On the other hand, we saw in discussing monetary policy in Part V that Fed watchers specialize in interpreting the Fed's actions. To cover the possibilities, we will consider two situations—anticipated and unanticipated monetary policy.

**Anticipated monetary policy** occurs when people expect the Fed to carry out a specific action and it does. Suppose the unemployment rate has been fluctuating between 7% and 9%, for example, and that the Fed has been shifting to an easy monetary policy every time the rate rises above 8%. When the unemployment rate again rises above 8% and the easy policy goes into effect, it represents anticipated monetary policy.

**Unanticipated monetary policy** occurs when people are surprised by the Fed's policy action. An example would occur in the situation just described if the Fed unexpectedly did not adopt an easy monetary policy until the unemployment rate reached 8.5%.

## The Policy Ineffectiveness Proposition

The distinction between anticipated and unanticipated monetary policy is central to the **policy ineffectiveness proposition:**

> *Anticipated* increases in the money supply raise the price level but leave aggregate output unchanged.

> *Unanticipated* increases in the money supply raise both the price level and aggregate output.

We will now look at the basis of this proposition.[2]

The difference between anticipated and unanticipated monetary policies is illustrated in Figure 26.5. Time is measured on the horizontal axis, with the dates—$T_0$, $T_1$, $T_2$—corresponding to the times at which the equilibrium points $E_0$, $E_1$, and $E_2$ in Figure 26.4 are reached. In both panels of Figure 26.5, easier monetary policy is initiated at time $T_0$.

[2] See Thomas Sargent and Neil Wallace, "Rational Expectations, the Optimal Monetary Instrument, and the Optimal Money Supply Rule," *Journal of Political Economy* 83, April 1975, pp. 241–254.

Panel A illustrates the case of anticipated monetary policy. Since the policy is anticipated to occur at time $T_0$, workers immediately negotiate higher wages and consumers immediately accelerate their purchases of goods. As a result, the price level immediately rises to the long-run equilibrium $P_2$, and aggregate output never changes from the full employment level $y_F$.

FIGURE 26.5
**The Effects of Anticipated and Unanticipated Monetary Policy**

A. Anticipated Monetary Policy

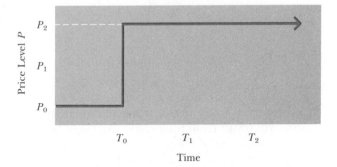

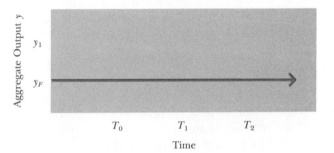

Panel B illustrates the case of unanticipated monetary policy. Because people are unaware of the new policy initiated at time $T_0$, they take action only when the policy is revealed by higher aggregate output. Workers then negotiate higher wages and consumers accelerate their goods purchases. This is why the price level rises to $P_2$ and aggregate output returns to the full employment level $y_f$ at $T_1$.

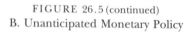

FIGURE 26.5 (continued)
B. Unanticipated Monetary Policy

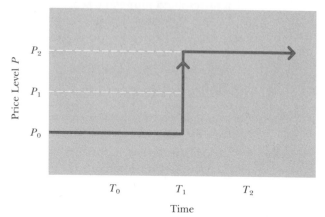

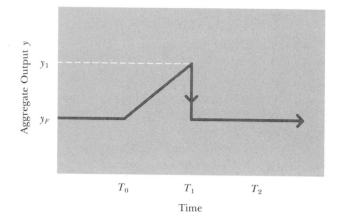

## The Effects of Anticipated Monetary Policy

The effects of *anticipated* monetary policy are illustrated in panel A of Figure 26.5. Because people expect easy monetary policy to be initiated at time $T_0$, they take action in anticipation of the higher price level that will result from the policy. That is, workers negotiate higher wages, and consumers accelerate their goods purchases. As a result, the equilibrium point $E_2$ and the price level $P_2$ are reached immediately, and aggregate output never changes from the full employment level $y_F$. Thus anticipated monetary policy immediately raises the price level and has no effect on aggregate output.

## The Effects of Unanticipated Monetary Policy

The effects of *unanticipated* easy monetary policy are illustrated in panel B of Figure 26.5. In this case, the easy monetary policy initiated at time $T_0$ comes as a surprise to people. Indeed, they will probably remain unaware of the policy until well after it is initiated, because the Federal Reserve is slow to release this information.

Only when people see that output is rising might they surmise that an easy monetary policy was initiated earlier. They will then—at time $T_1$—revise their rational expectations of the price level and act on this information. By this time, however, the monetary policy will have already caused aggregate output to rise.

Once they recognize that the easy monetary policy has been invoked, people will negotiate higher wages and accelerate their consumption purchases. At time $T_1$, therefore, the price level will rise to $P_2$ and aggregate output will fall to full employment output $y_F$. Consequently, unanticipated easy monetary policy affects aggregate output in the short run only, while in the long run (after time $T_1$) output returns to the full employment level and only the price level is permanently higher.

The new classical model predicts, therefore, that only unanticipated monetary policy has an effect on aggregate output, and then only in the short run. This has led economists to consider what other factors might account for the observed fluctuations in aggregate output, as recounted in the *real business cycle* debate in Box 26.3.

BOX 26.3 IN DEPTH

## The Theory of the Real Business Cycle

Fluctuations in aggregate output are usually described in terms of the *business cycle*—deviations in aggregate output from its long-run trend. The aggregate supply/aggregate demand model—developed in Chapter 25—indicates that aggregate output can fluctuate in the short run as the result of changes in any factors that shift the aggregate demand or aggregate supply curves. In particular, monetary policy has been considered a source of business cycles.

According to the new classical model, however, monetary policy has a limited effect on aggregate output. As an alternative, a **theory of the real business cycle** has been developed, attributing fluctuations in aggregate output primarily to shifts in the aggregate supply curve. According to this theory, technological innovations account for most of the observed fluctuations.

Another view—that of the nonclassical model, which we will look at shortly—is that wages and prices do *not* change as freely as assumed by the new classical model. In this case, monetary factors may still play an important role in explaining business cycles.

## The Federal Reserve and Anticipated Monetary Policy

The possibility that anticipated monetary policy will have no impact on aggregate output creates a quandry for the Federal Reserve. As with most large institutions, the Fed prefers to operate by established rules.

But if it uses rules for setting monetary policy, then people will learn about them and will anticipate the Fed's actions. As a result, the policy may have no effect on aggregate output.

Of course it is an exaggeration to say that monetary policy can be *perfectly* anticipated and that it thereby has *no* effect on aggregate output. Nevertheless, the new classical model represents a real challenge for the Federal Reserve. What can the Fed do about it? Unfortunately, not a great deal.

One apparently clever solution is for the Fed *not* to use any established rules. That is, it could determine monetary policy on a case-by-case basis. But for this to work, the Fed would also have to act in an *inconsistent* fashion. Otherwise, people could still figure out its implicit criteria and so anticipate its actions.

This may lead the Fed to design a *variable* monetary policy—at one time implementing a given policy under certain conditions, at another time implementing the policy under different conditions. For example, in using easier monetary policy in response to a rising unemployment rate, the Fed might sometimes initiate the easier policy when the unemployment rate reaches 7.5%, at other times when it reaches 8.0%, and at still other times only when it reaches 8.5%.

The problem with this approach is that if action is postponed until the unemployment rate reaches 8.5%, the Fed's lack of action at the time it was anticipated may actually cause *aggregate output to fall*. People would have expected the policy to be undertaken sooner—when the unemployment rate is 8%. So when the Fed fails to act at the 8% rate, the effect is *as if a tighter monetary policy* were being initiated at that time. Box 26.4 and Figure 26.6 illustrate this with a specific scenario.

The outcome is that easy monetary policy is either anticipated (in which case it may not affect output at all) or it is variable (in which case output may actually be reduced). What can the Federal Reserve do? Proponents of the new classical model draw a simple conclusion: the Fed should *not try* to use monetary policy to change aggregate output. Recalling the discussion of nonactivist and activist monetary policy in Chapter 25, this is the *nonactivist* policy conclusion of the new classical model.

## Anticipated Monetary Policy and Inflation Fighting

Although the new classical model indicates that monetary policy is *ineffective in changing aggregate output*, the same model indicates that monetary policy can be particularly *effective in fighting inflation*. Indeed, the more tight monetary policy is anticipated, the more effective it is for inflation fighting. This happens because monetary policy has its greatest effect on the price level when the economy reaches its long-run equilibrium. Since the economy reaches the long-run equilibrium most rapidly when monetary policy is fully anticipated, an anti-inflation policy will work most rapidly in this case.

BOX 26.4 MONEY MATTERS

## When the Fed Fails To Carry Out the Expected Policy

We have seen that the Fed's monetary policy can be ineffective—it can fail to influence aggregate output—if the policy is anticipated. A possible remedy is for the Fed sometimes *not* to carry out the expected monetary policy. However, a potentially serious problem can then occur: the Fed's inaction may actually cause aggregate output to fall.

Figure 26.6 shows a specific example. The initial equilibrium at point $E_0$ is based on the aggregate demand curve $D_0$ and the short-run aggregate supply curve $S_0$. Easy monetary policy would then cause the aggregate demand curve to shift to $D_1$. If people anticipated this policy, then the short-run supply curve would shift to

$S_1$, resulting in the long-run equilibrium at point $E_2$.

If the Fed fails to initiate the expected easy monetary policy, then the aggregate demand curve will not shift to $D_1$—it will remain at $D_0$. However, based on the *expectation of easier monetary policy*, the supply curve may still shift temporarily to $S_1$. A new equilibrium would then occur at point $E_1$, where the demand curve $D_0$ and the short-run supply curve $S_1$ intersect. At this point, aggregate output $y_1$ is below the initial full employment level $y_F$; so the Fed's action—or inaction—has the perverse result that aggregate output actually falls.

FIGURE 26.6
**Monetary Policy with Perverse
Aggregate Output Effects**

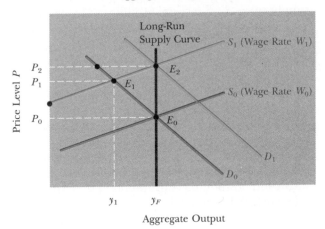

This process is illustrated in Figure 26.7. The initial position is point $E_0$, where the short-run aggregate supply curve $S_0$ and the aggregate demand curve $D_0$ intersect. Because the initial output $y_0$ exceeds full employment output $y_F$, there is initially pressure for the price level to rise. As a result the Federal Reserve may implement a tight monetary

The initial equilibrium at point $E_0$ reflects inflationary pressure, because aggregate output $y_0$ is greater than full employment output $y_F$. A tight monetary policy then shifts the aggregate demand curve leftward to $D_1$. If the monetary policy is unanticipated, the approach to the new long-run equilibrium will be relatively slow: the economy will pause at point $E_1$ before reaching the long-run equilibrium at point $E_2$. In contrast, if the monetary policy is anticipated, the economy will move immediately from the initial point $E_0$ to the long-run equilibrium at point $E_2$.

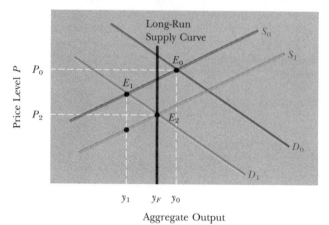

FIGURE 26.7
**Monetary Policy and Inflation Fighting**

policy in order to shift the aggregate demand curve leftward to $D_1$. A new long-run equilibrium will then be established at point $E_2$, representing a lower price level. The question then is *how rapidly* the economy reaches this long-run equilibrium. We will see that the answer depends on whether the anti-inflation policy is anticipated or not.

If the policy is *unanticipated,* the approach to the long-run equilibrium will be relatively slow. The economy will first move toward point $E_1$, where the aggregate demand curve $D_1$ intersects the short-run aggregate supply curve $S_0$. Since the economy is below full employment output $y_F$ at point $E_1$, wage rates will fall and the short-run aggregate supply curve will shift down to $S_1$. Following this shift, the economy will move toward the long-run equilibrium at $E_2$. Since each step takes time, the approach to the long-run equilibrium is relatively slow.

In contrast, if the policy is *anticipated,* then the approach to the long-run equilibrium will be rapid, perhaps even instantaneous. The reason is that people will know immediately that a new long-run equilibrium is to be established at point $E_2$. Thus, just as people immediately take action that increases the inflation rate when easy monetary policy is anticipated, they will immediately take action—reducing the pressure for higher wages and postponing consumption purchases—that lowers the inflation rate when tight monetary policy is anticipated.

Anticipated tight monetary policy has the further advantage for inflation fighting that aggregate output will not fall below the full employment level $y_F$. In contrast, as illustrated in Figure 26.7, unanticipated monetary policy first reduces output to $y_1$ (below full employment output $y_F$), before the economy proceeds to the long-run equilibrium at $E_2$. It is thus advantageous for the Fed to have people anticipate its policy. This might seem easy to accomplish: the Fed could simply announce its intention of carrying out tight monetary policy in order to reduce the inflation rate. However, such announcements also have to be *credible*—

## Inflation Fighting During the Early 1980s

When Paul Volcker became chairman of the Board of Governors of the Federal Reserve in 1979, inflation was already at double-digit levels and seemed to be escalating. So, as we saw in Chapter 20, he introduced a tight monetary policy with the goal of eliminating inflation.

Volcker recognized that *anticipated* tight monetary policy is advantageous for inflation fighting. So he publicly announced the goal of the monetary policy and indicated that it would continue until the federal government's budget was balanced—a realistic point that made the policy seem more credible. By 1982, the inflation rate was dramatically lower and an easier monetary policy was adopted.

The rapid decline in the inflation rate following Volcker's action shows that an anticipated and credible tight monetary policy can be very effective in fighting inflation. However, the deep recession that accompanied the tight policy during 1981 is not consistent with the new classical model. That is, according to the new classical model, anticipated monetary policy should not depress aggregate output below the full employment level.

people have to believe that the Federal Reserve will actually carry through with them.

Because tight monetary policy reduces aggregate output (even *anticipated* tight policy reduces output to the full employment level), people may suspect that the Fed will not carry through with it—the anti-inflation policy may not be credible. For a tight monetary policy to be credible and anticipated, the Federal Reserve must convince people that it will not discontinue the policy after aggregate output starts falling. Box 26.5 discusses this aspect of tight monetary policy based on the Federal Reserve's inflation fighting experience during the 1980s.

## Summary of the New Classical Model

We can now see why the new classical model is both new and classical. It is *new* because it assumes that people behave on the basis of *rational expectations*. It is *classical* because it assumes that *wages and prices can change freely*.

In the new classical model, *anticipated* monetary policy has a rapid effect on the price level, but a limited and possibly zero effect on aggregate output. Anticipated tight monetary policy is thus effective for inflation fighting.

In contrast, *unanticipated* monetary policy may have a significant short-run effect on aggregate output, while any effect it has on the price level is delayed. Unanticipated *easy* monetary policy may thus be effective for increasing aggregate output, at least in the short run.

# Rational Expectations in Nonclassical Models

Rational expectations are part of nonclassical models as well as new classical models. The difference between new and nonclassical models concerns the flexibility of wages and prices. In new classical models, wages and prices are fully **flexible**—they are free to change at any time—to restore market equilibrium. In **nonclassical models** wages and prices are "sticky"—they are not immediately flexible.

To learn about nonclassical models, we will first examine why wages and prices might be sticky. Then we will consider how monetary policy works in such models.

## Sources of Sticky Wages and Prices

*Sticky wages and prices* respond slowly to changing market demand and supply conditions. If there is high unemployment in the labor market, for example, then wage rates may decline gradually. Or, if the demand for a good falls, the relative price of the good may decline gradually.

Why do some economists feel that sticky wages and prices are a normal feature of the U.S. economy? *Long-term labor contracts* are the most commonly cited reason. For example, three-year contracts are common in many unionized industries. With long-term contracts, wages cannot change in response to new conditions during the life of the contract.

Labor contracts also tend to be *staggered* over time—they expire at different dates. Thus, during any given year only about one-third of all three-year contracts will expire, and during any given month only about 1/36 of these contracts will expire. As a result, if conditions in the economy change, causing all unions to want higher wage rates, most of the unions will have to wait a substantial time—even three years if they are unlucky enough to have just signed a new contract—before their contract expires and they can negotiate higher wage rates.

Although only about 20% of the U.S. labor force is unionized, major union contract settlements often set the standard for changes in the wage rates of nonunionized workers as well. So nonunion wage rates can be sticky in conformity with union wage rates. Also nonunionized workers and firms often act as if they had an *implicit contract*—an understanding about how and when wage rates can be changed—even though there is no legally binding agreement.

If firms determine product prices as a function of labor costs, sticky *prices* can occur as a result of sticky wage rates. For example, firms may use *mark-up pricing*—setting each good's price so that it exceeds the labor costs of production by a constant percentage. Although mark-up pricing is generally not consistent with full profit maximization, it seems to play an important role in the pricing policies of many firms. So, sticky wage rates may imply sticky prices.

Thus there is a plausible, if not decisive, case that wages and prices in the U.S. economy may be sticky when there is a change in economic conditions.

## Monetary Policy in Nonclassical Models

We will now look at how monetary policy works in a nonclassical model that combines rational expectations with sticky wages and prices. We will focus on how monetary policy influences the level of aggregate output and the price level.

### Monetary Policy and Aggregate Output

We will start by examining how monetary policy affects aggregate output in a nonclassical model. We will apply the same aggregate demand/aggregate supply model we have been using for the new classical model, but we will now include the effects of sticky wages and prices.

Easy monetary policy in a nonclassical model is illustrated in Figure 26.8. The initial position at point $E_0$ represents a long-run equilibrium determined by the aggregate demand curve $D_0$ and the aggregate supply curve $S_0$. Easy monetary policy then shifts the aggregate demand curve rightward, to $D_1$. What happens next then depends on whether the monetary policy is anticipated or unanticipated.

When the easy monetary policy is *unanticipated*, the results with the nonclassical model are basically the same as the results with the new classical model. The economy will first move to the equilibrium at point $E_1$, where the short-run aggregate supply curve $S_0$ intersects the aggregate demand curve $D_1$. As a result, aggregate output rises to the level $y_1$. Since output $y_1$ exceeds full employment output $y_F$, wage rates will rise, causing the aggregate supply curve to shift upward. Eventually the aggregate supply curve will reach $S_1$ and the economy will reach the long-run equilibrium at point $E_2$.

When easy monetary policy is *anticipated*, the results of the nonclassical and new classical models differ. With the *new classical* model, the economy immediately moves to the new long-run equilibrium—point $E_2$ in Figure 26.8—because people form rational expectations that the price level will rise to the new value of $P_2$. This result of the new classical model requires, of course, that wages and prices be flexible.

The initial equilibrium point $E_0$ is based on the aggregate demand curve $D_0$ and the short-run aggregate supply curve $S_0$. Easy monetary policy shifts the aggregate demand curve to $D_1$ and moves the long-run equilibrium to point $E_2$.

If the easy monetary policy is unanticipated, then the economy will adjust in the same way in the new classical and nonclassical models, with an intermediate stop at point $E_1$. If the easy monetary policy is anticipated, then the adjustment in a nonclassical model is slower than in a new classical model.

FIGURE 26.8

**Monetary Policy in the Nonclassical Model**

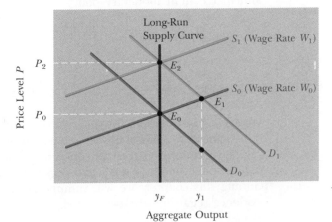

Aggregate Output

With anticipated monetary policy in a *nonclassical* model, people also form the rational expectation that the price level will rise to $P_2$. However, since wages and prices are sticky, the economy cannot move immediately to the new long-run equilibrium. Indeed, in an extreme case, the initial wage rate $W_0$ may not change at all. As a result, the short-run aggregate supply curve will remain at $S_0$ and the economy will move toward the short-run equilibrium at point $E_1$, the same point that is reached when monetary policy is unanticipated. This is the basis for the key conclusion of the nonclassical model—*anticipated easy monetary policy may raise the level of aggregate output in the short run.*

Of course, as labor contracts expire, wage rates will be negotiated at the level $W_1$ (corresponding to the long-run equilibrium price level $P_2$) and the economy will move to the long-run equilibrium at point $E_2$ (with output equal to full employment output). Thus, in both the new classical and nonclassical models, monetary policy cannot cause aggregate output to deviate from the full employment level *in the long run.*

### Inflation Fighting in a Nonclassical Model

We will now look at how sticky wages and prices affect inflation fighting in a nonclassical model. Recall that, for the new classical model, as long as tight monetary policy is anticipated (and credible), it will rapidly reduce the inflation rate, without reducing aggregate output (below full employment output). We will now see that in a nonclassical model, inflation fighting does not proceed this rapidly.

The problem of fighting inflation in a nonclassical model is that wages and prices are sticky. Staggered labor contracts illustrates the point clearly. If the Fed initiates a tight monetary policy, but new wage negotiations occur only periodically, then the inflation rate will only fall gradually. In addition, because tight monetary policy shifts the aggregate demand curve leftward, aggregate output may fall temporarily, as we illustrated earlier in Figure 26.6

These results of anticipated tight monetary policy in a nonclassical model—that inflation rates fall gradually and that aggregate output may fall—is the same pattern we saw earlier for *unanticipated* monetary policy in both the new classical and nonclassical models. The special feature of anticipated tight monetary policy in a nonclassical model is that sticky wages and prices limit the speed at which the inflation rate can fall.

## Rational Expectations Models: Evidence and Results

We have now studied two models that incorporate rational expectations—the new classical model and a nonclassical model—and have developed a number of results concerning the effects of anticipated and unanticipated monetary policy on aggregate output and prices. In concluding this chapter, we will summarize these results and look at the evidence regarding the two models.

## A Summary of the New Classical and Nonclassical Models

The effects of monetary policy in the new classical and nonclassical models are summarized in Table 26.1. The first part of the table shows how effective easy monetary policy is for raising aggregate output in the *short run*. We focus on the short run because monetary policy does not cause aggregate output to deviate from the full employment level in the long run in either model.

In both models, *unanticipated* easy monetary policy raises aggregate output. That is, easy monetary policy raises aggregate demand, and given that people are initially unaware of the policy, some of the increased demand is reflected in increased output. (In the long run, increased aggregate demand is reflected only in higher prices.)

However, the two models differ in the effect of *anticipated* monetary policy on aggregate output. In the new classical model, people form rational expectations of the new price level, and the economy immediately moves to the new equilibrium—so aggregate output never varies from the full employment level. In the nonclassical model, people form the same rational expectations of the future price level, but wages and prices are sticky, so some of the increase in aggregate demand is reflected in higher aggregate output in the short run.

The effectiveness of tight monetary policy in reducing inflation is shown in the second part of Table 26.1. We again focus on the short-run effects, because monetary policy has the same, strong, long-run effect on the price level in both models.

In both models, *unanticipated* tight monetary policy cannot eliminate inflation in the short run, because people are not immediately aware of the policy. For the same reason, unanticipated tight monetary policy may cause aggregate output to fall in the short run. (In the long run, of course, aggregate output will equal full employment output.)

**TABLE 26.1**
**Monetary Policy, Inflation, and Aggregate Output in the Short Run**

|  | Does Easy Policy Raise Aggregate Output? | |
| --- | --- | --- |
| Unanticipated monetary policy | | |
| New classical model | Yes | |
| Nonclassical model | Yes | |
| Anticipated monetary policy | | |
| New classical model | No | |
| Nonclassical model | Yes | |

|  | Does Tight Policy Eliminate Inflation? | Does Tight Policy Depress Aggregate Output? |
| --- | --- | --- |
| Unanticipated monetary policy | | |
| New classical model | No | Yes |
| Nonclassical model | No | Yes |
| Anticipated monetary policy | | |
| New classical model | Yes | No |
| Nonclassical model | No | Yes |

However, the two models differ in the effect of *anticipated* tight monetary policy on inflation and aggregate output. In the new classical model, based on rational expectations of the new equilibrium price level, inflation can be stopped immediately, and aggregate output never falls below the full employment output. In the nonclassical model, people form the same rational expectations, but wages and prices are sticky, so inflation continues in the short run and aggregate output may fall temporarily.

An evaluation of the new classical and nonclassical models can be based on either their assumptions or their results. We will first look at the evidence regarding their assumptions.

## The Assumptions

The two models differ in a key assumption: the new classical model assumes flexible wages and prices, while the nonclassical model assumes sticky wages and prices. Wages and prices in the U.S. economy might seem to be sticky because they are not always changing. However, it is not easy to tell whether wages and prices change sporadically because they are sticky (with factors such as long-term contracts acting as impediments to change) or because there is no reason to change them most of the time (they are already at the long-run equilibrium level). For these and similar reasons, it is hard to evaluate the two models on the basis of their assumptions.

## The Results

We have already summarized the results of the new classical and nonclassical models in Table 26.1. Most tests that try to evaluate the two models are based, in one way or another, on one key point of comparison:

According to the *new classical model,* anticipated monetary policy should *not* affect aggregate output.

According to a *nonclassical model,* anticipated monetary policy should affect aggregate output—easy policy should increase output and tight policy should reduce it.

To evaluate the two models on this basis, it is essential to determine whether each implementation of monetary policy is *anticipated or unanticipated.* Suppose that an easy monetary policy is initiated, for example, and that aggregate output appears to be rising as a result. If the policy were anticipated, then this outcome would provide evidence in favor of the nonclassical model. So to evaluate the models, we must be able to distinguish between anticipated and unanticipated monetary policy. Economists have developed statistical techniques to do this. Each actual change in the money supply is separated into two parts—the anticipated change (the change people were expecting) and the unanticipated change (the difference between the actual change and the expected change). It is then possible to determine whether anticipated changes are associated with changes in aggregate output.

Using this methodology, Robert Barro provided evidence in 1977 that supported the new classical model.[3] Barro's results showed that unanticipated changes in the money supply had significant effects on aggregate output, while anticipated changes had no discernible effects. This was strong evidence in favor of the new classical model.

However, in the large number of studies that have followed Barro's effort, anticipated monetary policy has frequently been found to have effects on aggregate output. So, the extent to which anticipated monetary policy affects aggregate output remains hotly contested.

Where does this leave us? The new classical model has had a major impact on how economists evaluate the likely effects of monetary policy. Most economists now consider rational expectations and the distinction between anticipated and unanticipated monetary policy to be central to macroeconomic analysis. However, these features of the new classical model are also part of the nonclassical model. So the dispute really centers on the assumption that distinguishes the two models—the extent to which wages and prices are flexible. There are two possible conclusions:

- Based on flexible wages and prices, anticipated easy monetary policy will not raise aggregate output.

- Based on sticky wages and prices, anticipated easy monetary may raise aggregate output in the short run.

We should also not forget that the new classical and nonclassical models agree on three other key features of monetary policy:

1. In the short run, unanticipated monetary policy can affect aggregate output.

2. In the long run, the economy will operate at full employment output.

3. Anticipated monetary policy will be more effective than unanticipated policy in inflation fighting.

[3] See Robert J. Barro, "Unanticipated Money, Output, and the Price Level in the United States," *Journal of Political Economy* 86, August 1978, pp. 549–580.

## Chapter Summary

1. Adaptive expectations of an economic variable are based on current and past values of the variable. Rational expectations are based on all available and relevant information. Rational expectations have two important features: (a) they are not biased (the average error in the rational expectation of a variable is zero); and (b) they depend on the structure of the economic system in which the expectation is being formed.

2. The new classical model is *new* because the expected price level is determined by rational expectations; and it is *classical* because wages and prices are assumed to be flexible. The policy implications of the new classical model depend on the distinction between anticipated monetary policy (which people expect) and unanticipated monetary policy (which comes as a surprise).

3. The main result of the new classical model is the policy ineffectiveness proposition: anticipated monetary policy does not affect aggregate output. However, anticipated monetary policy is more effective than unanticipated monetary policy for inflation fighting.

4. Nonclassical models combine rational expectations with the assumption that wages and prices are sticky. Long-term, staggered, labor contracts are the main reason that wages and hence prices may be sticky. In nonclassical models, anticipated, as well as unanticipated, monetary policy can affect aggregate output.

---

## Key Terms

Expectations:
  Adaptive
  Rational
January effect
Macroeconomic models:
  New classical
  Nonclassical
Monetary policy:

Anticipated
Unanticipated
Policy ineffectiveness proposition
Theory of the real business cycle
Wages and prices:
  Flexible
  Sticky

---

## Study Problems

1. Using *adaptive expectations,* how would a person form an expectation of next year's Treasury bill interest rate?

2. Using *rational expectations,* how would a person form an expectation of next year's Treasury bill interest rate?

3. Normally a company's stock price is expected to rise when the company announces higher earnings. Could it be consistent with rational expectations that a company's stock price falls when it announces higher earnings?

4. If you expected the price of a commodity to be sharply higher one month from now, what action might you take? How might your action affect the current price of the commodity?

5. According to the new classical model, the price level may rise rapidly following anticipated easy monetary policy. Why does this result depend on rational expectations? On anticipated monetary policy?

6. According to the new classical model, when can easy monetary policy affect aggregate output?

7. Comparing the *long-run* effects of easy monetary policy in the new classical and nonclassical models, what differences, if any, are there?

8. Comparing the *short-run* effects of easy monetary policy in the new classical and nonclassical models, what differences, if any, are there?

9. Indicate whether the following statement is consistent with only the new classical model, only the nonclassical model, or both: "The Federal Reserve should announce publicly a tight monetary policy when the policy is intended to reduce the inflation rate."

10. Indicate whether the following statement is consistent with only the new classical model, only the nonclassical model, or both: "The Federal Reserve cannot expand aggregate output beyond the full employment level in the long run."

## Recommended Reading

*In addition to the readings given in Chapter 25, the following refer to specific topics discussed in this chapter.*

*Rational Expectations and the New Classical Model*

Robert J. Barro, "Unanticipated Money, Output, and the Price Level in the United States," *Journal of Political Economy* 86, August 1978, pp. 549–580.

Rodney Maddock and Michael Carter, "A Child's Guide to Rational Expectations," *Journal of Economics Literature* 20, no. 1, March 1982, pp. 39–51.

Donald J. Mullineaux, "Efficient Markets, Interest Rates, and Monetary Policy," *Business Review*, Federal Reserve Bank of Philadelphia, May/June 1981, pp. 3–10.

John Muth, "Rational Expectations and the Theory of Price Movements," *Econometrica* 29, July 1961, pp. 315–335.

Thomas Sargent, "Beyond Demand and Supply Curves in Macroeconomics," *American Economic Review*, May 1982, pp. 382–389.

Thomas Sargent and Neil Wallace, "Rational Expectations, the Optimal Monetary Instrument, and the Optimal Money Supply Rule," *Journal of Political Economy* 83, April 1975, pp. 241–254.

Steven Sheffrin, *Rational Expectations*, Cambridge University Press, New York, 1983.

*Sticky Wages and Prices and the Nonclassical Model*

Stanley Fischer, "Long-Term Contracts, Rational Expectations, and the Optimal Money Supply Rule," *Journal of Political Economy* 85, February 1977, pp. 191–205.

John B. Taylor, "Aggregate Dynamics and Staggered Contracts," *Journal of Political Economy* 88, February 1980, pp. 801–823.

John B. Taylor, "Staggered Wage Setting in a Macroeconomic Model," *American Economic Review*, May 1979, pp. 108–113.

*The Real Business Cycle*

Edward C. Prescott, "Theory Ahead of Business Cycle Management," and Lawrence H. Summers, "Some Skeptical Observations on Real Business Cycle Theory," both in *Quarterly Review*, Federal Reserve Bank of Minneapolis, Fall 1986, pp. 9–27.

Carl Walsh, "New Views of the Business Cycle: Has the Past Emphasis on Money Been Misplaced?" *Business Review*, Federal Reserve Bank of Philadelphia, January/February 1986, pp. 3–13.

# Answers to Selected Questions

## Chapter 1

2. Beyond its normal uses for small transactions, currency is lost, hoarded, and used in the underground economy. More than half of the value of transaction deposits is held by business firms to pay for their purchases.

4. We saw in the text that if a family is paid monthly and spends all of its money each month, then its annual income velocity of money is 24. If it is paid twice a month, then on the same basis, the annual velocity of money is 48.

6. The quantity equation of exchange, $MV = Y = Py$, is an identity because velocity $V$ is defined as $V = Y/M$. To use the equation, we need to know which of the variables—$V$, $y$, and $P$— are likely to be constant.

8. When the price level and real income each rise by 3%, this means that nominal income rises by 6%. Velocity equals nominal GNP divided by the money supply. If nominal GNP rises by 6% and the money supply rises by 10%, then the resulting velocity will be about 60% ($= 6\%/10\%$) of its initial value, or 3 (60% of 5).

10. You will earn interest of $300 (6% of $5,000). The accumulated amount in the account will be $5,300 (1.06 × $5,000).

## Chapter 2

2. Based on $F = 12.5 - 0.75\ G$:
   a. If $G = 0$, then the maximum amount of $F$ is 12.5.
   b. If $F = 0$, then the maximum amount of $G$ is 16.7.
   Along the production possibility frontier, the maximum amount of $F$ or $G$ is 10.

4. Multilaterial trading requires a central agency to monitor trades, which is usually a costly way to arrange trade.

6. People use fiat money because other people will accept it, so it would be unusual to find some people using it and others not. The government would want everyone to expect that everyone else would use the fiat money; legal tender laws are one way to do this.

8. The bank has a reserve ratio of 60% ($=$ $60 of reserves/$100 of deposits). For a reserve ratio of 20%, the bank would need $20 of reserves. So it could make an additional $40 of loans ($60 $-$ $20). The balance sheet is then:

| Assets | | Liabilities | |
|---|---|---|---|
| Reserves | $20 | Deposits | $100 |
| Loans | $80 | | |

10. The Federal Reserve directly controls the monetary base because it prints the fiat money and creates bank reserves. The Federal Reserve can only control the transaction deposit component of the M1 money supply through its control of the monetary base (specifically bank reserves).

## Chapter 3

2. Since intrasector transactions cancel out, nothing happens if homes are bought and sold within sector 1.

4. $C_2 = 1100 + (1000 - C_1)\ (1.10)$. If $C_1 = 0$, then the maximum $C_2 = 2200$. If $C_2 = 0$, the maximum $C_1 = 2000$.

6. a. Saving rises.
   b. Saving falls.

664

c. Saving rises.

d. Saving falls.

8. From A to B: the marginal return *m* is 25% (= [1.25 − 1.0]/1).

From B to C: *m* is 10%.

From C to D: m is 5%.

These results illustrate a diminishing marginal return on investment. If the market rate of interest is 10%, the firm should invest up to a level of 3 (situation C).

10. a. Loanable fund supply rises; the interest rate falls.

b. Loanable fund supply falls; the interest rate rises.

c. Loanable fund supply falls; the interest rate rises.

d. Loanable fund demand rises; the interest rate rises.

## Chapter 4

2. Wealth is the accumulated amount of saving. Capital is the accumulated amount of capital investment. So, if saving equals capital investment, then wealth has to equal capital.

4. The size of a portfolio represents a person's wealth, which is increased by saving. If a person buys more capital or financial assets without saving, then the purchases must be financed by issuing financial liabilities (loans), so wealth is unchanged.

6. Babe Ruth's salary in 1967 prices was $200,000 ($100,000/0.50) while Reggie Jackson's salary in 1967 prices was $143,000 ($500,000/3.5). So the Babe had a higher real salary. A comparison of the two nominal salaries is distorted by changes in the price level over time.

8. The Fisher effect holds between years (1) and (2) and between years (2) and (3): in both cases nominal interest rates and expected inflation rise by the same amount.

10. a. *Consistent* with a neutral economy: unexpected inflation helps borrowers and harms lenders.

b. *Inconsistent* with a neutral economy:

people are changing their real behavior.

c. *Inconsistent* with a neutral economy: the stock market should be determined by real rates.

d. *Inconsistent* with a neutral economy: nominal interest rates and expected inflation should change by the same amount.

## Chapter 5

2. a. Increases the present value.

b. Reduces the present value.

c. Reduces the present value.

4. You should choose the highest value among:

> The rate of time preference.

> The marginal return on investment.

> The market interest rate available on other securities.

6. A lower bid-ask spread means that demanders pay a lower ask price and/or suppliers receive a higher bid price. If this happens, they will trade more, raising the quantity.

8. The formula is $PV_n = (\$1,000)/(1.08)^N$. So:

| N | $PV_N$ |
|---|---|
| 1 | $926 |
| 2 | $857 |

10. Other factors that determine the price of a security include:

> Its credit risk.

> Its liquidity.

> Its tax status.

> Other technical features.

## Chapter 6

2. To provide intermediation services, banks essentially "make a market in money," paying people who keep deposits in the bank a deposit rate and charging people who borrow money from the bank a higher loan rate.

4. The perfect market equilibrium does not

take into account the rate spread between loan rates and deposit rates. This spread is determined by bank operating costs, the degree of competition, and the extent of regulation.

6. A lower rate spread implies either a lower loan rate, a higher deposit rate, or both. A lower loan rate stimulates the demand for loans and a higher deposit rate stimulates the supply of deposits, both increasing the quantity of intermediation.

8. Banks will raise loan rates and lower deposit rates to balance the demand and supply of loanable funds. This also increases the quantity of intermediation.

10. Banks cross subsidize transfer services, paying less interest on account balances than they actually earn by investing the balances. As a result, people write a lot of checks, but try to keep low account balances. It would be better for banks to charge higher fees for transfers, while paying higher interest rates on the account balances.

## Chapter 7

2.

| | Security A | Security B | Security C |
|---|---|---|---|
| Expected Rate of Return | 10% | 13% | 10% |

Security B would be selected.

4. These people might be risk averse when they buy insurance, but risk loving when they gamble.

6. a. False: risk-neutral people *always* take fair gambles.
   b. True.
   c. False: risk-averse people *always* buy fair insurance.
   d. False: risk lovers want more risk, not less risk.
   e. True.

8. Risk-averse people dislike risk, so they have to be offered a higher expected return to hold a security with a higher level of risk.

10. Lenders (buyers of risk) will worry that the borrowers (sellers of risk) are concealing information about the nature of the risk being sold. Therefore, lenders will require a higher price of risk, which will limit the amount of risk transfer.

## Chapter 8

2. a. 8%
   b. 9.33%
   c. 8%.

4. Security sequence c would be chosen because it consists of a series of short-term, liquid, securities.

6. $r_{0,2} = 7\%$
   $r_{0,3} = 8\%$

8. a. Riding the yield curve fails under the PE theory.
   b. It works under the liquidity preference theory.

10. Nothing happens during the first year. During years two and three profits rise if there are more new loans than new deposits, and fall in the opposite case.

## Chapter 9

2. The country will sell—take a short position—in coffee futures to fix the price of its coffee sales. By doing so, the country would be indicating that it felt the current price was advantageous.

4. The arbitrage would be spot-to-future arbitrage. This would cause the futures price to fall and the stock market price to rise.

6. When the interest rates rise, its profits rise (by $10,000). To hedge its interest rate risk, it would purchase a long position in a financial futures contract.

8. The bank should purchase a long position in a financial futures contract, just as in Question 6.

10. The intrinsic value is $0 (the strike price is below the market price and this is a put option), while the time premium is $2 (which equals the total premium).

# Chapter 10

2. The Federal Reserve was supposed to manage its discount window to provide banks with enough currency to meet the needs of trade. The Federal Reserve failed to provide banks with enough currency during the Great Depression because it failed to recognize that the banks might need currency even though they were not making many new loans.

4. Bank holding companies are corporations that own one or more banks. Bank holding companies can carry out a wider range of activities than banks.

6. a. Given that all depository intermediaries had to meet the Federal Reserve's required reserve ratios, Federal Reserve membership was no longer an issue.

   b. With the elimination of Regulation Q ceilings, banks could compete for deposits by paying higher interest rates.

   c. Credit rationing of mortgage borrowers was reduced when usury ceilings on mortgage rates were eliminated.

   d. The cost of dealing with failing institutions was reduced by granting regulators increased powers to merge these institutions.

8. It was thought that investment banking created a conflict of interest for commercial banks.

10. Banking law generally defines a bank as an institution that attracts deposits *and* makes loans. A nonbank bank is an institution that does only one of these activities, but still carries out many banking functions.

# Chapter 11

2. With imperfect competition, a bank may be able to charge higher loan rates and to pay lower deposit rates, both of which can result in higher profits.

4. Required reserve ratios reduce the profit margin of a bank. Thus for the profit margin to be zero in a competitive industry, the loan rate must be higher and the deposit rate must be lower than would otherwise be the case.

6. Firms and consumers use credit lines to obtain funds from a bank, or to have a bank make payments on their behalf. As a result, a bank must hold liquidity for credit lines just as it does for checking accounts.

8. Liability management tends to be less costly than secondary reserves. That is, the bank can hold a larger amount of earning assets when it uses liability management; also the interest rate on new liabilities may be lower than the rate on secondary reserve securities.

10. Borrowing from the Federal Reserve is one form of liability management. However, the Federal Reserve only allows banks to borrow from it after all other sources of liquidity have been exhausted.

# Chapter 12

2. On the basis of a "customer relationship," a bank can obtain privileged information regarding a borrower's credit risk.

4. Target rate $r_t = 6\% + 3\% + 2\% = 11\%$. The bank would charge a prime—risk-free—borrower the target rate, 11%. The bank determines the contractual rate for the risky borrower, by using the formula: $r_t = r_c p_c + r_d p_d$, and solving for $r_c$: $r_c = (r_t - r_d p_d / p_c = (11\% - [-5\%] [20\%]) / (80\%) = 15\%$.

6. For a diversified bank, loan defaults are highly predictable, so the bank could anticipate the amounts, treating them as a cost of doing business.

8. Banks will raise the interest rates they charge *all* borrowers to compensate for the expected losses due to default. Honest borrowers have to pay these higher rates, unless somehow they can convince the bank of their true honesty.

10. Risky borrowers will not be so eager to borrow money at high interest rates when they have to place their own assets—the collateral—at risk.

## Chapter 13

2. Credit unions have a lot of information about borrowers because a credit union consists of a group of people with some common bond.

4. Shareholders buy and sell shares in an opened-end fund from the fund itself; whereas they buy and sell shares in a closed-end fund on a stock exchange. Money market funds invest in short-term debt securities; stock funds invest in common stocks.

6. Large investors can usually diversify their own portfolios, spread the management costs across a large amount of assets, and arrange for a sufficient cashflow that liquidity is not a problem.

8. Pension funds and insurance companies are financial intermediaries because they raise money and invest it in carrying out their business.

10. Poor underwriting experience means that the company has had higher losses on claims than it anticipated; poor investment experience means the company has not earned as much as expected on its investment portfolio.

## Chapter 14

2. Deposits $D$ are computed as the monetary base $B$ divided by the reserve ratio $d$:
$D = B/D = \$1,000/0.10 = \$10,000$.

4. $D_1 = (1/d_1)(B - C - R_e - d_2D_2)$
$= (10)(1000 - 300 - 100 - 10)$
$= 5,900$.

6. $E = (1 - d_1)D_1 + (1 - d_2)D_2 - R_e =$
$(.9)(5900) + (0.95)(200) - 100 =$
$5,400$.

8. The M1 money supply falls by a. 90, b. 100, and c. 50. The M2 money supply falls by a. 90 and b. 100; in c. the M2 money supply rises by 50.

10. a. If the discount rate falls, banks hold fewer excess reserves, so the M1 money supply rises.

b. If the time deposit interest rate falls, banks have fewer required reserves on time deposits, so the M1 money supply rises.

c. If the interest rate on investment securities rises, investors hold less currency, so the M1 money supply rises.

## Chapter 15

2. The interest rate elasticity of money demand is the percentage change in money demand relative to a given change in the interest rate. The elasticity is zero or negative:

| | |
|---|---|
| Classical quantity theory: | zero |
| Baumol-Tobin theory: | negative ($-0.5$) |
| Modern quantity theory: | negative (small) |
| Liquidity preference theory: | negative (large) |

4. The individual's periodic (monthly) income is $2,000, so the demand for money (average money held) is $1,000.

6. People must hold transactions account balances to make payments. The cost of transferring money from the investment account to the transaction account is an incentive to keep more money in the transaction account. The higher interest rate earned on investment account balances is the incentive to keep funds in the investment account.

8. According to the Keynesian theory, people will demand money as long as the reservation rate for bonds equal or exceeds the market interest rate. In the example, this is true for the four people with reservation rates of 7% or higher. So the demand for money is $4,000.

10. As a result of his use of a broad definition of money, Friedman finds a lower interest

rate elasticity of money demand than in most other theories.

## Chapter 16

2. When the monetary base rises, other things being constant, more reserves are available to support deposit expansion. When the opportunity cost of money rises, the reserve drains—currency, excess reserves, and required reserves on time deposits—tend to fall, causing the monetary base multiplier to rise.

4. When the interest rate rises, the money supply may rise, reflecting a movement *along* the money supply curve. However, by reducing the monetary base, the Federal Reserve can cause a shift in the money supply curve, restoring the money supply to its initial value.

6. Nominal income must rise enough to provide people incentive to hold the larger money supply. When the money demand curve is inelastic, nominal income has to rise more to create the necessary increase in money demand.

8. The real interest rate may fall due to the *liquidity effect*—a higher money supply reduces the opportunity cost of money— while the nominal interest rate may rise due to the *inflation effect*—if a larger money supply creates inflation.

10. In principle, velocity is positively related to interest rates: when interest rates rise, money demand falls, so the velocity of money rises. Between 1974 and 1981 both interest rates and the velocity of money rose; after that they both fell.

## Chapter 17

2. In principle, the main power could belong to any one of the three groups—the Board of Governors, the Regional Reserve Banks, or the members. The Board of Governors has the dominant power.

4. The Federal Reserve provides the federal government with an account to deposit government receipts and to write checks. The Federal Reserve also manages the auction sales of new Treasury securities that finance the government's budget deficit.

6. Since the Treasury/Federal Reserve Accord of 1951, the Fed has been explicitly independent of the administration. Nevertheless, the Federal Reserve may still respond to the political power of the administration.

8. The maximum employment goal is to make the unemployment rate as low as possible. A 4% rate is the current goal.

10. The goals of maximum employment and price stability are sometimes in conflict. If two policy instruments were available, then one might be assigned to each goal.

## Chapter 18

2. Defensive open market operations are carried out when external factors cause bank reserves or the monetary base to change. Dynamic open market operations are carried out in response to FOMC policy directives for a new monetary policy.

4. If people expect that a tighter monetary policy is in effect, they will immediately try to sell their debt securities, causing security prices to fall and interest rates to rise.

6. The Fed does not want banks borrowing for the purpose of profit, and it scrutinizes loan applications to stop this from happening.

8. With 100% reserve ratios, banks would not hold any excess reserves, so variations in excess reserves could not be the source of variations in the amount of bank deposits.

10. Stock margin requirements are directed at a particular class of securities—common stocks.

## Chapter 19

2. Each channel reduces the demand for one type of goods:
   a. People may consume less when the money supply is lower.
   b. Firms may invest less when the interest rate is higher.
   c. People may consume less when their wealth is lower.
   d. People may either consume or invest less if there is more credit rationing.
   e. People may consume less if they are less liquid.

4. With uncertainty about investment demand, the Fed cannot precisely determine the proper level for the interest rate. With uncertainty about money demand, the Fed will not know what money supply is needed to determine the interest rate.

6. Operating targets should be controllable with the Federal Reserve's instruments, such as open market operations. Intermediate targets should have a predictable impact on the realization of policy goals, such as the inflation rate.

8. Interest rates are both controlled by the Fed and have an impact on its policy goal variables. However, the Fed controls *nominal* interest rates, whereas it is only *real* interest rates that implement policy goals.

10. People will expect that tight monetary policy will raise interest rates, thus providing incentive for them to save more, and thereby consume less, of their income.

## Chapter 20

2. An accommodating policy provides the economy with enough money to carry out all desired transactions. If this occurs in an inflationary situation, the policy will accommodate—or validate—the inflationary pressures.

4. Free reserve tend to create a procyclical monetary policy in which the Federal Reserve accommodates increased bank lending—akin to the real bills doctrine.

6. Disintermediation occurs when deposits are withdrawn from banks because investors can obtain higher interest rates on other instruments. Banks must then reduce their lending. The 1980 legislation eliminated the Regulation Q ceilings that had limited the interest rates on bank deposits.

8. Monetary policy affects the stock market as investors reallocate their portfolios with regard to the returns to be made on stocks, bank deposits, and other securities. Stock prices may already reflect future expected monetary policy, however, and other factors may influence the price of a particular corporation's stock.

10. The Federal Reserve found it increasingly difficult to control the M1 money supply, particularly as bank customers switched their funds between different types of accounts. The M2 money supply is less sensitive to such switches.

## Chapter 21

2. U.S. capital inflows, which represent borrowing money from abroad, have reduced the net international investment position to the point that it is now negative.

4. The purchasing power parity (PPP) theory is that the exchange rate between the dollar and a foreign currency is determined by the relative price levels of the two countries. International commodity arbitrage may fail to occur due to high transportation costs.

6. The interest rate parity (IPP) theory is that the exchange rate between the dollar and a foreign currency is determined by the relative interest rates levels of two countries and the future expected exchange rate. International financial arbitrage may fail to occur because of exchange risks.

8. When the U.S. price level rises, the U.S. demand for foreign currency rises, while

the foreign supply of foreign currency falls. Both cause the exchange rate to rise—the dollar depreciates.

10. When the dollar is an international currency, people will want to hold it for purposes of international payments.

## Chapter 22

2. An increase in the U.S. price level would cause the dollar to become overvalued at the fixed exchange rate, forcing the Federal Reserve to sell foreign currencies in support of the dollar.

4. A dirty float means that the central bank intervenes in the foreign exchange market even though there is officially a flexible exchange rate system.

6. The advantage of a fixed exchange rate is that trading firms will have less uncertainty about the future value of the exchange rate. The advantage of a flexible exchange rate is that the domestic economy may be more insulated from international conditions.

8. A sterilized foreign exchange purchase combines a purchase of foreign currencies (for dollars) with the sale of Treasury securities (for dollars). Thus the net effect is that foreign currencies have been purchased and Treasury securities have been sold.

10. According to the gold standard, countries have to allow their money supply to rise and fall based on their gold flows. Little discretion is thus left for monetary policy.

## Chapter 23

2. Autonomous consumption expenditures will be $50 billion.
Induced consumption expenditures will be $400 billion.
Total consumption expenditures will be $450 billion.

4. Investment demand is based in part on the cost of financing or on the opportunity

cost of the funds invested. A higher interest rate raises these costs, thus reducing investment demand.

6. a. An increase in autonomous consumption expenditures raises aggregate demand by an equal amount.
b. A fall in the interest rate raises the investment demand component of aggregate expenditures.
c. An increase in government spending raises the government expenditures component of aggregate demand.
d. A fall in taxes raises autonomous consumption spending

8. First, easy monetary policy reduces the interest rate.
Second, a lower interest rate raises investment demand.
Third, higher investment demand creates a multiplier expansion of income and output.

10. To the right of (or below) the LM curve, the demand for money exceeds the supply of money—there is an excess demand for money. The interest rate must then rise to restore equilibrium in the market for money.

## Chapter 24

2. A steeply sloped LM curve occurs because the interest elasticity of money demand is low.

4. Fiscal policy is most effective when the slope of the IS curve is steeper and the slope of the LM curve is flatter. Fiscal policy is ineffective when the LM curve is vertical.

6. Expansionary fiscal policy raises income, raises the interest rate, and reduces investment demand.

8. Debt-financed expansionary fiscal policy causes the IS curve to shift to the right. Monetized expansionary fiscal policy causes both the IS curve *and* the LM curve to shift to the right.

10. In the IS/LM model, the IS curve represents the loanable funds theory of interest rates and the LM curve represents the money demand/money supply theory of interest rates.

## Chapter 25

2. The aggregate demand curve shifts to the right.

4. Wages rates rise, are unchanged, or fall, as aggregate output exceeds, equals, or is less than full employment output.

6. *a.* In the short run, the price level falls and aggregate output rises.
   *b.* In the long run, the price level falls and aggregate output rises if full employment output rises.

8. When the money supply is growing, the aggregate demand curve will continue to shift to the right, creating continuing inflation. A change in the money supply is the primary reason that the aggregate demand curve will shift on a continuing basis.

10. A negative supply shock—such as higher oil prices—will tend to reduce aggregate output. If the Federal Reserve accommodates the shock with easy monetary policy, then the result will be a higher price level. As a result, labor unions may try to raise their nominal wage rates, initiating a wage-push inflation.

## Chapter 26

2. Based on rational expectations, a person would determine an expected U.S. Treasury bill rate based on the projected demand and supply of Treasury bills.

4. You would buy the commodity now. This action would cause the price of the commodity to rise.

6. In the new classical model, *unanticipated* easy monetary policy can raise aggregate output in the short run.

8. If the monetary policy is *unanticipated*, then both models indicate that aggregate output and the price level may rise. If the monetary policy is *anticipated*, then the new classical model indicates that aggregate output will equal full employment output, whereas the nonclassical model does not.

10. This statement is true in both models.

# Glossary

**adaptive expectations** Expectations of a variable that are based on an average of past values of the variable.

**adverse selection** The situation when customers who are "bad" risks are more likely to buy insurance or take out loans than those who are "good" risks.

**aggregate demand** The total value of goods and services demanded for consumption, investment, government spending, and net exports.

**aggregate demand curve** The curve showing the inverse relationship between aggregate demand and the price level.

**aggregate demand inflation (or demand pull inflation)** Inflation created by increases in aggregate demand.

**aggregate expenditure function** The macroeconomic relationship between desired aggregate expenditures and aggregate income.

**aggregate expenditures** The total value of goods and services purchased in the economy. Aggregate expenditures comprise the components of GNP: personal consumption expenditures, gross private domestic investment, government purchases of goods and services, net exports of goods and services.

**aggregate income** The total payments made to the factors of production—wages to labor, interest and profits to capital and to entrepreneures, rent to landowners.

**aggregate output** The total value of goods and services produced in the economy.

**aggregate supply** The total value of goods and services supplied in the economy.

**aggregate supply curve** The curve showing the positive relationship between aggregate supply and the price level. Aggregate supply curves depend on the time available for wage rates to change: short-run supply curves apply when wage rates are fixed; medium-run supply curves apply when wage rates are changing; and long run supply curves apply when wages have no further tendency to change.

**"animal spirits"** The term used by Keynes to describe the willingness of entrepreneurs to carry out capital investment.

**annuity** A security with a series of equal payments at regular intervals.

**appreciation** An increase in the value of a currency under a flexible exchange rate system.

**arbitrage** Buying or selling a good in one market, while doing just the opposite in another market, to lock in a sure profit.

**asset** A item of value owned by a bank, firm, or individual, either financial or capital (tangible) property.

**asset management** Liquidity management using three groups of assets: primary reserves, secondary reserves, and earning assets.

**asymmetric information** A situation in which two parties have different information, such as when borrowers have knowledge concerning their own credit worthiness not available to lenders.

**autonomous expenditures** The part of aggregate expenditures determined by factors other than current income.

**availability doctrine** A theory of monetary policy in which the Federal Reserve controls credit availability—rather than interest rates or the money supply—in order to reach its policy goals.

**balance of payments accounts** An accounting of international trade and finance consisting of three main components: the current account measures the trade balance, together with smaller items such as net government grants and private gifts sent abroad; the capital account covers international financial transactions; and the statistical discrepancy reports errors in either the current or capital accounts.

**balance sheet** A listing of bank or firm assets, liabilities, and shareholder capital as of a particular date.

**balance sheet constraint** Total assets must equal total liabilities (including shareholder capital) for a bank or firm.

**bank assets** Assets owned by banks, such as cash, securities, and loans made.

**bank capital** The amount invested directly in a bank by its shareholders plus the amount of retained profits (profits less shareholder dividends) or losses the bank has accrued over time.

**bank costs** The costs of running a bank, including deposit interest and operating expenses.

**bank equilibrium** The situation when the demand for bank loans and the supply of bank deposits are equal.

**bank holding companies** Corporations, owning one or more banks, that are allowed to carry out activities closely related to banking.

**bank liabilities** Amounts the bank is to repay in the future, such as deposits.

**bank notes** A form of paper money issued by banks in lieu of deposits.

**bank profit margin** The interest rate earned on assets minus the sum of the interest rate paid on liabilities and the operating cost ratio.

**bank reserves** Bank assets which satisfy reserve requirements and from which deposit withdrawals are paid; see also reserves.

**bank revenue** Bank income consisting of interest earned on assets and services fees charged to customers.

**bank run** A situation in which people try to withdraw deposits rapidly because they suspect the bank is about to fail.

**banking principle** The principle that the *net* amount of deposit outflows can be small, even when gross deposit inflows and outflows are large.

**bankruptcy** The situation when a borrower defaults on a loan and the borrower's assets, except for some personal items, are distributed to the lender and other creditors.

**banks** Commercial banks and thrift institutions accept deposits and make loans. Investment banks act as brokers and dealers in primary markets to distribute newly issued securities.

**barter** Trade in which commodities exchange only for other commodities, either directly (all commodities received through trade are consumed) or indirectly (certain commodities are accepted and later traded for other commodities).

**basis** The futures market price minus the spot market price of a commodity.

**Baumol-Tobin theory** A money demand theory based on cash management policies. Its premise is that money demand is inversely related to the opportunity cost of money.

**bilateral balance in trade** Transactions between two traders that are balanced in value.

**Board of Governors** The seven chief executives of the Federal Reserve System.

**Bretton Woods Agreement** The 1944 agreement that established the International Monetary Fund, the World Bank, and the General Agreement on Tariffs and Trade.

**brokers** Financial institutions who bring borrowers and lenders, or buyers and sellers of securities, together.

**call options contract** Options contract on which the holder can decide whether or not to *take* delivery of the commodity.

**capital assets** Tangible, physical items, such as manufacturing plants and equipment, houses, and consumer durables.

**capital flows** International purchases and sales of capital assets and borrowing and lending.

**capital investment** Purchases of newly produced capital assets.

**capital ratio** The ratio of a bank's or firm's capital to its assets.

**cash management policies** Policies that people and firms use to determine whether to hold or invest their money.

**cashflow pattern** A security's pattern of payments (interest and principal).

**channels of monetary policy** The mechanisms through which monetary policy affect the economy.

**check clearings** In the process of clearing checks between banks, the bank receiving the credit has a favorable check clearing, and the bank receiving the debit has an adverse check clearing.

**Classical Quantity theory** The theory that money demand is determined by income (or another measure of transactions) and payments system factors (such as the frequency of income payments).

**clearinghouses** Cooperative arrangements used by banks to clear checks.

**closing transactions** The method of settling a futures or options contract that uses a second transaction to offset the first one.

**collateral** Assets owned by a borrower that become the property of the lender if the borrower defaults on loan payments.

**commodity exchange systems** Trading systems that use a commodity as the medium of exchange.

**compensating balances** Deposits that banks may require business borrowers to maintain as a condition for obtaining a loan.

**compound interest** The interest accumulated on a security when interest is paid on previously accumulated interest.

**Comptroller of the Currency** The office within the Treasury Department established under the National Banking Act to distribute currency and to charter federal banks.

**consumer price index** The price level of a typical consumer's "basket" of goods.

**consumption function** The macroeconomic relationship between desired consumption expenditures and current income.

**contractual interest rate** The stated interest rate on a loan contract that determines the amount the borrower is supposed to repay.

**correspondent banking** An arrangement in which large banks provide services, such as check clearing, to small banks.

**cost of carry** The expense of holding a commodity as part of an arbitrage transaction.

**cost-push inflation** Inflation that combines a leftward shift in the aggregate supply curve with an accommodating monetary policy.

**costs of trade** The costs, such as search costs and trading system costs, of arranging and carrying out trade in an economy.

**coupon bond** A security providing a series of annuity payments (coupons) and a single, larger, payment at maturity (principal).

**crawling peg** An exchange rate system in which a central bank maintains a fixed rate most of the time, but periodically changes it so that the rate does not become significantly overvalued or undervalued.

**credit crunch** An especially tight monetary policy in which the Federal Reserve restricts bank lending.

**credit rationing** The process when banks refuse to make loans, even though borrowers may offer to pay higher interest rates.

**credit risk** The risk that a borrower will fail to make the promised payments on a loan.

**credit scoring** Statistical procedures used to evaluate the credit risk of borrowers.

**credit unions** Depository intermediaries, with mutual ownership by the members, which specialize in making consumer loans.

**cross subsidization** A high price charged for one product to subsidize the low price charged for another product.

**crowding out** In the IS/LM model, crowding out refers to the reduction in consumption and investment spending when higher government spending raises interest rates. In the aggregate supply/aggregate demand model, it refers to the reduction in aggregate demand when increased spending in one sector of the economy causes the price level to rise.

**currency** The part of the money supply consisting of coins and bills.

**dealers** Financial institutions who "make markets" by buying and selling securities.

**debt financing** Government deficit financing in which the Treasury sells securities to the public—anybody in the economy other than government agencies or the Federal Reserve.

**debt security** A security representing the obligation of a borrower to make a specified payment on a specified date to the lender.

**delivery** The method of settling a futures or options contract in which the short position delivers the commodity to the long position.

**deposit expansion and contraction** Deposit expansion is the increase in deposits caused by an increase in the monetary base. Deposit contraction is the decrease in deposits caused by a decrease in the monetary base.

**deposit inflows and outflows** Bank account deposits and withdrawals of cash and checks.

**deposit insurance** Insurance provided by government agencies to depositors against loss of principal.

**Depository Institutions Deregulation and Monetary Control Act** The 1980 Act that deregulated banking by eliminating regulations, such as the Regulation Q ceilings. It also made all depository institutions subject to the reserve requirements of the Federal Reserve.

**depreciation** A decrease in the foreign value of a currency under a flexible exchange rate system.

**devaluation** A decrease in the foreign value of a currency under a fixed exchange rate system.

**dirty float** An exchange rate system in which the exchange rate is flexible and equals the equilibrium rate most of the time, but the central bank occasionally, and usually surreptitiously, intervenes to alter the exchange rate.

**discount loans** Loans made by the Federal Reserve to financial institutions through the discount window.

**discount rate** The interest rate used for time discounting, or the interest rate charged by the Federal Reserve on discount loans.

**discount rate changes (defensive and dynamic)** A defensive change occurs when the Federal Reserve discount rate is changed to match changes in market interest rates. A dynamic change occurs when the Federal Reserve discount rate is changed to initiate a new monetary policy.

**discount window** The Federal Reserve's facility for making loans to financial institutions.

**disintermediation** A situation in which banks or other intermediaries must curtail their lending because of deposit withdrawals.

**disposable income** The current income that remains after tax payments.

**diversified portfolio** A portfolio consisting of many small investments with independent risks, which reduces the overall risk.

**double coincidence of wants** A situation in which each of two traders wants to consume the good that the other trader wants to sell.

**double-entry accounting** A system of accounting in which each transaction is recorded by means of two balancing entries.

**dual banking system** The system of chartering and regulating banks at both the state and federal levels.

**equilibrium** In general equilibrium supply and demand are equal in all markets simultaneously. In partial equilibrium supply and demand may be equal in only one market.

**Eurodollar market** A market outside the United States, originally located in Europe, that deals in deposits and loans stated in dollars.

**exchange rate** The price of a currency of one country stated in terms of the currency of another country.

**expected holding-period return** The holding-period return based on expected interest rates for a security sequence that involves forward securities.

**expected interest rate** The interest rate investors expect to earn on a security that will trade at a later date.

**expected value** The summary measure of a series of possible values, computed as a weighted average of each of the possible values, the probability of each value being its weight. This measure can be used to compute the expected return on a security, the expected payoff on a gamble, or the expected loss due to claims on an insurance policy.

**expected value decisions** The decisions made by choosing the alternative that has the highest expected value.

**expenditure multiplier** The ratio indicating how much equilibrium income changes when autonomous expenditures change.

**federal deposit insurance** The guarantee of repayment of principal provided by federal agencies on bank deposits up to $100,000 per account.

**Federal Deposit Insurance Corporation (FDIC)** The federal agency, part of the Comptroller of the Currency, that provides deposit insurance for commercial banks.

**federal funds** The security used when banks borrow reserves on a short-term basis from other banks.

**federal funds rate** The interest rate charged when banks borrow reserves from other banks.

**Federal Home Loan Bank System** The federal agency that regulates savings and loan associations.

**Federal Open Market Committee (FOMC)** The Federal Reserve committee that determines monetary and foreign exchange rate policy.

**Federal Reserves banks** The twelve regional banks that manage such Federal Reserve tasks as check clearing and other business with member banks.

**Federal Reserve System** The central banking organization of the United States responsible for monetary policy, consisting of the Board of Governors, the regional Reserve Banks, and the member banks. It also provides services to financial institutions, banking supervision and regulation, fiscal agent services for the federal government, and economic research.

**Federal Savings and Loan Insurance Corporation (FSLIC)** The federal agency, operating as part of the Federal Home Loan Bank System, that provides deposit insurance for savings and loan associations.

**fiat money** Paper money and coins that are accepted in trade even though the intrinsic value of the paper and metal is negligible.

**finance companies** Nondepository intermediaries that specialize in making short-term, high-risk, loans that most other intermediaries avoid.

**financial assets** Securities, such as stocks, bonds, loans, and money.

**financial intermediaries** Institutions that raise funds by issuing liabilities and invest them by purchasing assets. Includes depository—commercial banks and thrift—institutions raise funds by attracting deposits. Nondepository institutions, such as insurance companies, mutual funds, and pension funds, that raise funds with nondeposit liabilities.

**financial investment** Financial assets purchased represent positive financial investment. Financial liabilities issued represent negative financial investment.

**financial liabilities** The debts of banks, firms, and people who have borrowed.

**fiscal policy** The level of government expenditures and taxes determined by Congress and the president.

**Fisher effect** The theory that nominal interest rates and the expected rate of inflation change by equal amounts (assuming the real interest rate is constant).

**fixed exchange rate** An exchange rate system in which central banks fix the exchange rate at a specific value by buying or selling foreign currency.

**float, bank** Arises when a bank credits a customer's account with a deposited check before the bank receives the corresponding credit from another bank or the Federal Reserve.

**float, customer** Arises when a bank delays crediting a deposited check to a customer's account beyond the date on which the bank receives the corresponding credit from the Federal Reserve.

**float, Federal Reserve** In the process of clearing checks, float arises when the Fed credits one bank before it debits another bank.

**Flow of Funds Accounts** The accounts, tabulated by the Federal Reserve, that record all financial transactions in the United States.

**foreign exchange market** The market in which foreign currencies are traded.

**foreign exchange operations** Federal Reserve purchases or sales of foreign currencies.

**forward exchange rates** The rates that are available when buying or selling forward contracts for a currency.

**fractional reserve bank** A bank that lends out some of its reserves, so that its ratio of reserves to deposits is less than 100%.

**free entry and exit** The situation in which new banks (or firms) enter the industry and existing ones exit the industry without cost.

**frictional unemployment** The form of unemployment that arises as people change jobs, which causes the natural rate of unemployment to be positive.

**full-employment output** The level of output that corresponds to the natural rate of unemployment.

**functional cost accounting** A technique used to estimate and allocate costs and revenues.

**functional cost analysis** An analysis carried out by the Federal Reserve to help banks allocate their costs and revenues.

**future value** The accumulated value of invested money.

**futures contracts** Securities that represent transactions on which the price is fixed immediately, but settlement is delayed, sometimes for as long as a year. Financial futures contracts are based on precious metals, foreign currencies, and debt and equity securities; interest rate futures contracts are based on debt securities.

**gambles** Gambles are favorable, fair, or unfavorable, as the expected payoff exceeds, equals, or falls below the amount bet.

**General Agreement on Tariffs and Trade (GATT)** The part of the Bretton Woods agreement calling for reduction of tariffs and other barriers to trade.

**Glass-Steagall Act (Banking Act of 1933)** The Depression legislation that created federal deposit insurance, prohibited interest payments on demand deposits, and separated commercial banks from investment banks.

**GNP deflator** The price level for all goods included in GNP.

**gold standard** A type of fixed exchange rate system in which there is a fixed conversion ratio between gold and each currency.

**government budget constraint** The constraint that government deficits must be financed either by issuing new Treasury securities or by increasing the monetary base.

**greenbacks** Currency issued by the U.S. Treasury to finance the Civil War.

**Gresham's Law** The concept that bad (or overvalued) money drives good (or undervalued) money out of circulation as the medium of exchange.

**Gross National Product (GNP)** The total value added for all goods and services produced in the economy annually.

**hedging** Transactions that involve taking a position in one market in order to offset the exposure to price changes that results from an existing position in another market.

**holding period return** The rate of return earned on a security or a security sequence for a given holding period—the period of time money is invested.

**hyperinflation** High inflation rates, often reaching several hundred percent per year, which invariably involve high growth rates in the money supply.

**income elasticity of money demand** The percentage change in money demand that results from a given percentage change in income.

**income—permanent and transitory** Permanent income is the part of current income that is expected to continue in the future. Transitory income is the remaining part of current income.

**indifference curves** Curves that show the level of satisfaction (or utility) a person receives from consuming alternative combinations of goods.

**induced expenditures** The part of aggregate expenditures determined by current income.

**inflation** An increase in the price level. Continuing inflation represents a continuing increase in the price level.

**inflation effect on interest rates** An increase in the inflation rate that raises the level of nominal interest rates.

**inflation rate** The percentage change in the price level, usually stated as an annual rate.

**inflation rate neutrality** The situation when changes in the expected inflation rate do not affect real interest rates.

**inflation tax** The reduction in the purchasing power of money that occurs when the price level rises.

**insurance** Insurance policies are favorable, fair, or unfavorable as the expected loss exceeds, equals, or is less than the premium.

**insurance companies** Financial intermediaries that provide insurance policies against various risks and hazards.

**interest elasticity of investment demand** The percentage change in investment demand for a given percentage change in the interest rate.

**interest elasticity of money demand** The percentage change in money demand that results from a given percentage change in the interest rate.

**interest rate** The percentage amount earned when lending money or paid when borrowing money.

**interest rate parity theory** The theory that the exchange rate between two currencies is determined by the relative interest rates of the two countries.

**interest rate pegging policy** The policy carried out by the Federal Reserve during World War II to keep interest rates on Treasury securities low in order to reduce the Treasury's cost of financing the war effort.

**interest rate risk** The risk that bank profits or investor earnings may change if interest rates unexpectedly change.

**intermediate targets** Variables such as bond interest rates and monetary aggregates that are used by the Federal Reserve to gauge the impact of monetary policy. Intermediate targets should be measurable and have a predictable impact on the policy goals.

**intermediation services** Services provided to expedite the transfer of loanable funds from borrowers to lenders.

**international banking** A form of banking that comprises trading foreign currencies, raising deposits through foreign offices, and making loans to foreign borrowers.

**international commodity arbitrage** Arbitrage that occurs when a commodity is purchased in a country (and currency) where its price is low and sold in a country (and currency) where its price is high.

**international finance** International trading of financial instruments and currencies.

**international financial arbitrage** Arbitrage that occurs when investors lend money in the country (or currency) that offers the highest interest rate, and borrow money in the country with the lowest rate.

**international investment position (for the U.S.)** Foreign assets owned by Americans minus U.S. assets (including loans) owned by foreigners.

**International Monetary Fund (IMF)** The organization created by the Bretton Woods Agreement to maintain the exchange rate system.

**international reserve currency** A country's currency that is held by other countries for international payments and to stabilize exchange rates.

**investment** Risky investments are rated favorable, fair, or unfavorable as the expected return exceeds, equals, or is less than the return on a riskfree alternative.

**investment deposits** Bank deposits, such as time deposits, with a fixed maturity and a relatively high interest rate on which checks can not be written.

**investment—desired** The chosen amount of capital investment based on the marginal return on investment and the interest cost of financing.

**investment function** The macroeconomic relationship between desired investment and interest rates.

**investment possibility frontier** The curve showing the amount of future goods produced for each given amount of capital investment.

**IS curve** A curve representing the equilibrium condition in the market for goods—that the demand for and supply of goods are equal.

**IS/LM interest rate theory** The general equilibrium theory in which the interest rate is determined by the IS and LM curves.

**Keynesian model** The macroeconomic model of Keynes based on the "income equals expenditure" approach and the expenditure multiplier.

**lags** Represent the time needed for monetary policy to have an effect on the economy. They can be long and variable.

**law of one price** The proposition that if a good is for sale at different locations, the same price will be charged at each one.

**leaning against the wind** A form of monetary policy in which the Federal Reserve tries to stabilize the economy.

**leasing** A bank activity, akin to lending, in which a bank purchases an asset and then rents it to a company or individual.

**legal tender laws** Laws that require people and firms to use fiat money.

**lender of last resort** Federal Reserve use of the discount window to lend funds to banks (and possibly to other firms) that have no other available source.

**liabilities** Amounts that a bank, firm, or person owes and must repay in the future.

**liability management** Bank liquidity management based on deposits and other bank liabilities.

**lines of credit** Bank commitments to make loans in specified amounts during specified periods of time.

**liquidity** The characteristic of an asset that can be sold on short notice at a price close to its full value.

**liquidity effect on interest rates** An increase in liquidity (such as an increase in the money supply) that reduces real and nominal interest rates.

**liquidity management** Bank policies involving assets and liabilities that are used to create liquidity.

**liquidity preference money demand theory (Keynes)** The money demand theory of Keynes that distinguishes three motives for money demand: a transaction motive, a precautionary motive, and a speculative motive.

**liquidity preference money demand theory (Tobin)** The money demand theory of James Tobin in which people hold money in order to lower investment portfolio risk.

**liquidity preference term structure theory** The theory stating that investors prefer holding short-term rather than long-term securities, other things the same.

**liquidity premiums** The higher interest rates on longer-term securities that occur according to the liquidity preference term structure theory.

**LM curve** A curve representing the equilibrium condition in the market for money—that money demand equals money supply.

**loanable funds interest rate theory** The partial equilibrium theory in which the interest rate is determined by the demand for and supply of loanable funds.

**long position** A security position in which the trader has the obligation (on futures contracts) or the option (on call options contracts) to take delivery of the commodity at a previously agreed on price.

**M1 money supply** The money supply defined as the sum of currency, travelers' checks, and transaction deposits.

**M2 money supply** The money supply defined as the sum of the M1 money supply and investment deposits.

**making the market** The process in which a dealer holds an inventory of a security and stands ready either to buy or to sell.

**managed float** An exchange rate system in which the exchange rate is usually determined by market demand and supply, but the central bank sometimes intervenes to alter the exchange rate.

**margin requirement** The amount of money a trader is required to keep on deposit with a financial exchange or with a broker.

**marginal propensity to consume** The ratio indicating how much consumption changes when income changes.

**market price of risk** The amount that must be paid by a risk seller to induce a risk buyer to accept the risk.

**market interest rate** The interest rate of return on a security, sometimes referring to a generic security for the economy.

**markets—primary and secondary** New securities are issued, in primary markets, and existing securities are traded, in secondary markets.

**market segmentation term structure theory** The theory that investors choose security sequences on the basis of maturity, not expected holding period returns.

**market trading line** The line indicating the combinations of goods that are available based on trade.

**maturity** The elapsed time between the moment a security is issued and the time the final cash-flow payment is made.

**maturity arbitrage** The process in which investors buy or sell securities of different maturities to obtain the highest possible return.

**maturity gaps** A measure of interest rate risk equal to bank assets minus bank liabilities at each maturity level.

**medium of exchange** A commodity, such as money, that serves as the means of payment for goods and services in an economy.

**modern quantity theory of money demand (Milton Friedman)** The theory of Milton Friedman that analyzes how people allocate their wealth among alternative investments (including money) on the basis of rates of return.

**monetarism** The macroeconomic school that believes the money supply is the main source of changes in the price level and nominal income.

**monetary base** The fiat money of the United States, consisting of currency outside of banks and bank reserves.

**monetary policy** Actions regarding the monetary base, money supply, and interest rates used by the Federal Reserve to achieve macroeconomic goals.

**monetary theory** The field of economics concerned with how monetary policy can affect real income and the price level.

**monetizing the deficit** Government deficit financing in which the Federal Reserve buys Treasury securities, thus raising the monetary base.

**money demand/money supply interest rate theory** The partial equilibrium theory in which the interest rate is determined by the demand for and supply of money.

**money illusion** The situation in which economic decisions are based on nominal variables (like nominal wealth or a nominal interest rate) when they should be based on real variables.

**money market funds** Mutual funds which invest in short-term securities.

**money supply** The quantity of money in the economy at a moment in time.

**money supply multiplier** The relative increase in the money supply created by a given increase in the monetary base.

**money supply targets** Growth rates for the M1 or M2 money supply that the Federal Reserve uses to gauge monetary policy.

**moral hazard** When people act to raise their risk level after they obtain insurance or a loan.

**multilateral trade** Trade, involving at least three traders, that has overall balance, but not bilateral balance.

**mutual fund** An investment company that raises money by selling shares to shareholders, who then own a prorated share of its assets.

**natural rate of unemployment** The unemployment rate at which labor demand and supply are balanced. This rate serves as a benchmark for determining whether wage rates are rising or falling.

**net asset value** The value per share of a mutual fund, determined by dividing the total value of its assets by the number of shares.

**net worth** The accounting term used to denote wealth.

**new classical model** The macroeconomic model that assumes (1) people use rational expectations and (2) wages and prices are flexible.

**nominal income** The amount of income stated in dollars (equal to the product of the price level and real income).

**nominal interest rate** An interest rate quoted in the normal manner, as the nominal amount of interest relative to the nominal amount borrowed.

**nominal and real magnitudes** Nominal magnitudes are expressed in dollars (or dollar prices). Real magnitudes are expressed in quantities, such as the number of units by weight or volume.

**nonclassical model** The macroeconomic model that assumes (1) people use rational expectations and (2) wages and prices are sticky.

**nonbank banks** Banking institutions that accept transaction accounts or make loans, but not both.

**offshore banking** Banking operations that are located outside of a country in order to avoid banking regulations.

**open interest** Futures and options contracts that remain to be settled.

**open-market operations** Federal Reserve purchases or sales of securities.

**open-market operations—defensive and dynamic** Defensive open-market operations are used to offset changes in bank reserves or the monetary base created by outside factors. Dynamic open-market operations are used to initiate a new monetary policy.

**operating targets** Variables like the federal funds rate, the monetary base, and bank reserves that are closely related to the Federal Reserve's instruments, such as open market operations. Since operating targets are linked with the Fed's instruments, they should be measurable and controllable.

**operation twist** An attempt by the Federal Reserve to combine easy monetary policy for domestic purposes with tight monetary policy for exchange rate purposes.

**opportunity cost of money** The interest foregone when holding money. It can be measured as the interest rate earned on investment deposits minus the interest rate earned on transaction deposits.

**options contracts** Contracts on which the option holder has the right, but not the obligation, to complete the transaction.

**output mix** The composition of total output among consumption, investment, government spending, and net exports.

**payments system factors** Characteristics of the payments system, such as the frequency with which income is paid and the form of money.

**pension funds** Financial intermediaries which manage retirement investments.

**Phillips curve** The inverse relationship between wage rate changes and unemployment rates.

**policy ineffectiveness proposition** The result of the new classical model that (1) anticipated increases in the money supply raise the price level, but leave aggregate output unchanged, and (2) unanticipated increases in the money supply raise both the price level and aggregate output.

**policy mix** The composition of macroeconomic policy between monetary policy and fiscal policy.

**political business cycle** The theory that monetary policy may be used to help reelect incumbent presidents, reflecting implicit presidential control of monetary policy.

**portfolio** The combination of capital assets, financial assets, and financial liabilities that a bank, firm, or person holds.

**preferred habitat term structure theory** The theory that investors hold securities with a maturity equal to their "preferred habitat".

**present value** The current value of a security's payments determined through time discounting.

**price level neutrality** The situation when changes in the price level do not affect real magnitudes such as real income and real wealth.

**prime rate** The interest rate that banks charge their most secure business customers.

**production possibility frontier** The curve indicating the amounts of two classes of goods that can be produced in an economy, assuming full use of all resources.

**proviso clause** The part of a Federal Open Market Committee directive that indicates a given policy should be carried out, *provided* that another goal is not violated.

**purchasing power parity theory** The theory that exchange rates between two currencies are determined by the relative price levels of the two countries.

**pure expectations term structure theory** The theory that investors choose the security sequence with the highest expected holding period return.

**put options contract** Options contracts on which the holder can decide whether or not to *make* delivery.

**quantity equation of exchange** The equation MV = Y, or MV = Py, (where M is the money supply, V is the velocity of money, Y is for nominal income, P is the price level, and y is real income).

**rate spread** The difference between two interest rates, such as the loan rate minus the deposit rate for a bank.

**rational expectations** Expectations of a variable that are based on all available and relevant information.

**real bills doctrine** The policy used by the Federal Reserve prior to World War II to operate the discount window, in which banks received discount loans as long as they presented "real bills"—sound business loans—for discounting.

**real business cycle** The theory that business cycles are due to factors other than monetary policy, such as technological change.

**real income** The amount of income stated in terms of purchasing power over real goods and services (equal to nominal income divided by the price level).

**real interest rate** The nominal interest rate minus the inflation rate. Ex ante real rates are based on the *expected* inflation rate. Ex post real rates are based on the *actual* inflation rate.

**real wealth effects** A two-step process in which (1) an unexpected increase in the price level causes real wealth to fall and (2) lower real wealth causes real saving to rise.

**redlining** The process in which a bank refuses to make loans to a particular group of borrowers.

**reflux ratio** The percentage of a bank's loans that are redeposited in the bank.

**regression line** A statistically determined line that closely fits a set of observations, such as a money demand curve.

**Regulation Q** The Federal Reserve power, in effect between 1933 and 1980, to set ceilings on savings and time deposit interest rates.

**relative price** The price of a good relative to the overall price level.

**repurchase agreement** A transaction involving short-term borrowing in which a security is sold, but the seller agrees to repurchase it at a set price at a later date.

**reserve drain.** A use of the monetary base that reduces reserves available to support transaction deposits.

**reserve multiplier** The relative increase in bank deposits for a given change in bank reserves.

**reserve requirements** Federal Reserve regulations specifying the reserve ratios for financial institutions.

**reserves** The amount of bank vault cash and reserve deposit accounts at the Federal Reserve.

**reserves available to support transaction deposits** The amount of the monetary base that is left after subtracting currency held by the public, excess reserves, and required reserves on time deposits.

**revaluation** An increase in the foreign value of a currency under a fixed exchange rate system.

**riding the yield curve** The investment strategy that involves buying a security with an initial maturity longer than the holding period and selling it at the end of the holding period.

**risk pooling** The process through which the risk level of a portfolio is reduced by including in it a large number of small investments with independent risks.

**risk structure of interest rates** The array of interest rates on securities that have different amounts of credit risk.

**risk transfers** The process through which a risk averse person sells a risk to a less risk averse person.

**risk-return tradeoff** The tradeoff in financial markets that securities offering higher expected returns usually also entail higher risk.

**saving (and dissaving)** Positive saving arises when current income exceeds current outlays for consumption. Negative saving, or dissaving, arises when current outlays exceed current income.

**saving (desired)** The chosen amount of saving based on current and future income, the market interest rate, and time preference.

**savings and loan associations** Depository intermediaries that specialize in making mortgage loans.

**second mortgage (or home equity loans)** Mortgage loans based on the excess equity value—the value of a house minus the amount of the first mortgage.

**securitization** A transaction in which a large number of loans are collected in a single package, and the package is sold as a security.

**security** A contract specifying the payments that will be made by one party to another party.

**securities—forward and spot** Forward securities will trade in a financial market at a later date. Spot securities trade currently in a financial market.

**security sequence** A series of securities that covers a given holding period.

**seignorage** The activity in which governments profit by minting coins.

**selective credit controls** Policies used by the Federal Reserve to regulate loan and deposit markets.

**settlement** The process of completing a security trade in which the seller delivers the security and the buyer pays for it.

**shadow price of loans** An implicit interest rate on loans, which is higher than the quoted market rate when there is credit rationing.

**short position** A security position in which a trader has the obligation (on futures contracts) or the option (on put-options contracts) to make delivery of the commodity at a previously agreed on price.

**speculation** Transactions that involve buying or selling a security in order to profit from an anticipated price change.

**spot (or cash) market** A market in which the settlement of trades takes place immediately (or as soon as the paperwork is completed).

**spot price parity** The theoretical value of a futures contract price that is equal to the sum of the commodity's spot market price and its cost of carry.

**stabilization policy** The use of monetary policy to strengthen a weak economy or to slow down an overly strong economy.

**standard of deferred payment** The monetary unit (such as dollars) that measures the amount to be repaid on loans.

**sterilized interventions** Foreign exchange operations in which the effect of the operation on the monetary base is canceled by an offsetting open-market operation.

**stock margin requirements** Federal Reserve selective credit controls concerning the percentage of a stock purchase that must be paid in cash.

**store of value** An asset which people hold to store wealth over time.

**strike price** The price at which an options contract can be exercised.

**supply shocks** Changes in input costs that shift short-run supply curves. Positive shocks (reductions in input prices) shift supply curves rightward; negative shocks (increases in input prices) shift supply curves leftward.

**supply-side economics** Policies that attempt simultaneously to increase output (and income) and to decrease inflation by shifting the aggregate supply curve rightward.

**synchronization** The coordinated timing of income receipts and consumption payments.

**synthetic loans** Loans that are modified by combining them with futures contracts. Synthetic adjustable rate loans combine a fixed rate loan with a long position in an interest rate futures contract. Synthetic fixed rate loans combine an adjustable rate loan with a short position in an interest rate futures contract.

**target cones and target tunnels** Geometric areas that illustrate the acceptable range of money supply growth rates for a year. Target cones provide a wider range later in the year, whereas target tunnels have a constant width for the entire year that is equal to the width of the target cone at the end of the year.

**term structure of interest rates** The array of interest rates paid on different maturities of a given type of debt security.

**thrift institutions** Savings and loan associations, savings banks, and credit unions.

**tier matching** The investment strategy of holding equals amounts of assets and liabilities at each maturity level to avoid interest rate risk.

**time discounting** The process through which future cash flows are converted to a present value.

**time inconsistency** The inconsistent behavior of the Federal Reserve when it announces one policy but then changes it because people change their behavior after the original policy is announced.

**time preference** The desire for current consumption relative to future consumption.

**trade balance** A country's exports minus its imports, which is a trade surplus when it is positive and a trade deficit when it is negative.

**trading system costs** The costs of maintaining the public facilities that are part of a trading system.

**transaction deposits** Bank deposits on which checks can be written without prior notice, including demand deposits, NOW accounts, and other checkable deposits.

**transfer agent banks** Banks (or gold merchants) who provide receipts that serve as the medium of exchange in economies.

**transfer services** The services banks offer with transaction deposits (checking accounts), which allow payments to be made by check.

**Treasury bill** A short-term security (maturity no more than one year) issued by the U.S. Treasury.

**Treasury bill interest rate** The interest rate that applies to Treasury bills.

**Treasury bond** A long-term security (maturity longer than one year) issued by the U.S. Treasury.

**Treasury bond interest rate** The interest rate that applies to Treasury bonds.

**uncertainty** A situation in which there are a number of different possible outcomes for an investment, gamble, or insurable risk.

**unit of account** The monetary unit (such as dollars) in which prices and wealth are stated.

**usury ceilings** The maximum interest rates that lenders may legally charge on particular categories of loans.

**variance of outcomes** A statistical measure of the distribution of outcomes that takes both the range of outcomes and their probabilities into account.

**velocity of money** The annual rate of turnover of the money supply, commonly measured as GNP divided by the money supply.

**wage-push inflation** A particular form of cost-push inflation in which the initial leftward shift in the aggregate supply curve is due to worker demands for higher wage rates.

**wealth** Nominal wealth equals financial and capital assets minus total liabilities. Real wealth equals nominal wealth deflated by a price index.

**wire transfers** A technique used by banks to transfer money instantaneously to other banks and their customers.

**World Bank** An international bank (also called the International Bank for Reconstruction and Development) that was initially established to foster the redevelopment of Europe after World War II. The bank now makes loans to developing countries.

**yield curve** A graphical representation of the term structure of interest rates for a given type of security.

**yield to maturity** The annual rate of return that would be earned on a security if it were held until maturity.

# Acknowledgments

**Part II**, page 155, portion of bill of sale (bottom right): Institute of Bankers

**Part III**, page 229, VISA, CLASSIC, and THE DIAMOND DESIGN are service marks of Visa International Service Association and are reproduced with permission; (bottom) Frank Lawrence Stevens/Nawrocki Stock Photo

**Chapter 5** Box 5.4, p. 113: Reprinted by permission of THE WALL STREET JOURNAL, © Dow Jones and Company, Inc. 1988. All Rights Reserved. Box 5.8, p. 124: Reprinted by permission of THE WALL STREET JOURNAL, © Dow Jones and Company, Inc. 1988. All Rights Reserved.

**Chapter 9** Box 9.1, p. 210: Reprinted by permission of THE WALL STREET JOURNAL, © Dow Jones and Company, Inc. 1988. All Rights Reserved.

**Chapter 10** Figure 10.1: Frank Lawrence Stevens/Nawrocki Stock Photo; Figures 10.2, 10.3 and 10.4: Nawrocki Stock Photo; Figure 10.6: The Bettmann Archive

**Part IV**, page 325, AMERICAN EXPRESS Card Design® and Gladiator Head® are registered service marks of American Express and are used with permission; (center and bottom) portions of bank note: Institute of Bankers; (lower right) portion of Silver Certificate: Frank Lawrence Stevens/Nawrocki Stock Photo

**Chapter 17** Box 17.1, p. 408: Reprinted by permission of THE WALL STREET JOURNAL, © Dow Jones and Company, Inc. 1988. All Rights Reserved. Box 17.4, p. 418: Reprinted by permission of THE WALL STREET JOURNAL, © Dow Jones and Company, Inc. 1988. All Rights Reserved. Box 17.6, p. 421: Reprinted by permission of THE WALL STREET JOURNAL, © Dow Jones and Company, Inc. 1987. All Rights Reserved.

**Chapter 18** Box 18.1, p. 444: Reprinted by permission of THE WALL STREET JOURNAL, © Dow Jones and Company, Inc. 1988. All Rights Reserved. Box 18.2, p. 445: Reprinted by permission of THE WALL STREET JOURNAL, © Dow Jones and Company, Inc. 1986. All Rights Reserved. Box 18.3, p. 446: Reprinted by permission of THE WALL STREET JOURNAL, © Dow Jones and Company, Inc. 1987. All Rights Reserved.

**Chapter 19** Box 19.4, p. 474: Reprinted by permission of THE WALL STREET JOURNAL, © Dow Jones and Company, Inc. 1988. All Rights Reserved.

**Chapter 20** Box 20.6, p. 498: Reprinted by permission of THE WALL STREET JOURNAL, © Dow Jones and Company, Inc. 1988. All Rights Reserved.

**Part VI**, page 507, details of currency from Angus, Ian (1974). *Paper Money*, New York: St. Martin's Press. Copyright © 1974 by Ian Angus. All rights reserved.

**Chapter 21** Box 21.1, p. 513: Reprinted by permission of THE WALL STREET JOURNAL, © Dow Jones and Company, Inc. 1988. All Rights Reserved.

**Chapter 22** Box 22.1, p. 539: Reprinted by permission of THE WALL STREET JOURNAL, © Dow Jones and Company, Inc. 1981. All Rights Reserved.

**Chapter 23** Box 23.2, p. 567: Reprinted by permission of THE WALL STREET JOURNAL, © Dow Jones and Company, Inc. 1988. All Rights Reserved.

**Part VII**, page 559, coins: Frank Lawrence Stevens/Nawrocki Stock Photo

# Index

*Figures are designated by the letter* f *and tables by the letter* t.